A WITCH'S HAND

Hau
Books

Director
Anne-Christine Taylor

Editorial Collective
Erik Bähre
Deborah Durham
Casey High
Nora Scott

Managing Editor
Jane Sabherwal

Hau Books publishes works for
the Society for Ethnographic Theory (SET)

SET Board of Directors
Kriti Kapila (Chair)
Janice Boddy
John Borneman
Frédéric Keck
Enrique Martino
Anne-Christine Taylor

www.haubooks.org

A WITCH'S HAND

Curing, Killing, Kinship, and Colonialism among the Lujere of New Guinea

William E. Mitchell

Hau Books
Chicago

© 2024 Hau Books

A Witch's Hand: Curing, Killing, Kinship, and Colonialism among the Lujere of New Guinea by William E. Mitchell is licensed under the Creative Commons license CC BY-NC-ND 4.0

Cover images (clockwise from top): Richard Thurnwald amid his boats and men on the upper Sepik River, 1914; a Lujere *na wowi* mask strides through the village to meet his patient, 1971; a map of the Yellow and Sand Rivers during German control, 1924.

Layout design: Deepak Sharma, Prepress Plus Technologies
Typesetting: Prepress Plus Technologies (https://prepressplustechnologies.com)

ISBN: 978-1-912808-45-8 [paperback]
ISBN: 978-1-912808-85-4 [electronic]
ISBN: 978-1-912808-46-5 [PDF]
LCCN: 2020951266

Hau Books
Chicago Distribution Center
11030 S. Langley
Chicago, Il 60628
www.haubooks.org

Hau Books publications are printed, marketed, and distributed by The University of Chicago Press.
www.press.uchicago.edu

Printed in the United States of America on acid-free paper.

This book is dedicated to all whose names
appear within these pages, both the living and the dead.
Each, in her or his way, helped me write this book.

Contents

List of Illustrations ... xix
   Figures ... xix
   Tables ... xxi
   Maps ... xxi

List of Abbreviations ... xxiii

Glossary ... xxv

Acknowledgments ... xxix

INTRODUCTION ... 1
   Beginnings ... 1
   Signposts ... 6

Part One: THE COLONIAL INVASION

Chapter One: GERMANY, THE LUJERE'S ABSENTEE RULERS ... 15
   The Colonial Cannibalism of New Guinea ... 17
   Richard Thurnwald, Pioneering Ethnographer and Explorer-Surveyor ... 21
      Thurnwald Encounters the Lujere, 1914 ... 25
      The Yellow and Sand River Excursions ... 26
      The Trashing of Thurnwald's Camp ... 32

Chapter Two: AUSTRALIA, THE LUJERE'S NEW RULERS — 37

From Australian Occupation to the League of Nations Mandate — 37
Constructing a Colonial System of Administration — 39
The Trade in Bird-of-Paradise Plumes — 40
The First Lujere Patrols — 44
Robinson's Pioneering 1929–1932 Patrols — 45
McCarthy's 1936 Patrol — 54

Chapter Three: THE JAPANESE INVASION — 61

The Fall of Rabaul, 1942 — 62
Guerrilla Warfare in the Upper Sepik Basin, 1943 — 64
The Lujere and the Mosstroops Guerrillas — 66
Steel tools at last — 70
Lujere memories of the war — 74
The Japanese Peril — 77
Japanese attacks in Lujereland — 78
The flight of the Mosstroops — 80
Operation Persecution: The Aitape Coast Recaptured — 83
The End of the War in New Guinea — 85

Chapter Four: AUSTRALIAN HEGEMONY RESTORED — 89

Return of the Patrol Officers — 90
Patrol Officer Gilbert and Father James's Patrol to the Sepik, 1949 — 92
Seeking a Yellow River Airstrip Site, 1951 — 94
Wakau's First Indentured Laborers — 99
The First Official Census of the Lujere, 1956 — 100
A Patrol Officer's Assessment of the Lujere Colonial Predicament, 1962 — 106
Here Come the Missionaries! — 107
The Sola Fida Mission and the First Regional Airstrip, 1958 — 107
The Christian Brethren Arrive, 1961 — 108
Wakau Village Makes a Move — 109

Chapter Five: COLONIAL TWILIGHT — 111

Establishing the Yellow River (Edwaki) Base Camp — 111
A Failed Attempt, 1968 — 111
Success, a Triumph of Local Politics, 1971 — 118
Here Come the Anthropologists! — 124
The Fast Track to Independence — 129

Chapter Six: THE SEARCH FOR A VILLAGE — 133

Gilbert Lewis's Lujere Experience — 133
The Search — 135
A Hasty Flight to Edwaki Base Camp — 136
Visiting Multiple Lujere Villages — 136
Narrowing the Options — 143
The Choice — 150
A temporary move to Edwaki Base Camp — 150
Settling in at Wakau village — 154

Part Two: WHO ARE THE LUJERE?

Chapter Seven: LUJERELAND — 161

The Lay of the Land: Low, Wet, Hot, and Humid — 162
Colonial Consequences — 164
"Isolated and Undeveloped" — 164
The South Wapei Census Division — 165
Indentured laborers — 165
Villagers' knowledge of the colonial government — 170
Councils and the Southwest Census District — 171
Jobs: An unfulfilled wish — 173
Rural Airstrips — 175
Hunting with Shotguns — 176
Scientific Medicine in the Bush — 178
Radios and Newspapers — 179
Trade Stores and Markets — 180

Tok Pisin Schools and Literacy	181
Yellow River Preparatory School	181

Chapter Eight: THE LUJERE VILLAGES — 185

A Muddle of Terms	185
Population and Gender	187
Lujere Regions	189
Leadership and Authority	191
Ancestral Origins	191
A Man, His Son, and Dog Go Up the Sepik	192
Male Initiation: Myth or Authentic History?	196
Talk, the Essence of Life	197
A Plethora of Papuan Languages: Namia's Neighbors	198
The classification gambit	198
Namia	200
Tok Pisin	202

Chapter Nine: OLD ENEMIES — 203

Traditional Enemies	204
Trading with the Enemy	205
Dressed to Kill	207
The Lujere Fight Shield	208
Slaying the Enemy	210
The Tsila Village Massacre	211
The Yellow River Massacre	213
Prelude to a Cannibal Feast	217
The Massacre	220
The Aftermath	223

Chapter Ten: WAKAU VILLAGE — 229

Wakau Local History	229
Cultural Impact of the Mission	232
A Pragmatic People	232

Cultural Changes Since Robinson's and McCarthy's Patrols	234
Dating Local History	236
The People and Households of Wakau	237
Betty Gillam and Jalman's Medical Clinic	237
Who Lives Where?	239
Women's Houses	241
Family Bush Camps	243
Men's Houses	245
The House as Cultural Metaphor	249
The Fieldwork Camp	249
The Lower Village: Dramatis Personae	252
Village Rhythms	254
Morning and afternoon	254
The evening dinner	259
Greetings, Old and New	260
The Ancestors' Stones	261
Taboos in Daily Life	262
Chapter Eleven: DISCORD AND DISSENT	265
Domestic Quarrels	265
Disputes Among Villagers	269
Colonial Offenses, Official and Unofficial	272
Klowi's Crimes	274
Patrol Officers and Villagers	276
Playing Politics	276
The Ten-Cent "Tax"	277
The 1972 National Election	278
The Power of the Patrol Officer	281
The Ethnologist's Rant	282

Chapter Twelve: CLANSHIP, KINSHIP, AND MARRIAGE — 283

   The Work of the Patriclans — 284

      Dual Clan Affiliation — 285

      Adoption — 289

   Economic Resources — 290

   Resource Transmission — 292

   Kinship Terminology — 292

      Wakau Kin Terms — 294

      Joking Relationships — 296

   Love and Marriage — 297

      Yaope Takes a Bride — 298

      Threatening Female Abduction — 299

      Tsaime and Nemia: A Turbulent Nuptial Scenario — 300

         An aborted elopement — 300

         A stick fight — 305

         The patrol officer's court — 306

         Klowi's stern lectures — 308

         The bow-and-arrow confrontation — 309

         A rained-out political meeting — 311

         The closing nuptial exchange — 311

      Nauwen and Kunai's Marital Woes — 312

Chapter Thirteen: INTO THE BUSH: THE QUEST FOR FOOD — 315

   Sago, the Lujere Staff of Life — 316

   Relentless Gatherers — 318

   Reluctant Gardeners — 318

   The Fervor of the Hunt — 320

   Ginger's Magical Power and Use — 324

   Hunting Dogs and Wild and Tame Pigs — 324

   Finding Fish — 326

   The Omnipresence of Food Taboos — 328

Part Three: MAGIC, MURDER, AND THE LUJERE IMAGINATION

Chapter Fourteen: STORIES FROM AN IMAGINARY PAST — 333
- Mental Worlds — 333
- The Storytellers' Tales — 336
  - *Why Dogs Eat Shit* — 339
  - *A Pond Python Eats a Mother and Her Baby* — 340
  - *Filial Love: The Cassowary Mother and Her Human Son* — 340
  - *The Turtle Moon and the Naughty Children* — 342
  - *The Selfish Husband and a Magical Skirt* — 344
  - *A Cannibal Demon and the Villagers' Revenge* — 345
  - *Wararu and the Spirit Woman* — 346
  - *The Origin of Frogs* — 346
  - *A Tale of Two Brothers* — 348
  - *Water-Snake Woman Is a Good Wife* — 350

Chapter Fifteen: THE LUJERE CURING FESTIVALS — 351
- Modes of Therapeutic Intervention — 351
- The Lujere View of Sickness — 353
- The Lujere Spirit World — 354
  - Souls, Spirits, and Ghouls — 354
  - Tracking Down the *Wowi* Spirits — 358
  - The Ways of Ritual — 359
- The *Wowi*-Spirit Curing Festivals — 360
  - *Mauwi's* Na *Wowi* Curing Festival — 361
    - Day one: Preparations — 363
    - Day two: The exorcism — 368
    - An outsider's perspective — 370
    - Ritual phallocrypts in the upper Sepik Basin — 372
  - *Mokadami's* Aewal *Wowi* Curing Festival — 377
    - Preparations — 377

The *aewal wowi* ritual horns	380
The concluding rituals	382
Wakau's Aewal Wowi *Curing Festivals*	384
The first curing festival	385
The second curing festival	388

Chapter Sixteen: 'SANGUMA': THE TERROR OF MAGICAL RITUAL MURDER IN OCEANIA — 391

'Sanguma' as Magical Ritual Murder	391
Sorcery and Witchcraft	392
Geocultural Distribution of 'Sanguma'	395
Ethnographic Descriptions of 'Sanguma' in Papua New Guinea	395
The first descriptions by Codrington and Seligman	395
'Sanguma' in the eastern islands	397
Hogbin's Guadalcanal description	397
Ludvigson's Espiritu Santo Island description	398
Fortune's Dobu account	398
'Sanguma' in the Sepik region	400
Bateson's Iatmul account	400
Roscoe's Yangoru Boiken description	401
Gesch's Yamuk village (Middle Sepik) description	402
Kulick's Gapun and Juillerat's Yafar descriptions	402
Scorza's Tumentonik village (Torricelli Mountains) description	403
Morren's Telefolmin description	403
'Sanguma' in Papua (former British New Guinea)	404
Knauft's Gebusi (Western Province) description	404
Burton-Bradley and Julius' Motu village (Port Moresby) description	404
Malinowski's Mailu description	404
'Sanguma' in the north coastal region	406
St. Lehner's Markham-Ramu plain description	406
Hogbin's Wogeo Island description	406
Koster's Banara (Bogia area) description	407

'Sanguma' in the Highlands	408
Berndt's Jate (eastern Central Highlands) description	408
Stewart and Strathern's Wiru and Hewa (Southern Highlands) descriptions	408
Ethnographic Descriptions of 'Sanguma' in Indonesia	409
'Sanguma' in North Maluku province	409
Bubandt's Halmahera Island description	409
'Sanguma' in West Papua province	410
Held's Waropen description	410
'Sanguma' in Papua province	411
Wirz's Marind-Anim description	411
Ethnographic Descriptions of 'Sanguma' in Australia	412
'Sanguma' in South Australia	412
Spencer and Gillen's Arunta description	412
'Sanguma' in Western Australia	413
Tokinson's Jigalong description	413
'Sanguma' in the Northern Territory	413
Reid's and Warner's Murngin accounts	413
Conclusion: The Cultural Extent and Mapping of 'Sanguma'	415
Chapter Seventeen: 'SANGUMA' AND SOCIETY	**417**
Lujere 'Sanguma'	417
The Apprenticeship of a 'Sangumaman'	418
Positive Roles of a 'Sangumaman'	420
The Origin Story of Lujere 'Sanguma'	421
An Iwani Sorcery Trial in Lumi	422
Etymology of 'Sanguma' and Its Conflicting Referents	425
Don Laycock and 'Sanguma'	426
Margaret Mead and 'Sanguma'	427
Is 'Sanguma' Real?	430
Father G. J. Koster's Accounts	430
F. E. Williams's Accounts	432

Dr. Becker's Surgical 'Sanguma' Patient	434
Iwani's Double 'Sanguma' Murder	436
The Queen v. three 'sangumamen'	436
The villagers' version of the murders	438
'Sanguma' and the Law	440
Reo Fortune's 1932 Critique of the Sorcery Ordinance of 1893	440
The Sorcery Act of 1971	441
'Sanguma' Witch Hunts in Papua New Guinea Today	442
The 2015 Repeal of the Sorcery Act	443

Chapter Eighteen: THE AFFLICTED AND THEIR CURERS — 445

Patients' Curing Options	445
Medical Services through the Administration and Mission	446
Litabagi's Wakau Medical Patrol	446
Home Remedies, Physical and Ritual	448
Pourame and Oria's Family Health Crisis	452
Magical Curers	454
Male Magical Curers	454
Female Magical Curers	455
Magical Curing Practices	455
Magical Curers and Their Patients	457
Klowi Treats Iwanauwi of Mauwi Hamlet	457
Menetjua Treats Tschorai	458
Eine's and Tschorai's Curer Treatments	460
A 'Sangumaman' Treats Ime	460
A Curing Clinic	463
Mangko Treats Kaukobu of Gwidami	469
Three Weari Curers Treat Klowi	471
Sickness, Curing, Placebos, and the Male Curers	473
The Curer Paradox and Self-Referential Magic	474
Psychosis or Devil Possession?	477

Chapter Nineteen: DEATH IN WAKAU   479

  Rampant Pneumonia   479

    A Hunting Camp Visit   484

    A Graveyard Ritual   485

    The Death of Ukai   485

      Ukai's wake   488

      Ukai's burial   490

    The Death of Kairapowe   494

  Saying Goodbye   496

  Magical versus Medical Curing   498

    Curing Modes and Techniques   499

    The Lujere Separation of Local and Introduced Curing Systems   501

    'Sanguma': Some Final Thoughts   502

Appendix: AI'IRE'S CHRONIC ABDOMINAL ILLNESS: A CASE-STUDY LOG OF MAGICAL AND MEDICAL INTERVENTIONS   503

References   507

List of Illustrations

Unless otherwise indicated in the text captions, all photos are by William E. Mitchell.

Figures

Figure 1. Richard Thurnwald amid his boats and assistants on the upper Sepik River, January 1914.	23
Figure 2. Richard Thurnwald's photo of Lujere men and boys on the Sand River, November 1914.	31
Figure 3. A Mosstroops photo of the Sepik River, marked up to show the seaplane landing area where men and supplies could be off-loaded.	69
Figure 4. A Lujere headman with a traditional pipe, as photographed by a Mosstroops member.	72
Figure 5. The Aukwom aid post orderly on the porch with some patients below.	139
Figure 6. A Lujere man stands on the porch of a traditional-style men's house (*iron*), one of two in Nami village.	145
Figure 7. Nakate and Manwai ready a canoe to cross the Yellow River.	147
Figure 8. View south from Wakau's upper village, looking over lower village roofs towards the 'kunai' plain, the West Range, and Victor Emanuel Range.	155
Figure 9. A Wakau village fight shield. Australian Museum, Sydney.	209
Figure 10. Aerial view of Wakau village, looking north.	230
Figure 11. Mothers visiting at Oria's wife's house, across from my office. Kwoien's wife Wariyeh with her newborn son is on the right.	231
Figure 12. Enmauwi smokes a traditional *mero* pipe as his daughter Wea plays with the stem of Nimo's *mero*.	236
Figure 13. Nurse Betty Gillam and the medical orderly Jalman set up for a medical clinic.	238
Figure 14. Wawenowaki (Klowi's wife, second from right) relaxes with family and friends on the front veranda of her traditional house.	243
Figure 15. K____ bush camp, a two-and-a-half-hour hike from Wakau.	245

Figure 16. Klowi's bush camp in the fens, across the Sand River. 246
Figure 17. The interior of Klowi's bush camp. 246
Figure 18. The abandoned men's house (*iron*) in Wakau, once the men's sleeping quarters. 247
Figure 19. The new men's house in the upper village of Wakau. 248
Figure 20. Villagers outside my office listening to a tape recording of a curing ritual. 250
Figure 21. My office, with its two indispensable and faithful assistants: an Olympia typewriter and an Aladdin lamp. 251
Figure 22. Wakau men returning home late afternoon with their hunting weapons. Note the old, abandoned *iron* in the background. 254
Figure 23. Wakau women returning home with firewood. 255
Figure 24. Boys spinning tops in the lower village. 257
Figure 25. Ai'ira's daughter Yawori holds a toy bow as boys spin their tops in the lower village. The path connects the lower and upper villages. 257
Figure 26. A boy astride an archaic grinding stone near the end of the upper village. 262
Figure 27. Breakfast with Joyce, Elizabeth, and Ned in my screened-tent dining area. 279
Figure 28. An Iwani villager receives a ballot from PO Lanaghan. 280
Figure 29. Ai'ire casts his ballot assisted by the Iwani 'luluai'; in the middle distance, women line up for a ballot. The house belonging to the 'kiap' is in the rear. 280
Figure 30. Leno striding angrily by the lower *iron*, bush knife in hand. 301
Figure 31. Tsaimi, face blackened to express his powerful emotions, holds the 'kiap' baton inlaid with the Queen's coin portrait to give to Leno. 303
Figure 32. Leno and Tsaime at PO Lanaghan's informal court. 307
Figure 33. Kairapowe washing sago by the Sand River with Oria's daughter Womkau. 317
Figure 34. Men carry a wild boar shot by Klowi to the 'kunai' house. 321
Figure 35. Klowi in the upper village with a recently shot Victoria crowned pigeon. 322
Figure 36. Mangko with boys and the cassowary he shot with his bow and arrow. 323
Figure 37. The boys and youths who created the *na wowi* masks. 364
Figure 38. Lijeria quietly awaits the beginning of his *na wowi* curing festival. 365
Figure 39. One of the *na wowi* masks approaches Lijeria, seated. 367
Figure 40. *Na wowi* mask carriers, Iwowari, Purkenitobu, and Katweli, practicing their moves. 369
Figure 41. A *na wowi* mask kneels next to Lijeria for the curing climax. 371
Figure 42. A *na wowi* mask parades across the village plaza, followed by chanting children and women. 375
Figure 43. Men playing *aewal wowi* horns encircle afflicted victims. The "grandfather" horn is the undecorated one and the others known as the "children." 380
Figure 44. Orana and Anwani are treated near the four *aewal wowi* placed on the ground. 383
Figure 45. Decorated *aewal wowi* horns perform for Maruwami's curing rituals. 389
Figure 46. Chest x-ray slide of victim's thoracic cavity with three casing wires. 435

List of Illustrations

Figure 47. Partial lineup of Wakau families for Litabagi's medical patrol; Mowal far left, next to Mangko and Kairapowe chatting. — 447
Figure 48. Aid post orderly Litabagi gives oral amodiaquine to Oria's sister's baby. — 448
Figure 49. Oria makes an *aewal wowi* curing bundle for his sick wife. — 450
Figure 50. Oria covers Pourame for the curing ritual. — 451
Figure 51. Warajak helps Oria complete the *aewal wowi* curing ritual for Pourame. — 453
Figure 52. Ime with K____ and Kowali, her mother's brother, holding a betel bespattered bundle. — 462
Figure 53. Yabowe, supported by her father, is treated by Ari. — 466
Figure 54. As Klene clings to a rafter for support, Ari tugs on his belly skin. — 467
Figure 55. Little Manwe is held down by his mother as Ari treats him. — 468
Figure 56. Ari explores Manwe's belly as his helper leans down with a curing bundle. — 469
Figure 57. Enaru squeezes Lijeria's flesh as his helper waits with her curing bundle. — 470
Figure 58. Men plan and prepare Ukai's gravesite. — 491
Figure 59. Two young women bring water to the gravesite for the men to wash the body. — 492
Figure 60. Meyawali and Mowal closing Kairapowe's grave with palm branches. — 495
Figure 61. The author with his cargo and two local boys on the Yellow River airstrip awaiting his MAF chartered plane to Lumi. Photo by Ray Lanaghan. — 497

Tables

Table 1. PO Oakes's Lujere village census data, 1956 — 105
Table 2. Lujere shotguns, radios, and male literacy in Tok Pisin — 180
Table 3. CMML Yellow River primary school students — 182
Table 4. PO Lanaghan's Lujere village census data, November–December 1971 — 188
Table 5. Lujere enemy villages by cardinal direction and language — 204
Table 6. Wakau population by marital status, 1972 — 239
Table 7. Wakau population by age and gender, 1956 and 1972 — 239
Table 8. Key to map 6, women's houses and men's collective houses in Wakau village — 242
Table 9. Iwani village males convicted of offenses 1955–1971 — 273
Table 10. Variability in Lujere curing modes and techniques, 1971–72 — 499

Maps

Map 1. The island of New Guinea, with the Sepik area framed in the center box. — 2
Map 2. The Lujere homeland and some of the Sepik cultures with ethnographic studies, 1972. — 3
Map 3. The Sand and Yellow (Gelb) river basins during German control. — 24
Map 4. PO George Oakes's patrol map of villages in South Wapei Census Division, 1957. — 101

Map 5. Lujere villages visited by Barry Craig on his 1969 collecting trip. 127
Map 6. Wakau village women's and men's houses in November, 1971. Drawing by Dan Holbrow. 241
Map 7. Oria's map of his land across the Sand River with sago stands and creeks. 291

List of Abbreviations

A$:   Australian dollar
ADC: Assistant District Commissioner
ADO: Assistant District Officer
AIB: Allied Intelligence Bureau
ANGAU: Australian New Guinea Administrative Unit
AN&MEF: Australian Naval and Military Expeditionary Force
CMML: Christian Missions in Many Lands
CPO: Cadet Patrol Officer
DASF: Department of Agriculture, Stock, and Fisheries
DC: District Commissioner
DDS: Department of District Services and Native Affairs
DORCA: Directorate of Research and Civil Affairs
FELO: Far Eastern Liaison Unit
JN: Joyce's typed field notes
Lang.:   Language
MAF: Missionary Aviation Fellowship
MBE: Member of the Order of the British Empire
MD: Author's typed diary notes
MN: Author's typed field notes
NAA: National Archives of Australia
NB: Author's field notebook
OBE: Officer of the Order of the British Empire
OIC: Officer in Charge
PNG: Papua New Guinea
PO: Patrol Officer
RAAF: Royal Australian Air Force
SVD: Society of the Divine Word, a Catholic religious order
SWCD: South Wapei Census Division
TP: Tok Pisin (Pidgin English, Melanesian Pidgin, Neo-Melanesian)

Glossary

Throughout this book, terms in the Tok Pisin language are indicated by single quotes; terms in Namia are indicated by italics.

Tok Pisin

'bus kanaka': unsophisticated, old-fashioned person (pejorative)
'hatwara': sago pudding
'haus kiap': patrol officer's rest house
'haus kuk': kitchen
'haus meri': women's house
'haus polis': police rest house
'haus tambaran': male ceremonial house
'kalabus': jail
'kanaka': Indigene, local, Native
'kanda': cane, rattan
'kapiok: bread fruit tree
'kaukau': sweet potato
'kawawar': ginger
'kiap': patrol officer
'kot': court; to be accused
'kulau': green coconut for drinking
'kunai': grass plains
'kundu': hand drum
'laplap': waistcloth or sarong
'limbum': flooring made from a palm trunk; pliable flower sheath of a palm sometimes made into containers
'luluai': top village official appointed by the 'kiap'
'mami': a type of yam
'maski': never mind
'meri': female

'morata': thatch shingles made of sewn palm leaves
'muruk': cassowary
'ofis': office
'ol i ranawe': everyone ran away
'pangal': sago palm stem
'popo': papaya
'Popi': Roman Catholic
'posin': sorcery
'ring moni': shell wealth
'saksak': sago
'sanguma' ('sangguma'): magical homicide
'sarip': small sickle for cutting grass
'satu': dice gambling game
'selmani': shell money
'sing-sing': festival usually including dancing and feasting
'sot win': shortness of breath
talatala: Protestant
'tok pilai': joking
'tultul': secondary village official appointed by the 'kiap'
'wailis': a radio transmitter
'wantok': person who speaks your language
'wanwok': person who shared your contract labor
'waspapa': a foster father, a guardian

NAMIA

aewal: stinging nettles
aewal wowi: stinging nettles bush demon
aijan aokwae: spirit associated with natural phenomena
amei: stone axe
anapi: bow
aokwae: spirit
aokwae bidami: spirit of dead person
aokwae naki: spirit of newly dead person
aokwae nebu: rainbow
Edwaki: Lujere central villages
ena aokwae: pond spirit
iju aokwae: stream spirit
imoulu: traditional male curer
iron: men's house
ithu wowi: water bush demon
lei aokwae: swamp spirit
Lawo: northwestern Lujere villages
mero: two-piece smoking implement
nakwolu: murderous male witch
na wowi: sago bush demon

Pabei: southern Lujere villages
paumei: sorcery
poketaiyup: a person's spirit or soul
tiramli: hand drum
walamaku: settlement
waniwani: wooden trumpet
Weari: eastern Lujere villages
wowi: bush demon

Acknowledgments

First and foremost, I would like to acknowledge the Lujere residents of Wakau hamlet of Iwani village, Aitape-Lumi Subdistrict, Sanduan (West Sepik) Province, who in 1971–72 and during my brief revisits in 1982 and 2000, generously shared their lives and stories with me. A few names warrant special mention, as their valuable contributions were so extensive: Oria, Kaiera, Nauwen, Arakwaki, Kunai, Klowi, and Waratchak, a boy in 1971 but on my return in 2000 a grown man called Jek.

I am deeply grateful for the generous three-year research grant awarded by the National Institute of Mental Health in 1970 that made it possible for me to live with the Lujere and collect the data upon which this book is based. I am also grateful to the Wenner-Gren Foundation for an earlier summer travel grant that brought me to Papua New Guinea in 1967 to join anthropologists Margaret Mead and Rhoda Métraux on the Sepik River.

I am also grateful to the following institutions and governmental departments for facilitative support, and to their staffs for personal courtesies: Carolina Academic Press; Christian Missions in Many Lands; Cornell University Library; Department of Anthropology and Sociology, University of Papua New Guinea; Division of Anthropology, American Museum of Natural History; Franciscan Friars of Papua New Guinea; National Archives of Australia; National Archives and Public Records Services of Papua New Guinea; Kreitzberg Library, Norwich University; Davis Family Library, Middlebury College; Morrisville Public Library, Morrisville, Vermont; Ethnological Museum of Berlin; New Guinea Research Unit, Research School of Pacific Studies, Australian National University; National Department of Health, Department of Social Development and Home Affairs, and Office of the Administrator, Papua New Guinea; University of Berlin Library; Bancroft Library, University of California, Berkeley; University of Michigan Library; Thomas James Rodoni Archive, University of Newcastle; University of Pennsylvania Museum Library; University of Sydney Archives; Howe Library, University of Vermont; Wenner-Gren Foundation for Anthropological Research; Sanduan (West Sepik) Province, Aitape-Lumi Subdistrict, and Edwaki Base Camp offices.

I am greatly indebted to the following individuals, some lamentably departed, who at very different times and in often vastly different ways each gave generously of their time and expertise to keep my research rolling along (listed alphabetically): Phillip Ace, Rosemary Ace, Alex Achjanie, Timoti Aliowoni, Bryant Allen, Dan Anderson, Janet Anderson, Ian Bean, T. O. Beidelman, Lauri Bragge, Peter Broadhurst, Ralph N. H. Bulmer, B. G. Burton-Bradley, Barry Craig, Kathryn Creely, Laurent A. Daloz, Diane De Terra, Jared Diamond, Mark Dornstreich, Stephen J. Duggan, T. Wayne Dye, May Ebihara, Harry Feldman, Tom Feldpausch, Becky Feldpausch, Oswald C. Fountain, Deborah Gewertz, Elizabeth A. Gillam, Risto Gobius, Robert Gordon, Phillip Guddemi, Eike Haberland, Karin Hanta, Robert Haynes, Alan Healey, Linda Hoffmann, Ian Hogbin, Heidi Horsely, Leo Hoy, Mary Taylor Huber, Peter Huber, Richard Hutchings, Adell Johannes, Dan Jorgensen, Bernard Juillerat, Christian Kaufmann, Antje Kelm, Heinz Kelm, Sander Kirsch, Ron Kitson, Raymond Lanaghan, Don Laycock, David A. M. Lea, Hope Leichter, James Leichter, Gilbert A. Lewis, Kay Liddle, Claudio Lomnitz, Joseph K. Long, Laura Marshall, Adrian Matthews, Shirley Matthews, Aileen R. F. McGregor, Donald E. McGregor, Marion Melk-Koch, Margaret Mead, David Merau, Rhoda Métraux, Wolfgang Mieder, Joyce Slayton Mitchell, Peter Moriarty, Lyn Wark Murray, Douglas Newton, George D. Oakes, Lita Osmundsen, Nina Parris, Cecil Parrish, Mary Parrish, Mark Pendergrast, Veronica Richel, Paul Roscoe, Jo Scanlan, Markus Schindlbeck, Meinhard Schuster, David P. Scorza, John R. Slayton, William E. Staley, Yvonne Starcheska, Andrew Strathern, John Sturt, Joseph Subasic, Nancy Sullivan, Pamela Swadling, Patricia Townsend, Edgar Tschadjin, Jacques Van Vlack, Beatrice Voirol, Annette Weiner, and C. S. Wigley.

During the actual writing of this book there are a few names already mentioned that deserve a separate shout-out for the many times they lent their expertise to my work: Bryant Allen, Lauri Bragge, Peter Broadhurst, Barry Craig, Kathy Creely, Stephen Duggan, Tom Feldpausch, Betty Gillam, Gilbert Lewis, David Merau, and Veronica Richel.

Lastly, a special acknowledgment and commendation is due the dedicated patrol officers who wrote the detailed reports I have extensively drawn from, and to their supervisors up the chain of command who added their own comments. Without making this "readerly pilgrimage" (Lomnitz 2014: xl) into the colonial past via these officers' comprehensive writings, all situated in time and place, I could not have enfolded my account of the Lujere into their long and deep history of foreign occupation. The patrol officers whose reports I gratefully cite are T. G. Atchison, Lauri Bragge, Merton Brightwell, J. K. Broadhurst, P. E. Feinberg, J. E. Fowke, Ric Hutchings, Frank D. Jones, Ray Lanaghan, J. Martyn, J. K. McCarthy, George Oakes, R. Orwin, G. F. Payne, E. W. Robinson, A. Stevens, M. E. Tomlinson, R. K. Treutlain, C. A. Trollope, F. J. Wafingian, P. B. Wenke, John White, A. S. Wright, and D. Young-Whitford.

Regarding Hau Books, my first thanks are to Hylton White, who initially appreciated the ethnographic scope and historical significance of my book about the Lujere people. The dedicated copy editors who worked on the book were Dan Holbrow (who also drew the charming map of Wakau village (map 6), Honora Perkins, and Julee Tanner; I owe a special thanks to Julee for all the laughs we had in Zoom meetings as we scrambled to finish the final editing.

Some of the material in the book was first presented in talks to the Anthropology Section, New York Academy of Sciences; Department of Behavioral Science, Pennsylvania State University College of Medicine; Department of Psychiatry, Tufts University College of Medicine; Department of Social and Preventive Medicine, University of Papua

New Guinea; and in sessions at the Ninth International Congress of Anthropological and Ethnological Sciences (1973); Seventy-Third Annual Meeting of the American Anthropological Association (1974); One Hundred Forty-Second Annual Meeting of the American Association for the Advancement of Science (1976); Wenner-Gren Foundation Ninety-Fifth International Symposium, "Sepik Research Today" (1984); and the Johnson State College lecture series, "The Creative Audience" (1990).

Introduction

The Sepik is a very large river.
Gregory Bateson (1932: 4)

Beginnings

Nostalgia is a troublesome sentiment. Like unrequited love, it is too self-serving, too wistfully sentimental, too intellectually sloppy. And it is usually only half of the story—the good half. Yet whenever I think of New Guinea and its Sepik provinces, as I did when beginning this book about the Lujere people, I inevitably succumb to nostalgia's seductive embrace. As I began to write, the faint whiff of tropical mold that even today clings to my old notebooks transported me back to the Lujere's swampy homeland and the "messiness and imponderabilia of fieldwork" (Dalton 2000: 291–92). Then the languid tropical air is suddenly suffused with voracious mosquitoes or angry bolts of lightning and torrents of rain transforming a pleasant afternoon into a hellish storm. It is the same when recalling the villagers with whom I lived. First, their personal warmth and gentle kindnesses towards one another and to me immediately jump to mind, and then I recall their obsession with the terrifying male witches—the nokwolu—who they said didn't hesitate to secretly attack and kill their neighbors.

Although nostalgic memories are a part of any author's ethnography, more important are the many hundreds of pages of handwritten and typed field notes, the boxes of taped interviews, hundreds of black-and-white and color photos, fragile decaying maps, stacks of film canisters and, today, video recordings and digital photos. Unlike nostalgic memories that uncritically gloss the past, a large corpus of clearly identified fieldwork materials critically jerks the writer back in time and space to specific persons and concrete events personally known or witnessed. Vague memories and even events long forgotten come scurrying back, leaping into one's consciousness, often with surprising vividness.

This book is about the Lujere people of Papua New Guinea as witnessed from the village of Wakau, where I lived with them in 1971–1972, a long time ago. I first heard about them when I lived in the foothills of the Torricelli Mountains, where I was studying the

Wape people in the village of Taute.[1] The Lujere were located about a three- or four-days' walk to the south. On a clear day in the right spot, I could see their wet grasslands far away in the Sepik River Basin; even farther in the dim distance were the Central Ranges on the other side of the hidden river.[2] Map 1 depicts the island of New Guinea and the Sepik area, while map 2 shows the location of the Lujere in relation to neighboring Sepik societies that had been the focus of ethnographic studies around the time of my research.

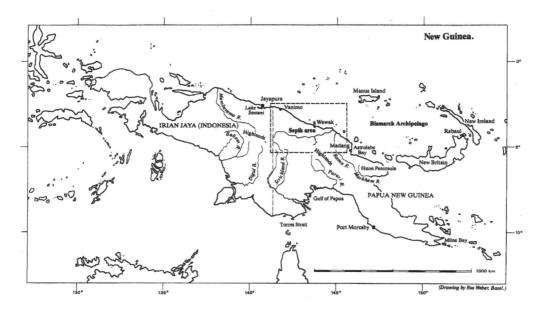

Map 1. The island of New Guinea, with the Sepik area framed in the center box. Reprinted from Lutkehaus et al. (1990: 664) by permission of Carolina Academic Press.

The government referred to the Lujere as "the Yellow River people," but the Wape called them 'ol man belong tais' ("the swamp dwellers"), usually adding with a look of scornful fear, 'Em i as ples bilong sanguma!' indicating that to them, the Lujere were the home of 'sanguma,' an old and dreaded form of ritualized magical homicide with, I would

---

1. When I first began to think about New Guinea as a field site for extended research with my family, I read an article by Eike Haberland (1965) on the areas in the Sepik region that needed ethnographic research and later talked with him personally at an anthropology meeting. One area was the Torricelli Mountains that lay between Aitape on the north coast and the Sepik River; the other was the area south of the Torricellis that Haberland (1965: 40) identified as "the river basin of the Yellow and Sand River." Neither had been studied ethnographically yet, although Gilbert Lewis was soon to do fieldwork among the Gnau in the Torricellis. As it resulted, I studied the Wape in the Torricellis, west of the Gnau, and the Lujere in the area of the Yellow and Sand Rivers.
2. Looking at map 2, the physiographic regions are the Northern Ranges of the Bewani, Torricelli, and Prince Alexander Ranges; the Intermontane Trough of the Sepik and Ramu River Basins; and the Central Cordillera of the West, Central, and Schrader Ranges (Löffler 1972).

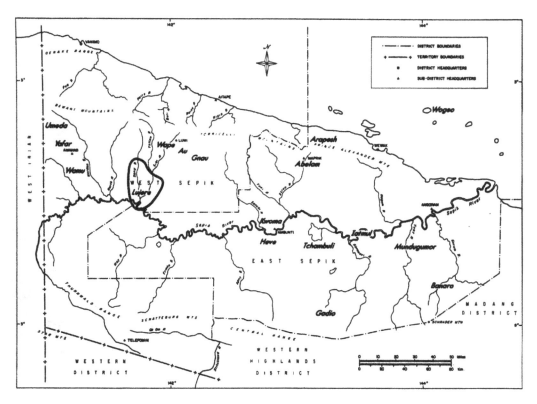

Map 2. The Lujere homeland and some of the Sepik cultures with ethnographic studies, 1972. Reprinted with permission from Mitchell 1975: 412.

learn, a wide cultural distribution in Oceania that stretched even into Indonesia and Australia and examined here in depth for the first time. On the rare instance when any Yellow River people happened to enter our village en route to the subdistrict headquarters in Lumi, word spread quickly as my neighbors and friends vanished into their homes. Everyone was afraid of the swamp people and their 'sanguma' witchcraft. Among the Lujere, 'sangumamen' are called *nakwolu*. In later chapters, you will learn why and how they are both feared and hated as killers but also respected and valued as curers called *imoulu*.

In 1962, Patrol Officer R. K. Treutlein made a fifty-six-day patrol of the villages between the Wape dwelling in the mountains and the Lujere in wet grasslands. He wrote:

> Once one goes further south the position changes, though, and the fear of "Sanguma" becomes very strong. Every sudden or unusual death, be it due to sickness or not, is blamed on Sanguma. The people are afraid to leave their houses at night, they barricade the doors at nightfall and will not come out except under the most dire circumstances, until daylight. Two cases of death allegedly due to Sanguma reported at Tubum village, were on investigation quite obviously pneumonia, yet the people blamed the Yukilos [Yukilo villagers] for having killed these two men by Sanguma. They said that this sort of thing has always been going on. (Treutlein 1962: 12)

For the Wape, 'sanguma' was called *numoin*, but the men who had that daunting power were no more; the last one in my fieldwork village of Taute died shortly before I arrived. But his death did not extinguish their formidable belief in 'sanguma' witchcraft or their mortal terror about the way they believed a victim was secretly assaulted and killed. First, a 'sangumaman' rendered his lone chosen victim unconscious by strangulation. With his victim now prostrate, if not dead, he made cuts in the body's fleshy parts, removed small bits of muscle; then, piercing the victim's armpit area, he drained some blood into a bamboo container. Once the bodily lacerations were finished, he magically closed them without scarring. His victim, who would have no memory of this murderous encounter, was then magically returned to life and sent home to meet his or her inevitable death in so many marked days. My neighbors' belief in 'sanguma' murders was thoroughgoing, but my thinking, so deeply grounded in Western rationalism, could not accept the details of a murderous 'sanguma' assault as factually possible. For one, human skin that has been sliced open in a tropical forest cannot be closed without a trace, and second, a dead person cannot be brought back to life. It seemed to me the belief in 'sanguma' murders was just a supernatural belief, a cultural "superstition" ungrounded in actuality, something the pioneering Sepik anthropologist Ian Hogbin (1952: 136) flatly declared "as almost certainly a figment of native imagination."

I made my first trip to the Sepik in the summer of 1967 to join Dr. Margaret Mead, my former Columbia University professor and dissertation advisor for my study (Mitchell 1978a) of New York City Jewish "family circles" and "cousins' clubs," and Dr. Rhoda Metraux, a former senior colleague on a multidisciplinary research project at Cornell University Medical College about Chinese students stranded in New York after the Communist Revolution (Hinkle et al. 1957). My task in New Guinea was to help Mead and Metraux with their American Museum of Natural History research in the middle Sepik Iatmul village of Tambunam, where Mead had worked with Gregory Bateson in 1938, and to explore where I might return with my family for extended research.[3] Having decided on the Lumi Sub-District of the West Sepik District, I secured funding and returned to Papua New Guinea in May 1970 from Vermont with my wife Joyce and our two preschool children, Ned and Elizabeth, for two years of fieldwork. The intent, as outlined in my grant proposal, was to study the therapeutic systems, both Indigenous and introduced, of at least two hitherto undocumented cultures in the West Sepik District. Compared to the highland districts, few anthropologists had worked there, so the region was rife with research opportunities.

My prior fieldwork with the Wape had been prolonged by the delayed climax of a great *niyl* curing festival that was essential to my research. Consequently, only a scant six months remained to study the Lujere, not a year as originally planned. Fortunately, I already had learned to live comfortably in the middle of a roadless jungle with no modern infrastructure, but I was also counting on my year and a half of fieldwork with the Wape to help speed my new research along. This would be solo work. Joyce and the children

---

3. See Silverman (2018: 192) for a despairing account of Tambunam village today, since the ravages of Sepik floods have destroyed its great ceremonial houses and swept much of its land into the river: "The river, once an asset, is now viewed by the Eastern Iatmul as a liability, while the bush, a former source of impoverishment, is seen as a source of prosperity [lumber!]."

would stay in Lumi, then go to Australia to be with friends. At the completion of my fieldwork, they would rejoin me in New Guinea for our journey home to Vermont.

The Wape told me that all the people living south of them toward the Sepik River had ceremonial lives different from theirs as well as numerous different languages. Two anthropologists from Germany, Antje and Heinz Kelm (1975, 1980), already had studied two of the villages, Kwieftim and Abrau that respectively spoke Ak and Awum. Joyce and I met them briefly in Lumi at a dinner given by the missionary physician Dr. Lyn Wark just as they were leaving and we had just arrived.

While still living with the Wape, in June of 1971, I began actively searching for my next solo field site. Joyce and I flew down to Magaleri, an Amal-speaking village near the Sepik that interested me, then we trekked westward through partial wetlands to visit several inland Lujere villages as well as two on the Sepik River. None completely met my research criteria, but there were a number of others unvisited and I remained optimistic.

The Assistant District Commissioner (ADC) in Lumi, Peter Broadhurst, generously volunteered to help me find my second fieldwork site and, from a set of questions I had compiled for him (Broadhurst 1970), made an anthropological survey while on a routine government patrol in May to a group of villages located on the lowland hills between the Wape and Lujere. Based on his survey and our discussions, in September, I set out to visit several Bouye- and Yis-speaking villages. While the Bouye speakers in Maurom village had especially interesting ceremonial lives, many men were away at plantation work making village life abnormal. Then a second solo reconnaissance trip to the Lujere towards the end of October, including a visit to the western Iwani hamlet of Wakau, convinced me of the aptness of my initial optimism. I would leave the interesting Bouye speakers for another ethnographer to document.[4]

The sweltering riverine ecological niche of the "Yellow River people," so very different from the Wape's mountains, as well as their different rituals, notorious reputation for 'sanguma,' and being both linguistically and ethnographically unstudied, promised plenty of research challenges, especially with my curtailed fieldwork time. Having spent the summer of 1967 on the middle Sepik River with Drs. Mead and Metraux, I already knew about the river's oppressive heat and legions of marauding mosquitoes. With the villagers' enthusiastic permission, I selected Wakau and their swampy domain astride the Sand River as my new home. It also had a special appeal because of a reputation for being more traditional, in both the positive and negative connotations of that term, not to mention that it was more like a two-hour walk, instead of two days, to a new government post, the Yellow River (Edwaki) Base Camp.

One way that my village research role would be different from many anthropologists was that my task, as already indicated, was to study both their own curative practices and those introduced by Westerners. Consequently, I would not be offering first aid assistance, as my methodological intention was to interfere as little as possible with the Wakau villagers' resort to curative practices. But I also knew that no European raised as I was could endure to witness severe suffering or death if s/he had the means for successfully intervening. As a result, I describe several health emergencies where I felt constrained to play a role, sometimes successfully, at other times with tragic consequences.

---

4. After I returned home, I promoted the Bouye as an interesting culture to study when speaking to anthropology graduate students, but they are still awaiting their ethnographer.

On November 3, 1971, I flew in a chartered, small Missionary Aviation Fellowship (MAF) plane with my equipment and supplies to the only usable landing field among the Lujere. It belonged to the Christian Mission to Many Lands (CMML) mission and serviced both them and the government's new station, the Yellow River (Edwaki) Base Camp, established the previous summer in part to deal with the 'sanguma' problem. Hot and humid, mostly flat and swampy, it was one of the country's more remote stations; the only way out was by a long boat ride down the Sepik, a hard two- or three-day hike up to Lumi or, if you had the money, in the mission's plane. For a patrol officer, it was one of the country's more undesirable postings. Ray Lanaghan was the patrol officer at the Yellow River Base Camp during my stay. After we both had departed and he was reassigned, he wrote to me from the high cool beauty of the Oksapmin Patrol Post, recalling "the heavy hot oppressive heat of Yellow River" adding with grim humor, "I will always look back on that place as a vermin-infested, mosquito-ridden, malodorous and ingravescent lair of inimitable iniquity."[5]

Signposts

Here I wish to alert the reader to some of the caveats for reading this book. Although the first Sepik anthropologists, such as Richard Thurnwald, Gregory Bateson, Margaret Mead, Reo Fortune, Phyllis Kaberry, and John Whiting, all used the term "primitive" to refer to the people they were studying, contemporary anthropologists have long since abandoned the term as they have "savages." As Rutherford observes, "For the most part, [even] politicians and pundits have learned not to call people *primitive*" (Rutherford 2018: 2). "Nonliterate" is a term frequently used to designate a society that did not develop its own writing system, a trait of all the societies of precolonial Papua New Guinea.[6]

When Margaret Mead (1938: 153) and Reo Fortune went to New Guinea in 1931 to work with the Arapesh they were unnamed and, as "the habits of English thought require that a people be named, we have called them the Arapesh, their name for *human beings*." Gregory Bateson (1932: 5), another Sepik River pioneer anthropologist who was similarly challenged, wrote, "I have adopted the name Iatmül as a general term for the people. But I doubt whether I am right in so doing." The people who are the subject of this book also had no word for themselves. Following naming conventions, I have called them the Lujere, a term in their Namia language that means "people."[7] But like Bateson, I too am troubled by the implied hubris such an editorial act implies and by David Napier's (2003: xxi) moral

---

5. Letter written at Oksapmin Patrol Post, West Sepik Province, January 9, 1973.
6. See Edward Dozier's (1956) article, "The Concepts of *Primitives* and *Native* in Anthropology," which explores in historical detail the changing currency of these concepts by anthropologists. The problem with the term "nonliterate," as Dozier (1956: 197) notes, is that it risks confusion with "illiterate."
7. My initial working term to refer to the Lujere was Lu, their term for man/men, which was also indicative of the level of my linguistic sexism in 1971. On a trip to Lumi at Christmas to see my family, Dr. Lyn Wark, an Australian medical missionary and friend, clued me into the fact that "Lu" could be mistaken for "loo," Aussie slang for a toilet. In mid-February 1972, while Yellow River missionary Ces Parish was an overnight visitor at my campsite, we agreed

injunction that in "so many societies naming is a powerful and often dangerous activity." Nevertheless, I took a similar semantic liberty in naming the Lujere's geographic area as "Lujereland." It is not an Indigenous concept nor an administrative one but simply a working construct of the ethnographer that allows me at times to make the occasional generalization regarding its inhabitants who share a language, cultural traditions, and a "safe" territory surrounded by former enemies, some of whom were headhunters and cannibals.

My 1971–1972 fieldwork with the Lujere was conducted in Tok Pisin, one of the official languages of Papua New Guinea, along with Hiri Motu and English.[8] While I collected vocabulary of their Indigenous language Namia, interviewed on Namia terms central to my inquiry, and learned phrases to amuse both them and me, I could not speak the language or follow in detail their verbal exchanges. At best, I knew enough vocabulary to sometimes have an idea what a conversation was about but no idea where it was going. Thus, I have tried not to clutter the narrative with Namia terms but, more often, have used the Tok Pisin term that they used to educate me. At various points in the book, I quote brief conversations with my informants, which I have translated from Tok Pisin. Villagers' discourse in Namia is also occasionally included, but as translated into English via a bystander's Tok Pisin translation.

While I have tried to standardize the spelling of Tok Pisin terms according to Father Mihalic's (1971) dictionary, this could not be done for place names, such as towns, villages, and hamlets, without distorting the historical record. For example, the same village appears on maps as: Worikori, Warukori, Warankori, and Walukali. Strange words pronounced by different villagers and heard differently by different colonialists receive diverse renderings. Most of the variances are in vowels and less frequently in consonants. To minimize confusion and advance understanding, I have at times followed a term with an alternative spelling in parentheses. Villagers' names were often pronounced differently (very differently!) depending on whom I was talking with, especially the vowels. I tried to standardize my spelling of their names in my written and typed field notes but didn't

---

on "Lujere," their term for "people," as an appropriate name for this group when referring to them in ethnographic contexts.

8. Since its inception, Tok Pisin has been controversial. As far back as 1921, Colonel Charles Monckton (1921: vii), a resident magistrate in British New Guinea, characterized the language as a "ridiculous jargon." On the other hand, Richard Thurnwald (1936b: 315), who was using it in the early twentieth century, wrote, "It is amazing to find how much can be expressed with it, when one gets used to it, with the help of intonation and gesture." But in 1931, Malinowski (1963: xxii) wrote disparagingly of "pidgin English," stating that "I never worked through this misleading and unpleasant medium," and in 1932, Reo Fortune (1963: 286) noted, "Pidgin is the legal language, if such it can be called." Fortunately, both Malinowski and Fortune were learning relatively easy Austronesian languages, not a difficult Papuan language of the Sepik area. While still in New Guinea, I took exception to this patronizing attitude in a colleague's article that obviously disparaged Tok Pisin as a language. I wrote a short article, "Use and Abuse of Pidgin" (Mitchell 1971), noting that "it is frequently treated as if it were a kind of broken English slang not really worthy of serious analytical consideration but, instead, a linguistic embarrassment," and cited some egregious examples and how to correct the problem. To my surprise, the article was reported on in Port Moresby's *Post Courier* (September 12, 1971) with the banner, "Research Worker: Attitudes to Pidgin Criticised." I have reread my article and, in the following pages, have tried to heed my youthful advice.

always succeed; I hope I have done better here. Throughout the text Tok Pisin words appear between apostrophes, and Namia words are italicized.

Regarding Namia terms, I followed the Feldpauschs' spelling if the term appeared in their dictionary (B. Feldpausch 2003).[9] However, some Namia terms I collected in Wakau village, especially ritual ones, do not appear in the Namia Dictionary. These words frequently had different pronunciations—the two brothers Nauwen and Oria I saw almost daily often pronounced a term differently—and I have made an arbitrary decision.

Apropos the multitude of New Guinea languages, researchers have frequently identified the same language by different names. Here I have adopted the name used in the comprehensive Ethnologue drawn up by the Summer Institute of Linguistics (Lewis et al. 2015). At first mention of a language, I try to give the Ethnologue name followed in parentheses by others. More detailed comments regarding the research languages are in chapter 8.

In what Bateson (1978: 77) called "the business of making anthropology out of fieldwork," and Diane Losche (2011) called "that remarkable but usually suppressed process by which fieldwork becomes ethnography," I have purposely tried to make this a multivocal ethnography including, whenever I could, the voices of numerous people of diverse status and concern. Thus, the narrative does not move smoothly the way a classic ethnography does when only the writer's summarizing objective voice tells the stories. The upside is that the narrative's sociocultural complexity in time, place, person, and purpose more authentically represents what I saw, heard, and read. Part 1 is mainly historical, while parts 2 and 3 are more ethnographic, and here I have tried to convey an understanding of the Lujere culture from the perspective of Wakau village as these were the people I lived with and knew best.

Unless I indicate otherwise, as in part 1, the temporal frame or "historical present" for my ethnographic findings is during my fieldwork in the early 1970s, the terminal phase of the colonial era just prior to Papua New Guinea's self-government on December 1, 1973, and full independence from Australia on September 16, 1975. At that time just over three thousand Lujere lived in fifteen (by official count) small, scattered villages and even more widely dispersed bush camps for hunting, gathering, gardening, and sago processing (Lanaghan 1971: 25).

I have referred to the men and woman, whether of the village or expatriates, who educated me in the ways of their society as "informants," the term's root signifying they were the ones who "informed" me when I sought understanding and knowledge. It is a term with a long, affirmative history among notable ethnographers publishing in English. I am aware that more recently, some anthropologists believe it too close to "informer," a term used for police collaborators, and have opted instead for "interlocutor"—apparently unaware that this term historically referred in the US to the actor posing questions in blackface minstrel shows, hence making it unacceptable to me.[10]

---

9. This accounts for the difference in spelling of some terms in my earlier Lujere publications before the Feldpausch's published their linguistic accounts of Namia in the 1980s and whose spellings I have adopted here.
10. See Merriam-Webster Collegiate Dictionary, 11th edition, for the entry *interlocutor*:

    1. one who takes part in dialogue or conversation

Introduction

As Andrew Strathern (1972: vii), an anthropologist who did extensive research in Papua New Guinea (PNG), notes, "It is an ethical question whether the anthropologist should identify his subjects directly." Don Kulick (2019: 271), who also worked in PNG, questions the use of pseudonyms, stating, "Whether such disguise always is necessary is debatable." Except in the case of a few notorious sorcerers, I have opted not to use pseudonyms but to use a person's name as I knew them—villagers, missionaries, researchers, and government officials alike. In the years between my fieldwork and the appearance of this book, many have died, including those who were my friends and generously made my research possible in myriad ways. It is to all of them, both the living and dead whose names appear within these pages, that the book is dedicated.

I have purposely placed the term "colonialism" in the subtitle of this book to emphasize that this was the cultural context of my research. Data on that historical context permeates the text from beginning to end, a context that Stocking (1992: 217) astutely observes was "a condition sine qua non of ethnographic fieldwork." Unlike early Melanesian ethnographers, such as Malinowski, who "either suppressed the presence of colonial powers and interests from his account of Trobriand life or represented them as disintegrative of *tradition*" (Asad 1991: 316), I include them as strategic players in my construction of Lujere society and culture. Indeed, it is impossible for me to reflect upon Lujere historiography without acknowledging how German, Japanese, and especially Australian colonialism impacted the Lujere. The latter personally helped shape how I perceived and understood my new Wakau village neighbors.

This book is a reflexive account of my research, whether conducted while living among the Lujere or after having returned to Vermont, emailing colleagues, reading patrol reports years later, or perusing my wide-ranging collection of notes, tape recordings, maps, photographs, films, and other data gathered during fieldwork. Consequently, I tend to be present much of the time in the text. Viveiros de Castro (2014: 39) asks the cogent question, "What do anthropologists owe, conceptually, to the people they study?" Regarding the Lujere, my answer is that I'm professionally obligated to present the actions and ideas of the people as accurately and completely as possible, acknowledging that it is but one individual's interpretation of their history and lifeways. For me, this book must be a reflexive account about the Lujere so there is no mistaking that it is but one American man's view of them in terms of their colonial past and how I understood their way of living and thinking in the early 1970s, a period shortly before independence.

In the preface to his book on the Maring of PNG, Edward LiPuma (2001: xi) cites a conversation he had with his professor and mentor, Roy Rappaport, who sagely advised him that, "The [ethnography] writer stood between two sets of subjects, those he had lived with and those he wrote for, and so he had a responsibility to honor himself and his profession by respecting both." That has been my ardent goal, but I would add another caveat. The more important of the two responsibilities is to the people, the Lujere, who generously and trustingly shared their lives with me and told me their stories.

Part 1 of this book, "The Colonial Invasion," initially surveys the Lujere's earliest colonial contacts via the Germans, who had assumed suzerainty over the northeastern part of

---

2. a man in the middle of the line in a minstrel show who questions the end men and acts as leader

New Guinea in 1884, calling it Kaiser Wilhelmsland. They briefly contacted the Lujere in the late nineteenth and early twentieth centuries but never colonized them. In 1914, the German ethnologist and explorer Richard Thurnwald was the first European who passed through Lujere territory while mapping the Yellow and Sand Rivers but, lacking a common language, his cultural observations were limited to what he saw. During World War I, the Germans were routed from New Guinea, and the Australians assumed control over the Lujere area. However, no government patrols entered a Lujere village until the early 1930s and no census was taken until the mid-1950s. In the early '30s, a few Lujere had returned from work elsewhere as indentured laborers, when they had learned the pidjin language known as Tok Pisin. As a shared medium of communication, this enabled the Australian patrol officers E. D. Robinson and J. K. McCarthy to record the first sociocultural data. Both men later would become New Guinea legends.

In World War II, the Japanese, in turn, routed the Australians from New Guinea's north coast and the Sepik River. Although they did enter Lujere territory via the Sepik to attack an Australian guerrilla post, they never actually visited any Lujere village. During 1943, the Australians had several roving guerrilla groups, the Mosstroops, in the Lujere area for five months, which had a profound technological impact: the Lujere replaced their ancient stone tools with metal ones acquired from the Australians. After the Japanese bombed the guerrillas' supply base in 1943, they quickly departed. The Lujere had no further pervasive foreign contact until after the war, when the returning Australians took control of the eastern half of New Guinea and commenced the first patrolling of Lujere villages in 1956. The coming of the missionaries and artifact-collecting anthropologists quickly followed. In 1971, the Australians' Edwaki Base Camp was established on the Yellow River, which allowed me to settle in the area and begin my study of the Lujere.

Part 2 of this book, "Who are the Lujere?" contains some of my ethnography findings about Lujere society and culture, including their adaptation to Australian colonialism, unusual attitude toward descent, their mode of traditional warfare, languages, subsistence and residence patterns, and kinds of discord among villagers. In this part, I continue to draw upon patrol officers' detailed reports to both deepen and expand the reader's knowledge of Lujere culture and society in the colonial era.

Part 3, "Magic, Murder, and the Lujere Imagination," concerns the imagination manifested by the Lujere in stories the men tell each other, the community curing festivals with ritual masks and horns, and in their beliefs and practices related to 'sanguma,' a type of terrifying ritual magical murder. 'Sanguma' has a wide Oceania distribution, stretching from the Moluccas in Indonesia, east across New Guinea to the Solomon Islands, and south into Australia, which, as already indicated, examined here for the first time. The last chapters explore sickness and the Lujere options for Indigenous treatments, mostly magical, including home remedies, curing festivals, and Indigenous healing practices, plus options introduced by Australia based on Western science and modern medicine. Paradoxically, the Lujere *nakwolu*, who are defamed for secretly murdering their fellow villagers with dreaded 'sanguma,' are also the society's prestigious and sought-after curers or *imoulu*. Predictably, it is via a *nakwolu*'s secret murders that he obtains the power to cure. When referring to these men within the text I eschew the awkward term *nakwolu-imoulu* that correctly denotes their two opposing statuses. More often I use the term *nakwolu*—the term I most frequently heard—unless they are specifically in a curing role as an *imoulu*.[11] A short section also examines the infamous witch hunts of contemporary PNG, where the term 'sanguma' has become a loose synonym for "sorcery." Toward the end, I compare magical versus medical curing within the context of Lujere society and the therapeutic techniques available to them and, finally, summarize my findings regarding 'sanguma.'

As this account of the Lujere is grounded in their years of colonial suzerainty, I have tried to create an understanding of the Lujere at a time of colonial twilight, when their ancestral heritage still resonated strongly within their thoughts and actions, and the future, even if they thought about it, was an unarticulated unknown.

---

11. Although *nakwolu* and *imoulu* are singular Namia terms, as plurals I would need to add a word like *kara*, "plural" or *kelo*, "many"; thus, to avoid cluttering the text with extra exotic terms, I have arbitrarily glossed them as both singular and plural (in the same way that *lu* can mean "man" or "men") and to denote possession add an apocryphal apostrophe "s."

PART ONE

The Colonial Invasion

Colonialism: A policy in which a country rules other nations and develops trade for its own benefit.
Encarta World English Dictionary

History tout court is something that we cannot do without.
Claude Levi-Strauss (1976: 49)

CHAPTER ONE

Germany, the Lujere's Absentee Rulers

It must be remembered that Papuans have no conception of subjection to a territorial power.
German Imperial Government Annual Report, 1902–03

The island of New Guinea—the second largest in the world—is anchored in the South Pacific just ninety-three miles north of Australia's Cape York Peninsula. It is over one thousand miles long from west to east and over four hundred miles wide from north to south. (Feldt 1967: 1). In 1606, the Spanish maritime explorer Luis Vaez Torres first sailed between the two lands and gave the strait his name. He was not, however, the first explorer to definitely have sighted New Guinea. Another Spanish navigator, Alvaro de Saavedra, has that distinction. Alvaro was leading an expedition prepared in Mexico by his cousin, Hernán Cortés when, while attempting in 1528 to return home from the Moluccas, he sailed east along New Guinea's north coast. But it was yet another Spanish navigator, Yñigo Ortíz de Retes who, in 1545, named the island Nueva Guinea.[1]

It took over three hundred years after the Spanish discovered the north coast of New Guinea before the Sepik River itself was first explored.

> It was Dr. Otto Finsch, a German scientist who had been commissioned by the German Neu Guinea Compagnie to locate suitable settlement sites, who found the entrance to the Sepik. It was mid-1885 and on this first occasion he was rowed in a whaleboat 30 miles upstream—to about the present position of Marienberg. (Townsend 1968: 75)

---

1. For a brief discussion of New Guinea's first European discoverers, both at sea and inland with a map of their exploits see Nelson (n.d.); a detailed exposition is provided by Jack-Hinton (1972). For an interesting museum's introduction to Papua New Guinea's prehistory, replete with color photos and maps, see Swadling (1981) and for a detailed scholarly appraisal see Swadling (1990).

Finsch named it the "Kaiserin Augusta Fluss" in honor of the Kaiser's wife and empress.[2]

Earlier, the French explorer, Jules Dumont D'Urville (1790–1842) sailing along New Guinea's north coast, gave it another name on his chart based on observing an inordinate amount of vegetative flotsam obviously emanating from a big river (Feldt 1967: 171): "Landing at Kariru Island, he pointed enquiringly at the debris going by. The natives answered *Sepik*, which is the name they gave to the current which runs past their island." Even in German times, the river's more popular name became "der Sepik" so that by 1916, the German geographer and explorer Dr. Walter Behrmann labeled his 12.5" x 11.5" colored map *DER SEPIK (Kaiserin-Augusta-Flusz) und sein Stromgebiet*, "The Sepik and its Basin."[3] This sprawling geographic area (see map 2) is often referred to as the "Sepik area" but as Margaret Mead (1973: 2), one of its pioneering ethnographers, emphasized, "The Sepik area is a geographically delimited area which does not correspond to any cultural, linguistic or demographic actuality."[4] With the advent of colonialism, what was once an expanse of primal terrain with primordial peoples living their own histories fell into political and economic vassalage under successive colonial regimes—German, Australian, Japanese, and Australian—as two World Wars decided their rulers.

The seven-hundred-mile Sepik River—PNG's second longest but largest river system—originates high in the Thurnwald and Victor Emanuel Ranges near Telefomin. It flows northwest before swerving in and out of the old Dutch border (now the Indonesian Province of Papua), enters the Sepik River Basin—one of Oceania's largest freshwater wetland systems—then continues its serpentine eastward flow to the Bismarck Sea free of bridges, dams, and industry. "Six thousand years ago much of the Basin was a vast saltwater embayment, that, over the next 5000 years gradually infilled to create the contemporary coastline" (Roscoe 2005: 558). The Sepik increases in size as it collects the waters and tropical debris of its many mountain tributaries then terminates in a great estuary on New Guinea's north coast spewing its brown, muddy waters and detritus far into the Bismarck Sea. Here is my favorite, more picturesque description of the middle and lower Sepik River by a former New Guinea patrol officer and leader of the famous World War II New Guinea Coastwatchers, Commander Eric Feldt:

> A coastal range, the Torricellis, runs along the northern side of New Guinea, leaving a wide valley between it and the central massif, a hundred miles to the south. In this lies the Sepik River, draining away the enormous amount of water precipitated in that country of high rainfall.
>
> And that describes the Sepik—a big, dirty drain, half to three-quarters of a mile wide, and thirty to forty feet deep, winding sinuously through a swamp two hundred

---

2. Finsch (Calaby, 1972), whom the northeast coastal town Finschhafen was named for, was one of the few towns not renamed after the Australians took control in World War I.
3. The map was published as a separate document to accompany his book (Behrmann 1917).
4. In spite of her comment, Mead (1978: 69) admits, "I myself have twice in the past attempted to characterize salient features of the region." The first time was in 1938, then thirty-five years later in a paper she prepared for the Ninth International Congress of Anthropological and Ethnological Sciences (Mead 1938: 157–201; Mead 1973). Her third and last attempt was in "The Sepik as a Culture Area: Comment" (Mead 1978), which is more of a critical reflection on the "culture area" concept, originally devised as a way to order museum artifacts

miles long by twenty miles wide. Its mouth is low and flat, passing through islands of black-trunked mangroves with poison green leaves, separated by still lagoons that were riverbeds once. . . .

In March and April, at the end of the north-west monsoon, the river is in constant flood, its marges covered except for slightly raised ridges on which the villages stand, houses built on high stilts so that the worst flood waters will run beneath the floor. In the center of the stream, which runs over three knots, the water hurries along. . . . It bears a procession of trees, branches, dead sugar-cane and other flotsam, all hurrying along in the brown water like traffic in a busy street. Sometimes an island of floating grass which has broken away from its home in a lagoon goes by—thick, green grass, sometimes an acre in area, so matted as to support small trees grown on water, without the aid of land, for nature practiced hydropony before man did.

The waters fall during the south-east monsoon, baring cliffs of mud at the side of the river. Mud banks appear on which crocodiles bask in the sun and on which birds gather in the hundreds. . . . Mosquitoes are in millions, as the swamps provide unlimited breeding grounds. By day they are a nuisance, swarming in the shadows, but by night they are a curse and a menace, deterred by nothing. (Feldt 1967: 171–72)

The Lujere homeland, far upriver, is bisected by the now narrowed Sepik River about three-fourths of the way up from its mouth. While there are a few small Lujere villages on the Sepik's south flank, most of the Lujere people live in the large area off the north bank that is bisected by the Yellow River and its tributary, the Sand River, that converge shortly before entering the Sepik.

The Colonial Cannibalism of New Guinea

The demands of nineteenth-century capitalism for new resources and wider markets resulted in the rapacious colonial expansion of the powerhouse Western nations throughout the world. The islands of the South Pacific were not excepted and became "part of the imperial scramble of the late nineteenth century" (Keenan 2015: 198). As the more obviously lucrative islands of the Pacific were claimed and then politically and economically dominated, New Guinea was coolly bypassed. Its reputation for aggressive inhabitants and lack of any easy commercial potential labeled it as an island pariah. The Dutch were the first to make a move; not that they saw any potential in the island for themselves, but by claiming the western half of New Guinea to the 141° east longitude in 1828, their neighboring commercially valuable "Spice Islands"—the Dutch East Indies—would be protected from encroachment. With no initial intent to colonize their new acquisition, they placed it under the jurisdiction of the Sultan of Tidore, whom they controlled. Asserting his power over some of the coastal villages, he demanded levies, including bird-of-paradise plumes and both male and female slaves.[5]

---

5. However, "In 1905 the legal fiction of Tidore's rule ceased when the Sultanate of Tidore lost its independence and was for the most part incorporated within the Dutch colonial state" (Swadling 1996: 279). For a discussion of the early slave trade in New Guinea see Rowley's (1966: 53–62) chapter on "The Papuan Slave."

As the Netherlands had claimed the western half of New Guinea, in 1884, the Germans annexed the northeastern section of the island and England claimed the southeastern section. The actual process was not as neat as just implied and Langdon (1971) gives a succinct account of the sometimes-awkward maneuvers of the competing colonial powers.[6] An exchange of notes between Germany and England fixed the boundary between their territories in April 1885. The British domain became *British New Guinea*, but negotiations for its transfer to Australia began in 1898, were finalized in 1906, and the territory renamed Papua (Mair 1970: 11).

Germany's New Guinea colony included not only the northeastern portion of New Guinea, named *Kaiser Wilhelmsland* after Emperor Wilhelm I, but also numerous islands to the north including the Bismarck Archipelago named for the Kaiser's powerful chancellor.[7] However, instead of directly administering the colony, the German Imperial government gave the responsibility to the newly formed Neu Guinea Kompagnie, a consortium of Berlin financiers interested in investing in the unexploited island and who had campaigned for the annexation.

The company was granted an Imperial charter by Chancellor Otto von Bismarck in the name of the Emperor in May 1885.[8] However, by 1896, inept administration, the difficult terrain and climate, tropical disease, personnel resignations and deaths, plantation labor problems, natural disasters, and simply bad luck[9] resulted in such large financial losses that the company began negotiations with the Imperial government to rescind

---

6. For a scholarly account complete with cited sources of the complex political partition of New Guinea, see Morrell (1960: 238–62).
7. See map in Buschmann (2009: 7). Germany's main colonial possessions in the Pacific were divided into two administrative units: (1) The "Old Protectorate" included Kaiser Wilhelmsland, the Bismarck Archipelago, Bougainville, Buka, and the Admiralty Islands; and (2) the "Island Territory" included Naru, and the Marshall, Caroline, and Mariana Islands. My discussion here is primarily confined to Kaiser Wilhelmsland. There is an enormous literature on German New Guinea, most of it in German but see Firth (1983), Griffin et al. (1979: 34–35), and Jacobs (1972: 485–48) for historical summaries in English. For a view of Germany's international colonialism, see Conrad (2011). Ian Campbell's book (1989: 1136–48) treats the Pacific islands as a historic whole, and his chapters "Melanesia: Missionaries and Colonists," "The Politics of Annexation," "Priorities in Colonial Policies," and "Colonial Consolidation" are especially helpful in placing New Guinea colonialism within a broader Pacific context.
8. See Moses (1969) for a translation of the charter and analysis of its inception as well as Biskup (1969) who discusses the latter in more detail.
9. The Neu Guinea Kompagnie's Annual Reports (Sack and Clark 1979) record in sober and substantive detail, year by year, the disastrous events and intractable situations that sapped the Kompagnie's financial and physical resources. Souter (1963: 74) takes a journalist's point of view:

    > The Kompagnie was unpopular with its staff, and, worse still, its operations were unprofitable. Its ships were wrecked in uncharted waters, its officers died of malaria and smallpox, and the local natives could not be persuaded to work. Nor did the Chinese coolies who were brought to the colony show much enthusiasm for manual labour; they deserted, and when recaptured and flogged they were inclined to commit suicide. One night six recaptured coolies who were confined on board a hulk in the harbour hanged themselves *en masse* from the taffrail. (Souter 1963: 74)

its charter. Finally, in April 1899, the Neu Guinea Kompagnie accepted compensation from the Imperial government and, in turn, surrendered its rights over the area. The German Imperial government assumed the onerous administrative responsibilities for Kaiser Wilhelmsland, freeing the Neu Guinea Kompagnie to concentrate exclusively on its commercial activities.

During the brief term of the Neu Guinea Kompagnie's control, the interior populations of the Sepik River Basin were scarcely impacted, and the Lujere not at all (Griffin et al. 1979: 44; McCarthy 1963: 140). It was a different story for the people of the coast and nearby islands. Lajos Biro, a Hungarian naturalist and ethnographer who lived and traveled in the German colony from 1896 to 1902 wrote about the German colonial relationship. He is especially vivid in his accounts of the German harshness and their "punitive expeditions" on local life and property after an attack by the local people.[10] As far as the scientific study of the Indigenous people was concerned, this was restricted almost exclusively to the collection of Indigenous artifacts by vigorously competing German museums. Today these artifacts form the basis of their great collections of precolonial New Guinea art.[11]

In 1886, the company's first Administrator, Vice Admiral Baron Von Schleinitz, explored two hundred nautical miles up the Sepik (Sack and Clark 1979: 7). Then in 1887, the Berlin directors of the Neu Guinea Kompagnie, influenced by the German banker Adolph von Hansemann, launched a hugely ambitious expedition to explore the country and collect scientific data. The leader was Dr. Carl Schrader, an astronomer, who was accompanied by a botanist and geographer with an ambitious plan of exploration to gradually open up the whole territory.

> The expedition . . . went up the Sepik beyond the point reached by Von Schleinitz and spent a few months on land near Malu, where the difficult terrain and the hostility of the local people posed insuperable barriers to exploration on foot. Their departure for Europe in 1887 put an end to von Hansemann's grandiose designs. There was no further exploration on the Sepik for twenty years. (Jacobs 1972: 490)[12]

Campbell 1989: 163) further notes that the laborers imported from Asia and elsewhere in Melanesia "were subject to such appalling living and working conditions and such severe punishments that by the time the company period ended, up to half of these imported labourers had died."

10. See Biro's (Vargyas 1986: 72–75) translated account of the brutal attack on little Ali Island just off the coast of Eitape (then Berlinhafen) after a surveying party was attacked with arrows injuring six of the party of ten who, as they escaped, shot and killed ten local men. The ship's crew returned in the afternoon, hacked to pieces the villager's canoes, burned their houses and chopped down their coconut trees. As the villagers fled in the night on makeshift rafts to neighboring Tamara Island, over two hundred were drowned at sea. "When the next morning the punitive expedition marched in there was not a soul on the island, except for a lad dying from a fatal wound."

11. For an enlightening discussion of the impact of Chicago's Field Museum of Natural History on the collection of New Guinea artifacts by Germany's museums see Buschmann (2009); see also Buschmann (2000) for an analysis of the tension between German ethnological museums and artifact-collecting commercial companies.

12. See the Kompagnie's Annual Report (Sack and Clark 1979: 7) for a fuller account of the expedition. The Kompagnie's Administrator, Vice-Admiral Baron von Schleinitz, also returned

In spite of their hasty return home, they did succeed in furthering the ascension of the Sepik to 380 miles and made some valuable scientific collections. Exploring by the Germans, however, was an end in itself, unlike the tradition in British New Guinea where it was accompanied with attempts at pacification and administrative control of the Indigenous population (White 1965: 93; Joyce 1972: 385). Although "a new station had been established at Eitape on the north coast in 1906 and during 1907 the first chiefs were being appointed" (Rowley 1954b: 826), the German Administrator's "Annual Report for 1907–08" states that in the northwest part of Kaiser Wilhelmsland from the mouths of the Ramu and Sepik rivers west to the Dutch border,

> There is no effective control whatever. In particular the powerful tribes in the two river basins of the Ramu and Kaiserin Augusta Rivers are neither open for recruiting nor under missionary influence or accessible to Government agents. It is not known whether or to what degree the inhabitants fight among themselves. (Quoted in Sack and Clark 1979: 277)[13]

In 1909 Chicago's Field Museum of Natural History Curator of Anthropology, Dr. George A. Dorsey, while in German New Guinea was invited to accompany the New Guinea Company's chief administrator, Georg Heine, on an inspection tour seventy-eight miles up the Sepik River in the company's steamer *Siar* (Dawes 1936: 53). Although Dorsey's collecting was constrained by the administrator's schedule, they went far enough up the Sepik for him to make an important early American collection of Sepik artifacts for the museum.[14]

The popularity and striking beauty of the Sepik artifacts engendered rivalry among the world's museums and stimulated any and all who found themselves on the Sepik to collect "curios" easily sold for a nice profit. The Hamburgisches Südsee Expedition was a large and ambitious scientific expedition from the Hamburgisches Museum für Völkerkunde whose director was Professor G. C. Thilenius. Working mostly in the Bismarck Archipelago, in 1909 the expedition finally ascended the Sepik some 262 miles in the Peiho. But the American Dorsey, "According to Thilenius, appears to have been bent on obtaining as many ethnological specimens as possible, for which he paid such high prices that people who came after him could get nothing at a reasonable value" (Dawes 1936: 53). Near the beginning of 1910, the expedition returned to Germany "with a rich

---

to Germany in June of 1887 on his regular leave and was sacked "at the wish of the Board of Directors, because differences of opinion had arisen concerning the management of the Company's affairs and the scale of expenditure" (Sack and Clark 1979: 22). An official from the German Post Office was granted temporary leave by Chancellor Bismarck to replace him.

13. Schindlbeck (1997: 35–36) describes a recruiter on the Sepik in 1910 who failed to attract recruits on his way up the river and then, to compensate for it, collected two thousand artifacts on the return trip to sell.
14. The *Siar's* captain, Heinrich Voogdt, was also collecting artifacts. See Welsch (2000) for the interesting story of Voogdt's collection and how it eventually went to Chicago's Field Museum. For a collection of Melanesian essays on the "ethnography of collecting," see O'Hanlon and Welsch (2000) and Kaufmann, Peltier, and Schindlbeck (2018) for essays focusing on the "materiality" of Sepik societies.

scientific booty, including 6,667 items in its ethnographic collection and 1,700 photographs, together with recordings of languages" (Jacobs 1972: 491). As German collectors and explorers continued to ascend further up the Sepik River, it was only a matter of time until they would reach the Lujere.

Later in 1910, a large government-sponsored German-Dutch expedition ascended the river to establish their common boundary. Professor Leonard Schultze of Jena University (a.k.a. Schultz-Jena) led the German group and reached a point six hundred miles upriver. Going and coming, the noisy motorized boats of these explorers, for the first time, passed the mouth of the Yellow River and transected the Lujere people's homeland on both sides of the Sepik. They obviously saw and interacted with the Lujere living in the vicinity of the mountain they called Mäanderberg on the south bank of the Sepik opposite the Yellow River. Kelm's (1966) book on Sepik art shows several shields collected by Schultz-Jena below the Mäanderberg in Lujere territory. It was a harbinger of the inevitable continued European contact to come.

Richard Thurnwald, Pioneering Ethnographer and Explorer-Surveyor

The most extensive and scientifically significant early twentieth-century explorations on the Sepik River were carried out in 1912 and 1913 by the Kaiserin-Augusta-Fluss Expedition. Sponsored jointly by the Königliches Museum of Berlin and the Deutsche Kolonialgesellschaft, this group of German scientists made a wide-ranging survey of the Sepik River Basin, although publication of their results was hindered by World War I.[15] The geographer Dr. Walter Behrmann photographed and published the first known picture of a Lujere man; he is striding in front of a typical house wearing a penis sheath and carrying a dugout canoe paddle (Behrmann 1917: plate VII).

Besides surveying and mapping the terrain, collecting artifacts, botanical and zoological specimens, and photographing the topography and people contacted, the two ethnographers Drs. Adolph Roesicke and Richard Thurnwald[16] also collected rudimentary ethnographic data necessarily limited by the number of unknown languages they encountered.[17] Thurnwald, who later attained international renown, previously had completed

---

15. Kaufmann (1990: 592–93) describes the expedition's sponsors in some detail and enumerates the names and responsibilities of its members and problems with some of the scientific collections. Also see Behrmann (1917: 3) for his characterization of the expedition's members and a detailed treatise of the geology of the Sepik Basin based on their explorations, and Behrmann (1922) for a popular account. It is unclear the extent of the problems the expedition had with the local people but John Whiting, studying the Kwoma near Ambunti in 1936, writes (1941: 19), "The first contact was in 1913 when the Kwoma killed a police boy connected with the Behrmann expedition, for raping one of their women. A Kwoma was shot in reprisal."
16. For a more detailed account of Thurnwald's Upper Sepik River explorations—from which I have borrowed heavily—see Craig and Winter's (2016) online paper, complete with many maps and Thurnwald's photos.
17. See Melk-Koch (1989: 321–22) for a list of Roesicke's New Guinea publications and Melk-Koch (1989: 326–51), Thurnwald's biographer, for a comprehensive bibliography including his New Guinea publications.

successful research with Melanesians on Bougainville Island.[18] His exploits with the Sepik expedition included three pioneering treks from the lower and middle Sepik River to the north coast through unexplored country with its primeval societies, accompanied only by local men, without mishap.[19] As the first White person to enter the Abelam area and report on their astonishingly high ceremonial houses and lavishly decorated facades, he was prompted to record in his diary, "The area I encountered on this excursion is the most interesting I have ever seen" (Melk-Koch 2000: 63).

At the conclusion of the main expedition, after most of his colleagues returned to their native Germany, Thurnwald remained in New Guinea to continue his research on the Bánaro society on the Keram (Töpfer) River in the Lower Sepik Basin and to explore the upper Sepik Basin. Besides being an experienced ethnographer, Thurnwald was an intrepid explorer with superb mapping and organizational skills, and talented in relating peacefully to uncontacted people. He spent most of 1914 in unexplored areas of the Upper Sepik that included cannibals and warring groups who had never seen a White person, but he had no adverse experiences. He always offered new contacts—even when faced with a drawn bow—trade goods like a coveted white glass ring that was especially effective in making friends.

Beginning in December of 1913, he traveled without government police protection—but with his own-armed men—up the Sepik with his machinist, Feodor Fiebig, the overseer of their motley array of motor-powered boats and dugout canoes that resembled what Thurnwald called "a floating gypsy camp" (quoted in Melk-Koch 1989: 191) (see fig. 1).

Thurnwald, an athletic forty-five—in Europe he skied, played tennis, and bicycled—and his machinist were accompanied by a group of loyal Indigenous men from the lower river, (including several with military-style caps and rifles), and others adept in manning canoes and carrying supplies, in an audacious year of exploring the upper Sepik River and its tributaries. This occurred in two forays. First, from December 1913 through March 1914, Thurnwald explored the Sepik to the international border and ascended the October, August, Green, and Yellow Rivers, mapping and collecting data on the way.[20] In February he and his crew of helpers ascended the Green River, almost to the Dutch border. "In contrast to the dullness of the inhabitants of the Upper Sepik [presumably the Abau speakers] . . . the people on the Green River revealed a greater vivacity, curiosity

---

18. His first trip to German New Guinea was 1906–1909 when he was thirty-seven. See Buschmann (2009: 97–117 passim) for data on his close relationship with the colony's second governor, Albert Hahl who, like Thurnwald, was not only interested in the colony's material culture, but in the natives' mentalities behind its creation. Both disparaged pidgin, believing that knowledge of indigenous languages was the only way to proceed. They both held doctorates in law and Hahl's special concern was to bring native and German views of justice into alignment. Thurnwald, because of the rigors of collecting artifacts including transporting and packing them in primitive conditions and his conflicting relationship with his museum's administrators, at times was antagonistic towards his collecting responsibilities (Melk-Koch 2000).
19. For a map of his treks to the coast, see Melk-Koch (1989:176).
20. See Thurnwald (1914: 341) for his map of the mountains and rivers of the upper Sepik territory.

Figure 1. Richard Thurnwald amid his boats and assistants on the upper Sepik River, January 1914. Courtesy of Marion Melk-Koch.

and interest."[21] He was especially impressed with the women who, instead of hiding or running away, always appeared together with the men. "The women initiate the conversations, carry up the sago, yams and tobacco to exchange for the glass rings, with which they decorate the little children." He describes their sex roles as seemingly reversed from traditional Western ones, prefiguring in an extreme way Margaret Mead's (1935) description of the Tchambuli (Chambri) of the Middle Sepik.[22]

He then momentarily left New Guinea, sailing to Sydney, Australia to rest for several months and to reprovision. Returning from Sydney in July 1914, he established a base camp at Mäander Mountain opposite the mouth of the Yellow River; then, in his most audacious exploring venture, ascended the Sepik to arrive near its source at Telefomin in New Guinea's Central Range on September 19 (Craig and Winter 2016; Melk-Koch 2000: 63). As he laboriously ascended the upper Sepik River mapping and naming its physical attributes en route, he memorialized his accomplishment by placing his name

---

21. Thurnwald quotations are from Barry Craig's research website, "Upper Sepik—Central New Guinea Research Project," with English translations of his two articles that pertain in passing to the Lujere and annotated by Craig, viz., Thurnwald (1914), http://uscngp.com/papers/26, and Thurnwald (1916a), http://uscngp.com/papers/27.
22. In the 1970s, Deborah Gewertz (1983) also studied the Tchambuli or Chambri people and established in her insightful, historically oriented ethnography that the sex roles Mead described were temporary artifacts at a time of great social turmoil.

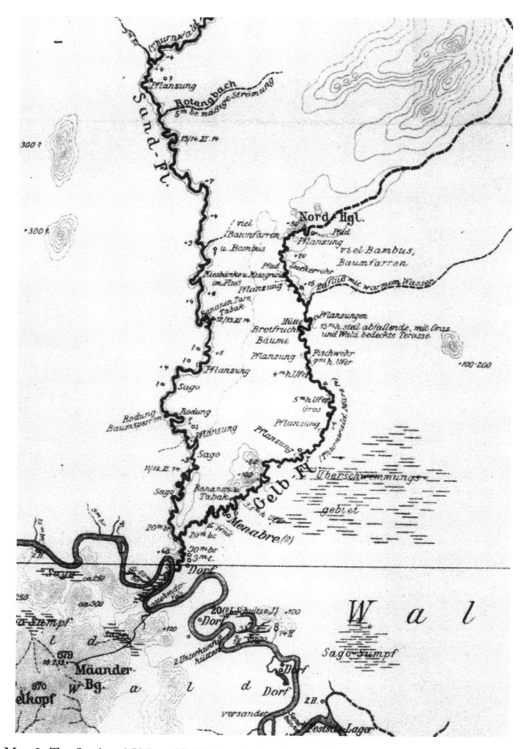

Map 3. The Sand and Yellow (Gelb) river basins during German control. Source: portion of Behrmann's (1924) foldout map, based on Thurnwald's 1914 expedition.

on a last adjoining mountain range, the only anthropologist whose name lays astride maps as well as books. Returning to his Mäanderberg base camp, he then explored up the Sand and North Rivers to the foothills of the Bewani Range. Few, if any, pioneering anthropologists have been as successful as an explorer and in New Guinea he is unique.

Thurnwald Encounters the Lujere, 1914

It was in the Mäanderberg area on the south side of the upper Sepik River opposite the mouth of the Yellow River and on his explorations up the Yellow River in March and the Sand River in November where Thurnwald would have seen and interacted with the Lujere. Thurnwald was the first European to navigate into the Lujere's heartland and to subsequently map and name the two rivers, the Sand and the Yellow (Gelb), that bisect their domain (see map 3). Thurnwald later described in detail how he proceeded in the Upper Sepik region, especially when contacting Native peoples like those on the Yellow and Sand Rivers who had never seen a White person:

> Each time I went up the main river and its tributaries I used the motorboat as far as I could, and from there on used the three canoes I had towed along. These were dugouts about twenty to thirty feet long and one and a half to two feet wide. They could be loaded with ample provisions and offered the advantage of a less conspicuous approach than the noisy motorboat. When the currents, rocks, trees, and other obstacles rendered the river impassable I left the canoes in the custody of one or two boys.[23] Then I climbed up to the crest of the nearest mountain range and proceeded along it for many days finding small hamlets at considerable altitudes.
>
> Unless we had been discovered by some chance meeting on the way, my arrival in the settlements was always a surprise, which made for safety if the natives did not become too much frightened. . . . Conditions were different on the middle and upper reaches of the river. . . . There the people never dreamed of meeting white men and sometimes had not heard a word of their existence. . . . When I appeared in such places, the first reaction was utter confusion and a wild flight not only of the women and children but also of the young men. Only two or three older men would remain to face me. I soon learned that it was best not to walk up to them but to stand still and make signs to them to approach me; sometimes I had to wait for ten or fifteen minutes before they would come.
>
> The same simple method of invitation worked successfully with the various tribes. I lured the men on by showing them beads or glass rings.[24] At our first meeting they

---

23. Colonialists even into the early 1970s usually referred to a native man in German, English, and Tok Pisin, as "boy," (Ger. Junge).
24. Maria Wronska-Friend has written an interesting article detailing the colonial production of these cheap glass and porcelain trade objects noting that,

> Their manufacturers expended much effort in producing close replicas of indigenous objects—usually personal ornaments—destined for customers in regions as diverse as the Middle East, India, Africa, Oceania as well as North America. . . . In Melanesia, the most common items seem to have been ceramic and, at a later stage, also plastic shell rings and discs, of diverse sizes and colours. In addition, replicas of dog teeth, pig

had no use for iron knives or ax blades, which they did not know and even refused to accept. After they had come forward I would give them beads or glass rings and offer some red powder, which I smeared on their forehead and cheeks. They liked this because of its magic association with the whiteman's features [Thurnwald assumes] and consequently his power—I was then sunburnt, and so looked red not "white." Next I showed them my watch and let them hear its ticking, and also used a small mirror to turn the reflected sun's rays on their eyes. These acts conveyed to the old men an impression of my magical power and also signified my good intention. Then the men would shout for the others, who were waiting near-by. The young bloods advanced hesitantly and suspiciously but also full of curiosity. When I gave them some presents too, the tension broke down into general merriment. The old men ordered some of the youths to bring me yams, taros, bananas, or coconuts—whatever was available. These not only added to my scanty store of provisions (rice and beans) and thus enabled me to extend my trips, but taught me the social importance of these customs. . . .In these encounters it was important to keep the people's interest alert, attract their attention to new phenomena, divert their suspicions, and not allow them too much time to talk the situation over. Taking pictures was always a good move. Pulling apart the tripod seemed to be the most impressive part of this proceeding. The camera itself did not attract them. In order to get my pictures, I first requested them to look through the camera at me and one of my boys, and then marked the spot where I had stood and urged them to change places with me, as if it were a game.[25]

I hardly ever met difficulties when I intimated my intention to pass the night at a certain place, although sometimes the people asked me as a foreigner to sleep in the village, while others wanted me to stay outside. The pitching of the tents, the blankets, the cooking utensils, the mosquito net, my washing and eating, and the lighting of the kerosene lamp, caused endless wonder. I felt, indeed, like the elephant in the zoo. When night came, I insisted, for safety, that visitors leave the camp. (Thurnwald 1936b, 319–20).

The Yellow and Sand River Excursions

In an early report in German, Thurnwald writes about his actual explorations up both the Sand and Yellow Rivers but rarely with the ethnographic detail one is yearning for. Even the pages of his diary that I consulted regarding these excursions were not as forthcoming as I would have liked.[26] Commenting on his trip up the Yellow River (see map 3), Thurnwald writes,

---

    tusks, dog whelks [small sea snails] and cowrie shells, as well as nose pins were manufactured. A popular item proved to be white buttons, perhaps because initially they were produced from mother-of-pearl shell. (Wronska-Friend 2015: 50)

The amusing irony is that these colonial imitations sometimes became part of museum collections of authentic indigenous objects.

25. Unfortunately, although Thurnwald took some excellent photos of the tribal groups he encountered, many of these were lost or damaged, especially of the Lujere, as explained later.
26. I am indebted to Barry Craig, as I am for myriad other research courtesies, for providing the relevant sections of Thurnwald's field diary on his Yellow and Sand River explorations.

> This river, with medium current, consists of limy yellow water, therefore I called it the Yellow River. It flows in endless meanders through terraced land crossed by low hills ten to forty meters high and sloping towards the Sepik. If you look northwards from a height near the river, these hills are scarcely noticeable. . . . The journey upstream in the canoes was monotonous. . . . The settlements have quite a different character here. One comes across actual villages with houses built in groups in a defined area. There are particular houses for the men, and the houses are not built in the unskilled manner that I have described above [i.e., societies he visited further up the Sepik]. The buildings, erected on posts one or two metres high, are not particularly artistic but at least they rest upon thick solid supports. The other cultural items are also richer and carved wooden figures and large standing slit gongs are found.[27] The villages do not always lie accessible to the river but are frequently somewhat inland. (Thurnwald 1914: 18–19)

Later patrol officers often forced dispersed peoples like the Lujere to build villages, but now we know from Thurnwald's brief description that, even at initial contact, they had villages with a separate men's house, as well as their dispersed homesteads and camps. Thurnwald saw slit gongs but there were none when the museum artifact collectors came just before I arrived. The Lujere, I was told, had slit gongs in the past that were struck only in celebration of an enemy killed; from Robinson's patrol report (see chapter 2) we know they still had them in the early 1930s. With the advent of the Pax Britannica, the slit gongs, unused and uncared for, apparently succumbed to tropical rot. The Wape, however, still used their slit gongs in the 1970s to send a roaring boom at curing festivals and for signaling in code, especially a villager's death or the approach of a patrol officer.

Thurnwald notes that the "upper village groupings" on the Yellow River spoke a different "dialect." This was probably Maurom village whose Pouye (Bouye) language is distinctly different (not a dialect) but, as part of the Sepik language family, is related to Namia, spoken by the Lujere. The Lujere had no tradition of carving wooden figures, so these were probably seen in Maurom, where in 1971 I saw carvings in their men's house. The following day he started back down the river.

On Thurnwald's return to the mouth of the Yellow River, he recorded little more about the Lujere, only that "the natives were again numerous and brought breadfruit, yams and sago."[28] At one point he was brought smoking tubes and gourds to trade for glass rings, but he did not say what the people looked like and wear. As he was an acute observer, there apparently was nothing unusual—like with the Green River people—that caught his attention except the following:

> I was never seriously attacked, although there were a few disturbing incidents. One of these occurred when we went in the canoe up the Yellow River, a tributary of the western Sepik. Warned by my boy, I noticed a [Lujere] man crouched in the wood with his bow bent and his arrow aimed at me. Putting up my arms, I waved to show that we

---

27. There is no evidence that the Lujere ever carved wooden figures; he is obviously referencing the Bouye speakers who did carve wooden figures, just north of the Lujere, where on his exploring trip up the Yellow River he apparently visited a single village, probably Maurom, and took photos of some of the men in the riverbed.
28. http://uscngp.com/papers/26, p. 19; English translation of Thurnwald (1916a).

had no wish to fight. The man understood, released the bow, and took out the arrow. (Thurnwald 1931: 321)

After exploring and mapping the Yellow River, Thurnwald sailed to Australia in April, as noted, to reprovision his expedition. As an Austrian, he would have been especially sensitive to the news regarding Europe's dangerous political disarray, including the June assassination of Archduke Francis Ferdinand at Sarajevo. Near the end of July 1914, he returned to New Guinea with supplies for two years and established his Mäanderberg base camp in Lujere territory on the south bank of the Sepik opposite the mouth of the Yellow River. Thurnwald resumed his explorations, both logistically and physically more challenging than before, to discover and map the headwaters of the Sepik, and would not have known of Germany's declarations of war on Russia, August 1, and on France, August 3 or, more seriously for him as an enemy alien, that Australia began its occupation of German New Guinea on September 11.

Having returned to his base camp after triumphantly ascending to the origin of the Sepik River, he learned about the war and abandoned a plan to cross the Torricelli Mountains to the coast, concerned that the Australians might take him into custody there and separate him from his hard-won research records and artifacts stored at his Mäanderberg base camp. As an alternative, he decided to continue his explorations in November up the Sand River, the Yellow's western tributary he had first seen and named in March (Berhmann 1917: 54). Once again, he would be traversing Lujere territory and interacting with the people.

On March 11, 1914, Thurnwald left his Mäanderberg camp with his noisy motorboat towing several canoes with probably a dozen or more of his men. Crossing and ascending the Sepik River slightly to enter the mouth of the Yellow River, they soon turned left into the mouth of the smaller Sand River. For the next two weeks, Thurnwald and his crew explored the river. Although it was the beginning of the rainy season, the Sand River soon became worthy of its name.

> In the beginning the water level was high and we proceeded comparatively quietly and easily along the countless windings of the forested banks. . . . Later the water level dropped and our canoes kept running aground on sandbanks. We would punt forward for several hundred metres without a hitch and suddenly jerk to a halt on sand again; we couldn't see the bottom through the muddy water. We went on for days like this. We met only a few [Lujere] natives along the banks.[29]

However, at his first night's camp on the Sand River (marked "11/12 XI 14" with a small triangle on map 3), Thurnwald indicates in his diary that his heart isn't in this trip up the Sand, writing that he is tiring of the hardships of exploring and wants to go home. The next morning he was awakened at 6:00 a.m. by voices calling. At some point, he was visited by a group of unkempt local men who did not appear with their bows and arrows and, from their demeanor, he assumes they must have heard about him from his trip up the Yellow River earlier in March. He further assumes that there are probably a number of villages in the area. Local people brought with them sago, betel nut, and coconuts; in

---

29. See http://uscngp.com/papers/27, p. 26; English translation of Thurnwald (1916a).

trade they wanted big porcelain rings, matches, tobacco, and colored beads. Trading easily ensued and he again mentions their unkemptness. It was ironically serendipitous that the land on which Thurnwald was encamped belonged to the grandfathers or great-grandfathers of the Iwani villagers with whom I lived and who would have been his disheveled visitors. As Thurnwald did not describe his callers beyond their state of grooming; it would have been a boon if he had photographed them as he often was wont to do. But for whatever reason, his tripod and camera lamentably remained unpacked.

Further up the river and out of Lujere territory, when the water became too shallow, Thurnwald and his men left their canoes and proceeded up the river on foot toward the hills. On November 19, at the serious start of the rugged hill country, he decided to end his exploration of the Sand River and encamped for two nights. The next day he climbed a small mountain just to the east of his river camp probably for surveying, named it Schlucht Berg (Gore Mountain) and on the way down learned of a commotion in his camp, but found it resolved by the time he arrived and boxed the ears of one of his men who apparently was at fault. Craig continues the story:

> He stayed a couple of days then turned back downstream where he was met at the place where he had left his canoes (at his camp of 18/19 November [noted on map 3]) by about 20 men with bows and arrows and short spears. The nearest present-day settlements are Pelama on the river about three kilometres north of this camp, and Yakoma five kilometres to the north-east. These people speak Seta, one of the Torricelli Phylum languages that straddle the Torricelli Mountains almost to the north coast. Among these men was one wearing a rattan cuirass and others, fight ornaments, including cassowary feathers, as if they were mammoth tusks, turned upwards in the nostrils. . . . Thurnwald made offers for string net bags, a cuirass and bows and arrows, in exchange for glass beads and rings. (Craig 2016: 55–57)

As Thurnwald was setting up his camera for pictures, some of his men returned to the camp frightening the visitors away. Thurnwald tried to lure them back but his diary is inconclusive.[30] Continuing down the river, Thurnwald and his men once again passed through Lujere territory. As on the ascent, the sandbanks slowed their journey, but this time people often appeared, undoubtedly well aware of these strangers in their midst. Thurnwald notes in his article that,

> Along the middle reaches of the river, large numbers of [Lujere] natives appeared, they provided ample supplies of breadfruit and sago. There seemed to be extensive settlement here. Undoubtedly among these people were some who knew of me from my journey up the Yellow River last year[31] and they treated me with friendliness. (Thurnwald 1961a)[32]

---

30. Craig (2016: 56–60) explains why he believes they returned and offers strong pictorial evidence.
31. "Last year" (*vorjährigen*) is an apparent error that he makes twice in this article. His explorations up the Yellow in March and the Sand in November were both in 1914. However, between the trips he sailed to Australia for respite and to resupply his expedition, which probably accounts for his temporal misperception.
32. http://uscngp.com/papers/27, p. 27; English translation of Thurnwald (1916a).

It is interesting that on this journey he paid more attention in his journal to nature, including animals and birds, than to the people he saw. For example, he has a rather lyrical description of a tall, black, beautiful cassowary with a red and blue neck and a green crown that strolled out of the woods one afternoon then, even more majestically, strolled back into the woods. But at a certain point he was so angered by one of his men that he struck him in the back of his head like "cement," knocking him to the ground. He was personally alarmed that he had done this but later noted, that the next camp was set up and broken down expeditiously.

I was singularly unsuccessful in discovering a single photograph of local people that Thurnwald made of the Lujere during his trips up the Yellow and Sand Rivers or at his Mäanderberg base camp. My colleague Barry Craig believes he has found one, albeit damaged, as he explains:

> There is an image in the Rodoni archives that we believe is Thurnwald's, showing six men and two boys standing on a pebble strand with a river behind. . . . The men are wearing relatively straight gourd phallocrypts, their bows and arrows are quite long and the man third from the left is holding a gourd lime container, all attributes of the material culture of the upper reaches of the Sepik River. They are not Mountain-Ok men who usually wear multiple loops of rattan around their waists and do not have gourd lime containers. . . .
>
> Nowhere since leaving Telefomin did Thurnwald come face-to-face with any local people. On his journey up the Sand River in November, he reports that at the stage where his canoes kept running aground on sandbanks, "we met only a few natives along the banks but on the way back downstream, along the middle reaches of the river, large numbers of natives appeared. . . . There seemed to be extensive settlement here" (Thurnwald 1916: 91). (Craig 2015: 58)

Confirmation that this photograph (fig. 2) was most likely taken on November 25 on the middle Sand River is found in Thurnwald's diary (p. 239) where he remarks: "After I had managed, before we departed the camp, to bring some natives in front of my lens, we went off in our canoes." He would have left it and any other photos he had taken on the Sand River at his Mäanderberg base camp when he left for his North River explorations, which would explain how it could have come into Rodoni's possession.

Again, although Thurnwald saw and interacted with numerous Lujere, he does not describe the people except noting there were a lot of them and that they were friendly. It appears from his diary that he did not leave the river to visit villages that, like on the Yellow, were usually inland. Except for the Lujere on the Sepik River, they generally are not a canoe people. Although Thurnwald's canoes went up and down the Sand River filled with his men and supplies, twice bisecting the Iwani villager's land and even camping overnight on it, fifty-nine years later when I lived with them, they had no cultural memory of such an auspicious event. Thurnwald's meager comments regarding the people indicate that the lack of a "wow" response was apparently mutual. It is probable that the Lujere he had the most interaction with were men from the hamlets on the Sepik's south bank, who would have visited his Mäanderberg base camp eager to trade.

Unlike the Abelam villagers' remarkable architecture he so admired, the Lujere's was modestly plain and, in contrast to the Green River people, the Lujere had no surprising

Figure 2. Richard Thurnwald's photo of Lujere men and boys on the Sand River, November 1914. Courtesy of Rodoni Archive, University of Newcastle, Australia.

sex role reversal to attract his attention. But there was one obvious feature of Lujere society that was impossible to ignore. While the Lujere, like many men of the upper Sepik Basin societies, sported an erect gourd phallocrypt as their startling primary attire, Thurnwald apparently viewed it as a ubiquitous regimental costume unworthy of comment. Unfortunately, if Thurnwald wrote more about the people living along the Yellow and Sand River than he recorded in his diary or published in his 1914 article, we will never know because much of his packed and stored research material was either maliciously destroyed, stolen, deteriorated, or lost in a sad saga of international administrative mischief and farce.

His next exploit—which turns out to be his last—was to explore in December the North River situated in the sprawling wet grasslands halfway between the Sand and Green Rivers. In the middle reaches of the North River, he entered the Yagroner Hills and found villages with houses similar to those of the Lujere but unlike the Lujere, the men wore cuirasses covering their hips, chest, and back. On Christmas Day, the river now too shallow, they pulled their canoes on shore and continued on foot in the riverbed to the territory of the Fas speakers in the Bewani Range. Everywhere the people were friendly and trading was easy.

By now the war in Europe was raging on three fronts, but on Christmas Day many British and German soldiers on the Western Front famously ventured into no-man's-land to spontaneously exchange greetings and gifts. It was an act of human nobility their commanders forbade repeating. On New Year's Day, 1915, the Germans torpedoed and sank the British battleship HMS *Formidable* in the English Channel, while in New Guinea, a heavy rain fell on Thurnwald and his men causing them to turn back before the river became too high to walk to their downriver, beached canoes. Once in their canoes, they continued down the river to a food depot they had stashed on the way up, only to find that it had vanished, a potent omen of a disaster yet to come.

The Trashing of Thurnwald's Camp

Australia, entering the war as Britain's ally, sent a military force, the Australian Naval and Military Expeditionary Force (AN&MEF) to New Guinea.[33] It quickly assumed power over the German colony and its capital of Rabaul on Neu Pommern (later New Britain).[34] In similar actions, New Zealand took possession of German Samoa and Japan seized Germany's Micronesian colonies. A contingent of the AN&MEF was sent up the Sepik to find and take the German research scientist and his German engineer assistant into custody. With bitter irony Thurnwald (1916a: 93) describes their "Krieg gegen meine Expedition" [their war against my expedition].

While Thurnwald was exploring up the North River, Commander Claude L. Cumberlege and his military patrol arrived on December 23 aboard the HMAS Nusa to the Mäander Mountain Base Camp (Townsend 1968: 238). Cumberlege writes approvingly about his trip up the Sepik to Thurnwald's base camp:

> Our voyage continued mile after mile through gorgeous forest and mountain scenery, until just before dusk one evening we descried a white boat some three miles ahead, secured to the bank. . . . We found here the Engineer of the Expedition and about 30 or 40 boys. A large village had been built, the forest cleared on the mountain side, and gardens planted. The professor, however, was further up the river in canoes, with the remainder of the police some 25 or 30 natives. (Craig and Winter 2016: 21)

Cumberlege left the following day to return to the coast with Thurnwald's engineer, Feodor Fiebig, and his personal property in custody. Major Martin stayed to continue to hunt for Thurnwald but after a week of no success, according to his own account (Craig 1997: 391), Martin and his men "loaded all the stores on the launch and two large flat-bottomed river boats which were there" and returned to Angoram. When Thurnwald

---

33. Much of this section is based on Barry Craig's (1997) exhaustive archival research tracing the byzantine fate of Thurnwald's research collections confiscated by the Australian military authorities in 1914 as well as Marion Melk-Koch's (1989, 2000) biographical writings on his career. Both were generous with their time in answering my questions for which I am grateful.
34. Australia, which had administered British New Guinea since 1906, renamed it Papua, thus solidifying control over the eastern half of the island. However, authority over the German section remained provisional until 1920, when the final treaty with Germany was signed and ratified. For an excellent early account of the Australian military occupation including the expropriation of German properties and the Mandate system, see *Official Handbook of the Territory of New Guinea* 1936: 59–76.

arrived back at his base camp on January 7, 1915, it was deserted and all of his boats, supplies, photos, equipment, and collections were gone.

It was Martin, according to Thurnwald, who raided his food depot on the North River. With undisguised sarcasm he adds,

> This action at any rate showed "military acuteness and boldness." His intention was to cause me to disappear into the stomachs of the natives! A heroic undertaking! Well, the natives had provided for me better than that and thanks to the provisions they offered me, I arrived safely at the main camp at Mäander Mountain.
>
> Here another surprise was in store for me . . . [the troops] had succeeded in storming my camp; everything not considered worthwhile removing was chopped into small pieces. Thus I found myself robbed of my pinnace and boats and deprived of gifts of barter and provisions. I had no choice now but to set out on my return journey down the Sepik by canoe. By mid-January, 1915, I arrived at the mission at Marienberg and learned there that my base camp at Katadjundo had suffered the same fate. . . that it had been plundered and robbed by the Anglo-Australian troops. (Craig and Winter 2016: 30).[35]

Thurnwald, with his camp trashed and robbed of his research collections, supplies, and boats and his own house on the hill pillaged and searched, was compelled to start down "the river on canoes with only a small quantity of beans left for me" (Craig and Winter 2016: 63).[36] His diary shows that his food plight was not as dire as his article indicated. He still had twelve canoes made by local people, so these were lashed together in two groups, and he and his twenty-nine men "set off adrift down the River on 8 January with beans and rice enough for 76 days. He arrived at Angoram on the 17th and at Marienberg the next day" (Craig and Winter 2016: 63).

Later, his machinist Fiebig told him that the soldiers broke into the store at night opening cases with axes and took seven or eight of them.[37] The next day they opened the store's door, searched the remaining cases, "taking away whatever they found: provisions, ethnological collections, skulls, knives and axes for trading, clothing, shoes, medicaments, etc." (Craig and Winter 2016: 63).[38]

On reaching Angoram, Thurnwald visited the British Police Station and was advised to stay at the Marienberg Catholic Mission. There he learned that after the soldiers had trashed his base camp on the lower Sepik River, local people had taken what was left but, with the intervention of the police, some items were returned to him. By early March,

---

35. http://uscngp.com/papers/27, p.30; English translation of Thurnwald (1916a).
36. For more details on the trashing of Thurnwald's camps, see Craig (1997).
37. Fiebig's fate was a sad one. He left the Sepik in 1919, unsuccessfully prospected for gold in Dutch New Guinea, and in December of 1923, committed suicide (Craig 1997: 399).
38. Thomas James Rodoni was a member of Cumberlege's force and took numerous photographs. His son donated his father's photographs to the University of Newcastle Cultural Collections and Barry Craig, with the help of Christine Winter (Craig and Winter 2016) translating portions of Thurnwald's field diary, has done some masterly sleuthing identifying a number of Thurnwald's photos within the Rodoni photo archive. How they got there is unknown, but one can surmise that as Rodoni was there when the base camp was trashed, he must have obtained them then.

Thurnwald was in Madang and had an audience with the Administrator, Colonel Petherbridge, who was visiting there. The Administrator was sympathetic with Thurnwald's plight and wrote to the Minister of State for Defense, dated March 9, 1915,

> Dr Thurnwald was in great distress when I saw him and was literally in rags and almost bootless. I instructed the District Officer at Madang to attend to his immediate wants, and procure for him a passage to Sydney by the next steamer. (Craig 1997: 392)

Thurnwald did not sail to Sydney just then but did before the year was out. Instead he appealed to the Madang District Officer, Captain W. M. Balfour Ogilvy, for permission to continue his ethnographic studies; this was granted with the caveat that he reside at the Marienberg Catholic Mission. Ogilvy, in advising his superior in Rabaul of his decision, noted that, "Dr. Thurnwald was not anxious to return to civilization and I am of the opinion that he is a perfectly genuine gentleman, wrapt up in scientific research work" (Craig and Winter 2016: 392).

Thurnwald attempted to collect for the damages inflicted on his property but was unsuccessful, although the Administrator allowed him £25 as rental for his pinnace. He returned to Marienberg near Angoram to work with two Keram River informants on his Bánaro ethnography.[39] In the meantime, Thurnwald's ethnographic collections that Major Martin had appropriated were stored in a Madang waterfront shed. Thurnwald finally left New Guinea, first sailing to Sydney, Australia, then on to San Francisco where he had friends at the University of California in Berkeley.

> Only 40 small boxes with field notes, phonographic recordings, equipment and some artifacts were in his luggage when he was eventually able to leave New Guinea in December 1915; 52 boxes with collections had to be left behind. (Melk-Koch 2000: 63)

At the University of California, according to the anthropologist and Columbia University professor Robert Lowie, a friend and fellow Viennese, Thurnwald had a pleasant stay after years of strenuous exploring, collecting, and fieldwork in New Guinea.[40]

> For a year and a half he lingered in Berkeley, hobnobbing with [anthropology professors] Kroeber and Gifford, indulging his athletic urges on the Faculty Club's tennis court, and preparing a treatise on the Bánaro. (Lowie 1954: 863)[41]

---

39. The Australian authorities were inconsistent in their expulsion of Germanic nationals allowing many planters and missionaries to remain. Malinowski, a Polish national, working in the Trobriands stayed to collect his data as a participant observer in village life changing the way anthropologists do field work.
40. In Thurnwald's obituary, Lowie (1954: 863) writes, revealing as much about himself as Thurnwald, that as a student at the University of Vienna, Thurnwald "displayed marked individuality in taking up bicycling and skiing. Even more aberrant was his advocacy of total abstinence [of alcohol], to which he adhered throughout his life."
41. Both Marion Melk-Koch (2010), Thurnwald's biographer, and Bernard Juillerat (2000), who worked in the upper Sepik area near the international border with the Yafar, have written critically interesting commentaries on his Bánaro fieldwork.

Thurnwald's (1916b) Bánaro monograph was the first in a cascade of ethnographic studies of Sepik River Basin societies of which this is, but yet, another.[42] In 1917, the United States joined the Allies in their war and Thurnwald, once again an enemy alien, was forced to move, this time back to Germany. But there was more bad luck; parts of his field notes were lost between Berkeley and New York (Melk-Koch 2000: 64). As his biographer noted, "Lack of his notes is the reason why Thurnwald never gave more information on the tribes" (email, M. Melk-Koch to W. Mitchell, August 28, 2014). So it was not an ethnographer who wrote the first cultural report on the Lujere but, as recounted in the next chapter, an Australian patrol officer. Nor did any of Thurnwald's Lujere artifacts, with perhaps two exceptions, ever reached a museum.[43]

---

42. Thurnwald (1921) later published in German a more extensive Bánaro monograph. German New Guinea's first ethnographer, however, was the twenty-five-year-old Russian scientist and explorer, Nicolai Miklouho-Maclay who initiated the first ethnographic fieldwork in 1871 on the north coast in the Astrolabe Bay area just over 100 miles east of the mouth of the Sepik River. See Mikloucho-Maclay (1975) for the translated diaries of his three visits to the Maclay Coast (now called Rai coast on most maps), and Webster (1984) for a detailed biography of his adventuresome life. An earlier and less detailed biography is by F. Greenop (1944).
43. Craig makes a convincing case on circumstantial evidence that Thurnwald collected a Lujere shield and hand drum now found in the Museum Victoria (Craig, Vanderwal, and Winter 2015: 135–39). For the tragic account of the fate of Thurnwald's Sepik collections, see Craig (1997).

CHAPTER TWO

Australia, the Lujere's New Rulers

This combination of judicial, administrative and police authority in one office is typical of government . . . in primitive areas.
C. D. Rowley (1958: 24)

German exploration of the Sepik River Basin had established that there was no easy opportunity for commercialism; consequently, the authorities designated it an uncontrolled area and then simply ignored it. Most of the commercial activity was on the islands of the Bismarck Archipelago or along the coast of Kaiser Wilhelmsland where the German settlers' plantations needed large numbers of laborers. These men, mostly from the Archipelago's islands or the Dutch East Indies, were usually indentured workers on a three-year contract. Laborers from the German held areas returned to their villages with knowledge of the trade language Melanesian Pidgin and the ways, often oppressive, of their White colonial masters. Flogging, with little administrative oversight, was a right given to any person who held the laborer's work contract.[1]

From Australian Occupation to the League of Nations Mandate

Australia governed German New Guinea from 1914 until 1920 as an occupational force with a military regime, the AN&MEF mentioned previously.[2] With the exception of

---

1. In 1915, Australia's military regime forbade flogging by employers, but they were allowed to impose fines and imprisonment for infractions. The courts, however, could order flogging until 1919, and hanging by the wrists was not forbidden until 1922 (White 1965: 96).
2. Rowley (1975b) discusses in interesting detail the transition from German supremacy to that of the AN&MEF. For a single volume that treats all dimensions of Australia's involvement with New Guinea, see Mair (1970).

recruiting laborers from up the great rivers like the Sepik and Markam, the Australian occupation had little impact on Indigenous life. In terms of government patrolling in the hinterlands, "There was no coherent policy of expansion: the government was far less known away from the immediate vicinity of the district office than in German times. The result was to leave the actual control of some important areas to enemy aliens" (Rowley 1958: 39).[3]

Although Richard Thurnwald was repatriated, some German planters and missionaries were allowed to stay in place to carry on their work and the Upper Sepik, where the Lujere lived, retained its "uncontrolled" status and remained closed to recruiters and prospectors. Even before the Sepik River's only police post at Marienberg on its lower reaches was attacked by villagers and closed in 1915—later to be reopened as just indicated—it was as irrelevant to their lives as was the closer and larger government station in coastal Eitape. Eitape was established as a German station in 1906 amid Indigenous peoples described as "completely uncivilized" and "extremely warlike."[4] It was taken over by the AN&MEF and was the only station on New Guinea's north coast between the mouth of the Sepik and the Dutch border, one hundred miles to the west. But the Lujere were separated from Eitape by a coastal mountain ridge, the Torricellis, and unexplored hostile territory that isolated them from any governmental intervention. Later, Eitape, renamed Aitape, became an important player in the Lujere's colonial history.

With World War I over and Kaiser Wilhelm II's German Reich defeated, the 1919 Treaty of Versailles stripped Germany of her colonial possessions. In December 1920 the British government, on behalf of Australia, assumed a mandate from the League of Nations to govern the former Kaiser Wilhelmsland and its associated islands.[5] Its new name was the Mandated Territory of New Guinea.[6] Wasting no time, in 1921 Australia began deporting most of the German settlers and planters they had initially allowed to

---

3. The occupiers, however, were not completely idle. In response to reports of native unrest on the Sepik River including a massacre of several hundred villagers, the Australians sent a peacemaking patrol up the river from February 3 to March 7, 1919, in a show of force to discourage fighting. It established an outpost at Marienberg on the lower Sepik consisting of "one soldier and four native police"; a planned patrol from the river to the coast was abandoned because of illnesses. The patrol's 560-ton SS *Sumatra* went 270 miles upriver to Jambon, one of the villages involved in a massacre, before turning back. The officer forwarding the reports to the Department of Defense in Australia comments proudly that offenders and guilty villages were punished but "without the loss of a drop of native blood, or the bodily injury of a single tribesman." From these reports ("Pacific Islands - Sepik River Expedition, 1919"), it is obvious no one knew that Thurnwald (1914) had explored the Sepik to its headwaters and published his results in German.
4. To establish the station, "It was necessary to clear a large site, on which work has now commenced on the construction of the permanent station buildings (quarters for the district officer, the police sergeant and the medical orderly, storehouse, barracks for the coloured [Native police] troop and a hospital)" (Sack and Clark 1979: 270).
5. The League of Nations gave another mandate to Japan to administer Germany's "Island Territory," essentially the islands of Micronesia.
6. As Errington and Gewertz (1995: 18) note, "Technically, no part of what became Papua New Guinea was a colony of Australia. However, practically speaking, Australia administered it as a colony."

stay who then suffered great economic losses when they were paid in devalued German Marks for their expropriated holdings.[7] Meanwhile, the Lujere were just as unaware that they and their lands were now under the hegemonic authority of the Australians as they were, thirty-eight years earlier, when the Kaiser assumed his rights over them. But this would soon change. Just as the Germans were wary to enter the country's hinterlands with police patrols to subjugate the people in the uncontrolled areas, it became a major objective of the Australians to establish the Pax Britannica throughout the Territory[8]. With the Bismarck Archipelago islands and the coastal areas of New Guinea already deeply influenced by the government, commerce, and the missions, the uncontacted inhabitants of the Territory's interior, often naked and wielding stone bladed axes, were the new focus of intervention.[9]

Constructing a Colonial System of Administration

A favorite method of colonial powers to establish control over a subjected people was by "indirect rule." This was a governance system intended "to allow the native to retain all of his traditional folkways which did not go contrary to the broad principles of nineteenth-century European morality" (Reed 1943: 138). This assumed there would be chiefs or other acknowledged cultural leaders with whom they could communicate. But many of the New Guinea societies the Germans had to contend with were egalitarian, with no obvious ranking leader to whom they could give orders or convey expectations. To facilitate their interactions with villagers they invented the 'luluai' and 'tutul' system; the former was appointed the village's leader, and the second originally as an interpreter.[10] Each was given a distinct cap to wear when in the presence of officials and it was one of the organizational programs retained by the Australians. With the ascendency of Tok Pisin during the Australian regime, the need for an interpreter became less important and the 'tutul' became more an assistant or deputy to the 'lululai.'

---

7. See Rowley (1958) for a detailed account of the years of Australian occupation. For his account of "Expropriation and Expulsion of the Germans," see pp. 317–25.
8. For the Germans, "The district officer's job was to make his district safe and profitable for Europeans." (Green et al. 1979: 40.)
9. This does not mean there were no labor recruiters entering this territory with armed assistants, some who were notorious for using aggressive tactics to force village men to sign on (Scaglion 1990, passim).
10. Biskup (1969), in an article on the genesis of German native administration in New Guinea, discusses the historical origins for the appointment of 'lululais' and the innovative role of the Administrator, Albert Hahl, whom Campbell (1989: 164) notes "was a liberal humanitarian, but he was still a servant of colonialism." Also see Buschmann (2009: 109) who emphasizes that Hahl invented the roles of 'luluai' and 'tutul' as a form of indirect rule by placing alleged indigenous elites in those positions. While that might have succeeded in chiefly societies or those with a 'bikman' tradition, it was less successful in the egalitarian West Sepik. See Rowley (1954) for a detailed historical discussion of the place and problems of German native officials, and Vargyas (1986) for a revealing portrait of the German colonial culture by Lajos Biró, a Hungarian naturalist and ethnographer who lived there from 1896 through 1902.

The executive advantage of the 'lululai' system was that it designated specific village individuals to whom directives could be given by administration field officers, usually the patrol officer or 'kiap' in Tok Pisin, who could then hold them accountable for their successful instigation. Unlike the ballyhooed doctrine of indirect rule by African colonial apologists, Mair (1970: 66) observes, "Indeed, if the equally ambiguous label *direct rule* is applicable anywhere, it is so in New Guinea. . . . The theoretical basis of the system was the idea that natives should do as they were told; and . . . to explain to the people that the orders given them were for their good." Regarding indirect rule, "At best, it was promoted as a seemingly convenient way to rule a large empire cheaply with only a handful of British administrators at the top" (Beidelman 2012: 2). The New Guinea irony is that in Australia's indirect rule, instead of a single designated rajah, emir, or chief, with thousands of subjects, each egalitarian village was its own "fiefdom," hence the administration had to appoint thousands of 'luluais' and 'tutuls.' But the direct power of the state remained firmly in the hands of the 'kiaps' "who led patrols of native police and acted as policemen, magistrates, government agents and gaolers" (Barnett 1972: 617).

The administration's "Native Regulations" were legion, covering all aspects of local life, and it was the responsibility of the 'kiap' to cite and punish violations. It was a fascist system of compulsion, since at no level were villagers involved in the construction or review of the regulations. As a colonial form of in loco parentis, the colonial state intruded with its assumed civilizing regulations to act in the best interest of those it considered "primitive." It can also be phrased as "enforced cultural change." Whatever it is called, it was of singular importance in the construction of the colonial culture in which my fieldwork was embedded.[11]

Beginning in the 1950s, the 'luluai' system was gradually replaced by democratically elected local government councils but not in the Yellow River area. In more recently contacted societies and remote areas like the Upper Sepik, it remained operative when I lived with the Lujere.[12] While each village had its own 'luluai' and 'tutul,' their authority was mostly manifest only in the presence of the powerful visiting patrol office; at other times for most purposes, they were just ordinary villagers.

The Trade in Bird-of-Paradise Plumes

Years before the Australian patrol officers penetrated the Sepik River Basin's backcountry, hunters from the islands of present Indonesia were making regular visits. These Muslim men, "Malays," were perhaps the first foreigners to enter the Lujere's homeland. Their quarry was the gorgeous plumage of the birds-of-paradise, the world's most extravagantly feathered birds, found only in New Guinea, the Moluccas, and the east coast of Australia. Most of its forty-one species are found in New Guinea's forests. An important

---

11. For a recent collection of articles that moves the discussion of White supremacy far beyond colonialism, see the "Special Section: Anthropology of White Supremacy" in the recent issue of *American Anthropologist* (2020: 65–162).
12. See Mair and Grosart (1972) for a detailed account of the development and history of introduced local government in Papua New Guinea and (Griffin et al 1979: 201–4) for some of its inherent problems.

luxury item of trade in the Far East, as early as the eighth century in Indonesia the Maharaja of Srivijaya presented bird-of-paradise plumes as tribute to the Chinese Emperor (Swadling 1996: 59).[13]

During German times, some administrative employees and settlers supplemented their incomes by hunting the birds in the coastal forests but more frequently hired local men to do the job. As the Government of German New Guinea's "Annual Report for 1911–12" notes:

> Hunting for birds-of-paradise has grown in importance. High prices and almost effortless profits have acted as powerful inducements to engage in this occupation, which became associated with a whole series of unfortunate features, reminiscent of a kind of *gold fever* on a small scale. On the other hand a number of small planters established their plantation ventures on the basis of hunting for birds-of-paradise. The actual hunting is usually done by coloured hunters in the employ of Europeans. In framing regulations to control hunting operations, the Government has endeavoured to take these various factors into account. A number of restrictions have been introduced. (Sack and Clark 1979: 346)

Apparently, the "restrictions" imposed were not sufficient. The alarmed officials noted in their report for the following year (Sack and Clark 1979: 366), "More stringent conditions have been imposed on this type of hunting, for the protection of the birds. The closed season has been extended from 1 November to 14 May, and three large reserves established, so that the preservation of all species appears guaranteed." What alarmed the officials was that Kaiser Wilhelmsland's major economic export in 1910–1911, was the plumes of 5,706 birds-of-paradise worth 171,000 marks. This amounted to 2,438 more birds than the previous year (Sack and Clark 1979: 346–47). Then in 1912–1913, the number rose to 9,800 birds killed and exported. But it wasn't only birds-of-paradise that were being killed; the hunters were too. Rowley (1954b: 826) notes, "The station at Eitape was busy with police reprisals for the murder of bird-of-paradise hunters."

Although the trade in bird-of-paradise plumes was centuries old, the impetus for this great increase in the demand for exotic feathers was European women's fashion.[14] For generations the hats and helmets of some European men of rank were bedecked with plumes, but it was the Queen of France, Marie Antoinette, who initiated the fashion craze for women to decorate themselves, especially their heads, with plumes (Swadling

---

13. When trade skins of the birds-of-paradise first reached Europe in the sixteenth century, they were without wings or legs prompting Carl Linnaeus, perhaps tongue in cheek, in 1758, to classify the Greater Bird-of-Paradise as *Paradisaea apoda*. It was initially assumed by many Europeans, since none had seen any live specimens, that the birds lived in the air, always turning towards the sun and never landing on earth until they died, for they had neither feet nor wings. These scholarly speculations caught the imagination of the general public. As a result, birds-of-paradise were painted by artists, sung about by poets and became the topic of edifying contemplation by theologians (Swadling 1996: 64).
14. See Pamala Swadling's masterly book (1996) with its numerous excellent maps and photographs that historically documents and discusses the bird-of-paradise trade, with special attention to New Guinea. For a well-documented general discussion of "Malays" in New Guinea, see Philsooph (1990).

1996: 83). The fashion spread gradually among the aristocracy of Europe and England, then to America and, finally, to any woman, regardless of rank, who could afford the luxury of a hat decorated with glamorous plumes.[15] And always, in an array of extravagant plumage that included egrets, ostriches, Victoria crowned pigeons, sea birds and even owls, the bird-of-paradise plumes were the most highly regarded and expensive.

The Malay bird-of-paradise hunters entering the Lujere's land came from Hollandia, the small Dutch settlement just across the border from Kaiser Wilhelmsland and the tradition continued after Australia assumed control in 1914.[16] From the 1890s until 1931, when trading in birds-of-paradise became illegal in Hollandia, its main business was exporting plumes from these birds; several Chinese stores facilitated in their export even after it was forbidden. Jock Marshall, a young Australian zoologist who spent 1936 wandering in the Sepik District behind Aitape, also visited Hollandia. He wrote:

> On sunny days long trestle-tables were slung outside the Chinese stores, laden with thousands of pounds' worth of plumes airing in the sun. Most of the feathers were the glorious sunset plumes of Paradisea minor, but there were also those of the exquisite little "King-bird," the famous blue-bird and other rare and less-known beauties. . . White Men all over the island were engaged in the trade: everybody, government officials, mission priests, planters and plain drifters, all dabbled in feathers and made easy money. Malay shooters from the Dutch side crossed the border and went far into alien territories, making friends with the natives, trading in beads and cloth and steel in return for feathers. (Marshall 1938: 198)[17]

Evelyn Cheesman, an intrepid Englishwoman and entomologist met Marshall in Hollandia and also wrote about the colonial town and the Malay hunters. Miss Cheesman was one of the most remarkable personages of this pre–World War II assortment of bold explorer-scientists.[18] In 1940 she was again in Hollandia. Having just walked forty

---

15. In my Kansas childhood I recall in my mother's wardrobe trunk of cherished sartorial items was a hat enfolded by the striking feathered beauty of a local pheasant.
16. The Malay bird hunters went even as far east as Yilui. Ward Oakley (1932: 5) on a patrol through uncontrolled territory reports that prior to 1921, Malays lived in the area for months shooting birds-of-paradise, hence recognized the power of firearms his police carried.
17. Marshall's (1938) book is the best one by a civilian on the early colonial West Sepik District. As a zoologist and acute observer of both the resident colonialists and indigenous people, he presents a vivid picture of the time and place.
18. Born in Kent in 1881, her ambition of being a veterinary surgeon was squelched when the Royal Veterinary College rejected her because she was female. By happenchance she became Keeper of the Insect House of London's Regent's Park Zoo, studied entomology for two years at Imperial College and launched an adventurer's career with eight remarkable solo expeditions to the South Pacific between 1924 and 1952, collecting over 700,000 natural history specimens mostly for the Natural History Museum including not only insects but reptiles, amphibians, and plants, many named in her honor as the discoverer. She wrote prolifically about her expeditions in an engaging, immediate style with an acute eye for important detail, including the geography and the local people she encountered. She knew how to explore, survive, and prosper under rugged circumstances and could write truthfully (Cheesman 1941: 183) after one adventure that the Native people "evidently ranked me as a true bushman." She

rugged miles from Hollandia to the Mandated Territory's first (then unstaffed) government station in Vanimo established to thwart the smuggling of bird-of-paradise feathers, she ventured inland on the plain toward the Bewani Mountains where she had promised the trustees of the South Australian Museum in Adelaide that she would collect insects for them. She worked from Krissa village where she met an old man and asked him if Malay traders ever came there.

> He was delighted to talk about the traders who came no more, only his generation remembers them. They were trading of course in paradise birds. One man came every year and stopped for a month at a time, while the villagers hunted birds for him, and he paid in beads, knives, cloth, cowrie shells, and tobacco—things that would cost a few shillings. I learnt that this was a regular trade route leading inland, and this same trader went beyond the Bewani Mountains. I asked whether the villagers like the traders. The old man beamed, there was no doubt about his feelings: "Abidi wai-ail" (traders good) he repeated several times. The old trading road crossed the [coastal] plain to the Bewani Mountains and beyond them to country inhabited by the Bendi tribe, a race of small natives [perhaps the people that Gell (1975) studied] of whom not much information is available. (Cheesman 1941: 184–185)

This undoubtedly was one of the main routes the Malay hunters took to reach the Lujere and beyond.

G. W. L. Townsend was a young patrol officer in Aitape immediately after World War I military rule was returned to civil administration. After recounting a story where he "unwittingly took part in the last large shipment of contraband bird-of-paradise skins from New Guinea to Hollandia" he adds,

> For several years after this our patrols in the hinterland of Vanimo crossed the tracks of Malay shooters from over the border and on two occasions Malays who were armed with bird guns were arrested. The guns they used were long-barreled, muzzle-loaders stamped on the stock with the Dutch Crown. They were the property of the Dutch Government, and were leased to a shooter for a fee of five guilders for the season. (Townsend 1968: 66)

As Marshall noted, the hunters entering the upper Sepik Basin spoke Malay, the precursor of Indonesia's official language, Bahasa Indonesia. A few Lujere men, as we will see, knew enough Malay from contact with the foreign hunters that they could communicate with the first Australian patrols that contacted them. But the hunters ventured far beyond the Lujere toward the east in the spreading wetlands, where the anthropologist Gilbert Lewis, on a patrol into the area, met local peoples who recalled that it was

---

treated with respect the native men she hired to help guide her and to collect, pack and carry her specimens as the experts they were on the local flora, fauna, and culture. Never adequately compensated, she lived frugally but in 1955 was awarded an OBE for her accomplishments and a modest civil list pension that eased her retirement years. She died in 1969 and London's Museum of Natural History, where she worked as a volunteer, made a video honoring her as one of their "heroes" (see https://www.youtube.com/watch?v=Vne43Pjg-gs).

in trade with Malay hunters when they tasted their first salt, saw their first matches, and were given the meat from birds after the feathered skin was removed.[19]

The First Lujere Patrols

In 1920, the military occupation of German New Guinea was terminated by the League of Nations and the area was mandated to Australia as the Territory of New Guinea. The Australians, using their occupation experience as a guide, divided the Territory into administrative districts and began the serious business of instituting civil authority. The sprawling Aitape District, the Territory's largest and named for its headquarters' coastal town, included the huge Sepik River Basin, then moved up and over the Prince Alexander, Torricelli, and Bewani coastal mountains northwards to the Bismarck Sea. One of the enthusiastic young men who came up from Australia to join the new civilian government was "Kassa" Townsend. Recently discharged from the Australian Imperial Forces as a lieutenant at the end of World War I, the 25-year-old Townsend came to Aitape in 1920 seeking new adventures. He rose from a patrol officer or 'kiap' to a District Officer then was a Lieutenant Colonel in New Guinea during World War II. At the end of his career, he writes in fascinating detail about how colonial Aitape looked and describes the collection of unique individuals he met and befriended there, from Chinese storekeepers and Indigenous policemen to various villagers and colonial officers (Townsend 1968). It is one of the best books ever written on the colonial system of the Territory of New Guinea.[20]

The sprawling size of the Aitape District was short-lived; in 1924, the area south of the Sepik River was withdrawn and named the Sepik District with headquarters at Ambunti, 250 miles upriver. In 1933, the two districts were rejoined as the Sepik District but with headquarters, at Townsend's suggestion, at Wiwiak, shortly changed to Wewak. Finally, in 1967, the district was roughly separated along the 143° east meridian into the West and East Sepik Districts with respective headquarters at Vanimo and Wewak. But within eighteen months, the West Sepik District's Ambunti Sub-District, was reassigned to the East Sepik District, acknowledging the administrative significance of keeping the major portion of the Sepik River within a single district (Lea 1972: 1030–1).[21] After

---

19. Email, Gilbert A. Lewis to author, April 10, 2014, regarding data gleaned from a patrol into the Wan-Wan area.
20. During World War II, Townsend (1896–1962) engaged largely upon intelligence and propaganda work among native peoples, for which he was appointed OBE" (West 1972: 1141). After the war he served from 1946 to 1956 at the UN in New York City in the Trusteeship Division. He retired to Queensland in Australia and a draft of his memoir was completed, except for his UN years, before his death. His editor Judy Tudor writes:

    Kassa Townsend was, in the Australian idiom, something of a loner. . . . He was that very rare thing in this century—a man of unblemished integrity, who put what he took to be his duty first; who could decide what he believed to be right and act on it, no matter what it cost. (Tudor 1968: 11–12)

21. Thus, those Lujere villages on the Sepik River, like Panewai, were in the East Sepik District while all the others were in the West Sepik District.

independence in 1975, the two districts were renamed the West Sepik (or Sandaun Province) and the East Sepik Province. No other administrative region in Papua New Guinea has undergone so many administrative permutations.

The three forms of colonial intervention in New Guinea with the most compelling impact on its Indigenous societies were: (1) labor recruitment; (2) government "pacification" patrols; and (3) religious missions. They usually occur historically in that order and the Lujere are not an exception. But it will take the 1929–1936 patrol reports of E. D. Robinson and J. K. McCarthy, to piece together the beginnings of this story.[22]

Robinson's Pioneering 1929–1932 Patrols

At this time the Sepik District was divided into two main subdistricts, namely, Ambunti and Marienberg. The district office was at Ambunti, 230 miles upriver, and it was from there that the Middle and Upper Sepik were administered. The only police post in the district was located at Marienberg, forty miles from the mouth of the Sepik, and the Lower Sepik and coastal area were administered from there. Keith McCarthy was the patrol officer at the Marienberg Police Post when Robinson was his superior as the district officer of the Sepik District. McCarthy, in another revealing book on colonial New Guinea, relates how he first met his new boss on the Yuat River (called Dörfer by the Germans), a tributary of the lower Sepik.

> The Yuat got narrower as its navigable limits were approached and at length [the pinnace] Osprey pulled into a collection of palm huts. This was where Robinson was camped with the gold prospectors. The District Officer was a Yorkshireman with a cheerful manner. He greeted me with a grin and said, "I hope you've bwought the gwog. We're all dying for a dwink." Because he could not pronounce the letter R, Robinson was known far and wide as "Wobbie." Luckily, I had brought the grog, so a case of warm beer was opened without delay. (McCarthy 1963: 46)

In the early 1930s, Gregory Bateson also was on the Sepik studying the Iatmul at the same time that Reo Fortune and Margaret Mead were studying the Mundugamor (or Biwat) on the Yuat and then moved further up the Sepik to study the Tchambuli (or Chambri).[23] In Bateson's foreword to *Naven* (1958: x), and Mead's acknowledgments in *Sex and Temperament in Three Primitive Societies* (1963: iv), both cite their indebtedness

---

22. The reports of patrol officers describing their visits to local communities have been a welcome source of detailed historic data on the colonial context of Lujere society. For a culturally comparative view of patrols and patrol reports in a very different part of Papua New Guinea at about the same time as my late-colonial fieldwork, see Errington and Gewertz (1995: chap. 1) on Karavar Island in the Duke of York Islands.
23. Fortune was supposed to write up their Mundugumor materials, but when he didn't, and Lévi-Strauss (1976) showed a theoretical interest in the data by sharing an early copy of his paper with her, Mead made plans for a Mundugumor monograph, however illness then her death in 1978 interceded. Nancy McDowell (1991: 26) "did extensive field work in Bun, the first group of people upriver from the Mundugumor," and, with access to the field notes of Fortune and Mead, plus her knowledge and insights into the region, wrote a compelling

to Robinson who, as the district officer, was in a position to facilitate their work and offer hospitality far from home.[24] In a letter from Tchambuli to friends dated February 1, 1933, Mead was even more expressive in her description of him:

> At Ambunti we stayed with the wholly adorable District Officer, Robbie, who is loved by and loves everyone. He had as a guest, chance-sent on a recruiter's pinnace, a most ambiguous female with a rattrap mouth, mascara eyes and a wholly suspicious and deadly restraint of manner, who was, I think, pretending to pretend that she wasn't a reporter or a spy from the League of Nations. . . . There was a mad proud recruiter and a slightly truculent little one and government officers—some good boy scouts and some not. Altogether it made quite an odd party. We played bridge, Reo and Gregory played chess, in between we discussed the functional method in anthropology or some such remote topic and at intervals Robbie interjected: "Stop it, I say, stop it!" (Mead 1977: 140)[25]

Mead also writes (1972: 210), "At ten o'clock our much-loved, jovial, and alcoholic host Sepik Robbie would say, 'We have had dinner, haven't we?'" Ambunti, the small rustic government station 230 miles from the Sepik's mouth, was Robinson's headquarters, and it was there that Mead, Fortune, and Bateson were his guests. From here, he made the first government patrol to contact the Lujere who, like the rest of the Upper Sepik cultures, were not yet under either government influence or control. In fact, the vast majority of the Sepik District was, from a European viewpoint, unexplored. In Robinson's "Annual Report of Sepik District 1930–31" to the government secretary in the Territory's capitol of Rabaul, he notes that the unexplored area consists of 18,086 square miles, while the areas under the government's (1) complete control is 2,532 square miles; (2) influence, 264 square miles; (3) partial influence, 1,110 square miles; and (4) penetration by patrols, 708 square miles (Robinson 1931: 5). Regarding the last category, he writes that seventy-one villages were visited on a recent patrol to the upper reaches of the Sepik River, adding,

> The patrol reached a point above the Haus River, then returned, visiting villages on the Haus, Mai [May] and Yellow Rivers. *All these villages were visited for the first time by any Official of the Administration,* [my emphasis] and friendly relations were established with the natives. (Robinson 1931: 8)

In another section of the report called "New Areas," he mentions that, regarding the Haus, Yellow, and Mai Rivers, "Owing to their distance from Ambunti, it is not possible to pay these people frequent visits" (Robinson 1931: 9). Then, regarding labor recruiting,

---

ethnography of the Mundugumor (McDowell: 1991), which also addressed the controversy about the "rope" kinship system.

24. In 1936, Richard Thurnwald (1936a) was teaching at Yale and gave a mixed review to Mead's *Sex and Temperament in Three Primitive Societies* in the *American Anthropologist*. According to Lutkehaus (2008: 141), a displeased Mead wrote a lengthy personal response to his criticisms.
25. Humorous stories abound about the good-natured Robinson. See also McCarthy (1963: 76, 136).

"Several Europeans have been engaged in recruiting throughout the District during the year. No complaints of their activities have been received" (Robinson 1931: 11). Robinson's comment was warranted as some recruiters were notorious for their labor abuses including recruiting in government "closed" areas, and even kidnapping men and youths by force to meet their plantation quotas.[26] The Territory, as a colonial regime of Australia, placed patrol officers in a politically sensitive situation. The government was obligated to open up the Territory to economic entrepreneurs, providing for their safety and cheap and obedient laborers. At the same time the patrol officer and district officer, while being the government's most strategic agents in accomplishing these goals, also were charged with the welfare of the local population under them. The competing interests could be difficult to navigate.

> The government made sure that labourers were available in tens of thousands. The number of New Guineans under indenture grew from 17,500 to over 41,000 between 1914 and 1939, as recruiters pressed further into the Sepik, Aitape and Morobe Districts. . . . The district officer who encouraged village cash cropping or kept employers to the strict letter of the labour laws could expect at best to be mocked by Europeans as a *kanaka man*, at worst to be demoted. (Griffin et al. 1979: 54–55.)

From a later report, we know that Robinson's first visit to the Lujere was in 1930 and he made revisits in 1931, 1932, and 1934. But with no knowledge of the many different languages or anyone to interpret for him, his first two visits were more "appearance" patrols than active ones. Robinson was just as linguistically limited in collecting cultural information as Thurnwald was seventeen years earlier when he first explored the Lujere's Yellow and Sand Rivers.

However, there was a groundbreaking difference when Robinson (1932) returned in 1932. Twenty-eight people, twenty-seven of them Lujere, had learned some Tok Pisin, the colonial lingua franca, enabling Robinson to gather data about their culture.[27] All were recently returned from three-year labor contracts working for the Catholic Mission of the Sacred Heart at Alexishafen, near present-day Madang.[28]

It is Robinson who gives us the first tentative account of Lujere culture. Because his 1932 patrol Report is so important in the Lujere's colonial history, I will report on it at length.[29] The area of the patrol was up the Sepik River "From Ambunti to the Sepik -

---

26. For a discussion of early labor abuses in the Sepik Basin see Scaglion (1990).
27. The language "Tok Pisin" is described in chapter 8, and the Lujere's Tok Pisin schools in chapter 7.
28. This was a large mission from German times that earlier had a strong reputation for establishing trade schools, teaching German, establishing health services, and planting large plantations of coconuts and *Ficus elastica* (Sack and Clark 1979, passim). As Mary Huber (1990: 198) notes, it "had not only a church, a school, a printing press, and a hospital but a coconut plantation, a copra factory, railway tracks, a timber mill, a carpentry, a machine shop, a tailor shop, a boot factory, a dry dock, and warehouse as well." Alexishafen is one of the few colonial German towns that retained its original name.
29. E. W. Robinson, "Patrol Report, A.4/1932–33" to the Director of District Services and Native Affairs, Rabaul, Mandated Territory of New Guinea, dated October 19, 1932.

Dutch Border and approximately ten miles of the Yellow River, and return to Ambunti." At that time he was the Acting District Officer for the Sepik District. The patrol lasted from September 7 to October 16, 1932, and "3 Native Police" accompanied him. The objects of the patrol were

1. To afford transport for patrol party of the Acting District Officer of Aitape [W. Oakley].
2. To pay my third annual visit to the upper reaches of the Sepik River and establish friendly relations with the natives, with a view to assist future patrols in bringing them under Government control.
3. To select a suitable site for a Government Post with regard to possible future operations. (Robinson 1932: 1)

Regarding Robinson's first objective, the acting district officer in Aitape, Ward Oakley, was accompanied by another European, Harry Eve, a surveyor with Oil Search Ltd., ever eager to survey new territory for the company's two local geologists, J. Montgomery and G. A. V. Stanley (Eve and Stanley we meet again in the following chapter). The patrol's first object does not concern us, except to note two things; had Oakley and Eve's patrol from Aitape over the Torricelli Mountains southward to the mouth of the Yellow River on the Sepik succeeded, it would have been the first overland government patrol into this uncontacted area that included the Oni, Bouye, Yis and Namia (Lujere) language groups. Second, because of the delay in waiting for the Aitape patrol that never appeared—this was before radio contact was utilized—Robinson spent considerable time with the Lujere villagers, enriching his understanding of their culture by talking with the recently returned contract laborers who had learned some Tok Pisin while away.

His government pinnace, the Osprey, left Ambunti on September 7, arriving at the mouth of the Yellow River on the tenth. As he was ahead of schedule and Oakley's Aitape patrol had not arrived, he proceeded upriver in a small, motorized boat to reinforce his previous village visits, returning to the Yellow River on the fourteenth. The following day he hiked the ten miles up the Yellow to the Lujere village of Mirijami (Miriyami), made camp there and lit a signal fire each night for the Aitape patrol as previously planned. On the nineteenth, he returned by raft to the mouth of the Yellow River and set up camp on the south bank of the Sepik at the foot of a thousand-foot hill called Kojabu (Kociabu, Kogiabu) that will continue to figure in the Lujere's colonial history. Here he again set signal fires to guide the missing patrol and continued to be visited by local peoples from many villages intrigued and curious about the unprecedented nightly fires. But Oakley's patrol, or even word about it, did not appear. Finally, reasoning that the patrol somehow had been aborted, he returned in the pinnace to Ambunti on October 2. Obviously concerned about the fate of the expected patrol passing through uncontacted territory and hearing nothing, he returned to the Yellow River and learned that the patrol had turned back at Maurom, a village in the foothills above the Lujere villages.[30] He then returned

---

30. The report that Oakley and Eve had turned back towards Aitape at Maurom village was incorrect. As noted in Oakley's detailed patrol report (Oakley 1932) his patrol purposely veered to the southeast and had to abort its goal a few miles north of the Sepik when it encountered impassable swamps. During its sojourn, the patrol was attacked several times, tricked

to Ambunti, arriving on October 16, and completed his patrol report on the nineteenth. A month had passed but Robinson used his attenuated waiting time well, as his report's ethnographic accounts on the "Upper Main Sepik Natives" and especially on the "Yellow River Area Natives" clearly show.

After explaining at length why he was not able to transport the Aitape Patrol to Ambunti, Robinson focuses his report first on the "Upper Main Sepik Natives." However, with no Tok Pisin informant from these villages to interview, his report relies on his visual observations that are mostly about weapons, clothing, and body decoration. Then his Lujere informants gave him some ominous data about their Sepik neighbors. "The Yellow River people tell me that these main river people are cannibals; I cannot vouch for this as the only reason the Yellow River people give for this statement is that whenever the main river people kill their enemies, they always take away the body." As I learned in fierce detail from my Lujere informants, their immediate neighbors across the Sepik River were, indeed, recently cannibals, as were the nearby May River or Iwam people.[31]

Robinson's patrol report is composed of four memoranda. Most germane is the one on the people with two parts: "Upper Main Sepik Natives" and, "Yellow River Area Natives." It begins with a succinct picture of the degree of government control on the upper river in October of 1932.

> The Sepik River has now been patrolled from the mouth to the Sepik-Dutch Borders; from the mouth to the village of Yessan, which is approximately 20 miles above Ambunti, the main river is now under complete Government control; from Yessan to the Sepik-Dutch Border the natives are not yet under Government influence. (Robinson 1932: appendix 3, 1; my emphasis)

Here is Robinson's verbatim report on "The Yellow River Area Natives":

> The Yellow River language [Namia] extends from Purami [village on south bank of the Sepik River] through the bush to both Yellow and Sand Rivers. In this area there are 27 men and 1 woman who can all speak a little pidgin. All have just completed 3-years contract at Alexishafen Mission. They are scattered amongst the following villages— Purami 5 men 1 woman; Panuai 3 men; Iremauri 2 men; Abriami 3 men, Mirijami 3 men; Yuani [Iwani] 3 men, Pabei 5 men; and Ibari (Main Sepik language [Abau]) 3 men. Owing to these people I was able to gather much useful information.
>
> As regards weapons, canoes, clothing, these people resemble the main river people, already explained.
>
> Here there are no Club Houses (house Tamboram) as on the lower main river; [instead] they have a "house boy" [Tok Pisin for men's house] where all married and single men sleep. The women have their own houses, which their husbands may use

---

by guides, and also ran into severe problems when the lessening population hampered the opportunity to buy supplementary food.

31. Phillip Guddemi's ethnographic study (1992: 138–48 passim) further verifies the custom of cannibalism by the Sawiyanō, the Lujere's enemies. Their eastern cannibal neighbors, the May River Iwam, were also Lujere enemies. See chapter 9 of the present volume for an account of the the infamous "Yellow River Massacre" of 1956.

during the day, and in which the women sleep at night; men and women do not sleep in the same house.

The clothing, as previously mentioned, is the same as the main river people [i.e., men wear a penis gourd, women wear fore and aft string skirts]. Here when a man's wife or child dies the man takes off his penis box [gourd] and puts a small pus-pus[32] around the top of the penis. This is worn until the man has killed pigs and made a feast for his dead [relative], when this has been done he again wears his penis box.

Marriage is by sister exchange only; should a woman run away with a man without the permission of her parents, both the man and the woman, when caught, are dealt with in the following manner—the woman's parents and relations assault the man with sticks and clubs and administer a sound thrashing, then the woman is held and speared with barbed arrows from the thighs down to her feet, neither of them are killed.

These people are not headhunters; when a man kills an enemy, he cuts off his victim's left arm at the elbow joint, failing this he cuts off a finger from the left hand. It was explained that the left hand or arm is always taken—never the right, because the right is the bow pulling hand, and as they have already killed their victim and have no desire to mutilate the body they only take the arm or finger as proof of their skill, they leave the victim his good hand.[33] This is then taken back to his village and hung up in the men's house and the men and women of the "killers" village visit and a big celebration follows; large wooden drums (Wei) [slit gongs] are fought with sticks, wooden horns (Woniguani) are blown and the natives of other friendly villages hearing this, all come to the dance and are shown the arm or finger as the case may be as proof that an enemy has really been killed.

Upon a male reaching the age of puberty nothing is done to celebrate this, no skin marking of any kind are practiced.

The men do all the hunting for game, all clearing of bush for gardens, build all houses and canoes etc; the women do all planting of native foods, and catch fish in the large round nets; fish are caught both inland lakes and rivers.

The following native foods are planted—taro, sugarcane, sago, native cabbage, bananas, and tobacco.

There are few coconut trees, and no paw-paws, in the whole of the area.

The following game is killed by the men—pig, cassowary, wallaby, opossum, crocodile, snake and various birds, all of which are eaten with relish by these people.

At my camps in both Mirijami and at the foot of the Kojabu mountain,[34] I was visited by natives from the following villages—Ibare, Yuani [Iwani], Mirijami, Abriami, Purami, Iremauri, Waiari, Pabei and Panuai, so that it can be easily seen that the natives are a friendly people. They all expressed a desire that an officer be stationed amongst them.

On my return visit I took up the following foodstuffs and distributed them amongst the natives for planting—paw-paw, pineapple, corn, yams and kau-kau. I also took

---

32. This is a bit confusing as 'puspus' means sexual intercourse but 'pus,' according to Mihalic (1971: 162), means "a sash, a scarf, a strip of cloth."
33. I did not know of or obtain access to Robinson's and McCarthy's pioneering patrol reports until long after I had returned to the US. The Lujere gave me the same data regarding a left-arm war trophy and the same rationale that was indicative of their profound human decency.
34. It is quite probable the Kojabu camp was the same as Thurnwald's "Mäanderberg" base camp.

6 coconuts, which I planted on the proposed site for a Post (Kreiwarr Mountain), I did not give these to the natives to plant as they have little high ground which the floods do not touch.

I brought a small monkey [boy] back with me to teach him pidgin. I intend to take him with me on patrol, and he will then see the various customs of the lower river people, and later he will be of great help in bringing his own people under control.[35] (Robinson 1932: appendix 3, 2–4)

Before continuing, the racism inherent in the term "monkey" to denote a human boy deserves comment. Michalic (1971: 130) argues that the pidgin term 'monki' was introduced by Malaysian traders, who themselves were colonized by the British in the eighteenth century. While no racist insult is intended when the Lujere use term (there are no monkeys in New Guinea), nevertheless, the term was adopted into Tok Pisin from "monkey," a term used by the Australian colonizers. Their long history of blatant racism toward non-White peoples, including the Australian Aboriginals, is amply documented, as reflected in this and other terms, like 'boi' ("boy") for an adult male, introduced into Tok Pisin.

Unlike many of the headhunting villages on the middle Sepik River who deeply resented the government's visits and remained decidedly unfriendly, the Lujere, as Robinson notes, were actually welcoming. But it wasn't just the young Lujere lad that Robinson envisioned helping him bring the Upper Sepik under government control. He had a grander plan that he submitted to the officials in Rabaul in another memorandum titled "Recommendations for future activities Upper Sepik":

All these time expired boys [contract laborers whose period of service had ended] are young and keen and can only speak a little pidgin, and I consider that if the river is to be opened up, now is the time to operate in the area, should it be left, then all these boys will shortly lose all the teaching of the "White Man" and lapse into their old state and so make the task of opening up the area doubly hard, in view of this I desire to recommend as follows:

1. That the land known to the natives as KREIWARR MOUNTAIN, situated on the right [south] bank of the Sepik River, opposite the mouth of the Yellow River, and rising to a height of approximately 150 feet, be appropriated by the Administration under the Lands Ordinance 1022 Section 68 (12).
2. That one European Officer with 20 Native Constabulary and 8 indentured labourers, or long service prisoners, be sent to establish a Post on Kreiwarr Mountain. I have cut roads and thoroughly inspected this site and consider it satisfactory in every way.
3. If I could be relieved of duties on the lower river for a few months I consider that it would be to the advantage of the Administration if I personally established the Post. My reason for thinking this is that I know the area fairly well, large numbers of natives of both the Yellow River and the Main Sepik Areas remember me from

---

35. According to my successful Yellow River cell phone conversation with David Merau of Yegarapi Village on January 24, 2015, the boy was Mamyowi from Ameni village. Later he signed on as a plantation laborer with a group of other young Lujere men and taught them Tok Pisin.

my previous visits, and I consider that after spending a few months with these people I should at least have a fair amount of their confidence and the Post could then be taken over by a Patrol Officer.

4. The cost of such a Post would not be great, a small pinnace would be necessary, as canoe work would be practically impossible owing to the strong [Sepik River] currents experienced in the upper reaches. The benefits it would return would amply repay any expenses incurred as it would be the means of opening a large area of at present unknown and possibly valuable country, and would possibly be the means of supplying an at present unknown quantity of labour. I shall be glad of advice with regard to these recommendations. (Robinson 1932: appendix 2, 1–3)

In July of 1934, Robinson, now the Assistant District Officer in Wewak, was again on patrol; this time to accomplish the first successful patrol from Aitape overland to the Sepik River—the same one that Oakley and Eve attempted two years previously but failed to complete. Crossing over the Torricelli ridge, he stopped to test and inspect an alleged gold find on Wini Creek that he correctly suspected to be the origin of the Yellow River. The prospector was Charlie Gough who was based in Aitape and owned the most popular trade store. He also was a labor recruiter and, on August 31, 1936, was speared to death over a recruiting incident in the Arapesh village of Ilihinga. Donald Tuzin (1976: 25–27) who worked in the nearby "enemy" village of Ilihita in the 1970s, reports this early incident and its meaning to his fieldwork.[36] Just then, Gough was hoping that the District Officer would declare his find a Gold Field, but that was not to be. Robinson and his nine policemen, medical orderly and thirty-four carriers continued down the Wini Creek to a larger river, hopefully the Yellow.

When they came to the foothill village of Kelnom just before the Lujere grasslands, one of the villagers who spoke Malay, as did one of Robinson's policemen, assured them that they were on the Yellow River. "Also, he told us that about five months ago two Malays and a party of natives were in the vicinity shooting birds-of-paradise and he was with them for two days" (Robinson 1934: 3). As noted earlier, although trading in bird-of-paradise skins was outlawed in Hollandia in 1931, it was obvious that in 1934 and 1936, there was a vigorous smuggling market.

On the 22nd of July, Robinson's patrol lunched in a hamlet of the Lujere village of Eiderwok (Edwaki) where about fifty men and women greeted them in friendship. Continuing, they passed Wei-ari and Papei villages inland on the Yellow's west flank arriving at Marajami late afternoon. "Here, many of the natives remembered me from before and

---

36. Townsend, told by McCarthy of the murder, went to investigate and gives a detailed account. Lehinga was deserted when he arrived, but he learned that nearby Ilahita village was harboring the murderers. "I called the Luluai of Illaheta in and told him that we would be moving camp to his village and that he would be expected to feed the lot of us" (Townsend 1968: 229–30). As there was over forty in Townsend's party, the culprits were soon apprehended. Jock Marshall (1938: 281–92), a young Australian adventurer and writer was a good friend of Gough's also relates the story from his perspective as do I (Mitchell 2012: 89–90). When I worked among the Wape in Taute village, the first men (thirteen of them) to leave the village to work for White people walked over the Torricelli Mountains down to Aitape to be recruited by Charlie Gough. Three were still alive during my initial fieldwork in 1970.

were very excited, patting me on the back saying, 'Kiap, Kiap'" (Robinson 1934: 4). The next day the patrol proceeded down the Yellow to the Sepik to meet the patrol officer from Ambunti, but there is no mention of a new base camp as Robinson envisioned. In 1934, the government officials in Rabaul obviously were not impressed with the need of establishing a new post in an area with little commercial potential.

Robinson became dangerously ill from a leech-induced internal abscess in his penis and was hospitalized out of the district in Madang.

> The narrow escape did not affect Robinson's sense of humour. The nature of the wound even appealed to his sense of the ludicrous and when he lay, bone thin and pallid, awaiting the schooner for Madang, he insisted that he would raise the question (at "the highest level") of officers patrolling the leech-infested grass country being issued with a "certain type of rubber goods" as standard equipment. (McCarthy 1963: 76)

Although Robinson was no longer the district officer, his scheme for a Yellow River government post had been broached; now it would take some commercial pressure to make it happen.

On February 10, 1936, "Kassa" Townsend returned from leave to New Guinea with his wife and infant son; his five-year-old daughter remained at boarding school in Melbourne. Docking in Rabaul, he met with the Administrator and the following day wrote in his diary, "Submitted Yellow River Post plans to Administrator."[37] On the same ship with the Townsends was PO James Hodgekiss.

> He was to open up a post on the Yellow River, a tributary of the Upper Sepik, a couple of hundred river miles beyond Ambunti, as Oil Search Ltd. had been pressing for years for permission to get into the uncontrolled territory accessible from there. It was necessary to have an experienced Government officer within reach of their activities and for this class of work there was no one superior to Jimmy Hodgekiss. His understanding of native thought and his acceptance of solitude and isolation were both absolute. (Townsend 1968: 224)

Robinson's October 1932 plan for a base camp at the mouth of the Yellow River was to become a reality—at least for a while. But the base would not be built on the little hundred-fifty-foot Kreiwar Hill as Robinson had suggested but atop the more commanding thousand-foot Kojabu (Kogiabu) Hill, where Robinson had lit his nightly bonfires to signal the wayward patrol of Aitape's ADO Ward Oakley and Oil Search Ltd.'s surveyor, Harry Eve. It is interesting to see the shift in purpose of the proposed base camp, from Robinson's acculturation goals for the local population, to Townsend's facilitating geographic access for commercial entrepreneurs, two different but intimately related sides of the colonial coin. Not only was the Yellow River (Kojabu) Base Camp opened in 1936 by Hodgekiss in part to facilitate Oil Search Ltd.'s quest for oil in uncontrolled territory, in 1938 Hodgekiss similarly opened the Green River Base Camp (off the upper Sepik River's north coast) and the Maimai Base Camp (northeast of the Lujere). But oil to

---

37. Personal communication from Laurie Bragge, who has the Townsend diaries.

warrant commercial production was never found; if it had been, the "development" of the upper Sepik Basin would have been a very different story.

McCarthy's 1936 Patrol

In June of 1936, Keith McCarthy, now the Assistant District Officer in Aitape, began a thirty-day patrol from Aitape to the "Sepik-Yellow River Base Camp" for general exploration and map-making, and to report on the possibility of a mail-running service between Aitape and the base camp.[38] As Molnar-Bagley (1980: 50) notes, "This base camp became famous as the most isolated posting in the Territory of New Guinea." Accompanied by ten police, two of whom spoke "pidgin Malay," and twenty-nine carriers, they followed the pioneering route taken by Robinson in 1934.[39] It was an uneventful patrol but McCarthy (1936) made the first detailed sketch map of the area between the coast and the Sepik as part of his patrol report.[40] He also notes that below the Wape villages Malay, as with Robinson's patrol, facilitated communication and "saved time for the people quickly gathered around when they heard our police speak [it]." His eleven-page patrol diary is that of a very observant person, and throughout it, he comments, like Robinson, on the friendliness of the people, an obvious contrast to other parts of the Territory where he had patrolled. Finally, after the patrol crossed the Sepik in local canoes lashed together, on July 9 at 9:00 a.m., they reached the base camp atop Kojabu (Kogiabu, Kochiabu) hill (1,000') established by Hodgekiss.[41] McCarthy (1936: 6) recorded that the people of

---

38. In those areas of New Guinea where there was no waterway or road, the mail between the district's headquarters and sub-stations might be carried by local "runners"—no man could actually "run" on these root-bound, wet, and rugged mountain trails—not unlike the western US pony express in the nineteenth century. McCarthy's plan was to have two police start at each end of the route—Aitape and Yellow River (Kogiabu) Base Camp— once every six weeks, exchange mailbags near its center (Talu village), and return home. He did foresee problems with men fearful to enter areas of their immediate enemies even when accompanied by two policemen. In fact, the two local men he selected to accompany him to the midpoint village turned back after two days, even though accompanied by the patrol officer and police, as they knew the next village, Maurom, was an enemy.
39. Although McCarthy follows Robinson's route and notes in his patrol diary Robinson's camp sites, in his book about his New Guinea years, he strangely writes, "On the southern side of the coastal range between Aitape and Vanimo (which, incidentally, was only twenty miles from the Dutch New Guinea border) the headwaters of the Yellow River had their rise, and to the best of my knowledge nobody had yet followed this river from its source to where it joined the Sepik" (McCarthy 1963: 161).
40. Robinson's and McCarthy's exploratory patrols of the area were indirectly recognized in the first *Official Handbook of the Territory of New Guinea* (1936: 369).

    In the interior, beyond the Torricelli Ranges, in the grass-covered country sloping into the Sepik valley, are larger communities of bush people, numbering several thousands, into whose territory patrols are now effecting penetration . . . and it is believed ere long the area will be under complete control.
41. McCarthy's (1936: 5) patrol report diary entry for July 9, 1936 says, "At 9 a/m/ we had reached the base-camp that had been established by J. W. Hodgekiss, P.O., on the 6th instant." Usually

Aidawok, Mariyami, Weari, and Pabei came with them to the base camp where Maraui from neighboring Purami greeted him. In November 1935, Maraui had accompanied McCarthy and the administrator, Brigadier General McNioll, on the latter's patrol across the Dutch border[42]. Hodgekiss had some local men at work clearing timber on Kojabu and, luckily for them in a steel-starved region, paid them with steel knives and axes.

The most significant part of McCarthy's patrol report is his "Notes on People, Customs, Etc." In his "Introduction," he distinguishes between "Two distinct types of natives we met with on the patrol—one of which I call the *Wipe* [Wape] type for want of a better name and the other the Yuan (or Yellow River people [Lujere].)" In this first identification of the Lujere as a people, McCarthy writes,

> The country further south from Talu and Maurel [Maurom] as far south as the Sepik River is inhabited by the folk of the Yellow River, or as I prefer to call them, the YUAN tribes. They know the Yellow River as the Yuan and in the absence of their tribal name I propose to call them the Yuan people. (McCarthy 1936: 12)[43]

He notes that the Yuan have a working knowledge of Malay Pidgin and, in his experience, "they are distinctive in being the only inland people who have adopted the tongue of the foreigners as a trade *talk*."[44] He further hypothesizes that the contact is ancient.

> For a Papuan people to know even such a simple language as Malay pidgin, which is at base Melanesian, means that long and constant contact has taken place between the two peoples. The visits of the Malayan bird-shooters are merely recent incidents of a trade route that has operated for probably centuries past. Long before the Malays entered the Sepik Basin the people of the Yuan had trading communication with those of the coastal areas north-west (Hollandia). (McCarthy 1936: 14)

There is no evidence that foreign traders entered the upper Sepik Basin for anything other than the plumes of the bird-of-paradise but as Swadling notes (1996: 51–63) the plume trade with Asia is ancient and could have commenced hundreds of years before the

---

this would mean the present or current month, i.e., "July 6," but in his book (1963:163), he says Hodgekiss "told us he had been waiting at his base camp for us for the last three weeks. His normal station was at Ambunti, and this base camp did not have an officer posted to it." This would indicate the base camp was established on June sixth. But there is further confusion when he (1936: 6) records in his diary "6th instant" again on July 14: "The *Thetis* [a government boat] had arrived on the 6th inst. [instant] and was expected to return from Ambunti on the 13th." (It actually arrived at the base camp around 3:00 pm on July 14).

42. See McCarthy (1963: 139–49) for a detailed account of this trip to the upper Sepik with the Administrator including an early description of Wagu village and two watery misadventures by McCarthy.
43. Had I been aware of McCarthy's patrol report while in the field, I might have been persuaded to follow his lead and called them the "Yuan" people.
44. Danilyn Rutherford (2012: 129), who worked on Biak Island in West Papua, Indonesia, emphasizes and documents the local blurring of linguistic boundaries within the country, noting "a dizzying variety of 'low Malay registers'" from which the national language, Indonesian, emerged.

modern craze of feathers in European women's fashion.[45] McCarthy has no discussion of the Lujere's own language, Namia, except to identify it as Papuan, for in 1936, none of the upper Sepik River languages were specifically identified. It would be another fifty years and after my fieldwork was completed before their language was actually studied in the field by linguists Tom and Becky Feldpausch. What follows are McCarthy's verbatim anthropological notes on the Yuan (Lujere) that complement and extend Robinson's 1932 observations. McCarthy usually puts Tok Pisin terms followed by "p." in parentheses. My occasional comments are interjected in brackets.

> Physical Characteristics: The people are of a dark-brown skin and generally well-formed. The men are slim and average about 5 feet 2 inches in height and are muscular although not heavily built.[46] Features of both sexes are not unpleasing although the practices of piercing the septum of the nose as well as slitting the tip does not enhance their appearance. A piece of bamboo or bone is generally worn in the septum while the slits in the nose sometimes hold an ornamental feather. The lobe and helix of both ears are usually pierced and small ornaments or trophies such as part of a pig's tail worn in them. Some of the men and women bore irregular scars on shoulders and back but cicatrisation is not generally practiced. Skin diseases were not common although some of the men were suffering from girili (tinea) [TP].
>
> Dress: The women wore small skirts of woven grass [corded string], short in the front but longer at the back. They were attached by a narrow cord and the flanks of the wearer were bare. Necklaces of red and white seeds threaded together and shell ornaments were worn by the younger girls. Large string bags (bilum p.) were carried and when heavily loaded were carried with the cord across the forehead and the bag slung behind.
>
> The dress of the men was the unusual type as worn by the people of the upper Sepik River. The penis is inserted in a gourd (kambang p.) which is sometimes carved. The shapes of the gourd vary and they are worn attached to a string around the waist. Both men and male children generally wear this peculiar covering.[47]
>
> Sometimes a belt of hollow cassowary bones, about 6 inches in length were threaded on cords with large seeds and worn around the waist. The bones are worn in threes and fours and are sometimes those of a crocodile. A headdress consisting of a forehead band of white threaded seeds was common and the younger men had the skin of the possum (kapul p.) on their heads. Small string bags were carried by the men. A pipe was usually carried. It consisted of the decorated gourd sometimes carved and covered with the skin of an iguana (pilei p.) with a short length of detachable bamboo inserted in the larger hole at the end. The tobacco is smoked green after a cursory drying over a fire and is rolled like a cigar and stuck in the end of the bamboo tube. The tube is

---

45. Mead (1938: 181), after a comment that the domestic fowl of the middle Sepik "are said to resemble Malay fowls," adds, "It must be remembered in this connection that there was once a Malay trade route from Dutch New Guinea over the Torricelli Mountains to the Yellow River."
46. In chapter 10 the height and weight of the Wakau villagers is reported; the average height of the males was five feet, four inches.
47. Village men explained to me that two small holes were made toward the bottom of the gourd and a cord was passed around the scrotum and another around the hips.

then held in the gourd and the smoker draws from a smaller hole at the other end of the gourd. Very often the cigar is smoked from the bamboo holder – the gourd is more common on the Sepik River villages.

Weapons: Bows and arrows are the principal arms of the men. The usual broad-bladed bamboo arrow is used for hunting pigs and cassowaries. The well-carved arrows used in warfare are barbed and painted red, black and white. The better carved arrows are sometimes wrapped with dried leaves to protect them. Bows are of hardwood and are about 5 feet in length. The arrow-heads are of hardwood . . . . At Aidawok [Edwaki] I noticed some of the men carrying unusually slender spears. They were of plain hardwood, pointed at both ends, some 4' 6" in length and about ¾ inch through at their thickest part.[48]

Houses: Houses are well-built rectangular affairs and are built on piles. Gable roofs are common but often a quarter-circle veranda is built in over the small doorways. A house at Kelnom [Yis lang.] was about 20 feet by 30 feet and was built on piles about 4 feet from the ground. The thatched roof was of sago palm while sides were of the same material. Flooring was of the limbong [PE] palmwood and the only decoration on the building was on the front. The palmwood and pankal [PE] planks were roughly painted in various designs in red, white, and yellow and black paint.[49] A larger house, evidently the house of the men, was noticed in a deserted [Lujere] village on 7.7.36. The houses were all extremely well-built.

Food: The staple diet of the Yuan people is sago and bananas [as it is today]. Small food plots are worked and in the Aidawok sweet-potatoes, pith, manioc and a little taro were seen. The gardens are situated on the hills near the villages or on the banks of the Yellow River. Game is plentiful in the area and all the streams contain fish. The smaller creeks are dammed and the fish caught in the shallow water.

Villages: There are no large villages although a considerable population in the plain lands nearing the Sepik River. The houses are in groups of a dozen or so and are built near the sago swamps. These hamlets are connected by foot-pads.

Large split gongs (garamut p.) were seen in all the villages. They varied in length and height from 3' x 1' to huge things of 10' x 3.'[50] At Aidawok I noticed the wooden hand-drums (kundu p.). They were of plain, uncarved wood and they had no hand-pieces worked on them. The tops of several were painted in red and white.

Disposal of Dead: A platform supported by poles about 18 feet in height is erected outside the house of the deceased. The body is placed on the top of the platform with certain belongings, such as bows and arrows, etc. No covering is made and the body is left to decompose in the open air. These platforms were seen at Aidawok and Pabwei hamlets. The stench from the decaying corpses was awful but the people of the places seemed surprised when we hurried from the vicinity—they did not seem to notice the smell. After the body has decomposed the bones are taken into the houses by the relatives of the deceased. At Aidawok I saw the skull of a man hanging on the wall near the door of a house – his former dwelling.

On 17.7.36, at a deserted [Lujere] village I noticed a heap of human bones on the ground outside one of the houses; they had evidently been discarded when the people

---

48. I did not observe these or see any among the Basel museum's artifacts.
49. In 1971–72, I did not see these painted planks in Kelnom or in any Lujere village.
50. In 1971–72, there were no 'garamuts' nor had any been collected earlier.

had evacuated the village some weeks previously. Such a frightful custom must spread disease and it must be one of the first practices to be abolished when the people come under some degree of control.[51] The ground on which the villages are built is firm soil and except for the peoples' present lack of tools there is no reason why burial (or cremation) should not take place.

Tools: *I would earnestly recommend the free issue of a certain number of steel axes and knives to these people* [my emphasis]. A few broken steel blades are jealously owned at some of the hamlets but the majority of the work of clearing and building houses has to be done by their primitive stone adzes. Trading will naturally ensue between the base camp and the various hamlets; food will be sold but it will be some time before the people learn to bring large amounts. They prefer to bring small individual portions of sago, etc. and these can be purchased for cheap (and for the most part economically useless) trade goods such as mirrors, beads, rings, etc. Steel tools should be introduced as soon as possible. But the people have not an abundance of food and for them to purchase an axe for its actual value in food is at the present stage an impossibility. Deliberately opposing the axioms of "never give a native something for nothing," etc, etc, I would recommend that half-a-dozen axes and knives be given to every village in the area. The population is not great and cost would be very small.

We endeavor to improve the position of a primitive people as soon as possible. They should not be denied a few knives and axes in order to support a doubtful principle----because the requisite number of pounds of sago is not available in exchange. With a few steel tools in the villages, future implements would have to be purchased. The natives must not be spoilt.[52] The system of flooding the native villages with rings, kauri shells, etc. should be avoided regardless of the value of such articles in the eyes of the people.

GENERAL: The population as seen by the patrol was not large. Patrols working from the Base camp will probably discover greater numbers of people to the west; towards the Sand River. I do not think that there are many villages east of the Yellow River [more than he imagined]. A large population will probably be found near the North River [it wasn't].

The people are the most peaceful that I have ever met. Patrols are welcomed as opportunities for trading and in fact they are more traders than warriors. The villages are all friendly towards one another. There was no mention of tribal fighting and in some cases men traveled without arms for two days outside the limits of their villages; an indication of general peace. They should quickly come under the control of the Base camp. (McCarthy 1936: 12–20)

---

51. Authorities demanded they switch to earthen burials. See chapter 19 for a discussion of their adaption of their traditional scaffold to the earthen burial.
52. This cold comment is out of character for McCarthy, whose reports and book otherwise indicate an official who was compassionate and respectful of the local people. The statement seems more a ploy to defuse the negative response to his request that he anticipated (and received) from some of his bureaucratic superiors. Still, the pioneer anthropologist Seligman (1910: ix) wrote that his main Koita informant, Ahuia Ova, "without becoming spoilt, has learnt to speak English and to write Motu extremely well."

McCarthy had reason to be impressed with the villagers' peacefulness. In 1933, he was in the eastern highlands west of the Bulolo goldfields when legendarily fierce Kukukuku warriors ambushed his patrol. "Seven Kukukukus were killed, a number of New Guinea police were wounded (one mortally) and McCarthy was struck by arrows in the thigh and stomach" (Nelson 2000). As to his compassionate plea to his superiors for some iron tools for the trade isolated Lujere, it fell on deaf ears:

> I felt that the trade or cash to buy steel goods would never be available to the people of the Yellow River and that the principle ["never give a native something for nothing"] was harsh when it applied to them, as to other equally isolated or desperately poor communities . . . In time the authorities thanked me for my exploratory work which was pleasing. On my appeal for iron implements they maintained a steadfast silence. The Yellow River was to remain as it was. (McCarthy 1963: 164)

And it more or less did. The transformation from stone and bone to metal tools did eventually occur but, as we will see, it was an ironic felicity of World War II.

Robinson and McCarthy both had extensive experience working with various New Guinea societies and their pioneering cultural observations on the Lujere are insightful as far as they go. Largely missing, however, is information on the Lujere's belief systems and social and ceremonial lives. 'Sanguma,' one of the problems that brought me to this wet grassland and for which the Lujere were regionally famous was, not surprisingly, never mentioned. A government patrol with multiple purposes moving quickly under arduous conditions from village to village amid a recently contacted people with no access to their language, is limited in what it can discover. In chapter 10, I reflect back on these first descriptions of Lujere culture by Robinson and McCarthy in light of what I later learned living among them.

CHAPTER THREE

The Japanese Invasion

> *Whatever the tide of the war in New Guinea ... it was*
> *in the end the native people who were most affected.*
> J. K. McCarthy (1963: 214)

On December 7th, 1941, Japan attacked Pearl Harbor, the Philippines, and Malaya, launching an unprecedented colonial conquest of the Pacific region. While World War I had little effect on the Indigenous population of New Guinea, World War II, or 'taim bilong pait,' had a devastating impact on numerous local regions. Peter Ryan, the Australian journalist who both fought against the Japanese in New Guinea and later wrote about the war, notes that

> For Papua New Guinea itself the war was the most cataclysmic event in the country's whole history. Between December 1941 when the Japanese struck and August 1945 when they surrendered, changes occurred or were set in motion which far exceeded in their effects the original coming of the white man (which had been local and gradual) or the results of any natural catastrophe of disease or volcanic activity. Hunger, hardship, captivity and violent death were the lot of many of the indigenous people. (Ryan 1972a: 1211)

Allen (1992: 55) also tells us that about 55,000 New Guinea men were employed or pressed into service by the enemy armies as carriers and laborers and that "between 1941 and 1945 over 170,00 Japanese died in Papua New Guinea, 14,500 Australians, 166 Papuan New Guinea soldiers and police, and an unknown number of Americans."

The Fall of Rabaul, 1942

Japanese forces swept swiftly through the Pacific Islands and Southeast Asia and in December of 1942, began their invasion of New Guinea.[1] "The Japanese came in with little violence, and the Europeans fled before them—or were taken, and sometimes butchered if they failed to get away" (Brookfield 1972: 93). Historians debate why the Australians were so woefully unprepared but one major factor was that New Guinea was a League of Nations Mandated Territory and under those provisions was not to be fortified or have a defensive force. Another factor was that many of Australia's armed forces were serving far away with the European Allied forces fighting the Germans and Italians. But there was another perhaps even more important factor. "Kassa" Townsend, who served in the war, writes scathingly about the shortsightedness and irresponsibility of Australia's prewar government:

> Ostrich-like, it buried its head in the sand although it could not possibly have believed that our potential enemies would respect New Guinea's [neutral] status.... As a result of this shilly-shallying no one, civilian or soldier, ever really knew the score; no one had any clear idea what to do in the event of an invasion; and, even when the Japanese bombs began to fall in January of 1942, no effort was ever made to get civilians out or to get military reinforcements in. (Townsend 1968: 250)[2]

What did not become clear until historians began writing about the invasion of Rabaul was that it was not just Australia's "shilly-shallying" but that a cold decision had been made to sacrifice the Rabaul garrison.

> In other words, the government wanted to preserve the illusion that Australia was capable of defending itself, and was prepared to expend the garrison for that purpose. As a result, no contingency plans were made to rescue any soldiers who might survive the pending invasion... There would be no relief, no miraculous Dunkirk. (Gamble 2014: 56)

The first bombs dropped were on New Britain in the poorly defended capitol of Rabaul. Then on January 23, the Japanese began an invasion with overwhelming military and naval might. The defense of Rabaul was short-lived and fell to the enemy in a matter of hours.

> Those in action escaped with what they stood up in—shorts and boots mostly, and a rifle.... The first impulse of all was to get away into the bush. But none of these men had been trained in jungle craft, few knew the kind of terrain they would meet outside the town limits of Rabaul and Kopopo. With the majority, the impulse to escape soon

---

1. For an overall picture of how the war impacted the Aitape-Lumi area, see Duggan (1979: 41–71). For a view of the Japanese occupation throughout the Melanesian area see Brookfield (1972: 88–97) and especially Allen (1982), whose article includes an excellent colored map.
2. Earlier, in late December 1941, White women and children had been evacuated from New Britain (Asian and local women were excluded) (Gamble 2014: 58–59).

The Japanese Invasion

gave way to despair and 900 to 1,000 surrendered or were eventually recaptured by the Japanese.

Probably 400 others continued their headlong flight into the New Britain bush. Of these a handful escaped under their own steam, but the majority were soon victims of hunger, dysentery, malaria, exposure and the unaccustomed roughness of the country. (Townsend 1968: 253)[3]

The men who did survive were helped to escape through the heroic actions of Keith McCarthy who, no longer assigned to the Sepik, was the Assistant District Officer at Talasea, three-quarters the way down New Britain's north coast from Rabaul. Like Townsend, McCarthy was highly critical of the administration's non-performance. In a letter of December 5, 1973, answering my queries regarding early administration records, he wrote:

> You know, I've often cursed the stupidity of the officials at Rabaul who lost all these valuable documents, including land records, when the Japs landed there in Jan, 1942. They had at least 6 weeks warning that the Japanese would eventually arrive; ample time to have shipped or hidden these records, but they did nothing. Knowing their love of Bumph[4] I would have thought they would have looked after papers better. I wish I could help you more and I regret not having all copies of my own patrol reports—however, the work of managing the escape of the 2/22 battalion from Rabaul made it essential that one had to move swiftly and only the bare essentials could be carried. I left them locked in the safe at Talasea and with a bit of luck the papers might have survived but a bomb landed dead on the house and nothing remained. (Letter from K. McCarthy to W. Mitchell, December 5, 1973)

Although McCarthy's personal papers were gone, by his bravery and enterprise he succeeded in rescuing more than two hundred soldiers and expatriates trapped on the island and leading them safely to Australia.[5] In recognition of his war deeds he was made a member of the Most Excellent Order of the British Empire (MBE) in 1943. It was not long, however, until he was back in New Guinea in a war role that directly affected the Lujere.

---

3. The infamous Tol massacre occurred at the Tol plantation where around 160 Australian men, mostly soldiers, unarmed and miserable, on 4 February 1942, had their hands tied by Japanese then were repeatedly bayoneted, slashed and shot, and left for dead. A few survived to tell their story. See Ryan (1972a: 1214) and especially Gamble (2006: 146–60) who also chronicles the successful escapes from New Britain. Rabaul became a Japanese bastion of strength and terror and one of the longest battles of World War II (Gamble 2010: 2014).
4. Bumph: "Useless printed instructions and manuals. Originated in England during World War II when English soldiers were overwhelmed with unnecessary printed materials and used them as they would toilet tissue or 'bum fodder.'" 50 cent crack dealer, UrbanDictionary.com, accessed July 31, 2003.
5. See McCarthy (1963: 189–213) for his personal account of this harrowing escape but see Gamble (2014) for his comprehensive history of the Japanese invasion of Rabaul based on both Allied and Japanese documents.

Guerrilla Warfare in the Upper Sepik Basin, 1943

After the fall of Rabaul and the rapid Japanese conquest of New Britain, all of the islands in the Bismarck Archipelago were in Japanese hands by the end of February. The invaders then moved towards New Guinea itself and eventually controlled much of the island's north coast.[6] The Japanese easily occupied Aitape on April 1, 1942 and set men to work building Tadji airstrip while Wewak became the strategic base for the operations of the one hundred thousand soldiers of Japan's 18th Army in mainland New Guinea under the command of Lieutenant General Hatazō Adachi.[7] The widespread social disruption caused by the Japanese invasion resulted in the collapse of civilian government in both Papua and The Mandated Territory of New Guinea. To restore order facilitating the war's objectives, they were merged into the single territory "Australian New Guinea" and a military government formed in April 1942, the Australian New Guinea Administrative Unit (ANGAU).[8] Although ANGAU's operational, administrative and production responsibilities were enormous, "It did not have access to government at high policy level, but remained a subordinate unit under command of New Guinea Force [i.e., the military]" (Ryan 1972b: 23). As the wartime organization with responsibility for the governance and welfare of the Indigenous population, it was essentially a military unit and has been accused as more concerned with the exploitation of Indigenous labor to advance the war against the Japanese than in addressing the needs of a population in wartime distress (Barry 1945).

While the Wewak to Aitape coastal area and the lower to middle part of the Sepik Basin were occupied by the Japanese entrapping some Europeans, the major fighting with the Allies was far to the east.[9]

---

6. The Japanese never succeeded in occupying New Guinea's south coast by sea or by successfully advancing over the central mountain range. See Campbell (2007) for a detailed account of the US 32nd Division's grueling campaign moving north over these mountains to engage and finally defeat the enemy on the north coast at Buna.
7. Santa Anna Mission operated Tadji Plantation, just east of Aitape. The copra plantation is no more but Santa Anna, now a Franciscan mission, is still active and the airstrip remains in use.
8. Even earlier in May 1941, the Australian military forces stationed in both territories were placed under a single command (Fulton 2005: 142.) See Ryan (1972) for a short authoritative account of ANGAU's purpose and organization, Powell (2003) for an account of its wartime exploits in New Guinea and Powell (1996) for the significant role of the Allied Intelligence Bureau.
9. Although some of the Europeans trapped in New Guinea joined ANGAU in the fight against the Japanese, others tried to make it back to Australia. One small group of six gold miners, a government clerk and a government medical assistant, escaped up the Sepik River then overland and down the Fly River to safety in the south coastal town of Daru. Led by one of the miners, J. A. Thurston, it was the first trip (April to September 1942) from the Sepik to the South coast of New Guinea. Clerk L. Odgers (1942) prepared the patrol report with its detailed diary. Also see Townsend (1968: 227–28) for a shocking account of the suicide of Assistant District Officer George Ellis at Angoram on the lower Sepik in 1942 and his rampaging policemen "who set out to kill every European still living on the River." First they shot and killed Patrol Officer R. B. Strudwick in Timbunke while he was eating, then further upriver killed a party of three miners and a Chinese carpenter before they were captured.

It was not until early 1943 that the people in the inland foothills villages had direct contact with Japanese troops. . . . Coastal men appointed as civilian officials by the Japanese, came inland and informed the foothills people that they were required to come out to the coast, to hand over their badges of office given to them by the Australians, to accept the rules of the Japanese administration and, above all, to contribute labour to the building of the coastal airstrips at But and Dagua. They moved back and forth to the coast until an outbreak of severe dysentery in mid-1943. (Allen 2006: 12)

The Japanese told the laborers to return home and stay there, but the epidemic of bloody diarrhea then spread from the coastal hills and into the mountains by the returning laborers killing hundreds of inhabitants and seriously depopulating some villages. In a detailed study of the epidemic and its population implications, Bryant Allen (1983: 234) believes that "The severe form of dysentery seems to have entered the inland from the Tadji area, near Aitape." While it seriously affected the mountainous Wape villages where I worked (Mitchell 1978b: 8) as well as in the mountains just to the east where Gilbert Lewis (1977: 230) worked in Rauit village, there is no evidence that it reached the swampy grasslands of the Lujere.

In 1943, the Japanese were in firm control of much of New Guinea's north coast as well and up past the middle Sepik River and were unsparing in their internment of international residents. An uncontested example of wartime Japanese brutality was the execution of foreign nationals aboard the Japanese destroyer *Akikaze* on March 18, 1943. Although Japan and Germany were allies, the ship's crew killed over sixty individuals, mostly German Catholic and Evangelical missionaries serving in the Sepik area, as they sailed from Manus to Rabaul. The Catholic missionaries killed were Bishop Joseph Loerks, ten fathers, and fifteen brothers. The adults, hung one by one by their wrists at the ship's stern, were then killed by gunfire and dropped overboard; the three infants were simply thrown into the sea. The Australian War Crimes Section in Tokyo investigated the atrocity, but no further action was taken.[10]

With tens of thousands of Japanese troops occupying New Guinea's north coast, it was the coastal villages that initially suffered the greatest exploitation for labor and deprivation. But it was not only the Japanese who demanded that the Indigenous population work for them; ANGAU also impressed thousands of local men as carriers and laborers in the areas they controlled to aid their fight. In the words of a New Zealand reporter who was there,

The objective now, of course, was no longer the extension of civilization but the maximum exploitation of native population for the purpose of waging war against the Japanese. All available males were conscripted for labour on military works, or for service as carriers, stretcher-bearers or workers on coconut and rubber plantations which had assumed new importance. (White 1965: 125)

So pervasive was the war in New Guinea that the Lujere, although far inland and far up the Sepik River, were eventually affected by the fighting. It was not over the coastal mountains that the war came to them but up the Japanese controlled Sepik. When I lived

---

10. https://en.wikipedia.org/wiki/Japanese_destroyer_Akikaze. Accessed March 2, 2016.

with the Wape who were nearer the Aitape coast, I heard many stories about the Japanese and the war. But while living with the more remote Lujere, I heard only a few war stories, as the Japanese never entered their villages. What little I did hear was as hard for me to make sense of as it was for them; it was only when I began this book and researched the World War II in New Guinea by delving into reports, books, and archives that I understood why and how the war found its way into their isolated domain.

The Lujere and the Mosstroops Guerrillas

An essential responsibility of ANGAU, the one that concerns us, "was to carry out patrols and organize the support and cooperation of the New Guinea people to assist the Army against the Japanese" (Fulton 2005: 140–141).[11] But there were other patrolling units, such as the Allied Intelligence Bureau (AIB) and Far Eastern Liaison Office (FELO), also working along enemy lines in all the occupied parts of New Guinea's north coast. They, like ANGAU operatives, were mostly Australian men with unique experience in New Guinea. The AIB men gathered intelligence on the enemy's activities from cooperating villagers or by stealth while FELO men as purveyors of propaganda were attempting to influence villagers to side with them against the Japanese. The distinction was sometimes more on paper than in practice. Common to all Allied patrols was that the Japanese knew they were out there somewhere and had the superior numbers to send out numerous patrols to find and engage them. Some lost their lives in guerrilla skirmishes with Japanese soldiers or in surprise attacks from villagers working for the enemy.

In 1943 the Allies' Joint Chiefs were eyeing an eventual offensive under the direction of General Douglas MacArthur against Japan's north coast New Guinea bases. Because the Japanese wielded power over large swaths of New Guinea and its residents, often extending far inland, there was interest in creating a stronger guerrilla-intelligence-propaganda presence in the extensive Sepik Basin that lay behind Japan's Wewak and Aitape coastal bases. A guerrilla force, code-named "Mosstroops," was the strategic outcome and it eventually materialized directly in the heart of the Lujere's homeland.[12]

Phillip Guddemi (1992: 37) mentions the "Mosstroops" in his dissertation on the Sawiyanō, the Lujere's cannibal enemies just across the Sepik. But it was not until my Australian colleague Bryant Allen alerted me to the hundreds of pages online, including twenty-seven field photographs in the National Australian Archives about the planning, operation, and termination of "Mosstroops," that I understood their significance in the Lujere's colonial history. Rather suddenly, my Wakau informants' cryptic comments about World War II began to make sense.

---

11. While ANGAU accomplished much in the war, some of Australia's goals and officers, especially General Sir Thomas Blamey, commander-in-chief of the Australian Military Forces, were strongly criticized (Grey 2008: 190). Peter Charlton (1983: 89) even titled his book, *The Unnecessary War*, noting, "The operations on Bougainville and around Aitape–Wewak were the very models of modern unnecessary campaigns." For an overview of the basic organization of ANGAU and its unique field services, including the expropriation of local labor, see Powell (2003). For a more succinct account, see Ryan (1972b).
12. According to the Oxford English Dictionary, the original Mosstroopers were groups of marauding bands operating in the English-Scottish border area in the mid-seventeenth century.

One of the first documents outlining the "Mosstroops" operation is dated April 29, 1943, marked "MOST SECRET" and titled "NEW GUINEA GUERRILLA FORCE." "Kassa" Townsend and Keith McCarthy, having put their pique against the Australian government behind them, were now both majors and, as undisputed Sepik experts, among the plan's architects and advisors, Townsend for FELO and McCarthy for AIB. It begins:

> As a result of discussions between Commander Proud and Lieut. Colonel Chapman-Walker, Major Townsend and Major Mccarthy (sic), the following points have been agreed and subsequently approved by the C-in-C [Commander in Chief of Australian Forces, General Sir Thomas Blamey]:
> 1. The creation of Guerrilla Patrols to operate in Japanese occupied territory is essential for the protection of Intelligence and F.E.L. Parties operating on the New Guinea mainland.
> 2. The organization, training and preparation of these patrols should be conducted by N.G.F. [New Guinea Force, i.e., the military].[13] As a preliminary estimate, it appears that it will be necessary to transport into the Upper Sepik River area a force of approximately 120 men with 100,000 lbs. of stores and equipment. In preparing detailed plans of this operation every effort will be made to reduce this number of men and weight of stores.[14]

Continuing, the document notes that the only practical wartime method of transport to the Sepik River is by "Flying Boat" (i.e., Catalina seaplanes); that Major H. M. Farlow should command the Force and, with the C-in-C's approval, he proceed to Brisbane, Australia to examine the detailed plans in preparation and agree on the personnel to be recruited. Farlow was with ANGAU and a former Assistant District Officer in Rabaul but with no Sepik experience.

The "Intelligence parties" the document alludes to were five small forward patrols operating along and, occasionally, within, the Japanese lines in the Sepik area. Their principal task, like the Coastwatchers, who were specifically interested in Japanese movements at sea and in the harbors, was to gather intelligence data on the enemy's land movements while other groups were more propaganda-oriented toward the villagers. Each patrol had a movable base with a wireless to send relevant information to their headquarters. According to the diary of the leader of one party, G. A. V. Stanley[15], the geologist with Oil Search Ltd. before the war but now a FELO agent, had his base for a time among the

---

13. In 1942, MacArthur placed all of the US and Australian units in New Guinea under the control of the New Guinea Force. See https://www.wikiwand.com/en/New_Guinea_Force.
14. Memorandum, "New Guinea Guerilla Force," 29 April 1943. World War II, Mosstroops Papers, National Archives of Australia, Canberra.
15. On September 20, 1935, the Wape area of the Torricelli Mountains had a devastating earthquake that Stanley personally experienced and published an account of (Stanley et al. 1935). So memorable was the severity of the '35 earthquake to the inhabitants that it was one of the few solid events by which I could correlate the time with a European calendar. Also see Cheesman (1949: 241) for her brief account of the quake related to her by another geologist who, like Stanley, was employed by Oil Search, Ltd.

Lujere at Edwaki (Edawok, Edawaki, Edoaki); both the name of the 705-foot hilltop and a Lujere village. In some areas, but not among the Lujere, these patrols faced villagers' hostility or attempts to capture them for the Japanese, who boasted to the locals that they would castrate any European captive.

> By 13th July [1943] a memorandum was produced in MacArthur's headquarters recommending the establishment of a base on Lake Kuvanmas in the Sepik area for the purpose of obtaining Intelligence, gaining meteorological information, favourably influencing the natives, reconnoitering for possible airfields, and protecting Intelligence parties operating in uncontrolled areas. (Dexter 1961: 260)

Although there was some strong opposition to the plan (Powell 2003: 60) it was adopted and ANGAU was designated as the supervising agency for all such intelligence-gathering groups. Keith McCarthy was appointed to the planning staff and ANGAU's Major H. M. Farlow was placed in command of the on-the-ground operations. Seventy-one men were recruited in Australia to help staff the operation. A Catalina seaplane began flying in men and by early August the Mosstroop's Lake Kuvanmas base camp on the middle Sepik was established. But as ANGAU's historian Alan Powell (2003: 61) writes, "From the beginning Operation Mosstroops went wrong." Two large and well-armed Japanese patrols came up the Sepik and attacked the camp. After an initial skirmish, the Mosstroops party retreated to a sago swamp but in the melee, some of the men were separated. Following a six-week arduous trek they eventually found safety at Wabag in the Highlands. In September, another Mosstroops group landed on Lake Yimas, just east of Lake Kuvanmas, and was attacked the same day. Local people had led the Japanese to them and in the resulting fight they killed or wounded nine of their attackers. Abandoning their stores, they also made the long trek to Wabag arriving the end of October. Here, the historian of the war in New Guinea, David Dexter, takes up the story:

> In spite of the unfortunate start and although the enemy was now aware that something was happening along the Sepik, it was decided to insert the balance of Mosstroops into the Sepik-Yellow River area. On 10th September Captain Milligan landed from a Catalina and established a base on the Sepik [near the mouth of the Yellow River] but on the same day the river became swollen making Catalina landings dangerous. A temporary base was then established at Lake Panawai, [a Sepik River oxbow] and the remainder of Mosstroops and stores were flown in. By the beginning of October, the movement was complete and the work of establishing a line of communication up the Yellow River and staging camps at Makeme, Birin and Abrau was begun. Advanced headquarters moved early in October from Lake Panawai to Pinnace Head [the limit of navigation up the Yellow River]. The Catalina unloading point for supplies was at Kochiabu [Kojabu] just downstream from the Sepik-Yellow River junction. Thus for a few weeks after their disastrous start Mosstroops had a chance to establish themselves. (Dexter 1961: 262–63)

By unloading supplies at Kojabu (Kochiabu), the site of the prewar Yellow River Base Camp, the Mosstroops sustained the government's importance of that area. But the exact history of the Yellow River (Kojabu) Base Camp after McCarthy's 1936 visit is as murky as the Sepik's waters. It does not even appear in a listing of all the government's stations opened from 1883 to 1963 compiled by McCarthy's (1964) own office when, much later, he was the Director of the Department of Native Affairs.[16] On Jack Fryer's World War II 1943 sketch map a defunct "Yellow River Police Post" appears atop Kojabu Hill so it is likely that the original Base Camp was down-graded to a "Police Post" when its 'kiap,' Jim Hodgekiss, moved on to follow the explorations of Oil Search Ltd.'s field staff. In 1942 the Police Post was closed when the Japanese occupied the North coastal area of the Territory and all of the government's alienated posts were abandoned.

All place names in Dexter's quoted text are in the Lujere area, with the exception of Abrau village, a traditional enemy whose villagers speak Awun. East Post, on the Sepik River below the Yellow River, was designated a "watching post" for the encroachment of the Japanese from down river. Ted Fulton, one of the men recruited for Mosstroops, has written about the experience (Fulton 2005: 209–14). A volunteer in the Australian Army, he was selected because of his long experience in New Guinea, first in government administration then as a successful gold prospector. In his words,

> Mosstroops were to collect information about Japanese operations, to help downed Allied aircrew, to bolster the morale of villagers by showing them we were still there in numbers and to arm and encourage selected village men to attack Japanese patrols in guerrilla warfare. (Fulton 2005: 211)

In hindsight, it was an ambitious agenda for a small group of men dependent on continual aerial supply support (see fig. 3) set against the sprawling Japanese army whose ruthlessness against non-cooperating villagers was well known.

Figure 3. A Mosstroops photo of the Sepik River, marked up to show the seaplane landing area where men and supplies could be off-loaded. Courtesy of National Archives of Australia.

The several hundred Mosstroops documents I have examined, while filled with logistic data, give little information regarding the troops' relations with or perceptions of the Lujere, a topic germane to my interests. One indicator of their thinking, however, lies in a "Mosstroops" report by their leader, Major Farlow. Here are extracts from a section titled "Handling of Natives" that reads like a guide to his officers:

---

16. I am indebted to Laurie Bragge for this information.

The native, never mind how primitive he is, sizes you up very quickly and your demeanour and every action is noted.

Before you can get him to assist you, you must first gain his confidence by showing him you do not want to cause him any inconvenience by your presence in his area and that you do not wish to interfere with his property.

If you wish his assistence you must pay him for it and it is always a good principle at first to be liberal with your payments. Once you have established values in the area do not alter them.

It must at all times be remembered that it is practically impossible to work in New Guinea without the natives' assistance. Therefore your dealings with him must be such as to impress on him that he will at all times be given a fair deal.

He is timid in most cases and will show no hostility to you. In fact he is quick to make friends. Do not treat him as an equal as he does not expect it.

Do not, on any account, have anything to do with his womenfolk, in fact, ignore them and discourage them from visiting your camp.

Learn Pidgin English. (Farlow 1944b)

The major's behavioral protocol succeeded as there are no recorded incidents of mistreatment of the Lujere by Mosstroops Europeans during their stay among them nor did I hear of any during my fieldwork. But Farlow, apparently comparing the Yellow River people to other populations where he previously was a patrol officer, found they did not measure up.

The natives living in this area are not many in number and are a very poor type of native. They are friendly but are very timid. They are nomadic and do not live in settled villages.[17] Hamlets are scattered throughout the surrounding bush where family groups live. They are without steel and very anxious to obtain tomahawks and knives. They will come into work but after a few days disappear. It is necessary to treat them patiently and wait for them to return and generally you will find that they have been away obtaining sac sac [sago].[18]

Steel tools at last

Fortunately for the Lujere, it was impossible for the Mosstroops's operation to go forward without the aid of local men to help relay their gear and supplies from camp to camp up the Yellow River and to provide food, especially sago, for the many New Guinea men, mostly police, they brought with them. This necessitated a big influx of trade goods flown in to secure the local food and labor they were dependent upon, an operational fact Farlow made explicit in his report:

TRADE. This is one of the most important items that a party should carry. Owing to the enemy having been in occupation of parts of New Guinea for some considerable

---

17. This, of course, is incorrect. "Nomadic" implies that a group has no fixed residence. The Lujere are best characterized as semisedentary.
18. "Mosstroops Report on Food Packs, Equipment, Weapons, Etc. by Major R. M. Farlow," n.d., p. 4, World War II Mosstroops Papers, National Archives of Australia, Canberra.

time the natives have become "trade hungry" and as trade is at present the only means of obtaining the natives' services, in the hinterland, large quantities should be carried. The items most sort [sic] after in the SEPIK area were: Tomahawks, Knives (all sizes), Beads, Mirrors, Plane Blades, Fish Hooks, China Beads.[19]

One actual drop of parachuted supplies towards the end of the operation from ANGAU headquarters to G. A. V. Stanley's camp recorded in the Mosstroops radio message log gives an indication of the amount and kind of trade goods that entered into the Lujere's region. The message in military parlance is from Farlow's Advance Base to ANGAU headquarters:

Stanley reports completed drop as follows (.) 3 btys, 1500 rds shot-gun can, 2 tins tropical spread each 3 lbs, 120 yards lap-lap [cloth], 1 gross matches, 1 gross mirrors, 36 hatchets, 2 gross small knives, 80 machettes, 100 plane blades, 2000 razor blades, 3500 buttons, 900 rings, bundles of stationery, 3 drums benzine, 1 drum oil, 3 drums sugar, 2 drums salt, 1 35 lb tin lifebouy soap, BOYS [Native police] soap, ditto mosquito net, 13 tins "C" rations, 50 Army packs, 1 OWEN gun, 4 globes, 4 topography SEPIK maps, 1 bottle herbs, 2 plaster.[20] [my inserted commas]

Remember, it was just seven years earlier that McCarthy made his compassionate plea to the government—a rare occurrence in a patrol report—for "half-a-dozen axes and knives be given to every village in the area." His superiors didn't bother to reply but now, in the name of warfare, the Australian government was finally giving the Lujere access to metal tools to replace their ancient labor-intensive stone ones, in trade for sago and labor. I like to think that McCarthy got as much ironic pleasure knowing this back then as I do now. It would take World War II and a Japanese invasion to accomplish it, but the Lujere finally had metal tools.

On October 6, Colonel Kenneth Wills, deputy director of military intelligence at Advanced Land Headquarters, landed on the Sepik at Kopiagu from Port Moresby for a progress report on the guerrilla operation from its leader, Colonel Farlow. He returned to Moresby the next day. While we don't have a record of his report, we do know that he carried with him a small collection of Lujere artifacts from Miriyami village consisting of two bows, two engraved bamboo-smoking tubes, and fourteen arrows, the barbed arrows for war, the plain blades for hunting. In March 1946, now a retired brigadier, he gave the collection to the South Australian Museum in Adelaide, his hometown. It is the oldest documented museum collection of Lujere artifacts.

Wills also had observed the people and a few comments are included in the artifact register, e. g., "Av.[average] Male height 5' 3," "Av. Female height 4' 6"; "Physique poor."[21] He added:

---

19. "Mosstroops Report on Food Packs, Equipment, Weapons, Etc. by Major R. M. Farlow," n.d., p. 3, World War II Mosstroops Papers, National Archives of Australia, Canberra.
20. Mosstroops Message Log, 0900 hrs, 11 Dec 1943, World War II Mosstroops Papers, National Archives of Australia, Canberra.
21. See chapter 10 for Betty Gilliam's statistics on the height and weight of Wakau villagers.

The males pierce the septum of the nose and wear a short bamboo therein, and puncture the front of each nasal passage so that a guria [Victoria crowned pigeon] plume or grass plume can be worn in upright position from each side of the nose.²²

When I arrived to live with the Lujere in 1971, this decorative custom was passé, but the nasal holes among older men were clearly visible. Finally, there were a number of photographs among the NAA's Mosstroops documents, but most concerned the members of the force. There was, however, one of a headman (fig. 4), who probably helped the Mosstroops recruit carriers.

Figure 4. A Lujere headman with a traditional pipe, as photographed by a Mosstroops member. Courtesy of the National Archives of Australia.

Information from the Mosstroops documents and my Wakau informants show the gradual establishment of their staging and patrol camps from the Sepik up the Yellow and Sand Rivers then easterly over the grass plains to Abrau and finally up to Mellip just before the hills begin. Some indication regarding the nature and extent of the patrols by the Mosstroops "and the intelligence groups" already active in the area, can be gleaned from the detailed daily radio log of messages sent and received. For the large number of men in the operation, my overall conclusion was that not a lot was happening on the ground.

Captain Bob Cole, whose group appeared to be more peripatetic than some, also kept a diary²³ of his whereabouts, for instance, on October 12 he was at Birin [a staging camp] and noted that Lieutenant G. A. V. Stanley was camped in the vicinity and met with him several times; on November 6 he was in the vicinity of Yilui village [not Lujere] and visited a bush camp where three other officers were camped and received supplies dropped by US bombers; and on December 6, he was at a bush camp when some of his men "came in with part of a drop [of supplies] which had been broken into and 4 of the 13 shutes

---

22. Artifact Register, "Brig. Gen. Kenneth Wills," South Australian Museum, Adelaide.
23. The following data are from a copy of a diary kept by R. R. "Bob" Cole, November 14, 1938– November 24, 1945, in the possession of Bryant Allen, who kindly gave me access to the quoted material.

recovered."[24] He then set out to recover the stolen cargo, inspecting the drop site on his way and in Makeme village recovered a rucksack, a knife and a bottle of herbs. Moving on to Yegaupi (Yegerapi) on December 10 in a three-and-three-quarter hour hike via Yaru and two other villages, he found each village deserted and all the houses closed. At six different places, the track was barred but he and his men broke through and moved on. Cole writes:

> It is apparent the kanakas realised their trouble. In YEGUAPI I found pilfered boxes and tins lying about. We camped in village and sent 2 local boys to EDAWOK hamlet for news. They returned with a little of the cargo and news that kanakas are scared of our reaction to the pilfering. Heard planes, appear to be Catalinas at *Round Water* [Panawai].
> Dec 11th Sat Remained at YEGUAPI and sent out locals and they returned with the headman and news that the rest may turn up tomorrow.
> Dec 12th Sun Sent 2 locals out and they returned late with the whole village and a little more of pilfered cargo—all slept the night there.
> Dec 13th Mon I calaboosed [locked up] all the marys [women] and children and sent kanakas back to get the stolen cargo. John Beatty [Mosstrooper] arrived from Advanced Base—gave us the local news—visited drop site and found broken drums and some cargo—marys and children escaped during the night by burning a hole in the limboom[25] floor. (R. R. Cole, unpublished diary)

While appreciative of Cole's dependency on the supplies dropped for him and his men, I was pleased when I read that the captive women and children burned a hole in the floor of the house and escaped. Then I learned that the locals involved had a slightly different version of this story. Tom Feldpausch, the American SIL-linguist who lived and worked among the Lujere from 1985 to 2008, emailed me this reply (September 10, 2014) when I asked him what the people in Yaru village where he lived remembered about World War II:

> They told us a story of how some Aussie soldiers were in the area and had arranged for an airdrop of supplies. But the drop was slightly off as far as location, and by the time the soldiers got there all the stuff was gone. So they rounded up all the villagers nearby and locked them in a house until they told the soldiers where the stuff was. The

---

24. There is strong evidence that some of the indigenous FELO agents working for Stanley used their status to exploit and sexually abuse the local population. In January of 1971, Ron Kitson, the Lumi recruiter and trader, gave me access to the first Aotei (Otei) Village Book, given to the village (located just north of Lumi) by PO Ray Stephen on September 2, 1939. These village books were kept by the 'luluai' and then consulted by visiting patrol officers who, in turn, left a brief report of their visits. (My typed verbatim copy of their comments is in WN, 481–82.) It is unclear when or how Kitson got possession of the book. The longest entry was by ANGAU Captain Donnell dated August 17, 1944. In it he alerts visiting officers that "Stanley's Felo agents" were "pulling" women of Sienam, Biem, Aueianak, Yankok and Yemnu villages. 'Pulim meri' is a Tok Pisin expression for the abduction or raping of women. None of the mentioned villages were Lujere.
25. Or 'limbum,' a type of palm bark used in strips for flooring of houses on stilts like the Lujere's.

shamans who were part of the group did magic that night to make it rain, and it did. Under the cover of the noise of the rain they pulled up part of the limbum flooring and all the people escaped. The next morning when the soldiers opened the door there was no one there! They realized they would have to do something else so they made some deals with the people; they got to keep so much for returning so much. This worked and the people returned some of the cargo, but got to keep some of the prized metal tools and machetes. (Email from T. Feldpausch to W. Mitchell, September 10, 2014)

Lujere memories of the war

During my fieldwork, I knew nothing about the Yellow River's Mosstroops or of their namesake, the seventeenth-century Scottish marauders on the English border. My Wakau informants indicated they were Australian soldiers of some kind but, as to why they were there and what they were doing, they were as mystified as I was. The Japanese, Australia's enemy, were fighting the war on the coast or far down the Sepik River, not in the Lujere's swamplands. As the Japanese were either on the north coast or far downriver, it was obvious to my informants that all of these young White men must be hiding from the enemy. It was a local understanding of the Mosstroops's purpose that might have vexed the planners back at the ANGAU headquarters.[26]

Below is a note I typed in the field on November 22, 1971, titled, "Early Contacts with Europeans." You will meet some of the men mentioned in more detail later.

> Most of this data from Arakwaki [the boss for building my house in Wakau] with added details by Oria [my best informant]. Arakwaki was telling the stories but he would look to Oria for details although the latter is younger. This was last night at my house; Arie and Nauwen [Oria's younger brother and my household helper] plus some . . . boys were there too. Masta Mak:[27]
>
> At the time of the war the Wakau people lived on two small hills not too far from the present site of the village that in turn, had been occupied at an earlier date. A European they called Masta Mak [surveyor, TP] lived with a long line of polis [police, TP] or soldiers near Iwani village atop Maui hill for a time; then they moved down to the bush on the Sand River near Wakau's kunai [grass plain]. For Wakau it was a momentous time: it was when the Wakau people got their first metal tools; the European traded these for sago for his men. The European's own supplies were dropped on the kunai by airplanes. First a fire was made on the kunai to show the area for the drop. The natives never helped with these drops; the polis collected everything. They were probably there about 5 months.

---

26. Allen's (2006) article makes an insightful summary of the war's impact on local life and includes the war memories of other Sepik area men. See White and Lindstrom (1989) for local representations of World War II on some of the other Pacific islands the war impacted.
27. "Masta" was the ubiquitous Tok Pisin term of colonial address and reference for a White man used by many New Guineans that both created and validated a class, almost "caste," difference. By the time I first came to New Guinea in 1967, younger male anthropologists preferred to be on a first-name basis with villagers and discouraged this practice. However, it could take months to accomplish and, while no one I knew would address me as 'masta,' I often overheard references to me with that term.

The Japanese were never in the area [i.e., in the villages] but they, the locals, describe the Europeans as hiding from them. . . The women were afraid of the foreign group and never went near them; only the men would occasionally go to them to trade. At this time, of course, none [of the Wakau men] had been to plantation [as indentured workers]. They still lived mostly in the bush in what appear to be isolated homesteads. . . Certainly, they say, they were more nomadic than today for they were hunters and sago eaters; gardens insignificant, even as they are today. (WN420)

"Masta Mak" was probably the thirty-three-year-old engineer and surveyor, Captain H. A. J. Fryer from Canterbury, Victoria, Australia, one of the men working in forward intelligence before the Mosstroops arrived and with long experience as a surveyor for Oil Search, Ltd. in New Guinea.[28] Considerate, fair, and well-liked by local men, Fryer wrote in his field diary:

It was humbling to realise that our new friends [Lujere carriers and laborers] had little or no vice, greed and lust, and no shame as we know it. Fear and anger, yes. What I particularly liked was their sense of humour. (Allen 1990: 189)

Fryer made a map I found amid the Mosstroops papers that shows he was encamped for a while at his clearly marked "D Base" near Yuani (Iwani) village atop Mauwi hill. The 'kunai' "drop site" where he received his supplies is also shown, as are the places on the Sepik and the two oxbow lakes near Purami village where the Catalinas could land. When Fryer and his men were in Wakau's area, either camping by the 'kunai' or living atop the hill at D Base, according to my Wakau friends, there were two men up in Iwani village, Kaiera and Yuwari, who knew Tok Pisin with whom Fryer visited.[29] They were probably two of the three men that Robinson had identified as Tok Pisin speakers from "Yuani" in his 1932 patrol report, recently returned from a three-year contract as laborers at the Alexishafen Mission. I was told that Wakau's old Leno had been one of his carriers. The Wakau men, none who then knew Tok Pisin, indicated there was considerable movement of the Whites and their men, mostly New Guinea policemen, frequently changing camps. Aiyuk told me that 'masta mak' (Fryer) finally left the area in a 'kanu' [dugout] with about ten men, some of them with reddish skins like some Papuans and, indeed, the Mosstroop records show they had a group of local men from the Royal Papuan Constabulary. Before Fryer left, one of his men got lost while hunting and somehow emerged near Wagu, an enemy village east of the Sand River and across the Sepik.[30] A Lujere man

---

28. Fryer's 1910–1993 papers, including extensive files of his years in New Guinea, are archived at the Australian National Archives. For a brief but penetrating discussion of the role and manner of Oil Search Limited's field staff see Allen (1990: 188–89).
29. This is not the same "Kaiera" you will meet in later chapters who was a sight-challenged, important informant.
30. The Wagu villagers spoke Abau. At contact the Abau people lived in large and rickety elevated community houses amid the trees some as high as forty feet, cool and mosquito-free. They ascended by ladder but could descend by long bamboo poles. See Behrmann (1917: 85, plate 5) for a photo, McCarthy (1963, 144–145) for a description of Wagu, and Craig (2008) for an interesting paper on Abau sorcery, healing, and sorcery death divination.

who had married a woman from there escorted him back to the 'kunai' and the 'masta,' in gratitude for guiding his lost policeman back, gave him a metal tool.

Menetjua, Wakau's oldest man, also had memories of the 'taim bilong pait.' He recalled three young White men coming up the Sand River in canoes when he was a youngster and watching them apprehensively from the shore. The people thought they were *aokwae* (spirits of the dead). His father and some of the other men traded sago with them for knives and rings. One of the men said his name was Wiski and that his companions were Markowa and Ari (possibly Harry Aitken, an AIB officer frequently with Fryer).[31] The strangers went on up the river to Gwidami village, where they spent the night and then returned down the river the following day, but the villagers did not know the purpose of their trip. Later, Wiski returned but this time came up the Yellow River, leaving canoes at the mouth of the Inarlit River and made a camp on the top of Mauwi hill (D Base). He and his policemen had guns and killed many wild pigs, cassowaries and Victoria crowned pigeons. Although Wiski and his men did not visit Wakau village, the Wakau men and youths were occasional visitors to their camp, usually bringing sago processed by the women to trade. Menetjua had a vivid memory of watching the strangers cook. They first put sago in a large drum, covered the sago with heated stones and then alternated layers of meat and stones to the top where it was capped.

Oria also remembered a story his father told him about Wiski. We were at one of the ancient axe-blade grinding stones where the old men more confined to the village, used to sit astride the stone to laboriously hand grind the villagers' stone tools. His father had brought some of his wife's sago to trade with Wiski and his men and received a prized adze metal blade for it. Later he showed me the old adze he inherited from his father with Wiski's piece of metal still intact within it that replaced the stone blade.

Like other Wakau men, Menetjua emphasized that the White strangers never caused trouble or bothered their women, adding that the Wakau women called these White men "*mo* 'bilong mipella,'" that is, "our mother" (in Namia, "mother" is *mo*). Menetjua could offer no further explanation, but I assume that like a generous and loving mother, these strange men provided the women with coveted knives and fishhooks plus "luxury" items like mirrors, rings, cloth, and colored beads for the first time. Although the Wakau men perceived this large peripatetic troop of young White men and their armed Black policemen living in their midst as frightened men hiding from the Japanese, their wives might have interpreted the presence of so many armed friendly men as protecting them from the encroaching enemy.

Then two days later I typed up another note titled "More on Early Times." I had been talking with four Wakau men, but it was Aiyuk, a rather slow, sickly man, and blind in one eye, who knew the most. Although he had worked in the goldfields of Wau in the Highlands for a year, he never learned Tok Pisin so Eine translated. He also reported that there were a number of Whites in the area during the war hiding from the Japanese. He mentioned "Masta Mak" then also remembered "Masta Waisan" [probably Mosstroop

---

31. I had access to only partial lists of Mosstroops names so have not determined the identity of these men. Most are identified in records only by their initials and last name. For example, the Mosstroops documents mentioning H. A. J. Fryer refer to him in that way or, more frequently, as "Fryer." Consulting his archived papers at the Australian National Archives I learned his full name was "Herbert Albinus Jackson Fryer" and that he was called "Jack."

officer Lieutenant Ray Watson] who was based on the Sepik, and remembered the name of another Tok Pisin speaker, "Meauwi," of Tipas village. According to Aiyuk, the first recruiter came up the Sepik River in a "lik lik sip" (small boat).

The Japanese Peril

While the Mosstroops units limited their patrols mostly to the Lujere's immediate region, the forward intelligence groups who preceded them into the area patrolled much farther afield to the east and to the north. One small group met with several violent deaths.

> A party led by Lieutenant Fryer and accompanied by a Dutchman, Sergeant H. N. Staverman of the Netherlands Navy, and an Australian radio operator [of Dutch descent], Sergeant [Leonard] Siffleet, arrived in the well-populated Lumi area south of the Torricellis in July. After reaching Lumi, Fryer and Staverman parted, Fryer to remain in the general Sepik area and Staverman to penetrate across the [Dutch] border into the hills behind Hollandia. Once again the unreliability of the [Wape] natives led to failure. Fryer's party was trapped [in Seinem village] by apparently friendly natives a few miles south of Lumi. The Australians managed to beat off the attack, but in the process their carriers deserted and seven weapons were lost. (Dexter 1961: 261)[32]

Fryer's party retreated south towards G. A. V. Stanley's camp off the Wagama (Yula) River just east of the Lujere's area. Staverman and Siffleet with two Ambonese privates, H. Pattwal and M. Reharing, and a line of carriers proceeded west towards the border. They had reached Wama, south of Vanimo, when Japanese, guided by unfriendly local people, ambushed Staverman and Pattwal on a reconnaissance patrol. After Siffleet radioed that Staverman was killed, he was instructed to take his party southward and proceed to Stanley's camp. Keenly aware that Siffleet and his companions were unfamiliar with the region, Fryer and twenty-nine- year-old Lieutenant Guy B. Black, from Queensland, Australia, set out to find and guide them to safety. Unsuccessful, they returned on November 23. Unbeknownst to them, their wandering allies had been captured by local men and given to the Japanese who imprisoned them in Aitape. At that time, the estimated strength of the Japanese army was Aitape 200, Vanimo 500, Hollandia 500, Wewak, 20,000, and 500 covering the Middle Sepik Area (Brown 2011: 125).

On October 24, 1943, Siffleet and Privates Pattwal and Reharung were taken to the Aitape beach and beheaded before a group of soldiers and New Guineans. Siffleet was buried on the beach below tide level and his body never recovered. The event is memorialized in a Japanese soldier's photograph of Siffleet later found on the body of a dead Japanese major when the war moved on to Hollandia in April 1944. The iconic photograph of Siffleet, moments before his death, blindfolded and kneeling in the sand with

---

32. Fryer's AIB group's code name was "Locust" and Staverman's "Whiting;" the latter Dutch group was under the direction of the Netherlands East Indies part of AIB later known as the Netherlands Forces Intelligence Services. See Richmond (2004a) for a more detailed discussion of this tragic patrol.

a Japanese officer holding his sword aloft, appeared in Life Magazine and elsewhere as evidence of Japanese brutality.[33]

Japanese attacks in Lujereland

Shortly before the coastal beheadings, the Japanese made their first attack against the Yellow River Mosstroops. The Japanese, obviously aware of the Allies' active aerial activity regularly flying supplies to the Yellow River area in their big Catalina seaplanes, sent two armed pinnaces up the Sepik on October 20, 1943, and attacked the Mosstroops's East Post. Major Farlow's account in his final report to ANGAU details the assault in dry military prose:

> At 1750 hrs, a party of the enemy in two pinnaces attempted to land at EAST POST. They were fired on by Lieut DOWNIE's party. The occupants of one pinnace were severely dealt with and it is estimated that 10 casualties were inflicted. The second pinnace landed a party of 15 and attacked the post from the land. Lieut DOWNIE and his 4 men were forced to withdraw. [The following day] Capt FIENBERG and party arrived from PANAWAI and proceeded to retake EAST POST.[34] The enemy had left taking with them the wireless set, 20 tins of ration and all personal gear. No 2 Fighting Patrol, under Capt GLUTH, were withdrawn from the L of C [line of communication] and dispatched to EAST POST. A further post *TOKIO* was established 2 miles further east [downstream] on the SEPIK RIVER. (Farlow 1944a: 4)

Lieutenant Downie and his men, outnumbered when the Japanese stormed their post, escaped through the swamps guided by one of the Native policemen. Although they lost equipment and supplies, there were no Mosstroops casualties and no Lujere were involved. But the attack clearly troubled ANGAU authorities. Two weeks later, on November 3, reinforcements—two officers and nineteen soldiers—called "Stop Troops," were flown in to relieve Captain Gluth's men at East and Tokio Posts. Heavy rains then raised the Sepik River forcing the abandonment of Tokio Post and withdrawal to nearby Purami village. The Panawai Camp on Lake Panawai was cleared of all stores and personnel thus eliminating one link in the laborious on-transfer of stores and supplies. A new initial staging area on the Sepik itself near the Iwani hamlet of Kociabu (one of Wakau's sister Iwani hamlets) was established and Gluth's "No. 2 Fighting Patrol" proceeded up

---

33. From a Japanese perspective, Siffleet and his comrades were honorably beheaded as enemies under the military's code of Bushido. The execution officer, Yasuno Chikao, was later tried for war crimes and his sentence of hanging was commuted to ten years imprisonment whereupon he returned to Japan. www.wikiwand.com/ov/Leonard_Siffleet. Accessed 24 May 2018.
34. D. M Fienberg (1916–1976), a native of Perth who later changed his name to Fenbury, led one of the most successful patrol groups in the Torricelli Mountains behind Aitape and was awarded the Military Cross. A forward-looking man like McCarthy, sensitive to the indigene's plight, he championed village courts and was openly critical of the government's policies. Consequently, in 1969 he was removed as head of the politically sensitive Department of the Administrator and appointed secretary of the new Department of Social Development and Home Affairs, a post he held until his retirement in 1973. http://adb.anu.edu.au/biography/fenbury-david-maxwell-10164/text17955, accessed online 10 May 2014.

the Yellow River to Pinnace Head, Farlow's headquarters, for onward movement up to Mellip, the terminal camp. Now there were twenty-one more men to feed, equip, and house.

The recruited Lujere carriers, earning coveted trade goods and steel tools in return for their labor and their wives' sago, were gradually moving the Mosstroops's gear and rations northward to Mellip via their camps at Makeme, Birin and Abrau. Then there was more enemy action November 11.

> On 11 Nov 43, Capt Ellis was in charge of Tokyo Post with two Ors and two native police. Three Japanese were met about 200 yards from the post and when sighted opened fire with automatic weapons and withdrew. Two days later a fairly large force of Japanese landed below Tokyo and also sent an additional force up river in launches. The Japanese attempted to cut off Tokyo, from East Post but the party at Tokyo managed to get through to East Post against which the Japanese again launched an attack. They were driven off and withdrew under cover of darkness taking their casualties with them. (Brown 2011: 127)

Then two days later the Japanese returned in force and mounted a new attack.

> Four (4) boat loads of the enemy landed at TOKIO [POST] at 1600 hours and attacked EAST POST just before dark. They were unsuccessful and it is thought suffered numerous casualties. Two canoes with Japs and natives were blown out of the water and at least 7 casualties were inflicted. (Farlow 1944a)

It was dark when the Japanese retreated with their casualties; one Mosstroop soldier was wounded. On November 21, Farlow received a radio message from ANGAU's headquarters ordering all field parties to stay in place and halting all patrols until further instructions. The same day, three more officers and twenty-one more soldiers were flown to the Sepik from Port Moresby to reinforce the Stop Troops. They were posted to Purami and to assist the East Post men patrolling downstream for the presence of Japanese activity. Across the river from East Post a new smaller post named North Post was established to prevent the Japanese from landing and establishing mortar positions. River patrols already had seen signs that the Japanese were trying to penetrate the swampy area just four miles below. The little war in the Upper Sepik was accelerating and it was obvious to all—except perhaps the Lujere who consistently read the presence of the Australians as "hiding" from the Japanese—that ANGAU's central command was concerned about the viability of its Yellow River guerrilla operation.

Farlow was recalled on November 23 to ANGAU Headquarters in Port Moresby for a personal report on the Mosstroop situation then returned the twenty-fifth to await the decision regarding further action. Compounding the Japanese–Sepik problem was that on December 2, Lieutenant Watson at the terminal Mellip camp had learned from friendly locals that the Japanese had occupied Lumi and that two White men had been seized by locals and handed over to the Japanese at Aitape. That both Staverman and Siffleet were already long dead indicates the paucity of ANGAU's coastal intelligence. But the implied threat that the Japanese might be planning to move a strong force down to the Sepik from Aitape into Lujereland was a real possibility. The Kelms (1980: 14) report in their book on Kwieftim and Abrau, both northern enemy villages bordering Lujere territory, that the Japanese once patrolled down as far as Kwieftim and then moved on to the west.

During the early planning of the Mosstroops guerrilla operation, a major concern of General Blamey was that too large an operation in the Sepik would bring attention from the Japanese and threaten the viability of the strategically valuable intelligence patrols. Writing to General Herring on June 28, Blamey wrote:

> The Japanese have very considerable forces along the coast in the area in which they will be working. Small patrols of ours, essential for the purpose of getting information, may get away with it, but if we make a show of force at all, say 20 or 30 men, the enemy could very easily and quickly bring a force of several hundreds or more against them. This would not only make it difficult for us to maintain observation in that area, but it could, with the superior force of the enemy, have the very effect on the natives that we want to avoid, and that is, that they would give allegiance to the stronger force. (Dexter 1961: 260)

It was a germane and prescient concern: the Yellow River Mosstroops operation now numbered over two hundred men. This necessitated a significant increase in the original supply plan that was dependent on air transport to the Sepik River and easily monitored by the enemy. General Blamey, in spite of his earlier view and the discussion by some authorities of a Mosstroops withdrawal, wrote on December 6 to General MacArthur that he was not willing to withdraw his men unless so ordered (Dexter 1961: 263). In the meantime, supplies and rations continued to be transferred along the camps with over one hundred tins of food moved to Mellip during the last week of November. At the same time, Farlow already had made evacuation plans if the Japanese invaded over land or up the Sepik:

> Lieut WATSON had been successful in recruiting labour and up to 100 labourers were being used. An emergency dump was established at WAGAU [Wagu], approx 10 miles upstream from KOCIABU. Two (2) good [water] landing strips were tested at YIBIRI and WAGAU.
> WAGAU dump comprised of 100 tins of ration, oil, benzine. In the event of the [Mosstroops] parties being forced back and A/C [air transport] not available, WAGAU was selected as a starting point for the party [to] move [on foot] towards TELEFOMIN. (Farlow 1944a: 5)

The flight of the Mosstroops

On December 5 at 5:30 p.m., a Japanese reconnaissance plane flying at fifteen hundred feet circled the main supply base at Kociabu on the Sepik. The following evening at 4:15, an enemy plane again circled the supply base completing six revolutions before withdrawing. The next event signaled the end of the ambitious Mosstroops guerrilla operation amid the Lujere in the upper Sepik Basin. Two days later, on December 8,

> At 1730 hours, two (2) enemy planes bombed and strafed KOCIABU. The attack lasted 40 minutes. Incendiary and HE bombs were dropped, destroying the camp

building and contents, which consisted mainly of personal gear of officers and Ors [orderlies] stationed at Stop Posts. One (1) [Chimbu] native belonging to Lieut AIKEN's line was killed. Lieut WATSON reported that enemy patrols had left Lumi and were within two (2) days journey to MELLIP.[35] He had destroyed the store's dump and withdrawn to BIRIN. (Farlow 1944a: 5)

That is the terse official account in Farlow's final report on the Mosstroops operation. Although a number of my older informants in Wakau village remembered the bombing—it was a first experience for them—Aiyuk was the most expressive in his memories of that night. He recalled four very loud bombs dropped—official record says five—and he imitated the terrifying sound of the strafing of the base that he could hear, but not see. He also noted that there was only one fatality, a policeman killed in the bombing, but another comment he made was inexplicable. He said that the 'namba wan kiap' or top officer shot at one of the two Japanese planes circling low over the area, then the other plane went under it and carried it away! I still remember expressing my amazement at hearing this account but the other men listening all agreed that was what happened. My typed notes say, "All give this version but seems impossible to me . . . So who knows what really happened. It was all new to them, and 25 [actually 28] years ago." Because of the Mosstroops documents in the National Archives of Australia, I have a better understanding today of what did happen; but as for Aiyuk's departing piggyback Japanese planes, that remains an enigma.

The day after Mosstroops main supply base at Kociabu was strafed, bombed, and destroyed, an official from Moresby flew down to assess the situation and inform the officers that air transport for future supply maintenance could not be guaranteed. Further, in the case of a Japanese invasion, air evacuation would be unlikely. Already known was the dangerous alternative of a long difficult retreat from Wagu, mostly on foot through rugged mountain terrain, towards Telefomin. Farlow, asked for his opinion, replied that under those circumstances there was only one course of action: recommendation for an immediate and complete evacuation.

This meant that the forward intelligence/propaganda groups in the area that headquarters relied upon exclusively before the Mosstroops arrived also would be pulled out. Fryer and Black went on leave just before the bombing and now Stanley, Cole and Aiken, all active patrollers and their men totaling fifty-two, were to be evacuated as well. Later Stanley would write,

From the standpoint of a local Native person, the effect of the bombing was astounding. One and all, the white men throughout the area abandoned their camps and stores and fled. It was quite impossible to reconcile the evacuation with the general propaganda which had been used by Lieuts. Fryer and Stanley from July to November. (Powell 2003: 63)

---

35. From notes kindly shared by Bryant Allen on Stanley's papers archived in the Library of the University of Papua New Guinea, there is reason to believe that the reported "enemy patrols" were fictitious to discourage the Mosstroops from moving north into the Wape area.

What Stanley didn't know was that the Lujere had the Mosstroops men figured out long before they fled the area. They were simply hiding from the Japanese and, when the Japanese found them, 'ol I ranawe.' But the running away wasn't logistically easy. On December 16, Farlow got his instructions that the evacuation was approved and the first planes would land at Lake Panawai. All parties were instructed to begin withdrawal to the Advance Base (Pinnace Head) for further movement down the Yellow River to Kociabu across the Sepik. On the sixteenth, three planes arrived, two at Panawai Village and one to Purami to begin the evacuation. On the seventeenth and eighteenth, three seaplanes were used each day, and on the nineteenth, four planes were allocated for the landings at Kociabu to complete the evacuation. It took twenty planeloads to transport the Mosstroops's 102 Whites and 127 New Guineans to safety in Port Moresby.

From the perspective of its goals, the Mosstroops guerrilla operation was a dismal failure. Here are the conclusions of Farlow's Mosstroops Report:

> The objects for which MOSSTROOPS were inserted were not attained for the following reasons:
>
> The enemy had located the general area of activity. It now became necessary to insert STOP TROOPS necessitating further A/C [air-lifts] being required to maintain them. These A/C were not available. Loss of security.
>
> Establishment of L of C [line of communication] between KOCIABU and ADV BASE had absorbed a third of MOSSTROOPS in the area.
>
> Pressure by the enemy necessitating a further party of MOSSTROOPS having to reinforce STOP TROOPS, leaving only one-third available to carry out the original plan.
>
> Lack of sufficient police and carriers. (Farlow 1944a: 8)

Lieutenant Ted Fulton, as an on-the-ground Mosstroops officer, was more direct in his assessment of the operation:

> The force carried out token patrols without achieving anything of importance. We were too far from any enemy action and the force was too large and had a severe supply problem. To supply the base it was necessary for Catalinas to come and go all the time. This constant air activity quickly drew attention. In addition, a high powered radio was on the air to Port Moresby most of the time... It would have been a matter of time before the slow Catalinas were shot down and the Mosstroops stranded, so it was fortunate that only equipment and no personnel was lost. (Fulton 2005: 211–12)

Fulton, expressing a Eurocentric colonial view, failed to note that one Mosstrooper New Guinean was killed in the bombing. There also may have been an unreported Mosstrooper fatality. While I was on a reconnaissance patrol visiting some Lujere villages east of the Yellow River before moving to Wakau, two local men, Manwai of Yegerapi and Nakaki of Alai accompanied me. Visiting as we hiked, Nakaki said that during the war when he was just a boy, there were five White men living along the Yellow River with policemen. One of the policemen had sex with a local woman and he was killed with a bow and arrow. After that, there was no more trouble. Interestingly, when I once mentioned

Nakaki's comment to some Wakau men while talking about the war, they were puzzled that they had not heard about the incident.

For ANGAU, the Yellow River Mosstroops's 1943 guerrilla operation was undoubtedly an expensive blunder. It is telling that neither Townsend (1968) nor McCarthy (1963) discuss or even mention the Mosstroops debacle in the war sections of their autobiographies, while Fulton (2005) derisively does. For the Lujere, however, it was a brief historic time—just over five months—when their tools went from stone to steel.[36]

Operation Persecution: The Aitape Coast Recaptured

Although the war in the Sepik didn't go well for the Allies in 1943, elsewhere in New Guinea it did. The Australians easily recaptured the north coast town of Lae by September 16 and then Finschhafen on October 2. But it was another six months before the next important Allied assault inaugurated General MacArthur's western New Guinea campaign. Strategically cartwheeling over Wewak to box in the Japanese Eighteenth Army, the Americans made simultaneous successful amphibious landings at Aitape and Hollandia on April 22, 1943. (Dexter 1961: 801–805). The immense two-headed invasion—a classic deception operation—termed Operation Persecution (Aitape) and Operation Reckless (Hollandia) consisted of 217 ships carrying 8,000 men with their equipment and supplies.[37] Brookfield comments about the massive scale of the Allied incursion into New Guinea and other regional islands.

> When war came back it came massively, swiftly and with great destruction. Material goods and men were hurled into the fray in unbelievable quantity and with seemingly reckless abandon. . . . The very numbers of men were startling. In 1941, the whole European population of Melanesia was not more than 30,000, half of these in New Caledonia. By the end of 1943 the USA had some 500,000 troops, probably more, deployed in Melanesia. (Brookfield 1972: 93)

The main troops making the amphibious invasion at Aitape were a United States Montana National Guard Regiment, the 163rd Infantry Regiment of the 41st Infantry Division. Also on board was "the ANGAU detachment that landed with them and they took up their familiar role; bringing villagers from the hills into the American perimeter, recruiting and supervising labour, leading patrols" (Powell 2003: 71). Not surprisingly, a number of the men who were a part of the Mosstroops operation were now part of the

---

36. The formal Mosstroops contingent was there from September to December 19, but logs and diaries show that other military patrols were already in the Lujere's area by July, e.g., Stanley arrived by a Catalina amphibian plane July 4 and others soon followed, which supports the five-month stay my Wakau informants remember. See Brown (2011) for the official history, acknowledged as possibly flawed, of the Mosstroops's guerrilla operations among the Lujere.
37. The "deception operation" by the Allies was the staging of strategic actions that led General Adachi to believe that the invasion would be in the Wewak or, further to the east, Hansa Bay areas. These strategies are detailed in Gailey's (2004) chapter titled, "Hollandia: The Great Leap Forward."

invasion detachment including David Fienberg, Harry Aiken, Ted Fulton and Jack Milligan, its leader. Earlier Fulton, who had walked the 90-mile Wewak-Aitape coast on prospecting and labor recruiting trips, was queried by United States intelligence officers at Finschhafen about the depth of the coastal waters around Aitape. Their information was that the waters were flat and shallow, but he assured them they were deep, speculating correctly that the planned invasion would be Aitape. Fulton describes the Aitape landing including a sighting of General McArthur:

> Daylight on 20 April revealed the sea full of ships with Navy planes overhead, a magnificent spectacle beyond description. The water was like glass and the weather hot with light cloud... On 21 April... In the evening officers and men were chatting, playing cards or smoking. It was the calm before the storm. There was a quiet confidence supported by the array of aircraft carriers and warships with Navy planes in the air all day.
>
> Next morning at 3.30 a.m. we moved into the ship's hold in the dark to wait the dawn. At 7.00 a.m. the warships commenced shelling the shore and Navy planes were bombing and raking the beach with machine gun fire. When we clambered down into a landing barge the din was terrific. Milligan and I, with the two NCOs, were in the first wave from our ship and the fifth wave of the invasion... The township and airstrip were occupied before noon and the beach became a scene of intense activity as the big landing ships dropped their ramps at the water's edge. The flow of the vehicles and DWKS (Ducks') [an amphibious truck] continued all day... Next day more ships carrying troops and equipment anchored. I saw a five-star general dressed in United States green service dress on the beach and recognised General McArthur. (Fulton 2005: 216–18)

The principal goal of the Aitape invasion was to capture Japan's Tadji Airstrips for the use of fighter planes to give support to the large base MacArthur wanted to build in Hollandia as he moved his armies north towards the Philippines. Expecting an attack on Wewak, the Japanese force at Aitape was less than a thousand. As the overwhelming number of American soldiers continued to come ashore at Aitape, the defense collapsed and the surprised Japanese retreated along the coast toward Wewak. In forty-eight hours of non-stop work including under lights at night, Tadji was ready on the twenty-fourth of April for planes to land.

In the Torricelli Mountains behind the Aitape coast, small patrols of the Allies and Japanese pursued one another in a grim guerrilla war gathering intelligence on each other and making surprise attacks. Both sides created intelligence networks using local peoples and demanded allegiance from those they contacted, thereby forcing them to participate in a conflict not of their own making.[38] "Traitors" who reported their positions or found to be disloyal were often summarily executed. The villagers "were pawns in the game and had to take their line from the party in the local ascendant" (Feldt 1967: 284). Fulton (2005: 226–38), in a chapter entitled "116 Days Behind Enemy Lines in the Torricelli Mountains," recalls patrols stalking the enemy and enlisting the locals' help. On one patrol he met a small ANGAU patrol led by Captain Jack Fryer (Wakau's 'masta mak'),

---

38. Richmond (2004b) describes the Japanese intelligence practices in New Guinea.

recently returned from leave, who earlier had liaised with the Mosstroops. Some of the jungle-savvy ANGAU officers like Fulton (2005: 229, 236–37), however, resented patrolling with the recently arrived American soldiers who, unschooled in the ways of the New Guinea bush and with no local language facility, made these large patrol groups slow, unwieldy, and to him, useless. Allen (2006: 22) gives an account of a patrol on June 5, 1944, when Fulton, accompanying an American Lieutenant, Ben Pascoe and his fifteen-man patrol, ordered the summary execution of a local man he thought was cooperating with the Japanese. Pascoe confronted Fulton with what he considered an unprovoked killing but Fulton, as an ANGAU officer, alone was responsible for all dealings with the "native people." Pascoe radioed a complaint against Fulton and submitted a report of the execution to his superiors, but no action was taken against him. Although Fulton (2005: 227) mentions the patrol led by Pascoe, he does not refer to his execution of a local man.

G. A. V. Stanley was another of the men evacuated with the Mosstroops who was back in action doing propaganda and intelligence work in the Sepik region as before. Originally scheduled to land with his party of Native police and agents on the upper Sepik River at the mouth of the Hauser River near the Dutch border, he discovered, during a flight dropping propaganda pamphlets over villages, that the Japanese had not occupied the Yellow River and Upper Sepik areas after the Mosstroops evacuated. Altering his plans, Stanley and his party were flown into a point about three miles below the Yellow River junction a few weeks before the Americans recaptured Aitape. His diary[39], however, indicates that his focus of attention was not the Lujere but the people to their east and the Wape to their north. Mosstroops had left a considerable amount of supplies in a number of dumps or supply-caches throughout the Lujere area, each booby-trapped with a loaded gun pointed towards the door. From Stanley's information, it is known that the Japanese raided some of these, but it is presumed that the Lujere successfully raided those that remained in their vicinity. Stanley's supplies were dropped or parachuted to him as before.

The End of the War in New Guinea

Two days after the Americans landed at Aitape and Hollandia, the Australians landed at Madang followed by Alexishafen on the twenty-fourth of April. Then on May 27, the Americans landed on Biak Island off the coast of Dutch New Guinea far to the west of Hollandia in a bloody campaign that lasted into August. Hollandia, however, was to be transformed into a major base to facilitate MacArthur's push northward towards the Philippines and Japan. Hollandia, once the little trading post for bird-of-paradise feathers that Jock Marshall visited in 1936, was quickly transformed into a military city of 140,000 men with a field hospital of 3,650 beds and a deep-water harbor that could accommodate an entire fleet. (Gailey 2004: 188–89).[40]

---

39. Stanley's wartime diary (box 1/6) is archived with his other papers at the University of Papua New Guinea Library. I am grateful to Bryant Allen for sharing with me his copious notes on Stanley's papers.
40. The folio-size World War II photo book (Bridges, 1945) presents a sweeping and, at times, stunning panorama of the war's violent progress with photos of both New Guineans and

Although the frontal thrust of the war had moved west and away from PNG, the fighting had not ended. General Adachi's 18th Army, hemmed in to the east and west and unable to receive supplies by land, air, or sea, was still strong enough to launch a desperate major attack against the Americans in Aitape from his garrisons in Wewak. The jungle engagement lasted a month and known in military annals as the Battle of Driniumor River, a small river about twenty miles east of Aitape, that was central in the bitter fighting. It was the last important offensive campaign mounted by Adachi's Army.[41]

> [Adachi] was not the man to let the Aitape landing go unchallenged. He could spare no more than 20,000 men, only 800 of them infantry, for his attack. He had no source of supply and could only move his troops on foot through the rugged coastal hills or up the inland route via the Sepik River and the harsh wilderness of the Torricelli Mountains. Not until the night of 10–11 July were his starved and disease-ridden troops ready to attack the American perimeter on the Driniumoor [sic] River. To get them there at all was a remarkable feat: to expect them to defeat superior numbers of well-armed, fresh American troops was too much. They fought magnificently, but were decimated. Starving bands of predatory stragglers wandered the mountains for months. The lucky ones reached Wewak. Thereafter, the 18th Army had no power to strike a major blow at the Allies anywhere on the north coast of New Guinea. (Powell 2003: 71)

The Japanese suffered 8,800 casualties while "The Driniumor River operation cost the Americans 597 killed, 1,691 wounded and 85 missing" (Taaffe 1998: 208).[42] For General MacArthur, in terms of the war's trajectory, PNG was now of slight importance as the remaining Japanese troops were in a miserable state in terms of health, troop strength and military options. With no supplies available by either land or sea and refusing to surrender, thousands of Japanese died gruesomely in the months to come. Ragged and starving—endocannibalism was not unknown—Japanese soldiers were forced to retreat

---

the liberating armies with accompanying maps. The photos of the north New Guinea coast include pictures in the Madang, Wewak, Aitape, and Hollandia areas including seven near-naked young Japanese prisoners at Aitape, troops fording the shallow Driniumor River on foot and in their armored vehicles, and Irving Berlin playing an upright piano to entertain a group of WACs and war correspondents at a Christmas party in Hollandia. The explanatory texts and picture captions were written by Professor A. P. Elkin, head of the Department of Anthropology at the University of Sydney and the ethnologist F. D. McCarthy of the Australian Museum. Also see Ryan's (1969: 185–98) insightful account of how after the war the Dutch attempted to build on the Americans' and Australians' elaborate wartime infrastructures to facilitate their influence—ultimately unsuccessful—in West New Guinea.

41. Edward Drea's (1984) account of the Driniumor Battle is especially accomplished as he consulted both English and Japanese accounts of the fighting as well as interviews with Japanese and Australian soldiers who participated in the fight.
42. According to Dexter (1961: 807) 450 Americans were killed and an estimated 8,800 Japanese killed from April 22 to August 25.

into the coastal hinterlands ravaging the villagers' gardens even as many died of starvation.[43] Ryan writes:

> [MacArthur] was prepared to let the impotent Japanese garrisons there wither on the vine, self-interned prisoners of war until ordered to surrender by their Emperor, and he gave no orders for major offensives to be mounted against them. General Blamey and the Australian government thought otherwise. (Ryan 1972a, 1222)

Because of Blamey's new campaigns against the decimated Japanese, it is this final epoch of the New Guinea war, controversial then, that remains controversial in Australia even today. After the Japanese defeat in the Driniumor Battle, the US Army command at Aitape was content to mount only defensive reconnaissance patrols and did not pursue the retreating enemy towards Wewak. Then beginning in September through October 1944, the American troops in Aitape were moved out to fight in the Philippine campaigns and replaced by the Australian Sixth Army, who had fought in the battles of Eastern New Guinea.[44] Australian forces also relieved the American Army on Bougainville Island and in both areas, the Australian command mounted offensive campaigns that, at best, were "mopping-up" actions.[45] The Australian journalist Peter Charlton, a caustic critic of General Blamey and the Australian government, writes regarding these actions that

> They were fought against an enemy already defeated, reluctant to fight, incapable of being evacuated or reinforced, forced to live off the land—'self-supporting prisoners of war,' one bitter veteran called them. The Japanese in the islands fought only when they were forced to. The Australians forced them to fight. (Charleton 1983: 1)

In doing so, these final offensives took over a thousand Australian lives via combat and disease before Emperor Hirohito's vinyl recording of his Imperial Rescript of Surrender was broadcast on August 15, 1945. Obeying his Emperor's edict, General Adachi handed his sword in surrender to Major General Horace Robertson on September 13, 1945, at Wewak's Wom Airstrip. Adachi was sentenced to life imprisonment for war crimes

---

43. Charlton (1983: 69) gives several first-hand reports of the starving Japanese eating their own dead, for example, "On one occasion a Japanese who had run from a hut was killed. In the hut was a frying pan in which meat was cooking. Under a white cloth was a dead Japanese from whom the meat had been recently cut." Earlier in the war when the Japanese were forced to retreat without adequate supplies across the Owen Stanley Mountains after their failed attempt to take Port Moresby, Ryan (1972a: 1218) reports that "cases began to be found where they were butchering both their own and Australian corpses for food." Tuzin (1983: 61–71) discusses the cannibalism of Ilahita Arapesh villagers in the Sepik River Basin by the trapped Japanese cut off from their supplies.
44. See Charlton (1983: 64–65) for Australian soldiers' comments on the "filthy state" of the Americans' camp, lack of aggressive patrolling and problems in their take-over from the American Army. But Charlton (1983: 66) gets it wrong when he writes "The Sepik rises in the Torricellis."
45. Gavin Long (1963) beginning with chapter 11, "Taking Over at Aitape," describes at some length the Australians' final skirmishes with the Japanese in the Aitape-Wewak-Sepik area.

performed by men under his command, including the killing of prisoners. While still held in Rabaul, on September 10, 1947, General Adachi committed ritual suicide with a paring knife.[46] Commenting on the final New Guinea campaigns, the war's Australian historian Gavin Long (1963: 387) summarizes that, "In both Australian and Japanese history the offensives of 1945 will endure as examples of splendid fortitude, but whether they should have happened seems likely always to be in dispute." Fortuitously for the Lujere, it was for only five months in 1943, that they became part of the historic saga of World War II.

---

46. Adachi left a letter to his surviving troops that Ryan (1972a: 1222) finds "is at once a moving document of soldierly loyalty and eloquent condemnation of the futility of war." It can be accessed on Wikipedia under Adachi's biography or in Long (1963: 387).

CHAPTER FOUR

Australian Hegemony Restored

> *It was an amazing adventure. But now with hindsight and a maturity of age
> I cringe at the arrogance and ineptitude of many of our actions.*[1]
> Former PO Ric Hutchins, 2015

The catastrophic war was over and the New Guineans were rid of the would-be colonizing Japanese but their former masters, the colonial Australians, were very much back in power and the cold fact that "The essence of the colonial system was despotism" (Mwakyembe 1986: 19) had not changed.[2] Initially this was irrelevant to the Lujere. They were left alone as the government reorganized itself in 1946 on a peacetime footing with the restoration of civil administration that responded to the devastation that many other New Guineans had suffered. One coastal patrol officer after the war reported,

> After the Japanese occupation of the Aitape Sub-District the people were included in a programme of supplying food and labour to the troops stationed on the beach. These demands told seriously upon gardens and man-power. . . [resulting in] Sickness, food shortages, declining population, lethargic condition of the native mind, lack of village organisation and leaders, migratory problems and, in general, an almost complete

---

1. Email, Ric Hutchings to author, March 29, 2015. In a later email, after some thoughtful comments about what the colonial personnel did and didn't do, he wrote, "Anyway enough of that. I saw my time there as an amazing experience and adventure for a kid of 21" (email, Ric Hutchings to author, March 31, 2016).
2. It is interesting that Australians, like Americans, tend not to see themselves as imperialists, as colonialists. Further, as the historian W. J. Hudson (1971: 1) notes, "Apart from small minorities alive to opportunities in the territory for economic exploitation and religious evangelism, Australians until recently have shown very little consciousness of Papua and New Guinea."

breakdown of prewar government influence upon villages and villagers. (Young-Whitfords 1946: 5)

As Roscoe (2005: 577) has observed, the events surrounding World War II devastated some local populations. The Lujere however, having never known government control of their villages by the Germans, Australians, or Japanese, simply continued living as they had for centuries; the major exception was they now had some metal tools and no longer depended exclusively on their stone, bamboo, and wooden implements to feed, house, and defend themselves. But some societal changes were in the offing; patrol officers were returning to visit and census the villages, Christian missionaries eventually found their way to the Lujere and, finally, the anthropologists arrived.

The only absent player in colonialism's intrusive panoply among the Lujere was the avid foreign entrepreneur. Once exotic feathers lost their fashionable allure, there was little in the Lujere fens the world's markets desired. In global terms—even in New Guinea terms—the Lujere like many of their remote upriver neighbors without roads, airstrips, and a modern infrastructure, remained in a cultural backwater. Politically, however, PNG was in the twilight phase of colonialism. Faster than most of the locals could appreciate or even know, the country was lurching awkwardly towards independence.

Return of the Patrol Officers

The New Guinea war made both the Australian government and the Australians themselves much more cognizant of the big island to their north and its inhabitants. Tens of thousands of Australians fought the Japanese on the beaches and in the jungles of New Guinea and their families had a shared intimacy with their experiences. New Guineans were no longer faceless "savages" but the men who performed the daunting labor (under ANGAU's enforcement) facilitating the Army's advance. The Australians' raised consciousness regarding New Guinea was constructively reflected in the Territory's postwar organization by the Australian government.

> War had shattered the perfunctory operation of the unenterprising peacetime Department of External Territories in Canberra [responsible for Native Affairs] . . . The inanition of the External Territories Department and the incapacity of Angau to cope with anything more than day-to-day administration left a policy vacuum. It was filled by a remarkable army unit, the Directorate of Research and Civil Affairs (DORCA). . . This unit advised . . . on all matters concerned with civil government in Papua New Guinea. It introduced a dynamism so far unheard of in Australian colonial affairs, and all the more astonishing because it was sponsored by the military. Not all its schemes were practicable and some were harebrained, but it assembled an impressive body of experts whose work wholly transformed the quality of Australian thinking on Papua New Guinea. (Ryan 1972a: 1223)

Three of the influential experts were the accomplished anthropologists Ian Hogbin, Camilla Wedgwood, and Lucy Mair, each with extensive fieldwork experience in the Territory. They, together with their colleagues that included among others a noted geographer, lawyers, and the agricultural scientist J. K. Murray—the first post war administrator of the combined territories—were instrumental in providing compensation to Native peoples for war losses, the consolidation of the two territories' laws, and innovative studies in, for example, education, forestry, Native labor, and administration. One eventual outcome of their work for DORCA was the Australian School of Pacific Administration that provided a higher level of training for officials, especially 'kiaps,' whose supervisory role had the most direct impact on the lives and well-being of local peoples.[3]

It was several years after the war's end in 1945 before an Australian 'kiap' on a census patrol visited the Iwani villagers. The Wakau story is that he came up the Sepik from Ambunti, disembarked at Tipas village, then walked to Bapei and on up to Yegerape where some visiting Wakau villagers brought home the news of his impending visit. After spending the night in Yegerape, he proceeded to Edwaki then, moving on, hiked up the 656-foot Mauwi hill to Iwani village with its sweeping views. There the 'kiap' lined up the Iwani men and women, including some from Wakau hamlet, to obtain a census count, but he did not visit Wakau itself. What mystified my Wakau informants—as it still does me—was that he read their names from a book and they couldn't imagine how he had obtained their names. A local man from Edwaki who spoke Tok Pisin accompanied the 'kiap' and they wondered if he had given their names to him. My notes (MN: 420) read, "They are still amazed at this but don't think he really could know their names 'nating' [without prior knowledge]." They recalled still being in traditional dress and that the 'kiap' walked back to the Sepik that same day, a very fast trip. I have been unsuccessful in locating the 'kiap's patrol report of this Iwani village census.[4]

While we don't know the year this Ambunti 'kiap' visited the Lujere after World War II, we do know that a 'kiap' and priest in tandem patrolled from Lumi through Lujere territory down to the banks of the Sepik River and back in September of 1949. This was PO Geoffrey B. Gilbert and the Franciscan priest, Fr. James O'Meara.

In May of 1949, Gilbert established the Lumi Patrol Post that later became the headquarters for the Lumi Sub-District as a part of the Sepik District with its post World War II headquarters still in Wewak. Now it was the Lumi 'kiap,' not Aitape's, who had administrative jurisdiction over the Lujere, the largest cultural group in the South Wapei Census Division. As explained in the next chapter, the Lumi Sub-District was divided into Census Divisions to facilitate the management and patrolling of a dispersed population in a tropical setting. But regardless of the district's bureaucratic structure, from the administration's perspective the Lujere were both a distant geographical and supervisory concern. Like the Wape, it was missionaries, not the government, who first established a resident base among them.

Before the war, Catholic priests and brothers of the Divine Word's mission in Aitape had penetrated over the Torricelli Mountains into the upper Wape area, making occasional visits. Then after the war, the Franciscans assumed responsibility for the Divine Word's Aitape mission work and established a new mission in the populous Lumi area.

---

3. Beginning in 1970, with independence imminent, the training of Australians was phased out and the training emphasis was directed toward New Guineans. See Grosart (1972a) and Campbell (2000).
4. I searched in both the Australian National Archives and the Melanesian PNG Patrol Report Archives at the University of California, San Diego.

Fathers James O'Meara and Denis Dobson were chosen to establish the new mountain mission but first their superior, Fr. Ignatius Doggett, made a visit with Fr. James. This was almost two years before the Lumi Patrol Post was established. Fr. Denis writes that

> In early November 1947, the Catholic mission plane from Madang (a Dragon Rapide) came to Aitape. It was piloted by Fr Glover (who later crashed and died in that same plane). The plane took Father Ignatius and Fr. James into Lumi. It made up its load with some essential supplies, including an all-important shot-gun and a case of cartridges, because Fr. James and I would be living to a large extent off the land and the game we could shoot.
>
> The airstrip proved disappointing.[5] It was hardly more than a clearing in the jungle and was extremely rough. But the plane managed to land safely and take off again without incident. It did not return to Aitape but headed straight back to Wewak on its way to Madang. (Dobson n.d.: n.p.)

Patrol Officer Gilbert and Father James's Patrol to the Sepik, 1949

The Franciscan mission had been built located on the south side of the Lumi airstrip and PO Gilbert established the Australian government's Lumi station on its north side.[6] Although Fr. James was not the first missionary to visit the Wapei, he was the first to visit the Lujere. I was still living in the Wape village of Taute in August 1971, when the Lumi priest, Fr. Gerald Walsh, kindly gave me access to a folder of the mission's historical papers. In it was Fr. James's diary of his Yellow River Patrol with PO Gilbert. Aware of its historical importance and still unaware of Robinson's and McCarthy's pioneering patrols, I typed a verbatim copy for my files (MN: 339–41), prefacing it with this comment:

> Note: This is a 5 page document, written in ink on separate sheets of tablet paper, in diary form of Fr. James's—the first priest to settle in the Lumi area—first trip to the tais [swamps]. It was also the first time a priest [or any missionary] had entered the area. Perhaps there had been government patrols there before—he was accompanied by Lumi's first kiap—but I do not know. Although there is no date on the diary as to year, from my earlier talks [in Lumi] with Fr. James, I know he made this patrol with the kiap in 1949. (MN: 339)

As Gilbert's patrol was a fairly long one (September 5–20, 1949), my guess is that Fr. James went along to survey the possibilities of establishing a new Franciscan mission station and I imagine Gilbert appreciated the priest's genial company. But, regardless of intent, it does evoke an especially strident form of sixteenth-century colonialism when Spanish conquistadors and priests proceeded in tandem to subdue, exploit, and convert an American heathen world.

---

5. According to the Franciscans' historian Stephen J. Duggan (1989: 73) "The airstrip cleared by European miners in the late 1930s offered the only safe landing ground for light aircraft throughout most of the Torricellis in 1947."
6. The history of the Franciscans in the West Sepik District, including the opening of their first station in the Wape area, is told by Stephen J. Duggan (1983).

The patrol began in Lumi with several police and about seventy carriers. They proceeded south toward the Sepik via Telote, Bulawa and Abrau before reaching Lujere territory. At most villages the 'kiap' lined up the villagers to make a census count and Fr. James said Mass.[7] They arrived in Abrau on September 10 at 1:00 p.m. "Old grass-covered village. Strong opposition to taking us to Nami [a Lujere village]—at war." The following morning, Sunday, he wrote:

> Mass in open for all to attend. Catechist leads the prayers. Kiap lines natives [for village census] while I say office. Get boys to work on [air] strip. Buy plenty of sassak [*sic*] [sago for carriers]. Abrau, 160 [people]. Very hot afternoon. 7 gurias [Victoria crowned pigeons] brought in by police-boy. Decided to push down to Edawaki [Lujere] on Tuesday.[8]
>
> Monday, Sept. 12th
>
> Mass and breakfast. With help of catechist give school to about a dozen young lads, few of whom can scarcely talk Pidgin. Visit village and work on [air]strip. Police boy brings in a pig. Buy a few pulpuls [Native skirts in TP]. More sacsac [sago in TP] comes in and ensures our setting off for Edwaki tomorrow.
>
> Tuesday, Sept. 13th
>
> Mass, breakfast. Set off about 8:15 for Edwaki, kunai [grass plains in TP] and bush [forest in TP][9] alternately. Cross Yellow River at midday. Up and on after boys have a wash in the river. Many natives waiting at first group of houses, owing to fact that one man had been in Abrau and went on ahead to make ready about 2 p.m. On further to village about 3 p.m. Fortunately two houses in construction suitable for our accommodations. Seem to be a willing crowd, but real bush-kanakas, unable to speak Pidgin[10]. Settle in, dine and into bed about 7:30 (terrific headache).
>
> Wednesday, Sept. 14th
>
> [Still in Edwaki village] Rise about 8 a.m., Mass, breakfast. Rain last night but fine today. P. O. [Patrol Officer Gilbert] lines village. Long impressive line. See practice of all in putting dead upon bed or scaffolding. Give a little school to young lads. Edawaki 160 (prob.[ably] 300 when all in [village]). (Fr. James O'Mera, unpublished diary, cited in MN: 339–41)

The next day the patrol left Edwaki, crossed the Yellow River to Pabei, saw "scattered houses," and continued on to the Sepik River. "No village, but a few houses about. Settle in under rough shelter. Enjoyable swim." In the morning they counted about eighty men and a few women, many from "back in bush. A pretty wild, unintelligent crowd.

---

7. Based on figures in Oakes's (1956) patrol report's "Village Population Register," the only villages that Gilbert made an initial census was in Wokien, Abrau, and Yukilo.
8. The fact that Fr. James had help from a catechist and got the Abrau men to work on the airstrip indicates that he and/or Fr. Dobson, his co-Lumi priest, had made previous visits to Abrau and counted it as a Catholic village. The airstrip was eventually completed and used by the Franciscan pilots and government charters, especially for maternal and child welfare patrols.
9. PNG's Australian expats generally used the term "bush" to refer to a forested (jungle) or wilderness area. In TP it is written 'bus.' See Mihalic (1971: 79) or Volker (2008: 14).
10. Mihalic (1971: 71) defines "*buskanaka* = a wild, uncivilized man (an abusive term)"

Kiap lines them but not adequate to take census. Take a few photos. Very hot." On the seventeenth, the patrol was back in Edwaki and by the nineteenth, Fr. James was out of wine—"no wine, no Mass"—then passing through Galgatu and Kamnum villages, he arrived home in Lumi on the twentieth.[11]

The patrol's camaraderie expressed between the government and the church Is interesting but not unusual. One of the obligations of the colonial government's field staff was to facilitate the work of visitors, be it missionary, miner, petroleum geologist, or anthropologist, approved to enter the country or particular area. There also is nothing in Fr. James's diary to indicate he found the Lujere to be a particularly appealing population or would recommend Franciscan proselytizing to his superiors.[12]

In the late 1950s, members of two Lujere villages, Akwom and Worokori, built airstrips for the Catholic mission's plane, but it never landed at either one. It did, however, periodically land at the Abrau airstrip Father James mentions during his 1949 visit. Retired Franciscan priests whom I contacted while writing this book said they were unaware of any early intent of their order to proselytize among the Lujere. It remains a puzzle what motivated the men to expend such tremendous effort to build airstrips by hand with no assurance of their being used unless they misconstrued the mission's intent. "Cargo-cult" thinking, of course, comes immediately to mind as a motivation, but there is no recorded evidence of cargo-cult attitudes in the area. It is certain, however, that Fr. James returned to Lumi with a deep appreciation of the Lujere's oppressive climate. While the Catholic and Protestant missionaries competed among the mountainous Wape, sometimes ruthlessly, for their souls, this would not be the case among the Lujere.

Seeking a Yellow River Airstrip Site, 1951

Late in 1950, the Sepik District's Acting District Commissioner, J. R. Higby, sent CPO R. Orwin on an extended patrol from Lumi Patrol Post south towards the Sepik with two objectives: attempt to find a direct route from Lumi to Green River Patrol Post far to the west, and locate and inspect possible airstrip sites in the Yellow River area. Higby was considering opening a Yellow River patrol post to be serviced as a short extension flight by Lumi's weekly plane. This could avoid the logistic hassles of servicing such a Post by long boat trips up and down the Sepik as for the prewar Yellow River Police Post.

---

11. Although Gilbert was, at least in part, conducting a census-taking patrol and would have filed a patrol report with his superior in Wewak at the Sepik District Office, again, as in the Ambunti patrol to Iwani village mentioned earlier, no archived report has been located although Gilbert's patrol reports exist for 1948 when he was assigned to Ambunti. According to George Oakes's 1956 patrol to the Lujere villages, he notes that he made the first censuses of their villages, with the exception of Edawaki. Although Fr. James writes that Gilbert lined up the Edawaki locals, Oakes's (1956: 2) report cites their first census by the Green River patrol officer W. Crellin who "passed through part of the Edawaki area in 1951." Gilbert also attempted to line up the people living at the Sepik—probably Tipas village—for censusing but eventually gave up.
12. According to Duggan (1989: 71–72) the Franciscans' leader, Fr. Doggett intended to establish numerous Franciscan missions south of the Torricellis. It is interesting that none were established south of Lumi but were placed to its East and Southeast.

As Orwin's patrol fortunately was recalled before he could explore a land route to Green River,[13] his main task was to locate a favorable area for an airstrip and, by implication, adjacent land for a possible Post. It was a big assignment for a rookie patrol officer; besides, he would be in the bush for New Year's Eve.

On December 28, 1950, he left the Lumi Patrol Post at 9:40 a.m. with an unusually large contingent of police, eleven constables in all. Apparently the DC in distant Wewak wished to assure the safety of a patrol led by a junior officer in an area where most villages had never been visited by a patrol officer. It's of interest that Orwin's Patrol Report indicates that he was unaware of Gilbert's 1949 patrol from Lumi or McCarthy's 1936 patrol from Aitape, both through the Yellow River area to the Sepik, and cites only Robinson's pioneering 1934 patrol down the Wini, Sibi and Yellow Rivers to the Sepik (Orwin 1951: 2). By New Year's Eve, a Sunday, the patrol was in Maurom but it was just another day. "Prepared cargo for move-off in morning. Heavy rain fell during the day. Slept night." (Orwin 1951: 3)

By January 7 they had reached the Lujere village of Dauwo (from his map, probably a hamlet of present-day Norambalip) where he counted fifty residents and bought food with trade goods. The following morning, he

> Left DAUWO Village at 8:30 and with a native guide from MAUWI [hamlet], IWANI group, followed a native track through dense jungle. Small settlement of MAUWI natives seen and visited. Reach southern extremity of small mountain at 11:30. Followed track North West up along the mountain. Passed through old settlement of MAUWI and finally reached MAUWI.[14] Fair sized village and about 70 natives seen here. Patrol rested for a short time and then proceeded along a track on top of the mountain in a North West direction. [Descending the mountain,] Followed a jungle track for about two hours until the SAND river reached. Numerous houses of the IWANI people seen along river banks. (Orwin 1951: 4)

When I lived in Wakau, there were no houses along the Sand River. One thing I learned about the Lujere from reading patrol reports covering a forty-year span of their history from 1932 to 1973 was the extent of their labile settlement patterns: over time, families abandoned hamlets and hunting camps, moving on, to make new ones, then sometimes, years later, returning. When I was walking along a bush track with an alert and knowledgeable Lujere informant, the seemingly static tangled jungle became socially alive as he recalled the old hamlets, camps, and gardens, unseen by my I eyes, that in his

---

13. The area between the Yellow River area and the Green River Patrol Post is a vast sparsely inhabited wetlands roughly forty miles wide and fifty miles long from the Sepik to the Bewani Mountains. I'm guessing that bush pilots clued the Sepik Acting District Commissioner that a long, arduous trek through wetlands by a large patrol with little access to local food might not pay off with a viable track, so he jettisoned the idea.
14. The terminology can get confusing here. This little mountain or hill is called Mauwi by the locals and the hamlet on top, is also sometimes referred to as Mauwi as well as Iwani, while the government administration sometimes uses "Iwani" to refer to all of "Iwani's" hamlets. There is no consistency of usage at all. It was on top of this hill where the Mosstroops had one of their bases.

memory lay all around us. Orwin's patrol report especially names numerous hamlets or villages, for example, Dauwo and Wagabu, that were unknown to me.

At one of the Iwani's riverside houses on the Sand, Orwin met a man, Kawi, who spoke Tok Pisin and whom he obviously liked as he persuaded him to join the patrol as interpreter and guide. Later commenting on the paucity of "native" dugout canoes, he noted that Kawi had a canoe and took regular trips down the Sand to the Sepik, undoubtedly to fish or visit relatives. The patrol would have traversed the 'kunai' where one of the Mosstroops groups camped that lay between an abandoned Wakau village site and the Sand River. Then after sloshing through a sago swamp for about an hour, they came to a hamlet, Wagabu, on the edge of a small kunai where the patrol spent the night. The next morning, the ninth of January, Orwin and two of the police found a larger 'kunai' about an hour's walk away with possibilities for an airstrip. The patrol moved to the new 'kunai', erected temporary quarters, and luckily the following day, fourteen men from Iwani presented themselves for work, were hired, and began cutting the grass for an airstrip.

During the next few days, Lujere residents from Iwani, Wagabu, Dauwo, Arami, and Karami settlements brought food to be purchased for trade goods, including metal tools. On the twelfth, Orwin recorded in the patrol diary that he was troubled with two bad "leg sores" or tropical ulcers, the painful and flesh-damaging bane of tropical inhabitants. He also sent a message with two of the police to the 'kiap' in Lumi advising him of his movements and to be passed on to the DC in Wewak. Day after day, the Iwani men continued the laborious cutting of grass with their indispensable bush knives while torrential rains came and went, as did an airplane that was heard passing over to the north of the campsite probably looking for the patrol. Aiendami villagers brought food to trade for the first time. Another day, two Tok Pisin speakers from Edwaki visited and said they would return with villagers bringing food. It is obvious in Orwin's report that in 1950 there were not many good Tok Pisin speakers in the area as he emphasizes that facility.

On the seventeenth, his workers burned off part of the 'kunai' revealing the soggy consequence of the heavy rains and were unsuccessful in draining off the surplus water. This waterlogged 'kunai' could never be an airstrip; after ten days of concentrated labor, Orwin abandoned it for a large 'kunai' that he and four of the police, whose superior grasp of the tropical conditions he would have appreciated, had located to the northeast. Natives from Abliami to the north visited his camp for the first time, and on January 20, he records,

> Line of natives sent to new camp site to build temporary quarters. Another line also sent to commence cutting the grass on the proposed airstrip site. Constable KOMBO reported that an aircraft, presumed to be an Auster, was seen to the East of the new camp site. Did not see the natives working on the airstrip. EDWAKI natives returned as promised and brought in a plentiful supply of all types of native foods. Of their number four or five spoke reasonably good Pidgin. These natives very enthusiastic over our being in the area. Showery afternoon. (Orwin 1951: 5)

Orwin's patrol with his eleven police would have been big news throughout Lujereland and probably beyond. The Edawaki men were able to articulate clearly to Orwin in Tok Pisin what most of the Lujere probably felt. It was the first time since the Mosstroops and FELO and AIB operatives were airlifted out of the Lujere's homeland at the end of 1943 that a European officer with his armed Black police had settled down among them. After a seven-year hiatus, their sago, labor, and talent were once again valued and needed providing them, in return, with coveted goods and tools otherwise generally unobtainable.

Work continued on the new quarters and grass cutting for the new airstrip site while individuals from three new settlements (Moukam, Megoindam, and Eilam) made initial visits with food to trade. However, Orwin writes, "Trade goods, especially small knives, razor blades, etc., in short supply. Still experiencing some trouble with leg sore" (Orwin 1951: 5). For the tropical ulcers of a 'kiap' to appear twice in a patrol report was now a serious problem.

On Tuesday the twenty-third, Pabei villagers brought in sago; in the afternoon, his two police returned from Lumi with a letter from its 'kiap' requesting that "three fires be lit and be kept smoking to enable planes leaving Lumi to fly direct to present camp site without the necessity of making wide sweeps over other kunais to locate camp site" (Orwin 1951: 5). Recalling the superior planning in 1932 by the OIC requesting Robinson to light a nightly fire to guide the Aitape patrol to the Sepik, one senses some slippage in professional acumen by Orwin's Acting District Commissioner of the Sepik District who ordered the patrol. The Lumi 'kiap' was only a conduit for messages between the two as this was before Lumi became a subdistrict with its own ADC and patrols.

The following day Orwin moved his camp to the new campsite and lit the requested smoking fires. Late that morning a Norseman plane was seen east of the camp that, circling once, flew towards the camp where it circled several more times before dropping a bag of rice, with a note saying a drop of rations would be arranged as soon as possible, and some precious penicillin, with which he immediately commenced treating his bad leg sores. Work intensified on the airstrip and, on the twenty-fifth, he bought two pigs and the Karami villagers brought in sago. Shortly after noon the Norseman plane returned and began dropping rations. Especially welcome was more rice and meat for the police and labor lines as well as some personal mail for himself. He must have been both startled and elated when he read the District Commissioner's message to him:

> A memorandum from the District Commissioner instructed me to abandon the attempt to walk through to Green River and to return to Lumi by the shortest route. Natives from MIRIYAMI passed through camp on their way to a native "sing-sing" [festival], at one of the villages to the north of the camp. Paid off the local natives who had been employed at the camp. Also paid, by medium of axes and knives, the natives on whose ground the camp had been made. Satisfactory arrangements reached over this payment to the natives concerned. (Orwin 1951: 6)

The next day he spent readying the cargo for the patrol's return to Lumi, recorded that his leg sores showed considerable improvement, and paid Kawi, his Iwani interpreter. Apparently eager to get back to Lumi, on the twenty-sixth, a Sunday and usually a rest day for patrols, he struck out for Lumi with three police, ten carriers and a guide; the rest of the patrol were to follow with the bulk cargo. After four full days of arduous trekking, he arrived back in Lumi on January 31 at 6:30 p.m. He had succeeded in locating a possible site for an airstrip and his labor line already had cleared a width of 150 by 800 feet. We never learn why DC Higby jettisoned the Lumi-Green River exploratory trek or terminated Orwin's patrol when work was just beginning on the best airstrip site his patrol had located. Was it concern for the young cadet's health? Did he have a more urgent assignment for him? Whatever the reason, in retrospect, Higby's setting two such major patrol goals for a very junior officer seemed overly ambitious.

Orwin's report is of ethnographic importance as he gives us an interesting early picture of the Lujere in 1950–51, some twenty years before I arrived. They were predominately in traditional dress, not unlike McCarthy's 1936 description except the men wore more feathers.

> The males wear a gourd affixed to the penis and fastened around the stomach with a cord. The females wear a short grass skirt.[15] It was noticed that some of the males were not wearing a gourd but had their penis fastened with only a cord. Enquiries revealed that this was done as a mark of mourning for the death of the man's wife.[16] The feathers of the gouria and bird-of-paradise adorned the hair of most of the males. In some instances they also daub themselves with a red clay paint. The teeth of various animals as well as strings of shells are worn either round the neck or stomach. Apart from a few strings of shells the females wear very few ornaments. (Orwin 1951: 9)

However, there had been important cultural changes. From Orwin's perspective, the administration's emphasis on peaceful intervillage relationships appeared especially effective between the Lujere and the enemy villages to their north but not to the west across the Sand River.

> There is a good deal of intermingling with the natives from the North, around MAUWWUL [Maurom] and YEFDIN [Kwieftim], and some of these natives, more especially the EDWAKIS, visit LUMI on infrequent occasions. . . . As far as could be ascertained they do not have much to do with the natives towards the West and appear to be frightened of the natives from here. (Orwin 1951: 9)

Orwin established good relations with the Lujere and obviously liked them, especially his interpreter, Kawi, and had no adverse complaints about them as some other 'kiaps,' we soon see, had regarding them.

> These natives are a particularly friendly type and rendered the patrol a great deal of assistance in the supplying of native foods, work on the station and carrying cargo at various times. There are a quite a number of light-skinned natives scattered through the area.
>
> In a number of cases, especially with the EDWAKI natives, pleasure was expressed that the Government was in their area and these natives stated that they would do anything in their power to render assistance to the patrol. No acts of hostility were met with during the time that the patrol was in the area.

---

15. In 1971–72, their fore and aft string skirts reached to about the knees.
16. As reported earlier, McCarthy first observed this custom in 1936. In 1971, I did not observe it as most men wore cloth shorts. Whether it was continued out of sight I do not know.

At least ten of the native males seen had been away to work prewar. They had been taken out by pinnace from the Yellow along the Sepik. Of particular note was one KAWI of IWANI who was employed as interpreter. He understands practically all the local dialects and has a good knowledge of local conditions. It would not be a very hard job to bring these natives under full Governmental control with the minimum of effort. (Orwin 1951: 9)

In spite of his patrol's recall, Orwin completed his report as if a Yellow River area airstrip were a serious concern to the administration or, at least, his DC, by presenting detailed data on the viability of the activated site. In addition, he wrote that "Mr. R. H. Gibbes of Gibbes Sepik Airways has inspected the site from the air and has informed me that, in his opinion, it is one of the best sites for a future airstrip that he has seen so far" (Orwin 1951: 11). He was referring to Bobby Gibbes, the most highly decorated World War II ace in the RAAF.[17] After an inordinately long and unexplained delay, on June 15 DC Higby forwarded Orwin's Patrol Report to the DDS's Director with a covering memo that is noteworthy for its two-sentence brevity. After indicating the attached report, he writes, "It is hoped that, eventually, we will be able to construct a D.D.3 aerodrome in the area covered by the patrol" (Orwin 1951: 13). Somewhere in the colonial hierarchy his hope was vetted then abandoned. There would be no airstrip. Orwin's search, finding, and work on an airstrip site was in vain. Again, the Yellow River area would remain more or less as it was.

Wakau's First Indentured Laborers

While the world still was not beating a path to the Lujere's domain, the Australian colonial economy had kicked back into gear after the war and indentured workers again were in demand. Lujere men were leaving home for the first time in increasing numbers to sign on as laborers. The major labor recruiter in the Lumi Sub-District was Ron Kitson, based in Lumi and an acquaintance of mine in 1970–72, who traveled throughout the district seeking men for specific labor assignments, e.g., on copra plantations or in the gold fields.

In the 1920s and 1930s, the Wau goldfields in Morobe Province were a main destination for Australians coming to New Guinea to get rich (Healy 1972). But gold production was thwarted by World War II and in 1943, the same year that the Mosstroops were based among the Lujere and the Japanese raided their East Post, the Battle of Wau was fought. Again, it was the soldiers of General Adachi's Eighteenth Army, this time advancing inland from Lae attempting to capture Wau, a strategic base. In January they were successfully repulsed by the Australian Army, and then again in June in a final failed attempt. After the war, gold mining never attained its prewar level of production. It was sometime after the war, probably in the early 1950s, when recruiter Kitson signed on Wakau's first indentured laborers. Their destination was the Wau goldfields in the Morobe District.

There were three Wakau men still alive during my fieldwork from that indentured group: Aiyuk, who then lived in Mauwi, Eine, and Luritsao. Aiyuk remembered the

---

17. See www.wikiwand.com/en/Bobby_Gibbes, for more information about Gibbes's successful postwar career in aviation and hostelry in New Guinea.

names of all the others who left with him including four men still alive—two in Mauwi—and five who had died. The twelve men walked up to Lumi wearing little more than their penis sheaths, where Kitson signed them on and gave each a 'laplap' or waistcloth to wear.[18] From Lumi they flew to Wewak, then Lae and by land up to Wau where they worked in the goldfields for one year.[19] Aiyuk explained that they worked dredging boxes in the brooks looking for gold. It was, he said, hard work that they didn't like, especially as Christmas Day was their one and only holiday. For the year of strenuous labor, they received one 'fuse' and one 'paun.'[20] From that time on, some Wakau men have always been away from home, usually for several years at a time.

The First Official Census of the Lujere, 1956

Although Wakau men recalled a 'kiap' coming up the Sepik River just after the war and lining some of them in Maui hamlet to be enrolled and counted, the first hard evidence for a census of the Lujere villages was by PO George Oakes in June and July of 1956 coming down from Lumi to the Lujere lowlands. Oakes, born in the Territory on the island of New Britain and the son of Methodist missionaries, was evacuated in 1941 as a boy of seven with his mother and younger brother before the Japanese attacked and invaded New Britain in 1942. His father, the Rev. Dan Oakes, died on the Japanese prison ship Montevideo Maru when it was torpedoed in July 1942. As a youth Oakes was a survey draftsman in Sydney then, returning to the Territory, became a patrol officer in 1954. He patrolled extensively in the Southern Highlands when in 1956 at the age of twenty-two, he was transferred to the relatively new Lumi Sub-District.[21]

A number of the Lujere villages had never been visited by a 'kiap' and none appear to have been lined up and formally censused. Other than Robinson and McCarthy's 1930s pioneering patrol reports and Orwin's 1951 "airstrip" patrol, they remained administratively unknown. Although the Lujere were the largest linguistic group in the South Wapei Census Division's humid swamps, they were easily overlooked because their population was sparse, dispersed, and far from Lumi compared to the administrative needs of the subdistrict's sizable population in the Torricelli Mountains. The South Wapei Census District had its first census in 1956, and Oakes was charged by Lumi's ADC Frank D. Jones to carry it out. Map 4 shows Oakes's map of the South Census Division villages,

---

18. It was similar with the first Taute villagers who worked as indentured laborers. This was before World War II and the creation of the Lumi Patrol Post, so to sign on they had to walk over the Torricelli Mountains to the coastal town of Aitape. Wape men were traditionally naked and my informant, Tongol, laughingly recalled how they had to pick up a big 'kapiok' leaf to shield their genitalia from the view of the town's two or three White women. Thus began their acculturation to Western notions of shame.
19. Several retired 'kiaps' told me that contracts were usually for three years; it is unclear why the one for Wakau men was for a single year.
20. A 'fuse' was one hundred shillings (five pounds) wrapped tightly in paper. The 'paun' (pound) in 1955 was valued at A$2.
21. The biographical data comes from W. T. Brown (2012) and from George Oakes (email to author, March 11, 2012), who had contacted me from Sydney via the University of Vermont after reading my book about the Wape, *The Bamboo Fire*.

including the part of his larger map of the Lumi Sub-District. Note that Wakau is west of the Sand River.

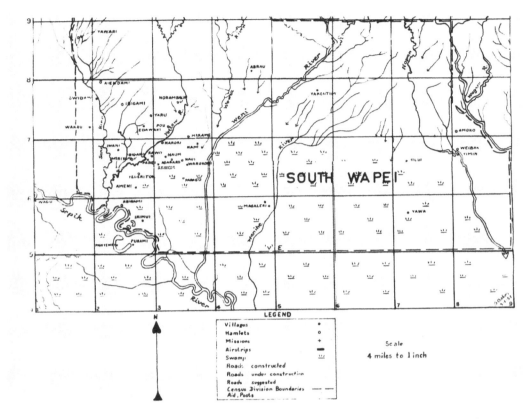

Map 4. PO George Oakes's patrol map of villages in South Wapei Census Division, 1957.

To maximize access to villages, Oakes's patrol began purposely in the dry season on June 13, 1956. In his "Introduction" to his patrol report Oakes (1956a: 2) cites PO Gilbert's "Aitape Patrol Report of 1949/50" (with Fr. James) but tells us no more, only adding that "Since this patrol, PO Mr. W. Crellin of Green River [Patrol Post] passed through part of the Edawaki area in 1951, E.M.A. [European Medical Assistant] Mr. G. Blythe of Lumi, did a medical patrol through part of the Edawaki area and Abrau in 1952. . ." but again, the relevant records, like that of Gilbert's, could not be located. Oakes also mentioned that two Europeans recently had been in the Edawaki area, viz., Ron Kitson, the Lumi labor recruiter and Mr. K. Knight, who had a mission station in the Torricelli foothills by Kamnum village.

Oakes's patrol lasted over a month as he also was instructed to census the villages in both the South and the South East Wapei Census Divisions.[22] Because of the size of his

---

22. T. G. Aitchison, DO of the Sepik District, comments in his cover letter with the patrol report (Oakes 1952a) sent to the Director of the Department of Native Affairs that, "All of the villages with the exception of those on the Sepik River were visited and censused during 1940."

assignment, he was kept on the move through what he characterized as "leech-infested forest" so there is a paucity of cultural information either in his daily diary or summarizing comments; we learn little about the Lujere or their villages compared to a patrol he did later in October in the Torricellis where he was able to spend one night in each village. However, for the first time we do learn interesting population figures for the different Lujere communities. He also carried an altimeter so the altitudes of some, but not all, of the villages are given. Oakes was accompanied by four police officers, one Native medical orderly, and about twenty-five carriers recruited from village to village. No translator was needed because all of the villages, including those not previously visited by the administration, had returned laborers speaking Tok Pisin. He also noticed that it was not unusual for young boys to have picked up some Tok Pisin from their "older *traveled* brothers."

Moving south into Lujere territory from Abrau he first visited the villages east of the Yellow River including Nami, Naum, Worukori, and Akwom, then Pabei on the lower Yellow and was impressed with the extent of the wild game, for example, "Saw numerous Goura [*sic*] Pigeons, Birds-of-paradise, and other tropical birds, wild pigs and cassowary on the trip" (Oakes 1956a: 4).

In Pabei a large contingent of villagers had gathered including from the Sepik River villages of Tipar (Tipas) and Irimui, plus Panewai from across the Sepik. The Sepik villages had come on their own volition as they had heard the patrol would not visit them.

The next day the patrol moved to Tipas and encamped while Oakes hiked an hour and five minutes to inspect a hamlet and then returned. This was the first census of these Sepik River villagers, and many would never be counted again. Six weeks later toward the end of August they were killed and eaten in a cannibal massacre, described in chapter 9, by their deceitful May River neighbors. Oakes, by then patrolling up in the Torricelli Mountains, once again would make the long and swampy trek down to Tipas, this time to join the administration's investigation of the massacre. But on Thursday, June 28, 1956, Oakes reports,

> Broke camp from TIPAR and in light rain, proceeded mainly through sago swamps towards MIRIYAMI (altitude 300 ft.) Forded the YELLOW RIVER at MIRIYAMI, inspected MIRIYAMI hamlet then proceeded to IWANI. After inspecting the IWANI hamlet of DWORIDO climbed steeply to IWANI village [Mauwi hamlet] where camp was made. (altitude 800 ft.)[23] During afternoon sent two policemen out to tell the natives of IWANI, who were in sago swamps nearby, to assemble tomorrow at IWANI for recording of census. (Oakes 1956a: 5)

The next morning it rained heavily but "Rain finally eased off after lunch when inhabitants of IWANI (IWANI, DWORIDO and MIRIYAMI Hamlets) and WAKAU (WAKAU, LEUBANAGI and UWALAMU Hamlets) were lined up and censused.

My search of the early patrol report archives did not find such a census or even a 1940 patrol and Oakes's (1956) "Village Population Register" cites each Lujere village as an "Initial Census" except Edawaki that he cites as "First Census since 1951." These data, plus my fieldwork, makes it possible that DO Aitchison misspoke.

23. The 1974 Papua New Guinea 1:100,000 Topographic Survey (Yellow Sheet) Map shows Mauwi as 656'.

IWANI village inspected" (Oakes 1956a: 6). He mentions seeing Wakau's old site—the site where I lived with them—and then wading across the Sand River, obviously shallow, and continuing to walk northwestward to Wakau's 1956 village site comprised of two of the hamlets, viz., Leubanagi and Uwalamu.[24]

> Departed IWANI and descended down the north-west side of the IWANI Hill. Three quarters of an hour later we entered a patch of kunai grassland which was crossed in 15 minutes. [an old Mosstroops camp area] Passed the old site of WAKAU Village [on his right]. Ten minutes after leaving the grassland we forded the SAND River. The western bank of the river was then followed upstream for 25 minutes when we headed westward to WAKAU over a track passing through rain forest and sago swamps. Inspected WAKAU. Then proceeded to GWIDAMI (altitude 400 ft.), a hamlet of AIENDAMI, along a similar type of track. (Oakes 1956a: 6)

His walking time from Iwani to the 1956 Wakau site was two hours. Having already censused the Wakau villagers in Iwani, he had only to inspect what must have been an almost empty village for the state of its houses and latrines. In 2012, I was startled to receive an email forwarded by my university from George Oakes, then retired in Australia, introducing himself and noting he had read my book, *The Bamboo Fire*, about the Wape. When I learned that he had made the first census of the Lujere villages I had hopes that he might remember his visit to Wakau village from the dozens of villages he had visited on that patrol so long ago. Not surprisingly, nothing came to mind. After all, he had lined up and censused the Wakau villagers in Iwani then, crossing the Sand River, just walked through the village for an official "inspection" and continued right on to Gwidami (Mokadami).

As in his "inspections" of the other villages, we learn nothing specific about Wakau as a physical place (not even its height). But the census figures of the villages in his report's "Village Population Register" are statistically helpful as shown in Table 1.[25] Nine Wakau men were away as indentured laborers, far under the one-third of adult males the administration tried to limit as a way to minimize a village's social disruption while still providing cheap labor for the Territory's entrepreneurs. The fact that Wakau already had a rest house on the administration's first visit indicates the villagers' ready accommodation to the administration's learned wishes, so perhaps more than just a handful of men had been away to work.[26]

---

24. The names of the two hamlets as pronounced by Oria were Lubanaki and Yoluamu.
25. His "Village Population Register" shows that he visited eleven Lujere villages but not Yawari and Montopai in the northwest corner of Lujereland. Yawari, the northernmost village was a twelve-hour walk away from centrally located Yegerapi and he probably was unaware of its existence.
26. "I was surprised to find that every village visited was equipped with a Rest House" (Oakes 1956a:14) This is the strongest evidence possible that these Lujere villagers, some never visited by an Administration patrol, were positively oriented to the presence of the Australian 'kiaps' and their New Guinean policemen, and the influential impact that returned laborers could have on their fellows. That was the Administration's hoped-for consequence of the indentured labor experience for men in areas not under their complete control but, as we will

Eine, one of the men who first left Wakau to work in the goldfields, told me a brief side story about their men's house that I found scribbled on a kinship chart. Before any of them had gone away to work and were still wearing penis sheaths, but after Lumi station was established in 1949, Leno (in 1971, one of Wakau's oldest males and a man of arguments) set fire to their men's house and to the houses of Newai and Mitchaki's wives and everyone "ran away into the forest," obviously to their camps. This clearly demands a follow-up story but, in lieu of that, it is relevant to Leno's rampaging response to Tsaime's attempt to elope with his daughter Nemiai during my stay, as reported in chapter 12.

From table 1, we learn that slightly over one-third of the adult Lujere males were away as indentured laborers. All of the other figures probably err on the side of under representation as the initial census of a dispersed population. Regarding the Lujere's overall population, the figure of 2,318 is at best an estimate as the Lujere villages across the Sepik were not included nor Yawari on the upper Sand River. Oakes (1956a: 13) writes, "Inhabitants of two villages, Irimuri and Panyewei, which are on the north and south side of the Sepik River respectively were censused at Pabei where they were waiting for me." Although he included the Irumuri census in his report, he did not include Panyewei's.[27] It is also interesting that Oakes's population tally shows that the number of males is significantly higher than the number of females, a finding that is explored in chapter 8.

Writing generally, Oakes notes that most of the villages did not have cemeteries and instructions were given to make them. The instruction must have paid off because Oria, then a boy, remembers the cemetery. While Oakes did not report seeing any decaying bodies aloft on scaffolds, Oria recalled seeing a funerary scaffold with a woman's body at a camp, but not in the village. As it was the dry season, Oakes found that "the drinking water for these people was mostly foul and stagnant," but also observed that few mosquitoes were seen (Oakes 1956: 13). But "In nearly all villages visited, the environs of hamlets were cluttered with rubbish and overgrown by bush. It was stated that in future all rubbish must be collected and placed in a clearing near the village and burnt" (Oakes 1956a: 12). He found the general health of villagers to be less than favorable, not surprisingly for a people with no modern medical facilities. The patrol saw numerous bad cases of yaws, tropical ulcers, scabies, malaria, and pneumonia as well as many sores. His medical orderly did what he could, but they soon ran out of penicillin and other medicines, as the fresh supplies anticipated had not arrived before the patrol set out. Oakes's report recommended that aid post orderlies be posted in Aiendami, Edawaki and Pabei knowing, like McCarthy's plea for metal tools, that recommendations were often just that and were dead on arrival. But no patrol report was complete without lamentations regarding

---

see in chapter 9, for the Iwan on the May River, their indentured labor experience did not alter their traditions of headhunting and cannibalism.

27. Oakes rightly believed that Panyewei was in the Ambunti Sub-District and that perhaps was the reason he didn't include it. He unsuccessfully recommended that Panyewei and other villages, e.g., Purami, on the river in that immediate area "be incorporated with those of the Edawaki area" noting that they will not travel to Ambunti as they must pass through enemy territory. Although he also correctly assumed that the southern side of the Sepik was uncontrolled territory and out of bounds for labor recruiters, he noted that some men already had been recruited as laborers "as all the inhabitants of Panyewei, that were seen, were clothed in 'laplaps'" (Oakes 1956a: 13).

Table 1. PO Oakes's Lujere village census data, 1956

Name of village	Children		Adults			Total village population
	Male	Female	Male		Female	
			Resident	Absentee*		
Nami	43	28	57	24	60	212
Worukori	37	23	50	20	62	192
Naum	33	26	57	25	65	206
Akwom	32	13	32	17	38	132
Pabei	30	24	62	18	62	196
Ameni	11	13	35	12	42	113
Irimui	13	9	23	1	26	72
Iwani	33	28	77	13	74	225
Wakau	20	13	35	9	33	110
Aiendami	83	80	128	40	123	454
Edawaki	10	57	131	24	184	406
Demographic total	345	314	687	203	769	2,318

* Absentee men were away working as indentured laborers for colonial enterprises.

the construction and use of latrines (six feet deep). "Most of the villages in the South Wapei area did not have latrines, and in the few that did, I strongly suspect that the females' latrines are seldom used. All villages without latrines were told to construct them and it was stressed over and over again that they must use them" (Oakes 1956: 12). His survey of their food supply was more positive.

> Sago is the staple food for these people. Other vegetable foods of these natives include sweet potato, yams, taro, mami, pawpaws, bananas, tapioca, and breadfruit but in smaller quantities. Cocoanuts also give variety to their diet.
> There is no shortage of animal foods as the bush abounds in game such as wild pigs, cassowary, possum, wild fowl and a variety of wallaby. Fish also supplement the natives' diet. These are caught on pronged spears, in nets, or in baskets set in timber dams across the streams. (Oakes 1956: 13)

And what were the Lujere wearing in 1956? In answer to my email, Oakes replied, "In 1956 many of the Yellow River people still wore traditional dress. It was interesting that when I came to do a census everyone had a lap-lap on!" (email, April 3, 2015). Men, especially those who had worked several years for Europeans, sported their modern attire, that is, 'laplaps' or shorts, however shabby, when confronted with administration formalities. On the fourth of July, Oakes visited his last two Lujere villages, Yaru and Norambalip. The following day his patrol preceded across grasslands to the Yellow River where they forded it up to their waists and, leaving the swamp villagers behind, headed north to the Torricelli Mountains.

A Patrol Officer's Assessment of the Lujere Colonial Predicament, 1962

Just six years later, a patrol by PO Treutlain in June and July 1962 to the South West Wapei and South Wapei Census Divisions found that there was "an unsatisfactory state of affairs in the Native Situation notably in aspects of village maintenance, census attendance, and settlement patterns" (Trollope 1962: 1). This necessitated a follow-up patrol from November 4 to December 7, 1962, by PO C. A. Trollope, based in Lumi, with four police and a medical assistant to provide smallpox and antiyaws vaccinations. Trollope's initial evaluation was that:

> The South Wapei communities [primarily Lujere] had in most instances carried out the instructions issued by Mr. Treutlain. However, it is quite noticeable that villages are only partly lived in. Token effort prior to impending patrols presents usually a good picture. The people of this region are essentially hunters and not gardeners which of course lends itself to the nomadic habit. Sago is the staple and in most cases is worked from natural stands. There is evidence however, in a number of cases, of attempts at taro planting and subsidiary crops on a garden basis but the inevitable complaint is that pigs root these out whilst the owner is away on some hunting expedition. . . . The people in each instance were addressed on the advantages of living in permanent and collective settlements and strongly urged to attain this condition. (Trollope 1962: 1)

Village absenteeism for a census patrol is always a vexing circumstance for the patrol officer as it is, in a reverse way, to the family away in a bush camp working sago and fishing or hunting who must walk several hours to the patrolling site, often not their own village. Some of the Lujere villages were especially culpable in this respect.

> For years certain communities, more notably, YAWARI, AIENDAMI, IWANI, and AMENI (TIPAS), have had as much as 50% absenteeism at census taking. . .villagers were asked in each of the above villages to locate these absentees and present them to the patrol. Within no more than 24 hours all but a few had been brought to the patrol. . . Deliberate evasion was obvious and a number of convictions [were] made contra census regulations. The people of these groups are perhaps more primitive in habit than the remaining South Wapei communities and no doubt their persistence in this condition is due to the lack of [European] contact. (Trollope 1962: 2)

PO Trollope then commented on the positive impact the missionary Johansen family who established the CMML Yellow River mission in 1961 were having on the central Lujere villages, discussed in the following section. He ends his patrol report with an interesting summation of the Lujere people and their environment nine years prior to my fieldwork and before the imminence of self-government and independence overshadowed all administration officers' thinking.

> The South Wapei people vary in state from primitive to semi sophisticated. TIPAS village adjacent to the SEPIK River for instance is a strange mixture of men anxious to build up business ventures through copra production and selling crocodile skins and others in the same age group still in traditional dress and unable to converse in 'pidgin.' Whole groups of essentially primitive natives contrast with other communities

influenced by repatriated labourers and consequently showing some signs of change in outlook. The reason for this continuing primitivity [*sic*] is isolation. Small communities in vast areas of flat swamp country make inter group contact difficult . . . The region is nearly impassable during the wet season. Sorcery pervades thought throughout and will be a major obstacle in cultivating new outlooks. The immediate solution to this region is raising the people from their present state is regular Administration patrolling, endeavoring particularly to gather them into central settlements. (Trollope 1962: 2)

It was a thoughtful assessment of the current situation, but herding the people together in bigger settlements as a mode of modernizing them was far off the mark. It seems that "development" in the Western mind is often associated with creating larger social units and, when governing wayward small groups, always is. However, the Lujere's evolved residential arrangement of small villages plus satellite family bush camps was a perfect fit for their ecological zone; it provided both a community for sociality and defense as well as dispersed work camps to facilitate subsistence. The tragic mistake Australia made centralizing the Aborigines in villages was not one they would repeat in the Upper Sepik wet grasslands.

Here Come the Missionaries!

Nine years after Father James's Lujere visit, the first Protestant evangelical missionaries came to live and proselytize among them.[28] The Lujere, having only one religious domination seeking to convert them to Christianity, were spared from the Wape experience of witnessing the initial rancorous contention between the Catholic Franciscans and Protestant Christian Brethren over village exclusivity. Also, unlike Oceania's Polynesian cultures where the arrival of "Europeans were taken as envoys of the gods" (Strathern 2017: 226), among the animistic Lujere, Europeans were seen pragmatically as potential sources of work and wealth.

The Sola Fida Mission and the First Regional Airstrip, 1958

The Lujere's first residential missionaries were a young Australian couple John and Val Watkins of the Sola Fide (Latin, by faith alone) Mission, a tiny poorly-funded independent Evangelical group. They brought their ministry to the Lujere in 1958 where they built a house and bush material church by the sago swamp near Yegerapi village and where their baby was born.[29] Earlier they had joined Ken and Norma Knight, Baptists from

---

28. For information about the Protestant missionaries who have worked among the Lujere I am indebted to Ces Parish, Betty Gillam, and Kay Liddle, all New Zealanders and pioneer CMML missionaries in the West Sepik District. Kay Liddle also contacted several former missionaries, including Mary Parish, Lyn Wark Murray, and Dan Anderson, then shared their information to him with me. I also consulted the Thorp's (2004) informative history of Christian Brethren missionaries in Papua New Guinea. A few of the dates obtained from the different sources are conflicting and I have done my best to be as accurate as possible.
29. The dates for the Sola Fida Mission are primarily from Ces Parish, WN660–1.

Sydney, Australia, in Kamnum village (Autu language)—located between the Wape and Lujere—then briefly worked in the isolated village of Guriaso (Autu lang.) to the west on a tributary of the North River, before deciding to establish their missionary work among the Lujere.

The Sola Fida missionary couple's major and lasting contribution to the Lujere, however, was not their evangelical message, but John Watkins's construction with local men of the area's first airstrip. It was symptomatic of the Administration's back-burner view of the swamplands people that it was a mission that successfully built the first airstrip, although initially few planes landed. Six years after DC Higby's aspirations for an airstrip in the Yellow River area and CPO Orwin's search for a suitable site, Watkins located his site just east of Edwaki Hill. Lacking documentation of its construction, one assumes because of the mission's poverty that the local men volunteered their labor for its construction, as did the men of Worikori and Akwom for their airstrips also built in the 1950s. Although there is no record of the date when the first plane landed at Yellow River, early on, a one-engine Cessna 182 piloted by Sepik Robie flew in with oil and flipped over, severely damaging one wing. A new wing was transported up the Sepik to Tipas village where local men carried it to the crash site for the plane's repair. The strip, albeit enlarged, still serves the area providing the Lujere with access to the global world.[30]

After the airstrip was completed, Valerie Auwardt, a nurse from Sri Lanka, who trained in England and then went to Australia, joined the Watkins to provide the first medical services to the mission's immediate area. But the Sola Fide Mission's stay was short-lived; faith alone was not enough to sustain their work. With insufficient funds to even provide themselves with adequate food, after eighteen months the Watkins were forced to leave in December 1959 because of his serious heart condition. The Knights came down from Kamnum to fill-in for four months, then they, too, left. Auwardt remained for a time to run the mission where she also had a Pidgin Literacy and Bible School.

The Christian Brethren Arrive, 1961

Another evangelical Protestant mission was ready to step in and provide the continuity the Sola Fide Mission couldn't. This was the Christian Missions to Many Lands (CMML), a Christian Brethren group with members mostly from New Zealand.[31] The CMML already had a mission in Lumi and in several other ostensibly 'Popi' (Roman Catholic) Wape villages, spiritual incursions unappreciated by the Franciscan Catholics. The Lujere's first CMML missionaries were Roland and Margaret Johansen who arrived with their small children towards the end of 1961. The extension of the airstrip in 1962 was a major physical accomplishment as was relocating the mission atop breezy

---

30. That is to say, "access" when the planes fly. In 2000, for example, my charted plane was delayed three days in coastal Vanimo while we waited for the radio to be repaired and returned from Goroko in the Highlands. Today, I am told, there still are no scheduled flights to or from Yellow River and chartered flights are rare. A Lujere villager wanting to visit the coastal provincial capital of Vanimo must first take a motorized canoe up the Sepik to Green River, then go by foot and truck via Amanab to the coast involving several days travel.
31. See Fountain (1999: 3–20) for an overview of the CMML's work in the 1960s. For a more detailed account of the Edwaki missionaries see Thorp (2004: 30–32).

Edwaki Hill just west of the airstrip, the latter for reasons of Margaret's health. But with her health problems persisting—they had left PNG in 1959 because of them—in January 1963 they moved to Rabaul. Roland had found work there with the Department of Forests, but the move was initiated to improve Margaret's health condition and so their children could attend the International School. Ces and Mary Parish, already seasoned missionaries among the Wape, came to replace them. Sickness, it seemed, was a hazard of mission work in the Yellow River area.

It was not until the Parish's arrival with their two small daughters in January 1963 that a mission presence was firmly established among the Lujere. Jack McNab, another New Zealander, joined them and helped build the mission relocated atop the hill. Mary, a nurse, provided health services and Ces was a strong and energetic patroller carrying his pastoral message to many villages.

Bruce and Margaret Crowther joined them for part of 1963, built a house, and stayed until the end of 1965, when they returned to Australia with an ill son. In the meantime, in September 1964, Violet Goff, a nurse, joined the mission staff and the Parishes had a years' furlough in Madang, where Ces was helping with the Tok Pisin translation of the New Testament. In 1966, Betty Gillam, a New Zealand nurse and another strong and energetic patroller, helped pioneer the maternal and infant welfare patrols among the Lujere, as did nurses Heather McIntosh, Olive Westerman, and Shirley Stevens from other CMML missions. On occasion, they were helped by Lumi Hospital's only physician, Dr. Lyn Wark, an Australian who had befriended Joyce and me while we worked among the Wape.

The Parishes returned to the mission in July 1966 and, finally, in November 1969, a young New Zealand couple, Rosemary and Phillip Ace and their two small children, joined the Parishes. Both families, as noted earlier, were serving the Lujere community when I arrived in 1971. The frequent staff changes and transitions just described are more typical of the Evangelical mission stations staffed by families with their more unpredictable familial circumstances, than a Franciscan mission staffed variously by single priests, brothers, and nuns.

Wakau Village Makes a Move

PO Treutlein's patrol map shows Wakau still west of the Sand River in July 1962, so it was probably later in 1962 or 1963 that the Wakau villagers returned to their old village site just east of the Sand River where I lived with them. Arakwake told me it was he who initiated the move. He first learned of the mission's arrival while walking back home from Lumi after being returned from Dylup Plantation as an indentured worker.[32] Stopping in Edwaki, he first learned about the new missionary 'masta.' Back in his village, many were dying of 'sotwin,' probably pneumonia or flu, but 'sanguma' was blamed and Arakwaki

---

32. Dylup Plantation, located near Madang, was established in 1904 by the German New Guinea Company and was where many Sepik men like Arakwaki were indentured as copra workers. More recently the old coconut trees were used to make furniture, and now the Madang Provincial Government has purchased the property for a vocational school. See http://asopa.typepad.com/asopa_people/2010/10/big-future-for-coconut-timber-in-png.html (site accessed May 18, 2016, but later discontinued.)

decided to move back to Wakau's old site near Iwani. Some of the men who came with him were Eine, Yaope's and Tsaime's fathers, and Kwoien. The site had returned to forest, but the towering old coconuts were still there. They cleared the area, built houses and gradually the rest of the villagers joined them.

My Wakau neighbors mostly ignored the CMML mission, while it was of varying importance to villagers nearer to it. It appeared that the disregard was mutual. I had the distinct impression that the mission viewed the Iwani hamlets as especially driven by Satanic forces and even as frightening places. Visits by the mission men were infrequent and only after I moved into the village did a maternal and infant welfare nurse visit it. As one nurse explained to me, they did not visit because of fear after hearing "such horrible stories about the place"—stories of 'sanguma' atrocities—told by their villager friends near the mission. There were no committed Christians in Wakau during my stay; their visits to the mission were limited to its health services and its small trade store for essentials like salt.

CHAPTER FIVE

Colonial Twilight

In the end we shed our colonial burden with almost indecent haste.
The Honorable L. W. Johnson (1983: 264), the Territory's last administrator

Establishing the Yellow River (Edwaki) Base Camp

Eight years after the Japanese departed New Guinea in defeat, Patrol Officer P. B. Wenke lamented in his report on a patrol from Ambunti to between the Maimai area and the Sepik River that

> Ambunti is too far away and inaccessible to provide a good base camp for patrolling and administration [of this area]. Undoubtedly the MAI-MAI and Yellow River Posts will be re-opened again some day but until then these people will remain more or less as they have been for centuries. (Wenke 1953: 9)

A Failed Attempt, 1968

Fifteen years later in June 1968, the first postwar action was taken to open a new Yellow River government post in the South Wapei Census Division (SWCD)[1]. It proved, however, to be a colonial calamity of misunderstandings and misplaced hubris, with the Lujere the most deeply affected. The initiation for the new government station would not come from Ambunti, but from the Lumi ADC, J. E. Fowke. The paper chase begins with his May 27 to June 14, 1968, patrol (Fowke 1968: 31) whose objects were "General familiarization and assessment of area potential. Assist with seting [*sic*] out and location of Yellow River camp site." Fowke visited most of the Lujere villages including Tipas,

---

1. Lumi Sub-District was divided into discrete areas to facilitate the taking of administrative censuses of each village. The SWCD is discussed more fully in chapter 7.

located on an island in the Sepik, and even Panewai village on the opposite side of the river, formerly in close contact with the Mosstroops men. While they did not leave their opinion of Panewai village, Fowke disparagingly did: "The most depressing, filthy and fear ridden village on the whole patrol" (Fowke1968: 24).[2]

For the new camp, Fowke had selected Edwaki Hill, rising dramatically from the soggy grasslands, on a saddle about 1,000 yards south of CMML's mission station (1,100 feet high) while the government's site was about 400 feet lower. He marked out the dimensions for both the 'haus kiap' and 'kalabus' [jail] to be built of bush materials and, meeting with the villagers, explained to them their construction obligations if the base camp were to be a reality.[3] Down the hill and just to the east was the airstrip. Although the government could use the mission's airstrip, the mission's motorbike track to the airstrip was on mission-eased land, thus necessitating a separate motorbike track for the government to access the airstrip and for general ingress and egress.

Immediately upon return from his patrol, Fowke gave written instructions to the young CPO Ric Hutchings, indicating he would be accompanied by three police officers of the Royal Papua and New Guinea Constabulary.[4] He added,

> The objective of this patrol is to assist the local people in the planning and erection of a set of buildings in the Yegerapi-Yellow River area which will be in the nature of a Base Camp and Rural Police Post. All adult male residents of the mentioned [South Wapei] census district have voluntarily donated one month of their time to the completion

---

2. On October 7, 1970, PO John White (1970) visited Panewai; when he ordered some houses in disrepair to be pulled down the villagers refused. White had no police back up so had to retreat without carriers. ADC Laurie Bragge's patrol report comment stated that he, White, and six policemen would visit Panewai first week of December to settle the villager's dispute with the Administration. Panewei, being on the south side of the Sepik was not in Fowke's Census Division, although linguistically and culturally it is a Lujere village. There was talk of placing Panewai in the SWCD, but a May River Patrol Post officer, M. E. Tomlinson (1969: 14) who visited Panewai on April 14–15, 1969, wrote, "Discussions with people as to whether area be administered from May River or Lumi—adamant in wish to remain in Ambunti Sub-District." Their wish prevailed.
3. His Patrol Diary notes that in each village he had "lengthy discussions" with villager leaders and, while he does not mention the nature of their discussions, this obviously was when he explained the new base camp and sought and received their cooperation in its building.
4. During World War II, the previously separate police forces of the Territories of Papua and New Guinea were combined in 1942 under the title Royal Papua Constabulary and New Guinea Police Force. In 1953, Queen Elizabeth II approved the name Royal Papua and New Guinea Constabulary. In 1964 the uniform was approved that was worn during my fieldwork. It consisted of a light blue shirt, dark blue shorts, dark blue knee stockings with red garter flashes, black boots with puttees, a black belt and a distinctive dark blue beret with the affixed Constabulary badge of chrome with the bird of paradise depicted on a red enameled background. Non-commissioned ranks were also issued a .303 short Lee-Enfield rifle they carried on patrol. In a cultural environment where the locals wore little clothing and the expatriates wore nondescript tropical clothing, the members of the police force were a striking sartorial contrast that commanded, and was given, attention and respect by all. For an extended discussion of the New Guinea police see Grimshaw (1972).

of this task. It will be your job to co-ordinate the periods of voluntary labour so that at any one time there is not an excess of volunteers with a resultant lack of efficiency.

Buildings to be constructed include a secure Lock-up, two native materials Police Houses, a cargo shed, two intransient houses, and a good Rest House. (Hutchings 1968: 20)

Besides the station's buildings, Hutchings was instructed to build a motorbike track from the CMML airstrip up to the new station. He also was told to conduct a "Problem Census," explained later.

Hutchings's patrol report diary begins with Friday, June 21, 1968, and records the project's daily progress and the number of men volunteering their labor each day. His summarizing table shows the number of men available by village and the number of volunteer laborers per week for June and July (Hutchings 1968: 14). Iwani village, and by implication Wakau as one of its hamlets, was not a big contributor. By comparison Magaleri, as one of the most distant villages with a similar number of available men as relatively nearby Iwani, volunteered twice as many men, 31 to 16. Hutchings's workday for the volunteers was a long one, 7:00 a.m. to 5:00 p.m. By July 1, work on the 'kiap's house was going very well, and the men completed thatching on one side. His diary then notes,

In p.m. I spoke with the A.D.C. Lumi via the mission radio concerning the situation regarding K____ as the local people were becoming a little concerned for their safety. I was instructed to sit tight and only act if further trouble arose, and then to send K____ and the interested parties to Lumi. (Hutchings 1968: 5)

K____ was a notorious 'sangumaman' from Iwani village. Remember his name.[5] You will eventually come to know him well. The next day the men covered the house's other side with thatch, but,

In the afternoon while twenty odd men were on top of the house, the house collapsed, several injuries were received. The three worst cases were treated at the mission aid post and entered the house sick for observation. Work ceased for the day at 3.30 p.m. (Hutchings 1968: 5)

When Hutchings later checked the injured, he found them "comfortable." The most seriously injured man was Kwolyen (Kwoien) of Iwani village (Wakau hamlet) who broke an arm and two ribs; the other two men suffered badly bruised hips and had difficulty walking for several days. The following morning Hutchings was surprised to see all the men show up for work except those injured; the 'haus kiap' was dismantled and work began on the 'haus kalabus.' Then that night at 1:30 a.m., one of the two constables with Hutchings was awakened in the 'haus polis' by a small fire that was quickly extinguished. The work continued on the 'haus kalabus' and without explanation, he writes, "Today a

---

5. In public records his name is spelled in various ways. Since accusations of being a 'sanguma' can be inflammatory, I have replaced the names of some of the most infamous ones with initials, as in the case of K____.

marked difference was noted in the attitude of the men. They are now much happier and working well" (1968: 5).

Sunday, July 7 was not a workday so Hutchings walked up to Norambalip village to watch a curing ceremony for a sick man but provides no details. He also spent a lot of time talking with the locals, obviously seeking data for his "Problem Census" and it was almost midnight before he returned to the Yegerapi 'haus kiap.' On Tuesday he had his gear moved up the hill to the nearly finished 'haus kalabus'; by Wednesday it was completed and on Thursday work began on the reconstruction of the 'haus kiap.' However, the design was changed, and he planned to build it as a very large A-frame house similar to the design of the Lujere's men's houses, whether on his own initiative or with the permission of the Lumi 'kiap,' he doesn't say.

One of the research delights of the digital age is the ability to access information and people all over the world almost instantly. This book could not have happened otherwise. I had luckily located Hutchings in Australia and in a March 20, 2016 email, I got my answer.

> I started building a normal style house and it was while the men were putting the morita on the roof that the whole thing toppled. The result of that failure, led me to build the A-frame design with its inherent stability, so the debris was cleared and construction resumed on the original platform. The man and meri post were erected as in their building style . . . With the variation of the lifted portion of the roof to give that million dollar view of the Sepik plains. No doubt that is where you drank many beers with Ray! (Email from R. Hutchings to W. Mitchell, March 20, 2016)

We'll catch up with PO Ray Lanaghan and those beers later. Right now, with the men's help, he planted nine support posts, six that were twenty feet long, and three that were thirty-one feet long. In the meantime, at the beginning of the third week he and a work crew began work on the motorbike track earlier laid out by the government interpreter from Magaleri, Makau Papkai, a knowledgeable, energetic and controversial (with the expats) political advocate for the area who also had supervised clearing the track's brush. This was the project that gave Hutchings the most trouble; first the heavily rooted trees had to be removed then the planned track built.

> Work of removing the large trees for a width of 40 feet the length of the road was a large job as many of the trees exceeded 80 feet in height. This occupied a line of 35 men for three weeks, and appeared to be the only job the locals had any aptitude for, or interest in. (Hutchings 1968: 10)

After that backhanded compliment, when the actual cutting of the track began, Hutchings was even less generous in his comments.

> This [track] started at the station end. I realized that there is only one other road in the area and that the people are not used to road work, however I feel that the standard of work was very poor. The men claiming they did not know how to make a road. It is more probable that because it involved some hard work they naturally were unable to gain any knowledge of how to do it. In one week of six days 20 men managed to half

complete 150 yards of motor bike track. An average of 3 ½ feet per man per day. The second week was just the same, so a total of 240 yards has been completed. (Hutchings 1968:10)

Evaluating the men's work overall, Hutchings emphasized it was voluntary labor noting that village men between the ages of sixteen and forty-five had volunteered to work for one month. While acknowledging that there were good workers and poor workers, "On the whole I would say that the quality and quantity of the work was poor" (Hutchings 1968: 13). Then he makes his most damning criticism colored by a common colonial complaint.

Road work appears to be there [*sic*] greatest dislike and they seem incapable of gaining any understanding of how to work a road. This could be due to the fact that it involves a little hard work, which is against their nature. (Hutchings 1968: 13)

Finally, as indicated earlier, his report was obliged to contain an answer to the "Problem Census" his ADC set for him regarding the local view regarding the area's lack of development. One of his most telling comments follows, "On many occasions during my talks I gained a definite feeling that these people do not wish to develop economically, or rather they can not be bothered to make the effort" (Hutchings 1968: 15).

He begins, however, with a reference to a World Bank survey that "suggested that economic development of the May River and adjacent similar areas be forgotten, due to the lack of prospects" (Hutchings 1968: 15).[6] The Lujere knew that their soils wouldn't successfully grow crops like coffee or rice and, even if they did have a commodity the world wanted, the expense of getting it to market in their isolated domain probably would be prohibitive. He reports that the Lujere saw the answer to their economic woes as the establishment of a Yellow River government station. Why else would they have worked so hard for such long hours in such crushing heat for no pay?

Again and again in answer to my leading questions as to why the people did not pursue various methods in attempting to help themselves economically I was met with the answer, that first of all they must work to build the station up and then when this is finished they will grow food etc, and sell it to the station. Also I gained the impression that many men think there will be ample work available for them as labourers. This combined with their theroies [*sic*] concerning the Govt school [they felt would follow the Base Camp] led me to think that they expect a ready made "Lumi" to evolve and bring with it its economic wealth.

If this is so, it again shows that the people expect development to come easily to them without much hard work on their part. This was also apparent in the standard of work done by the men and the quantity put out by them, during their week of voluntary service.

---

6. I searched for this "survey" online but was unsuccessful in locating it. That does not nullify the sentiment in the Territory at the time of my field work that, as Hutchings indicates, the Upper Sepik area had little economic potential, hardly surprising as the first colonial occupiers made that decision in the early nineteenth century.

> It is apparent that the people are aware of the fact that there is no possibility of great economic development to this area and that they are waiting for the Govt to enter the area to solve this problem. This hope has been fulfilled by the establishment of a base camp at Yellow River, however I consider the people are going to be greatly disappointed, for they are expecting to [*sic*] much. (Hutchings 1968: 16)

The Lujere were "greatly disappointed" but for quite another reason as we soon learn. In Hutchings's other comments on the potential economic development of the area, he criticized them for not fencing their gardens against marauding pigs and not seriously hunting crocodiles for their valuable skins. Hutchings's station-building patrol was an especially onerous one. I cannot help but think that this young inexperienced cadet patrol officer was elated when it was over and he returned to Lumi to write up his report, after which he had a leave of three months in Australia.

One of the interesting aspects of patrol reports for the researcher is that the submitted report is but the first of several steps with each successive step collecting further information on the relationship between the Native populace and their colonizers. In this instance, we not only get an especially intimate glimpse of the hierarchy between the colonized and colonizers, but also of the internal hierarchy of the colonizers themselves. CPO Hutchings submitted his report to his immediate superior, ADC Fowke in Lumi, who, adding his generally favorable comments, forwarded it to his superior, District Commissioner J. E. Wakeford in Vanimo, who then forwarded the report with his comments to Mr. Tom Ellis, Director of District Administration in the Department of the Administrator, in Konedobu (Port Moresby).

ADC Fowke approved of his cadet patrol officer's work, writing, "All objectives were achieved, and Mr. Hutchings has done an excellent job in furthering the establishment of Yellow River as a Base Camp" (Hutchings 1968: 26). He also comments on the role of 'sanguma' in the camp's establishment and on the men's volunteered labor.

> Sorcery or "sanguma" is rife throughout this area and would be the greatest single hinderance [*sic*] to the areas development as a knit society. In most cases allegations can not be substantiated due to the indefineable [*sic*] nature of the complaint.
>
> The problem is real and one of the main reasons for the seting [*sic*] up of the Yellow River as a Base Camp. Regular staffing of the Camp will considerably break down the sorcery element . . . A total of 418 men donated one week of their time over a period of six weeks. It is very gratifying to know that the Administrations [*sic*] presence in the area is desired by the people. (Hutchings 1968: 26)

However, the response by the District Commissioner to Hutchings's report and Fowke's forwarding comments was hardened indignation. Acting within a tight bureaucratic structure more military than civil, the ADC apparently had stepped out of line. Directing his memorandum to the ADC, on point after point, he chastised Fowke. But his clincher was that, during a meeting of the House of Assembly in early June 1968, Tom Ellis, the powerful and experienced director of district administration and thus where the buck stopped, replied to a question by Jakob Talis, house member for the Lumi and Yellow River area, by saying that the administration would not give consideration to establishing a patrol post or base camp in the Yellow River area. The reason given was,

"The Yellow River area is sparsely populated and with the present shortage of field staff, establishment of a patrol post there cannot be considered for the near future. The area is not too far from Lumi and is adequately patrolled from there" (Hutchings 1968: 21). Continuing, the district commissioner unreservedly laid down the law.

> Because of this categorical answer from the Director and in conformity with instructions . . . all construction work at Yegarapi [he means Edwaki] will cease immediately. The new Rest House will remain as such and the building which you term a "detention" house will become the barracks fro [for] patrol personnel. Furthermore the terms Base Camp or Patrol Post will no longer be used . . . It was, is and will be only a Rest House centre and must be referred to as such. (Hutchings 1968: 21)

Then his syntax begins to falter:

> It is obvious . . . that both Mr. Hutchings and the local population anticipate this centre to be manned by Field Officers. Your remarks regarding the effect that regular staffing of the camp will have on the practice of sorcery confirms this I fail to see how this could be effected without prior approval from this Office being received. As stated above there will be no regular staff based at Yegerapi [he means Edwaki]. You must inform the village officials and people of this. It must be done promptly and the explanation must not embarrass the Administration otherwise there could well be a loss of confidence in the Administration and its officers. (Hutchings 1968: 24)

Finally, speaking more directly about Hutchings's report, DC Wakeford writes that,

> Despite the fact that the objectives of the Patrol are no longer valid the patrol was not entirely wasted as Mr. Hutchings should have gained valuable experience in the handling of large groups of relatively primitive people.
> (ii) Mr. Hutchings should pay more attention to the manner in which he presents future reports. In this report there were:
> (a) Some untidy erasers;
> (b) Some incorrect word usage. For example "sight" for site, "to" for too.
> (c) Some spelling mistakes. For example "therories" for theories, "azette" for economic. (Hutchings 1968: 23)

A further paragraph censures Hutchings on the use of abbreviations like "Govt," and instructs him to avoid the use of words like, "House Kiap" ['haus kiap'] or "House Kalabose" ['haus kalabus'] and, finally, "it would pay Mr. Hutchings to obtain a book on Pidgin English in order that he knows the correct spelling of Pidgin English words should it ever be necessary for him to use them in the future" (Hutchings 1968: 23). It is sobering, however, to know that patrol officers usually typed their own reports in the field under difficult circumstances on manual typewriters with several carbon paper duplicate copies long before computers and the brilliant "spellcheck" were available.[7] A 'kiap' friend of

---

7. While an ADC and certainly a DC had access to secretarial help, a patrol officer usually didn't. When the acting director of the Department of District Services and Native Affairs

mine who knew Wakeford before he died in 1987, recalled him as "an efficient but 'crusty' individual" (email, Laurie Bragge to W. Mitchell, October 8, 2014). If queried, Hutchings might have chosen more pointedly impolite adjectives.

As I learned more details about the history of the creation of Yellow River Base Camp while writing this book, I better understood the sometimes bitter and unyielding views some of the Wakau men had of the government administration. Sixteen Iwani men had volunteered their labor to build the base camp including Kwolyen (Kwoien) of Wakau hamlet who sustained the most injuries when the 'haus kiap' collapsed, breaking his arm and two ribs. Now there would be no Yellow River Base Camp. How could that possibly be locally explained without embarrassing the administration or 'govman' when the Lumi 'kiap' himself publicly arranged for the men's volunteered labor and personally pegged the dimensions of its major buildings? 'Ol I giaman mipela' [they lie to us] was a phrase I occasionally heard in reference to the administration during my stay; this unfortunate, but farcical "undoing" incident, I now understood, must have been an important component of that mistrust.[8]

Success, a Triumph of Local Politics, 1971

Even jungle bureaucracies, like their urban counterparts, have a way of morphing hard policy into new, often reverse directions. More than two years after Ric Hutchings completed his patrol to supervise building the abruptly aborted Yellow River Base Camp, on October 7, 1970, Hutchings, now a full patrol officer, began another patrol to the South Wapei Census Division, the Lujere's home. It would have resounding implications for the future of the seemingly irrevocably canceled base camp that both District Commissioner Wakeford and Director Ellis of the Department of District Administration had earlier abandoned with dogged resolution. But there was a new officer in the bureaucratic mix: ADC Fowke was gone and the present Lumi ADC was Peter J. K. Broadhurst.[9]

Broadhurst's instructions for Hutchings's three-week patrol indicated that a hospital orderly, an interpreter, and a constable, all New Guineans, would accompany him. Among the written tasks he was specifically charged to carry out were to take a census of each village and spend at least one night at each village rest house, investigate villagers' complaints, check all shotgun licenses, promulgate political education, inspect for the

---

    chastised a patrol officer for smudged copies of his patrol report, his superior, ADC Rigby of the Sepik District, replied back to the acting director in his defense.

> The reason for the smudged copies is that Mr. Feinberg cannot be supplied with an office typewriter. The only one available for issue to him is a rather ancient portable which can only take two copies at a time. . . . More typewriters are still required. Green River has none, Telefomin and Vanimo have only portables, and several typewriters in this District sadly need overhauled by a technician. (Feinberg 1951)

8. The topics of trust and mistrust have a long and important history in the analysis of humans and their social institutions. See Carey 2017 for a recent pithy analysis.
9. Peter Broadhurst was the Lumi ADC from January 1969 until December 1971; during my fieldwork among the Wape in the Lumi Sub-District, he and his wife Helen—who also had two preschool children—were helpful friends to Joyce and me as he was when I lived alone with the Lujere and then in the writing of this book.

medical condition of yaws, and collect service data on the villages' 'lululais' and 'tutuls.' He also was charged to prepare a "Situation Report," a document that was especially helpful to my understanding of the area in 1970, the year before I began my Lujere research. Hutchings was further ordered to

> Pay particular attention to any manifestations of cargo cult and sorcery you may discover and report fully thereon. Vague reports that sorcery is rife throughout the area has been reported to this office by C.M.M.L. personnel. Nothing definite is known and I want you to undertake a thorough investigation of this aspect and discuss the problem with the various Mission personnel stationed in the area. (Hutchings 1970: 55)

There also was a growing concern regarding which subdistrict should administer the area that is indicated by this unusual charge:

> At each village conduct a survey to ascertain whether the people of each village wish to remain in the LUMI Sub-District or be transferred to the Ambunti Sub-District and be administered by the May River Patrol Post. Until a road is built from Lumi to the C.M.M.L. station Yellow River... it is doubtful that the people of the South Wapei will be allowed to join the Wapei Local Government Council. (Hutchings 1970: 2)

Showing his preference Broadhurst adds, "It would appear to me that their natural communications are towards the Sepik River and by boat up and down that river for supplies. By joining an Ambunti Local Government Council, equipment for projects could be brought to them by river" (Hutchings 1970: 54).

To initiate the patrol, Broadhurst arranged for two flights chartered by MAF flights to transport Hutchings, his personnel, and their gear from Lumi to Kwieftim, the airstrip nearest to the northernmost Lujere villages. After a fifteen-minute midday flight on October 1, they were greeted on landing with heavy rainfall and insufficient local men to carry their gear onward. The next morning, having secured enough carriers, the patrol began a three-hour rugged walk in more heavy rain to the Lujere village of Yawari. Having sent word for the Montopai villagers to come to Yawari, Hutchings lined them up for a census count and then counted the Yawari villagers the next morning. Once the patrol's tasks were completed, they set out at 10:00 a.m. for Aiendami village, moving southward just east of the Sand River. But the village's rest house was in poor condition, so they continued fifteen minutes more to Gwidami (Mokadami) village where the patrol finally dropped its gear after a seven-hour rain-soaking hike.

The next day, October 4, the hospital orderly found his first cases of yaws. Antiyaws medication was given to each villager necessitating the patrol's personnel to work until long after dark. Yaws, a bacterial infection, thrives in moist climates and is easily transmitted by the fluid of an infected person's lesion. If not treated, it may lead to chronic disfigurement and disability, especially if the feet are affected.

Aiendami and Gwidami are both located just north of Wakau village along the Sand River, so we will have reason to revisit them in parts 2 and 3. Leaving Gwidami the following morning at 8:00 a.m., the patrol most likely, although unmentioned, passed through Wakau en route to Iwani village atop its imposing hill. In his patrol diary, Hutchings writes,

> 8000 Departed for IWANI, arriving at 1000 p.m. [*sic*; a.m.] Place in shambles, [only] 1/10 of population in village. House [for] police fell over when used, so supervised removal and began constructing of new house. Walking time – 2 hours. Slept IWANI. (Hutchings 1970: 2)

Hutchings found Iwani village such a challenge to his patrol that he wryly queried if it even should be azette as a "village." Consequently he kept his patrol there for three nights to attempt constructive changes. The second day he notes that more people had returned to the village and, undoubtedly, some were from Wakau; as an official Iwani hamlet they went there to be counted.

> 7th October
> Still at IWANI. It was considered worthwhile to spend 3 nights in this (village?) as they are the least contacted in the area. The whole time work was in progress [rebuilding the rest house for police] the 3 officers furthered the education of these people by merely talking on many and varied topics. I doubt if they have ever been together for such a length of time doing something as a village project.[10] Slept IWANI. (Hutchings 1970: 3)

The following morning after Hutchings completed his census, he hiked down Iwani's hill and over to and up its higher sister hill where he examined the old base camp site and stopped for a visit at the mission station. He then continued his patrol visiting the other Lujere villages and to several non-Lujere villages also in the South Wapei Census Division, spending a night in each and seeking the information he was charged to collect. The patrol, ending at Abrau, made a short flight back to Lumi on October 22. Hutchings had a similar impression of the Abrau villagers as he had of the Iwanis.

> Inspected the village, very poor, similar people to IWANI (very primitive). . . . Awareness of people similar to that of IWANI. So time spent in general conversations and demonstrating better way of construction re[garding] houses etc. (Hutchings 1970: 4)

While Hutchings had an adverse view of the Iwani villagers with their village "in shambles" and absence of knowledge on the workings of government beyond the visit of a 'kiap,' his overall opinion of the Lujere people after visiting most of their villages on this patrol was highly favorable. It also was quite at odds with his initial view of the Lujere two years earlier, based on his sometimes-trying experience with them in the building of the Yellow River Base Camp. Now, based on his more extensive experience in the Lumi Sub-District he found them intelligent, strong, diligent workers. "The I.Q. of these people is by far, greater than their neighbours in the Lumi Local Area" (Hutchings 1970: 12). "By their nature and physical stamina these people are a better type of worker than is to be found in the remainder of the Sub-District" (Hutchings 1970: 9).

While it is interesting to see how Hutchings's view of the Lujere changed, what is most immediately germane in his report are his comments regarding a new Yellow River

---

10. He was unaware that socially crucial events, such as funerals or a curing festival, could quickly bring the villagers together.

base camp. He cites the villagers' feeling of governmental neglect as validation of a need for one and writes at length to explain this to his superiors.

> A peculiar political situation exists throughout the South Wapei where approximately 90% of the adult male population has worked for two or more years in other parts of the Territory where the indigenous population enjoys a much higher standard of living and has achieved more general political awareness. . . . On returning to their home area which is particularly isolated and lacks any immediate economic development, they find it difficult to correlate in their minds the Administration policy of general advancement of all indigenous people of the Territory to their home area. As a result of this a certain feeling of neglect by the Administration exists with the people. . . . No real solution exists to this feeling of neglect other than through more intensive patrolling, construction of a Base Camp at Yellow River, and the implementation of any feasible economic development scheme regardless of how small the project or return might be. . . . The people demonstrated their willingness to work and faith in the Administration in July, 1968, when they donated some 22,500 man hours of work in the construction of a base camp at Yellow River. They received no pay for this work and even after the project ceasing in view of departmental policy they still do not want pay if a base camp is established.
>
> If a base camp is not established in the area, rumors were heard that the people would no longer have anything to do with the Administration and that they would go back to their traditional ways and culture—a threat which I feel is a probability as they are not so far removed from this stage at the present time. Sanguma is rife throughout the area and many persons expressed the view they wanted a Kiap to help them protect them from themselves. (Hutchings 1970: 5–6)

He also wanted to make it abundantly clear to his superiors the extent of the villagers' lack of political awareness in a country that was being pushed rapidly toward independence and the importance of the administration's positive intervention.

> Radios and newspapers are non-existent, information of the outside world minimal. As such, the awareness of political matters is practically negligible. No person knew who the M.H.A. [Member of the House of Assembly] for his area was.
>
> Generally there is no political awareness among the people on the central or local government level, and only a limited understanding and appreciation of the Administration in the village, however this will not always remain so. Discontent is growing with the return of indentured labourers and stories of developments in other areas. . .It is now an opportune time for the Administration to step in and cultivate the present good will of these people before it turns bitter; which is within the foreseeable future. (Hutchings 1970: 7)

Hutchings then moves his argument into the national political level by critically discussing one of the Wapei-Nuku open electorate's two elected Members to the House of Assembly.

> Apparently Mr. Jacob Talis, M.H.A., canvassed this area to gain support for his proposed personal Patrol Post at Anguganak [a major CMML mission station east of

Lumi]. Violent reaction was received against this proposal by all persons in this area. (Hutchings 1970: 7)

If such a post were approved for Anguganak, Hutchings avers that the administration, by "satisfying one person, has gained the distrust of 4,664 frustrated and more deserving people" (Hutchings 1970: 8).[11] Finally, he asserts the Yellow River missionaries are avidly in favor of establishing a government station.

> The Mission at Yellow River has come to realise its limitations as far as providing services and assisting the people to develop. They are keen for the Patrol Post to be established at Yellow River as they feel the lack of law and order in the area warrants it. Incidences of Sanguma are numerous, thus acting as a barrier to development in any sphere. (Hutchings 1970: 12)

Hutchings submitted his report to Broadhurst who, in turn, forwarded it to DC Wakeford along with his comments to Hutchings. Broadhurst's document is missing in the archives but is alluded to as commenting incisively on the issues raised by Hutchings, especially regarding a Yellow River Base Camp. Wakeford's comments, while seemingly in favor of a base camp, suggest a procedural disagreement with his boss Tom Ellis.

> The Departmental Head [Tom Ellis] made it clear to a question by Mr. Brere Awol, M.H.A., recently that a Post at Yellow River would not be established. However this is a matter for the Administrator's Executive Council to decide, not an individual. I suggest that you make a case and I will see that it goes before the Council during their visit to this District in January [1971]. (Hutchings 1970: 4)

With Ellis away, the Acting Departmental Director, S. J. Pearson, "a very senior and competent officer" (email from P. Broadhurst to W. Mitchell, February 4, 2015), replied to Wakeford on December 10 with copies to Hutchings and Broadhurst. After acknowledging receipt of the documents, Pearson strongly compliments Hutchings's detailed report then emphasizes that a Yellow River station is "a Departmental matter" and, by inference, not the concern of the Administrator's Executive Council. Then he comments on Hutchings's report.

> An Informative and well presented report documenting local problems and attitudes, as well as giving a thoughtful account of the present situation in the area.
> Submissions by the A.D.C. [Broadhurst] or yourself [Wakeford] will be considered by the Departmental Head.
> Please let me have your submissions under separate memorandum. (Hutchings 1970: memorandum, n.p.)

The memoranda the acting department head requested, ostensibly championing a Yellow River government station, were forthcoming from Broadhurst and Hutchings

---

11. The population figure Hutchings cites was for the South Wapei Census Division of which the Lujere were the largest group.

but lost as they are not archived as part of Hutchings's patrol file.[12] Fortunately, Peter Broadhurst, now retired from a second career in Australia, and I were in communication. Although he could not locate his missing memorandum among his New Guinea papers, in reviewing his field officer's journal and personal papers, he remembers the approval for the Edwaki Base Camp this way.

> I am sure that the change of heart for the establishment of the Base [Camp] was because Jacob Talis, the local member [of the House of Assembly] was agitating for its establishment. At this time the Administration was bending over backwards to accommodate the wishes of the Legislative Assembly and local members. (Email from P. Broadhurst to W. Mitchell, January 31, 2015)

Thus, both of the area's members in the House of Assembly, Jacob Talis and Brere Awol, were advocating for a Yellow River government station. With the country racing towards self-government in 1973, Broadhurst writes, "I think the department wanted as many areas as possible under control and contact" (email from P. Broadhurst to W. Mitchell, January 24, 2015). Eventually, "The hot potato was left to me to make a decision and I recommended that a Post be established at Yellow River and this was accepted, in that it would start as a Base Camp so it really wasn't a Patrol Post. . . . Pearsall was the Acting Head and . . . Ellis approved of the action taken to establish Yellow River on his return" (email from P. Broadhurst to W. Mitchell, February 4, 2015).[13]

Member Talis not only achieved his desire for an Anguganak (Yangkok) patrol post but a base camp for Yellow River as well, thus retaining his large pool of South Wapei Census Division voters. Ironically, by the time of the next election in 1972, although the Lujere remained within the South Wapei Census Division, for elections to the House of Assembly they were transferred from the Wapei-Nuku electorate to the Upper Sepik Electorate and Member Talis could no longer represent them. This was a point of confusion for some, including me, considered later in the chapter. Regardless of the administrative details, it was significant to the Lujere that after an earlier bitter disappointment, they finally would have a government station with its own resident police and patrol officer.

By 1963, expatriate patrol officers were no longer recruited on a career basis but on a six-year contract and, with the increased emphasis on the localization of public service positions, by 1970, an Indigenous 'kiap' was not a novelty. On April 10, Broadhurst sent Patrol Officer Charlie Ali, a Native New Guinean, to begin establishing the newly approved base camp. Broadhurst recorded in his field officer's journal on April 20, "Packed my own patrol gear for departure tomorrow for Yellow River for inspection of Edwaki

---

12. In a memorandum that is part of the file from DC Wakeford to the Departmental Director referencing Hutchings's patrol report and dated January 29, 1971, he writes, "Forwarded herewith please find the following: Copy of memorandum of 17/12/70 from the Assistant District Commissioner at Lumi [Broadhurst] together with copy of memo from Mr. Hutchings," apparently making the case for a Yellow River government station.
13. The new Edwaki (Yellow River) Base Camp was similar in status to the administration's pre–World War II Yellow River police post on the Sepik River, which also never achieved the status of a "Patrol Post."

Base Camp," using the term it eventually would be called. Then, "22.4.71 [I] departed Lumi 1:30 p.m. with CPO W. Swan per Helio aircraft for Yellow River CMML airstrip. Met by PO Ali who has been establishing the Base Camp at Edwaki" (email from P. Broadhurst to W. Mitchell, January 20, 2015). But there were to be more bureaucratic stratagems before this newest of government stations was firmly staffed.

While still at the base camp helping Ali in its establishment, Broadhurst received radioed instructions on the twenty-fourth from the deputy district commissioner in Vanimo that he and Ali should proceed to Lumi then on to Vanimo. Broadhurst notes that, "Apparently the Departmental secretary [Ellis] in Port Moresby instructed [Vanimo] that he wanted an Overseas Officer [a White man] and not a Local Officer [a Black man] at Yellow River. (I recall that there was nothing sinister in this move and that it was done to protect the Local Officer.)" However, there was a complicating incident related to the proposed staff change. Broadhurst writes,

> On the removal of Patrol Officer Charlie Ali on Saturday 24.4.71, we were met at the airstrip by a group of 30 rather hostile and frustrated natives who demanded that Mr. Ali remain at Yellow River as their "Kiap." Informed them that this matter was out of my hands, however I stated that I would leave Mr. Swan at Edwaki to continue on with the work undertaken by Mr. Ali. The people accepted this but requested that Mr. Ali be returned to Yellow River. (Email from P. Broadhurst to W. Mitchell, January 31, 2015)

While in a Vanimo meeting with District Commissioner Wakeford and his deputy, Broadhurst learned of the decision that Ali was to be transferred to the Green River Patrol Post further up the Sepik River and its present officer in charge, PO Ray Lanaghan, transferred to Edwaki Base Camp. It was a decision that piqued District Commissioner Wakeford, who later wrote,

> I still think it was a mistake to have taken Mr. Ali away from the area. I doubt if the communication between the people and the present officer will be as effective as it was with Mr. Ali, although he was only there a short time. (Broadhurst 1971: 17)

On the twenty-seventh, Broadhurst and Ali flew to the Green River Patrol Post where Broadhurst picked up Lanaghan for the return flight to Vanimo then on to Lumi. Finally, on April 13, the new base camp's new 'kiap,' Ray Lanaghan, flew down from Lumi to take charge of the camp's further completion.[14] The Edwaki Base Camp, complete with police and a 'kiap,' thanks to some grassroots maneuvering in a colonial bureaucracy knowingly soon to end, was at last a staffed reality.

Here Come the Anthropologists!

The anthropologist, wherever she or he works in the field, is a very different creature from the 'kiap' or missionary who has entered the bush to intervene as a change agent or enforcer in the lives of the local people. These 'kiaps' and missionaries enter an unknown

---

14. This paragraph is based on an email, Peter Broadhurst to author, January 31, 2015.

environment, often unfriendly, committed to their interventionist role as a civilizing influence in transforming the society into a version of their own Western one. It is not easy work, and they frequently spend their entire career dedicated to the task. The anthropologists of my generation were seldom activists in the field; we came to learn, not to change. Although I was the first and only anthropologist to settle down and live with the Lujere, I was preceded by a distinguished succession of anthropologists including the pioneering Richard Thurnwald and a later group of both female and male anthropologists making collections of cultural objects for the world's museums.[15]

After Thurnwald made his cursory "first contact" exploring visits to the Lujere up the Yellow and Sand Rivers in March and November of 1914, it was almost forty-five years before another anthropologist visited them. Between the late 1950s and my 1971 arrival, several anthropologists, namely Alfred Bühler and Meinhard and Gisela Schuster from Switzerland, Barry Craig from Australia, and Antje and Heinz Kelm from Germany, made brief artifact-collecting patrols among the Lujere. In 1959, Alfred Bühler was on the Sepik River collecting for Basel's Museum für Völkerkunde. Low water prevented him from entering the Yellow River, but he collected at the Lujere village of "old" Tipas (Sipas, Sipat, Ameni) inland from "new" Tipas on the north coast of the Sepik and just east of the Yellow River's mouth (Fyfe 2006: 2–3). There he collected 186 items plus shields he apparently bought from a trader further down river, probably in Ambunti.

In 1965, Meinhard and Gisela Schuster, also from Basel's museum, now renamed Museum der Kulturen, traversed the Sepik River on a small houseboat extensively collecting Sepik artifacts (Schuster 1967). They visited the Lujere villages of Bapi, Yegerapi, and Iwani and purchased 197 items. During a 2017 trip to Basel, I received from the museum's retired director Meinhard Schuster and retired curator Christian Kaufmann, a copy of the recent catalogue of their Lujere objects and the present curator, Dr. Beatrice Voirol, kindly showed me the Lujere artifacts collected by the Schusters and Bühler, all expertly stored off-site.[16]

Antje and Heinz Kelm who, as noted earlier, worked in Kwieftim and Abrau villages in 1969–70, made a collection for Berlin's Museum für Völkerkunde. Both of their field site villages bordered traditional enemy Lujere villages to the south. The Kelms collected in Yegerapi, Norambalip, and Ali (letter from H. Kelm to W. Mitchell, September 20, 1972). Dr. Antje Kelm, in an email message to the author, September 17, 2014, mentions their trek from Abrau to Norambalip village: "From Abrau we only once visited the village of Norambalip along the Yellow River to see their material culture and to buy, if possible, some of their items. We were able to get some shields there." They were, however of recent origin made in the 1960s with iron tools. "Older shields from colonial times were not to be had among the Yellow River villages when we were there." Other than collecting for the Berlin museum, they also gave some Lujere artifacts to the PNG National Museum and Art Gallery in Port Moresby.[17]

---

15. For an anthropologist's perception of the critical views of anthropological fieldwork in their country expressed by Papua New Guinea university students, see Gordon (1981).
16. In 1984, the museum was the site for the Wenner-Gren Foundation's international Sepik symposium (Lutkehaus et. al. 1990) organized in part by Schuster, Kaufmann, and me.
17. Since the Germans first went up the Sepik River in the late nineteenth century, the art and crafts of the local people have been collected and then taken abroad to be displayed and stored

Barry Craig, today the doyen of Sepik art, was a Sydney University graduate student in anthropology when he made his second artifact-collecting trip to the Sepik region, having just finished his master's thesis on the Mountain Ok (Craig 1969). On June 30, 1969, he flew to Yellow River in a six-seater Cessna 185 plane, the largest plane that could land there, and for the next seven days assiduously collected Lujere ethnographic data and artifacts. The CMML missionary Bruce Crowther, who had returned from Australia, met Craig's plane and helped orient him to the culture. He also gave him information about how long it took to walk between villages, which was especially useful when one's time was limited and energy might be flagging. He camped in Yegerapi's 'haus kiap' then next morning climbed the steep motorbike trail to the mission atop Edwaki Hill to get A$40 in coins to facilitate his buying. Craig, a dedicated trekker, visited Yegerapi, Alai, Naum, Nami, Walakori (Worikori), Akwom, Bapi (Pabei), Iwani, Wakau, Mukudami, Yaru and Norambalip (see map 5).[18]

Twenty-two pages of his collecting expedition's report (Craig 1972) are concerned with the Lujere and is the first publication about them. As their language had no analysis other than its classification until 1986, when Tom and Becky Feldpausch of the Summer Institute of Linguistics (SIL) came to live in Yaru village, Craig collected Namia word lists as well as cultural and social data. While of importance, his most original data are those he collected on Lujere designs via shields and men's designs painted for him. While in Bapi he photographed eight Lujere shields and also made a detailed sketch of each one noting its timber source and identifying the symbolic meaning of its component designs (Craig 1972: 10). In both Naum and Iwani, where he spent the night, he gave men marking pens to draw their shield designs on paper and his notes follow their work, including their mistakes made in a non-correctible medium.[19] Several men might begin working on a single design, hoping to access Craig's monetary reward. His conclusion in Iwani on their aptitude to work with this new medium was this:

> Despite the tentative marks to guide the application of colour in the left hand end of the second design, it was done incorrectly and attempts to correct it were not successful. It is evident that most of the men are not competent artists at all – probably only a few men are sufficiently aware of what they are doing to do a really good job. Identification of such men is difficult without knowing the language and it would be necessary to overcome the inappropriate motives [being paid] for everyone claiming he was a good artist. (Craig 1972: 31)

---

in the world's museums, great and small. In 1982, Michael Somare, born and raised in the Sepik River Basin and Papua New Guinea's first Premier, was in New York City to address the United Nations and to receive the first Pacific Man of the Year award in a ceremony at the Metropolitan Museum of Art. In his comments accepting the award, he said he would use the $10,000 accompanying it towards establishing a museum on the Sepik River. It didn't happen, but the National Museum and Art Gallery contains collections of the Sepik River Basin artifacts and, since 1986, the Michael Somare Gallery for temporary exhibits.

18. Craig's excellent map shows all of the Lujere villages during my fieldwork except Yawari and Montopai up high on the Sand River, and Purami and Panawai on the south side of the Sepik River.

19. The "lapse-time" progress of the joint painting by men of three shield designs, one in Naum and two in Iwani, is shown in illuminating detail in Craig (1975: 431–37).

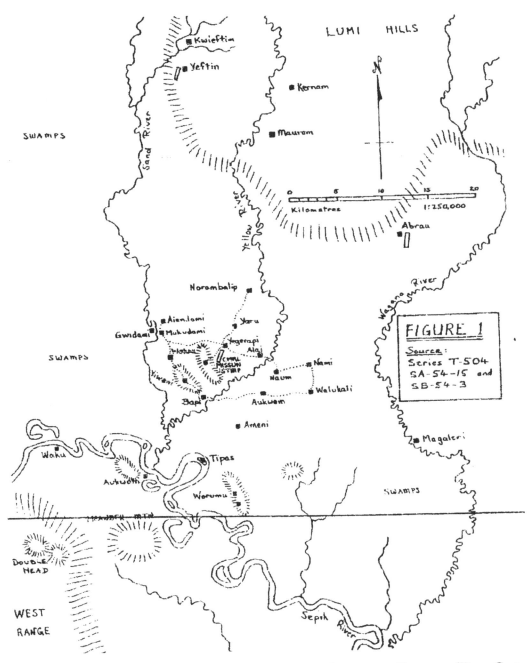

Map 5. Lujere villages visited by Barry Craig on his 1969 collecting trip. Courtesy of Barry Craig.

Although not entranced with some of the Iwani male's artistic prowess,[20] Craig (1972: 27) was captivated, as Joyce and I were later, with Iwani's locale on Mauwi hill: "Wonderful view to all points of the compass. . . . Smoke rising from a bush camp below. . . the sunset emphasized the deep blue silhouette of the jagged Yagroni Hills." After buying about fifty objects and having lunch, he and his carriers started the hike down Mauwi hill towards Mukudami at 2:35 p.m. At 3:10, they stopped at Iwop Creek, about six feet wide, so the carriers could take a five-minute bath and arrived at Wakau at 3:35 p.m. Singularly unimpressed after Iwani's panoramic views, he matter-of-factly notes: "Purchased several objects at Wakau, including a shield and departed at 3.55 p.m." With the equator's short afternoons, he wanted to reach Mukudami long before dark so he could pay off his carriers, set up his camp, wash and eat before the sun dropped out of sight. For Craig, twenty minutes in Wakau was just right and it was time well spent. His feat was collecting a rare old Lujere shield made in the 1920s by Weima for Sydney's Australian Museum (Beran and Craig 2005: 77).[21]

By the time he returned to Yegerapi he needed seven carriers for his purchases. The last villages he visited were Yaru and Norambalip. Craig, hiking back down to Yegerapi on Sunday, July 6, his last full day with the Lujere, stopped in Yaru for a half hour to purchase artifacts before arriving in Yegerapi at 4:20 p.m. He writes:

> Got artifacts ready for flying out tomorrow and departed at 5.30 p.m. for the Mission, arriving 6.10 p.m. Had been invited for a meal and had a warm bath – delicious! I found out later that a 'tumbuan' ceremony [probably *na wowi*] had been organized at Norambalip for this evening but I was not told about it whilst I was there. . . Rose 6.50 a.m. Had everything carried down to the airstrip shed: ten shields, two 'tumbuan' [masks] . . . four small rice-bags full of objects, two patrol boxes, two rucsacs, a bundle of fish nets, a bundle of sago-pounders, two bundles of arrows and one of bows. . . . Waited for plane from 9.20 a.m. to 11.30 a.m. Loaded and took off at 12 noon (AMAF Cessna 185); arrived Green River c. [circa] 12.20 p.m. (Craig 1972: 34)

After collecting in villages further up the Sepik River near the international border, he traveled back down the river, stopping in Aukwom and Tipas in mid-July to make his final purchases of Lujere artifacts. In all, Craig collected 499 Lujere objects.[22]

---

20. Lujere's artistic concerns, compared to the societies of the middle Sepik, e.g., the Kwoma's (Bowden 1983) elaborate carvings and painted art creations, were relatively slight. I kept in my 'ofis' [office] while living with both the Wape and the Lujere, paper and a box of crayons that were available to anyone who wanted to draw or make pictures. The Wape, unlike the Lujere, tended to be avid amateur artists with a strong sense of design and color. Only four Wakau youths and two adults, Oria and Samaun, made any drawings, just twenty-one in all. Usually only a single or at most two crayons were used in making repetitive marks or simple drawings covering the page.
21. See chapter 9 for a photograph of the shield and more information on the Lujere fight shield.
22. Craig's collecting expedition was financed by the Museum für Völkerkunde, Berlin; the Rijksmuseum voor Volkenkendek, Leiden; and the Australian Museum, Sydney. The objects were distributed to these museums and Port Moresby's National Museum and Art Gallery.

The Fast Track to Independence

While the remote Lujere seemed light years away from the political ferment in the Territory's national scene, this time marked "the closing of the colonial frontier" (Bracken 2007: 206), a nationwide period of tremendous governmental turmoil that rarely, if ever, entered into the consciousness of men and women like the Lujere located on the fringe of national life. But the changes underway would, sooner than later, impact the lives of New Guineans living in the country's rural backwaters as sure as they would the lives of the urban dwellers. We already have seen a suggestion of it in the saga of the Yellow River Base Camp.

Following World War II, many of the world's colonial dependencies began to seek independence from their current rulers, but not the Territory of Papua and New Guinea (with the two prewar territories now combined and administered as one). With the Japanese gone, the Australians were back in force, both politically and commercially. When I began my Lujere study, the expatriate population reached its peak of over 50,00 in 1971 (Lipscom, McKinnon, and Murray 1998: 19). The road to the country's independence was initiated by neither the Australian rulers nor their Indigenous subjects but by external world opinion, especially from the UN. "A visiting UN mission in 1962 stressed that if the people weren't pushing for independence, then it was Australia's responsibility to do the pushing" (1998: 19).

Knowing that self-government and then independence were inevitable, the tenor and active concern of the Australian government towards their colonial territory gradually shifted as the establishment of the Edwaki Base Camp demonstrates.[23] "Nativisation" (Rowley 1966: 9) or "localization"[24] of the expats' public service roles became an overriding concern as not only the government, but the missions began to train and prepare local men and woman to assume new authoritative positions even as the expats debated whether to remain in New Guinea or explored new lives back home or elsewhere.[25] The inevitable project of decolonization was clumsily underway.

The sixties were a time of social turbulence felt most acutely in the areas where towns had grown, and lawlessness was on the increase.[26] Some rural young men with a rudimentary education but few marketable skills migrated to the towns seeking work that was unavailable and fell into marauding gangs that coalesced at night to rob and rape. Commonly referred to as 'raskols' in both Tok Pisin and English, they continue even today as a community threat and social problem indicating the persistent disjuncture between the country's economic and educational infrastructures. But the Lujere, with no towns or

---

23. Wolfers (1971) discusses in detail the Territory's political development from World War II to 1970, focusing on the process and problems of decolonization as does Rowley (1966), whose time frame for the impact of colonial rule is more sweeping.
24. By the time of my 1970s fieldwork, "localization" had become the preferred term to use, and "natives" was gradually being replaced by "locals."
25. Papua New Guinea's national newspapers, e.g., the *Papua New Guinea Post Courier* "Letters to the Editors," often decried a rush to independence that the editors headlined in the June 18, 1970, edition, as "Territory is still not ready for independence."
26. L. W. Johnson (1983), the Territory's last Administrator, ruefully reflects back upon these changes.

roads, a single small elementary school, and little connection to national media, remained peaceful and as quietly unaware of impending "self-government" and "independence," just as, over a hundred years earlier, they had been unaware of the Kaiser's suzerainty over them.

To appreciate the lack of the Indigenous population's political influence in the colonial government and the rapid rate of political change envisioned, a look at the role of the Territory's Legislative Council established after World War II is helpful.

> Throughout the 1950s the Legislature Council had consisted of 29 members: 16 officials, plus the Administrator as chairman; 3 Europeans elected by an exceedingly apathetic expatriate population; 6 other non-indigenous, nominated non-officials (including three mission representatives to look after Indigenous interests); and 3 *nominated indigenes* [my emphasis] (by custom, one each from Papua, the New Guinea mainland, and the New Guinea islands). The indigenous nominees were comparatively quiet, moderate, progovernment men, accepted as leaders of their people probably by no more than a few villages in each of their vast "constituencies." The Australian government was pledged to change this structure only in accordance with indigenous demands, and then only in the direction of increasing the indigenous component in the legislature. (Wolfers 1971: 147)

While slight changes in the Legislative Council were made, the administration's major preoccupation was with the "grassroots" development of local government councils throughout the Territory that brought groups of villages together into a democratic local government with the power of taxation. The administration toyed with the idea of developing a local council for the Lujere but were convinced the Lujere were too remote and economically disadvantaged to sustain the financial obligations. It is significant that the Lujere themselves resisted this progressive change, preferring the prewar system of direct rule, a legacy of the Germans' nineteenth-century regime, with the 'kiap's appointment of 'luluais' and 'tutuls' who were usually blithely ignored except during the 'kiap's rare visits. But, as we have seen, they did want a local government station that, to them, offered the possibility of local jobs, and policing of the perceived rampant 'sanguma' scourge.

In 1964 the Territory's first House of Assembly replaced the Legislative Council as the country's legislature. Like the previous Legislative Council, it was subordinate to the Australian government and, within the country, subordinate to the Administrator, a non-elected executive appointed by Australia's Governor General who, in turn, was appointed by the Queen on advice of the Australian Prime Minister. Despite the House of Assembly's royal colonial trappings, its composition was a major step towards a democratic legislature.[27] Ten of its sixty-four members were nominated by the Administrator and appointed by the Governor General. The remaining members were elected, thus providing a majority of Indigenous women and men. Membership in the 1968 House was increased

---

27. Grosart (1972b) provides a full account of the establishment and composition of the 1964 and 1968 House of Assembly. For a sympathetic but wry account of the struggles with the idea of a representational government by House Members and their constituents see Mair (1970: 44–57).

to ninety-four, of whom Jacob Talis was one, with ten appointees. During my fieldwork in Wakau, there was another national election in April 1972, reported on in chapter 11.

In 1965 the House of Assembly created a "Select Committee on Constitutional Development" and in 1971 they recommended, many thought rashly, that the Territory prepare for self-government. In the towns and larger stations like Lumi, locals and expats alike were acutely aware of this accelerated thrust towards self-government and discussed and argued exactly how and when it should be accomplished. However, when the Lujere's aspiration for a government station was achieved early in 1971, their political concerns appeared to shrink back to the social affairs of everyday village life and to most the idea of self-government was just an abstract, even meaningless, foreign phrase. That was the local situation while I lived among the Lujere.

Regardless of the Lujere's lack of attentiveness to their country hurtling towards nationhood, on the first of December 1973 the Territory became self-governing followed by independence on September 16, 1975. To mark the latter occasion, the Queen sent her son, His Royal Highness Prince Charles, to represent her and he was joined in the main ceremony in Port Moresby by Sir John Kerr, governor general of Australia, Australian Prime Minister Gough Whitlam, and Michael Somare, chief minister of Papua New Guinea, who was born and raised in a village on the lower Sepik River and became the country's first prime minister. As a constitutional monarchy with membership in the British Commonwealth, the new nation of Papua New Guinea joined the United Nations on October 10, 1975. While many of the local citizens of Port Moresby, towns, and larger stations were undoubtedly aware of these historic events, with few radios or newspaper readers among the Lujere, even had they known, these events were as relevant to their daily activities as snow is to making sago jelly.[28]

---

28. The lack of any form of modern media was one of the defining characteristics of Lujere society during my tenure among them. The observant patrol officer Ric Hutchings (1970: 13) who made several patrols to Lujere villages wrote, "Radios and newspapers have no role to play in the lives of these people. At present this social structure is basically as it was traditionally, therefore not requiring such aids to entertainment."

CHAPTER SIX

The Search for a Village

> *It is best to choose for the first centre of study a locality well
> removed from the main focus of foreign influence.*
> Notes and Queries on Anthropology, 1951

Scientifically, it is one thing to have museum collections of a society's material culture, but quite another to have an ethnographic account of its way of life. Both are important but obviously very different. The former is usually done expeditiously, moving quickly from village to village as we saw in the last chapter, while the latter demands the anthropologist to stop, settle down, and smell the smoking fires. I too made a collection of Lujere artifacts for the American Museum of Natural History in New York[1] just before I returned home, but in June of 1971, the Lujere were still unknown to me. I was living with the Wape in the Torricelli Mountains knowing only that I soon wanted to study one of the undocumented cultures south of them toward the Sepik River. I could only discover which one by scouting their villages to find a welcoming one that was compatible to my research. Having found my Wape field site village comparatively easily, this would be a tougher undertaking than I expected. But I was not the first ethnographer to explore the Yellow River area for a research site.

Gilbert Lewis's Lujere Experience

In November of 1967, Gilbert Lewis arrived in Lumi from London for two years of research and in need of an appropriate village. Lewis already had a medical degree from

---

1. Photos of the Lujere objects I collected for the American Museum of Natural History in New York City, may be accessed online from their website. I also gave objects to the Papua New Guinea National Museum and Art Gallery, and University of Vermont's Fleming Museum.

Oxford, but his study of a Sepik society would be the basis for his doctoral thesis in social anthropology at the London School of Economics; his supervisor would be Anthony Forge, who had worked with the Abelam of the Middle Sepik Region. Lewis was still new to Lumi when he had a felicitous opportunity to fly down to Yellow River on an MAF plane. Some of his gear had not arrived in Lumi but the CMML missionary Ces Parish, who welcomed him, loaned him a mosquito net and daypack, and then found two guides to accompany him. Lewis recalls,

> I spent a few days in the Yellow River area when I was an absolute beginner . . . I couldn't speak pidgin. . . . It was my first trip [to find a village] just after introduction to Lumi. Yellow River is to me a slightly dream-like sudden jump into Sepik fieldwork, the noise of a flock of hornbills . . . Sepik faces saying things to me but I couldn't understand. And I remember big stripey-legged mosquitoes. (Email from G. Lewis to W. Mitchell, April 10, 2014)

He visited Iwani's Mauwi hamlet, then Akwom and Naum villages east of the Yellow River. He also remembered

> walking in sometimes water logged bush, pulling off leeches, stopping in at least two villages overnight, the rectangular square ended houses, rather empty villages, people a bit shy but coming with curiosity, not understanding what they said, picking up bits of pidgin, trying saksak [sago] for the first time, sharing [my] tinpis [canned fish] and rais [rice]. (Email from G. Lewis to W. Mitchell, May 2, 2014)

Leaving the sweltering grasslands, Lewis returned to mountainous Lumi and, like Fr. James before him, never came back. Within weeks he had located a village in the southern foothills of the Torricelli Mountains east of Lumi where he settled among the Gnau. His village of Rauit sat atop Anguganak Bluff with both views and breezes and no leeches or "stripey-legged mosquitoes." The following May his wife Ariane and toddler son Jerome joined him.[2] The family remained based in Rauit until mid-November of 1969, when, with his two years of productive fieldwork completed that included his mastery of both Tok Pisin and a challenging unrecorded Papuan language, they returned to London.

In early March of 1969, I was planning my grant submissions for fieldwork and, learning from the Man in New Guinea Newsletter of Lewis's presence in the Lumi Sub-District where I hoped to work, I wrote him a page-and-a-half single-spaced letter filled with searching questions, as the area was anthropologically unknown. To my elation, in early May I received a six-page single-spaced letter complete with a small sketch map of

---

2. Dr. Gilbert A. Lewis and I remained in correspondence until shortly before his lamented death in 2020; his son Jerome Lewis continues the anthropological tradition with a 2002 PhD in anthropology from London School of Economics, research on the hunter-gatherer people of Central Africa, and as a lecturer at University College London where he is co-director of the Extreme Citizen Science Research group, co-director of UCL's Environment Institute, and Director of Anthroscape Ltd.

Lumi Sub-District for orienting his detailed remarks—a nascent fieldworker's treasure.[3] It was a meticulous introduction to the sprawling area, replete with historic, geographic, climatic, environmental, ethnographic, missionary and administration data—a precious document of strategic facts gleaned from his many months of on-the-ground experience. I spent hours poring over its contents trying to absorb its knowledge and becoming familiar with its exotic names, places, and ideas. For example, his letter was probably the first time I had seen a definition for the occult word 'sanguma,' a concept I focus on in chapters 16 and 17 of this book and is a conspicuous thread of inquiry throughout the text.

Knowing that Lewis also was a physician and in the field with his wife and toddler son, I again prevailed on his kindness with questions on how to keep a family healthy in a tropical environment and for any tropical housekeeping advice he and his wife could give Joyce and me. As if his encyclopedic letter was not a sufficient gift to a fieldworker colleague, shortly after they had returned to London in early January 1970, I received another superbly detailed letter regarding health hazards and how to hopefully avoid them or treat them, with special medical concerns regarding children and an addendum by his wife Ariane, with astute comments on the care of her little son and advice on ordering supplies from Wewak, local food available, lighting, cooking, and keeping clean in a forest village with no modern infrastructures.

The Search

Eventually, to our great relief and jubilation, we learned that our research grant was funded, and we could begin to actively benefit from the Lewis's generous help. On April 1, 1970 (April Fools' Day), Joyce, Ned, Elizabeth, and I flew to London from Montreal on the first leg of our journey to PNG. We were delighted to spend a day with Gilbert and Ariane Lewis and their young sons in their London home to personally thank them for their diligent help and learn in even more astute depth about the encounter before us.

At that meeting I had no idea that I would be studying the Lujere. But, as Gilbert talked about the different cultural groups he knew, he touched upon his brief visit to the "Yellow River people," apologizing for his lack of cultural information about them as he was just learning pidgin. I scribbled in my notebook that they were long, tall people, probably sorcery-ridden, were famous for their now rare but beautiful shields, women even at the mission station wore traditional string skirts, and that one missionary told him the Iwani villagers were the "wild" ones. This was the first information I learned about the Lujere, all substantiated by my research except that I found the Lujere much shorter than he recalled. Lewis's research among the Gnau was primarily on illness and ritual. Like the acclaimed English anthropologist W. H. R. Rivers, also a physician, Lewis was a prodigious fieldworker and talented linguist who learned the language and had a physician's critically nuanced eye that is abundantly evident in his richly detailed books (1975, 1980, 2000, 2021) and articles on the Gnau.

---

3. Among others to whom I wrote for information who worked, or had worked, in the West Sepik District and were generous with helpful information were Drs. Jared Diamond, Leo Hoy, John Sturt, and Lynette Wark.

A Hasty Flight to Edwaki Base Camp

In early June 1971, Lumi's ADC Peter Broadhurst asked if I would like to accompany him and the Acting District Commissioner from Aitape, Trevor Bergin, on a government-chartered inspection flight to the Edwaki Base Camp (see fig. 5) and then to the Yankok Patrol Post near the Anguganak airstrip, both recently approved and constructed administrative bases. Also aboard were Police Inspector MacDonald and H. Muller, the latter from the Department of Agriculture, Stock, and Fisheries (DASF). They had official business to pursue, but Peter knew I was planning to make my next research village somewhere in the area south of the Wape and this would give me a chance, for free, to have a whirlwind fly-over look at the Yellow River area and visit the new base camp. This thoughtfulness of Peter was typical; he was a good friend and a good 'kiap.'

On June 10 at 10:13 a.m., we took off and landed thirty minutes later at Yellow River. While they conducted their business, I visited the CMML mission and, fortunately, both resident missionary couples were there. First I had a cold drink with Rosemary and Phillip Ace at their house, then coffee with Mary and Ces Parish at theirs. I also had a chance to visit the new base camp and briefly meet the resident patrol officer, Ray Lanaghan, a tall red-haired young Australian I immediately liked. Lanaghan had interrupted an initial patrol (Lanaghan 1971) of the villages he was now responsible for to return to the base camp to meet with Broadhurst and the other administration officials. Although we later became good friends, it is ironic that he does not mention meeting me that day in his patrol report and, in my field diary, I note meeting him but couldn't recall his name.

At 12:30 p.m. we left the base camp for the airstrip, and at 1:00, we took off for Anguganak, landing twenty minutes later, where we visited the Yangkok Patrol Post, and by 3:30, we had returned to Lumi. It had been a very important day. Although I had previously met the missionaries in Lumi, if I decided to move to this area, I had now established friendly relations with the five strategic people I might need to call on if health or other problems arose. Yet, I had scarcely interacted with any Yellow River locals except for the 'tultul' from Yegerapi, with whom I visited while hiking up to the mission from the airstrip. The single note in my notebook verifies this dearth of contact: "YR people: (a) thin mouths (b) more open faces (c) thin faces." Pathetically meager as this was for an initial observation, it stood the test of time.

Visiting Multiple Lujere Villages

In the months following I made two patrols to the Lujere villages to search for a suitable research site. From July 19 to 23, Joyce and I visited seven villages. Then, in a solo patrol October 21–25, I visited four new villages and revisited two I had seen. Joyce's brother John Slayton was visiting us from the Netherlands where he was teaching so Joyce and I, leaving Ned and Elizabeth in John's care, flew from Lumi on July 19 to Magaleri (see map 5) in MAF's Cessna, landing at 5:30 p.m. We should have arrived earlier but the pilot, having flown there but once, couldn't locate the isolated village's airstrip in the flat-fens countryside, even though Joyce and I also searched out our windows for it. This necessitated flying south to the Sepik River, then back north toward Abrau, before he finally spotted it. I wrote in my notebook, "Magaleri is really in the middle of nowhere." It is not a Lujere village and is the only village that speaks the Amal language. Because of its large size, linguistic singularity, and geographic isolation, I wanted to start our patrol from here just in case it was the "perfect" village. Fortunately, it wasn't.

We toured the large village of approximately six hundred people, and later I spent over an hour at the 'sutboi' [shotgun hunter] Yuwi's house getting cultural information from him and others who came in. Twenty-two men were away as contract laborers and the mission's influence was surprisingly strong for such a distant village, both negative factors as a research site. Ces Parish, the CMML missionary, had convinced them to destroy their large men's house where curing rites and feasting occurred and hunting trophies, for example, pig and crocodile skulls, had been displayed. Whereas before all males except babies and small boys lived in the men's house and women had their own houses, married men now lived with their wives and single males lived together in a 'hausboi.' While interesting as a large endogamous village with only one woman married in from a Sepik (Lujere) village, male initiation seemed to be abandoned and they claimed they never had 'sangumamen.' However, they assured me that Worikori village, a traditional enemy, where Joyce and I were to trek the following morning, had plenty of them.

The long tedious walk to Worikori was reason enough not to live in Magaleri. We left with four young men, each to get five shillings, who took turns carrying our two backpacks. We started at around 8:30 a.m., stopping only for a brief lunch, and it was after three before we arrived, very tired and dripping sweat. In an emergency, it would be an even longer hike on to the base camp. Instead of bringing my canvas golf shoes with sharp cleats to hike in, as I had done in the mountains, I unwisely brought my untried tropical boots. All day we walked through forests and swamps. I wrote,

> The walk, however, was flat but through a long stretch of sago swamp walking on logs. Several of the many log bridges (single logs!) were very high above the water and slippery. On two I got half way and had to finish on my hands and knees! Rather ignominious to be sure! But JM [Joyce] with her cleats, trotted over them all. (MN: 287)

Worikori, a Lujere village, was situated park-like on both sides of a winding creek.

Several boys grabbed our dirty shoes and socks to wash in the creek and we began a conversation with Au'uro, a young single man who welcomed us and was my main informant. As usual, other men joined in. We were, after all, a novel distraction in an otherwise very predictable day. I hired Wario, another young man, as our personal assistant—later I learned he and Au'uro were brothers—who brought water so we could take much-needed sponge baths. The village had a bush material church that apparently was originally Catholic but now overseen by a man placed there by CMML who was from Amanab near the Indonesian border. There were just two houses in the old style with 'limbum' (palm bark) slats, tied together with 'kanda' (rattan) allowing breezes into the house; others all had a 'pangal' (sago palm stem) front and back. Only four men were away as contract laborers. From Au'uro and the others, I collected a lot of detailed ethnographic information—my first on the Lujere—but was too wiped out from the long hike to take notes. At 8:00 p.m., the 'lululai' paid us a call, but Joyce and I were in our sleeping bags and asleep before 9:00.

The next morning, I was up early and at 6:30 a.m. energetically writing in my notebook as much of the precious ethnographic data I could remember from yesterday evening. I would need it when I began a book like this and wanted to compare Lujere village customs and ideas. The most important thing I learned was that the Lujere villages, that is, all Namia speakers, have always been on friendly terms and never fought each other but, it was not until I had returned to Vermont and read McCarthy's 1936 patrol report that this was historically verified. Their traditional enemies were Magaleri, Yilui, Yawo, and Bulawa villages. Several villages would join in an enemy raid; the forearm of the dead was taken as a trophy for a victory celebration. However, neither they nor their immediate neighbors were cannibals. It was also interesting that they claimed 'sanguma' was new; now they have a lot: "Not traditional, old men did not do it, nau tasol" (MN: 288), but it was a view of 'sanguma' not replicated elsewhere in my Lujere research. Regarding sorcery, if you wanted to make a person sick, you took the ground where they had stepped, wrapped it in leaves, then hung it where branches of two separate trees touched and rubbed in the wind making a noise.

All of the Namia speakers were said to be descendants from Iwani village and marriage was by both sister exchange and bride wealth, usually thirty or forty Australian dollars. Wario, who had just returned as a contract laborer, paid four 'stik,'[4] or forty Australian dollars, for his new wife. Traditionally a corpse was placed on a raised platform in front of the house; the body was covered with sago palm leaves, but the head was kept exposed to the elements. Later the bones were collected, placed in a net bag and brought into the house where the spirit of the deceased watched over the occupants. They had no menstrual huts, as menstruating women slept in a corner of their house. Sago was the main food, but gardens were not important as the pigs always dug them up. The village had three shotguns and lots of game; one would not eat sago unless there was a bit of game to go with it. For luck in hunting with a bow, the hunter rubs ginger on his face then talks out to his ancestors. Neither they nor, as I would learn, any of the Lujere ever made pottery or imported it. Regarding puberty rites, they had none now and but inconclusive data, as I would get for a couple other villages, regarding the past—very vague data that in the distant past boys were brought into the men's house and later emerged decorated with feathers and danced in the plaza—but I couldn't discern if this was actual history or part of a myth. As for clans, they just had two. Au'uro and his brother belonged to the 'wail kokonas' (wild coconuts) clan through their father.[5]

After I finished my notes and had breakfast, we started for Tipas, walking via Naum and Akwom villages. The brothers Au'uro and Werio were our congenial guides and carriers. The first Naum hamlet, totally empty, had only four houses and a small but beautiful men's house in which were stored ceremonial paraphernalia, just some shell rings and a few bows and arrows. Then we entered Naum, a rather strung-out ramshackle place scorched under a blazing sun. Its only inhabitants appeared to be some children at the far end of the village; my guides said the other villagers were probably hunting or making sago and that fourteen men were away as contract laborers. In the center of the village a large men's house was being built, its framework mostly in place and the 'morota' (thatch shingles) piled on the building's 'limbum' floor waiting to be attached. Later, living in Wakau, I became accustomed to, if not pleased with, an empty daytime village with

---

4. One *stik* is a role of one hundred shillings.
5. I later learned that clan membership, which I describe in chapter 12, was more complicated than this.

Figure 5. The Aukwom aid post orderly on the porch with some patients below.

everyone away in the bush working or hunting—so different from most Wape villages where there were always some adults around that I could talk to and children playing.

With no one to talk to in Naum, we moved on, passing a big garden that Au'uro said was made by the people of two hamlets. It had many bananas, some manioc, 'kaukau' (sweet potato), taro, and lots of 'pit pit' (wild sugarcane). It was strictly slash-and-burn gardening, no fences or weeding, with pillaging pigs always a problem. Shortly we arrived at Akwom's aid post, a comparative beehive of activity, where I met the CMML male appointee for the Worikori church, and the friendly orderly who showed us around (see fig. 5). Entering the aid post, I took pictures where the 'doktaboi' or orderly sees and treats outpatients, then we visited his little 'haus sik' or "hospital" where we saw several malnourished babies who were languishing because he had no powered milk to give them.

It was oppressively hot, and someone kindly brought Joyce and me 'kulaus' (green coconuts) to drink, filled with cool, refreshing coconut milk. Then after a short thirty-minute walk we were in Akwom proper, a small, scruffy-looking village with no traditional houses but whose house facades were assembled from *pongal* (sago palm stems). Thirteen men were away as contract laborers. Perhaps it was the heat, but I immediately eliminated Akwom as a possible village and we moved on.

Like Worikori, Akwom had an unused airstrip the villagers made, I later learned, under the planning direction of the 'Popis.' After all of that arduous village labor, no plane had ever landed at either one, a fact that initially puzzled me enough to wonder if they were part of a cargo cult and the airstrips were for flying in riches from the ancestors. But when that was also ruled out by various conversations with those who knew the Lujere's immediate history, I really forgot about them. After starting this book, I contacted pioneer Catholic and Protestant missionaries and administrators who might have information about their origins. Other than being constructed in the late 1950s, I have not been able to discover the name of the person who laid them out or exactly why.

At 12:30 p.m., we stopped for lunch in a new little hamlet our carriers had not known about. We ate in an open-sided 'hausboi' while two men, four women, and fourteen children climbed in to watch us. Heavily conditioned by our long stay with the Wape, we turned our backs to them, eating our food privately so as not to embarrass them by seeing us with our mouths full, chewing. They must have thought our behavior very peculiar because the Lujere, I would learn, have no mannerly restrictions on eating in front of others like the Wape do.

After our thirty-minute luncheon break, we struck out, and by 2:00 p.m., we were on the north banks of the great, muddy, legendary Sepik River. Tipas, our destination, was on a small island so some nearby men called over to the island to bring a canoe. There were some dugout canoes around with carved traditional crocodile prow heads, but one had an unusual fish head prow that I photographed. Joyce settled down on a house veranda near the river's bank with the carriers for an hour until two older women finally arrived in a dugout to ferry us across. Tipas was a bushy, odd place with about ten good houses and only very young coconut trees. There were lots of women and children about but very few men. Near each house was a rude platform for smoking fish over a smoldering fire. Everyone seemed to be eating fish and sago; so much fish! Still, we saw two of the most malnourished children we had ever seen. Joyce (JN 80) wrote they were "about 4 years old with red thin hair, no buttocks, huge stomachs (spleen) and hardly able to stand up." We also saw some really fat babies but there was a lot of tinea, a common tropical fungal skin infection exacerbated by warmth and high humidity, that is easy to get but often hard to eradicate.[6]

Joyce and I camped in the 'haus kiap' that was about ten feet from the Sepik with a cool breeze. then suddenly, a legion of mosquitoes arrived. We quickly applied some insect repellant and ate in the open. After dinner I had an interview next door that Au'uro had arranged for me on his own initiative in the 'haus polis' (police resthouse). Just then his village of Worikori seemed a likely candidate for my new research, as he was the kind of bright, interesting, and resourceful researchm assistant one hopes for. The men I interviewed included Kanauwi, the licensed shotgun hunter, two older men, a man who had tagged along with us from Akwom, and several boys. We squatted around a clay hearth with a fire of dried 'pit pit' of which there was a lot on the island. Real firewood and drinking water had to be ferried over. Although I obtained a lot of solid data, the interview was sometimes difficult as they had trouble with what are usually simple things. When I asked about clans and who belonged to what, they would have discussions before they would come up with an answer. I also had to give them a lot of examples of the Wape to get them talking on things.

Kanauwi finally said he was of the 'banana' clan, and the others were 'kapiok' and 'banana,' but since it took an inordinate amount of discussion to reach these decisions,

---

6. Serjeantson, Board, and Bhatia (1992: 218) note that "*Tinea imbricata* is common in the low-lying and coastal areas of Papua New Guinea, where it may affect 10–20 % of the population, but is rarely seen in the highlands."

which at best seemed tentative, I knew I did not begin to understand their descent group system. Part of the problem, I thought, might be that some of the men had never left the village so they had very poor Tok Pisin, but in the other Lujere village interviews, I also had trouble getting any clan data that I felt was solid and dependable. The Tipas men were far more articulate when describing their former cannibalistic enemies in the mountains across the Sepik, the Sawiyanō, where Phillip Guddemi (1992) did field work in the 1980s. They gave me graphic, imaginary descriptions of how their enemies would cut up their victims, throwing the parts on a fire to be cooked and eaten. But the verbal clarity vanished when I asked about male initiation. Like in Worikori, boys apparently had been secluded in the men's house then brought out wearing a headdress of many feathers, such as bird-of-paradise, Victoria crowned pigeon, and white cockatoo, for the women to see. But I was unable, as in Worikori, to elicit further clarification as a discussion ensued regarding whether women were allowed in the men's house as Kanauwi had alleged. When the man who came with us from Akwom voiced an emphatic "no" to the idea, Kanauwi seemed to change his view. I was, however, left again with a very vague notion of Lujere male initiation. (Unfortunately, I had not seen Robinson's 1932 patrol report where he unequivocally reports they had no male initiation.) So it was rewarding to write in my notebook something as concrete as seeing three large newly carved shields in a little shed belonging to an Ambunti man who had bought them to sell downriver in Ambunti to artifact dealers and collectors who don't venture up to the remote upper Sepik Basin.

Kanauwi had agreed to take Joyce and me by canoe the following morning to Aukom, an Iwani hamlet, on the south bank of the Sepik just above the mouth of the Yellow River. There we would get someone to take us on to Iwani. We were all ready to leave at 7:40 a.m. when a storm came up with heavy rain and a cold wind. Finally, when the storm had subsided, with much persuasion by me to Kanauwi who seemed to be wondering how he had agreed to this venture, Joyce and I waded into the Sepik to climb into a typical Sepik canoe, a long, slender, and tippy dugout with an elegantly simple crocodile head prow. Kanauwi had recruited two teenage youths to help him paddle the canoe upstream against the current and at 9:45 we were on our way. It was not a pleasant morning, cloudy and misting on the river. Unknowing, we passed the old locations of Richard Thurnwald's base camp that the Australian soldiers had raided in 1914, and the old Yellow River Police Post Hodgkiss had opened in 1936 that became the Mosstroops's Kociabu base the Japanese bombed in 1943.

After a little over an hour and a half we were at the mouth of the Yellow River and in five or ten minutes more we were disembarking at Aukom. It sat on a little hill rising steeply from the south bank and consisted of six houses; only one family was home. Kanauwi led the boys and me into the house—Joyce by choice stayed outside—where the family was eating cooked bananas that they generously shared with us. The hamlet, we learned, was almost empty because everyone else had gone by canoe up the Yellow and Sand Rivers to Iwani to bury a man who died yesterday. There apparently was some discussion in Namia about his death because I heard the Tok Pisin term 'poisin' (sorcery) mentioned but not 'sanguma.'

I now had a problem. Kanauwi had brought us to Aukwom but there was no one here to take us on to Iwani. Kanauwi and his young helpers were stuck with us, and it was clear they, especially Kanauwi, didn't like it. He was insistent on taking us to the Sepik's north shore across from Tipas, and from there Joyce and I could start the long solo walk to find Iwani. Not bloody likely, I thought. I was just as insistent, maybe slightly bullying, that we had to reach Iwani today, which was true. I don't recall what I offered him, but we left Aukom hamlet at 12:10 p.m. After a shaky crossing of the Sepik, with water slopping into the narrow tippy canoe and his yelling can we swim or not, we proceeded up the Yellow River. Joyce broke out some sardines and crackers with lime juice—from a US plastic lime-shaped container—that were delicious. We shared our treat with our three companions, hoping this would bring Kanauwi into a better humor. The storm was long gone and the sun was blazing.

Eventually Kanauwi decided to leave the boat on the shore, and we struck out on a path next to the river. As no one knew the path, there were several false leads before we hit the main one. All of this indecision was making Joyce anxious. We traveled very fast as it was midafternoon, and Kanauwi and I were also getting anxious, afraid we would be caught hiking after dark on an unfamiliar and very narrow winding trail. At last, we came to the Sand River, a good sign of progress, and must wade or swim across. Kanauwi suggested I go first but knowing the danger of crocodiles lurking under the water and not experienced enough to read the depth, I demurred. After a pause and a close perusal of the area he started across and we all trailed behind him wading just thigh deep. From then on, we slogged through sago swamps until late in the afternoon when we heard wailing. To my relief, Kanauwi said we were near the Iwani hamlet just beneath the mountain and where the dead man lay. He then explained as a way of warning, it was their custom for men and women to take off their clothes when mourning. As we approached the hamlet a woman saw us and ran off. By the time we arrived at the impressive men's house, the largest one I had seen, everyone was wearing a bit of Western clothing and cordially welcomed us; the most cordial welcome we had had. The old men were smiling, there was much shaking of our hands, and children crowded about taking it all in.

To our surprise, it turned out they were expecting us. Ray, the Yellow River 'kiap' who knew of our plan to be in Iwani tonight and fly back to Lumi tomorrow, had sent 'mulis' (oranges) and onions over to Iwani for us and the word spread that a White couple was coming. Joyce, they said, was the first White woman to enter the hamlet. Joyce and our boat crew climbed on up the hill to the main Iwani hamlet, but I stopped to visit with the people. This lower hamlet, (Iwariyo), had only four houses. The body was in the men's house and I was told women were in there too. Then I started getting conflicting reports; some said he was buried, others said not until tomorrow morning. This wasn't helpful; feeling tactfully aware of my alienage, I decided to join Joyce on top, all the while thinking this might be the only funeral I will see during my fieldwork, and planning to return after I had dinner.

The trail was steep and the red claylike soil slippery but on finally reaching the top I found Joyce standing in the hamlet's plaza; it was like being on top of the world. There were fabulous views in every direction. It was sunset and the sky was aflame; we had never seen anything quite like it and we both agreed—this is it. The immensely tall coconuts defined Iwani's antiquity; it was later confirmed by others as the original ancestral home to all the Lujere villages. But there was no men's house, just the old worn house poles that outlined a former one. We saw some wildflowers in bloom and the setting was almost alpine with occasional stone outcroppings.

It was a spectacular spot, certainly the most desirable place physically I had seen on the patrol for my new fieldwork. The 'haus kiap,' our camp for the night, was very removed from the hamlet so we descended the ridge a bit then walked along the trail until we found it. Writing today, I imagine the Mosstroops's Iwani camp was probably located in the same area, but back then, I did not have the knowledge to ask. Our new Iwani assistant, Bie, and his sidekick, Arian, were already there, both from Iwani and recently married. After a dinner with Ray's cooked onions to enliven our dreary canned fish and his exotic oranges for dessert, we went out to look at the stars and found the Southern Cross. I decided not to return to the funeral; I couldn't overcome my feelings that I was an insensitive intrusive stranger just barging in. Then there was that slippery trail down and the climb back up in the dark. We crawled into our sleeping bags and easily fell asleep after a day, for us, of high adventure.

After breakfast I interviewed Bie while he was cleaning up, but did not feel that he was a reliable informant—not in the sense that he was intentionally dishonest, but in the sense that he seemed to paint a more modern picture of his people that was in line with his own personal aspirations. A projection of personality to a culture, you might say. On male initiation he drew a total blank and had no details on curing rites or clans. Joyce and I walked through the hamlet a couple of times to take photos, then headed for Edwaki, the Yellow River Base Camp, arriving in just under two hours. We had an animated lunch with Ray, thanked him for his gustatory gifts, then Joyce visited Mary Parish and Rosemary Ace at the CMML mission while their husbands, Ces and Phillip, came over to visit with Ray and me. When it was nearing time for our plane to Lumi, the men, who would be meeting it on their motorbikes, gave us an easy lift down the hill.

On our flight back to Lumi on the administration's scheduled charter, Vince, the pilot, kindly circled our Wape village of Taute twice so I could photograph it. That evening I had a chance to chat with Father James, ever gracious, at the expat's clubhouse. The following morning before returning to Taute I interviewed him at the Catholic Mission about his early years in Lumi with the Wape, unaware that in 1949, he was also the first missionary to visit the Lujere.

Narrowing the Options

On October 21, I flew in the CMML plane to Yellow River to continue my search for a research site. Ray was away on patrol, but had offered me the hospitality of the base camp. The base's two policemen, Tabinum and Wai (the latter from Tambunam village on the middle Sepik, where I had worked the summer of 1967) welcomed me, as did Makau, the base's interpreter from Mageleri village. Ray had appointed Manwai from nearby Yegerapi as my assistant and carrier/guide. New voting boundaries had placed the Yellow River area into the Ambunti election precinct (not in Lumi) for choosing its member to the national House of Assembly and the present member, Nauwi Saunmabi from Ambunti, was there to meet some of his new constituents. Men had gathered in the dirt plaza between the base camp's office and the policemen's building for a meeting that began around 5:30 p.m. and continued for several hours.

After the talk by the House of Assembly member, he asked to hear the people's concerns. Makau was the first to speak and among his comments he voiced the need for a 'dittiman' (agriculture officer) to help resolve the area's economic plight and the need for more schools, teachers and teaching supplies. Litabagi, the aid post orderly in Yegerapi and a Lujere resident, had some strong thoughts about the deadly assaults of the 'sangumamen' and wanted them all thrown into prison until they died. He also complained that the locals did not help supply his family with food or keep the grass cut around the aid post, both nominal expectations of villagers with a resident orderly. This aroused the member to say he would report this concern to the health authorities and, if the villagers didn't give more support to the orderly, he personally would place him in a village that would. Of course, he didn't have that power, but the locals did not know this so there was more discussion and rehashing the same topics over and over. Hungry, I went up the ladder into the base camp and continued to listen while I ate. There were about twenty-five men at the meeting, which finally ended at 8:15 p.m., when someone, I couldn't see who, made a single loud clap. The only woman present was the wife of the aid post orderly. Later I learned that she was one of his several wives, a very unusual circumstance among the Lujere.

Earlier Makau, a locally knowledgeable and helpful man, and I looked at some of Ray's local maps, and I decided to cross the Yellow River near Alai village the next day, then continue on via Naum, which I had already visited with Joyce, to Nami village where I would spend the night. The next morning before breakfast, I had coffee with the two policemen and Member Nauwi where there was more conversation condemning the 'sangumamen.' Nakaki, originally from Alai and now living in Naum, joined Manwai and me to be my volunteer guide for the day. By 8:45 a.m., we were underway. For some reason I decided to bring only my Leica camera dedicated to Kodachrome film. We did not stop in Alai as it was not a research site candidate, being too close to the mission and government stations. At 10:00 a.m., we crossed the very brown Yellow River in a canoe and at 11:40 a.m. entered Naum village. En route there was more talk about 'sanguma' as the scourge of the area. One of the men had a bamboo jaw harp that he said was traditional, not new.[7] I also asked about marriage and other customs, but it seemed that every topic inevitably returned to 'sanguma.' I photographed the large newly completed men's house I had photographed in its initial stages in July. Inside there were bloodstains on the center pole. Someone gave me a refreshing 'kulau' to drink and I visited with the 'luluai' while we waited for Nakaki's mother to bring us some sago. The village had about fifteen houses, mostly old style and a few with no sides, scattered randomly along and around the large open area.

It was here that I first heard about the small groups of White men with Native policemen—the Mosstroops, I much later learned—during World War II, and the locals' killing one of their policemen who had sex with a village woman; this then morphed into a story of a 'masta' being killed and eaten in the mountains across the Sepik. There were more remembrances of 'masta mak' during the war and seeing their first White men. After the war, a recruiter came down from Lumi to recruit laborers, the first to leave from the Lujere villages northeast of the Yellow River.

As we talked, I was aware of many annoying flies, the first I had experienced in such numbers, and that several of the men had a type of aquiline noses I couldn't recall seeing among the Wape. The sago arrived and, because it had been cooked on a stone, tasted delicious, at least in comparison with to the large gelatinous boluses or 'hatwara' sago

---

7. I also collected several for the American Museum of Natural History, but see the jaw harps from Papua New Guinea on display at the National Music Museum: http://collections.nmmusd.org/Oceania/1438PapuaNewGuineaJewsHarp/JewsHarps1438-1442.html.

Figure 6. A Lujere man stands on the porch of a traditional-style men's house (*iron*), one of two in Nami village.

that are preferred by many Wape but that I find, groping for a polite term, unacceptable. Our conversation continued and I was delighted to see the men eating openly together, not turning away Wape-style to eat unseen. Like other New Guinea men who have adopted cloth clothing but without money for the luxury of soap, their dingy shorts and 'laplaps' (waistcloth) bore stains and grime that water alone couldn't remove. While cloth clothing, regardless how shabby, identified them as modern men, it was not necessarily an improvement in style, hygiene, or simplicity over their forefathers' jauntily elegant phallocrypts.[8]

Leaving Naum at 12:25 p.m., we arrived in Nami, named for its creek, and at 2:00 we headed for the 'haus kiap' where I would sleep, and we appreciatively drank a 'kulau.' Nami was one of the newest Lujere villages and its founder came from Alai. Apai, a strong and humorous man, greeted me and had his pregnant wife Bodtwai, bring two 'limbums' (shallow buckets made from a palm's flower sheath) of water so that I could wash up. But I was more interested in seeing the village than getting cleaned up—there were two large, well-constructed men's houses (fig. 6)—besides, with the sweaty heat, it

---

8. "In 1971–1972 the Indonesian government [in New Guinea] launched Operation Koteka ("Operation Penis Gourd") which consisted primarily of trying to encourage people to wear shorts and shirts because such clothes were considered more "modern," but the people did not have changes of clothing, did not have soap and were unfamiliar with the care of such clothes so the unwashed clothing caused skin diseases."

was too early. As we rested Nakaki joked with Apai, obviously his friend, and as others came in the conversation (all in Tok Pisin) was about work and wondering when the 'kiap' would return, with the implication that when he did, there would be paying jobs at Edwaki complete with a local boss who would oversee the work. It was the perennial dream of these men: a money-making job near home with family and friends.

Nami village was similar to Naum, with its flat Kansas-like surroundings and its houses generally spaced far apart in a relaxed spaciousness, unlike Wape houses, which were tightly clustered together around a small central plaza on a narrow mountain ridge. The Wape-type village, while crowded, makes fieldwork easier as one is privy to much that is happening without even trying. It was becoming clear to me that collecting data among the Lujere could be more of a challenge, what with the dispersed village layout and the villagers' prolonged absences in the bush.

Throughout the afternoon I informally interviewed the men with me and listened to the 'luluai,' a big, pleasant, and "old-fashioned" man, tell me about his people's origin, hunting lore, fight lore and garden lore, but I especially enjoyed my more animated conversations with Apai and Mitahki, a young short man, and Talakebluwa, middle-aged, the latter two from the same men's house. Finally, after 5:00 p.m., I had a much-needed sponge bath with Bodtwai's water, had something to eat, then Nakati and Manwai joined me for their gobbled-down dinner of 'hotwawa' and smoked pork. We joined the men gathered on the house's veranda, and I mostly listened as they recalled their experiences as indentured laborers far from home, discussed problems with shotguns, and debated village councils (they didn't have them), among other topics I didn't write down. Energetic and articulate, seeming to delight in conversing in Tok Pisin, they kept bringing up new topics mostly related to their common experiences with work and the government. 'Sanguma,' to my surprise, was never mentioned. By 9:45 p.m., this Lujere "male bonding" session ended, and the men departed. I had collected more basic data here than in all other places combined. I began to write down some summary notes about this interesting and productive day, at 10:30 p.m., I could still hear an occasional voice from the nearby men's house speaking in Tok Pisin.

Writing from what I knew right then about the Lujere, I hypothesized that it was a relatively "new" culture when compared to with the Iatmul (on the middle Sepik River) and Wape (in the Torricelli Mountains) with whom I had lived, basing my hypothesis, rather precariously, on the data that the Lujere appeared to have far fewer rituals regarding hunting and curing and, overall, the culture seemed less complex. Regarding the Lujere men, I wrote,

> Men are more expansive and humorous. Not as cool as the Wape, more spontaneous. . . . Boys are quiet but big men talk and play, e.g., Nakate funniest and wittiest kanaka [local man] I have ever met. Like an American; he called me "Kanaka Bill"! Very fast on the uptake and a straight man, droll humor; I love it! (MN: 667)

The following morning, I was up at 6:30 a.m., and at 7:45, Nakate, Manwai, and I left Nami to return to Edwaki. As we walked, Nakate gave me a much more nuanced view of Lujere curing rites and its Namia vocabulary, especially regarding *wowi*, their only curing 'singsing.' At 10:30 a.m., we paddled across the Yellow River (fig. 7) and at 12:15 we were atop Edwaki Hill at the base camp.

Figure 7. Nakate and Manwai ready a canoe to cross the Yellow River.

It was hot, but there were clear views of all the mountains. I went over to the CMML Mission and Rosemary Ace, always friendly, offered me two cold drinks and two teas and cookies. Then she generously gave me bananas and a pineapple. While we visited, I met the Norambalip store-keeper and the Iwani 'tultul.' The latter's wife and baby were in the 'haus sik' and the mother had worn out Rosemary by sitting on her doorstep asking for food. Neither the mission nor government hospitals had funds for a food budget, so patient's families had to bring them their food and provide care. At first I was surprised that Rosemary did not know that the local member of the House of Assembly had been on the station for two days, but it is easy to see how treating the sick, teaching a pidgin literacy class, and caring for a husband and two small children kept her mission bound.

Returning to the base camp, I took advantage of my access to the government's patrol reports and spent the rest of the day and the following morning busily reading them and taking notes. The only reports available were recent ones for 1970–71, but they were especially helpful for statistical village data. It was not until I left the field that I learned of the existence of Robinson's and McCarthy's pioneering patrol reports, and it was another year before I obtained copies from Australian archives and read with excitement the valuable "first contact" Lujere cultural data they had recorded.[9]

---

9. Stopping in Port Moresby en route home in 1972, I visited the government's new National Archives Office and, in lieu of actual patrol reports they did not have, I was shown a reference guide to patrol reports dated to 1941. Once home, I wrote to the director of the Commonwealth Archives Office (now the Australian National Archives) in Australia and later to

With the patrol reports safely returned to Ray's files, at 10:00 a.m. Manwai and I started for Iwani's Mauwi hamlet where I planned to spend the night then return to the base camp for my flight back to Lumi—hopefully having decided about my Lujere fieldwork site. But before I hiked up the hill to Mauwi, I intended to stop in Wakau, the only Iwani hamlet I had not visited. It was a clear sunny day and in about an hour we came to a creek with a downed tree for a bridge that was about a foot and a half under water in the middle. Somehow in crossing the underwater bridge I lost one shoe, but Naminum of Mauwi, who was bathing there with a little girl and boy, rescued it before it disappeared downstream. Then he and the children joined us as we proceeded to Wakau. At 11:50 a.m., we walked into the hamlet.

Wakau is situated in the forest on a rise at the edge of a wide-open 'kunai' plain that almost abuts the hidden Sand River (shown in fig. 13 in Part 2). I admired the old coconut trees towering above the hamlet and made a rough count of twelve houses plus a men's house and another much larger one recently abandoned. Although not high like Mauwi hamlet, there still was a beautiful view of the distant mountains, savanna, and forest (see fig. 11). I wrote in my notebook, "Really a good spot." Other than Mauwi, it was the only place I had visited where I felt an immediate physical connection to the locale. It was midday and the hamlet was mostly empty except for a few men who came out to greet our group, including a boy who brought the inevitable *kulaus* to refresh us. I then walked the length of the hamlet visiting and asking questions of whoever was around. Kunai was the only unforgettable Wakau man I met that day, both slight and slightly goofy and pop-eyed; it makes me smile to recall him even now.

However, like Barry Craig on his collecting trip to Wakau, I too was eager to move on. I wanted to get up to Mauwi to spend the rest of the day in hope of finding some village enthusiasm for my moving there and access more closely the quality of informants necessary to instruct me in their customs. Before 1:30 p.m., Manwai and I were on our way. In fifty minutes, we were on top and at the 'haus kiap' where I would sleep. I walked over to the almost empty hamlet, admired the stunning views as I had with Joyce in July, and surveyed the village as a place to work and talked to whom I could. I took a number of photos of the houses, a man with several children, even a shot of Wakau's 'kunai' plain, and settled on a place to build a house if it were agreeable with the villagers. It was not a good omen when Manwai and I had trouble getting enough water to wash up and cook dinner. Before dinner I visited with the 'luluai' and Dian, a strong young man who had returned to the village five months earlier after plantation work. Nanum, another man, was holding a barbering session as we sat around watching and talking. I talked about my coming to live in Mauwi but was offered no encouragement and even had difficulty in getting the names of enough men to carry my camp cargo to Mauwi if and when it arrived.

---

the National Archives of Papua New Guinea requesting copies of over a dozen reports that I thought could be relevant to my research with the Iatmul, Wape, and Lujere groups. Thus began an oft-tortuous correspondence with both archives that continued over twelve years before I received the last requested report. (Later all of the patrol reports became available through the University of California Library in Santa Cruz, which was my always-helpful source for reports while writing this book.)

Neither the 'lululai,' while pleasant enough in a remote way, or Dian, while an intelligent and attractive young man, appeared to have sufficient interest in his customs to be a good informant. After dinner I was in a pessimistic mood. I wrote, "Having 2nd thoughts about this place. Enough men here to make a house, to be informants? I wonder. Maybe Nami is better. Don't see a single good informant in the place!" (NB #21). It was raining slightly when Manwai left at 8:40; no one had come during the evening to talk with me. Before turning out my light I made a final note, "I'm a bit disarrayed; not quite the reception I'd expected. Not like Taute, anyway. They seem to care less!" (NB #21).

I spent a miserable and spooky night inside my insect net listening to the mosquitoes' incessant hum then, finally falling asleep, awakened frequently by pigs rooting around under the house. The rain slashed noisily against the 'morota' roof, the wind howled, and I dozed with ridiculous thoughts of 'sanguma,' as if I were eight years old again remembering a scary ghost story we children might tell one another on a hot Kansas summer's night. I was glad to hear Manwai's morning arrival as he carried a big stick to threaten the two marauding Mauwi pigs that didn't hesitate to attack humans. But it was a quiet morning. One boy came to see me and a man called out a greeting as he went by on his way to Aiendami village. Breakfast finished with a hot cup of tea at hand, I began scribbling down my thoughts, thinking out loud as I was finding the present situation insupportable.

> People talking in the houses, slight [rain] shower, 'lululai' gone to the bush—What a place; I think I will have to give it up—just not tuned into me enough. Not unfriendly, but just don't give a damn!
> And these pigs that are after you all the time, I just can't take—at least two everyone is afraid of. Crazy. How could the kids [Ned and Elizabeth] cope with that?
> Man-eating pigs and Sanguma, what a hellish combination.
> 9 [a.m.]—Rain has stopped now or just about. Sun trying to shine. Think I must see Pabei [village] and maybe settle on Nami although it is a 4 hour walk away [from base camp]. Nami seems relatively untouched by the mission and some literate people there anyway.
> Also little Alai [village]—might try it for a while, then move on. But who for . . . [an assistant]? Change all the time? [Just] live in haus kiaps? A rugged life, I fear. But [I] could carry a little tent but no refrig[erator] or could I? Maybe here [Mauwi] awhile, then Alai and Bapei—or just stay on the plains, that's probably better.
> And certainly, the kunai hamlet [Wakau] is more promising than this place. That might be a possibility. I think this place is hopeless. . . . Two months there then on to Nami for a few months or a month or 2 in each place. Problem here is getting enough decent informants to tell me what is going on. (NB #21)

Those notes make clear that, in spite of my energetic ruminations, I returned to the base camp without a final decision about my next fieldwork site. This was not an entirely new experience as I had patrolled extensively before I settled in Taute. What was new was selecting a field site—the Iwani hamlet of Mauwi—only to discover it was a bad choice. Back at the base camp, Rosemary Ace and Mary Parish invited me to lunch with them and their children, providing a needed and pleasing change of pace. Then in the afternoon the policeman Tubiman told me in considerable detail about a lurid Mauwi 'sanguma' killing, and Manwai, who was listening, followed with a related update he had heard just yesterday regarding a planned payback killing in a village on the Sepik. Late Monday afternoon after paying Manwai for his help, my mission plane arrived and I returned to Lumi, eager to ready my gear and move to the Yellow River 'tais.' Exactly where, I still didn't know.

The Choice

The next morning, I hiked out to Taute and for the next three days did little else but organize and pack up my supplies and equipment. Kumoi, my main informant and major domo, organized the carrying and by Wednesday the men we had selected began moving my cargo to Lumi. On Thursday evening I was finally finished, and I gave out presents to my best friends who had stood by me the year and a half I lived there and helped when the going was rough. Friday, my Taute fieldwork with the Wape finished, I joyously hiked into Lumi. After greeting Joyce and the children I washed up and we went to the Broadhurst's to pop a bottle of champagne to celebrate my exit and impending move to Yellow River. Perhaps that helps to explain the over-the-top note I typed in my diary that night.

> Finished packing cargo; closed up the house and departed Taute. WHOOPEEEEEE!!! A few tears were shed by the women; men shook their heads and wondered how soon the masalais [bush demons] would move in on them now that I'm gone. Sad, really. But I am thrilled to GET OUT and start something NEW. (MD: 55)

Their rationale for assuming a swift return of the bush demons to the village after I left was their belief that the strange smell of my families' bodies—I like to think it was from the soap we showered with daily that they could not afford—frightened away the demons and accounted for so few village deaths while we lived among them.

A temporary move to Edwaki Base Camp

The Taute men were to bring the last of my cargo to Lumi on Saturday but by Sunday afternoon they had not arrived. I was seriously concerned as my MAF charter flights to Yellow River were for Monday morning. It was very unusual and worrisome that no word was sent telling why they hadn't come. Then late in the afternoon when I was about to cancel my chartered flights, the Taute men came trudging into Lumi. Included in their cargo was the small but heavy kerosene refrigerator, our most precious camp possession that kept food from spoiling and could even freeze two tiny, treasured trays of ice cubes or, on special occasions, make ice cream for the children. It wasn't Ben and Jerry's, but in the jungle it was a tasty cool treat. The men said they were delayed because old Taolefe had died, and they stayed in the village to mourn his death. No one blamed me outright for Taolefe's death, but it was unpleasantly ironic that the day after I moved out of the village the last survivor of Taute's oldest patrilineal clan died.

Most of my cargo for Yellow River was already locked in the 'kiap' storage shed on the airstrip, but this new load needed extensive reorganization. Joyce had invited the Broadhursts for dinner, but they left early so we could start working. Even then we were up at 5:30 a.m. working feverishly in case Colin's plane arrived early in the morning. By

7:30 we had loaded the hospital's pickup and were starting off to the airstrip when we got word that the charters would be in the afternoon. I chucked away the banana I was having for breakfast and Joyce and I returned home for a relaxed breakfast.

There were to be three charters: two were mine and the other one Peter's to replace the two policemen at the Edwaki Base Camp. Twice during the day Colin landed, we loaded the plane, and then he soared away. It was around 6:00 when he landed to get the last load of cargo and me. But he quickly apologized that my charter was canceled because the MAF inspector had landed on the airstrip and closed the field because of the wet conditions. It would be Wednesday at the earliest before he could come back for me. My first concern was about my two planeloads of equipment and supplies already unloaded but he assured me the policemen had taken care of them. Instead of being disappointed, the delay delighted me; I was worn out from the work and tension that a major bush move entails, and landing on an isolated grass airstrip at dusk with my gear dumped around me was a depressing thought. Now I would have a mini-bonus holiday with Joyce, Ned, and Elizabeth before my move.

I was pleased that the new base camp had been approved and I looked forward to the occasional companionship and help of its young and, I speculated, iconoclastic 'kiap.' While the two Yellow River missionary families were generous and quick to provide a meal or meet any perceived need, they appeared to be weighed with work and responsibility. I doubted that they appreciated the ridiculousness of our intrusive roles with the Lujere who, until we arrived, were quietly minding their own business.

A primary difference among those who intrude into the lives of the colonized is often the motive that brings them there, varying from seeking wealth, power, knowledge, souls, or adventure, to providing healing or learning. But regardless of motive, the common bond among them—and it is an immensely strong one—is the touch of nuttiness, you might even call it "colonial madness," that they all share—trader, miner, patrol officer, missionary, anthropologist—of forsaking the "known" for the "unknown" in a remote land. It is a strange kind of bond.

When Colin and I landed Wednesday afternoon on the Yellow River airstrip, I found all of my cargo safely stored in a nearby locked shed. Ray was away on patrol but had invited me to stay in the base camp 'haus kiap' until I settled on a village. Phillip Ace, ever helpful, met me on the airstrip and helped arrange to get all my cargo carried up the steep hill to the base camp. The carriers were local men who had volunteered to repair the airstrip, and some of Phillip's youths in his Tok Pisin school, all pleased to earn a few shillings where such opportunities were rare. Later I joined the Aces for dinner with another New Zealand missionary couple from Anguganak who were soon leaving the Territory for good. I wrote, "Pleasant evening but there is little humour in these CMML New Zealand missionaries; pretty heavy going" (MD: 55). Fortunately, many New Guineans have a wonderful sense of the absurd so I knew my life in the village would have its share of laughs.

Makau, the administration's interpreter, found me a personal assistant named Towi, a man from nearby Yegerapi who had worked for Ces Parish. The two of us set to work organizing my stuff in Ray's big, somewhat jumbled A-frame 'haus kiap.' I previously had told the Iwanis that I was interested in living in one of their hamlets, but we needed more discussion and if interested, to meet my plane. When I didn't arrive on the day expected, I had hoped that on hearing the plane land today they might have assumed my arrival and try to contact me. But it was obvious that the Lujere, especially the Iwanis, were not standing in line competing for the residence of this odd 'waitskin' who wasn't going to open a trade store in their village, but just wanted to learn about their way of life.

Towi and I organized a credible temporary camp within the sprawling A-frame and I erected a small umbrella tent I had brought for the children and, very tired and ready for sleep, crawled into it for protection from the mosquitoes. I was sleeping soundly when one of the worst storms I have experienced in New Guinea or anywhere began about midnight.[10] It obviously was the thundering start of the rainy season. The howling wind and savage rain swept through the houses' large openings, I supposed for viewing sunsets, tossing the 'kiap's gear hither and yon and drenching some of my boxes and trunks. I escaped from the dripping tent and in the flashes of brilliant lightning and booming claps of thunder I raced around trying to rescue the most vulnerable items. The only dry place I could find was Ray's little personal office and, finally surrendering to the disarray, I collapsed into a damp sleep as the rolling thunder echoed further and further away.[11]

It took Towi and me most of the next day to dry things and restore some livable order after the storm. I was eager to decide where I was going to live, so Sunday morning Towi and I headed for the two Iwani hamlets, Mauwi, atop its long hill, and Wakau, down below near the 'kunai' plain. The hike from the base camp to Mauwi's 'haus kiap' was a short hour and fifteen minutes. There was only one man in the hamlet and he explained that everyone was in the bush hunting or finding food, not unlike the situation when Hutchins's patrol visited the previous year. He also said the Iwani men had gone to meet my plane Monday but when I didn't arrive, decided that it must be next Monday. I walked around the hamlet and noticed that two new houses had been started but the area Joyce and I had selected for my house, if I moved there, was still empty. Nevertheless, as much as I delighted in the hamlet's beautiful and breezy location, I was convinced that Mauwi was not for me. There were too many young men working away at plantations and there was no genuine enthusiasm for me to live there. Now everything depended on my visit to Wakau. With some trepidation, I, with Towi leading the way, started down the hill towards Wakau and its 'kunai' plain, where the Mosstroops Lieutenant Fryer and his men had camped.

As we walked on a well-trod path through the 'kunai,' I saw men gathering in the hamlet and walking to its edge to greet us. I relaxed. I knew this was the place. What a relief! There were at least twelve men in the hamlet, most of them young and very friendly to me, insisting, in a nice way, that I come live with them. They had, in fact, sent three men to Edwaki just that morning to contact me but we missed them when we went up to Mauwi. (We did meet them on the way back, however, in the camp by the river.) It seemed as if all of the women and children were watching and smiling at me; not timid

---

10. Once in Wakau, I would learn that the wind was called *waweli* and some men knew the magic spell to create a fierce wind; in Wakau it was Meyawali.
11. Thurnwald (1914) provides a hair-raising, accurate picture of the Sepik Basin's rainy season storms. For a translation in English see USCngp.com/paper/26 'Discoveries in the Basin of the Upper Sepik." But my favorite description of a tropical rainstorm is by Rodney Needham (1967: 281) that echoes my experiences. Thus, "Thunder, both in Malaya and Borneo, is an appalling natural phenomenon, seeming to crack and reverberate menacingly on the very surface of the forest canopy and shaking the guts of the human beings cowering underneath."

but apparently pleased and interested in my presence. I saw only one woman wearing a Native skirt, and she had thrown on a blouse. Everyone, as during my previous visit, seemed to have jumped into cloth.

I visited the drinking water spring just a few minutes' walk from the village, a shallow spring—about a foot or a bit over deep—but perhaps ample. It could, of course, be dug out larger as was the one in Taute. The water where the people bathe and wash clothing was a creek crossed on a log about ten minutes or so before you enter the village. Presumably my clothes would be taken there to be washed. It certainly wasn't a clear creek, quite muddy but no darker than the Sepik.

I walked through the village a couple of times, talking with the men; I was especially interested in the big old abandoned men's house as a temporary dwelling while my house was being built. The village was laid out on a more or less northeast-southwest axis with the 'kunai' to the southwest, then the unseen Sand River hidden behind a narrow band of forest between the 'kunai' and the river with the serpentine Sepik River beyond. On the horizon lay the West Range, actually a northern spur of the Central Highlands that the Sepik wrapped around at the Indonesian border in its descent to its great west to east flow to the coast. The village's first house sat out on the 'kunai,' the next three were on a rise above the 'kunai,' then about fifteen or so feet higher was a long, level, L-shaped rise with the rest of the houses scattered on both sides along an open central plaza. At the far end, the rise disappeared into forested swampland; there were a few towering coconuts (a sure indication of an old village site), and many younger ones. In all, there were about sixteen houses including two being built.

I had a meeting with the men at the new men's house in the upper village and told them I would come to live with them. They agreed to fix up the old men's house so I could move the following Friday when they would come with the Mauwi men to carry in my cargo, adding that the women would also come to carry the smaller articles. Interestingly, they said they would need only two men to carry a trunk; this was some different from the Wapei who insisted on four men rotating in twos to carry a trunk. We set no pay. I made a point, however, that I was not a businessman and explained how they would have to teach me their ways.

The only *tok* about my bringing money to them came from Kunai, a peculiar man with intense poppy eyes I immediately recognized from my first visit and, I surmised, a bit addled. Draped around his waist was an old orange 'laplap' topped with an old orangeish shirt. On his head was an odd cloche hat with *guria* [Victoria crowned pigeon] feathers in it. And, as before, he clung closely to me and did a lot of the talking.

It was he who mentioned his poor clothes and that with me there he would be able to buy new trousers and a shirt. He was probably saying what was on every one else's mind. He had, it seems, no censor and in that way he might be a good informant to get leads about what is going on. But I would find him difficult to work with regularly. A bit too nutty. He also had the habit of frequently gripping my upper right arm between his thumb and fingers when he was talking. No one else did this. Tautes did this sometimes but what was different was how he gripped gently then released and then kept repeating this that was odd. I am sure that he is an odd ball. What I didn't like was that in his enthusiasm to convince me regarding the charms of Wakau, some of the more stable young men were reluctant to compete with him so I heard a bit too much from him. But I did like the men, the directness of their gaze, their smiles, and handshakes. They genuinely made me feel welcome and you must have that if you want to live happily among a foreign people (MN: 410).

While I was in the village, two men entered, one bearing a small pig that had been killed by his dog, not with a bow or gun! One of the men was from Gwidami and his face was painted black. Towi told me later that he probably was in mourning although he did not know the details. Towi was greeted by the villagers, some shook hands with him as with me, and he was given a small package of gelatinous sago dumplings[12] and a piece of smoked pig. They had killed a pig just the day before. When Towi and I returned to Edwaki, Makau, the interpreter, had a wild pig he had shot laid out and was butchering it. Never had I seen so much wild pig in one day, plus all of the wild birds the police were boiling and a rack of wild pig they were smoking.

The two police assigned to the base camp were from the Lumi police detachment and they rotated monthly in pairs. When the 'kiap' was away on patrol, as he often was, they supervised the building of the road to the airstrip and heard villagers' complaints. The older was from Manus Island where Margaret Mead had earlier worked and the other, whom I knew best, was William, a Tolai from New Britain Island. One morning they came over to the 'haus kiap' to visit in Tok Pisin as they looked through my field glasses; it was the first time while in the bush that New Guineans had initiated a discussion on world events, and I enjoyed it immensely.

Topics that they introduced were the atomic explosion in Alaska that morning (William brought this up); what were the Japanese up to these days; the Vietnam War and, for local variation, 'sanguma.'[13]

Regarding 'sanguma' they said they did not have this in their own villages and seemed a bit puzzled by it. Was it true or just a belief as William suspected? After all, he said, they aren't Jesus, they can't work miracles like cutting up a man, taking out his flesh then sealing him up as if nothing had happened. The Manus man was sick of the whole thing, it was all they seemed to talk about. Both asked me about it, and I agreed with William that magically sealing the wound must just be a belief.

Settling in at Wakau village

The reason I set Friday to make my move from Edwaki to Wakau was because Joyce and I had a close friend, Marge Behrens from New York City, coming to visit us. Marge and her friend Janet Sacks from Chester, Connecticut, would spend a few days in Lumi with Joyce and the children and then on Monday, a charter would fly all of them to Yellow River, and they would spend two nights with me in Edwaki at Ray's 'haus kiap' (Ray was still on patrol) and they would return on Wednesday. Although I was eager to begin my

---

12. What I refer to as a "sago dumpling," is also called "sago jelly" (Gillam 1996: 30), "sago pudding," and 'hatwara' (Mihalic 1971: 96).
13. While the Vietnam War was an unknown phenomenon to the Lujere, I can't emphasize enough how important it was to my thinking during my Lujere fieldwork and I followed it as best as I could via the weekly Port Moresby newspaper and an occasional late-night, static-prone, short-wave-radio news report. See Rio and Bertelsen (2018) for a brilliant summary of the tumultuous political and cultural events of the 1960s and '70s and their impact on anthropology.

Figure 8. View south from Wakau's upper village, looking over lower village roofs towards the 'kunai' plain, the West Range, and Victor Emanuel Range.

new work, I also wanted Joyce, Ned, and Elizabeth to see where I would be living while they were in Australia (fig. 8).

I went into "bush-host" mode readying the camp but have no memory or notes as to how I found beds and mosquito nets for five visitors. On Tuesday, the six of us took off to visit Wakau, the children astride the shoulders of two young men. The day was oppressively hot. Marge and Janet, both older than Joyce and me, were motivated good sports but not in shape for steamy tropical hiking; it took a grueling full day going and returning with just a couple of turn-around hours in the village to sightsee and rest. We were all warmly welcomed; I knew the villagers would enjoy seeing my family in the flesh, especially the children, and it would give me a more fully human presence in their village in the months ahead living alone as a known husband and father. Nonetheless, I later was offered, with her permission, the most comely young woman in the village as a wife, an offer I politely refused, explaining our custom of monogamy. Having recently made a village census and counted many bachelors, I was aware of the magnitude of the offer. Had I accepted the offer without a sister to exchange, as is their custom, they obviously expected a hefty "bride-price" from their new American neighbor.

Next day, Joyce's plane arrived midafternoon as planned, and my family and friends flew back to Lumi. I slowly walked uphill to Ray's big empty house. That evening I had a rare feeling of loneliness. As much as I liked speaking Tok Pisin, I had thoroughly enjoyed rapid-fire conversations in English with so many lively Americans and two of them from New York, my favorite American city. Their responsiveness and vivaciousness had excited me, and Ned and Elizabeth had been a delight. Now I was back to hanging out at night, mostly alone; the only daily English I would hear would be in my head when I typed up my notes. On Thursday, I readied the patrol boxes, trunks, and boxes containing my equipment and supplies to be carried to Wakau, making some changes to distribute the weight more evenly. On Friday morning the men and women of Mauwi and Wakau began assembling at the 'kiap's house and the laborious transfer of my cargo to Wakau got underway. But the trails were good and the creeks low. Near the end of my fieldwork, we once had to slosh through one of the creeks waist-deep in water.

The men, like the Wape, were leanly muscular and not tall. Since I was also not tall, I could savor the uncommon experience of being relatively taller than others while in the field. The men also appeared to be more energetic than the Wape and perhaps stronger; instead of lashing a box or case for four men to carry like the Wape did, they needed only two men, as I mentioned. And rather than my hearing complaints about how heavy the loads were, there was a lot of smiling and whooping as they set off for Wakau. One man, however, irritated me and, as I learned later, also irritated most of his fellow villagers. I had given Aria a bundle of planks to carry but I was disgusted to learn he took the bundle apart and gave the planks to four little girls to carry. Still, if all went more or less as planned, I would be sleeping in Wakau that night, embedded within a new sociocultural milieu, the object of my new research.

All day the Iwani men and women carried my cargo to Wakau and dropped it in the ratty, old, abandoned men's house as I arranged it and dug out the things I needed for my temporary camp. It somewhat bothered me that the thatch on the back of the big empty house was either gone or decayed with little boundary between its rotting posterior and the encroaching forest. But with logic that defied me, ignoring the house's gaping rear, the men made sure that I could secure the front entrance from a murderous 'sangumaman.' Unlike the Wape, who believed that Europeans were immune to 'sanguma' attacks, the Lujere apparently thought otherwise. As a stranger in the village, it was a disquieting thought. We erected my umbrella tent and, strictly on intuition, I chose a temporary personal assistant, Nauwen—clean, quiet, single, and pleasant—from several young men who presented themselves, but Nauwen was so easy to work with that he continued to assist me throughout my stay. As we interacted daily, he was invaluable in keeping me abreast of village events, but he was not a teacher. With no intellectual interest in his culture, I had to look elsewhere for ethnic enlightenment. Interestingly, it would be his brother who would fill that role.

After I had eaten and Nauwen and I had put things away, a group of men stayed to watch and visit as we all swatted at mosquitoes. But our conversation was rather slow-going; even slower initially than with the Taute village men. By using the bug repellent "Off," the mosquitoes weren't too annoying, and we visited until about 9:00. My visitors were adamant, however, that I not sleep alone, further intoning the terrors of 'sanguma.' I thanked them but brushed aside their idea to protect me. While by definition a fieldworker's privacy is limited, I drew the line at bedtime; the idea of a nightly 'sanguma' minder was untenable.

Gradually the men filed out of the old rotting house declaring that if I heard any odd noises, I must yell loudly, and they would rush out with bows and arrows to attack or rout the intruder. What sane 'sangumaman,' I thought, would wander around outside this dilapidated house when he had a wide-open entrance from its forest end? I blew out my kerosene lantern and eventually went to sleep. But at some time before daylight, I was frightened awake by a crashing rustling sound on the sloping 'morota' roof just above my head. Sitting bolt upright, I also heard a chicken's desperate cackling. I listened intently for any other sounds from the house's dark gaping posterior. Assuming it must be an errant roosting fowl that tumbled off the roof, when all was quiet, I warily lay back down. Closing my eyes, I wondered what the hell had I gotten myself into.

Several weeks later after moving into my new house I began to grasp why my new hosts were so concerned about a 'sangumaman' attacking me. Ray sent me the following handwritten note that he knew, while it might alarm me, would also make me laugh:

> Bill,
> Have just heard an interesting story: A certain gentleman from IWANI (an tap) [Mauwi hamlet atop the hill] T____ (brother of deceased TULTUL) has threatened to DO YOU IN!! for reason as yet unascertained. (Yu no ken frait masta, GOVMAN i stap clostu!) [Don't be frightened sir, the government is nearby!]
>
> Not necessarily shall you meet your doom per medium of Sanguma, but could be by the rather common instrument of destruction, a tomahawk.
> Cheers,
> Ray
> Will investigate more thoroughly AFTER the act. (Letter from R. Lanaghan to W. Mitchell, n.d.)

But I made my own investigation and Nauwen said they had heard the story. T____ was one of Mauwi's accomplished 'sangumamen' who thought Wakau 'sanguma' had killed his brother, the 'Tultul.' In retaliation, he had threatened that Wakau's new 'masta' may not be with them very long. Some men thought it was a double-edged threat because they also had enticed me to live in Wakau instead of Mauwi.

PART TWO

Who are the Lujere?

They are more traders than warriors.
ADO J. K. McCarthy, 1936

They are more hunters than agriculturists.
Lumi ADC J. E. Fowke, 1968

CHAPTER SEVEN

Lujereland

> *Facilities for education within this area are at a deplorable level. There are no agricultural economic developments whatsoever throughout the area.*
> PO Ric Hutchings (1970)

> *The people show a complete lack of interest in anything that is going on in the outside world.*
> ADC Peter J. K. Broadhurst (1970)

In the late 1950s, when I began graduate school in anthropology at Columbia University, it was customary for many ethnologists to present their fieldwork account as more or less definitive: an "objective" and "true" account of a people's culture. Today, anthropology having survived the postmodern turn and, becoming both more mature and enlivened by it, takes a humbler approach to ethnographies. Thus, this account is but one version of Lujere culture and society, a version skewed not only by my training and personality but also by my association primarily with the villagers of Wakau and male informants; I was not allowed linguistic access to the women. This should not be interpreted as an apology that my data are not more inclusive (although I wish they were, one never has all the data) but simply a statement of what this ethnographic account is: one American man's descriptive interpretation of Lujere culture in the early 1970s from the perspective of: (1) an examination of its colonial history; and (2) my living in Wakau village as reflected in the twilight of Australian colonialism.

The Lay of the Land: Low, Wet, Hot, and Humid

Luckily, as long as I'm in a tee-shirt or less, I like to sweat; in the Sepik's atmosphere of optimal humidity, it can be done without even moving. In northern Vermont one's skin is often dry and scaly; in the Sepik it is always moist and plump. A hot, humid July day that can drive a native Vermonter almost to tears is a welcome pleasure to me. The Lujere temperature ranges from nighttime lows around seventy degrees Fahrenheit to a daytime high of around ninety-five degrees in both the wet and dry seasons. That was different from the Torricelli Mountains I had just left where the low was a "chilly" sixty-five degrees with a high of eighty-five degrees.

The Lujere habitat is covered with a mixture of swampy grasslands and tropical rainforest. While good garden land is at a premium, game (including pigs, cassowaries, and Victoria crowned pigeons) is plentiful, and the waterways abound with fish. There are no roads or towns, no plumbing or electricity. Villages are located on relatively high ground and the level of wetness in surrounding areas rises and falls precipitously. One might leave a village on a muddy track and return a few days later thigh deep in water. A semisedentary people, the Lujere spend days, even months, hunting, fishing, and working sago while living in bush camps where related families might live together in a single flimsy structure. Village houses are traditionally inhabited by a woman and her children, while men and youths sleep in a large dormitory-style A-frame structure.

I arrived in the Yellow River area toward the beginning of November 1971, at the start of the rainy season that averages around ninety inches of rain and lasts into April when the rains diminish. The wet season brings heavy rains every three or four days with up to seven inches in a single day and the occasional high wind and spectacular electrical storm like the one that greeted my arrival at the base camp. Storms of that intensity with gale-force winds were a special concern to my Wakau neighbors who, frightened that their roof would collapse, or a tree fall on it, might vacate the house and shelter on the ground beneath its stronger 'limbum' flooring. Indeed, Klowi's wife's old house, just below mine, fell in during a big windstorm. Some men know a secret ritual to make fierce winds; in Wakau only Meyawali knew how.

The dry season persists from April into late October or early November with rains on the average once or twice a week and rarely over three weeks apart. The roughly six-month dry season averages sixty inches of rain. The level of humidity drops a bit in the dry season just as there are more clear skies than during the rainy.[1] Apparently, the reason neither the Namia language nor Tok Pisin has a word for "humidity" is because it is a climatic constant. A day of nil humidity was unknown. Referring to a "dry" and "rainy" season is actually a misnomer—some expats facetiously call them the "wet" and "wetter" seasons. As Gillam points out about the Lujere climate,

> Though people try to define an actual wet and dry season, there are simply high rainfall and low rainfall seasons. In other words rainfall is a matter of degree and the dry season is simply a period of less rain. (Gillam 1983: 59)

---

1. My climate information is augmented by the Feldspauch's (1988: 4) records for the area.

Lujereland lies in the lowlands between the Torricelli Mountains and the Sepik River. The landscape is one of rainforests and vast natural grass plains on poorly drained soils intersected by wooded creeks and two major rivers, the Yellow and the Sand, rising in the cloud-bound Torricelli Mountains, then flowing southward to unite before entering the Sepik. The grassland soils are leached, sandy loams with poor nutrient values and kangaroo grass (*Themeda* spp.) is the most common ground cover. The rivers are bordered by tall open forest; sago palms (*Metroxylon* spp.) dominate some of the more inland watercourses while rushes (*Juncus* spp.) and bracken (*Pteridium*) predominate in the marginal and wet areas.[2]

The area traditionally occupied by the Lujere villagers runs roughly from the Sepik's south bank area (home of three villages) at the mouth of the Yellow River for about twenty-five miles northward, while its east–west axis of habitation extends for about eighteen or so miles from the immense fens west across the Sand River opposite Wakau, east to Worikori's land, or about 475 square miles. The geographic elevation of the region ranges from around one hundred to three hundred feet along the rivers with the Edwaki hill system seven hundred to a thousand feet high. This embraces Mauwi hill, on top of which Mauwi hamlet of Iwani village sits, and the other slightly higher Edwaki hill just to the east, where the CMML Mission and Edwaki Base Camp are situated. Other than these twin tropical monadnocks, the terrain is relatively flat except for a small hill southeast of Tipas village near the Sepik. On the Sepik's south bank before the abrupt mountain rise are also several small hills within the Lujere territory, including Kojabu (Kociabu), where Robinson burned his signal fires in 1932 and the Japanese bombed the Mosstroops supply base in 1943. The southernmost Lujere villages situated on the south flanks of the Sepik River are Aukwom, visited by Joyce and me, and to the east, Panewai and Purami located near the Mosstroops' Catalina water landings. Behind them the mountains rise steeply towards the domain of the Lujere's traditional cannibal enemies, the Sawiyano, and, during my fieldwork, the recently built Ama airstrip of the Seventh-Day Adventist Mission.

Footpaths of varying width and oft-challenging conditions connect all the Lujere villages and camps with the ease of travel greatly dependent upon the amount of rain that had fallen, necessitating administration patrols to be scheduled in the dry season. During the rainy season log bridges over a creek might wash away and some foot trails could disappear into the mud of a spreading swamp, while the torrents of tropical rain coursing down the Yellow and Sand Rivers can make them impassable. There are no bridges over either the Sand or Yellow Rivers and, although the prime habitat of crocodiles, they must be forded on foot if no dugout canoe is available, which is often the case. A felled tree sometimes bridges a large creek that otherwise would be impassable after a heavy rain. Small barefoot children learn at an early age to navigate the various demanding surfaces they daily encounter, developing a sure sense of balance with feet that are tough, strong, and amazingly dexterous with enviable toe-gripping power.

One aspect of a tropical equatorial locale that is very different from a Vermont perspective is the relative consistency of daylight hours throughout the year. Because New Guinea lies directly south of the equator, there is very little variation in the time of sunrise and sunset regardless of the month. While I lived in Wakau, the sun—when you could

---

2. These paragraphs have benefitted from the data compiled by Ian Bean (1971).

see it—plunged quickly over the horizon around 7:00 A.M. and, without any lingering twilight, the nights were long and dark, unless the moon was out. Because of the fear of 'sanguma,' villagers were normally confined inside their houses after dark. Wakau at night was mostly a silent, solemn, even slightly ominous place. As I usually spent my evenings typing up notes in my screened work tent by lamp light until late, I missed the sound of my Taute friends visiting on their house verandas or the happy sound of a clutch of women's raucous laughter.

Colonial Consequences

Once a land is seized and colonized by a foreign power, it is transformed in both subtle and severe ways. But compared with some other parts of New Guinea, Lujereland in 1971 looked much the same as it did when Thurnwald made "first contact" on the Yellow and Sand Rivers in 1914. An exception was that the omnipresent penis sheath that heralded a man's approach was disappearing, at least in the presence of expats. The houses, fabricated from the forest and bound with cane, were mostly unchanged, and hamlets and villages were still connected by a crisscross of native paths; the sago-oriented cuisine and pace of living remained very similar. Yet colonialism had irrevocably altered both the psychological context of everyday life and the individual consciousness of each man, woman, and child. Of marked importance was that personal biographies, once experientially constricted, had differentially expanded as most men left for several years to work far from home for foreigners while women at home had to take up the slack. Missionaries brought new stories and explanations about life they were eager to share; 'kiaps' brought new rules and forms of punishment hitherto unknown; medical patrols and aid posts brought new, often amazing therapies and radical ideas about sickness and its prevention; anthropologists wandered through villages buying old handmade crafts and ritual items or even moved in to record their way of life and ancestors' stories. Regardless of the villager, their awareness of the world was, depending on the individual, impacted by their experiences with colonialism.

"Isolated and Undeveloped"

Whenever an administration official referred to the Lujere's homeland, the terms "isolated and undeveloped" would appear like a sacred mantra. Lujere villagers eyed the world from a somewhat different cultural perspective. While they might disagree with the term "isolated," feeling to be in the *center* of the world they knew, few would argue against the term "undeveloped" if translated into Tok Pisin ('no gat wok bisnis'). Colonialism had raised their consciousness regarding money and development, contemporary concerns previously unknown to them. There was a very good reason why the only expatriates who lived in the South Wapei Census Division were missionaries and the local 'kiap': there was no way to make money. Lujereland was one of the last places an enterprising colonial entrepreneur would choose to be. What Karl Heider (1970: 297) wrote for the Dani of Irian Jaya—"The Dani have nothing and produce nothing which the world wants"—could also be written for the Lujere.

The South Wapei Census Division

From the Kaiser's reign to Australia's, Germany's nineteenth-century style of colonial bureaucracy persisted as a marvel of imposed administrative nesting divisions striding over a multitude of culturally alien societies. As already seen, the Australian system, like the former German one, was highly hierarchical both internally and in its imposition on the subjugated populace. It could be argued that Anglo-Saxon colonialists stress the value of numbers and counting, especially when so much else is culturally elusive. Counting and recording a village's residents by name was a continuing responsibility of patrol officers—an indispensable colonial ritual. After assembling villagers in a line, preferable a very straight one, the patrol officer sat at a small table under a hand-held umbrella taking roll call in the village book with several uniformed and armed policemen in attendance. Toddlers learned early who were the rulers and the ruled.

Since this book is about the Lujere, it is also about the Australian colonial realm in which they were embedded, and the South Wapei Census Division (SWCD) was the administration's smallest unit that enfolded their villages. Among the Lujere, probably only a handful knew what the SWCD was and how it pertained to them. Most Lujere were simply unaware of the Australian colonial bureaucratic structure that tightly overlaid their looser primordial society. Their knowledge of the administration and its forms of governance was in strictly personal terms: a politically powerful 'kiap' with armed policemen who visited the village every year or two. If villagers were away in the bush hunting or making sago, as they often were, they could easily miss a few 'kiap' sightings. Although the Wakau villagers had come under the Kaiser's foreign suzerainty in 1884, it would be seventy-two more years before a colonial official, an Australian 'kiap,' entered their village and took a census of the residents. As described in chapter 4, PO Oakes mapped and took the first census of Wakau and most of the other Lujere villages in June and July, 1956.

When possible, the Australian authorities attempted to create census divisions by common language and geography to facilitate patrolling and the collection of statistical information. Among the Lumi Sub-District's thirteen census divisions, the SWCD was by far the largest in geographic area with more than 730 square miles and by far the smallest in population density at six persons per square mile. Its population was forty-six hundred with the Lujere a majority at just over three thousand.

None of the Australian patrol officers who visited the villages of Lujereland and knew the area up close had any positive or encouraging words about either its present or future. The conclusion of PO R. K. Treutlein's 1962 report, written nine years before I arrived, is typical:

> A very backward area, in all fields, the South Wapei is going to be a great problem in the near and distant future. Advancement of these people will be severely hampered by their great dispersion, the difficulty of the terrain, which becomes well nigh impassable in the wet season, and the lack of an assured economic future. (Treutlein 1962: 25)

Indentured laborers

In the early 1970s, the only sure way most Lujere men gained access to money was to sign a contract as an indentured laborer and work on a distant plantation or mining project.

Their patrol officer (Lanaghan 1972: 4) wrote, "These people have become professional Plantation Labourers—with some going back for their 2nd and 3rd terms." While they still had the 'selmani' [shell money] of their ancestors, they coveted the introduced Australian coins and bills that could buy foreign things. During my fieldwork, 33 percent of the SWCD's males were working as indentured laborers in other parts of the country (Lanaghan 1972: 2). That was a high proportion of the male population but characteristic of native areas once they came under the administration's influence and eventual control as an essential part of the colonial economy. This partial absence of adult males in village life is one of the defining attributes of almost all New Guinea anthropological studies of village life. It is why I tried to find a village that had enough men in different statuses at least to give a sense of the normal rhythms of everyday life.

Ric Hutchins characterized the economic contribution of SWCD returned laborers in a 1970 patrol report, noting that

> These men can be expected to earn a gross $23,000 between them during a year. At the completion of their two years contract each man will return to his village between $20 and $30 cash apart from goods such as axes, clothing, saucepans and other trade store goods.
>
> From this source approximately $10,000 of "new" money enters the area each year. Most is buried in tins etc. only to be produced on the occasion of a marriage taking place or some unforeseen circumstances arising such as a Court fine having to be paid. . . . By tradition these returning labourers bring with them some article of clothing for each of their immediate relatives. (Hutchins 1970: 46)

The administration's indentured laborer strategy had a two-pronged advantage: first, cheap labor was recruited for maximum economic returns often to the degree of exploitation, and second, the men recruited were brought into totalizing work situations subjecting them to a regimented and severely truncated version of "civilized" society. The experience was thought by authorities to be personally transformative by replacing savagery with a worker's colonial civility. But there was tremendous diversity in how men experienced and interpreted their years as an indentured laborer. While many a man's consciousness was altered about what a life could be as they became intimately involved with alien ways and learned a new language, Tok Pisin, there were many others, as we meet in chapter 9, who returned to their village, itself little changed, with their ancestor's active stances on warfare and cannibalism vividly intact. The pioneering Sepik anthropologist, Ian Hogbin (1943), is one of the few experienced fieldworkers who have written critically regarding the multiple negative aspects of the indentured laborer experience.[3]

Very little has been written about the indentured experience, but these men frequently were an anthropologist's principle informants as they could speak Tok Pisin that was

---

3. Hogbin writes, for instance,

> Maintaining that a few years spent in European employment "is the most hopeful means of introducing the natives to civilization," the Administration systematically encourages them to leave home for the plantations and goldfields. . . . however, the "introduction to civilization" which the labourer receives can scarcely be called beneficial. (Hogbin 1943: 134)

especially important among the societies with difficult, unrecorded Papuan languages.[4] Often, most of a plantation's or mine's indentured workers were segregated, ghetto-like, to work and sleep with men of their own village and/or language for ease of worker–boss communication and to avert inter-group hostilities. Workers' free time usually was very restricted with little opportunity for learning beyond their rudimentary job skills. Some, like Aiyuk of Wakau, returned home without even learning Tok Pisin. My experience was that village children, especially boys, appreciated the trendy cachet of Tok Pisin and picked it up quickly as a second language. Labor contracts, as noted, could be for two or three years and some men returned several times as the one sure way to get the White man's money that was rapidly supplementing, if not replacing, traditional wealth in cultural exchanges and to secure a wife. Like a college student who returns after spending her junior year in France, a returned laborer had prestige in contrast to the 'buskananka,' the "wild uncivilized man" who had never left the jungle. The anthropologists Ian Hogbin and Camilla Wedgwood (1943), who both had done fieldwork in the territory and knew firsthand the exploitative problems of the indentured laborer system, wrote a scathing twenty-nine-page pamphlet indicting it.[5]

> Claiming that a few years spent in European employment is "the most hopeful means of introducing the natives to civilisation," the Administration in Mandated New Guinea systematically encourages them to leave home for the plantations or goldfields, a policy which has also been adopted in Papua and the Solomons.... Labour recruiters are permitted to enter new districts immediately after tribal fighting has been stopped, and, as it is rarely possible for the natives to obtain the necessary money for the head tax, which is imposed on all able-bodied men, the young people with fewest responsibilities are forced to make contracts.... The minimum period of indenture is three years in New Guinea, two in the Solomons, but contracts are generally renewed, the average period of absence being six years.
>
> Inquiry reveals, however, that, despite the claims of the New Guinea administration, the laborers are not "introduced to civilisation." On the contrary, the information they obtain about Western culture is vague in the extreme and usually inaccurate, the tasks carried out in no way enrich their outlook, and the elementary hygiene picked

---

4. On March 29, 1971, I wrote a letter to the manager of the Dylup Plantation near Madang, where thirteen men of the Wape village of Taute that I was then studying were working. After introducing myself, I wrote in part,

   > I have decided that anthropologists are never going to understand village culture unless they have at least some kind of first hand understanding of the villagers' experiences on plantations. Certainly in my work these experiences loom as the most important and interesting in a man's life. And I think they have a profound influence on the structure and quality of village life—not only for the men but for their wives and children too. (Letter from author to the Dylup Plantation, March 29, 1971.)

   I asked that I be able to visit informally with the Taute villagers and their supervisors and assured them that I would not abuse this privilege. My letter was not favored with a reply.

5. See Lutkehaus (1995: chap. 10) for a detailed discussion of Wedgwood's participation in various organizations involved with Australia's civil policies for the Pacific, in particular New Guinea.

up is quickly forgotten. It is difficult to see how the native can discover much about us when all but a small—though notable—minority of island employers look upon him as a "stupid kanaka" or a "bloody n_____" and, far from cultivating his acquaintance, do not learn to speak to him even in correct pidgin English. (Hogbin and Wedgwood 1943: 5–6)

Their tract is an important historical document as it develops a detailed critique of the system from its impact on the sexual behavior of young men isolated for years at a time from meaningful contact with young women,[6] to its opposition

> of educationists and others interested in training them for self-government. All sorts of excuses are made for discouraging the establishment of schools, for example, and even medical services are in some quarters frowned upon as unnecessary pampering. "As soon as the natives here are made to work the healthier they will be, and the less call there will be for the expenditure of the Government on large quantities of medicine for the curing of native ailments, which are nothing more than pure laziness on the part of the kanaka," wrote a commentator in the Rabaul *Times*. (Hogbin and Wedgwood 1943: 7)

Although in the 1970s racism was still a major factor in some expat–local relations even within the administration, it had of political necessity gone more underground and was no longer an accepted stance, as espoused by the writer to the Rabaul *Times*, that could be self-righteously publicly shouted.

Even though the indentured worker's opportunities were usually constricted, there were instances where workers from different societies did become friends during their work period and, if proximity permitted, even maintained their friendship after returning home. Just as persons who share a language are called 'wantoks' in Tok Pisin, those that share a work experience are called 'wanwoks.' These 'wanwok' friendships also display the importance the plantation experience had in establishing intercultural relationships among men who, ordinarily, never would have met. Such was the case of Tuai and Biai—a Lujere and Wape man—who met on New Britain Island while working copra on Kapit Plantation near the town of Bainings.[7] What follows is the tragic story of the only relationship I knew about between two men from the two cultures in which I carried out fieldwork from 1970 to 1972.

Tuai was from Yawari, the northernmost Lujere village I never had visited, and Biai was from Taute village, my Wape research base in 1970 and 1971, and I knew him and his family well. The two men had remained friends and occasionally visited each other.

---

6. Hogbin and Wedgwood (1943: 9), espousing a 1940s view that homosexuality was a "maladjustment," report, "Exile in labour barracks gives rise, too, to much sexual maladjustment. The labourers are at an age when desire is most urgent, and the savage punishments meted out by the courts have done nothing to check the inevitable increase in homosexuality. A study of Solomon Islands records reveals that even the sentencing of a youth of seventeen to seven years for 'unnatural behavior' brought no diminution in the number of cases heard."
7. Lewis (1975: 213) also indicates the importance of the 'wanwok' relationship for the Gnau in the Torricelli Mountains.

Their relation also had an interesting economic aspect that highlights a significant difference between the two societies. The Lujere bush, while infamous for 'sanguma,' was renowned for its wildlife—its quantity of wild pigs, cassowaries, and other birds—while the Wape bush was just as well known for its poverty of hunting opportunities. The Wape area was always much more densely populated than Lujereland, but originally had sufficient game for occasional successful bow-and-arrow hunting. However, the introduction of the gun, first by the Franciscan priests in 1947, to find their dinner, then by the 'kiaps' and police in 1949, to find theirs, began to impact the wildlife breeding population. Then this dwindling game population seriously worsened after it became legal in 1960 for village men to apply to the 'kiap' for a hunting license and own a shotgun.[8]

Hence the interest the Taute villagers had, via their contact with Tuai, in 1966 to invest in a new gun for Yawari village. Altogether, five Taute males and one woman advanced ten dollars towards its purchase. However, as far as getting the wild meat they wanted, it wasn't a great success because Yawari was several days' walk away. Nevertheless, villagers had on occasion made the trek and returned with meat and one of Taute's two licensed gun owners also had taken his shotgun down to hunt in the Yawari bush. But it was considered a dangerous excursion and Biai was occasionally warned that he could be killed with 'sanguma.'

Inevitably, the Yawari villagers' notorious reputation for 'sanguma' became a problem in Taute village. The incident began when Biai, angry with his wife, yelled at her to go fuck her *faf*, (her mother's brother), a heinous insult. She then told her *faf*, Wamala, and he, in turn furious at the insult, accosted Biai on the village dirt plaza and, in his railings, accused Biai of bringing Tuai, who was then visiting, to Taute to kill him with 'sanguma.' The dispute was eventually more or less resolved but, in November of 1970, when the incident occurred and I typed up my notes about it, I was unsure of the location of Tuai's village and totally unaware that this would be my very first data on the Lujere. Biai, however, eventually paid a tragic price for his friendship with his 'wanwok' Tuai. When I returned to Taute village in 1982 for a short visit, I learned that Biai was dead—attacked by 'sanguma' in the Yawari village's bush—and his Lujere friend Tuai was implicated.

The story was that he had been hunting with Tuai who had shot a cassowary and, while Tuai continued to hunt, Biai was to plant some sago for him. Biai was approached by two men who asked to borrow his knife, but Biai saw them hide theirs and told them so, whereupon they attacked him and cut several places on his left side to take his blood. When they began to close the cuts, two pregnant women appeared and the last cut wouldn't close. Biai fought the men who then ran off and he somehow made it to Kwieftim, but his Taute companions had to carry him on to the aid post in Wilkili near Taute. Once home he reported the attack in Lumi and his attackers and Tuai apparently were apprehended and put in jail. Although his "sore" became dry, it was still wet on the inside causing his death; at least this story was how some of the Taute villagers understood Biai's death as the result of the earlier 'sanguma' attack.

---

8. For the moral implications among the Wape regarding the introduction of the shotgun, see Mitchell (1973).

Villagers' knowledge of the colonial government

One of the pervasive complaints that runs through the Lujere Patrol Reports is the officers' dismay at the Lujere's lack of knowledge and understanding of 'gavman'—that is, the regional and national government, albeit totally foreign and unseen—and their lack of awareness about the Territory's impending rapid conversion towards self-government and then independence. Thus, the following negative summary comments from two of their patrol officers: "Generally speaking there is no political awareness among the people on the Central or Local Government Council level and only a limited understanding and appreciation of the administration in the village" (Fowke 1968: 20), and "A universal lack of knowledge, relating to anything political, is common throughout the whole of the South Wapei" (Lanaghan 1971: 23). I can only agree, at least for the Lujere.

It is difficult for a Westerner raised in a complex, industrialized, and urbanized country to project himself into the mind or thinking of a Lujere man or woman: a person whose parents and relatives were born, lived, and died in a society lacking the social, economic, religious, and political institutions we take for granted and that shape everything we do. But if it is a psychological stretch for us to grasp their cognitive world—and it is—it seems obvious that we are a bigger mystery to the Lujere than they are to us. We at least have the advantage of seeing them in situ in their home habitat; they see us out of our Indigenous context as exotic and mysterious isolates in theirs. For them, we are the invading Martians from another planet they can only wonder and guess about. Without schools, literacy, newspapers, radios, and political educational patrols to inform them in a sustained way, they have no entry route into our cognitive worlds of organization. They cannot even frame the question. So it is no wonder the Lujere were in the dark as to how their village fit into the administration's political divisions of "District" (West Sepik), "Sub-District" (Lumi), and "Census Division" (South Wapei) or the nature and work of the "House of Assembly" in relation to their right to vote.

Another factor caused outright confusion in local thinking as it did in mine initially: the names and boundaries of the House of Assembly Electorates. PO Wafingian wrote the following after completing a patrol of the SWCD:

> The people are confused as to the fact that their representative to the House of Assembly is from the AMBUNTI Sub-District; whom the people had voted for. But the South Wapei Census Division is still part of the Lumi Sub-District, therefore are also still part of LUMI [Sub-District]. They stated that if they are still part of LUMI Sub-District, why did they have to vote for a man from the AMBUNTI Sub-District. This I was not able to answer, and stated that, I would seek the truth and tell them later. (Wafingian 1972a: 1)

The "truth" the patrol officer might have known was that the Territory is divided into House of Assembly Electorates that may be different from the Sub-Districts. In the 1968 election the SWCD was part of the Wapei-Nuku Electorate, but for the 1972 House of Assembly election, was part of the Upper Sepik Open Electorate.[9] I didn't discover the

---

9. It is impressive that in this election 75% of the registered voters in the SWCD cast a ballot (Fowke 1968: 20).

change until a local candidate from Ambunti came to Wakau to campaign. Wafingian, admittedly new to the Edwaki Base Camp, seemed unaware of the administration's division of the Territory into assigned electorates that were independent of district and subdistrict boundaries.

After all, 'gavman' to most Lujere was not an abstract concept but the boots on the ground of the 'kiap' and his 'polis.' These men had direct influence over their lives and did not hesitate to exert their power when they felt it was necessary to carry out their duties. Fortunately, and to these men's credit, I saw very few blatant abuses of that power while living in New Guinea, but the ones I did see were egregious ones. Although the 'lululai' and 'tutul' were, from the administration's perspective, an indispensable part of their government, the Lujere villagers did not share this view. As their patrol officer (Lanaghan 1971: 16) expressed it, "Most everyone pays lip service to Luluais and Tultuls. They don't possess any real authority."

Councils and the Southwest Census District

After World War II, the Australians began to plan how the indigenes could be involved not only in a representative national governmental body, but also at the local level. The results were the Local government councils that in the 1950s were an experimental idea.[10] However, after the Local Government Ordinance 1963–71 came into operation on January 1, 1965, they were an increasing reality. In 1965 there were 114 councils covering a population of 1,250,000 and by 1970 the number had increased to 146 councils serving 2,068,000 people; some 90 percent of the population was under locally elected government councils (Grosart, 1972c: 268). These councils functioned as a form of local government similar to a village or town government in the United States with some legal power. Depending on the community, they had various responsibilities that could, for example, include building and maintaining roads, bridges, parks, aid posts, airstrips, water and power services, and community markets, and may make rules regarding, for example, public health, school attendance, livestock control, and the levying of taxes at a flat or graduated rate. But just as the Territory's administrator was subject to Australia's prime minister, so were the councils subject to their 'kiap.' Mair cites an administrative ruling that states,

> Whenever possible [the officer] should refrain from giving direct orders. He should endeavour to induce the village council to see the advantages of the course he would like to follow so that they themselves initiate the desired action. Only when it is impossible to persuade the Village Council to undertake action itself should the administrative officer make use of his authority to issue instructions. (Mair 1970: 82)

In the Sepik hinterland, a local government council usually consisted of several culturally related villages whose population exceeded 5,000 and, most important, had some economic base so that taxes, albeit sometimes nominal ones, could be collected. The

---

10. Mair and Grosart (1972) provide a lucid history of local government in Papua New Guinea including the origin, formation, and challenges of local government councils. Also see Mair (1970: 81–111) for a much more detailed discussion on their origin and history.

administration encouraged the formation of these local councils since "council experience is regarded as a significant element in the political education programme and councils are indispensable agents in all aspects of the rural development programmes" (Mair and Grosart 1972: 658). The Wape had a local government council that was especially important to villages near Lumi, although to Taute villagers across the Sibi River where I lived, the council became a topic of concern, it seemed, only at tax collection time. Still, undoubtedly the local government councils were a significant initial approach to raise the thinking of villagers regarding representative government and bringing them into a politico-economic universe greater than their village.

There was also a distinct economic advantage in having a local council as they were eligible for governmental grants, especially the job-making infrastructure construction projects. But the SWCD was in a catch-22: without a crop like coffee or rice that necessitated transport to market, there was no compelling need to construct roads thus providing employment. Perhaps the strongest argument against a council for the SWCD was that there was not sufficient local lobbying for one. After a patrol of the SWCD villages, PO Lanaghan reported,

> In a follow-up of the last patrol, people were again asked, how would they receive the implementation of a low budget council, with perhaps Government subsidy. . .the answer was an emphatic "No." (Lanaghan 1971: 24)

The administration's patrol interpreter Makau Papkai and the Yegerapi village aid post orderly, Litabagi, were both active supporters of a council for the area and used their voices and influence toward establishing one, but the fact that everyone would have to pay taxes to maintain it was a powerful negative argument; the wide support necessary even for the administration to consider one was never forthcoming.[11] As ADC Broadhurst acutely observed,

> The only genuine political pressure exerted by the people as a group has been to place before the Administration their desire to have a Patrol Post established in the area near to Yellow River. This year the Administration approved the establishment of a Base Camp at EDWAKI, the station currently being staffed by a Patrol Officer. (Broadhurst 1971: 8)
> DC Stevens summarized the overall situation succinctly when he wrote that,
> I regard the provision of at least a limited economy and communications system as an essential pre-requisite to the establishment of a Council. Apart from the fact that the people do not want a Council, the system would presently create many more problems than it would solve. (Stevens, in Lanaghan 1971: 8)

The SWCD had achieved a base camp for the Lujere but, to the satisfaction of most villagers, there would be no local government council hounding them for taxes.

---

11. PO Wafingian (1972b: 4) reported that the people he had talked with wanted a local government council in their area, even if it were a low-level one, then notes that "it was the voice of only three villages" but doesn't name them.

Jobs: An unfulfilled wish

A common question that dominated the thinking of both the administration and Lujere villagers was about "development" or 'wok bisnis.' There also was no other concern that had such a bleak if not impossible prospect for successful achievement. When a society occupies a compromised ecological zone with no market-desired natural resources or crops plus lacking an economically feasible infrastructure to move it to market if it did, the possibility for new wealth approaches the realm of the surreal. Here is a case in point:

When the Lumi ADC J. E. Fowke made his patrol to the SWCD to initiate the new Yellow River Base Camp, the section of his report "Economy of the Area" stated that

> There was no agricultural economic development whatsoever throughout the area at the time of the patrol. Such activities as the planting of perennial crops, market gardening or animal husbandry for monitory return are not practiced. Approximately eight months ago one Makau of Magaleri, an Administration Patrol Interpreter at Lumi, cultivated a small patch of rice from which he harvested approximately half a ton of paddy rice. 600 lbs of this paddy rice was airfreighted to Lumi at cost of $15.00 where he sold the rice to DASF for three cents a pound representing a net profit to him of $3.00. The balance of the crop has been allowed to rot beside the Magaleri airstrip.
>
> This was the first attempt anywhere in the Census Division at economic agricultural development. Being a leader in the area and a very influential man it can be expected that no further rice plantings will take place until some more realistic marketing facility is provided. (Fowke 1968: 21)

Harvesting crocodile skins had been tried and a few men did make some money selling skins to traders, if and when they came up the river, but it was not a dependable source of income for more than a few, if them. A man in Worikori planted a cacao tree that had born fruit, establishing viability as a crop, but at the time there was no economic incentive to plant more. The base camp, as already described, was an economic hope as a source for local jobs but while I lived in Wakau, it remained just a hope. There were schemes for building a road to Lumi but, being thirty-five miles away as the cockatoo flies and with swamps, rivers, and rugged mountain terrain, it was cost prohibitive. Even project money to hire men to build a road to the Sepik, a feasible task, wasn't there. The administration, always struggling with tight budgets, was not about to squander precious funds to build a road to nowhere.

As previously mentioned, the only dependable money the Lujere men could earn was as indentured laborers and this was considered an insufficient economic base for establishing a council. The SWCD was similarly economically stigmatized, but because of its proximity to Lumi, it was allowed to join the Wapei Government Council. Lumi's ADC J. E. Fowke, who you recall got in trouble in 1968 for fostering a Yellow River station, was one of the few administrators to even speculate about establishing a local government council for the SWCD. He was well aware of the "isolated and undeveloped" argument against a council, as well as the administration's current policy to "consolidate rather than expand in this field," yet he thought that by growing rice it would be practical to establish a subsidised Low Level Council in the South Wapei with a tax rate of fifty cents. With this resultant revenue a project such as the setting up of a rice polishing factory and purchase of river transportation equipment could be embarked on. (Fowke 1968: 8)

The district commissioner's two-paragraph comment on Fowke's idea began with an admonishment:

Before there is any native encouragement or fostering [*sic*] of business ventures in the South Wapei census division by Administration officers it will be necessary for full submissions to be presented to the District's Co-coordinating Committee for approval. (Fowke 1968: 29)

And the next paragraph outlined more discouraging requirements. Of the numerous administration officials whose usually thoughtful comments I read regarding the economic and political development for the SWCD, none were optimistic about the area's immediate potential for success. Only money—unrealistic amounts of money—might do the job. According to Lumi ADC Broadhurst, for

Political, Economic and Social Development of the area. . . the Administration would have to commit to the area a tremendous amount of financial aid. This would take the form of numerous Political Education Patrols. . . and the posting of an Agricultural Field Assistant to EDWAKI to assist the people in economic development, which would be centered around the crocodile industry, rice, lowland coffee and cocoa. Transport of produce to outside markets is a problem and consequently costs to undertake development would be astronomical. (Broadhurst 1971: 2)

Considering the area's small and dispersed population, constricted government finances, and an administration soon to be devolved with independence, any real economic development for the SWCD was imaginary—in Tok Pisin, just 'tok win.' But even in the economically walloped Upper Sepik Basin, "Hope springs eternal in the human breast" (Pope [1733–34] 2016). Shortly after I returned home toward the end of April 1972, Ray Lanaghan was transferred and replaced by PO F. J. Wafingian who, with the eagerly volunteered labor of Lujere men, began a nine- to ten-mile road to the Sepik. He writes in his "Road Construction" Patrol Report that

In four weeks, some 60 men have turned up and had completed 1 mile of road already. The people are brought to work on a village to village basis. They work for two weeks. Then go home and a fresh 30 men take over. To show their willingness the workers had never complained of long hours they work. The supervisory job is done by the author aided by MAKAU the Government Interpreter. They even carry out orders without hesitation, and they do not complain even if it is hard work. Work starts at 7 a.m. in the morning, with a break for lunch and goes on til 4 o'clock in the afternoon. . . . An application for Rural Development Board has been put in already. However if this application fails, could the Administration consider giving us aid in supplying more tools. (Wafingian 1972: 1)

Wafingian reasoned that with the plentiful timber, bridges could be constructed over the six to eight small creeks and swampy sago patches, but his main concern was building a proper bridge over the more formidable (especially in the wet season) Yellow River. Optimistically he added, "More advice would have to be sought on this matter at a latter date. I presume this could be one of the Army Civic Aid Projects if necessary" (Wafingian 1972: 1).

ADC Wright noted in his comment on Wafingian's report that, while the application for administration support money was not granted, the requested tools to help build the road would be forthcoming from Lumi. It was an example of bureaucratic compassion that had been in such short supply in 1936 when McCarthy's request for a few axes and knives for the steel-deprived Lujere was ignored. From the District Commissioner's comments on the report, the odds on completing the road project looked grim:

> Developmental Departments have been loathe to encourage economic development in this area due to its isolation and lack of adequate communications. It is thought that this area has potential for rice, cattle, coffee, copra and tobacco. Due to the low population however (5,500 is the entire South Wapei Census Division) this project has received a low priority on the District R.D.F. [Rural Development Fund] programme. (ADC memo, in Wafingian 1972)

Or, in more direct parlance, "forget about bridging the Yellow River." To this day, there isn't one. The last comment on Wafingian's road building report was, as usual, by Tom Ellis, the secretary of the Department of the Administrator. His comment was more avuncular than critical. He knew from experience the local problems in raising unrealizable hope.

> Mr. Wafingian is obviously a keen young officer who undertakes his duties with enthusiasm; however enthusiasm must be tempered with discretion otherwise there could be an adverse reaction from the village people. (Ellis memo, in Wafingian 1972)

As I write today, now well into the twenty-first century and well over a hundred years after Schultz-Jena's 1910 ascent of the Sepik River first transected Lujereland, the area remains "isolated and undeveloped."

Rural Airstrips

The location of airstrips in remote areas was one of the most physically visible and non-controversial legacies of the colonial years. While airstrips brought some advantages to the local people, such as the possibility of an airlift to a hospital, the primary beneficiaries were the territories' resident expatriates, such as government administrators, businesspeople, miners, missionaries, and anthropologists, all now enabled to work in isolated places with the advantages of swift ingress and egress and the rapid transfer of mail and valued commodities. The SWCD's four minimum-category Delta airstrips were located at Yilui, in the far eastern area; Magaleri, into which Joyce and I flew; Abrau, which Father James helped supervise its readiness in 1949; and Yellow River, Lujereland's only licensed airstrip and operated by the CMML Mission. In 1968, PO Fowke reported that in the SWCD

Three other airstrips are under construction at Yakiltim, [northeast area, Awum language] Akwom, and Warukor [Warikorwi], the first two mentioned are supervised by CMML and the last by the [Lumi] Catholic Mission.

All construction work on these strips has been done on a voluntary unpaid basis while, regular maintenance is performed similarly. With the exception of Yellow River, the land on which the 'strips are located is owned by the village people.' (Fowke 1968: 16)

When patrolling, PO Fowke heard a complaint from the Magaleri villagers that, while it was their labor that built the airstrip on their land, the CMML Mission permitted only their CMML planes to use it. Villagers, he was told, had assembled a load of fresh meat to be back-loaded and sold at Lumi but the CMML plane was diverted for mission business and the meat, about eighty dollars' worth, could not be sent or sold locally at a good profit. A Catholic mission aircraft was available but, because of CMML's restrictions, could not be used.

While PO Fowke was told that the Akwom airstrip was supervised by the CMML, when I visited Akwom and Worikori in 1971 with Joyce, I was told that their rudimentary airstrips were built for the Catholic mission's plane, but it had never landed at either one. However, I knew from Joyce that their plane flew medical workers routinely to the Abrau airstrip to conduct health patrols. Trying to better understand the rationale behind the unused airstrips, while writing this book I contacted retired Franciscan priests who said they were unaware of their mission's involvement with the airstrips or of any intent to proselytize among the Lujere. It remains a puzzle what motivated the men to expend such tremendous effort to build airstrips by hand with no assurance of their being used unless they misconstrued the mission's intent or were misled. There is no evidence that the airstrips were the result of "cargo cult" thinking, that is, preparing a landing strip to facilitate the arrival of deserved foreign riches from their ancestors.[12] Rather, like their generous contribution of labor to build the Yellow River Base Camp, I assume they thought that an airstrip seemed like a smart thing to do if they wanted to develop 'wok bisnis.' I generally found the Lujere, excepting some of their supernatural beliefs that we'll examine later, to be a very pragmatic and levelheaded people.

Hunting with Shotguns

Every Lujere man had a black palm bow and a few arrows, and he seldom left the village without them, ever ready to shoot game. In those areas of Papua New Guinea where wild game is available, shotguns are an important weapon augmenting the traditional bow and arrows. However, in a relatively densely populated area like around Lumi, the introduction of the shotgun contributed to a great diminution of game. This was not a problem in Lujereland because of the small, scattered population and immense acreage with an abundance of game.

A license to hunt with a shotgun called a "Certificate of Registration" was secured through the 'kiap'; he decided who got a gun and how many per village, usually dependent

---

12. Lanaghan (1972: 6) notes in his patrol report that, "The well publicized TURU Cult did not noticeably effect the environs of the South Wapi nor is there any sign of cult behavior or unrest evident among the S.[outh] WAPEI'S."

upon its size. In some of the Lujere villages, as among the Wape, villagers pooled their money to buy a gun. Although only the licensed hunter could use the gun legally, others might borrow the gun to hunt covertly. Women and men with the money bought a shotgun shell or two and gave it to the licensed gunman, gambling he would kill game with it. One of the tasks of the 'kiap' when on patrol was to see that each license was current and that the gun was in working order; a defective gun could be confiscated and destroyed. His tally shows that all Lujere villages had shotguns and that most of them had three. They were all single-shot and most were Winchesters. While villagers could not be licensed to own a rifle, the CMML missionaries, Cecil Parish and Phillip Ace, each had licenses for a .22 rifle. The only other guns in Lujereland were those of the police stationed at the base camp.

A villager owning a shotgun (called 'sutboi' in TP) with a 'laisens' (license) from the 'kiap' was perceived by villagers as in a superior relationship with the administration. Although the 'luluai' and 'tultul' also had a unique relationship with the administration, from a villager's perspective it was more of a "gofer" role, while the licensed gun owner enjoyed a more prestigious status among villagers. The special military-style caps given by the administration to the 'luluai' and 'tultul' were usually only worn when in attendance with the 'kiap.'[13]

One of the three Iwani shotguns belonged to Klowi of Wakau, the village's most interesting man. Villagers gave him shells and he actually hunted, more or less, for the whole village. He also was a very good shot, as I recorded early in my stay in my typed notes:

THE ABUNDANCE OF GAME
There is no doubt of it, this bush is filled with wild life. Until five months ago, the Wakau men had never owned a shotgun; all game had to be killed by bow and arrow. Now with Klowi's 12-gauge shotgun, he seldom goes out without bagging something. Yesterday before lunch he shot one pig, one cassowary and five [Victoria] crown pigeons. In the afternoon he shot another cassowary and a 'kokomo' [hornbill]. Everyone had plenty of meat to eat last night! (MN: 34).[14]

The Wape men were allowed to purchase shotguns in the early 1960s but the Lujere not until later because of the administration's assumptions regarding their "primitiveness." PO Treutlein wrote in his patrol report,

A number of villages, both in the SW [Southwest] and South Wapei approached the patrol about shotguns. While the South Wapei natives [the Lujere] could make good use of guns in their areas of bush, they are still far *too primitive and ready to resort to blood-shed in settling their differences* to allow any guns into that area. (Treutlein 1962: 15; my emphasis)

---

13. This prestigious status of the 'sutboi' was clearly recognized by the administration officials. ADC Broadhurst (1971: 2) noted, "In some cases his sphere of authority is accepted by the people as being greater than that of village officials, particularly if the village officials are not strong characters."
14. As indication in Part 1, MN is an abbreviation for my typed-up fieldnotes.

Of course, this was a totally specious assumption, since the Lujere, even when first contacted by the 1930s Australian patrols, were at peace among themselves; McCarthy, you will recall, reported, "The people are the most peaceful I have ever met" (McCarthy 1936: 20).

While most of the game presented a hunting challenge, the stunning Victoria crowned pigeon, docile and as large as a small turkey, was too easy to kill. Like the northern New England spruce grouse or the Galapagos blue-footed booby, it was more a ground-dweller than a flier and often indifferent to human presence. Occasionally Klowi would bring me one and, although I might feel an initial tinge of guilt for eating such a hapless and beautiful bird, it was too delicious to refuse.

Scientific Medicine in the Bush

Colonialism has been a whipping boy for every other kind of -ism, but it is rarely faulted for its introduction of scientific medicine to a preliterate society. In the West Sepik Province, the administration worked closely with the missions in establishing medical services. The CMML hospital at Anguganak was directed by Dr. John Sturt, a New Zealander, and the administration's hospital in Lumi was directed by Dr. Lyn Wark, the CMML medical missionary from Australia already mentioned; both were assisted by several expat missionary nurses and local medical orderlies. Anguganak was also the site for one of the Territory's hospitals for training aid post orderlies, the men who provided most villagers with their only immediate access to Western medicine. These men, literate in Tok Pisin, completed a two-year training course of didactic lectures and supervised work on hospital wards and in clinical laboratories. They were trained in basic medical techniques and treatments as well as in hygienic village practices to prevent illness. Their training in first aid procedures included the treatment of wounds, burns, fractures, asphyxia, shock, hernia, fits, fainting, dislocations, sprains, and bruises, as well as in the diagnosis and treatment of tropical diseases of the skin, malaria, respiratory and gastrointestinal illnesses. In reply to my email query, Dr. Sturt wrote,

> I started the medical work at Anguganak in 1959 and was there until the end of 1969. One of the major activities was training medical orderlies to work in the hospital but later to go out and run aid posts. The nurses trained local girls to work in the Infant Welfare ward and to go on trek with them to run [village] clinics. We didn't have a separate name for the Aid Post training school. We named the hospital 'Haus Laip' [life] and referred to it that way rather than 'Haus Sik.' . . . I think the mission still owns the hospital but Government is responsible for staff. (Email from J. Sturt to W. Mitchell, July 21, 2015)

The Lujere had access to two of the aid posts run by the administration's Public Health Department, whose orderlies were trained under Dr. Sturt's supervision; one in Akwom that Joyce and I visited on our patrol, and the other in Yegerapi near the mission's airstrip that replaced in 1969 the service previously provided by the CMML Mission. Litabagi was the aid post orderly at Yegerapi and during my fieldwork worked closely with the mission's health services provided by Rosemary Ace and Betty Gillam, both trained nurses. Litabagi also did Bible training in 1968–69 but, as the CMML historians Dennis and Barbara Thorp observe, "His place as a teacher of the Bible has been made difficult by his marriage to four wives" (Thorp and Thorp 2004).

Aid posts were first aid stations dealing with any and all health complaints presented to them.[15] They also had several beds for inpatients but at the aid posts, as in the two hospitals, patient's families were primarily responsible for their food. Depending upon the evaluation of a patient by the Yellow River CMML missionaries, a seriously ill or injured patient might be evacuated to the hospitals at Lumi, Anguganak, Vanimo, and Wewak on an AMAF plane. An aid post orderly was paid fortnightly, and villagers were expected to help with his food and maintain the structures; both requirements could become an occasional contentious issue.[16]

Most months one or two CMML nurses from Lumi flew down to Yellow River and patrolled some of the Lujere villages giving "Maternal and Infant Welfare" clinics with special attention to lactating mothers and their babies and the physical development of toddlers.[17] While I was in the field, Betty Gillam was the lone patroller; later she made two valuable nutritional studies among the Lujere (Gillam 1983, 1996).[18]

Radios and Newspapers

By now there should be no surprise that the Lujere were neither participants nor interested in the national culture of Papua New Guinea. Newspapers were not a part of their community life except as paper for rolling cigarettes. I earlier mentioned the lack of radios or 'wailis' owned by Lujere villagers; as table 2 indicates, only six villages had radios and only three, Alai, Naum, and Yegerapi had working ones. PO Lanaghan (1971: 15) observed after a patrol of all the villages that more radios were being brought back by laborers returning from coastal plantations but that "Lack of care and protection from insects render most radios inoperable soon after the original battery supply has expired."

---

15. Given to each orderly was *The Aid Post Medical and Hygiene Training Book* (Fowler 1960), a 171-page manual in Tok Pisin produced by the Public Health Department that uses text, drawings, and diagrams to discuss a wide range of topics a medic might have to treat. It also was my first-aid bible while in the field.
16. Some points of strain in the colonial Aide Post Orderly (APO) system are discussed by Mitchell (1968). In 1965, the Department of Public Health decided to phase out the APO health role and closed the government's training schools. However, missionary medical facilities, like at Anguganak, continued to train some APO's. The closing of the schools was widely criticized by some of the country's health officers, such as Radford (1971:14), saw the APO program as "a top priority in planning the allocation of resources for a successful future health service." After I left the country in 1972, the government reversed its policy and reopened one of the APO training schools at Mt. Hagen.
17. Denoon's chapter on "Women and Children Last" in a book on public health in Papua New Guinea (Denoon, Dugan, and Marshall 1989) documents that it was not until 1948 that the Public Health Department began to initiate special attention to the medical needs of mothers and infants.
18. I deal with some of these findings in chapter 12.

Table 2. Lujere shotguns, radios, and male literacy in Tok Pisin

Village	Shotguns	Working radios	Nonworking radios	Literate males
Aiendami	3	0	0	2
Akwom	3	0	0	0
Alai	3	2	0	1
Gwidami	1	0	3	5
Iwani	3	0	0	10
Mantopai	2	0	0	1
Nami	2	2	0	0
Naum	3	0	1	5
Norambalip	3	0	0	10
Pabei	3	0	1	1
Tipas	2	0	0	2
Worikori	3	0	0	4
Yawari	2	0	0	3
Yegerapi	4	4	1	20
Totals	37	8	6	64

Source: Abstracted from Lanaghan (1971)

I had a strong AM radio with an antenna wire strung high between two trees that I played mostly at night in my 'ofis' screen tent and tuned to a distant classical music station I sometimes could pick up. Once it was dark most villagers were inside their houses with doors shut tight. But after dinner I lit my Aladdin lamp that gave a bright, soft light and went to work typing up notes, the notes that made this book possible so many years later. Once in a great while, one of the men or an adventuresome youth would come by and quietly watch me type, ever ready to help me understand what had happened that day. If I wanted New Guinea news, I might tune in to Radio Wewak, a Tok Pisin station, but it was unusual for anyone to comment on what we heard. It seemed to have the same grabbing interest as a local broadcast from Bismarck, North Dakota would have for me.

The radio was recognized as a purveyor of music and talk, but the sole local function of a newspaper was, as mentioned, as a coveted form of cigarette paper. My weekly *Post Courier* from Port Moresby, while sometimes loaned to the missionaries or 'kiap,' was usually returned to become valued currency for buying local foods or rewarding a helpful informant.

Trade Stores and Markets

The CMML mission ran a small trade store that carried the basic commodities, such as salt, tin fish from China, sweets, batteries, fishhooks, line, kerosene, men's shorts, and women's blouses and skirts. A trade store usually consisted of a shed with an outside high counter and merchandise on the shelves behind the salesperson. In January of 1971, Makau, the administration interpreter, opened a competing trade store near the Edwaki Base Camp and its Wakau visitors said the new store had cheaper and fairer prices. Kerosene was twenty cents for a full bottle; the mission's kerosene was also twenty cents a bottle but not filled to the top. Makau's store also sold trade tobacco and newsprint for wrapping cigarettes, which the mission store didn't. Sometimes a villager would try to establish a small store, as in Norambalip, but it was unusual for them to last.

A regular community market was organized that January and, according to the 'kiap' Ray, it had come about by chance. Some locals had approached him with produce and he bought some for the jail, but told them to return the next week and they would have a market. That's the gossip we heard in Wakau, so I went in with Nauwen and with Oria who had spent the previous afternoon in the bush getting betel nuts he would try to sell. But we did not get to the base camp until almost noon and the market unfortunately was over. Ray said about one hundred people had come but with just him and the police as dependable buyers, most returned home with what they had brought, just as Oria had. His plan now was to have a single village bring produce each week; next week it would be Norambalip village as they had come the farthest. Eine and Arakwake's wives also had brought food they tried to sell to Rosemary at the mission with no luck. Rosemary, incidentally, didn't know about Ray's weekly market plans, which was typical of the regrettable lack of communication between the two expat institutions.

Tok Pisin Schools and Literacy

Ces Parish and Bruce Crowther both had devoted considerable time to small ad hoc Tok Pisin Bible Schools advancing literacy with Bible-oriented materials, as did Phillip Ace during my PNG fieldwork. While most men who left their village to work for the European returned speaking fluently in Tok Pisin, far fewer were also able to read and write it. In most villages, as in Wakau, there were no female Tok Pisin speakers, and those who were literate in the language were still rarer. An exception was Yegerape village near the mission. Ray Lanaghan's statistics in table 2 are only for males, and Yegerapi village had by far the most literate males just as it had the most attendees in Bible Schools as well as the most shot guns and radios. But two of the Lujere villages Ray visited, Akwom and Nami, had no men literate in Tok Pisin and three had only one literate man. Reading in Tok Pisin was mostly restricted to religious material while writing was almost exclusively in missives to relatives away at work or to an anthropologist friend. As noted earlier, except for a few New Testaments, there was little, if any, national literature, such as books, magazines, or newspapers, in the villages.

Yellow River Preparatory School

Bruce Crowther, with the CMML Mission as sponsor, began the first English language school at Yellow River during his and his wife Margaret's stay from August 1963 to towards the end of 1965. After building his family's house atop the hill, he and local men built the classrooms and school desks from local materials below the mission's hill station for easier student access. Crowther also taught classes in Tok Pisin and had about one hundred students in all.[19] With Crowther gone, Violet Goff, another adherent of the Australian Christian Brethren, took over the mission's commitment to the school. In 1968, as discussed in chapter 5, the Lumi ADC J. E. Fowke made a patrol of the SWCD, then spent several days based in Yegarapi village to mark out his proposed administration station atop Edwaki hill, also home of the CMML Mission. Although his patrol report does not mention conversations with the missionaries, it is obvious from his report he did have contact with them, as the following quotation about the lack of educational opportunities for children indicates:

> Efforts have been made over the past seven years by the CMML at its Yellow River station to establish a preparatory school, with little success. Children from several of the nearby villages, within walking distance, have attended at irregular periods but it has not been possible to keep them at school to a stage when they can read or write. The main reason for this failure is the all consuming fear by the parents of sorcery or 'sanguma' which they state will attack their children while on the way to school. . . . Approximately two years ago a child was "lost" while traveling to school and to this day no trace has ever been found. Since this incident no local children have attended the Yellow River school. (Fowke 1968: 12)

However, in October 1970, PO Hutchings reports that

> Children are again attending the Primary T School at Yellow River even though incidences of "Sanguma" in the area are high. This indicates the importance placed on education, if parents are prepared to risk their child's safety for the sake of education. (Hutchings 1970: 12)

Hutchings then makes the point that the facilities for education "within this area are at a deplorable level," citing the "abundance of small children" within the SWCD: 594 from six to ten years old; 684 from one to five years old; and 286 under one year of age. As table 3 indicates, only 97 Lujere children of school age (16 percent) attended school.

Table 3. CMML Yellow River primary school students

	Girls	Boys	Total
Standard 2	5	15	20
Standard 1	14	24	39
Preparatory	11	27	38
Totals	30	66	97

Source: Hutchings (1970).

---

19. Lyn Wark Murray, email to author, July 30, 2015, based on her phone conversation with Margaret Crowther.

When PO Wafingian patrolled the Lujere villages in July 1972 after both Ray and I had left the Lujere, he included a brief report on "Education" but without any enrollment figures:

> There is only one proper school where English is taught. This is looked after by the C.M.M.L. Mission and is staffed by 3 teachers. The classes range from standard 1 to 4. The successful students proceed to Angugunak (*sic*) for their higher primary education. Besides that we have a few pidgin schools [that] also are supervised by the C.M.M.L. Mission.... Only a few students, (4) have succeeded from the English school at Yellow River, and are undergoing training for jobs or tertiary education. (Wafingian 1972: 8)

The ADC's comment on Wafingian's education report was, "The educational facilities are reasonable having regard to the remoteness of the area and the scattered settlements of local population" (Wafingian 1972: 9). But here is what's odd: in June 1968, there is no Yellow River school, but in July 1972, four years later, the PO says there is an English language school with standard (elementary grade levels) 1–4 and that four students have finished and moved on. Thus in 1968, when there was no school, four children would have been in attendance to move on by 1972. One or both of the 'kiaps' seem to have things mixed up a bit.[20]

---

20. I thought I might be able to sort things out if I got the term schedule so on July 27, 2015, Sister Jo Scanlan, who at the time in question was a teacher in the Lumi school, emailed me from Australia to provide the following data regarding the schedule for the three terms: (1) mid Jan, Feb, March, April, followed by first term holiday; (2) May, June, July, August, second term holiday; (3) September, October, November, mid December, then six weeks holiday. Unfortunately, this did not resolve the discrepancy.

CHAPTER EIGHT

The Lujere Villages

> *The villages are all friendly to one another.*
> ADO Keith McCarthy (1936)
>
> *Very few people live in the village all the year round.*
> PO R. K. Treutlein (1962: 14)

A Muddle of Terms

The administration generally used the word "village" as a collective term for several geographically separate but culturally related clusters of houses called "hamlets." A single 'luluai' and 'tultul' was appointed for the "village" regardless of the number or size of its "hamlets." This nomenclature system of "villages" and "hamlets" was a colonial organizational shadow imposed on the Lujere's own Indigenous sense of organization and generally was ignored by them except when the government interrupted their lives. More confusing when consulting maps or texts, there often is no lexical consensus on a settlement's spelling, hence the custom of placing alternative spellings in parentheses. Also, a tropical village constructed of bush material is not securely fastened in place with nails and mortar so if cultural or environmental events necessitate a move, it is easily done. Although the villagers remain the same, the ground or area where the village is newly placed has a different name and so might the village. That is usually the situation when you notice on a map or in a text two very different names with one—usually the old name—in parenthesis, such as Mokadami (Gwidami) or Ameni (Tipas). On some maps, both the old and new names will appear separately. Furthermore, as already noted, a village may have many hamlets, each with a different name. In the initial 1956 census, PO Oakes recorded nine hamlets for Aiendami and three hamlets for Wakau village: Wakau,

Leubangi and Iwalamu. To show that there is no consistency in naming practice, when Wakau moved back across the river to its earlier World War II site where they had traded with the Mosstroops, the administration retained its name of Wakau but, while it had been mapped as a "village" when west of the Sand, it was now considered a hamlet of Iwani village in the census.[1]

For the Lujere, unconcerned with maps and printed texts, settlement naming is a simple oral task. They do not have comparable terms in Namia to distinguish "hamlet" and "village";[2] each separate cluster of dwellings is considered a distinct settlement called a *walamaku* (*wala* = house, *maku* = group) and each *walamaku* has a distinct name. As mentioned earlier, it is usually the name of the ground on which the settlement sits. To the Lujere, each *walamaku* is a social entity to itself, beholden to no other *walamaku*, and held together based on cognatic and affinal kinship ties that, in turn, links it to other *walamaku*.

In practice, the administration, especially in censuses, sometimes muddled the concepts "village" and "hamlet." I also tend to use them interchangeably unless I am making a specific organizational point. Although Wakau was considered an Iwani hamlet in the 1972 administration census, I usually refer to it as a "village" using that word as a synonym of "settlement." There also is no specific number of Lujere villages; it all depends on the patrol officer who is doing the counting and how he categorizes a specific settlement or *malamaku*. For example, in 1956, George Oakes's initial administration census of the Lujere (see table 1 in chap. 4) counted Wakau as a separate village (which included Leubanagi and Uwalamu hamlets), but after they all moved back across the Sand River in the 1960s to an old site (where I lived), Ray Lanaghan's 1971 census (see table 4 below) reclassified Wakau as a hamlet of Iwani village. So, to maintain equanimity, it is best to be linguistically adaptive when discussing Lujere settlements. For the record, however, my Wakau informants taught me that "Iwani" consisted of four related settlements: *Mauwi*, ostensibly the oldest atop the hill of the same name; *Iwarwita*, tiny and near the southwest base of the hill; *Wakau*, just off the 'kunai' northwest of the hill; and *Aukwom*, the newest, on the far (south) bank of the Sepik near the mouth of Yellow River.

A source of perennial confusion for me concerning all of Namia speech was that I could not discern a clear-cut tradition on how words should be pronounced, even in a small community like Wakau. If I were working with more than one informant, pronunciation of the same term could vary. Most vexing was that Nauwen and Oria, raised in the same family, sometimes contradicted each other on pronunciation of a Namia term

---

1. The linguist couple that studied Namia in the 1980s render "Wakau" as "Wagou" in their publications (Feldpausch and Feldpausch 1988: 48). In terms of Namia vocabulary, I follow their renderings (Feldpausch 2011), but in proper names including villages, I use the pronunciation I heard in Wakau or the spelling used by one of the village men literate in Tok Pisin. I have mentioned elsewhere that there was no clear consistency in the pronunciation of many proper names and my decision was an arbitrary one.
2. This is a common practice in Melanesia; for instance, Scott notes that the Solomon Islands' "Arosi do not verbally distinguish between villages and the smaller hamlets which they comprise, but use the same word, *'omaa*, to refer to both" (Scott 2007:39).

or the name of a person or village. Although I never attained even rudimentary fluency in Namia, I never ceased my study of the language.

Population and Gender

A little over a week after I moved to Wakau, Ray Lanaghan began a patrol of all the SWCD villages that included the Lujere villages north of the Sepik River. In early January of 1971, we heard he would take a census of the Iwani hamlets on the ninth and, as his girlfriend was visiting him from Australia, I invited them for dinner in Mauwi hamlet after the census concluded. The villagers knew about his impending visit and were well aware that a 'kiap' would be annoyed if a village looks untended with tall grass on the path. Arakwaki had cleaned up the upper part of the village where his wife's house was located, but the rest of the village by contrast looked abandoned. It was an awkward time for me. I never interfered in village affairs, but I was concerned that Ray might scold them or even send a few to the 'kalabus,' so, late in the afternoon on the eighth, I finally voiced my concerns about the impending visit of the 'kiap' to a few of the men; about ten minutes later I saw some taking turns cutting down the wild grass with their 'sarips.' These men were so different from the Wape who, if they had an inkling that a 'kiap' would be coming to their village, not only did the grass get cut but also any old unoccupied house was burned to the ground. But the Wakaus could not be more blasé regarding colonial authority.

Based on Ray's late 1971 patrol census (Lanaghan 1971: 25), the administration recognized fourteen Lujere villages in the SWCD (see table 4), with a total population of 2,847. However, if the Lujere across the Sepik River in the May River Census Division were added, it would come to just over 3,000.[3]

The most interesting information revealed by the census is the disproportionate ratio between males and females. There are 250 more men than women and 119 more boys than girls. These lop-sided demographics infer there will be a significant number of men who will not marry and have families. As the Lujere are a society where the preferential form of marriage is sister exchange, the demographic consequences are most severe for sisterless males.

---

3. There are three settlements across the Sepik in the East Sepik Province: Panewai, Purami, and Aukwom (Aigum, Augam). In 1972 the census for Panewai was 108 (Stevens 1972). I found no census figures for Purami and Aukwom. Aukwom does not appear in censuses of either the East or West Sepik Districts for the reason below. PO Payne writes regarding Aukwom that

> A group from 'Mowi' [Mauwi] village in the same census division [SWCD] have also made a camp at the mouth of the Yellow River known as Aigum [Aukwom, Augam], they claim they hope to move in permanently. Their location may give rise to some confusion in the future, but at present they are lodged between the Sepik-May and Rocky Peaks C/D, and it was thought unwise to attempt to include them in either of these C/D as Tipas and Aigum are only 4 hours walk from Edwaki Base Camp and most of their ties are with people from this area. (Payne 1972:1)

Table 4. PO Lanaghan's Lujere village census data, November–December 1971

Name of village	Children		Adults			Total village populations
	Male	Female	Male		Female	
			Resident	Absentee*		
Aiendami	46	36	35	30	45	192
Akwom	57	34	41	14	45	191
Alai	21	19	31	8	28	107
Gwidami	58	39	60	22	69	248
Iwani	64	72	79	23	90	328
Mantopai	26	18	25	23	24	116
Nami	53	36	52	29	54	224
Naum	32	32	42	16	43	165
Norambalip	55	44	75	8	59	241
Pabi	55	49	50	21	46	221
Tipas	27	30	31	9	31	128
Worikori	40	27	45	19	38	267
Yawari	58	49	51	26	56	240
Yegerapi	75	63	69	7	63	277
Demographic totals:	667	548	686	255	691	2,847

* Absentee men were away working as indentured laborers for colonial enterprises.

For both the world and Papua New Guinea, the ratio of males to females, favors males. However, if there is a marked gender disparity in a society, cultural attitudes towards children must be examined for the possibility of female infanticide. I did not personally obtain any direct evidence from the Lujere on this practice; I did, however, hear rumors from the expatriates about female infanticide—never males—but without hard data. The closest is when the linguist missionary Becky Feldpausch, who lived in Yaru village with her husband Tom, reported:

> One man told us that 15 years ago [when I lived in Wakau], a father intended to kill his newborn daughter because he had no son and this was his 5th daughter. Another man intervened and said not to kill her but to consider her as his. So the father did not kill her and she is considered the intervener's adopted daughter. (Feldpausch 1988:18)

In another incident, PO C. A. Trollope reported a case of female infanticide with a more tragic outcome and submitted the following report to the Lumi ADC:

> AKWOM VILLAGE A native [named] AIDO was arrested from this village on the suspected killing of his new born daughter. The man had ordered his wife to hang the

child in a basket from a tree and leave it there until its death. The wife, WEINI did so under her husband's compulsion. Several hours later, moved with emotion for her child, she took it down and was seen doing so by AIDO. He took the child from her and buried it apparently alive. Preliminary hearing has been completed and AIDO committed for sentence. (Trollope 1962: 2)

The two authenticated incidents just cited seem to indicate that female infanticide occasionally was attempted but of themselves, are insufficient to hypothesize female infanticide as a definitive answer for the gender discrepancy. A comparison of the 1956 and 1971 censuses offers an interesting historical picture of the problem. Of the 2,847 Lujere in the 1971 census, 1,608 were males and 1,239 females or, at a one-to-one ratio, a surplus of 369 males. For comparison see table 1 for data from the first census of Lujere villages made by PO George Oakes in 1956.[4] In his 1956 census, of the 2,318 Lujere accounted for, 1,235 were males and 1,083 were females or, at a one-to-one ratio, a surplus of 152 males. In other words, the ratio of males to females in 1971 was 1.3 and in 1956, 1.14. The "Absent Male" column refers to indentured laborers.

Compared to the male-to-female gender ratio for Papua New Guinea of 1.05, or 1.01 for the world,[5] the gender imbalance for the Lujere was substantially higher. While I can't tease out the factors to account for this robust disparity between the sexes, its obvious cultural consequence is to make marriage a more challenging act for males than females. Besides, the mature male's disadvantaged status position when he is wifeless with neither sons nor daughters and often motherless exacerbates the problem of who will feed him.

Lujere Regions

While the Lujere have no word comparable to "region," they mentally arrange their villages into four geographic regions with the affective feel of the American idea of a "region" or "district," indicating recognized social, even historical, ties. The four regions are each distinguished by the name of the ground it occupies: Lawo, Edwaki, Weari and Pabei. No distinctive cultural or dialectical differences exist among them, nor is there a known reason to group the villages together beyond sharing in common a named ground whereby their proximal locations facilitate social interaction and, formerly, both defensive

---

4. Aukwom, a small community, is presumably censused with Iwani village. So, if Panewai had a population of 108 and Purami was a similar size, my estimate for the 1972 Lujere population would be just over 3,000. Aukwom was the Sepik River village Joyce and I visited en route to Iwani village and Mauwi hamlet.
    A patrol report for PO Gilbert's 1949 patrol to the Sepik from Lumi with Fr. James could not be located in any archives. However, Oakes' (1956) patrol report notes that a census for the village of Wokian (Pouye lang.) was done in 1949; it was one of the villages Gilbert visited with Fr. James. He also notes that Edawaki had a census in 1951 by a Green River Patrol Officer. All the other Lujere villages Oakes visited are cited as an "Initial Census," so it is a safe assumption that Gilbert did not officially census any of the Lujere villages.
5. See www.wikiwand.com/en/List_of_countries_by_sex_ratio (accessed August 16, 2015).

and offensive warfare. That a "region" might also be the name of a "village," such as Pabei, is not a concern. Like other aspects of Lujere culture, this was not a hard and fast typology.[6]

The Lujere do not have terms for the cardinal positions to indicate direction as in English, but the named regions are one way to orient oneself or others. The four regions and their constituent villages are

1. Lawo: The *northwest* villages of Yawari (Yuwari), Montopai, Aiendami, and Gwidami;
2. Edwaki: The *central* villages of, Yergarapi, Yaru, Norambalip, and Alai;
3. Weari: The *eastern* villages of Akwom, Naum, Nami, and Worikori;
4. Pabei: The *southern* villages of, Wakau, Iwani, Pabei, Tipas, Aukwom, and Panawai.

An individual may be identified by her regional name, such as Weari, as well as by her village, for instance, Worikori. It is probable—although the historical research has not been done—that a district's villages are historically closely related as various factors generated the departure of villagers to create a new community, as they continue to do today. Both my and the Feldpausches' informants attested to more extensive social and marriage relations with those within their district although this is not fully substantiated by the empirical evidence. For example, Wakau residents had stronger social ties with nearby Gwidami and Aiendami villagers (Lawo District) than with more distant Pabei or Panawai villagers in their own Pabei District, at least during my fieldwork. Still, villagers referred to Panawai, located across the Sepik, with a sense of social closeness that for a long time puzzled me until I became aware of the regional identities.

One of the most interesting facts about the Lujere, just as the perceptive McCarthy determined on his 1936 pioneering patrol, is that "The villages are all friendly to one another." My Wakau informants were adamant that Namia speaking villages never engaged in warfare with one another. This is an unusual phenomenon as many New Guinea language groups, certainly in the Sepik area, engaged in internal warfare; the Wape, all Olo speakers, certainly did. In my pondering why the Lujere had internal peace, I wonder if they are a young society with insufficient history to routinize and valorize intervillage strife, a point supported by the lack of regional dialects. There is the further point that all the Lujere villages see themselves as historically relating back to Iwani village as the original "Mother" village.[7] Whatever eventually can be established to explain Lujerland's

---

6. Toward the end of my fieldwork, Oria named six regions adding "Iwani" and its constituent hamlets, and "Amani" and the Tipas related hamlets. Also see Feldpausch (1988: 3-4) for their discussion of the Indigenous grouping of villages as viewed by their informants in Yaru village. In an even later paper (Feldpausch 1999: 1) they place Iwani, Wakou, Aukwom (Augam, Aigam), and Panawai into a separate "Southwest area" called "Iwani" with the "Southern area" identified as "Ameni" or "Pabei" with six villages, namely, Tipas (Ameni), Elmoli, Pabei 1, Pabei 2, Panewai, and (Panewai 2). Probably part of the reason for the areal differences is that there is no consistent geographic point for viewing the "areas."

7. The Marind Anim are a society over three times as large as Lujere that also appears to have an ethos of peace among its villages. Van Baal's ethnography of the ten-thousand-strong,

lack of internal warfare, the fact remains that a 'sangumaman,' in Namia a *nakwolu*, is believed not only to furtively kill in his neighboring villages but within his own village as well. While the Lujere did not war among themselves, it was believed that a *nakwolu*, did not hesitate to secretly attack even his fellow villagers.

Leadership and Authority

PO Lanaghan writing about the Lujere notes that "Generally speaking there is no traditional 'leader' in respect of an all-powerful individual. Occasionally there may appear a man that could wield more influence than was the normal case, but this gentleman still needed support from his compatriots" (Lanaghan 1972:16). Just as there is a laissez-faire attitude among the Lujere settlements vis-à-vis one another, so there is towards "local authority" that is primarily based on kinship statuses and roles. As already noted, the administration's appointed 'luluais' and 'tultuls' had unquestioned authority only in the presence of the 'kiap.' The concept of a single authority figure over all the Lujere villages did not exist until the 'kiap,' supported by his armed policemen, demanded compliance. Between a 'kiap's visits, there could be months, even years, when local life immediately returned to its egalitarian ways. And, as we saw in chapter 2, the Lujere did not protest the pioneering patrols by Thurnwald or the administration's patrols by Robertson and McCarthy. Instead, the patrols were shyly welcomed as bearers of exotic and desired trade objects, which the locals eagerly obtained in exchange for the sago given to feed the European's entourage of police and porters.

Ancestral Origins

In Warikori during my patrol with Joyce I first heard that all the Namia speakers traced their origins to Iwani village. That certainly was the view in Wakau. One of my main informants in Wakau was Kaiera, a quiet thirtyish man whose mother, born in Wakau, had married a man from Mauwi where she still lived. Kaiera, born in Mauwi, was afraid of Mauwi 'sanguma' and, via his mother's connection—plus his mother's brother's daughter was Klowi's wife—had moved to the men's house of Wakau's upper village where he felt safer and did not have to climb up and down Mauwi's steep hill. A partially blind bachelor with a left eye that swung around wildly, he spent most of his time in or near the upper village's men's house. However, he had enough vision to find his way around the village, gather a little firewood and tend a small garden just below my house. He also had made friends with Nauwen, my 'mankimasta,' and was often sitting quietly in my 'haus kuk,' so I saw him frequently.

---

warlike Marind Anim located across the international border on New Guinea's south coast, notes, "Most remarkable of all is that, in spite of absence of intervillage authority and organization, they managed to maintain relatively peaceful conditions among themselves" (Van Baal 1966: 24).

Then Friday, after our hardly having ever exchanged more than a hello [for three months], he came to my office and was watching me type in the afternoon. He said something about his telling me stories sometime so I said now is a good time. I turned on the Uher [recorder] and away he went, first singing war songs that I had never heard, one after the other with volunteered translations, source, etc.; an anthropologist's dream informant. So we worked for about two hours until I was too tired to go on. (MN: 539)

That afternoon I learned, among many things, why the Lujere no longer had 'garamuts' and the origin story of the Lujere people. The 'ofis' Kaiera and I were sitting in was a screen tent protected from insects and rain under a 'morota' roof that also covered a couple of low benches for visitors. Newai, a teenage boy, later joined by Klowi, occasionally added a detail to Kaiera's story, or laughed at its lewder events. It was a long story with occasional backtracks and corrections. The following version of the Lujere origin story is Kaiera's but, as retold by this listener, is considerably leaner.[8] In chapter 14, we will examine more stories and their place in the life and imagination of the Lujere.

A Man, His Son, and Dog Go Up the Sepik

According to a Lujere traditional story, the Lujere ancestor was a man named Walwin, who went up the Sepik River in a canoe with his son and a big male dog named Mauwi, which was a great hunter. [Kaiera infers that Iwani's mountain was named after this dog, adding that they still "have" the dog as they have not lost his name.] While they go up the river the father decides to go hunting with his dog and tells his son to wait for them. The dog kills a pig and a cassowary, and the father brings their carcasses back to the canoe and they continue to paddle upstream until it gets dark. Then they cut and eat the game, the boy eating with the dog. Every day they do this, the dog kills the game, and they rest at night and eat.

Finally, the three of them came to the mouth of the Iwan (Yellow) River and go up a ways until they come to the mouth of the Taun (Sand) River. The son wants to go up this river but his father says, "You can but I'm not," and they continue up the Iwan River until they come in sight of the little mountain Mauwi. The father climbed the hill and saw the Inarlit River.[9] He notices that its water was different—that it is red and that it is a very good river that he thinks comes from the mountains. When they get to the Inarlit River the son wanted to follow it but the father says no. Then they go up the Milyar tributary as the father wanted. Finally, they beach their canoe and begin walking. The father goes ahead until he sees Mauwi mountain, returns for the boy and dog, and they all go up the mountain and continue to a small grassy area where they

---

8. For the Lujere, like most New Guinea societies, there was "a lack of concern with the origins of the universe in general or of the earth as such" (Berndt 1972: 824). Indeed, the idea of a "universe" or "earth" was not a part of their Indigenous consciousness. Many New Guinea societies do have stories about *human* origins but, if the Lujere have such a story, as they could, I did not learn of it.
9. This is the main river or creek that flows between the two highest hills that lie between the Yellow and Sand Rivers; Iwani village sits atop the west hill and the CMML Mission and Edwaki Base Camp atop the east hill.

make a little house and, after eating the dog's game, go to sleep. The next morning, they find another grassy area named Ireno with a large ironwood tree in the middle and they start building a house. A single woman named "Wind Woman" or in Namia, "Oroble," lives up in the tree where she would rest on one of the branches and call out. After Walwin and his son finish building their house, they sleep there.

On the very top of the hill is an ironwood tree, the kind with the fruit that falls down and cassowaries and pigs like to eat. It stands in the center of what is now the central plaza of Mauwi hamlet. Walwin, on seeing many pigs and cassowaries gathered around this tree, says, "I can't shoot them all because they might kill me." Then he shoots the biggest pig there. It is as big as a cow. Then all the pigs and cassowaries run away; some go down to Bapei, some towards Iwareyo, some towards Edwaki, some down towards Wakau, and some towards the big bush to the west. Walwin follows the injured pig he has shot until he finds its dead body. He says, "Oh, I'm not strong enough to carry this pig, it's not a small pig I could carry." Then he covers the pig with leaves and returns the next morning with his son to butcher it.

The woman who lives in the ironwood tree returns and sits down on a branch of this tree. The branch stood up just the same as a man's erect penis, and when she sat down on it she made this sound: "Loble, loble, loble." The branch goes into her vagina, and she bled as if it were water. Walwin looked at her and says, "What's going on? I think this is a spirit woman, not a real woman."

Walwin then cuts some branches and vines and makes a bed in the tree just beneath the branch she has fucked. He measures the branch and thinks that his penis was just as big. Then he chops off the branch and it falls to the ground below; now his penis stands erect just as the branch had [much laughter]. In the afternoon it rains and when it has almost stopped, Walwin tells his son he is going up in the tree now; his son ties a rope around his father's waist, who then climbs up into the tree and lies down on the bed he has made. The wind begins to blow and Walwin says, "I think she will come with the wind." He then instructs his son to hold fast to the rope around his waist.

Walwin lies down on the bed and his penis is already erect when he hears the woman's "loble, loble, loble." She comes and sits down on his erect penis as if it were the branch. As they are having sex, they both fall out of the tree down to the ground. As they lie on the ground they continue to have sex. They continue on, and on, and on, and on, and on, and on, and on, until the woman is pregnant. But Walwin does not take his penis out of her but keeps it in and they continue to have sex. Finally, the baby that is inside of the woman wants out, so she shoves Walwin's penis out of her way and the baby girl is born.

The Wind Woman speaks another language and does not understand Walwin's language. After she has the baby girl, she uses hand signals to tell Walwin that she would like to try some of their food, such as sago dumplings, cooked sago, meat, grubs, fish, and all the different kinds of food she points to. First, they give her sago and she likes it; then she tries sago dumplings and likes them too. Then she tries meat, grubs, fish, eggs, Victoria crowned pigeons, hornbills, birds of paradise, lizards, and she likes it all.

Then they begin having sex again and this time she has a baby boy. She decides she wants to learn how to make sago dumplings and they teach her. Then she learns how to cook sago with a hot stone. She tries cooking meat and says, "This kind of work is very good." She learns how to get grubs out of tree trunks and cook them, how to catch fish and to butcher the stomach of a pig. She also learns how to pick up the pig's shit. Then she learns how to cut firewood and to wash sago. Walwin and his son teach her all these things. And she continues to have babies, alternating between a girl and a boy. After she had learned all these different tasks, Walwin said that she is now a real woman, not a spirit woman and tells his son, "You can stay with her, she won't eat you now. She is a real woman and understands all of the things we do."

Walwin, his son, and the dog finish killing all the game on the mountain including all the young game. Walwin then goes to the top of the mountain where the ironwood tree stands and all the game has earlier gathered and clears the area and builds his house there. The ground on the top of the mountain is wet and muddy because so many animals have walked about there, but once he cuts down all the trees and bushes, the sun shines on the ground and it is dry. All the children of the Wind Woman also live up there.

Once, when Walwin is walking in the forest, he finds two men. He discovers them on the side of the mountain where Iwariyo hamlet [the "funeral" hamlet Joyce and I passed through] is now. These two men live inside the earth; neither is married nor has any children. They walk around underground breaking firewood [Kaiera imitates the sound]. Walwin said, "Who is that making that noise underneath the ground? What is it? Is it a spirit man or a spirit woman?" He goes home but decides to return the next day and dig a hole in the ground to see who is there. During the night he whispers to his son, "I think tomorrow you and I will go and find what it is I heard making the noise inside the ground."

The next morning, they go to the place where Walwin heard the noise and each cut down a tree, sharpen both its ends, then begin digging into the ground. They dig the hole down, down, down, down, down, until they saw the house of the two men. They ask, "Who would live here? Are they spirit men? Who would live underground like this?" The two men look up and see Walwin and his son standing there and say, "Who are you standing there? We hope you aren't spirit men." Walwin and his son reply, "We are not spirit men, we are real men. You are the spirit men!" They continued back and forth accusing each other of being spirit men until Walwin and his son ask the men to come up on top, but the two men keep asking Walwin and his son to come down where they were. Finally, the underground men get their way and Walwin and his son go below and sit down with the two men.[10]

The two underground men eat dirt and their shit is abnormal. They eat meat but with dirt, not sago. They think sago is not good to eat. The men smoke some grubs and fish and give it to Walwin and his son to eat. After eating, the four visit, smoke, and chew betel nut. Walwin and his son eventually say they must go back to their own house, that they have ruined the men's house by digging the hole, so the two men go up

---

10. Stories of hidden underground people are rather common in Melanesian societies and they always enchant me. In the Solomon Islands' Makiran culture they have "cargoistic and millenarian aspects" that Scott summarizes:

> wonder discourses about the underground envisage that, when the army emerges, true Makiran language and *kastom* will be restored, the hidden riches of Mikira will bring fabulous prosperity, sexual immorality will run rife, and Makira will become an autonomous superpower. (Scott 2016: 489)

with them, take wives, and have children by them. Walwin's son also takes a wife from one of the Wind Woman's daughters and he also has children.

Now there are many people on the mountain and it is completely covered with houses. Finally, some of the people leave the mountain because it is too crowded and make new houses in Bapei. Others make houses at Iwariyo, while others go down and make houses at Edwaki, some go to Lawara, and others to Epoumu. Some of the people eat meat, but others go to bed hungry so they continue to move into other areas to live. Some go off to Gwidami and Aiendame, others Yuwari, others to Tipas. More time passes and Walwin's son's children now must move out. One, however, stays in Mauwi, but the rest leave: one goes to Gwidami, one to Edwaki, one to Tipas, then some to Magaleri and others to Wagu. It was only later the people moved to Wakau.

Just when I was beginning to think that this story could go on endlessly tracing migrations, like the First Book of Chronicles in the Old Testament traces who "begat" whom, Kaiera rather abruptly said the story was finished. It was after 4:00, extremely hot, and the cicadas were droning monotonously. I wanted to ask Kaiera how Namia speakers settled Magaleri and Wagu as neither village speaks Namia today, but I lacked the energy. A different line of questioning revealed that another name for Walwin was Mais, but what interested me most about the story—besides the riotous marathon sex scene that ends with his infant daughter pushing his penis out of her way so she could be born—was the relationship between her mother and father that provides a rationale for the female division of labor. It is her father who instructs her mother, a spirit woman, at her own request, not only about all the father's foods but how to prepare them, besides other female tasks like collecting firewood and, of course, picking up pig shit, that civilizes her into a real woman. Initially, according to the story, males had to do *everything*, until females came along and opted to help.

It goes without saying that Lujere men invented these stories, and they are told over and over in their men's houses. Kaiera learned them as a growing boy in a Mauwi men's house, as did Newai and Klowi in a Wakau men's house. When local news and gossip was insubstantial, telling stories—a term I prefer to legends or myths—in the darkness of a men's house during the long nights was the main form of entertainment. Some of the stories were so long they could be classified as sagas; Yaope told me one about "Snake Woman" that lasted over two hours. The mental "worlds" of these Lujere males, if compared to a contemporary Westerner privately accessing an array of digital devices to discover all information and images throughout the known universe, are both geographically and culturally acutely localized. But that is part of the intellectual and emotional excitement of fieldwork: liaising with minds whose workings are in some ways so vastly different from one's own.

As Kaiera was telling the story, I thought I might also learn about the origin of men's houses but there was nothing special about males except the bonding of the father and son, and the peaceful encounter between them and the two underground men. Unlike some Lujere stories, this one was totally absent of violence, something I became acutely accustomed to in Wape tales. Instead, there was the scene of the underground men feeding the strangers Walwin and his son, then their visiting, smoking, and chewing betel—just like Lujere men did when I lived with them—before the underground men were taken home and given Walwin's daughters for wives. At no point was there any indication of a man having more than one wife—Walwin's only spouse was the Wind Woman—or any suggestion of sister exchange as a preferred form of marriage. It is also interesting that Walwin's son married a half-sister, but this anomalous tie is ignored.

A related point to the story's absence of violence is that the fissioning of the villages and resultant migrations were due to depletion of the local food supply, not because of internal fights or arguments. Whether this was completely true or not, it is the way the Wakau men view their past in terms of their origins story.[11] What is significant is the historical fact that the Lujere villages did not wage war or raids on one another. Finally, it is noteworthy that Walwin and his humanized wife appear to be of equal genealogical standing; there is no heavy emphasis in the story of one line—female or male—over the other that, up to a point, is echoed in my findings. While it is true that both parental sides of a Lujere person's kin network are of great social and emotional importance and, significantly, postmarital residence is highly flexible, the overall system, as discussed in chapter 12, is patrilineally skewed with strategic resources transmitted through males. Finally, there is the inevitable emphasis in a story invented by males that Walwin's Wind Woman, like Adam's Eve, owes her humanity to her male consort.

Male Initiation: Myth or Authentic History?

In my second and third patrols among the Lujere when I was searching for a village on which to base my research, men in both Worikori and Tipas villages spoke about male initiation, but in inconclusive ways, indicating it had existed in the distant past. From my work in Wakau, I had decided that it did not exist now or probably ever. Then Kaiera told me an interesting story about the initiation of young boys into manhood. The story, as in all the Lujere folktales I heard, was related as if the events had actually happened and perhaps was the source for the earlier inconclusive stories I had heard. Here is the story, which was told in Tok Pisin and which I have edited only slightly.

> A long time ago, even before our grandparents were alive, all the young men from all of the villages used to go into one great big house when they were about to mature into men. The house was completely enclosed, and the doors were fastened so the boys

---

11. Betty Gillam had another less sexually overt version of an origin story from villagers she knew near the Edwaki CMML Mission. I suspect, but don't know, that perhaps it was cleaned up for telling a woman missionary.

> The legend has it that Wilaki and Krenmau as fully grown men suddenly came to life by coming out of the ground on the top of Edwaki hill near the Sepik River. These two brothers built a shelter there. Wilaki was the adventurous brother who took to wandering around the other hills and swamp land. On the hill called Mauwi [location of Iwani village] which is in close proximity to Edwaki, Wilaki observed some beautiful pigeons. There was one special female pigeon he became attracted to. To befriend it he built a pigeon house on the top of an ironwood tree and tried to lure her inside, which he did after waiting a long wait. Kremau, being a good brother, built a house for them at Edwaki. There Wilaki and his pigeon wife lived and brought up two children. Wilaki continued to wander through the area and claimed it as territory for his descendants. (Gillam 1983: 10)

could not go outside. They were kept there from five to twenty years old. Their bodies were rubbed with thorns from the sago palms and 'kanda' and other thorns as well as the jaws of pigs and crocodiles, and the bones of snakes and other animals. When their bodies were scraped, the boys would yell and scream, and the men would beat on the 'garamut' and their 'kundus.' All the rubbish from the great house would be put beneath it and burned, creating a tremendous amount of smoke. No weapons were kept in the house to prevent the boys from trying to run away.

While the boys were in seclusion, their mothers and fathers made decorations for them to wear when they exited the house for the festival. The women made huge amounts of sago and the men went hunting for game, and other food was gathered for the male initiation festival. All of the boys from many different villages would be in one big house, for example boys from Gwidami, Aiimdani, Bapi, Wiere, Mauwi, and Tepas would be together. The reason for scrubbing their bodies was to make them bleed so the old blood would leave them, and the new blood would come into them so they would grow big and strong. When the boys first went into the house, a banana species called *aralt* was planted, and the boys were not allowed to leave until it bore fruit. Then they would leave the house for the great festival; the men and women from the surrounding villages would all bring their food to the big men's house.

However, this time the boy's parents had all gone into the bush to get food but stayed a long time. The boys became very hungry then very angry. They collected all the 'apike' [a green] and bananas, made a fire, then burned the bananas and put the black skins on themselves. Then they used the 'apica' leaves to make wings, finally they cut their skin and bled. Now they became giant fruit bats.

When the parents returned with food for the boys, they knocked on the door to give it to them, but the boys had made a hole in the roof and had flown away. They were hanging up in all the village trees, the breadfruits, the mangos, the betelnuts, and the coconuts. When the parents saw what had happened to their sons, they began to wail and cry, saying it was all their fault; "We were gone away too long and our sons were hungry." So the villagers lost all of their young men. (MN 1971)

Kaiera told me that this was a Mauwi story but that they never had male initiation in his time, his father's time or in his grandparent's time but, he added, before then they might have. The term he associated with this story was *mariaita* but said there was no translation for it.

Talk, the Essence of Life

Talking and listening, listening and talking, make humans unique in the animal world; language is an essential part of being a sentient human being. As Lamont Lindstrom observes for Melanesian societies, "Here are people who define humanity by the capacity to talk" (Lindstrom 1990: xiv). This is related, of course, to the fact that none have devised a form of writing, thus prioritizing oral communication. Nowhere in the world have there been people as actively engaged in inventing new languages as on the island of New Guinea. In the Indonesian western half, formerly Irian Jaya, there are over 300 languages and in the eastern half, Papua New Guinea, there are over 850 languages, and these are different languages, not dialects (Lewis et al. 2015: 201). New Guinea is the world's second largest island but with over a thousand languages spoken on the island, no other area of the world for its size comes close in terms of linguistic multiplicity.

A Plethora of Papuan Languages: Namia's Neighbors

New Guinea's Upper Sepik Basin has the highest concentration of different languages and variety of major language families on the island and perhaps in the world.[12] For example, while the Lujere have their own language, Namia, they are surrounded by thirteen other vigorous languages: Abau, Ak, Ama, Amal, Awun, Bouye, Guriaso, Iwam, Iteri, Kwomtari, Odiai, Yale (Nagatman), and Yis. These languages, in turn, are variously members of four different major language families: Arai (Left May), Kwomteri, Sepik, and Torricelli, except for the Odiai and Iteri languages that are "isolates" with no known genetic relationship to other languages. According to Steer, "The Sepik catchment exhibits a degree of genetic diversity unequaled anywhere in the world. . . . [and] the upper Sepik has diversity commensurate with this" (Steer 2005:5).

The classification gambit

All the above languages are classified "Papuan," as are most of the other languages of Papua New Guinea except a few coastal languages newer to the island classified as "Austronesian." The term "Papuan" does not presuppose a genetic tie among languages so labeled but distinguishes them from Austronesian and Australian languages. Sidney Herbert Ray (1892), a member of A. C. Haddon's famous 1898 Cambridge Anthropological Expedition to the Torres Strait, originated the important distinction between Papuan and Austronesian languages.[13] Joseph Greenberg and Stephen Wurm made early attempts at large-scale classifications of the numerous Papuan languages but more recently Malcolm Ross, building in part on their work and using newer findings has classified all the known Papuan languages as a work in progress, updating Laycock's (1973) preliminary classification of the Sepik languages. The comprehensive and authoritative *Ethnologue: Languages of the World*, published by SIL International, uses Ross's classification of the Papuan languages, as do I in these comments.[14]

---

12. The online *Ethnologue* has the best mapping of the Upper Sepik Basin languages. See http://ethnologue.com/map/PG_3 and http://ethnologue.com/map/PG_5.
13. Ray was born and raised in tough East London of working-class parents and attended a teacher's college. He was a self-taught linguist, at a time when linguistics, as Stocking (1996: 116) notes, was of "marginal status" in the emerging science of British social anthropology. Despite his accomplishments as a published linguist, he taught in an elementary school in East London until retirement. Haddon tried, as did other distinguished British anthropologists including Oxford's Edward B. Tyler, to find an academic or museum post worthy of him, even in Australia, without success. See Wells' (1999) brief biography of Ray as a poignant case study of the rigidity of the Twentieth Century British class system.
14. SIL International, a faith-based organization, was formerly named the Summer Institute of Linguistics. *Ethnologue*, edited by M. Paul Lewis (2009), may be viewed online: http://www.ethnologue.com/. For hardcover see Lewis (2015). Also see Pawley, et al. (2005), a sprawling book examining the Papuan-speaking peoples' cultural, linguistic, and biological histories; for

The first attempt to classify the languages of the upper Sepik Basin was by Loving and Bass (1964), while the first attempt to classify all the known languages of the Sepik Basin was by the Australian linguist, Donald Laycock (1973). Much of Laycock's pioneering work has stood the test of time but Ross (2005), on the basis of his analysis of pronoun paradigms, separates Laycock's "Sepik-Ramu" phylum into two groups, "Ramu-Lower Sepik" and "Sepik," the latter to include the languages of the middle and upper Sepik River Basin area.[15] He also suspects that the most promising candidate for an external relationship with Sepik languages, including Namia, is with the Torricelli language family, not the Ramu. Interestingly, Don Laycock, in a long letter to me of June 1, 1976, mostly about 'sanguma,' had some thoughts about the Lujere having formerly spoken a "'Torricelli' [phylum language] that was absorbed to the extent of adopting a Middle Sepik language." If Ross and Laycock's suppositions were true, that would presuppose that the Lujere's ancestors came from the north and over the Torricelli Mountains, instead of up the Sepik and Yellow Rivers as their mythic origins attest. Following Allen (2005) writing more generally on the migration of Sepik inhabitants, I find the evidence more convincing that some ascended the Sepik then down the Torricelli's south flowing rivers into the lowland fens.

There are fifty-six languages in the Sepik family that are spoken from the middle Sepik west to the Indonesian border, south into the Southern Highlands and, spilling north over the Prince Alexander Mountains, to the coast around Wewak and even into the Bismarck Sea and a part of Mushu Island. There are even several Sepik family languages in the coastal vicinity of Vanimo. The Sepik languages are characterized by simple phonologies and few consonants, are rarely tonal, and usually have a three-vowel system that recognizes only vowel height.

Ross, as well as Laycock, places Namia, Ak (83 speakers), and Awun (384 speakers) in a "Yellow River" subdivision of the Sepik family, indicating they are more similar to each other than to other languages.[16] Ak, as mentioned earlier, is spoken only in Kwieftim village, a traditional Lujere enemy, and Awun only in Abrau and Yakeltim villages, also traditional Lujere enemies.[17] One can only presume that the remote ancestors of the present Ak and Awun speakers either left or fled from the remote ancestors of the contemporary Lujere because of some enmity. an enmity only relaxed from retributive homicide after the colonial law of the 'kiaps' was established. Evidence shows (Steer 2005, 27) that Namia has a distant genetic link to Iwan that "corresponds to a separation of at least 3,000 years."

---

an excellent detailed review of the book's important contributions, see Terrill (2007). For an earlier seminal linguistic analysis of the Papuan languages see Foley (1986).

15. While Laycock's (1973) and Steers' ([2005] 2011) hierarchical rationale uses the traditional nomenclature of phyla and stocks, the *Ethnologue* eschews this usage.
16. Steer, however, is skeptical because of the dearth of data on Ak and Awun languages, noting "at least as far as the public record is concerned, the place of Ak and Awun in the Yellow River family is a matter of faith" (Steer 2005: 27).
17. According to Antje Kelm (1972: 447) who did fieldwork in Abrau, they referred to the Lujere as the Kari.

Namia

When I began my Lujere fieldwork in 1971, Laycock had only roughly classified their language.[18] It was not until Tom and Becky Feldpausch, American linguists with the Summer Institute of Linguistics, intensively studied the language that it became well-documented. Their research base was in Yaru village from 1985 to 2008 and my comments about Namia are based on their extensive research.

The first study of Namia was a sociolinguistic survey by missionaries Ronald and Doris Pappenhagen (1981). Their linguistic informants indicated that four regional dialects of Namia existed. However, neither they nor the Feldpausches discovered any substantial empirical evidence to substantiate the presence of dialects and their "dialect" areas appear to refer to the Lujere "regions" already discussed. The Feldpausches' dialect survey (1999) established that the words from every area were 98 percent cognate. They also indicate that

> The richness of the Namia language is found in its verbal affixes and phrases. The Namia people make fine distinctions in the categories in which they view situations. They mark almost every statement with their view of reality. They can make different types of commands, and make negation in multiple ways. The study of tense, aspect, and adverbials and mood in Namia has been rewarding to understand more fully how the Namia people view their world. Their use of duration and transitivity give much more information about the event than a tense system could give. When an event starts, ends, or is accomplished, are also more important than time, and are all shown by aspect suffixes. (Feldpausch and Feldpausch 2003: 26)

Like many languages, Namia has several words with multiple meanings: *naki* means "new," "neck," and "vine," and *wei* means, "ripe," "red," and "slit-drum." Namia is the most frequently spoken language in Lujereland; unlike Papua New Guinea's towns, theirs is not a polyglot society with many linguistic migrants. Very few Lujere speak or understand another Indigenous language. However, many of the men and youths, as noted, speak Tok Pisin. Except near the mission, it is rare for a woman to have learned it; none of the Wakau women spoke it. Sometimes, when I hung out in a Wakau men's house (*iron*) at night, I often overheard men's conversations with a mixture of Namia and Tok Pisin and, sometimes for a short interval, just Tok Pisin, especially if it concerned a contemporary political issue with the administration.

As Namia has no concept of a Western week with its seven named days, it borrows Tok Pisin's weekday names as it does many other terms for alien concepts, items and actions. It is interesting that two of my best informants in Wakau, Oria and Kaiera, were men rejected from labor recruitment for physical reasons, but both had learned Tok Pisin in the village, and Oria also was literate from attending Phillip Ace's mission literacy classes for a while. Tok Pisin had the cachet of modernism and, as the lingua franca of Papua New Guinea, Lujere males could easily communicate with other Tok Pisin speakers regardless of their mother language whether it was Papuan, Austronesian, or English. However, if one is a Tok Pisin speaker and doesn't speak Namia, there can be lexical glitches listening

---

18. Foley (1986: 242) critically discusses Laycock's earlier proposed Sepik sub-phylum that contained a large grouping of Sepik languages including Namia.

to a Lujere man's Tok Pisin. Namia has no voiced or aspirated stops, such as [b], [d], [g]; and there are no alveolar fricatives, [s] and [z]. This can make Tok Pisin at times sound oddly accented to an English speaker. While in the field, it seemed that the village of "Tipas" was never pronounced the same way twice, not to mention numerous other words, alerting me to phonological particularities of Namia that were beyond my linguistic skills to codify long before the Feldpausch's research. In hearing Namia spoken while I lived there, it also seemed that there were an inordinate number of "l" words or "l" sounds lapping through the air. Indeed, in checking Becky Feldpausch's (2003) Namia Dictionary, there are more words beginning with "l" than any other letter. In speaking Namia, it also appeared to me that, compared to the Wape I lived with or the English-speaking expats, there was very little lip-work—a visual lack that frustrated my attempts to learn it.

One of the instructive papers the Feldpausches have prepared on the language considers the rules for translating the Namia language.[19] Here is a brief sample of their findings. The most common word order is Subject-Object-Verb (SOV), such as *Loko-tanalwa taplu-pnowe* (He gave food to his son). Sentences with time and place are usually ordered as Subject-Place/Time-Object-Verb, such as *On-apo-kali lomon-ija*, (I will now tell a story.) In sentences that describe something, the word order is Pronoun-Noun, such as *Loko-lu* (He is a man) or Noun-Adjective, such as *Loko-walei* (He is tall).

> In her *Introduction to the Namia Dictionary*, Becky Feldpausch writes,
> Typologically, Namia has the following characteristics. Basic word order is SOV [subject, object, verb], it uses postpositions and has no switch reference, medial verbs nor absolute tense. The morphology is agglutinative (with aspect, mood, and direction markings required on verbs). . . . But it does not have person markers on indicative verbs. For this reason it uses free pronouns instead. Number is not marked in the nouns, there are few adjectives and no comparative words like 'bigger' or 'smaller.' Reason clauses normally occur before result clauses. There is no grammatical marking for direct quotations. (Feldpausch 2011: 2)

Namia, like Tok Pisin, has no plural ending for nouns and I have followed that convention in my use of Namia nouns, for example, *lu* signifies both "men" and "man." Namia has no tone and accent is predictable on the penultimate syllable. It also has six phonemic vowels and shares lexical similarities with the languages of the Lujere's traditional Sepik enemies: 13 percent with Abau and 12 percent with the May River Iwam (Lewis et al. 2015: 235).

> Namia, as is typical of many Papuan languages, has high inflection on the verb with up to seven orders of prefix and up to five orders of suffix. There is verb serialization but no clause chaining nor switch reference. The tense system is unusual with nonfuture (past and present), definite future and indefinite future as marked categories. Also perfective vs. imperfective aspect can be marked on the verb. . . . Namia also has a limited gender system, marking male and female gender on certain third person singular forms. (Feldpausch and Feldpausch 1992: iii)

---

19. See "Rules for Translation in the Namia Language" by Becky Feldpausch, November 2008. http://www.sil.org/resources/archives/31078.

The gender of all animals and birds is determined by suffixes: *amowabu* for females and *aibagi* for males. Namia is the child's first, and often, only language. Everyone living in Lujereland, except for expats and police, spoke Namia. Today, thanks to the Feldpausch's dedicated work, Namia is one of the most comprehensively studied languages of the Upper Sepik Basin and their numerous papers are all accessible online.[20]

Tok Pisin

Tok Pisin, the second most spoken language in Lujereland, is a creole language and, like English and Hiri Motu, an official language of Papua New Guinea.[21] As the country's most popular language, Tok Pisin's word sources are mostly from English, just over 80 percent; from German, nearly 5 percent; from Spanish, Portuguese, Latin, Geek and onomatopoetic words, nearly 5 percent; from the Pacific area, nearly 7 percent; and unknown, about 3 percent (Steinbauer 1969: 6). As de Groot notes,

> The people of Papua New Guinea use the language of Tok Pisin every day to communicate, to teach, to command, to pray and to express whatever they want. Tok Pisin is a living language, continually expanding and changing, and characterized by regional differences. (de Groot 2008: i)

The regional Tok Pisin of the Lujere was that of the country's northwest coast and the Sepik River Basin. This is the version of Tok Pisin used in the cited dictionaries—that is, Mihalic (1971) and Volker (2008). The Tolai language of New Britain is an important source of Tok Pisin's grammatical structure (Foley 1986: 36). Tok Pisin's simple syntax facilitates mastery and easy communication among those using it as a second language; it is not a "broken" English but a language that can accurately reflect a speaker's "thoughts, feelings and emotions" (Volker 2008: i). I have no gift for languages but was fluent after my summer stay on the Sepik in 1967. Today it is usually classified as a creole rather than a pidgin as it increasingly becomes a first language replacing an Indigenous one, as Kulick (2019) has documented for Gapun village in the Lower Sepik. Most Lujere men were fluent in Tok Pisin having learned it as indentured workers. Even some men who hadn't worked away picked it up as had some women near the base camp and mission, as well as some children, especially boys.[22] For Lujere youths, speaking Tok Pisin had connotations of both modernity and mature masculinity, while in the nation, especially in the multilingual towns, it was a language of personal and commercial expediency for both sexes.

---

20. Also see Thomas and Becky Feldpausch (1993) regarding phonology essentials and (2000) for Namia orthography. The Feldpausch's numerous Namia papers can be accessed at http://www.glottolog.org/resource/languold/id/nami1256.
21. Tok Pisin, the accepted term today for the language, has been called variously "Pidgin English," "New Guinea Pidgin," "Melanesian Pidgin," "Neo-Melanesian," and "Tok Boi." For an enlightening discussion of the origins, history, and usage of Tok Pisin see Foley (1986: 30–41). For Tok Pisin dictionaries see Volker (2008), Steinbauer (1969), and especially Mihalic (1971: 1–54) for his detailed linguistic analysis of the language.
22. For information on Tok Pisin literacy among Lujere men, see the discussion related to table 1.

CHAPTER NINE

Old Enemies

> *The reason for cannibalism itself has been given by natives as the simple desire for good food.*
> F. E. Williams (1930: 171)

> *"You managed not to get eaten, then?"*
> Prince Philip, questioning a Papua New Guinean hiker, 1998.

At first contact, the Lujere villages were at peace with each other but not with their linguistically different neighbors. A bordering village that did not speak Namia was an enemy, and the enmity was mutual. Inhabitants of enemy villages could at any time and in almost any circumstance feel free to kill any member, male or female, young or old, of an enemy village. "Warfare" in egalitarian societies like the Lujere consisted of retaliative surprise raids. As Fried has observed, "military organization in such societies indicates a complete absence of command or coordination: every man stands and fights or runs away by himself" (Fried 1967: 104). In lowland New Guinea, the payback killing or running feud characterized intervillage hostility. Knauft describes it as follows:

> The goal of most such raiding parties was to capture and/or kill one or more enemies in retribution for previous killing. It was usually of little consequence if the person(s) were men, women, or children. Frequently, the raiders would try to surprise their target village or obtain victims unaware on its periphery. Ideally a victim could be obtained without raising the general alarm, thus allowing the raiders to return successfully to their own territory without resistance. In many cases, the killing of a single victim by the attacking force (without themselves sustaining a loss) was tantamount to a "victory." (Knauft 1999: 102)

The nature of this kind of "warfare" is clearly demonstrated in the section below on "the Tsila Village Massacre." In culture areas like Lujereland without chiefdoms or other Indigenous over-arching political institutions, small independent hamlets like Wakau often made alliances with neighboring groups to mount retaliative killing raids.[1]

One of the most interesting facts about the Lujere was that on first contact they did not raid within their language group, that is, other Namia speakers. I have no compelling explanation for this unusual phenomenon in the Sepik region. Because they did not evolve more culturally complex institutions such as initiation and regional exchange systems, as well as their overall ethos of keeping life simple, I hypothesize that they are a younger culture than some of their neighbors and that time has not eroded the original amity among villagers as population pressures caused a sequence of people hiving off from the mother village of Iwani to establish new villages in the easily available land. It is, however, just a guess.

Traditional Enemies

The Lujere's enemies were the foreign villages that surrounded them, but a Lujere village usually clashed only with the alien villages in their immediate area. The most important enemy villages are shown in table 5 along with the language spoken and their cardinal direction from the center of Lujereland. The ten enemy villages surrounding the Lujere spoke eight distinct languages, all members of the Sepik language family. While according to Laycock (1973: 23) Bouye (Pouye), Awun, and Namia are more closely related as members of the Yellow River family, this relationship is challenged by Steer (2005: 27) and others and is discussed later.

Table 5. Lujere enemy villages by cardinal direction and language

Village	Direction	Language
Maurom	North	Pouye
Wokien	North	Pouye
Kwieftim	North	Ak
Abrau	East	Awun
Yakeltim	East	Awun
Magaleri	East	Amal
Wanimoi	South	Iwam
Wapoulu	South	Ama
Wagu	West	Abau
Tsila	West	Yale

1. Shaw (1974: 14–15) in the context of Papua New Guinea discusses the factors contributing to the functioning of a society including the role of alliances. For a critical summary of warfare in both precolonial and colonial New Guinea, see the chapter "Warfare and History in Melanesia" in Knauft (1999: 89–156).

There is an interesting story about Wagu told to me by Kaiera. He said that Iwani, tired of Wagu's homicidal raids, made peace with them before the Europeans came and were like 'wanblut' [one blood], visiting back and forth. When they made peace, the Wagu's came in canoes and the Mauwi villagers walked to the river (MI: 151). If true, it makes the marriage of an Iwani man to a Wagu woman, as espoused in chapter 3, plausible; I did not get Kaiera's story confirmed but such voluntary truces did occur. The Wape village of Taute where I lived made peace with the enemy villagers of Kamnum before the 'kiaps' came. When men became contract laborers before 'kiaps' exerted direct control over them, it was the returned laborers who sometimes were the catalyst for peace.

Trading with the Enemy

As the Lujere were also dependent on their enemies for much of their trade goods, exchange partners were an ironic necessity. Parts of New Guinea, especially the north coast and offshore island societies with sailing craft, developed complex systems of symbolically linked trade like the famed *kula* of Malinowski (1922), but not the Upper Sepik societies. There, trading with the enemy was a simple, stark transaction. Not every man had a trading partner in an enemy village, but those that did provided the conduit through which desired objects and products flowed across borders. When Tok Pisin became the common *lingua franca* for trade between enemies, exchange was facilitated but it could still be, as we soon see, a risky encounter.

Shell valuables were in sufficient number that they reached the Lujere from the north coast's Bismark Sea, passing over the Torricelli Mountains into Wapeland and down to the villagers of Kwieftim and Maurom where the Wakau men gave them smoked meat and sago grubs in exchange. But metal tools were so scarce and prized that, as McCarthy clearly realized, they rarely, if ever, were obtained in trade. The shells received by the Wakau men and other Lujere were, in part, then traded with the Sawiyano cannibal villages[2] across the Sepik in the mountains just above the Lujere villages of Panewai and Purami. In return for their shell valuables, the Lujere received very thin spears with beautifully carved tips for killing humans, "fright" attack wigs of women's hair worn over a warrior's forehead and eyes, bird of paradise feathers, tight net bags (unlike the Lujere's looser style), and an aromatic bark. Scrapings from the bark were mixed with ginger, skinned betel nut, betel pepper vine, then folded into betel vine leaves and rubbed back and forth until it turned red. A prized charm, it was fed to a man's son or dog for hunting luck. The trading was often done at the Sepik River where both groups presumably would meet in peace.

Phillip Guddemi (1992: 152–53) relates a fatal incident he was told by the Sawiyano during his 1986–1988 fieldwork, an incident initiated by customary trade that ended in cannibalism. Waliyaupei was a Lujere man from Panewai village who, under the protection of his Sawiyano trading partners, was visiting their ritual houses associated with

---

2. My Mauwi-born informant Kaiera said the Namia name for them was *woniablu* (WN:113) while Oria of Wakau said we had no name for them. The men were of similar age, both excellent informants, but because of Kaiera's sight impairment, he had spent much more time than Oria sitting in the men's house soaking up tradition and was an endless font of the old stories.

male initiation, a custom not practiced by the Lujere. The incident had occurred after the Sawiyano men had begun work as contract laborers and Guddemi spoke with several older men still alive who had participated. Waliyaupei's opportune visit struck one Sawiyano man as an excellent time to "avenge general and particular slights coming from the region of Panewai," and convinced others they should kill him. Waliyaupei's protectors protested by asking the avengers where they expected to get their shell valuables if they killed off their trading partners, but the men in favor of the killing were adamant; the others, afraid they would miss out, acquiesced. Waliyaupei was ambushed, killed, butchered, divided, and eaten. When Guddemi asked some of the senior men of Panewai about the incident,

> They mentioned that it was not by accident that Waliyaupei had been killed. He had been caught in adultery by another man, who prepared a potion of magic plants and uttered spells into it . . . so that Waliyaupei would find death. The death might have taken place in many ways; as it happened, he found death at the hands of the Sawiyano. Thus, in 1988, it is maintained in Panewai that there was never any anger over Waliyaupei's killing, he was already meant to find death. (Guddemi 1992: 153)

Consequently, the Panewai people never reciprocated Waliyaupei's death, so it became the Sawiyano's last recorded cannibal feast.[3] This did not mean that the implicated villages became fast friends. In 1987, Guddemi heard rumors of a letter sent by some Panewai men to the Sawiyano threatening death by 'sanguma' if they did not stop encroaching on their territory. Thus, even though traditional enemy villages may no longer murder one another, the feeling of enmity lingers even as it does between some Vermonters and New Yorkers across Lake Champlain, aware of their colonial history.

Tsila [Tila] village[4], another traditional enemy of the Iwani hamlets, is a day's walk into the sprawling wet lowlands west of the Sand River and today the Wakau men still trade with them, but trade is limited usually to their hunting charms in exchange for shell rings or money. Their hunting charm called *keri* is composed from a bush hen's egg, sago beetles, and wild ginger wrapped together in aromatic leaves. Wakau also received from them some of the curing rituals and artifacts discussed in chapter 15. One January morning shortly after hearing a radio broadcast of President Nixon's new budget, I met the Tsila 'luluai' Wapia who happened to be in Wakau and we sat down for a short visit. The name of his hamlet was Era and the other hamlets or villages he named were Marakwani and Nagatiman, all speakers of the Kali [Yale, Nogatman] language that is a major linguistic conundrum. Classified as an "isolate" it has been compared with languages in a

---

3. A Sawiyano origin myth (Guddemi 1992: 67) also concerns the Panewai people. The ancestors of the Sawiyano lived in a large magic ginger plant that was aggressively encircled by ancestors of the Panewai villagers who came in twelve canoes. Not surprisingly, the Panewai of the story were vanquished. "The magic-ginger-plant turned into men and these twelve canoes were finished, killed altogether" (Guddemi 1992: 67).

4. This is not the Tila village that is on the Horden River as it is too far to the west but probably Dila or Hila village—or a hamlet—whose lands could logically border those of Wakau. As I have observed elsewhere, there was a lot of variation in the pronunciation of village names not to mention how they were recorded.

radius of about a hundred miles and shows no traits to justify inclusion in any of them.[5] Knowing this fact I spent most of a short time with him getting a long word list and numbers in Yale. It would have been more helpful to my research, for example, to elicit historical information on trade, vendettas, and curing customs. I did learn that only single males sleep in their men's house, that they have a ten-month male initiation, and they never had the 'garamut.' They have several different curing ceremonials and he sketched in my notebook four headdresses or masks—difficult to tell which—but none were similar to the *na wowi* mask said to come from there. When I tried to find out if they have lineages or descent groups, I struck out completely. No ethnologist had before, or since, attempted to collect cultural data on this small group, isolated both geographically and linguistically and with hindsight I regret I did not dig deeper. Oria and I and others had planned a visit to Tsila, but it never happened.

Dressed to Kill

Oria startled me one day with a dreadful face decoration of matted human hair that his stepmother had given to him after his father's recent death. He didn't want it and hoped to trade it for some newspaper to roll cigarettes. As I received a weekly newspaper from Port Moresby and had the only supply of newsprint in the village, we made a trade. The hair was from women living across the Sepik in the Western Range, the Sawiyano, the Lujere's traditional enemy. It had been purchased with shell rings by a now dead Mauwi man who knew their language, although it was not clear to Oria how he had learned it as neither parent came from there. The hair ornament comprised four bundles of matted hair from five to eight inches long, tied together with 'tulip' twine decorated with Job's tears grass seeds.[6] It was worn tied around the forehead, the matted hair falling over the face. Only men on the warpath or sorcerers out to kill could wear it. Oria then tied it on his forehead to demonstrate its fierceness. Without a doubt, it was a weirdly scary kind of facemask. He said that when women saw a man bedizened with one, they simply fainted from fright.

A warrior's costume also consisted of a waist string and upper armbands draped with shredded sago and wild coconut leaves. His face was painted black with ashes mixed with water and a half-shell ring was thrust into the hole in his nose septum. If he had killed any enemy except a baby, he could place the feather of a young cassowary into his nostril holes extending upward. Another homicide badge consisted of crocodile teeth; old Menetjua had four holes in the top of his nose, with the two outer ones for the insertion of the teeth. The decorations were worn in an attack and in a victory celebration. The long claw of a wild bird, the *ewara*, was also sometimes worn at the celebration. A warrior's wife's decoration consisted of the skin and feathers of a small bird attached to her ear and a small shell nose ring.

---

5. For references to the relevant linguistic research on Yale, see Steer (2005: 41–43).
6. The item was part of the collection of Lujere artifacts I presented to the American Museum of Natural History and can be viewed in their online catalogue as catalogue # 80.1/6464 of the Lujere items, Papua New Guinea, South Pacific Collections of the Anthropology Division under "Our Research."

During the 1940s and into the '50s, all the Wakau men and women had the two nostril and single septum holes, just as McCarthy and the Mosstroops inspector Colonel Wills earlier reported. The holes were made in early adolescence before secondary hair growth appeared. Depending upon the bravery of the person, the holes were made all at once or singly. Like piercings in America, there was no attached ritual and anyone could do it. After the piercing, the holes were filled with bits of wood; for the septum, the plug was gradually increased to the size of hole wanted. These piercings were made only during the rainy season when the flesh was believed to be softer, thereby lessening the pain and chance of infection. All the older men and women of Wakau had some of these piercings but they already had ceased decorating them before I arrived. Once Eine inserted part of a pig's tusk into his septum to show me how he used to look.

The Lujere Fight Shield

A Lujere warrior's largest and most decorative fight implement was his shield or *wali*.[7] Until the Mosstroops introduced metal tools, they had been laboriously hacked from the imposing buttress root of the ficus tree with a stone adze. Barry Craig, whose 1969 collecting trip is described in chapter 5, published the first article on the Lujere. His article (1975) on the art style of Yellow River is based on the analysis of twenty-nine Lujere shields. During his visit he photographed seventeen shields, ten of which he collected. Most were recently made for sale to outsiders except the older one he collected in Wakau; it was made in 1922 by Weima (see fig. 9) but the design was reworked about 1966.[8] He also was able to photograph six more Lujere shields owned by a collector in Ambunti.

Most important were the five precolonial shields now in Berlin's Museum für Völkerkunde, collected in 1912–13 by the German expedition that Thurnwald joined. These shields, all carved with traditional tools before they had metal, came from "Unterhalb Mäander-Berg" or below Meander Mountain, roughly the same area where the Mosstroops established their initial base camp in 1943. One of the expedition's ethnologists, Dr. Roesicke, photographed a sixth shield from the same area. The shields were shaped into wide, flat, rectangular boards about four and a half feet high and a half inch or so thick, an appropriate size for a Lujere man whose average height was about five feet four inches.[9] "The carrying strap is strung horizontally through two holes, one at each edge of the shield, so that it can be slung over the shoulder, leaving the hands free for using the bow and arrow" (Craig 1975: 430).

---

7. The C-14 dating on a Lujere shield in the Jolika collection at the de Young Museum in San Francisco is 1490–1670 (93.7% probability) (Peltason, 2005: 141, plate 357). If the dating were correct, the design for the Lujere shield would have been achieved between three hundred and five hundred years ago.
8. Abrau village, a traditional Lujere enemy bordering to the north, had shields very similar to the Lujere. See Plates 28 and 29 in Kelm and Kelm (1980) for photos of the traditional fight stance of a warrior with shield and a pulled bow and arrow. Also see Beran and Craig (2005: 76–77) for a summarizing discussion of the Yellow River shield. See Craig (1988: 62–67) for relationships of neighboring styles of design.
9. See chapter 10 for more detailed information about the size of the Wakau villagers.

Figure 9. A Wakau village fight shield. Australian Museum, Sydney, E64932. Photo courtesy of Barry Craig.

Based on the design and appearance of the twenty-nine shields pictured in his article, Craig abstracted the characteristics of the Yellow River style in terms of form, technique, composition, and motifs. The relief bands that shape the design are black and the interstitial areas variously white, red, brown, or yellow. "The commonest arrangement of motifs is around a lozenge shape with spirals at top and bottom . . . or around an X-shape with spirals at top and bottom, turning either outwards or inwards" (1975: 430). Craig also notes "that there is a distinct boundary between the Iwam style of the Sepik and May Rivers, and the styles of the peoples of the West and Central Ranges and of the Sepik upstream from Meander Mountain" (1975: 439). The ethnographic irony Craig has identified is that, while the Lujere's Namia language is more closely related to the Iwam language than, for instance, the Mountain Ok's, in terms of art designs, the reverse is true.

When I began collecting Lujere artifacts for the American Museum of Natural History at the end of my fieldwork, there were no fight shields available, not even new ones. However, the men of Wagu village just up the Sepik from the mouth of the Yellow had carved several new ones on speculation and brought them to the Yellow River Base Camp in several canoes in hopes of finding buyers. They were well crafted and similar in design to the Lujere shield and I bought several. But with Yellow River far off the tourist route and with no expat community, most had to be carried back to their canoes.

Slaying the Enemy

One hot, laconic afternoon when most of the villagers were working in the bush or living at a bush camp, Kaiera wandered down through the empty village to my 'ofis' screen room tent and began telling me stories and singing songs, actually more like chants, about former enemy attacks. His visits became frequent and as I recorded our interviews on my Uher tape recorder, he occasionally asked to hear a song and I would replay it to his smiling satisfaction. As usual, he voluntarily translated into Tok Pisin. Kaiera was an excellent teacher, a tutor really, and I his only student. He was especially proud of his paternal ancestor Komtri, a successful warrior. In Mauwi's continual war with Epai village (which the government called Wagu), a number of Lujere had been killed by the Epai warrior Aubou, who was greatly feared by the Mauwi villagers until Kaiera's ancestor Komtri killed him. Kaiera then sang the chant celebrating Komtri's killing of their fierce enemy. Among the Wakau men who had participated in raids, he said the only ones still alive were Aiyuk, Ukai, Leno, and Menetjua.

When the Lujere ambushed and killed an enemy, they cut off the left forearm and returned with it to their village for a celebration. It was always the left forearm; to take a man's right arm, his indispensable bow arm, would be an unnecessarily cruel, even dishonorable act, what we might call "overkill." As Kaiera told it, the rest of the body was left at the spot where it had fallen. Before leaving, the warrior chewed ginger and spit it on his dead foe. Then when his relatives came to carry the body away, they would not be angry and want revenge.

Once home, the trophy arm was heated over a fire with parts of a ginger plant and then held or hung aloft while the warriors paraded victoriously around it. Eventually the arm and the fingers were mutilated with many small cuts. The ritual of the heated ginger was to make the enemy forget about the murder and not pursue them, as were the songs the men sang as they celebrated the killing. Kaiera sang some of the songs—actually more like chants—for me: one ordered the enemy to "stay on your mountain just as the tree trunks do!" Another song was, "You people must stay on your mountain like the stones do. I killed a man, but you must stay there as the stones do!" I learned from others it was the one time they beat their big wooden slit-gongs in celebration of an enemy's death.

In Tipas I was told that when they killed one of their Sawiyano enemies across the Sepik, they too cut off the forearm as a trophy, cooked it, and hung it up. If a child did not grow well or a man or woman was sickly, they would be fed a bit of the cooked flesh of the victim's arm. But, my informant emphasized, 'lik lik,' a very tiny amount. It was the only Lujere example of ritual cannibalism I learned of other than associated with 'sanguma.'

According to Kaiera they called the cannibals across the Sepik the "Woniablu" who referred to them as the "Iwani," but their ethnographer Phillip Guddemi (1992: 35) wrote that they called the Lujere the "Sonamo." Regardless, Kaiera had another fight song for me about two cannibal men, Akaru and Imari, and he sung it so slowly it seemed more like a lullaby. Before I could query him, he launched into an intense description of how the cannibal men, women, and children all eat the victim including the blood. He claimed they brought their sago, 'tulip,' and 'apica' leaves with them to eat with their victims' raw flesh. What they didn't eat in situ, he added, they carried home.[10]

Kaiera had never seen his village attacked but his account was a detailed child's nightmare image of the cannibal enemies across the Sepik, undoubtedly echoing the grisly stories he heard from his parents and others growing up. I recall another informant telling me, as if it were yesterday, how the attacking cannibals would truss up a victim to a pole and carry them home like a pig to butcher and eat. In all the local cannibal accounts I heard, I could never distinguish between what was a nightmare fantasy or real. The last cannibal feast of Lujere villagers—a bloody massacre reported even in the *New York Times*—was just fifteen years before my fieldwork, so memories and fears of their anthropophagic neighbors were still acute and vivid. But the story Kaiera wanted to tell me just then was not about their cannibal enemies across the Sepik, but their fierce enemies in the sparsely occupied swamps sprawling westward across the Sand River whose lands bordered theirs. My genealogies are testimony to Tsila's raids with an occasional relative killed by a Tsila warrior: for example, Klowi's maternal grandfather's sister and her two children were attacked and killed in the bush, as was Oria and Nauwen's father's youngest brother.

The Tsila Village Massacre

While the Lujere's cannibal neighbors were literally bloodthirsty, the Lujere were bloodthirsty in a more symbolic sense but, in terms of delight in killing the enemy, just as spirited. The Iwani hamlets made a brutal attack on a hamlet of Tsila village west of the Sand River sometime between the devastating earthquake of September 20, 1935, and the end of World War II. Again Kaiera, one of my best informants for detailed historic events, gave the following account.

One time both the men of Iwani and Tsila were in the bush en route to raid each other. The Iwani men saw some of the Tsila men's tracks headed towards Iwani but said, "We won't worry. None of the women are in the village so they won't get killed," and proceeded to Tsila. When they neared the village, they stopped to put on their fight decorations

---

10. At contact, cannibalism was widely distributed throughout Melanesia. According to Knauft (1999, 103-04), on New Guinea it was found variously along the south and north coasts, the southeast highlands, the Sepik region, Strickland-Bosavi area, and the Star Mountains area. On the adjoining islands of the Bismarck Archipelago cannibalism occurred in the Admiralty Islands, the southern Massim area, northern New Britain, the Solomon Islands, northern New Hebrides, New Caledonia and, further to the east, Fiji. Obeyesekere's (2005) book *Cannibal Talk* is primarily on Polynesia and takes exception to colonial and popular accounts of cannibalism in that cultural area while not denying that it existed in places.

and then began yelling and loudly hitting the trunks of trees. Once decorated, the men's faces were somewhat concealed. The Tsila women thought that it was their men returning triumphantly home. Two old men who had remained in the village came out of the men's house and began to hit their 'garamuts'[11] to celebrate. One of the main Iwani men on the raid was called Biauwi; one of the main Tsila raiding men was Wauri. Tsila was filled with women waiting for the return of their men, but a third old man had remained inside the men's house.

As the Iwani men approached the village some of the women began to doubt if these men were their own warriors, then, as they came into view the men began singing their victory song. Then they ran to encircle the women to keep them from escaping. Kaiera told me that they murdered every single woman and child that was there. Some of the children were killed inside their houses. They killed the two old men beating the 'garamuts' and their bodies fell over their drums. Kaiera smiled at the thought of so many enemies being killed. The only person that the Iwani men did not find was the old man who had hidden himself in the men's house. Victorious, the Iwani men returned towards home.

The thwarted Tsila men were returning home when they heard some sounds in the forest. First, they thought it was cassowaries. Then they decided it was Iwani men striking the trunks of trees and realized their own village had been attacked. Afraid of what had happened to their families, the men began to run towards their village. When they saw the tracks of the Iwani men they knew their families had been murdered. Entering the village, they saw only dead bodies. One man on entering his house saw his murdered family and called out, "All of my children and wife are killed, every one of them; not a single one escaped."

They found the old man who was still alive, and he told them about the raid, how all of the women were outside waiting for their men so that none of them escaped. Finally, they buried all of their children and wives. Then Kaiera remembers this was before the 'kiaps' came and says that they built scaffolds for the dead, and then correcting himself a second time, said that would have been too much work so the men carried the dead into the houses and abandoned the village. The name of the hamlet where the massacre occurred was Woarani. The account ends with Kaiera adding that the men cut off the forearms of their victims and brought them back to Iwani as trophies for a celebration.

Although there are some logical glitches and questionable firsthand details in Kaiera's version of the tragic event, it was, at least to the Iwanis, a real event. Unfortunately, my interview with Wapia, the Tsila 'luluai,' was in January 1972 and it was the following March when Kaiera told me about the Iwani's massacre of the Tsila hamlet. Had the dates been reversed I could have questioned Wapia about the massacre's authenticity and his version of it, hopefully yielding significant new data.

Another bit of enemy fighting data I regret not having is Hodgekiss' patrol report when McCarthy met him at the Yellow River [Kogiabu] Base Camp in 1936. Regarding Hodgekiss, he wrote,

> His own arrival there hadn't been quite as peaceful as ours had been. He had turned up during a full-scale battle between the Mariyami [old Lujere village on lower Yellow

---

11. In my Wakau interview the Tsila 'luluai,' if you remember, told me they never had 'garamuts.'

River] and the [Abau] villages of the Sepik. Hodgkiss [*sic*] had simply announced that he intended to camp on their battle-ground and that he advised everybody to cease fire and go home. The warring sides watched Hodgkiss' [*sic*] party pitch its tents, then shrugged their shoulders and took his advice. (McCarthy 1963: 163)

Because McCarthy did not witness the "battle" (both he and Hodgkiss were new to the cultures), and Hodgekiss' patrol report cannot be located, I assume that McCarthy's account, written so many years later, misconstrued Hodgekiss' report. None of the relevant Sepik cultures engaged in face-to-face skirmishes as famously reported by Heider (1970), Gardner and Heider (1968), and Mathieson (1969) for the Dugan Dani in what was then West Irian. Lujere "warfare" was limited to clandestine raids—never traditional combat—so it is hard to visualize a "full-scale battle" on the "battle-ground" referred to. McCarthy's patrol report (1936) mentions nothing about the Lujere's fight style but emphasizes their peacefulness; nevertheless, enemy villages with whom they fatally feuded surrounded them.

The Yellow River Massacre

Unlike Kaiera's account of the Tsila massacre or McCarthy's alleged "battle," the following massacre account does not rely on one man's narrative but on a bulging file of documents labeled "Tribal Fighting—Lumi—Sepik District, 1956–1957" in the Australian National Archives and for years closed to public access.[12] On August 22, 1956, the front page of Sydney's *Morning Herald* carried the sensational three-column headline, "HEAD-HUNTERS KILL 28 IN NEW GUINEA MASSACRE" and, continuing the story on an inner page, couldn't resist the two column headline, "CHILDREN'S HEADS CHOPPED OFF."[13] The *New York Times* recognized the uniqueness of the story but relegated it to page four with a one-column heading, "28 SLAIN IN NEW

---

12. I initiated access to this voluminous file in May 1978 and received an apologetic reply in July 1979 that it was "completely within the closed period" and that "Special access is usually only given for projects of national importance or cases such as a minister of the Crown wishing to refresh his memory." Still, I was invited to apply for special access and did. In the meantime, when in Lumi I was able to make a chance perusal of Brightwell's report in 1982 from the recruiter Ron "Kit" Kitson's old copy, but with time only for a few cursory notes. (He was recruiting laborers in the Yellow River area when he learned of the massacre). After much correspondence the old-fashioned way, I was notified by a letter from the Director General of the Australian Archives dated 24 January 1984 that my request for special access to Commonwealth records relating to the Yellow River Massacre of 1956 had been granted and a copy of the file was sent to me. It was over a five-year wait, but the data were worth it, and I wish to again express my appreciation to the officers and staff of the Australian Archives. Without direct access to Brightwell's superb reports and the Archive's accumulated records regarding the Yellow River Massacre, I could not have told its story. Today the Archives' file on the Yellow River Massacre is in "open access."
13. Most of the data for this section are from the large file on the Yellow River massacres in the Australian National Archives (CRS A518 [Department of Territories] EU840/1/4, Tribal Fighting—Lumi District, 1956-1957). See especially Merton Brightwell's masterful (1957a)

GUINEA," while the *Los Angeles Times*, totally ignoring the event, observed on page sixteen that "French Slay 50 Algerian Rebels." Killing one's enemies is a universal phenomenon, but the New Guinea story had a difference, the victims—Lujere men, women, and children—were eaten.[14]

The following day the *New York Times* had another one-column story titled, "HEADHUNTER TOLL RISES" and reported that ten more bodies of "cannibal headhunters' victims" were found by a district officer in the Telefomin area in the mountains southwest of the earlier report. More germane was that the Lujere massacre also was having international political repercussions. The *Times* article concluded with the following paragraph:

> The Melbourne Herald assailed the United Nations Trusteeship Council today for advocating self-government for New Guinea in view of last week's massacre of twenty-eight natives by cannibal head-hunters. The newspaper branded as "nonsense" a recent 8-to-6 vote of the council calling on Australia to set a "target date for self-government of its trusteeship territory."[15]

Such politically motivated comments by the Australian press were a principal reason the Territory's government responded so quickly. The administrator, politically sensitive to criticism from the homeland and always strapped for money—thus especially parsimonious with "wild" uneconomic areas like the Upper Sepik—hurriedly responded with visits from high officials, augmenting the local field staff, sending additional patrol equipment, and establishing a new patrol post. A murder, especially lots of them, even without the added infamy of cannibal headhunters and international press coverage, was often a sure path to augmented government services.

The massacre, usually referred to as "the Yellow River massacre," occurred on a Sepik River sand bar on August 9, 1956. Two male survivors traveling via canoes and footpaths took a week to reach the nearest patrol post at Lumi to report the calamity. On August seventeenth, the Lumi ADO Frank Jones notified his superior, Sepik District Commissioner Tom Aitchison, that

> A report has reached this office [Lumi] of a massacre of South Wapi people by members of an uncontrolled people. . . . The massacre occurred approximately ten days ago, and the people murdered were from the villages of AMENI (TIPAS), IRIMUI, and PANYEWAI. These [Lujere] villages were recently censused by PO Oakes in an initial

---

"Report of Investigation of Massacre of Yellow River Natives," and his follow-up reports on seven short patrols (1957b) during the investigation of the massacre.

14. There is a huge bibliography on cannibalism; see especially Goldman (1999) for a critical view of the anthropological literature, Sanday's (1986) examination of cannibalism as a cultural system and Lindenbaum's (2004) review of the changing anthropological approaches to cannibalism. For a contrasting psychohistorical stance towards cannibalism see Sagan (1983), and Prinz (2007:173–214) for a philosopher's wide-ranging discussion of the concept of moral relativism and practices such as cannibalism, infanticide, human sacrifice, and honor killings. Not surprising, cannibalism is also a lucrative hook for some tourist tours; for instance, Mar (2016) describes a tour to the "Cannibal Caves" of Fiji.

15. "Head-Hunter Toll Rises," 1956, New York Times, August 23, 1956.

census.[16] . . . Of the men who came to report the matter, two had spear wounds which were healing. They reported that the killing was done by tomahawk and limbom spear only. . . AMENI canoes were used to help the raiders remove the dead, and the report states that the dead were eaten. Two bodies [actually five] were left at the point of the massacre, as the canoes were overloaded, but the heads were removed from these two bodies by the raiders. . . . It is expected that more information will be obtained in the next few days, but this basic information is forwarded by today's courier urgently, as it is felt this is probably the worst native massacre reported for some years.[17]

Later it was reported that the massacre messengers to Lumi carried bundles of 'pitpit' stems denoting the number of male and female deaths and, to authenticate their account, one finger each cut from two of the bodies left behind. ADO Jones's initial report to his district officer started a procession of memorandums, radiograms, and international phone calls up and down the chain of command from the ADOs of Lumi and Ambunti in the bush to Australia's capitol, Canberra, and the Minister of External Territories, Paul Hasluck.

PO George Oakes, who had made the first census patrol among the Lujere just weeks earlier, was again on patrol when his superior Frank Jones sent a message that he was to proceed to the village of Tipar (Tipas) in the South Wapei Division to join him (Oakes 1956b: 5). Hiking via Abrau and the Lujere villages of Nami and Naum, he liaised with Jones on the twenty-seventh. An ironic footnote to the Yellow River massacre is that an Australian woman went to jail because of it. Patricia Robertson, an expat Teletype operator in Port Moresby employed by the Department of Post and Telegraphs, illegally disclosed the massacre contents of the government's official radiogram to an Australian newspaper and was sentenced on a Friday, August 31 to three months in jail. As the Territory had no accommodation for a jailed White woman, she spent the weekend at the jailer's residence with him and his wife, until housing was readied at the Bomana Gaol (Brown 2012).

The government's reaction to the horrific event was, considering the challenging environmental circumstances, both administratively effective and compassionate to victims and slayers alike and makes a good case study of a colonial regime in critical action. Yes, compassion to the slayers up to a point, as the officers knew that the administration had not yet exerted political control over the killers who, simply put, were faithfully following the respected precepts of their ancestors: you kill us, we kill you and eat you.

---

16. See Oakes (1956). On the morning of June 26, 1956, Oakes carried out the census of the Pabei hamlets: Ina, Yegiratok and Ibigami. He adds, "The inhabitants of IRIMUI and PANYEWEI Hamlets and the AMENI Hamlets—TIPAR [Tipas] and ABIRAMI further to the south near the SEPIK River had also gathered at PABEI on their own volition" (Oakes 1956). They had heard he did not plan to visit them and were partially right. Oakes correctly believed that as Panyewei was situated on the south side of the Sepik it was not in the Lumi Sub District, but in the Ambunti Sub District.
17. Frank D. Jones, memorandum, August 17, 1956 (CRS A518 [Department of Territories], EU840/1/4, Tribal Fighting—Lumi—Sepik District, 1956–1957), Australian National Archives, Canberra.

By August twenty-first, DO Aitchison, keenly aware of the massacre, sent a two-page memorandum to his immediate superior in Port Moresby, A. A. Roberts, director of the Department of Native Affairs. It contained one new bit of information and the administration's plan of action:

> It now seems practically certain that the raiders were members of the IWAM people on the MAY RIVER.... A patrol lead by ADO Jones is leaving LUMI within the next two days to proceed to the scene of the alleged murders. He will be accompanied by 12 Police. Mr. PO Oakes who is at present on Patrol will join ADO Jones immediately on completion of this Patrol.[18] ADO Brightwell will proceed from Ambunti to arrive at the Sepik, Yellow River junction not later than the 29th August. He and ADO Jones will liaise. ADO Brightwell will take over the investigations. Should it be deemed necessary a further Patrol Officer will be made available to ADO Brightwell. [The trawler] M. V. THETIS is proceeding to Ambunti where it will be joined by myself [obviously flying to Ambunti], and proceed to the Yellow River Area. It is expected no further information will be available for ten days.[19]

Mert Brightwell was appointed Cadet Patrol Officer (CPO) in 1947 after having served in World War II as a Royal Australian Air Force (RAAF) wireless operator and air gunner. In 1954 he was posted to the Ambunti Patrol Post when it was still a part of the Angoram Sub-District and was knowledgeable of the Sepik area as far as the Dutch border. When the Ambunti Sub-District was created in June 1956, he was placed in charge. Bill Brown, a fellow officer, notes that

> He had wide shoulders, a barrel chest and no neck—attributes he credited to his long line of furniture-removalist forebears. But, despite his stature, Mert was light on his feet and the life of the party when he would sashay from behind a screen, straw boater in one hand, cane in the other, tap dancing through his own sung-rendition of *Father In His Life Was Ne'er A Quitter.* (Brown 2012)

On August twenty-seventh, Aitchison boarded the *Thetis* in Ambunti and proceeded upriver toward the massacre site. The following day the Ambunti workboat, *M. L. Mala*,

---

18. As noted earlier, George Oakes contacted me via email March 11, 2012, after reading my book, *The Bamboo Fire: Fieldwork with the New Guinea Wape*. To my happy surprise he wrote,

    > In 1956 I visited and censused every village in the Lumi area.... Six weeks after I had visited and censused the Yellow River people word got out that about 30 of them had been killed and eaten by May River people. I joined the ADO from Lumi and went down to the Sepik River where we met the ADO from Ambunti and did an initial investigation into the deaths and also travelled on the 40 ft. workboat [Mala] to Ambunti and back. Later a fellow Patrol Officer Tony Redwood, was given the job of rounding up the cannibals and caught over 40 of them. Tony Redwood is now living in retirement in Florida. [I was unsuccessful in contacting him.]

19. T. G. Aitchison, memorandum August 21, 1956 (CRS A518 [Department of Territories] EU840/1/4, Tribal Fighting—Lumi—Sepik District, 1956–1957), Australian National Archives, Canberra.

with a four-man boat crew likewise departed with Brightwell accompanied by seven police and a medical orderly. They passed the Ambunti-based labor recruiter R. C. Mackie moving downstream with forty-three new recruits and early in the afternoon overtook the *Thetis*. After a run of eleven hours, the *Mala* moored and after dark the *Thetis* arrived and moored astern the workboat. River fog delayed an early morning start but later they passed fifty men in their canoes taking crocodile skins to sell in Brugnowi, just above Ambunti. Stopping at Iniok village, Brightwell made inquiries about the massacre, and learned they had seen bodies floating down the river and that a neighboring group had told them about the attack. Now there was no doubt that the perpetrators were the May River Iwam.[20]

On August thirtieth, the river was again in heavy fog necessitating the *Mala* to reduce its speed until, near the mouth of the Frieda River, visibility was almost zero and they had to stop for a half hour before moving on. Eventually the *Mala* passed the mouth of the May River, and at 1:20 P.M. Brightwell saw the following chaotic scene:

> Abandoned canoes sited at left bank; went ashore and found four temporary houses of rude construction—there were string bags hanging with their contents and empty ones lying about. Several fishing nets were scattered about and washed sago. Fires had been used to burn pigs teeth ornaments and a human jaw bone was found in one fireplace. Several meat tins were scattered about. Broken bows and arrows were found and two spears and four fishing spears. One bush knife. There were razor blades, mirrors, and lap laps, trade paint, a rucksak and odd native ornaments broken and scattered about the place—some partially burned. Many lime gourds were lying about, all of them smashed. THETIS arrived at 1330 [1:30 P.M.] and D.O. Aitchison came ashore and inspected scene. Gear collected and put aboard THETIS. Obviously this is the camp of the Yellow River people and the scene of the massacre. (Brightwell 1957b: 2)

He was almost right. While it was the victims' camp and where the survivors expressed their grief afterwards, the massacre occurred across the river on a bloodied sandbar now swept clean of both blood and the few bodies left behind. Brightwell's ensuing investigation into the massacre was extensive, taking months to complete. By diligently interviewing the Lujere survivors and Iwan attackers he gradually grasped the nature of the murder plan, its execution, and its aftermath. It is one of the most complete and authoritative accounts of a large New Guinea cannibal massacre to be recorded.

Prelude to a Cannibal Feast

The Wanimoi villagers (Iwan language speakers), living in an uncontrolled area far upriver from the nearest patrol post in Ambunti, had little contact with administrative officers. According to them, Westerners had visited them only three times: by "Sepik Robbie" in the 1930s; in May 1942 by a party from the administration boat *Thetis*; and in April 1952 by the Ambunti-based labor recruiter R. C. Mackie. At some time beyond living

---

20. See Yoshida (1987) for data on the migration routes of the Iwam to the May River based on their myths, Schuster (1969) for a discussion and photos of their palm-leaf sheath paintings, and Rehburg (1974) for a description of their social structure.

memory, the Wanimoi people lived on the Sepik at the mouth of the May River then moved eighteen miles up the May apparently to distance themselves from their Lujere enemies. The animosity between the May River Iwan and the Sepik River Lujere was an ancient one. Brightwell reported that

> Each side recognises the other as a traditional enemy and each can give hazy and mutilated reports of past killings and retributions as related by the old men. Some stories relate as many as 12 people being killed at a time whilst other old men say they could not count how many had been killed in their lifetime as . . . the killings formed a continuous [back and forth] process. (Brightwell 1957: 2)

Brightwell's findings regarding the massacre begin with the 1950 killing by the Iwam of Nanau, a Lujere man of Tipas village. Revenge came late in 1953 when eleven Lujere men in two canoes from Tipas and Abirami villages, apparently looking for trouble, paddled down the Sepik and intercepted two Iwam canoes carrying three men and a married couple. They pursued both canoes but the one nearest the right bank escaped into the May River. The other canoe, cut off by the two Lujere canoes, was forced toward the left bank where the two Iwam men, Kwaso and Nabreik, scrambled ashore. Nabreik escaped into the bush but Kwaso, hindered by elephantiasis in his large swollen leg, was quickly run down by eight of the Lujere men and easily killed, his body pin-cushioned with arrows. Before they left, Kwaso's left forearm was severed and taken home to display in a victory celebration. But the price of victory meant it was now the Lujere's turn to fearfully wonder when and where the Iwam would attain their retributive homicide for Kwaso's death. Who the killer might be was easier to ascertain; Kwaso was from Wanimoi village and it would be his Wanimo mates who would avenge his murder.

In March 1954, labor recruiter Mackie in need of indentured workers, signed on twenty Iwam men to work copra at the Tomlabat Plantation on New Ireland, and eight Iwam men to work at the Numanuma Plantation on Bougainville, all for two-year contracts. Of these twenty-eight men, eleven were from Wanimoi village. During their contracts, the men did not leave the plantation and were housed and worked only with other Iwam men. Their lone opportunity to see the Territory's towns and have any outside contact with other islanders was during transport to and from the plantations. When their contracts were finished in April 1956, they were returned to Ambunti and then borrowed canoes from the ADO for the long paddle home up the Sepik and May Rivers. The station's ADO Brightwell later commented,

> It was remarked upon at the time these repatriates were landed at AMBUNTI how little they had learned whilst they were away at work—there was not one of them that spoke reasonable pidgin—the best was a broken rather crazy and rather unreliable grasp of the language whilst the majority of them could not talk even mutilated pidgin. It was remarkable that they had learned so little and regrettable that better use had not been made of the two years. . . . Apparently the IWAMS had little more contact with Administration and more advanced natives than they would have in their home village and the effect of these conditions was most apparent on their repatriation; they had learned little, some nothing. (Brightwell 1957a:10)

The returned Iwan laborers were some of the first to experience extended contact with the allegedly "civilizing" Australian colonial regime and Brightwell was eager to follow up on this meager beginning. As the *Mala* was then attached to the Ambunti Patrol Post, he decided to visit all of the upstream villages including Wanimoi. Brightwell was in Wanimoi village the fourth and fifth of May and asked the repatriated laborers to return the canoes he had loaned them. They arrived in Ambunti on the ninth of May with the borrowed canoes and all started home the following day except one young man, Nari.

Brightwell was selecting a man from each of the returnees' villages to live on the station for a time to improve their Tok Pisin, thus giving the administration someone to communicate with in every Iwan village. He planned to return each man with a 'tultul's hat as the administration's first step in exerting control over the Iwam. For Wanimoi village he had selected Nari who seemed to have some initiative and whose Tok Pisin, while not really intelligible, was the best of the village's eleven returnees. On May 29, an Iwam canoe voluntarily visited the station, the first time this had happened, and on June 2 Brightwell allowed Nari, although his Tok Pisin was not much improved, to return to home. He intended to give him a 'tultul' hat but the only ones he had were ridiculously large.

> Shortly after NARI arrived back at WANIMOI an old man named NANI, a clansman of the murdered KWASO, brought to the attention of the young men that KWASO'S death had not been avenged during their absence and it was about time something was done about it. NARI advised the villagers against this and suggested that they forget the whole thing. He told them that the YELLOW River people were more advanced than the IWAMs and that such action would make the Government cross and lead to trouble. . . . At this indication of non support NAHI turned on NARI and told him that he would never give up the obligation to avenge KWASO and that NARI knew nothing about Europeans, Government or Government officials; and if NARI knew so much about these things then he should go to AMBUNTI and have the Government Official adopt him and look after him. This remark caused NARI great shame and he made no further opposition and appears to have thought it necessary to do something to re-establish himself. (Brightwell 1957a: 4–5)

But an epidemic of whooping cough started moving up the Sepik and May Rivers resulting in five Wanimoi deaths, so it was not until the end of July that Nari broached his scheme that could regain his respect. His idea was to go to the Lujere and, under the deceitful guise of friendship, arrange a meeting to end the enmity between their villages, at which time they would avenge Kwaso's murder. His plot gathered enthusiasm and on August 4, two canoe loads of men, five in one canoe, and nine in the second, were on the Sepik headed upstream towards the Lujere when they eyed two Lujere canoes with twelve people aboard moving downstream.

> The YELLOW River canoes on sighting the IWAM canoes made off upstream but NARI called out to them in his pidgin that they need not be afraid or run away, that he wanted to shake hands with them and be friends. The use of pidgin overcame all the traditional distrust and the YELLOW River canoes came down to the sandbank where the IWAMS were waiting. NARI spoke pidgin to one of the YELLOW River

men named IROLAI saying that all the fighting of the past was finished and that they should be friends as they all had native officials and had progressed from the old conditions. Spears were broken as tokens of friendship, betel nut and food was exchanged and consumed. (Brightwell 1957a: 4)

They agreed that villagers from the two groups would meet together in five days after they all returned home at a particular sandbar chosen by the Lujere a bit downstream named Ausin. There they would feast each other to celebrate forsaking their old warring enmity for a new relationship of peaceful amity. Irolai in Tok Pisin told his new Iwam friend, Nari, that on the third day his Tipas group would go down to Ausin to make shelters and prepare food for the Iwam's arrival on the fifth day. On August 7, the Tipas villagers started down the Sepik arriving near the meeting sandbar on the eighth where they built shelters and began fishing and making sago. As newcomers arrived, their eventual group numbered forty-two people from four villages; the majority, twenty-eight, were from Tipas, eight were from Irimui village and three each from Abirami and Panawai villages. Of the forty-two, nine were children, the youngest a three-year-old boy from Abirami; the rest comprised eighteen females and fifteen males.

While the Lujere were busy preparing for the unprecedented peace parley, Nari was arranging revenge. At a meeting in one of Wanimoi's men's houses, Nari asked how many should they kill to avenge Kwaso's death, one or two? Some of the younger men thought one death was enough when the aged Nahi, strongly disagreeing, said, "I am against that, I want them all killed. They are always killing us off—if we only kill one or two they will continue to kill us—I want them all killed and that will finish the matter and we will be free from further attack" (Brightwell 1957a: 6). In the discussion following Nahi's suggestion of a mass slaughter, it was agreed that they would arrive a day early knowing that their true Tipas enemies would be there, in case on the fifth day, Lujere villagers they don't fight were present and they would be outnumbered. The plot was settled: they would arrive a day early and kill everyone. Nowhere in the record is it mentioned that a massacre would provide a generous feast for all the villagers.

The Massacre

On August 7, the Wanimoi villagers started down the May River in twelve canoes with their prepared food. They numbered forty-four men, and two aged women, one of whom was Kwasho's mother, apparently eager to witness the gory revenge for her son's murder. Before they got underway on the morning of the ninth for the nearby Ausin sandbar and the Lujere's rendezvous with death, old Nami gathered the group. He told them he would give the signal to commence killing by saying to Nakuno, "Nakuno, I want to eat sago now."

It was still early morning and the Lujere were busy with food preparations when the twelve Iwam canoes slid into view downriver, canoes that were not expected until the following day. They were definitely surprised and probably embarrassed as their food for the celebration was not ready. The Lujere camp was on the north bank, but the Iwam grounded their twelve canoes on a sandbar just across from them. Going ashore with some of their provisions, they called across the sprawling Sepik to their new friends to come over and shake hands. Completely trusting, without weapons, they—with the exception of a young wife and two young girls—complied; men, women, and children climbed into the long, narrow, and tippy canoes that standing men adroitly paddled to the Iwam's sandbar killing field. Nari greeted them in Tok Pisin extolling their newfound friendship and, to memorialize their goodwill to one another, spears were broken and lime gourds smashed.

> NAMI then told NARI and the others to pair off with the YELLOW River men—but did not mention the women and children. The YELLOW Rivers did not have food with them so they were taken by their IWAM partners and provided with food. Many of the YELLOW River people were sitting in the IWAM canoes with their IWAM partners attending to them. Food was distributed to the YELLOW River men who shared it out to their women. (Brightwell 1957a: 7)

Naini, a married Wanimoi man with two wives, also gave some of the Lujere women sago and fish, six of whom with two of the children then returned to the Lujere camp. Their rationale is unknown but whatever it was, it saved their lives. The two aged Iwam women fraternized with the remaining Lujere women and, if ten of the fifteen Lujere men were in a canoe being served by their Iwam host, that left thirty-four Iwam men standing around free to attack the remaining thirty-four Lujere of which only five were men. While the food was being distributed, Woripa, the only man from Panawai and a boy from Tipas got into a canoe and pulled away upstream to bring back some Lujere men who were working in an area called O'gwibira and missing out on the big occasion. Seeing this, Nari told his guest Oralai to call them back as their leaving might make the Iwam suspicious or afraid, as indeed it had. Oralai innocently complied and the two returned to the sandbar and certain death. The Iwam, now convinced that other Lujere men were nearby, felt compelled to hasten their attack.

While the former enemies were enjoying the improvised brotherhood feast in comparative quiet as so few Iwam knew Tok Pisin, the Iwam alone knew that they were actually dining with their next meal. Then old Nami, speaking in Iwam, spoke the arranged signal, "Nakuno I want to eat sago now." Nakuno did not reply but immediately speared his partner Paidei, a young single man from Irimui; Nari without a pause ran a spear into his alleged friend Irolai killing him, and N'habe, after spearing Abai of Abirami, cut off his head. The terrified screams of unarmed men, women and children being chased, caught, speared, and axed to death carried easily across the Sepik and the women and children in the Lujere camp fled in terror into the bush, sure they would be next. On the bloodied sandbar, victims tried vainly to escape the slaughter by running into the tall grass only to be speared or axed from behind. As the victims one by one fell dead or dying, three fell into the river and their bodies were swept away. Tipas, with the most people present, suffered the most casualties with eighteen dead. Wolali, his wife, and his seven-year-old son were all killed, as was Nawepogo and his young wife. Taigwe of Tipas, who carried the news of the massacre to Lumi, dashed safely into the bush with only a spear wound to his arm, but both his wife and two young daughters were killed and carried away. There were only two other survivors of the massacre, both agile youths of Tipas: Wunibei, who like Taigwe escaped death with just an arm wound but whose father was killed; and Youneri, the only survivor who miraculously vanished into the tall grass unscathed. The Iwam's twenty-nine victims numbered thirteen women, twelve men, and four young boys, including the three-year-old.

The attackers, having killed every enemy in sight and still spooked by Woripa's earlier starting upstream, were anxious to be gone before any Lujere canoes would appear and, seeing evidence of the attack, try to overtake them. The Iwam readied their twelve canoes and seized two of the canoes the unsuspecting Lujere had used to cross the river, like proverbial lambs led to slaughter. They quickly loaded eighteen of the bloody bodies lying about as well as two heads from the corpses left behind.[21] As a witness to the treacherous carnage, Masio, Kwaso's old mother, must have felt triumphantly revenged for her son's death as she settled into a departing canoe. Leaving at top speed they vigorously pulled their canoes downstream to the May for the eighteen-mile row upstream, arriving at Wanimoi village about 5:00, well before dark. After the Lujere bodies were lined on the ground outside one of the men's houses, the village drum was sounded, and the women and children who missed the murderous adventure came to admire the trophies. The bodies were first decapitated then butchered into portions and distributed to all the villagers to consume at their leisure. Unlike the Aztec, here the eating of human flesh was a feast, not a sacrifice to seek communion with the gods (Sahlins 1978).

The heads were collected and carried up into the men's house where they were cooked, and the sacred flutes blown for a village-wide celebration. Eventually the men ate the flesh from the heads and the initial celebration finally ended at dawn. Later the skulls were hung in the open to dry and then individually decorated by the killer.[22]

Once the Iwam were clearly out of the vicinity of the massacre, two of the Tipas females from the Lujere camp—Aiyenali, about twelve years old, and Yegei, the young wife of the murdered Wariso—canoed across and joined Wunibei to survey the tragedy. This would have been an especially horrific experience for Yegei. Of the five bodies the Iwam left on the bloody sandbar, one was her husband, Wariso, still wearing his blood-soaked checked shirt and black shorts. Brightwell's report notes that "WARISO had an axe wound through the back of his neck but had died of a spear wound which was not noticed because he was wearing a shirt. The axe wound was inflicted later by MOM" (Brightwell 1957a: 8). Also lying among the murdered was Yegei's mother-in-law—Wariso's mother Owinawaki—who "had a spear wound just below the ribs through stomach" (Brightwell 1957a: 8). The three other sandbar casualties were the speared and beheaded bodies of Abai and Palei and the body of an old woman, Yemiei, who had been speared through the chest and had an axe wound on her back.

---

21. Rune Paulsen who lived with the May River Iwam for two years in the late 1980s, says the Iwam did not take prisoners but after a massacre, "If the river and canoes were located nearby they would carry all the corpses back to their village" and their extensive food taboos were lifted for a cannibal feast. "Everybody was allowed to eat food from everybody else and that people even took food from each others mouths—a thing which is unthinkable at all other times" (Paulsen 2003: 44). Cannibalism, he writes, was "a very complex and large-scale ritual extending over several weeks" (Paulsen 2003: 45).
22. See Van Baal (1966: 745–51) for a more detailed grisly comparative account of a head-hunting massacre, home coming "merry-making," and cannibalism among the Marind-Anim of the southeast coastal section of Irian Jaya's Merauke district. It is ironic that Arens' (1979) book calling cannibalism a "myth" was published so near the time it was still a fact in New Guinea.

Yegei and Aiyenali canoed back to the Lujere camp where they joined the other women and girls in breaking, smashing, scattering, and burning their possessions in a frenzy of hysterical grief, creating the chaotic scene Brightwell witnessed. As it was still early in the day, the thirteen survivors eventually started upriver to O'gwaibira where the Lujere men who missed the deadly celebration were working. Two of the men there retrieved the bodies of Yegei's husband and his mother and placed them in a house in O'gwaibira. The other three bodies left on the killing sands were carried away by the rising river. Five days later Abai's headless torso was lifted from the Sepik 175 miles downstream.

The Aftermath

Once Brightwell had located the site of the massacre on August 13, inspected it with the District Officer, and removed evidence to the *Thetis*, his investigation of the incident continued. The following morning there again was heavy fog. By nine-fifty when the *Thetis* with DO Aitchison had not arrived, Brightwell returned downstream to find the *Thetis* stuck on a sandbank. After lashing the *Mala* to the side of the *Thetis*, with all engines in reverse, the *Thetis* was liberated and the DO decided to return to the scene of the massacre. Brightwell continued upstream to Tipas, home of some of the massacre survivors whom he wanted to interview as possible witnesses, and where, as prearranged, he met Lumi's ADO Jones and PO Oakes.

> Remained overnight and had general discussions on ADO Lumi's investigations and enquiries. Decided to move Yellow River witness[es] down to massacre site and carry out investigation on the spot. . .0630 [6:30 A.M.] left Tipar [Tipas] with ADO Jones and PO Oakes and Yellow River survivors of massacre. . .[At] O'GWAIBIRA [the officers] went ashore and inspected the bodies of WARISO and OWINAWAKI [killed in the massacre] and had them identified.[23] . . . 1110 [11:10 A.M.] came upon THETIS moored in stream just below massacre site. Carried out investigating of happening preceeding [sic] and at time of massacre in the YELLOW River camp—a very poor account given by the survivors—their story changes and they do not seem to be very clear on rather obvious points—there is also some difference in their accounts of movements. Will make very poor witnesses. Remained with THETIS overnight. General discussion with District Officer [Aitchison], ADO Lumi [Jones] and self. THETIS damaged and will return to AMBUNTI with District Officer. . . ADO Jones broke up his party—some to return overland to LUMI and others to come to AMBUNTI on MALA. (Brightwell 1957a: 2–3)

---

23. George Oaks, who is retired and living in Australia, sent me via email two photos from August 1956 from "the trip to check on the cannibals with Frank [Jones] and Mert [Brightwell]. (These two unfortunately passed away years ago). As a matter of interest, the Wewak District Officer . . . was Tom Aitchison who had been a Patrol Officer in the Sepik for several years before the war and I think then visited the Yellow River area. He had been patrolling over quite a bit of NG by 1956—he retired shortly after." The photos were one of the two bodies brought to O'gwaibira after the massacre, now gutless and partially mummified, and a photo of the small workboat *Mala* approaching to pick up Oakes and Jones. (Email June 19, 2012, from George Oaks to author.)

By September fourth, Brightwell was back in Ambunti—but not for long, as his next task was to apprehend some of the eight repatriated laborers involved in the massacre to get their account of the attack and, through them, exercise influence on bringing in the other offenders to stand trial for murder. He sent a message that the ex-laborers should meet him at a designated site but, while about a dozen of the Wanimoi men came, only a few of the ex-laborers appeared. Still, his discussion with them about the massacre was gratifying as they openly admitted to it. He first learned that "The massacre was deliberately planned and cleverly executed with nobody in opposition to it" (Brightwell 1957a: 4). The following morning, he proceeded up the May in the *Mala* to Wanimo village with several of the Wanimoi men aboard.

> As arranged yesterday the skulls of the victims were produced and handed over. Also as arranged yesterday five of the repatriated labourers who are involved in the massacre prepared to proceed to AMBUNTI. At the last moment one of them was a little reluctant and it was necessary to raise the voice and firm the features in ordering him aboard whereupon he complied. . . . Two drums of fuel were left at WANIMOI village as a reminder of the Government and also to serve as an indicator of their attitude towards it—should the drums be destroyed, looked after as instructed, or ignored. . .The people did not run away when the patrol entered the village but gathered around. Their attitude was quite good but every precaution was taken. There was some crying and pleading by the women and old men about taking the five repats and if the matter had been unduly prolonged difficulties would have arisen. (Brightwell 1957a: 4–5)

The Territory's administrator, Brigadier General D. M. Cleland in Port Moresby, was kept updated on the investigation by DO Aitchison and sent several radiograms regarding the massacre to his superior in Canberra, the Minister of the Department of Territories, Paul Hasluck. Administrator Cleland's August 21 radiogram to Minister Hasluck, which contained part of DO Aitchison's action plan, had an interesting added typed note: "Rec'd by phone from Mr. McCarthy 8:30 pm 21.8.56."[24] McCarthy had made a substantive evening phone call regarding the massacre to the Minister's Canberra office. Once again, Keith McCarthy, now executive officer in the Department of the Administrator, had a tangential role in the Lujeres' affairs. By September 3, some of the action plan was being realized as described in Director of Native Affairs Roberts's dispatch to the administrator:

> Following upon my earlier discussion with Your Honour, I left for the Sepik District on Thursday, 23rd August, 1956, and in conjunction with the District Officer [Aitchison] visited AMBUNTI and the May River area. . . Patrols from LUMI by road [ADO Jones] and AMBUNTI by river [ADO Brightwell] have met at the YELLOW River approximately 60 miles upstream from the May River Junction. The District Officer [Aitchison] has also taken M.V. 'THETIS' to the area and is in radio communication. He will advise what will be the final course of action after investigation,

---

24. Copy of Administrator Cleland's radiogram to Minister Hasluck, August 21,1956. (CRS A518 EU840/1/4, Tribal Fighting—Lumi—Sepik District, 1956-1957), Australian National Archives, Canberra.

on the spot, where the murders occurred. . . . I do not anticipate any real result for at least one month.[25]

Apparently, Director Roberts flew to Wewak, was joined by Aitcheson, and flew on to Ambunti where they met with ADC Brightwell. The three men made an extensive aerial reconnaissance over the May River area to estimate the population and to hunt for an aerodrome site for a possible new patrol post to deal with the crisis. They observed seven village groups all in swampy country on the lower May, some miles in from the Sepik River. Women and children were seen in the villages and men in their canoes, but no possible site for even a small airfield was seen. The officers' aerial patrol was simple and easy; the hard work for coming to grips with the massacre was now on the land and rivers. Only there did the details of the massacre come into focus.

By October 16, Administrator Cleland had enough information from the field investigators that he sent a two-page foolscap report to the Department of Territories in Canberra for Minister Hasluck's attention. In it he noted that an experienced patrol officer, A. L. Redwood, had been posted to assist Brightwell in the establishment of a base camp on the May River twenty-one miles from its mouth and in the capture of the men still at large. Twelve additional police, including a sergeant and a lance corporal, were also assigned to assist in an unrelenting program of patrol work to continue until all who had killed during the massacre were apprehended. To facilitate the patrols, two outboard motors suitable for canoe patrolling in the Sepik and May River backwaters and swamp canals were delivered to Ambunti. Already, the administrator noted, the men's vigorous investigations were paying off.

> At Wanimoi Village eighteen (18) freshly decorated human skulls were recovered by Assistant District Officer Brightwell, and these were claimed by the people of Wanimoi . . . to be the skulls of some of the victims of the attack on the Yellow River people. Five of the Iwam Group who took part in the August attack have been apprehended, and are at present at Ambunti.[26]

Most of the attackers had disappeared into the May River swamps and it was a tedious and lengthy project rounding them up to stand trial. But by November 24, Brightwell, who was at the May River Base Camp, reported in a radio conversation with the DO that only sixteen of the murderers were still at large, as were seven uncontacted witnesses. Throughout the rounding up of the attackers, as well as the Lujere and Iwam witnesses, the administration showed concern for the villages losing many residents and ensured that children with absent parents were cared for. Because the Iwam had actively predacious enemies, the Mianmin, on the upper May River, one of the reasons for the new May River Base Camp was to protect the women and children of Wanimoi village,

---

25. A. A. Roberts dispatch to the Administrator, September 3, 1956. (CRS A518 EU840/1/4, Tribal Fighting—Lumi—Sepik District, 1956–1957), Australian National Archives, Canberra.
26. Administrator Cleland's report for Minister Hasluck's attention, "May River Patrols—Sepik District," October 16, 1956. (CRS A518 EU840/1/4, Tribal Fighting—Lumi—Sepik District, 1956–1957), Australian National Archives, Canberra.

now devoid of warriors, from Mianmin attacks. Another reason was to send a strong message to the Iwam that their raids against the Lujere had to stop.

While there could be no trial without the accused, the Lujere witnesses were essential for the State to make its case. On the fifteenth of November, Brightwell was in Tipas and sent out a message that all the survivors of the massacre should meet with him the next day. Of course, little happens that quickly in New Guinea and only a handful appeared. He did choose three interpreters who could translate Namia to Tok Pisin for the court.

> 17th November. Remained at TIPAR [Tipas] and interviewed all survivors of the massacre selecting six as the best possible witnesses. They are very difficult as witness[es] are bound to give much trouble in the box. They will return to AMBUNTI in MALA. 18th November. . . brought the following Yellow River witnesses; females AIYENALI, YEGIEI and ARUKOMIE, and males TAIGWE, WUNIBEI and YOUNERI. Interpreters SAMBEN, MINIA, and AMI – not a very bright lot but about the best available. (Brightwell 1957b: 7)

That night they stayed at the base camp and the following day PO Redwood returned with four more prisoners and the last of the attackers was caught on December 1. With all the parties to the case eventually in Wewak, the lower court hearing against the Wanimoi village men was heard in January and the Supreme Court Hearing was heard in February. The result was predictable. An International Telegram was sent to Canberra from the administrator on February 11 with the fateful outcome: "FORTY NATIVES FOUND GUILTY [in] WEWAK OF WILFUL MURDER BY MR JUSTICE GORE AND DEATH SENTENCE RECORDED."[27]

The forty death sentences for the Lujere's mass murderers were later commuted to seven years in prison. The post-war application of law in the Territory was changing. In earlier times seven Kimindimbit men from the central Sepik who took the heads of twenty enemy villagers were hung at Ambunti on separate gallows until dead.[28]

But what about the six Lujere witnesses and three interpreters who had been commandeered by the administration in November? After being away from their families for over three months, they finally returned to Tipas accompanied by Brightwell on March 8.

> The witnesses and interpreters returned home. The 18 skulls of the victims of the massacre which had been recovered from WANIMOI were handed over to the villagers

---

27. Australian Archives ACT CRS A518 Item EU840/1/4. Canberra.
28. Nari, who had originally been groomed for a local leadership role but became one of the massacre's ringleaders, reappears in a 1969 patrol report of the Sepik-May Census Division by ADO M. E. Tomlinson (1969). Having served his sentence and returned home, Nari is mentioned in Tomlinson's report under the section on "Leadership" as "pro Administration," apparently more for his name recognition than leadership skills. Hence,

    > He has made unsuccessful attempts at growing rice in the IEMOMBUI area and is now believed to be growing coffee in conjunction with people in the Lumi Sub-district. NARI is noted in his area for his pugnacious attitude towards outsiders, but otherwise has no real influence over his people. (Australian Archives ACT A518 Item EU840/14. Canberra: 7)

for burial. Those men who were responsible for the killing of KWASO of WANIMOI were told that no action would be taken against them under the circumstances – but no future killings would be tolerated. (Brightwell 1957b: 9)

Brightwell had learned of two other skulls of Tipas villagers killed by the Wanimoi men some years before and these too he collected, along with several human teeth bracelets from the victims of the recent massacre and returned them to the village. Finally, he returned Kwaso's skull to his Wanimoi kin.[29] Wanimoi village, a primal nemesis of the Lujere, was no longer a threat. With its warriors in prison the two big men's houses looked abandoned and, with so many of the prisoners' families gone to live with relatives, the village now was more dead than alive. The colonial rule of the 'kiap' was altering everyday life in multiple ways. For one, the Iwam's ancient tradition of a cannibal massacre and feast seemed to be over. But not for the bordering Mianmin.

In December 1956, they attacked the Atbalmin, killed and ate eighteen men, women, and children, and carried off two young women. The killers, like the Iwam, were arduously tracked down, captured and tried. Then in 1957, Mianmin men attacked a village near the May River Patrol Post. The new station that was supposed to deter the Mianmin as well as the Iwam was not doing the job.

> The Mianmin—garbed only in narrow cane waist bands, 15 centimetre working-dress phallocrypts, testicles in the breeze—considered the May River people to be underclad "bush kanakas"—their attire being a small marine shell perched snail-like on the end of the penis. Some six months after [Patrol Officer] Aisbett's patrol had passed through [from Telefomin to May River] a group of Mianmins made the next foray, selecting the small settlement of Suwana in the Abaru group near May River Patrol Post. . . . The Miamin surrounded the village at dawn, killed three men and one woman, cut up the bodies and set off for home with seven female captives and butchered bodies—leaving only the heads and entrails behind. One of those women had difficulty keeping up so she was killed and parts of her body taken to be eaten. (Brown 2012)

One of the abducted women escaped and reported the raid to the OIC at May River Patrol Post, Jack Mater, who, along with PO Jim Fenton from Telefomin, an interpreter, and police, sped up the May in outboard-motor-powered canoes.[30] Entering the rugged hills, on the patrol's fourteenth day they reached the Mianmin village and surrounded it. At dawn they captured the killers without incident.[31] Among the police, Constable

---

29. Brightwell's next assignment was to the Okapa Subdistrict in the Eastern Highlands. Here again he was involved with cannibalism—not the exocannibalism of the Iwam, but the endocannibalism of the Fore related to the famous neurological disease of kuru (Glasse 1969:18; Lindenbaum 2013). For a zoologist's recent, if often cheeky, review of the research on kuru and other transmissible spongiform encephalopathies, as well as a probing discussion of cannibalism across natural species, see Schutt (2017).
30. For a fuller account of this raid and its aftermath see Gardner (1999: 31–34) who quotes extensively from Mater's patrol report.
31. See Dornstreich and Morren (1974), who both did field work in the Sepik Basin, for a careful examination of the nutritional value of cannibalism. Morren (1986) did fieldwork with the

Augwi alone arrested nine of the fifteen murderers. In an adventuresome life of extremes, in 1953 Augwi had been in London as part of the Territory's contingent for the coronation of Queen Elizabeth. While these clashes indicated that cannibal strife remained rife among some of the Upper Sepik societies, at least for the Lujere it had come to an end.

Mianmin, raiders of the Iwam. For an authoritative discussion of the history and regional systems of the Mountain Ok or "Min" who reside in the central mountains above the Iwam, see Jorgensen (1996).

CHAPTER TEN

Wakau Village

> *One comes across actual villages with houses built in groups in a narrow area. There are special houses for the men and they are not built in the unskilled manner.*
> Richard Thurnwald (1914: 347)

> *For our house is our corner of the world.*
> Gaston Bachelard (1964: 4)

Wakau Local History

According to local belief, Wakau village had its origins atop Mauwi hill when a group decided to move down to the rise of land called *wakau* just north of the 'kunai' plain, hence the village's name. At some point, the villagers moved southwest across the Sand River to the area where the 'kiap' first visited Wakau in 1956 and, since a census was taken it was recognized as a component, albeit minuscule, of the Territory of Papua and New Guinea. Then, sometime between when the Sola Fida missionaries arrived the middle of 1958, built their mission station and airstrip, and departed in December 1959, the Wakau villagers returned to their old village site just east of the Sand River where I lived with them. Arakwake told me it was he who initiated the move. He first learned of the mission's arrival when walking back home from Lumi after returning from Dylup Plantation[1] as an

---

1. Dylup Plantation, located near Madang, contains 2,300 hectares and was established in 1904 by the German Niugini Company. Later it became a copra plantation where many Sepik men like Arakwaki were indentured workers. More recently the old coconut trees are used to make furniture and the Madang provincial government has purchased the property for a vocational school. See http://asopa.typepad.com/asopa_people/2010/10/big-future-for-coconut-timber-in-png.html (accessed May 18, 2016).

indentured worker. After overnight stops in Kamnum and Wokien villages, he first heard about the new missionary 'masta' in Edwaki.[2] Back in his village across the Sand River, many were dying of 'sotwin,' probably pneumonia or flu, but it was blamed on 'sanguma' and Arakwaki decided to move back to Wakau's original site. Some of the young men who came with him were Eine, Yaope's and Tsaime's fathers, and Kwoien. The site had returned to forest, but the towering old coconuts were still there. They cleared the brush, built houses and gradually the rest of the villagers joined them. And that is where I found them in 1971 (see fig. 10).

Figure 10. Aerial view of Wakau village, looking north.

When an ethnologist takes the audacious step to move into a strange village to learn a new way of life, the ardent hope is that the choice of village was a wise one. With no control over how one's education will evolve, the personal charge is to keep wholly open to people, ideas, and events while relentlessly trying to document a record of it

---

2. There is the problem, however, that PO Treutlein (1962) shows Wakau on his 1962 patrol map as still west of the Sand. Although his patrol path shows him closely circling Wakau, which is odd, rather than passing through it as with the other villages, he explicitly notes, "WAKAU: This village used to be censused separately also, is now a part of IWANI." (1962: 25). Therefore, he took a census of the Wakau villagers at Iwani just as Oakes did in 1956. So, it is doubtful that Treutlein visited Wakau or even knew that it had moved its location. Tellingly, there is no indication in his day-by-day patrol diary regarding his walk from Aiendami village to Iwani that he and his patrol crossed the Sand River *twice*, a messy wet necessity, to visit the Wakau on his map.

all. Ethnographic fieldwork is an enveloping experience of humble surrender, giddy exhilaration, and restless trepidation like no other I know. It continues 24/7 from the day one moves into a village, until the day you move out.³ Fortunately, Wakau village was an excellent choice with the exception that I could not communicate with the women. Most villagers grasped the nature of my work and generally tolerated—even at times encouraged—my eccentric questioning and occasional imprudent intrusion into local affairs. But there were boundaries. Some were those they imposed on themselves, like most of the women all in cloth—but still topless--after I moved in. I had lived in Wakau almost four months before I started seeing many women in their traditional string skirts or, sporadically, just with a pubic covering (fig. 11). I wrote in my notebook, "I'm just part of the scenery at last!"

Figure 11. Mothers visiting at Oria's wife's house, across from my office. Kwoien's wife Wariyeh with her newborn son is on the right.

---

3. But living alone in a radically different alien culture can definitely challenge your senses. How else can one account for the following amazing—weird, really—comment I found in one of my field notebooks?

> Marvelous dinner of lamb chops, thyme rice, succotash, and beer, then finished Maugham's *Cakes and Ale*. The most civilized fun evening I've had since coming to N. G.! Enchanting book. (NB #24)

It also indicates how deep the "field" experience can become as a life zone in and of itself when working solo.

Only once during my stay did they impose a boundary on me of which I was aware. While attending a nighttime funeral wake at the very end of my fieldwork, I was abruptly asked to leave the house of mourning. The ancient custom of many mourning nude as an expression of their sorrow was inhibiting some of the visiting women—embarrassed by the White man's presence—from fully expressing their grief. I, chagrined and internally grumbling, quietly departed.[4]

Cultural Impact of the Mission

Although the Wakau villagers appreciated the mission's small trade store for essentials like salt, and a mother with a critically sick baby knew that Rosemary's help was available, overall, my neighbors paid little heed to the mission's presence. It also appeared that the disregard was mutual, not in any hostile sense, but I had the distinct impression that the mission viewed the Iwani hamlets as especially Satanic-riven and even frightening places compared to the villages where some had accepted their Christian teachings. Wakau had no committed Christians during my stay and until I moved into the village, a maternal and infant welfare nurse had never visited. They did not visit, I was told, because of fear after hearing "such horrible stories about the place"—stories of 'sanguma' atrocities—repeated by their villager friends near the mission. In reference to the CMML Mission's influence among the Lujere, ADC A. S Wright commented, "They do not appear to have made a great impact on the spiritual beliefs of the people" (Wafingian 1972).

A Pragmatic People

One of my first research tasks was to make a map and census of the village. It took me two days, and I had no sooner completed it than there were important changes. It was my first indication—although I did not know it then—of the suppleness of Lujere society and culture. I gradually learned it was a society very unlike the Wape, where one's behavior and choices were strongly constricted by cultural customs. Instead of being driven by cultural fiat, Lujere customs were guidelines indicating preferred ways to do things while acknowledging that extenuating circumstances were important considerations that determined what actually happened. This was a society where the exigencies of life, not customary principles, usually took precedence. During my fieldwork, over and over again, I recognized the Lujere inclination to prioritize practice over principle. Related to this generally practical approach to life, they were disinclined towards altered states of consciousness; trance was not practiced, and hallucinogens and alcohol were unknown. Many villagers, however, were avid chewers of betel nut, a mild stimulant comparable to caffeine.

Overall, Lujere culture also appeared to have very little formal learning like among the Iatmul, where men's lengthy ritual chants were explicitly taught. But just as Lujere children picked up their native language from hearing it, they mostly picked up the gendered

---

4. At the time it never occurred to me that if I had removed my shorts and tee-shirt, I may have had the moral right to have stayed.

skills they needed by accompanying their parents and observing them. The only specialists in Wakau were Klowi, the licensed shotgun owner, who had learned to use the gun for hunting by trial and error, and the *imoulu* healers who, after their initial initiation as *nakwolu*, already knew their overt healing moves by watching other *imoulu* curing their neighbors as well as themselves since childhood.[5]

It was not that the Lujere did not have traditions, but theirs were more open and pragmatically situated with seemingly more choices than I was accustomed to, having lived in two much more tightly organized New Guinea societies—that is, the Wape and Iatmul. In the Iatmul village of Tambunam, the women's only path through the village, for example, was behind the houses along the forest and latrines; the men's path was in front of the houses and along the always-interesting Sepik River where the canoes were beached and visitors arrived and departed. It was the difference between an urban alleyway and a grand boulevard. Women could walk down to the river but had to return to their path to traverse the village. By comparison, in Wakau a person, female or male, could walk anywhere irrespective of gender; to an outsider like myself the Lujere appeared to have a relatively relaxed approach to life. For certain, they were easier to live among than the Taute Wape. In one early letter to a friend, I described them as "loose, wicked, and warm." My view of Lujere culture was initially influenced by the continual movement of villagers in and out of the village, seemingly at will. The Taute villagers I knew so well were like most peasants everywhere; regardless of where they were during the day, in the evening they came home to supper and bed. The Lujere, however, were much more peripatetic, they could walk away from the village to a forest camp and stay for days, weeks or even months at a time.[6]

This fluidity in their residential patterns seemed to reverberate into other aspects of their behavior. Attention could wane when I began going for detailed data on, for example, kin terms, descent lines, land tenure, inheritance, and marriage. This part of the research was often challenging and frustrating, as few men cared much about this kind of knowledge. Unless a man knew his father's and mother's parents personally, he might not know their names, and this in a culture that casually called relatives by their given name, not a kinship term. A Wape man would suddenly leave the group in abject shame if he inadvertently uttered a relatives' tabooed name; a Lujere man would not. There were no similar naming taboos. Nor was Lujere society like that of the Iatmul, with deep genealogies and ritual experts who took pleasure in teaching a culturally naive outsider. While the Lujere were *ideologically* patrilineal, maternal ties might take precedence if the situation warranted. What mattered to my Wakau friends was not a life that slavishly followed cultural precepts, but an emphasis on the present and tomorrow in terms of a practical, workable existence.[7] To me, at least, that seemed to be the kind of society their ancestors—and the environment—had created for them.

---

5. Their therapeutic techniques are described in chapter 18.
6. This is a characteristic of some of the societies of the Upper Sepik Basin. For example, Jorgensen writes of the Mountain Ok speakers in the mountains of the Upper Sepik, "Even where there are permanent villages, people commonly have alternate residences to which they move for longer or shorter periods of time" (Jorgensen 1996: 192).
7. In reading an essay by Margaret McArthur about the Kunimaipa of the Goilala Subdistrict north of Port Moresby after finishing this section, I empathized with her comment: "I do not know why these people are prepared to take for granted many features of the human

British anthropologist Phyllis Kaberry, who did pioneer fieldwork on the middle Sepik with the Abelam in 1939–40, has commented on what she calls "The Plasticity of New Guinea Kinship." She specifically calls attention to publications since World War II noting, "many writers have emphasized the *flexibility* [my emphasis] with which rules of recruitment to kin and local groups are applied in many New Guinea Societies" (Kaberry 1967: 106). She makes the further point that this kind of plasticity or flexibility was also a characteristic of prewar studies, particularly referencing patrilineal descent, and cites as examples two Sepik societies, the Arapesh (Mead 1947: 182) and the Abelam (Kaberry 1941–42: 88–9). Lujere society, as shown in "Clanship, Kinship, and Marriage" in chapter 12, is but another more recent example.[8]

Cultural Changes Since Robinson's and McCarthy's Patrols

Lujere villages in the 1970s, especially those like Wakau with no colonial structures such as an aid post or church, looked outwardly much the same as they had when Robinson and McCarthy made their pioneering patrol reports in the 1930s. An important difference, however, was that in precolonial times a Lujere village was more lost in the forest, encased in trees, shrubs and grasses. The idea of a 'ples klia,' a clearing or open plaza amid the village houses, was a standard 'kiap' expectation, but also an expectation by some returned workers who had spent a couple of years on colonial stations where large open areas importantly symbolized modernity and the opposite of an overgrown 'ples bilong buskanaka,' a village of wild uncivilized persons. Most returning workers spoke Tok Pisin, thereby giving them verbal access to Westerners and other New Guineans that helped establish and burnish a new identity of a 'man bilong nau'—a modern man—not a 'bus kanaka.'

The traditional A-frame style house assembled from natural materials without nails remained popular throughout the region but now there were some houses with very low sides. As noted earlier, there was considerable variability in the appearance of a village's houses, especially as they aged. Wakau's tattered and abandoned men's house, the largest structure in the village, was obviously an impressive presence in its prime. While house styles had changed some, gone completely were a village's funeral scaffolds holding decomposing bodies whose stench swiftly drove McCarthy and his men from a village. Now as a health precaution the government had long ordered the dead to be buried as soon as possible. However, if death came at a distant bush house where 'kiaps' never trod, a traditional funerary scaffold might be raised.

Most notably, dress also had changed. Unless a man was in the bush—or a European entered a village unannounced—a phallocrypt gourd was seldom seen. Cloth shorts, however threadbare, were generally preferred. As men usually wore the same shorts day

---

condition that in other societies fire men's imaginations. . . The emphasis of their society is on the here and now" (McArthur 1971: 189).

8. Kaberry's excellent article (1967) also provides a searching review of a number of Highland societies, such as the Chimbu, Mae-Enga, Bena Bena, and Kuma, summarizing their characteristics and documenting their organizational plasticity as well as critiquing Barnes' (1962) article.

after day, it was a big aide in helping me learn their names. The women were generally topless, wearing either a shapeless faded skirt or sarong; both seemed to be winning out over the traditional and elegantly simple brown string skirt that Lujere men found graceful and alluring.[9] McCarthy described their skirts as short in front and long in back but, according to what I saw and was told about the past, their skirts were long in both front and back. It was in the Wape area that the women's skirts were short in front and long in back.[10] Little children were still naked and girls began wearing clothing before boys. At any government activity that involved the 'kiap,' like voting or census taking, it was seemingly mandatory for everyone except the youngest to jump into cloth of some kind.[11] The 'kiap,' of course, could have cared less how they dressed as long as they were present.

Body decoration had also changed. Traditionally, piercings of the nose, ear lobe and helix were fancied, but these fell out of fashion sometime after men began to leave as contract laborers. Now some men and women had small "homemade" tattoos, often on the face. Men such as Nauwen, having seen the elaborate keloids of the Middle Sepik men while working as indentured laborers, occasionally attempted less extensive ones on their bodies.

A man's armory of bows and arrows was essentially unchanged from precolonial times, except that arrows for killing humans were no longer made. The shotgun was a new weapon, but only a select few men were licensed by the government to own one. Wakau village, as noted earlier, did not have a shotgun until five months before I arrived. Food getting, such as gardening, hunting, and fishing, had also changed little from Robertson and McCarthy's reports, except for the introduction of basic metal tools and plastic fishing line to facilitate these activities. Although the 'garamut' or slit gong that celebrated an enemy's death were gone, the small wooden hand drum or 'kundu' was still made, as was the traditional two-piece smoking pipe (*mero*) also popular in other parts of the Upper Sepik (see fig. 12).[12] Composed of a narrow length of incised bamboo inserted into a

---

9. There could be slight stylistic differences among villages: for example, the women of Gwidami had some yellowish strings over the darker ones.
10. In 1972, I collected and donated to the American Museum of Natural History in New York City 198 Lujere artifacts, such as skirts, penis sheaths, body decorations, pipes, tops, jaw harps, whistles, lime pots, bone tools, bows, arrows, and net bags. To see images of the articles, go to https://anthro.amnh.org; narrow your search by choosing "Collections Database," then "Pacific" for Collections Area; "Ethnographic" for Collection Type; "Papua New Guinea" for Countries; and finally, "Lujere" for Cultures. This is a rather quirky database, so play around with it.
11. George Oakes, the Lujere's first census 'kiap,' in an April 13, 2015, email to me wrote, "In 1956 many of the Yellow River people still wore traditional dress. It was interesting that when I came to do a census everyone had a laplap [waistcloth] on!" It was customary for a returning indentured laborer to bring gifts to important family members and essential were cloth skirts, waistcloths, and shorts. The same was expected of me, plus watches, when I returned to the Wape or Lujere.
12. According to McCarthy the Lujere hand drum at contact had no handle but my village photos show only hand drums with handles, a style they probably picked up as plantation workers.

long gourd, both men and women used these striking smoking devices.[13] Native tobacco, as initially observed by McCarthy, was still smoked relatively green by many after a brief drying in the sun or over a fire. Hand-decorating a *mero's* bamboo stem that held the tobacco was still an appreciated skill.

Figure 12. Enmauwi smokes a traditional *mero* pipe as his daughter Wea plays with the stem of Nimo's *mero*.

Dating Local History

Establishing an accurate timeframe for events among a preliterate people, like the Wakau villagers, is a research challenge. While several men in Wakau were literate in Tok Pisin, they did not have the Western obsession with dates. Many, however, had memories or knowledge of significant events, if not of the year. The two oldest events I could date precisely and use as markers with informants to establish the relative date of other events were the great Torricelli earthquake on September 20, 1935,[14] and 1943, which marked

---

13. See Craig (1990) for a comparative discussion of Namia smoking tube designs and pictorial representations.
14. Wakau villagers had no stories about what causes an earthquake. Oria's father, however, told him about this one. His father was in the bush near the Sand River 'sovalim pis' (scooping up

the Mosstroops' visit. Other established dates were more recent: for example, 1956, the Yellow River Massacre and Wakau's first census by PO George Oakes; 1960, Iwani's double 'sanguma' murder; 1965, six-week jail terms for twenty-five Iwani men (mostly Wakau) for "disobeying a lawful order" related to the village being in disarray; and 1968, the building of the Yellow River Base Camp.

The People and Households of Wakau

Betty Gillam and Jalman's Medical Clinic

There were no overweight people in the whole of Lujereland. It was by luck that I was able to collect the height and weight of the Wakau villagers, the only Lujere group so studied. The CMML nurse, Betty Gillam, who had visited the Lujere from Lumi since 1966 to conduct infant and maternal welfare patrols, had never visited any of the Iwani hamlets; she had been intimidated by the frighteningly negative stories she had heard about them. Joyce and I knew Betty as a friend from our Wape fieldwork, so I invited her to bring her health patrol to Wakau and she accepted. She had assisted Dr. Wark in her growth and maturation studies of the Wape people (Wark and Malcolm 1969), so she had both the implements and knowledge to assess the overall health of the Wakau villagers, especially the children, and to record each individual's height and weight.

Betty came to Wakau with Jalman, a medical orderly, and we had the clinic ready the morning of January 17, which took almost two hours (see fig. 13). The clinic was held at my 'haus kuk' with the adults and children standing on Betty's kilogram scale and her measuring stick marking the height in centimeters. The babies were weighed in a cloth attached to a hanging scale and, as usual, they did not like it. This was a new experience for the villagers, so the mood was more festive than just dutiful; the only outright refusal to participate was Samaun's. Jalman helped to place the people on the scale, Betty adjusted the marker stick, and I recorded the figures she called out. I was surprised that Betty, who had done this routine many times among the Wape and other groups, seemed rather nervous and her movements quixotic. Once she pushed the metal marker completely up and off the top of the height measuring stick almost stabbing old Leno. And when they did not stand up just so, she pushed and pulled them in place. Most surprisingly she did not speak to them in her fluent Tok Pisin but in English! Which means, I guess, that an ethnologist's 'wantoks' may at times be just as puzzling as the locals he is studying.

---

stunned fish) when the quake hit. Trees fell down as he ran back to Wakau. The frightened villagers were also afraid of a flood and then hiked up to Mauwi hamlet to be safe. Coastal villages have good reason to be frightened of a tidal wave, but it is puzzling how they, so far inland, got this belief. The only explanation is that when Robinson returned up the Sepik in 1932, twenty-seven Lujere indentured laborers had returned from the coast and brought the knowledge of the association of earthquakes and tsunami home with them. The date of the quake also establishes that in 1935 they had yet to move across the Sand River to where PO Oakes visited their village in 1956.

Figure 13. Nurse Betty Gillam and the medical orderly Jalman set up for a medical clinic.

Overall, Betty found most of the villagers in good health and, happily, no childhood malnutrition, a more frequent finding among the Wape and occasionally among the Lujere as well. After the weighing and measuring, a few people came up to her for a shot for 'sotwin' (shortness of breath), having learned the power of the aid post orderly's penicillin injection. She was a bit reluctant to get involved but I pressed her into it, knowing most would not go to the aid post and could get dangerously worse. She did not, however, give any inoculations to the children, as she doubted that she would patrol here again for the booster shots. But she did treat Leno, Menetjua, Luritsao, Ai'ire, and Kairapowe, Ukai's wife, all in various stages of pneumonia, as well as Sakome, whose fever Betty thought was from malaria, and Wolwar's wife Nauware, who had a very fast pulse and bronchitis. As one shot of penicillin was not always enough to achieve a cure, I volunteered to continue treatment of the sickest ones with my own tetracycline capsules, and Betty instructed me on their follow-up medication for the next few days. As the villagers knew I was just following her instructions and she was leaving, it wouldn't get me into the medical business. After all, I was there to study their therapeutic systems, not to become one myself. As you will later see, their propensity for pneumonia challenged my original intentions.

We collected data on 113 villagers present, but here I will give data only on the adults, of whom there were 33 men and 22 women.[15] The height range for the men was from 4' 11" to 5' 7," with an average height of 5' 4." For the women, their height ranged from 4' 10"

---

15. All of the data were collected in terms of centimeters and kilograms then converted into feet and pounds.

to 5' 4," with an average height of 5'. The men and women's short height and lean frames also accounted for their low weights. The men's weight range was 82–126 pounds, with an average weight of 107 pounds. The weight range for the women was 71–109 pounds, with an average weight of 95 pounds. At 5' 6" and 135 pounds, I was—for probably the only time in my life—always one of the biggest guys in the room.[16] Size, of course, is relative. When Ray entered the village on one of his rare visits with his tall, lanky Australian frame striding in long steps across the plaza past my neighbors, my perception of our "normal" village instantly shifted to one populated by a diminutive people with miniature houses.

Who Lives Where?

The day after I moved to Wakau, I began to take a census of the households and roughly map the village. I had lived in the village for over three months when I did another census and, as I feel more secure with this one, it is the one I will report on. Table 6 shows the marital breakdown of Wakau's population on February 25, 1972.

Table 6. Wakau population by marital status, 1972

Status	Males	Females	Totals
Single	11	4	15
Married	26	26	52
Children	24	24	48
Widowed	3	2	5
Totals	64	56	120

In table 6, the discrepancy in the ratio between males and females is major only among the single adults. Table 7 compares the male–female population of Wakau's first census in 1956 (table 1) with my 1972 census and shows that the numerical relationship of females to males had slightly increased.

Table 7. Wakau population by age and gender, 1956 and 1972

	1956		1972	
	Male	Female	Male	Female
Child	20	13	24	24
Adult	44	33	40	32
Gender totals	64	46	64	56
Village totals	110		120	

---

16. Arakwaki, Enmauwi, and I were the same height; only Oria, at 5'7," was an inch taller.

In 1956, there were sixty-four males to only forty-six females, while in 1972, the female count had gained by ten, but the male count stayed the same. However, with eleven men and four women unmarried it meant there were almost three times the number of unmarried men to unmarried women. The ratio of girls to boys, however, was equal, possibly indicating a more favorable forecast for Wakau's future bachelors. Of the single adults in the village, all their parents were dead except for one woman and one man. Two of Wakau's forty-eight children lived with a parent who had remarried, nine lived with a single parent and two, who were not born in Wakau, lived with adopted parents. Ten of the twenty-six married couples had no children, but they were young and mostly newly married. Two of the couples were married by proxy after the husband left the village as an indentured laborer and one couple, Ukai and Kairapowe, were older and childless.

While I lived in Wakau, six men were away working, but in the years since the men began leaving the village for contract work, only three men took jobs and never returned home. However, one who was a driver in Kokopo, East New Britain, returned before I arrived and left with a widow as his wife. When I made the February 1972 household census, there were ten bachelors; from their perspective as men, it was possible they might never marry if they had no sister or other woman to exchange. Of those, only Poke, Kunai, and Aria not only had no woman to exchange, but were considered by all, including themselves, as too old to marry and were confirmed bachelors. Mangko was an interesting exception. He was a lively and attractive young man, an excellent hunter and *nakwolu*, and had a woman to exchange. I was told that Mangko did not want to marry, 'Em i no laik long marit!' But he ultimately succumbed. When I returned to Wakau briefly in 1982, Mangko was a married man.

Most of the men spoke fluent Tok Pisin. Only the two old-timers, Menetjua and Leno, had no facility with the language, while Aiyuk and Ukai, two other older men, had a limited hearing knowledge but not speaking.[17] Four men, Klowi, Kwoien, Waniyo, and Meyawali had some facility with the language but were not fluent. There were also several men who, besides being fluent, were more or less literate in Tok Pisin: Oria, Unei, Kairapowe, Nakwane, Yaope, and Tsaime. Villagers kept in touch with men working away with letters and sometimes sent brief missives to the 'kiap' with a request.

In any Lujere village, there are two kinds of houses: a number of small houses and one or two larger ones. The former are the women's or family houses, while the latter the men's houses. The size difference is because the men cluster together into dormitories while their wives live either alone or with one or two other wives and their children. Marital couples also have one or more rudimentary bush camps where family members go singly or together to get food. Women making sago would never stay in a bush camp overnight without their husband, but a hunting husband might spend several days in a camp, especially if he were hunting with other men. For extended stays, the family packed up and went as a group. The men did all house building, agnates usually helping one another.

---

17. I never heard Aiyuk speak any Tok Pisin; Ukai did speak to me a few times in Tok Pisin, but haltingly as if he had first worked out what he was going to say.

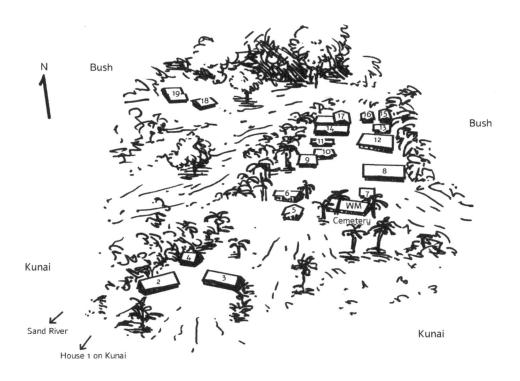

Map 6. Wakau village women's and men's houses in November, 1971. Drawing by Dan Holbrow.

Women's Houses

Most of the houses in a Lujere village are those where one or more women—the wives of related men—live together with their children. These houses are devoid of partitions and there are no raised beds to sit or sleep on; all life is lived on the strong 'limbum' floor that spreads out in wide bark sheathings like planks in an old farmhouse. Although the husband builds the house for his wife with the help of clan mates and other village men, it is her home where she cooks and cares for her family. If she is pregnant, it is also where she might bear her child attended by other close women unless in a bush camp. Depending upon the number of women residents, there are usually one to four clay hearths level with the floor where cooking is done, each woman with a hearth of her own. Wawenowaki's house (fig. 14) was in the traditional A-frame style, but a newer style had low side walls made of sturdy sago palm stems as did the upper village's *iron* (see fig. 19, below) which, while was not as elegant a design, was roomier. At night, the women and children sleep around the hearth, infants in their mother's arms, hence babies don't fall off a bench into the fire as can happen among the Wape. Whereas Wape babies are carried within a house because of the dirt floor, the Lujere baby is allowed to crawl on the 'limbum' floor exploring her or his environment.

Husbands usually sleep in the men's house where their wives bring them their food. That is the tradition, but the Lujere play with tradition and adapt it to their needs and whims. For example, sometimes I saw men having their evening meal of sago, cooked

Table 8. Key to map 6, women's houses and men's collective houses in Wakau village

House	Occupancy
1	Elewa (*Waniyo*), Aiidwapi (*Nimo*), Debrai (widow)
2	Miwali (*Ai'ire*); Wowire (*Aiyuk*)
3	Wawenowaki (*Klowi*)
4	Lower men's house
5	Pourame (*Oria*)
6	Abandoned, *Oria's* widowed mother's (remarried) house
7	Irowe (*Ino*), Waluware (*Luritsao*)
8	Abandoned men's house
9	Maiteniya (*Enwauwi*), Noloware (*Wolowar*)
10	Sakome (*Waripe*) [*Wauripe*]
11	Yaopowe (*Mari*)
12	Idet (*Akami*), Talai (*Eine*)
13	Wariyeh (*Kwoien*), Apewaki (*Mowal*)
14	Upper men's house
15	Alitowi (*Arakwaki*), Auwe (*Nakwane*)
16	Being built by *Arawaki*
17	Being built by *Nakwani*
18	Kairapowe (*Ukai*)
19	Being built by *Nauwen*

Note: Wife's name appears in regular case; husband's name appears in italics.

greens, and usually some form of meat at their wife's house while playing with their children. A man also might choose for a time to sleep in his wife's house, a finding I had for other Lujere villages. In Worikori village I was told that all the married men slept in their wives' houses. This type of a woman's house is different from the first only in that the husband often builds himself a raised bed in one corner, similar to the kind he would sleep on in the men's house with a smoldering clay hearth underneath primarily to drive off mosquitos. I have also been in a Wakau house where two husbands (who were brothers) partitioned off a small room for themselves with raised beds while still having a bed in the men's house. While these were purportedly women's houses, village males, at least to me, always referred to them by the husband's name or, if two brothers' wives occupied the house, by the oldest brother's name. I don't believe their privileging the husband's name was a sexist put-down; rather, by referencing the husband, it facilitated communication with me, as it was the men I knew well and could communicate with, not their wives who only knew the Namia language. When referring to a village house I generally have followed their lead.

The Lujere did not have a separate house for menstruating women. Menstrual blood, as in much of Papua New Guinea, has alleged powers to diminish a man's prowess. So, if

Figure 14. Wawenowaki (Klowi's wife, second from right) relaxes with family and friends on the front veranda of her traditional house.

a man's wife were menstruating, he would probably sleep at the men's house and someone else would prepare his food. Not to respect this taboo supposedly could result in early aging and jeopardize his hunting competency. However, how slavishly this custom was followed varied.

Family Bush Camps

The bush camp was a more rudimentary dwelling built in the forest for hunting and making sago where families, as indicated, might stay for days, weeks, or even months. Formerly, villagers might leave their village home for six or more months at a time if their bush camp were a several hours' walk from the village. A few camps in the great fens west of the Sand River might be nearer the "enemy" Tsila hamlets than to Wakau. Some families might have more than one camp if their resources were scattered.

One February day at random I made a count of the whereabouts of all twenty-three husbands or "household heads" that included Soukene, whose husband was away as a contract laborer and who lived alone with her children (WN: 516). Nine of the men were in forest camps with their families; another was visiting in Mokadami with his new wife; another was at the aid post with his sick daughter. Soukene, who had gone with her children up to Mauwi, her natal village, because the bachelor, Samaun, harassed her for sex. In sum, twelve household heads and most of their families were not in the village that day, leaving eleven married men and their families in and around Wakau. Most of the bachelors, as usual, were home except Mangko, who was hunting with two youths from the lower men's house, and the bachelor Aria, who was helping Luritsao in his garden to assure some dinners from his wife, Waluware. It's interesting that the day I took the count the number of families was almost evenly divided between those home and those away, but that ratio could vary wildly.

Most forest camps were relatively isolated and very casually built; some even jettisoned the A-frame style and were little more than a roof over a raised 'limbum' floor open on several sides. Considering their genuine fear of lurking 'sanguma' murderers, it was a persistent enigma to me how they logically justified such a vulnerable house style (see fig. 16) in the middle of a jungle with no immediate next-door neighbors to call on if help was needed. Small paths crisscrossing the forest and swamps provided access to friends' and relatives' camps thus maintaining social ties and keeping up on each other's news, hence the encamped families were not as socially isolated as some 'kiaps,' and I originally, believed them to be.

The family bush camps, while of significance to the social and economic life of the village, were ad hoc affairs with fluctuating residents. Their egalitarian composition also was different from either type of women's village houses. In the bush all the members of a family plus visitors slept in the same house regardless of whether they were married, unmarried, old, young, male, or female. Occasionally a small hut for youths might be built semi-attached or nearby. At no time did I hear any complaints about going to a bush camp or living there; in fact, it seemed families enjoyed the change in location and daily tempo, not unlike an American family on a camping trip.

The rainy season that was more or less November through April was also the hunting season when families moved to their bush camps for weeks at a time. The first bush camp I visited was K____, on a cloudy morning in early February. The hike from Wakau with Oria, Mangko, Alomiaiya, and Newai was about two and a half hours into the forest but included a short stop at old Leno's "hamlet" about forty-five minutes out of Wakau. He had built a village-type house—not a bush camp—in an open area that provided a retreat for his often-truculent temperament. On reaching Klowi's bush camp, I was surprised to see that it was much higher off the ground than a village house (fig. 15). The front was closed but the back was open, and the sides had strips of 'pongal' laid up halfway providing an atmosphere of air and light. The wives and children of K____, Kwoien, and Luritsao, a grown daughter of K____ by an earlier wife, and a couple of youths were scattered around the several active cooking hearths. Ai'ire, with his wife and little daughter, was the only man present. Visiting ensued, with some horseplay between Newai and Mango, and a tasty lunchtime snack of pork and sago cooked in a long green leaf. We returned to Wakau by 2:30, hot and tired.

Klowi had asked me to visit him at his hunting camp across the Sand River so on the last day of March, Oria, Nauwen, and I, together with Samaun, Kworu, Nakwane and his wife Auwe, and Marawame visited his camp about an hour's walk west of the Sand River. The river was high from heavy mountain rains, so we had to ferry across in a dugout canoe. The trail, like most bush trails in the wet season, was abysmal; I was sloshing through shallow muddy swamps with leeches climbing up my boots and heading into my socks. We passed through Ai'ire's new garden with bananas, some taro plants and sweet potato vines then through an old garden of Klowi's, now new bush. We passed a big murky pond where a large python was killed a few months earlier. Klowi's camp (figs. 16 and 17) was minimalist at best, with only a roof and a 'limbum' floor, no sides, but there were several

Figure 15. K____ bush camp, a two-and-a-half-hour hike from Wakau.

hearths, the welcoming smell of smoke and food cooking, and people and possessions (including at least one dog) lying comfortably around. Attached to the camp was a small lean-to where the youths slept.

As we visited, Oria, Nauwen, and I ate the snack offered to us of sago and edible greens. Mangko, who was ill, was quietly sitting up by a hearth and, although he looked better, said that his chest still hurt. Leleware, Porken's widow, came in saying that Warajak wasn't around and Tsaime and his wife went to find him. She was afraid that a 'sangumaman' might attack him, but there was no general alarm; a fact was presented, and action was taken: typical Lujere behavior. I visited with Ai'ire who was still chronically ill, chatted with the youth Kairapowe, always smilingly upbeat, who had come from Yaope's nearby bush camp to see me. Later, when a few of us were on the ground and leaving, Klowi returned from hunting, still full of vigor, and with a beautiful Guria pigeon slung over his shoulder that he insisted was for me. I refused outright, but it was useless. Klowi passed the bird to one of my party and, moving on, we sloshed back through the leech-infested swamp towards home.

Men's Houses

The Namia term for "men's house" is *iron*, and Barry Craig (1972: 34) had visited, photographed, and sketched one in Norambalip that was as proud and handsome as our old abandoned one once had been but that now sat defeated and battered (fig. 18) It was a classic Lujere A-frame about twenty-nine feet wide and fifty-three feet long, with an

Figure 16. Klowi's bush camp in the fens, across the Sand River.

Figure 17. The interior of Klowi's bush camp.

inside apex of twelve feet. The beds lining each side were about eight feet long by three feet wide, and stood two feet above an in-floor clay hearth that was two and a half feet square, which, when smoking, provided warmth and, hopefully, kept the mosquitos away while sleeping.

Figure 18. The abandoned men's house (*iron*) in Wakau, once the men's sleeping quarters.

With their old *iron* falling apart plus some partially disclosed tensions among members, the Wakau men built two new smaller ones; one in the lower village section, and the other one toward the middle of the village's upper section, as seen in map 6 of the village. The upper village *iron* (fig. 19) was the larger one, measuring twenty-three feet wide by thirty-one feet long with a five-foot front veranda, while the lower *iron* was fifteen feet wide and seventeen feet long. Some men, like Oria, now spent more time at their wives' houses, even sleeping there instead of in their *iron*. From their comments I surmised this sometimes was related to fears of a 'sanguma' attack from a fellow *iron* resident. When I moved to Wakau, construction of a large new *iron* to house all the village men was underway. Already a large platform frame was completed on the 'kunai' near Waniyo's wife's house, but as long as I lived in the village, that was as far as it got. No one would give me a direct answer why work had stopped but I gradually became mindful of interpersonal animosities and aware that the 'sanguma' fears among some of the men from different clans had not diminished but intensified. These seemed answer enough. For whatever reasons, the traditional separation of Lujere husband and wife to sleep in separate houses when in the village was apparently changing. When Joyce and I visited Worikori village, married men, as indicated earlier, said they slept in their wives' houses. Nevertheless, two sturdy *irons* in the village indicated that, like in Wakau, married men could and probably did maintain a space in the *iron*. Again, in Tipas I was told the same thing but, in neither village did I have the time to verify assertions as I could in Wakau.

Figure 19. The new men's house in the upper village of Wakau.

A Lujere *iron* is more than just a dormitory for village men; it is also a center for male learning, storytelling, gossiping, healing, and community sociality, including dying. It should not, however, be confused with a 'haus tambaran,' a men's ceremonial house where sacred objects are housed and celebrated. In the Middle Sepik among the Iatmul these are large ostentatious buildings, while among the mountain-dwelling Wape they are small, plain, and functional. But there are no comparable ritual structures among the Lujere, correctly indicating that Lujere ritual life was not as rich and complex.

In Wakau's upper village *iron*, each man had a bench or bed of his own although Poke and Kunai, two older inveterate bachelors with no sister to exchange in marriage, slept on one together. Sons, as soon as they can leave their mothers, go to sleep with their father in his *iron*. As boys mature, they eventually leave their father's beds and sleep in clusters on the floor with light blankets if they are lucky or on empty beds. This *iron* also had rudimentary plumbing; a long bamboo tube extended from the house to the outside, averting the inhabitants from leaving to urinate at night or during a rainstorm. When I first took a census of the upper *iron* there were twenty-two men and youth inhabiting it. However, it was rarely, if ever, fully occupied as families came and went, alternating their time, as just implied, away in bush camps. Which males lived together in a specific *iron* was related to the Lujere patrilineal clan system discussed in chapter 12 and the nature of the ties between specific clans. When Wakau was located across the Sand River they had three *irons* then, when they moved back across the river, a single large one, abandoned for the two smaller *irons* during my stay. Women and older girls rarely entered an *iron* but little girls had total access especially if their fathers were there. An exception during my stay was when a male villager lay dying in the upper *iron* and his wife and one or two other female mourners sat with him. After his death his body was removed to his wife's house for the customary mourning period before burial.

The House as Cultural Metaphor

The house is not necessarily a metaphor for a particular culture, but for the Wape and Lujere they appear to be. The mountain-dwelling Wape traditionally was a more closed and secretive society with food eaten privately within a house built directly on the ground; a single door and smoke hole in the center top were the only openings. Family members slept on slightly raised beds made of 'pangal' stems with the father's bed partially separated by a 'pangal' wall and another separated section for a menstruating female. Youths slept in a separate communal house or 'haus boi.' Neighbors and visitors were free to join a family member on the house's roomy front dirt veranda, but only close family and perhaps an ethnographer who also was a personal friend, were invited into the house.[18]

In contrast, and reflecting the Lujere's more open culture, the Lujere houses had at least two doors and sometimes even a separate door for dogs. Villagers, male and female, were usually (but not always) welcome into each other houses; for instance, although little girls came to the *iron* if their father was there, other females usually entered only if involved with a curing treatment. For me, who had lived in both societies, the difference was almost like night and day.

The Fieldwork Camp

My base in Wakau as built of native materials, open on most sides and measuring forty by sixteen feet, that sheltered one large tent with an attached screen room of the same size, my living quarters, and another large screen room tent, my 'ofis.' It was strategically situated toward the middle of the village, and easily provided both visual and walking access to community events and daily activities. The front of the house (see fig. 20) bordered the main path and contained my office, which had a view of many of the village's houses and offered a mosquito-proof work and interview area. The inside space fronting the screen room had low benches that welcomed anyone to come in and hang out while I was there working with an informant or typing up my notes (fig. 21). Like all Lujere dwellings, it was several feet off the ground.

---

18. This closure of the Wape domestic unit ironically reminded me of Metraux's (2001) description of *le foyer* for the French family.

Figure 20. Villagers outside my office listening to a tape recording of a curing ritual.

As I was the only exotic entertainment the village provided, there were occasionally—albeit not as frequently as in Taute village—a few men or youths present with whom I could clarify data, seek new information or just casually converse.[19] The back of the house had a large area for my sleeping tent and personal supplies with an equal size attached screen room for dining and relaxing that looked over the adjacent cemetery and glimpsed the 'kunai' beyond. This was the same versatile tent I slept and worked in when I joined Margaret Mead and Rhoda Metraux in 1967 on the banks of the middle Sepik in the Iatmul village of Tambunam. Outside this tent and under the same roof was a pantry area and a small, attached bathing area for a bucket shower; a separate 'haus kuk' or kitchen was behind and to the side of the house to minimize the hazard of fire, and Kunai's splendid outhouse was further back near the forest.

Building a house from bush materials in a strange village is an excellent way to begin fieldwork; by becoming gradually acquainted with the village men's work skills and distinct personalities, I also began to learn the cadence and cares of the community. I

---

19. As Craig has written, "It is hard to escape the feeling, when in a fieldwork situation, that it is the *anthropologist* who is on display to the villagers, rather than the other way around" (Craig 1975:10). You might also recall from chapter 1 how Thurnwald said he felt "like the elephant in the zoo."

Figure 21. My office, with its two indispensable and faithful assistants: an Olympia typewriter and an Aladdin lamp.

chose Arakwaki as a supervisor to oversee the house building. He had returned to the village several months earlier after a period of indentured labor and seemed steady, mature, strong, and with a ready smile. But building a house among the Lujere was a far different task than among the Wape. When I outlined the kind of house I wanted to the Taute men, they set to work following my plan with very few questions. Not the Lujere. First, unlike the Wape, they were not as familiar with carpentry tools. The village had no saws and only two hammers. Their universal tool was still the 'busnaip' or machete introduced by the Mosstroops and, for their building needs, it served them well. However, my pantry called for a counter and shelves and, with no planed lumber, its construction was definitely a challenge. The low sides of the office area for my screen tent were to be just vertical pieces of sago palm stems or 'pangal' thirty inches high. Simple? I thought so.

I cut them two 'pangal' pieces the required length to use as models. But when they lined the 'pangal' they had cut, it was sometimes long and sometimes short, a motley hodgepodge of lengths. They had mostly ignored my stick models, but then they weren't using their eyes either as the low wall was a wildly jagged affair. When I explained anew the sticks had to be the same length so that long finishing pieces of 'pangal' would cover the rough ends on top, they nodded good-naturedly and, I imagine, inwardly rolled their eyes. Years later when I read Ric Hutching's travails with the Lujere men in building his much more ambitious Yellow River Base Camp, I felt a retrospective pang of compassion for him.

Compared to some of the Lujere villages I had visited, most of the Wakau houses were old and rather sloppily constructed with spindly supports, tattered 'morota' roofs and drooping eves. But my new house was handsome. The men, twenty-eight in total, were undaunted by my occasional critiques and suggestions in house building, persevered jauntily, and speedily finished it in twelve days. I could see why the labor contractors liked to recruit in the Yellow River area; the Wakau men were definitely strong and willing workers. But the biggest building surprise was Kunai's outhouse for me, a job he took on single-handedly. I had to reevaluate my view of his goofiness when I went to look at it. Constructed without any guidance, for what it was and what he had to work with it was a splendid latrine.

I was very pleased with my new camp, which was both functional and comfortable if far from anything familiar. But that is the point of fieldwork. Much later, Iwi cut a tree that was blocking my view of the base camp's hill. If it were a clear night without driving rain or fog, I might see a distant speck of lantern light from the 'kiap's camp; a tiny welcome sign of urbanity.

The Lower Village: Dramatis Personae

Because the lower village was just down a slight rise from my house, I tended to interact more with its residents, especially the men, several of whom are key players in this narrative. I will introduce some of them here in more detail to increase your familiarity with what may seem, as it did to me, a flurry of strange names. Fortunately, you don't have to hear the varied pronunciations I heard but only see the pronunciation I opted for. I had one advantage in learning their names that I did not have as a professor. While my students in the US wore an array of clothing, most men in the Lujere villages had a single pair of shorts each and, if the cloth for each pair had a distinctive pattern, it further simplified my task of learning their names. It was also convenient that the lower village (see map 6) had only three homes and one *iron* and that all the men, except Aiyuk, belonged to the Elamoli clan through their fathers.

House One was the village's southernmost house and located a good walk away on the 'kunai' near the floor frame for the proposed new *iron*. It had more household members than any of the others, nineteen in all. Village men, as explained earlier, referred to it as

"Waniyo's house," thus prioritizing the household's senior male. Three brothers made up the nucleus of this household: Waniyo, Nimo, and Engwe. Waniyo, about forty, lived withhis wife Elewe and their three children. Nimo, about thirty-two, lived there with his childless wife. Engwe, about twenty-seven, was a bachelor (he finds a wife in chap. 12), They lived there together with their widowed and childless sister, as well as with old Leno's daughter, Nemiai, who ran away to live here because her father forbade her to marry (she also finds a mate in chap. 12). Others who lived there were the family of Debrai, a widowed affine with two sons both away at plantation work, one son's wife, a married daughter whose husband was also away at work, and four younger sons. Without any young sisters to exchange in marriage, prospects that these sons would find a wife were dim.

House Two was Ai'ire's wife's house and they had one little daughter. Ai'ire was a thoughtful, smart man in his early thirty's, a good friend, but ill during my entire stay. He is mentioned frequently in the text as I followed his illness and report in detail on his case in Appendix. Ai'ire's parents died when he was small and he was raised by Klowi and his wife, as Ai'ire's father was Klowi's mother's brother. In a similar way, when Klowi's parents died while he was still a boy, his mother's other brother took care of him.

Ai'ire's two orphaned half-sisters were also household members, as was Mangko, a thirtyish bachelor recently returned from indentured labor, and his two younger brothers, one who was away working, and his young sister, Wabe. Another household member was the youth Newai who came to Wakau as a little boy from Mauwi to live with Mangko, his mother's clansman. Klowi said that Mauwi village killed their children with 'sanguma' so he would help Mangko look out for him. Aiyuk, who moved his wife and five children to Wakau because he was afraid of the 'sanguma' in Mauwi, were also attached to this house for a time before moving to Arakwaki's wife's house in the upper village.

House Three belonged to Wawenowaki, the wife of Klowi, the feared 'sanguma' killer, popular healer, and licensed shotgun owner, as well as the most charismatic and unusual man in Wakau. They had four children; the youngest was an adopted boy, Pipia, whose name in Tok Pisin means trash or something you throw away. Apparently sickly and rumored that he was a 'masalai's child, his parents didn't want him and they gladly gave him to Klowi to raise.

Also, part of this household were four siblings whose father was dead and whose mother, Mamau, had remarried Anwani, a Gwidami man who was Eine's wife's brother. In exchange for the widowed Mamau, Anwani gave his twice-widowed sister Aidwapi to Nimo (House One), well into his thirties and still wifeless. In the next chapter, we learn about Nimo's negative feelings about this match. Anwani was very sick and the plantation where he worked broke his contract and sent him home; his mysterious illness and attempts to cure him are discussed in chapter 15. The four siblings who did not follow their mother Mamau to Gwidami were the bachelor Tsaime, in his late twenties with a warm and expressive personality and whose nuptial misadventures are followed in chapter 12; his sister Wabe; their bright fourteen-year-old brother Warajak; and younger sister Womie. Klowi and his wife also took in and fed the orphaned youth Unei, an alert youth with extensive tinea.

House Four was the clan's *iron* where all the single males slept, and often the married men like Klowi and Ai'ire were there too. With so many youths and young bachelors, it was a lively house when they were around, and their enthusiastic voices were easily heard from my house when they played their game of spinning tops in the open plaza. It was my favorite place to hang out. After one evening visit to the *iron* I wrote, "These men are great—so much easier to live with than the Wape—and generous. I really like them; all lolling about, talking, smoking, chewing betel and little girls in the house too!"

Village Rhythms

Morning and afternoon

In the morning, if a family was in the village, a married man was usually up and off to find food or perhaps going to the forest with his family. The husband carried his bow and arrows, a large knife and maybe his axe over a shoulder. While his wife processed sago, he might hunt, fish, or work in his small garden. Babies, toddlers, and girls were with their mother while sons accompanied their father. During the day the village was mostly empty, but from around four thirty to six, the villagers began returning. The husband usually returned first, his wife and children afterwards. He would carry his weapons and any game he may have shot (fig. 22). Sometimes he might also carry some firewood on his shoulder, but he would never bring water. Or he might bring a few bananas or some garden plants for transplanting to a new little garden. His wife and daughters would be much more heavily laden, carrying sago, garden foods, and abundant firewood (fig. 23). Then the wife or a daughter would make a separate trip to bring water for cooking sago dumplings, the preferred dining staple.

Figure 22. Wakau men returning home late afternoon with their hunting weapons. Note the old, abandoned *iron* in the background.

Figure 23. Wakau women returning home with firewood.

But the *iron's* single men, especially the older ones whose fathers are dead, slept late, as did the widowers. They had no family to feed so they slept in, arising leisurely about eight or nine, maybe later. Perhaps they would go, usually in twos, to find fish, or work a bit in a small garden. Early in the afternoon they returned to the *iron*. Or perhaps they would spend the entire day in the men's house lazing about with a faraway look in their eyes, smoking or chewing betel. They did not talk much. Their lives were quite restricted, and they had little responsibility except for themselves. They also had little status.

A single man does not always know who is going to bring him his dinner sago, especially if he has no mother or married brother or sister in the village. Some evenings several women will give him sago; sometimes no one. Whether they are given sago for an evening meal depends upon their relationships mainly with their male married relatives whose wives provide them with food, especially if they have helped in gardening or house building. If a bachelor was a good hunter like Mangko and occasionally provided his relatives with pig and cassowary meat, they will more kindly provide him with sago and greens. Otherwise, any food is given perfunctorily and, when in short supply, not at all. Or if the bachelor is suspected of sorcery or other anti-social behavior, his married male relatives have the supreme sanction of cutting off his sago supply from their wives as they did with Aria. Then he goes to bed hungry, and the day is spent scrounging in the bush for food. And no one brings him water or firewood. Other men in the *iron* might take pity on him and give him a bit to eat. There is a myth about men who don't share; the man not fed disappears, thus weakening the group as a punishment to the selfish. Even at best, the position of a bachelor is not an enviable one.

So, the usual atmosphere of a men's house during the day is a desultory one. Only the village drones or sick are within, dreaming away. But when a visiting curer, an *imoulu*, arrives and the house is crowded with men and boys, things liven up. It is the same in the evening after eating when the men and youths, visiting with one another, catch up on the local events and gossip as they smoke and laugh. It was my favorite time to visit an *iron* and, as I always arrived carrying a kerosene lantern, was warmly welcomed into the darkness. Smoking tobacco was enjoyed by both men and women but compared to the Wape, there was much less betel chewing with its red spittle decorating the landscape.

The mood at the lower *iron*, which was smaller and had several younger men and youths, was, as already indicated, usually more upbeat. In the afternoon around 4:30, the youths and younger men might gather outside the *iron* to play a lively game of spinning tops. The tops were composed of a small coconut shell disk with a wooden spindle through its center. Some disks were beautifully carved and painted.[20] Stout low sticks were set up about a foot or so apart—gradually replaced by empty tin cans from my kitchen—then standing back several yards, the player, sometimes leaping into the air, would send a top spinning towards the cans, hoping to hit one (as in fig. 24). One afternoon I filmed them playing when Akami, Newai, Iwi, Kworu and K____ visiting son, Yaunuo, were on one side, and Unei, Warajak, Alomiai, and Aka'u were on the other. There was no sense of them being two teams. It was simply a fun-game. Although skill and a certain amount of athleticism were required, no score was kept and the opportunity for competitive comparison among the players was ignored.[21] Similarly I watched boys stage a mock fight just for play after being up all night at a curing festival. The only other toys I saw were small bows with arrows like Ai'ire's little daughter Yawori holds in figure 25.

One thing that was unusual after I'd lived so long with the Wape was the general expressiveness of the villagers, best described in an extract from a letter to my mentor and friend, Rhoda Metraux.

> This is a much more assertive society than the Wape. The parent-child relationship is incredible after the placid tempo of the Wape. Children swear at parents, throw their belongings about, throw away food they have been yelling for, bop their parents and throw big sticks at the houses. It is very startling. Of course parents aren't just taking all of this and they bop children on the head (always the head!), yell at them and drag them off to the bush when the child wants to stay in the village and play. In Wape, if the child didn't want to go to the bush, the *entire* family stayed home with him! Yet there is great affection too. . . . I do miss the Wape wit that so beautifully veiled their hostility. But it is easier to live here where things are open and there aren't schemes afoot that are hushed up. There is scheming here but it seems to be mostly out loud. (Letter from W. Mitchell to R. Metraux, February 13, 1972)

From my house, as mentioned earlier, I had a good view of much of the upper village, so I was a witness to little children playing together quietly in the dirt as well as to

---

20. The carved and painted surface of some tops and the incised terminus of a *mero*'s bamboo tobacco holder were the only everyday objects I observed that were expressively decorated.
21. According to Beatrice Blackwood (1935: 279ff.), on Bougainville Island boys and men play a game with similar coconut tops but compete to see whose top spins the longest.

Figure 24. Boys spinning tops in the lower village.

Figure 25. Ai'ira's daughter Yawori holds a toy bow as boys spin their tops in the lower village. The path connects the lower and upper villages.

some of their tantrums. I rarely knew what they were upset about as the houses were not that close to mine. My account in the letter above of the boy throwing sticks was about Wolwar's son and he was hungry, so he let everyone know. I recall another little boy crying loudly and throwing away his sago to the chickens. It is not that children weren't fed as they were well cared for. I attributed the childhood storminess to the general openness of the culture; adults also were expressive of their feelings, resulting in frequent discord, as detailed in the next chapter.

In an early notebook entry regarding motor activity, I wrote, "Movements of men and women are slow and deliberate; graceful but rather pokey. But the heat has me slowed down in activity and motions too! Not as invigorating as in the Torricellis (not that that is Vermont)." Wape men strolling around the village more often than not walked with their right hand behind their back holding their left arm, but I only occasionally saw this posture among the Lujere. Another difference was that a Wape man holding his bow in his left hand signaled shooting an arrow by slapping his right thigh while a Lujere man would snap his right-hand fingers. Men carried small children around on their shoulders and babies in their arms but rarely, if ever, in a cloth sling as Wape men and women and Lujere women did.

Although it appeared that women had a much heavier workload than men, they did have leisure time when they enjoyed each other and the children, especially the households with several wives who might gather with their children on the front veranda to visit, smoke, and chat with a passerby (as in fig. 18). From my office vantage point, I frequently saw several women, especially younger ones with babies, standing together visiting (as in fig. 14) and, like children everywhere, the Wakau youngsters, although toyless in Western terms, found ways to entertain themselves like playing in the village's sandy dirt.

Most bathing, which was frequent, occurred for the men in the creeks and the Sand River. A male waded naked into the water casually shielding his genitals, rubbed his body to remove the mud, and then submerged his head to rinse his hair. Soap was a luxury they did not have. If his shorts were muddy, he would wash them at the same time, as some men owned only the shorts they wore. The females bathed in two water holes for their exclusive use. The holes were about four feet in width with a small log placed across the top. To bathe, I was told, a woman would lower herself nude into the water from the pole.

Because I lived in Wakau, the villagers seemed to wear more cloth than in some of the other villages I visited nearby where on entering, I often saw traditional string skirts and the occasional penis sheath, but if I stuck around they might be quietly replaced with cloth. This was not a 'kiap's expectation or mine but a projected local view of appropriate attire when around Europeans. I assumed it was a form of embarrassment avoidance related to the same psychology when Europeans feel constrained to dress up or dress down in a social situation to feel at ease and has little to do with the others' sartorial expectations. My dropping in at a bush camp was different; no one was concerned with what they were wearing, and a penis sheath or string skirt never came off. It was always "casual Friday" in the bush.

Appraising another's perception of time is difficult as it can only be inferred. I know my sense of time changed radically after moving to Wakau and living alone without my family's different schedules, for instance, Ned was schooled by Joyce on weekdays and our weekend was marked off behaviorally if not always as forcefully as at home. The Wape also were adherents of a weekly routine and on Saturday night the men often gamboled at 'satu,' a dice game. But in Wakau, there was a sense of timelessness with days and weeks drifting into each other. It was fascinating, and delightful, to gradually be aware of my loosening sense of time. I wrote to my colleague and close friend May Ebihara,

> Unlike the Wape, they treat every day like the other. They know about weeks from their plantation experiences but they haven't brought the weekend concept home with them. The European week has so much finality to it and you are always feeling guilty because you got so little accomplished. But here the days just tumble along with few, if any planned climaxes. Like the biggest thing that has happened around here for quite a while was that a dog was found dead under the abandoned men's house today. (Letter from W. Mitchell to M. Ebihara, January 14, 1972)

The evening dinner

Dinner took place from 6:00 to 7:00, just before sunset, being the main mealtime and an occasion of great activity, with villagers walking around with food, women and girls carrying it to the *iron*, and young men walking together as they ate their dinner of meat or fish and sago, maybe with some greens, while somewhere a child was yelling out for more food. Eating was not a private activity, as with the Wape who ate their sago and greens closeted inside their houses, rarely with any meat to share. Eating in Wakau was a lively public activity, probably because they had access to an enviable amount of meat.

Early one evening, sick of typing up notes and limp from the humid heat as well as feeling isolated from the village activities, I impulsively took off into the village without notebook or pen; the idea of having to do another single bit of work right then was intolerable. Feeling genially liberated, I walked through the hamlet headed towards the upper *iron* where I visited a bit and learned that Kunai was cutting up the pig that Klowi had shot yesterday. He had wounded it but it had not fallen so Mangko and a few others from the lower *iron* had tracked it down and Mangko had killed it with an arrow. I found Kunai sitting on Arakwaki's veranda with part of the butchered pig in front of him in a 'limbum' basket and cutting it into smaller pieces with his rather dull knife; the youth Kairapowe was helping him. Standing by the open door I glanced inside and was smilingly invited to come in.

The house was occupied by the wives of two sets of brothers: Arakwaki and Nakwane's wives, Alitowi and Auwe, had the hearths in the front of the house, and Luritsao and Enewan's wives Waluware and Abuwe, who were also sisters, had the two hearths in the back of the house. When I went in, all four wives were sitting on the floor at their hearths preparing the evening meal. Two dogs were also wandering around and Kairapowe pointed out their own little entrance opening to the porch. Auwe, Nakwane's wife, was making sago dumplings and she offered me one on a leaf that I ate with a bit of freshly cooked pork that Kunai gave me. Auwe was putting six to ten dumplings onto separate leaves then wrapping them; later they would be taken over to the *iron* for the men to eat. To make the dumplings, she mixed sago flour with hot water in a 'limbum' basket. The water was warmed by dropping into it hot stones heated on the hearth. After removing the stones, she added the sago flour and a grayish viscous mixture soon formed. To make the dumplings she took a small stick in each hand, reached into the mix and, twirling the sticks, lifted out a portion that she twirled a few more times to make it about eight inches long, then placed it on a leaf. The dumplings were then eaten with the fingers. Auwe also placed several dumplings on a leaf for the two dogs, but they totally ignored the dumplings. being only interested in the bounty of pig meat that Kunai had brought into the house and placed by Alitowi's hearth.

Alitowi then began to prepare her evening dish of pork with sago cake and cooked greens; 'tulip' and 'apika' are favorites. First, she placed several long vines on the floor that she covered with palm fronds then added a layer of bright green banana leaves. After covering the banana leaves with a thick layer of sago flour about two and a half feet square, she added pieces of the butchered pig with the skin intact. By this time the stones heating in a wood fire on her hearth were hot, some red hot, and they were placed atop the pig meat producing an immediate scorched aroma that excited the dogs more than me. Then more pig pieces were set atop the hot stones and a few more stones were placed around the food mound and on top. Greens were placed over the entire sizzling and steaming mound then a final layer of palm and banana leaves. With assistance from one of the women she pulled the vines up around the bundle, tightly closing the leaf enwrapped food, and then securely tied the vines. Picking up the bundle she placed it on the hearth's wood burning fire where she had heated the stones. I didn't stay for the cooking—I went home to type up what I had seen—but Kunai said she eventually would turn the bundle on another side to cook and, when she had decided the food was done, she would remove the bundle from the fire, open it, and her one dish dinner of sago, pork, and greens would be distributed and appreciatively devoured.

Traditionally, the Lujere had no access to true salt for seasoning but today they can buy it from the mission trade store. However, if they don't have the money, the old way of seasoning food is still practiced. Leaves of the rattan plant or the stem of a sago palm leaf are dried in the sun then burned to the ashes that are used for flavoring.

Tropical evenings near the equator are short so when the sun drops over the horizon and nightfall descends, most villagers have eaten and already are in their dark houses lit only by a hearth's glowing embers, the doors fastened tight against any 'sangumaman's incursion. But the nights were not always quiet ones. Children would awaken and cry out. Oria's five-year-old daughter Womkau who lived across from me was notorious for awaking then launching into an attenuated wail until someone quieted her with a bit of sago. However, the most disturbing nighttime sound was the indescribable crying of an infant suffering with cerebral malaria.

Greetings, Old and New

A villager's daily comings and goings were usually unceremonious with no ritualized "hello" or "goodbye" Namia greeting of any kind, a convention I never was comfortable with. However, the relation between strangers or between expats and locals who spoke Tok Pisin was usually recognized with 'moning' (good morning), 'apinum' (good afternoon) or 'gutnait.' The traditional colonial greeting to an expat was 'moning masta' (master) or 'misis' (Mrs.), but I insisted to be addressed by my first name, "Bill," which yielded a greeting that sounded like 'moning Beal.'

Although there was no Indigenous everyday greeting in Namia, there was a behavioral one when a villager met or left someone who lived far away or wasn't often seen. Once in a neighboring village with Eine, I saw an old man recognize another man and grabbing each other with hands on each other's shoulders, they put their faces very close together and nodded back and forth, rubbing noses. It was a joyous embrace full of happiness reflected in both of their faces. Later that day in another hamlet, Eine saw a relative and they repeated the same joyous greeting. It was a unisex greeting and a very old tradition, but was going out of fashion, especially with some of the younger villagers.

The Ancestors' Stones

Lujere villages are ephemeral creations that can quickly burn down, rot away, suffer severe wind and rain damage, or be abandoned for a new site. Constructed of bush materials in a harsh, humid, and storm-prone environment, homes were not long-lasting; no bride went to her new husband from the house whence she was born. Material permanence was limited to small, hard things like shells, girdles strung of bone, a boar's tusk, and the stone blades of axes. Large objects or monuments constructed in perpetuity, so familiar to Western communities, didn't exist. Or so I thought.

Near the end of my fieldwork Kunai, in need of newspaper for his cigarettes, brought me two old stone axe blades, and we made a trade. Earlier I had wondered where their axe blades came from and who made them but, like so many questions, had never pursued it. Had I thought to ask Kunai right then as we made our swap, I'm sure he could have told me. But later that day, knowing that only twenty-eight years ago a stone axe or *amei* was all they had for chopping, I asked Oria. He surprised me by saying that one of the big stones where village men used to sharpen the stone blades for their axes was up near Arakwake's wife's house, so we went to have a look. Indeed, there was not just one big stone but three. Then he showed me a taller stone covered by jungle vines at the end of the village near Nauwen's unfinished house.

One of the stones was about a foot and a half off the ground and three or so feet long. This was a big rock and, except for the other grinding stones, there were no others around and the village's slight rise from the 'kunai' tapered to perpetual forested wetlands. The mystery to me was how did these big "ancestral" stones, these monuments to an ancient past, get there in a primeval society without the wheel or beasts of burden. No one knew. 'Mipella no savi.' Then came the predictable retort, "They are to do with our ancestors of a long time ago." Perhaps, I thought, they had lain there for centuries but no one had invented a story to explain their presence, as surely an Australian Aborigine would have done. The Lujere imagination, it seemed, was not prone to performing the anomalies of nature. Their creative métier, something we have only sampled but explore more deeply in part 3, was in generating unseen terrors and inspired visionary tales.

The job of grinding the blades was done by the old men who sat astride a stone as they shaped and sharpened the blades by hand while the younger men were, as today, out hunting, fishing, finding food or goofing off in the *iron*. The craftsman sat astride the rock, as the boy imitates in figure 26, and ground the blade against the rock to shape and sharpen it, obviously a slow tedious task. The grinding scars were still very evident on the vine-free rocks. The Lujere had two basic types of stone blades. The large *aruwa* blade was used in an adze to cut down trees; the pointed cylinder shaped *yauna* blade was used to fell sago palms. Women also sometimes used the *yauna* blade when processing sago. Both types of blades were secured into a conventional wooden axe handle found throughout New Guinea.

Figure 26. A boy astride an archaic grinding stone near the end of the upper village.

Oria showed me a traditional adze that belonged to his father, but the stone had been replaced during World War II by a piece of metal. It was a swap his father had made with 'Whiski' for his mother's sago to feed, we now know, the Mosstroop's policemen. Back then, boys had small adzes with stones in the *aruwa* shape as well as the small bows and arrows still made in 1972. The small adzes were also used for jobs like cutting pig bones. I also wanted to know the source of the stone blades, so we found old Menetjua and with both Oria and Wauripe translating, learned that the stones came from far up the Yellow River. This was possibly up in the Wape area where the Wape got their stones from the local riverbeds. There was also a mountain just across the Sepik River where the Lujere also acquired stones from its streams; as an alternative source, Wakau villagers might also obtain them from Edawaki in exchange for shell rings.

Taboos in Daily Life

The innumerable taboos the society has acquired through time and applies relentlessly is one of the inescapable factors in being a Lujere. The taboos reside, however, primarily in the individual's consciousness and a central part of Lujere socialization is learning what actions are tabooed and the negative consequence if broken. First, "Taboo is not a thing. Being taboo is a condition" (Bracken 2007: 1). As taboos vary according to one's age, gender, and societal situation, acquiring this information is an extended learning duty from childhood to old age. Throughout the book I occasionally mention specific taboos, but it would be impossible for me to list all of these, as they are legion—and enormously tedious—and I was still acquiring new ones when I departed. There is, however, a short discussion of food taboos in chapter 13 because they are believed to importantly impact a villager's health. I mention the topic of taboos, not to provide closure on it, but to emphasize that it was a complex and pervasive factor in how villagers interacted and of which I had only partial knowledge. Below, is an example regarding a tabooed behavior and the serendipitous way much of fieldwork proceeds.

In February, Mowal's wife Apewaki had a baby daughter and, several days after the birth, I asked some of the men if I could see the new baby. But I was told "no" because it would harm me if I did. If I, a man, would see the mother and baby before they both had bathed, I would lose weight, become skin and bones, and always be hungry. Girls and women could visit them without incident, but even little boys were tabooed. Only the father could interact with the baby and her mother without fateful results. I thought it was curious that the father was immune, while the rest of the village males were not. No explanation was offered. I could only surmise that the mother's husband was somehow ritually inoculated against proximity to her vaginal bleeding that, whether from menstruation or childbirth, was deleterious to a man's well-being. A few days later I learned that they had bathed and, when I dropped by, Apewaki proudly showed me her tiny pink infant who she had named Kairapowe, which I came to recognize as a "unisex" name.

CHAPTER ELEVEN

Discord and Dissent

Domestic disputes and marital problems were many.
PO Ray Lanaghan (1971: 7)

Annette Weiner (1984) writes about the cultural constraints in a Trobriander's mind that inhibited the expression of anger towards a fellow villager. The Lujere behavioral temperament was very different. In a society where individuals were as publicly expressive as the Lujere, dissension was a common occurrence and sometimes was brought to Ray for mediation. While verbal assertiveness was common, physical aggression was unusual. Although there are instances of interpersonal conflict throughout the book, here I will (1) offer some incidents demonstrating the range of village conflicts; (2) examine the administration's colonial record of civil and criminal offenses for Iwani villagers; and (3) review the liaison between 'kiaps' and villagers.

Domestic Quarrels

These first examples are domestic clashes. The most common were between children and parents; as several appear in the text here is one more with implications for wider emotional assumptions. One morning early in my stay, I heard a commotion coming from Ai'ire's house in the lower village. It sounded like a child or young person yelling out in anger. Then I saw Aiyuk come out of the *iron* carrying a big stick in his right hand and a shorter one in his left hand. He hurried across the plaza and went into Ai'ire's house where his family lived. The noise continued, the boys in the plaza playing with tops stopped to watch the excitement, and I called to Nauwen in my 'haus kuk' to join me to see what was happening. Then Klowi emerged from the *iron* and he too entered Ai'ire's house. Soon the loud commotion ended.

What had happened was that Aiyuk's oldest boy was angry because he wanted some money to buy a pair of trousers and either his father wouldn't give him any or didn't have any, hence his yelling and tumultuous behavior that had included throwing some of his mother's belongings around. Aiyuk had intervened with his threatening sticks and then Klowi intervened to keep the father and son from fighting. Gradually, the commotion in the house subsided. Klowi emerged calmly carrying an axe. A short while later, Aiyuk also left the house, but the boy remained inside. It was interesting that the boy wanted trousers, called 'trausis,' not shorts, as no expats in the Yellow River area ever wore long pants because they were too hot. However, 'trausis,' like sandals, were definite status symbols among more acculturated New Guinea males, and apparently he was aware of that. It made me more attentive to how the seemingly isolated Lujere culture was changing in odd little ways. Aiyuk's sole attire as a youth was a small gourd penis sheath that he chose from the forest and styled for himself, but his son's sartorial imagination and desires were influenced by global capitalism and commodity fetishism.

Wakau parents were, I thought, very tolerant of their small children's ofttimes demanding behavior. Womkau, Oria's little daughter and immediate neighbor, I observed the most. When she did not get what she wanted, she never hesitated to express her dislike orally and often physically as well. One morning she wanted some 'apica' (green leaves) to eat. Her busy mother's response was to holler at her to fetch some water. Womkau then began to wail loudly and repeatedly struck the side of the house with a stick, actions both of her parents ignored. It reminded me of Wape parents who rarely responded to a child's temper tantrum but let the child exhaust themself.

Around noon I went down to the lower *iron* and there was Aiyuk sitting by a clay hearth in his never-never land, calmly smoking his Lujere style pipe. When his son came in he sat down near his father. I looked him over well and saw no bruises, and he smiled when our eyes met. This father-son quarrel prompted recall of a similar argument when I lived in the Wape village of Taute, between Moala and his son. In Wakau the angry boy was physically combative toward his parents, in Taute the angry boy threatened suicide; their contrasting actions seemed to highlight the difference between the Lujere and Wape cultures in the handling of anger. With the Lujere there appeared to be less sublimating of anger and turning it back on oneself than among the Wape; for instance, I heard of no cases of suicide or attempted suicide while with the Lujere, but among the Wape it was not unusual. At the risk of severe over-simplification, one could venture that the Lujere tended to "vent" their frustrations and that the Wape tended to "sublimate" theirs.

I also noticed when small children misbehaved or did not follow instructions they were bopped on the head, not painfully, but jarringly. While in my 'ofis' working I had a good view of several houses up-village and, consequently, casual village behavior. One late afternoon I saw Kwoien, whose house was just across from the upper *iron*, bop his little son Aleowaki on the head, not too hard, but I didn't know why. (Perhaps it was related to his son's earlier behavior when he and another little boy were throwing things at a child in a house.) Kwoien then grabbed his son by the arm and pulled him up to the house veranda, bopped him again, then walked over to the *iron*. Aleowaki did not fight back, nor did I hear him cry. It was a typical miniature parent-child altercation. Late one morning Irowe, whose husband Ino was away as an indentured laborer, went past my 'ofis' pulling her complaining little daughter along. Finally, as they started down the short incline to the lower village, Irowe stopped to slap her daughter's head and smack her body with the blunt side of her bush knife; then continued to pull the child along. The child's argument was that she wanted to stay in the village instead of going to the bush to work sago with her mother.

Most spousal arguments are commonplace and dreary to the outsider; here is an exception to that presumption. Luritsao's family lived in the house just north of mine, House Seven but, two days after I had completed mapping the village and taken a census of each household, he tore the house down. He and his oldest boy continued to sleep in the upper *iron* while his wife and other three children, one a baby, moved in with Arawaki's and Nakwani's wives in House Fifteen.[1] I was in my office screen room one morning getting organized while a few youths were sitting just outside visiting and having a good laugh. I asked them what was making them laugh but no one would give me a serious explanation and I was too busy to push them for it. Later I asked Oria what the joke was, and he explained that it was an earlier argument, audible to all, between Luritsao and his wife that occurred at the abandoned *iron*. The argument concerned Luritsao's baby boy who was sick again. He was running a fever and Luritsao's wife wanted to take him back to the 'haus sik' where she already had spent several days. Luritsao was emphatically against it and told her absolutely no—probably because he again would have the responsibility for the other two young children including feeding them during her absence. She persisted and he, in his anger, broke her sago container. Furious, she replied that the reason the child was sick in the first place was because he couldn't abstain from having sex with her. Furthermore, she said, if he didn't let her go to the 'haus sik,' she would take a knife and cut up her vagina so he never could have sex with her again! That, of course, was what the youths had been laughing about. Oria explained that the child was sick because Luritsao continued to break the taboo of having intercourse with his wife until the child was several years old, two at the very youngest. Oria added that his son was one year old last month, so he had a big taboo on intercourse, hadn't broken it, and didn't intend to. But Luritsao's last children, he said, were too close together, as the toddler was carried about most of the time and, if walking, had to have a hand.

When Eine's wife Talai went to the new Edwaki market and then to the mission to sell food without success, Eine was furious when she returned with no money to give him and yelled at her insultingly in both Namia and Tok Pisin. Her response was not to respond in kind as Luritsao's wife did, but to simply walk up to Arakwaki's wife's house and spend the night there. But that didn't quiet Eine. The following night he began another rant about her stupidity while sitting on Oria's porch holding a burning torch. The next morning the entire family returned to Oria's house where they had been living or, if Oria spoke English, he might have said "squatting." I'll return to that quarrel in the next section.

In many New Guinea societies, the status of women was low and wife beating, while a civil offense, was locally approved and endemic (Counts, Brown, and Campbell 1999). In such societies, wives are viewed as controlled by others. A wife is an obedient chattel and, when not, is to be physically punished. However, the Wape villagers I lived with disdained violence towards women; if a husband and wife were in a loud escalating

---

1. Luritsao's mother's father and Arakwaki's and Nakwani's father's father were brothers that, in terms of Lujere ideas of kinship and descent, made for a close tie that should become clearer in the next chapter.

argument, the women neighbors would surround the house until tempers cooled or the woman came outside (Mitchell 1999). But that was not the Lujere way. Compared to the Wape I knew, the Lujere were more open to violence but, by New Guinea standards, still on the light side.

I only knew of four incidents of physical wife abuse while in Wakau and one of those was by the Mauwi man K____, first mentioned in chapter 5. I learned of it one evening while at the lower *iron* visiting with Unei, Klowi, and Iwi, his grown adopted son. Iwi initiated the conversation saying that a couple of days earlier K____ had attacked his wife with a bush knife striking her across the forehead. The blood flowed and she was knocked unconscious. She was born in Wakau, was Kwaien's sister, and known to everyone including me. The story was that she had taken her child to the 'haus sik' for treatment but K____ was angered, like Luritsao, when she stayed too long. Because he was a feared 'sangumaman,' no one, especially not her brother, soft-spoken and mild Kwoien, would report the attack.

Tsaime said if it were his sister he would go to the 'kiap' and have K____ jailed. There were different versions as to how long she had remained unconscious, which was not surprising, as it was a neighboring village. It happened near the end of my stay in Wakau and I already had a negative view of K____, based partly on the adverse talk that accompanied his name but more specifically on my watching his treatment of a Wakau girl, discussed in chapter 18. About a week later I saw K____ entering the village with his wife and two children; obviously, she had survived the attack and life moved on. In this next incident of wife bashing, I had an active first aide role.

Early one Monday morning when I was mixing up some pancakes and cheerfully anticipating the Vermont maple syrup we had brought from home, Waniyo's wife Elwe came up to my house with blood dripping from her upper left forearm and from the area just in front of her right ear. There was also blood on her thigh and in one hand she carried a bloody piece of firewood. With Oria and Nauwen translating, I learned that she and Waniyo just had a fight and he had struck her repeatedly with the firewood. She had come to me with the hope that I would report the incident to the 'kiap' but Oria explained that the rules for filing grievances were that she, being the aggrieved party, must personally take her grievance to the 'kiap.' Here is what she told Oria had happened: she was getting ready to go to the bush to make sago when Waniyo accused her of making the sago for an *aewal wowi* curing festival for Ai'ire, our neighbor, who was sick. But apparently, he was really angry at Ai'ire and Klowi for not helping him with food for the two *aewal wowi* curing festivals (discussed in chap. 15) that he gave for a sick member of his own household. Elwe protested that the sago would be for their own household, but as he did not believe her, they began to fight. Oria said that before I came to the village, he occasionally hit her but not since I had arrived. I dressed her arm wound, an ugly jagged affair, and put antibiotic powder on her cheek cut, a bloody mess but not as deep.

The third instance of wife abuse surprised me as they were my neighbors and seemed very compatible. I had lived in the village almost two months when one evening just after dark I heard a loud commotion near the men's lower *iron*. I went down to investigate and Klowi was striding around the plaza railing against Tsaime's marriage, as discussed earlier. But a concomitant commotion had been that Ai'ire had struck his wife Miwali. He was angry because she regularly went to Waniyo's wife's house after dark. But, according to Oria, the real reason was that Ai'ire and Klowi (Ai'ire's dead father's brother) were shamed, or humiliated, when Leno accused them of always eating his sago, thus implicating the men in cutting his sago palms and their wives in processing the flour. The insult was that the men could not provide for their families. For some reason Miwali apparently was punished, you might say scapegoated, for this. But, if true, the exact dynamics escaped me; it was one of numerous examples where my understanding was left dangling.

The last case of spousal abuse was, like the first, by a Mauwi man of his Wakau born wife. Turai, the licensed shotgun owner in Mauwi, was married to Oria and Nauwen's sister, Note, and when he shot a cassowary, his wife gave some of the meat to her brothers. This so angered Turai that he burned his wife's backsides with a piece of glowing wood. In retaliation, she had come down to Wakau with her son and wanted her brothers to report her husband to the 'kiap.' The source of her husband's anger was that on a recent visit to Wakau, Oria had not given him any meat although Oria had received some pig meat when his father's brother's dog had killed a little pig.

Disputes Among Villagers

As the Lujere had a surfeit of land and a small, dispersed population, land was not a major source of dissension, as it was in more densely populated areas of the country. But the distribution of resources could excite passions if someone felt unfairly treated. Such was the response when Oria felt cheated on a pig distribution.

Oria and other men had gone to shoot a pig that was loitering near the Kaigu Creek. Oria killed it with a spear and, as the slayer, would get a good cut. Although the hunter was tabooed from eating his own kill, at least his family could. The next day, Oria and I went to the base camp to see the new market Ray had organized; when we returned, the pig had been dressed and distributed at Waniyo's house. Oria had been given only the tail! The following morning, while Oria and I were working together in my screened room, his wife occasionally called over to him with comments that seemed to make him increasingly edgy. Finally, at 11:50, he went out to deal with his allocation of the insulting pig's tail and gave an explosive lecture to all and then had his little daughter carry the tail to the upper *iron*, making it clear that he wanted none of that pig's tail. (Later I heard from Nauwen that he wanted the jaw). But there was a further dispute about who had killed the pig. Waniyo claimed that Mangko had shot it first, but Nauwen said that Mangko claimed that he had missed the pig. I wasn't a witness to the further details but eventually the dispute was resolved and there seemed to be no residue of bad feelings from Oria toward the other men.

A more serious quarrel erupted between Eine and Oria after he moved his family into Oria's house. Eine was a mature knowledgeable man, a good hunter, with a wife from Gwidami and four children. He was also a shameless scrounger. While I lived in Wakau, he did not have a village house for his family but, taking advantage of both his and his wife's kinship ties, moved his family into other men's wives' houses. He was also the only villager who made innumerable material requests from me, the rich newcomer. When Nauwen returned from working on the coast, he was infuriated to discover that Eine had cut a line of his sago palms. After I moved to Wakau, Eine also cut some of Wolwar's sago palms so angering him that in a burst of fury he threatened to burn down Eine's house, momentarily forgetting that he didn't own one.

In Eine's partial defense, it was only when I began to collect the villagers' genealogies that I came to better appreciate one factor contributing to his scrounging behavior. His was a worst-case scenario for a son whose father dies relatively young without planting adequate food resources for his progeny. Eine's mother and father had three children: a daughter, a young son who was killed in a Tsila raid and Eine, still a baby when his father died. His mother then married Purkan who was one of Oria and Nauwen's father's (Limeritjo) three younger brothers: Ukai, who I came to know, Purkan, who became Eine's stepfather and now long dead, and Sitwaui, slain in the same Tsila raid that killed Eine's brother. Purkan took his young stepson Eine with him into his large bush, shared in part with his two brothers, to cut sago, hunt, and fish. Then, while Eine was still a little boy, Purkan died, as did his mother; now an orphan, Limeritjo and Ukai took care of him. Thus, while still a child, Eine became a putative agnate to the younger Oria and Nauwen, whose mother helped feed him, giving him the putative rights and obligations as a patrikin with a common grandfather.

Nauwen was the first to challenge this interpretation when, after Eine had cut sago Nauwen considered his, he pointedly told Eine that they did not have the same grandfather and he had no rights to the sago palms, thus discounting Eine's status as Purkan's stepson. It was also true that Eine had inherited sago palms from his own father, but they were in another area of the forest and, presumably, not convenient to the village. But it was his rift over housing with Oria that finally disrupted the relationship between the putative paternal cousins.

After Oria's father died, he moved his family into his mother's house after she remarried and moved to her husband's village, and Eine's family moved into Oria's old, dilapidated house. It wasn't long, however, before Eine's family moved in with Oria's family and Oria's old house was torn down. Both houses were near mine, so I observed some of these changes. Earlier I cited a domestic quarrel Eine had with his wife, but there was additional tension in the joint household when their daughter, about ten or so, repeatedly would sit on Oria's porch and wail for sago. I knew indirectly that Oria resented Eine bringing his family to live in his small house and as putative close agnates it wasn't necessary for Eine to ask permission. While I was not aware of any open quarreling between the households, I was aware of the increasing tension and of the tension developing between Eine and me because I would not comply with his many querulous requests. To everyone's relief, one morning the family departed, Eine resentfully, to a bush camp. Oria later told me that Eine could not come live with his family again; his house was taboo to him.

Just as Elwe wanted me to report her husband to the 'kiap' for striking her, others sought my intervention in quarrels although I had been very vocal that the 'kiap' wanted to hear complaints from the actual aggrieved person, not from me. One evening just before dark, K____ arrived in the village with his family. He almost immediately went to my 'haus kuk' and talked with Oria and Nauwen. Oria was initially evasive when I asked what he wanted, then said K____ had asked if I had written a letter to the 'kiap' at Ariawani's suggestion. A couple of days earlier, Ariawani had asked me to contact the 'kiap' and report that K____ had threatened him with 'sanguma' after Ariawani had accused him of cutting his sago palms. I told him I couldn't, and hadn't; of course, Oria already knew that.

Stick fights were sometimes fought between villagers or between men in neighboring villages; always the intent was to chastise but not to kill. I witnessed one of these on the 'kunai' just west of Wakau. It concerned a Wakau father who did not want his daughter to marry and is described in the following chapter. On a more mundane level, there was much more contention and disgust with pig feces within Wakau than in Taute where there might be some grumbling, but never a yelling match as in Wakau. Waniyo allegedly built his house down on the 'kunai' to avoid pig feces, and Klowi said he would build a new *iron* on the 'kunai' and Enewan already had started a house down there for the same reason. One "pig shit" yelling match occurred near my 'ofis.' Late one morning I saw Aiyuk poke his head out of the lower *iron* and begin yelling. Next, I noticed Sakome carrying her baby walking down towards my house where she stopped, faced down towards the *iron*, strongly called out a few sentences, then turned calmly back up the village path. Eine, translating, said Aiyuk was angry about the feces from Waripe's pig and wanted his wife Sakome to have it shot, but she wasn't about to comply.

Gossip and quarrels are closely related. Here is a case of gossiping that skidded around on the edge of a quarrel. Eine was visiting with me one hot afternoon at the 'ofis' when we observed Menetjua crossing the 'kunai' after bathing. Next, we heard him talking just below us; he obviously had stopped at the *iron* to voice his complaint. Eine said he had named Samaun as responsible for casting the spell that was causing so many villagers to have a very bad cold including him, and that he did it in retaliation against the women who were not sending him enough 'sacsac' and 'hotwara' (two sago preparations)—but, Menetjua added, they were. When I questioned Eine about the spell, he said that Samaun wasn't a *nakwolu*, but that his brother Meyawali was, and he probably had instructed him in the ritual. I heard other complaints about Samaun as the cause of all the coughs, runny nose, and chest pains but as far as I could learn, he never retaliated with a strong denial. I supposed that the negative gossiping at his expense might have got him the food he wanted.

When I returned from Lumi after being in Lumi for Christmas with my family, several of the men came by and we were lounging in the evening on my little back veranda, and I asked what had happened while I was gone. Silence. I was back on Wakau time, always a physical and mental shock after several days of being on active family and expat time. I gradually shifted into local mode and, as we sat swatting the occasional mosquito with only the light of a little hanging kerosene lantern, an event was presented, discussed listlessly, then silence until another event was presented. It was a slow and gradual revelation over a couple of hours of the life of a little New Guinea hamlet; an attenuated pace that would drive some people nuts. Had I gone inside to my 'ofis,' as was my strong initial inclination, instead of restfully surrendering to the silences and slowing down, I would have learned nothing.

Relevant to our topic of discord, Yaope had hit Aria when Luritsao, Aria and Yaope were all sleeping in the old, dilapidated *iron*. Men sometimes sleep naked and, on this occasion, Yaope had put his light cover aside. Aria, seeing this, attempted anal intercourse with him. This was, incidentally, the first time I had heard a mention of sex between village men among either the Wape or the Lujere. From the matter-of-fact way the incident was related I wondered if sex did occasionally occur among Wakau's single men; there certainly was a large number of mostly enforced bachelors. Anyway, Yaope struck Aria hard as he threw him off. A few days later Aria went to the base camp and told the police that the Wakau men wanted to kill him with 'sanguma.' When he returned to Wakau the next day, he was roughed up by Nauwen and Mangko and told to get out and move up to Mauwi, which he did. As everyone seemed to dislike Aria, I was surprised to hear Nakwane speak up for him and say he was an innocent victim of Samaun's suggestions and held Samaun as the real culprit regarding his going to the police. The minutia of life, any life, is staggering. There obviously was another thread to this story but I didn't pursue it as Arakwaki mentioned that Yaope also took a wife while I was away and this was an event, reported in chapter 12, I was eager to learn about.

Colonial Offenses, Official and Unofficial

While in Lumi at Christmas, I examined the "Gaol Register" published by the subdistrict, which recorded all the inmates in the Lumi Correctional Institution (LCI). The register began in 1951, and I checked from then through December 1971 for the individuals jailed from Iwani village's four hamlets including Wakau. The offender's name was given first followed by a slash then his father's name. Spelling, as usual, was challenging and the administration's "official" name for the offender also could be different from his popular village name. Back in the village I sat down with several of the men, and we figured out from my detailed notes who most of the Iwani offenders were and the men specifically from Wakau. With the offender's name was his legal offense but not always its substance, the sentence imposed, the date the sentence began, and the release date. Offenders charged with capital crimes like murder were committed for trial by the Supreme Court in Wewak and their trial records were kept elsewhere.

Although the Gaol Register was begun in 1951, the administration, as we know, did not begin patrolling all the Lujere villages until George Oakes's 1956 pioneering patrol that included Wakau when it was located in the sprawling fens west of the Sand River. The total number of offenses committed by Iwani villagers in the twenty years up to and through 1971 was sixty-two, all by men, although if a woman didn't show up for census, it was her husband who was punished, not her. The type, number and percent of the different violations are shown in table 9. Of the nine violent offenses, one was an October 1960, three-month sentence to Saime, a Wakau *nakwolu* and Mangko's father, for "unlawful assault," unspecified, and five for "willful murder" including three related to a 1960 'sanguma' double murder in Iwarita hamlet involving the Iwani 'sangumamen' K____, S____, and A____ whose case and trial is discussed in chapter 17. In table 9, K____, also accounts for "escaped from custody" two times and the "theft" conviction.

The other two convictions for "willful murder" were in 1955 before any government official had visited the Iwani hamlets. The convicted murderers were two Wakau men: Waribe, and Tiai, the father of Arawake's wife Alitowi. According to Oria and Kunai, they speared and killed the Bapei man Nemano while he was in the bush collecting sago grubs with his small son. This was apparently in retaliation for Tiai's child being killed by 'sanguma.' Tiai and Waripe were tried and sentenced to prison in Wewak for four years and, according to the Gaol Register, were respectively, forty and thirty years old. They were the first Wakau men to be jailed by a colonial regime. At the time Kunai was a laborer on Buka for two years but he recalled Tiai returned from his imprisonment looking like an old man and died soon afterwards.

Table 9. Iwani village males convicted of offenses 1955–1971

Offense	Number convicted	Percentage of convicted
Violent	9	15
Disobeyed lawful order	29	47
Escaped from custody	10	16
Aided prisoner escape	2	3
Failed to appear for census	7	11
False report	2	3
Child neglect	2	3
Theft (in prison)	1	2
Totals	62	100

The other violent convictions were rape (one), "unlawful assault" (two), and "did lay hold of a woman" (one). The last offense concerned Klowi's adopted son Iwi, twentyish, who was the only Iwani villager convicted of violence close to my time in Wakau. In April of 1971 Iwi served three months in the LCI for the citation: "On 23 of April at Edwaki laid hold of and forced to the ground and removed her dress of IPAI / NERIAU of Iwani." She [Ipiyai] was an older woman making sago when he attacked her, but she broke loose before he could rape her. She told her husband and when Oria who was at the mission Bible school learning Tok Pisin heard about it, told the new local 'kiap' (that Ray replaced) who sentenced Iwi to three months. According to Oria, Iwi did not take offense to his reporting him to the 'kiap.'

Most of the Iwani villagers' offenses—47 percent—were for "disobeying a lawful order" or "failure to comply with instructions," common charges by a patrolling 'kiap' who found a hamlet in disarray. This is what happened in Wakau on August 31, 1965, when a patrolling 'kiap' sentenced sixteen Wakau men—Aiyuk, Akami, Eine, Aria, Engwe, Enuk, Limeritjo, Luritsao, Meri, Mowal, Nauwen, Oria, Poke, Waniyo, Wauripe, and Wolwar—to six weeks in the LCI because the trail to the village was not maintained, the grass was uncut where villagers line for census, and the brush was not cut back from the village. Eine, as Iwani's 'tultul,' was held partly responsible and had his 'tultul' hat removed that same day.

Table 9 also shows seven men were charged with failing to appear for census; for instance, in October 1960, Meyawali was sentenced to one month of jail time for not appearing. The Lumi records indicated that Klowi was one of the two men convicted of "child neglect." On December 5, 1962, he was sentenced to three months in jail for disobeying PO C. A. Trollope's order to take his five-year-old daughter for medical treatment, as it was "readily accessible" at the "CMML Mission Hospital." But he and three other Iwani men, while being escorted by the police to Lumi to serve their sentences of census evasion, escaped at Abrau the following day. Klowi was captured January 24, 1962, and his fifty days at large were added to his original sentence. He again escaped for six weeks but was soon back in the slammer and finally released June 5, 1963. Keeping Iwani villagers in custody once they were committed was sometimes a problem for the administration, as there were ten charges (17 percent) of escaping from custody and two charges (3 percent) of aiding a prisoner to escape.

There were also two charges for "false report" related to a 'sanguma' case I observed in Lumi before I lived with the Lujere and describe in chapter 17. Overall, the Iwani people, as a village of over three hundred people with only nine violent offenses (albeit five murder convictions) known to the administration since they began patrolling, were by comparison to some Highlands societies a nonviolent people. That is an outsider's view. But a villager who believed that most of her co-villagers' deaths were caused by the violence of 'sanguma' might make a different judgment.

While discussing law and order from an administration perspective, it is significant that not all violations were of an official nature, but some were by the unofficial fiat of the 'kiap.' At the more rural stations, the 'kiap' was a king-like figure with police to back up his orders, and 'kiaps' varied on how they exercised this power. The 'kiap' at Yellow River was in an unfortunate catch-22. While he was expected to maintain the station, he was not provided the funds to keep the grass and jungle from re-engulfing the laboriously cleared land, work that the Lujere men had provided gratis to build the station. Afterwards they expected jobs but there weren't any.

In Lumi it was easier to keep the station looking good. The Wape men were devotees of an illegal gambling game called 'satu' so, when the large airstrip's grass needed cutting, as it almost constantly did because of the high rainfall, the police would go to a village where they knew 'satu' was being played and legally bring in the men for several weeks of cutting grass by hand with their 'sarips.' The Lujere, however, were not gamblers. In Yellow River, the 'kiap' had to be more creative to secure his free labor, for example, when the people were coming to the base camp to vote in the 1972 national election, he immediately put the early comers to work cutting and digging grass, but when three took off, which was their right, he sent the police after them and they had to spend the rest of the day—except when they voted—cutting grass until 6:00. Or, when he was taking the census for Iwani, a man's wife did not appear as soon as he thought she should, so he put the husband to cutting grass at the station for a couple of weeks. The 'kiap' was aware that these capricious practices were all outside the law—although locals didn't know it—and a regretful way to keep his station in shape.

Klowi's Crimes

Klowi was to me something of an enigma. On the one hand he was righteously authoritative, a feared 'sanguma' killer and alleged murderer of two fellow female villagers. On the other hand, he seemed sensitive and caring, was a popular curer or *imoulu*, and one of the most amiable, personable, and interesting men in the village. I liked him immensely. But I remember his stopping alone by my 'ofis' late one dark night and, as he watched me type, soberly saying in his limited Tok Pisin, "Mi man nogut," that he was a bad person. He spoke it calmly, almost ruefully. I don't recall my response, but that quiet nighttime admission is seared in my memory.

From different people I had learned that he was the only man who had openly killed fellow villagers. Eventually, I learned more pointedly about his crimes in an interview with Oria and a chance one with Mangko, Klowi's paternal nephew. They said the murders occurred when Wakau was located across the Sand River. The first murder was of Unei's mother, but I do not have any reliable information regarding it except it was some informants' belief and that Klowi took responsibility in raising her son Unei.[2] Had I asked an old-timer like Eine, I might have gotten the full story. The other alleged murder was of his stepdaughter Manwe whom he desired. After Klowi's first wife died, he married Wea who was widowed and came to him with her daughter Manwe. Her apparent murder was during an *aewal wowi* curing festival held for Arakwaki and Nakwane's mother (later Oria and Nauwen's stepmother).

Oria began his account of the murders by recalling that he had just shot a very large pig, his second one, then named the number of pigs several other men had killed (e.g., Arakwake, three pigs; his father's brothers Ukai, five pigs and Purkan, two pigs; Kwoien, two pigs) but that his father had been unsuccessful—in fact it had been a very long time since his father had shot a pig. It was an odd preamble to a murder story but did authenticate, again, the importance of hunting to Lujere men: Klowi was enamored with Manwe; she was a plumpish young woman with high pointed breasts and Klowi wanted to marry her, but she wanted to marry another man, and this angered him. They apparently argued, even fought, in his hamlet. Then she ran away to Oria's hamlet where the curing festival was being held and hid in Ukai's house. Oria said he and his friends were just youths and did not know what was happening. The villagers celebrated all night. At daybreak, Tsaime and Warajak's father asked Engwe and Nimo why Klowi had battered Manwe. Klowi, who was hiding in Arakwaki's older brother Luman's house, came out brandishing his bush knife and went up on Ukai's veranda and called out, if you want to argue with me, come on! He then went into Ukai's house and Manwe ran out quickly followed by Klowi, but she ran back into the house, chased by Klowi. Once inside, she went out the back door that was on a slope and fell. In the darkness Klowi couldn't see her at first, but when he did, he struck her three times around the head with his bush knife. She didn't scream but was covered with blood that ran like water and some of the villagers saw this. In Oria's account, it is unclear where and when she died but the horrific part is that he allegedly cut off her lips and ate them raw. At some point her body was placed on a scaffold in the forest and not in the village as done traditionally, apparently so a patrol officer would not see it, as burial was now the law. That is the story I got from villagers. But when I made a study of the Lumi Gaol Register, I came upon the following contradictory data:

KARAUWI [Klowi] / NANAMIAR [father's name]
July 28, 1960
That on or about the 14th day of September 1959 at Wakau, Karauwi [Klowi] a male native of Wakau in the Lumi Sub-District did unlawfully strike Manowai [Manwe] / Tiora [father's name] a female native of Wakau.
Given 6 months at Lumi Correctional Institution by [PO] J. Martyn

While my local data were all over the place regarding exactly where and when she died, my informants agreed Klowi murdered—not just assaulted—her during the *aewal wowi* festival. How do you reconcile that surety of local village data with the documented

---

2. It is possible that Klowi was thought to have murdered her via 'sanguma.' Unei, as shown in the next chapter, also had a special kinship tie to Klowi.

fact of PO Martyn's Lumi record that Klowi "did unlawfully strike" her in September of 1959 and was sentenced in July 1960, to six months jail time in Lumi? That was only twelve years before I arrived, not a generation or two that could account for faulty memories. And why the ten-month hiatus between the alleged attack and Martyn's sentencing? The confusion only increases. I once thought that the reason I got such conflicting accounts regarding when and where she died, was that she initially survived the attack then succumbed to her injuries, but when I read PO Martyn's citation written ten months after the attack that seemed less plausible.

I had first heard about her death from Mangko when I was hanging out in the lower *iron* one afternoon as he cooked the toes and leg bone of a cassowary, Aiyuk slept, and Iwi strummed his toy guitar. I asked Mangko to tell me about the times that Klowi had been in jail. He said it was when Klowi killed the single girl Manwe; when he killed Unei's mother, Auwowe; for 'sanguma'; and for 'bikhet,' being disobedient. He then told me a shorter story about the murder of Manwe; it was not a 'sanguma' murder as people saw him openly attack her at the curing festival.

However, no record exists in the Lumi court records of him killing either woman, only the citation in the Gaol Register of him "unlawfully striking" Manwe that contradicts the local memory of her murder. There was no record of any type of an illegal action toward Auwowe by Klowi. Perhaps her demise was a 'sanguma' death that was attributed to Klowi, or perhaps her death wasn't reported to the 'kiap' as a murder. Questions abound. Based on the conflicting information, I have given up on solving these dilemmas. In Wakau, Klowi was unique as a man with a mystique of violence—not just 'sanguma'—surrounding him.

Patrol Officers and Villagers

In my hundreds of pages of typed field notes, there are numerous headings or paragraphs involving the Lujere men's disapproval of administration policies or officers. Some examples of this discord, an inherent quality in any large bureaucratic structure, already have been presented. Here are several more where I also have included my take on the problematic situation.

Playing Politics

I had slept only five nights in my new Wakau house when Peter Broadhurst, the Lumi Assistant District Commissioner, totally surprised me by walking into the village just after lunch. He told me that he and the District Commissioner, Bob Bunting with his wife Nan, had flown down to inspect the Edwaki Base Camp and were flying back to Lumi tomorrow. They would return on the plane that Joyce and the children would arrive on to see my new Wakau digs, and I could spend a few days being a father and husband again. Peter insisted that I return with him to the base camp to meet the Buntings; as Ray was there, we could all party, then I'd meet Joyce's plane tomorrow. Peter and I arrived at the base camp late afternoon and, after meeting Bob and Nan Bunting, Ray quickly confided that he had to break into my food order from Wewak that arrived on the Bunting's and Peter's government-chartered Cessna. There wasn't a single beer in the camp but, he enthused, the beer in my food order could save the day. And it did. The five of us—four White Australians and one White American—talked, ate, laughed, and drank beer until 11:00 p.m. It was an affable group of colonialists partying in the bush, but it was a class of humanity rapidly coming to an end in New Guinea. The administration's Australian officers already were starting to disappear; only the anthropologists would survive independence. At most, we anthropologists viewed ourselves as inadvertent and peripheral agents of colonialism, sometime-visitors who adjusted to our social milieu, whether in an Indigenous village or a colonial base camp, to get on with our important research work.

Part of my work that convivial evening was to give both the district commissioner and Peter a better understanding of how the base camp was viewed by the locals. I wanted them to have some idea of how the locals felt ripped off by the administration. What better time than when we were all having fun and enjoying each other over a few beers. But I had to tread carefully as I didn't want to offend Ray, as he was both my friend and a helpful ally for my research. I emphasized how the Yellow River locals had enthusiastically agreed to give their labor free to establish the base camp, but their expectation was that this would then be a station that could give them some jobs. But there were no jobs. Nothing had changed. They still were expected to give their labor for free. They were no better off than before; if they wanted money, they still had to leave their families to work on the plantations. I even mentioned that I had seen women with babies helping by carrying rocks to the airstrip. The DC was surprised that no pay at all was given, adding that they would do something.

During our lively evening, the subject of missions came up and it was clear that the DC's wife thought that missionaries' trade stores for the locals were funding their trips around the world. I pointed out that, at least in Yellow River, no missionaries were traveling for pleasure from their little trade store's profits. In fact, it was a generous service for the people as the volume was so small that no expat trader would open a store down here. The mission's store, a counter, actually, was the only place at that time where locals could buy basics like salt and matches, as well as kerosene, batteries, clothing, and other articles. Ray, who had no particular fondness for missionaries, backed me up on the frugality of their lives.

The Ten-Cent "Tax"

Makau, the base camp's interpreter, had an idea to get money for shovels by requesting each man to donate one shilling, about ten cents. He sold the idea to Ray and on their patrol a couple of weeks later, in each village Macau made the pitch for each man to give a shilling. Of course, most men did. When Peter at Ray's dinner party, told me with pride and amazement that Ray had collected over fifty dollars on his patrol, I stated my reservations because there is an implied coercion when the law tells you it wants some money. The man who can jail you should not be asking for money. Peter, of course, could immediately see it from the villager's perspective. Ironically, the next day before Joyce's plane arrived, Ray told me that the Wakaus had brought in their donation of four dollars and thirty cents. The DC was so impressed, Ray said, that he gave the station money to buy shovels. But there is one more angle to this little story.

Back in Wakau with my family, I learned that all the adult men of Wakau had donated a shilling to go to Makau, or to the government, or exactly where they weren't sure. Some spoke of it as a tax. They had heard about it from a Gwidami man visiting a relative in Wakau. They got the preposterous idea that the money was to buy the shame they had given to a Mantopai man who wanted to be council member, but everyone was against it. But there were no councils in the South Wapei! Nevertheless, somehow the government got entangled in it, so they gave the money but no one, absolutely no one—not even the most intelligent men—knew what it was about. They knew they must pay it or 'go long kalabus,' be jailed. I was annoyed that they had been taken in without understanding anything regarding their donations. Some of the men wondered if Macau got the money and the more they thought about it, the nuttier their observations got. I finally intervened and said that the government couldn't jail them for such a thing. Not paying taxes, yes, but not for giving to a voluntary fund for shovels. But I'm not sure how much sense that made to them either. At least money to help buy shovels had a concrete observable outcome, unlike taxes.

Joyce's visit with the children to my Wakau camp gave us five days to reconnect as a family; in fact, this would be their only visit. Two of those days would be involved in the hot humid trek from and to the station. Both children, accustomed to the more temperate climate of the Torricelli Mountains, found the lowlands climate physically oppressive. They didn't complain but their afternoon lethargy and damp flushed cheeks were sufficient evidence. I suspended formal anthropological work while they were there and joyfully concentrated on them. It was great to have all three with me and gave the villagers a chance to see and interact with them, thus getting a fuller awareness of who I was (fig. 27).

In the evenings Joyce and I discussed her plans for their living in Australia while I continued to work with the Lujere and, with great eagerness, our plans for our leisurely trip home through Asia and Europe after two years away. On Saturday night we celebrated our being together with a bottle of champagne Joyce had brought. At midmorning on Monday, we were en route back to the station. First, we had refreshments with Mary and Ces Parish while Ned and Elizabeth played with their children, Martin and Wesley. Their baby Christine was asleep. Then Ces heard on the mission's radio that the plane was late so Mary made lunch for all of us plus Rosemary Ace and her children Adrian and baby Laurel. Finally, midafternoon in intense heat and humidity, my family with Ces started down the little mountain to the mission's airstrip to meet the mission plane. Joyce and the children were already dying of the heat and terribly flushed and the long walk down the unshaded road to the plane almost finished them off. As they crawled into their seats, I know all three couldn't fly back to "gloomy Lumi" fast enough. The Yellow River area—for a lot of reasons—wasn't for everyone.

The 1972 National Election

March 1972 was the third national election since the House of Assembly, the national legislative body, was established. Wakau villagers had voted for the first time in the 1968 election but then it was just a voice vote. This would be the villagers' first paper-ballot election and there were photographs of the candidates they could choose from. Around 6:30 on the morning of March 8, most of the villagers who were going to vote had headed for the base camp. Norambalip villagers would vote ahead of us, so I left with a second group of voters at 9:00 A.M., and we were atop the base camp's hill at 10:45. As I looked around, everyone was in cloth; there was not a penis sheath or string skirt in sight and very few bare bosoms.

It was an unusually hot and humid day, the base camp was devoid of shade trees and there was no breeze; the sun was blazing, and it promised to be an especially grueling day

Figure 27. Breakfast with Joyce, Elizabeth, and Ned in my screened-tent dining area.

for everyone, especially those waiting, seemingly forever, to vote. The clerk (who checked the name of each voter once he located it with a local's help) and Ray (who then handed out the ballots) each sat under an improvised cover of palm branches that provided a bit of protection. Not all of the Wakau men came to vote: Kwoien was sick with a painful abscess that Klowi had lanced the night before, Kworu had a fever, and Kaiera stayed home because of his visual challenges. No reasons were offered why Mangko, Unei, Menetjua, Samaun, Meyawali, and others didn't come. I was sitting in a narrow strip of house shade with Enmauwi and Oria's daughter Womkau when Ces Parish greeted me and said he was here instead of in Warikori as planned; he had gone and come back the day before, a nine-hour trek. It was almost 12:30 when they finally called for the Iwani villagers to come and vote.[3]

Makau, the administration's interpreter, gave very brief voting instructions in Namia to the assembled villagers and the voting began. Once the clerk had approved the voter's name, they moved over to Ray's desk where they indicated their choice by pointing to the candidate's photo. Ray marked the ballot and handed it to the villager (fig. 28), who then walked over to the ballot boxes, where the Iwani 'luluai' stood in his official hat, and dropped it in (fig. 29). The padlocked metal ballot boxes were marked "Upper Sepik Electorate, Yellow River Base Camp." By 2:30, the voting was finished and those who hadn't already left started back to Wakau. Seventeen Wakau men and sixteen Wakau women voted, representing 53 percent of those eligible to vote.

---

3. Iwani's Aukwom hamlet had voted earlier. When Ray found them lined up at Tipas to vote, he agreed to let them vote there.

Figure 28. An Iwani villager receives a ballot from PO Lanaghan.

Figure 29. Ai'ire casts his ballot assisted by the Iwani 'luluai'; in the middle distance, women line up for a ballot. The house belonging to the 'kiap' is in the rear.

Ray had invited me to stay overnight, and we would have dinner and some beers. I asked him what he thought of the Iwani voters, did they know what they were doing? He replied that about half were "donkey votes," his term for uninformed, but the rest, he said, seemed to know who they wanted. After dinner our roving conversation was mostly local, about the area, people, mission, guns, and government. He told me that he had received $750 from the DC. It was a result of my telling the DC at Ray's bush dinner party for his bosses that the natives had made the base camp with no compensation whatsoever.

In the budget the DC's money gift was apparently listed for the camp's building materials. Ray wanted to use it all for a road from the station down to the Sepik but figured the money would only be enough to clear the brush and dig the ditches, all by hand labor. He felt he should give some of the money to the workers who built the station but had no idea how to distribute it fairly because of the number of people involved and the different levels of commitment they gave to the project. I told him that if he wasn't going to give it outright to the base camp workers, which I reluctantly agreed would be a daunting if not impossible task to get it right, an immediate need was some kind of footbridge over the Yellow River to connect the eastern Lujere villages; when the river was in flood, which was often, it was impassible. Ray also reminded me that we didn't know if the station would remain or would be closed when the new patrol post [Ama] in the hills just across the Sepik eventually opened. Right then they were still having problems locating a proper airstrip. In early June, Ray planned to go on a three-month leave and was sure he wouldn't return to the base camp but to another West Sepik post, rather than to his personal choice of Manus Island—far from the Sepik—with its tropical beaches and cooling sea breezes.

The Power of the Patrol Officer

One of the reasons I stayed overnight after the voting—besides Ray's lively company and the respite from village life—was to see if I could convince Ray to give Wakau a second shotgun as their bush was huge and there was no problem of overkill. In January, when all of Wakau went up to Mauwi for the annual census, Oria and the men asked Ray for permission for a second shotgun, but his reply was a brisk, "No!," adding that Wakau had not been eager to come to work at the station—for free of course—so he would return their behavior. I heard him say it. Besides, he added, his policy was one gun to fifty men. This was not a policy of the administration, but his policy to protect the villagers' game so they wouldn't shoot it all like in the Lumi area. As he and I discussed the gun issue that evening, it was obvious that it disgusted him that the men didn't get out with their bows and arrows more but wanted to depend on the gun for their protein. I disagreed, saying that the Lujere men loved to hunt almost more than anything else and that it was unusual to see a man leave the village for the bush without his weapons. (Of course, there was always the *iron* drones, but I didn't mention them.)

One of my arguments that night was that in a village like Wakau with only one shotgun—some villages I knew had two or three—the licensed gun owner gets no meat as there is a taboo against a hunter eating what he kills. Ray did not know this, was astounded, and began to think that perhaps two guns should be allowed per village. He, incidentally, had not issued the multiple gun permits, as the Lumi 'kiap' issued those before Ray arrived. I told him there were villages smaller than Wakau with multiple guns, so his system looked blatantly unfair to villagers. But Ray was not interested in bringing about a uniform distribution of gun licenses. What had been given, he said, had been given, right or wrong. His concern was the future and what he had to do. So, I totally lost our gun debate, although he did say that he would put in his next report about the custom of hunters tabooed from eating what they kill. When I later told Oria about my losing conversation with the 'kiap'—as it was he who wanted and was saving for the gun—he said he would wait until the 'kiap' went on leave then go up to Lumi and ask the 'kiap' there.

The Ethnologist's Rant

Once back in Wakau, I had to get off my chest what was annoying, even exasperating me with the administration's approach to the Lujere, and the only place I could do that safely was at my typewriter. Even there, I tried to control my ire:

> The overall problem with the YR base camp in its relations with natives is that the gov't has not made a permanent commitment to the place. They established it under unusual circumstances accepting the natives' offer to build the buildings if they would put a kiap there. But the people never expected that they would continue to work for nothing; the point in having a station was to bring them a way to get money! Instead they find they are working for nothing; some station!
>
> This has caused them to move away from the gov't who they see as just exploiting them for free work and, as they have pulled away, the kiap has become more authoritarian to get his work done. Schismogenesis[4] has set in as the gov't and natives move further away from each other with increasing antagonism. . .Far better to bring in the council [system], let them get up their own taxes and let the men work off their taxes to build, [road work] etc. And it would get the kiap off the hook and get some of the responsibility onto the people. Then they can bitch at their own [council rules] and change them if they wish. Now they just have to take whatever the gov't and the kiap dish out. (WN: 543)

I know I felt better with all that banged out on my sturdy typewriter and partially banged out of my system as well. I knew, of course, that the council system had been rejected because the area's economic base was considered so miserable that there wasn't enough money generated to work with. But I still think that a weak, struggling council would have been better for everyone than the rancor I witnessed.[5]

---

4. Schismogenesis is a term coined by Gregory Bateson (1972: 68) that refers to the behavior of two oppositional forceswhen responses intensify a progressive negative differentiation and eventual breakdown:

   > If boasting is the reply to boasting, that each group will drive the other into excessive emphasis of the pattern, a process if not restrained can only lead to more and more extreme rivalry and ultimately to hostility and the breakdown of the whole system.

5. Other than me (to myself privately), no one else espoused a local government council for the Lujere except PO Wafingian, voicing the locals' wish in his patrol report (1972b), made after I had returned home. His ADC, A. S. Wright, predictably shot down his suggestion.

CHAPTER TWELVE

Clanship, Kinship, and Marriage

New Guinea societies, on the other hand, seem to be characterized by a considerable degree of optation.
J. A. Barnes (1962: 7)

The most important social unit for replicating Wakau society was the nuclear family with its members located variously in the women's and men's houses and the bush camps. But the social unit that owned the village's land and dominated the economic, political, and formerly warring spheres of village life was the patrilineal clan, or "patriclan" (Murdock 1949: 69). What is unusual about these patriclans is that, while wealth is transferred exclusively through males, a boy or girl belongs to both their father's and mother's paternal clan, a finding explored below. That sounds very straightforward here, but it took me a *very* long time to "get it." The Wape I had lived with for eighteen months before moving to the Lujere had classical patrilineal descent groups that everyone seemed to understand so, when I began patrolling the Lujere villages seeking a research site, I was mystified when answers to my queries regarding descent groups was met with pauses, confusion, group discussions, and muddled responses. I was slowly learning that descent as a dogma was alien to their thoughts and lives.

The classic article on unilineal descent groups, based primarily on African materials, was Meyer Fortes' (1953), "The Structure of Unilineal Descent Groups." A corollary classic is J. A. Barnes (1962), "African Models in the New Guinea Highlands," which offers critiques of the African models of descent groups in "what we might call the African mirage in New Guinea" (Barnes 1962: 5). He cites eight characteristics of Highland societies to substantiate their distinctness from the African models. I will cite three of these that are especially representative of the Wakau version of Lujere social organization:

(c) An adolescent boy, and even an adult man, has some choice in deciding whether he will adhere to the local group in which his father is an agnate or to some other group to which he can trace non-agnatic connection. He may be able to maintain multiple allegiance or to shift his affiliation.
(d) A married woman neither remains fully affiliated to her natal group nor is completely transferred to her husband's group but rather sustains an interest in both.
(e) Many individuals who assert a mutual agnatic relationship are unable to trace out their connections step by step and are uninterested trying to do so. (Barnes 1962: 6).

Evidence for my highlighting these three features appears in the following pages. Anthropologists who entered into the debate regarding the differences and/or similarities between African and New Guinea Highland descent groups included Salisbury (1964), Sahlins (1965), Kayberry (1967), Strathern (1972), and La Fontaine (1973), among others. My intent here is not to belatedly enter into this debate but to acknowledge some of the apparently unique aspects of descent groups in New Guinea, not only in the Highlands, but in the Sepik lowlands as well.[1]

The Work of the Patriclans

There were numerous patrilineal clans or patriclans within Lujereland,[2] named mostly for animals or plants, such as *Abi* (cassowary), *Ewo* (lesser bird of paradise), *Kinarwi* (large bush rat), *Polami* (a bee), *Amtolami* (pandanus), *Walili* (ironwood tree), *Eindami* (a tree species), *Wek* (rat), *Itwaru* (crocodile), *Luwepan* (opossum), and *Pargret* (wallaby), whose members were scattered among the different Lujere villages. Wakau had five clans, *Elemoli* (breadfruit tree), *Apelami* (wild coconut), *Iwaridami* (a tree species), *Wolo* (rattan) and *Naroli* (a banana species). From the clans I knew, there were no prohibitions, behaviors, or totemic implications of any kind related to a clan's cultural icon, such as crocodile or cassowary. When questioned, informants would reply, 'em i nem nating,' "It's just a name." This struck me as quintessentially "Lujereistic"; here was something they could have culturally elaborated upon in numerous symbolic ways like many societies do, but they, typically, kept it simple. They did, however, have an idea that clans should be exogamous, but bowing to Lujere practicality, it was not always honored.

The social implications of clan membership were more extensive for males than for females; for instance, village males who were members of the same clan, as already noted,

---

1. During the years my late wife Annette Weiner (1992) was thinking about and writing *Inalienable Possessions*, I benefited greatly from our exchange and kinship discussions, probably because the Lujere data were so different from what she was examining.
2. Like West (2005) and his confused understanding of Muedan sorcery (*uwavi*) in Mozambique, I was never satisfied with my clan data from my first field trip. It is frustrating when "Knowledge gained one day was lost the next as I gathered contradictory evidence or became aware of disparate perspectives" (West 2005: 10). So, on my brief return trip in 1982, I worked with Oria and others including Warajak, now grown, to clarify and augment my initial data. The interpretation in this chapter is based on my 1971–72 and 1982 fieldwork.

slept together in the same *iron* creating a corporate residential kin group. In Wakau, for instance, male members of the *Elemoli* clan slept in the lower *iron* while the male members of the other four clans—that is, *Aplami, Iwaridami, Naroli* and *Waro*—slept in the upper *iron*.[3] This does not mean that males exclusively slept in the *iron*, as husbands slept with their family when at a bush camp and a few like Oria slept in their wife's village house almost exclusively while maintaining a bed in the *iron*.[4]

Dual Clan Affiliation

My Wakau informants declared unequivocally that a person, male or female, was a member of *both* his or her parent's patriclans. When I would describe the Wape patrilineal clan system stating that a person, male or female, belonged *only* to his or her father's descent group, they were emphatic that this was *not* their way. Yet, when I asked Oria to give me the clan names of all the Wakau men, he gave me only the name of the man's patrilineal clan, not his mother's father's clan that she was born into, so the Lujere's descent group ideology was a point of confusion to me for a very long time.

First, this definitely was not a case of double descent where Ego (in kinship parlance, "Ego" is used as a word for the person who serves as the focal point from which all other kinship relations are determined) belonged to both a *matrilineal* and *patrilineal* descent group. There were no matrilineal descent groups among the Lujere. Nor was it an ambilineal system with multiple descent groups that Ego could affiliate with. Barry Craig, during his 1969 artifact collection trip among the Lujere, became aware that this was not just an ordinary patrilineal descent group society. He wrote, based on his visit to Naum village on the first of July,

> I was told by informants that it is not uncommon for a man to work both his wife's, and his own, land, living in her village alternately with his own. His children thus become familiar with both father's and mother's land and may elect to inherit rights to their mother's as well as, or instead of, their father's land. Thus the system would appear to be cognatic, at least with respect to land rights, and the "clans or sub-clans" may not be unilineal groups at all. (Craig 1975: 420)

Craig's informant certainly provided an interesting, even startling, example of optative residence and inheritance. My data are that the circumstances of a man inheriting land rights from his mother's patriclan are very unusual and highly variable as explained below. Thus, my Wakau-based research did not confirm his hypothesis that the Lujere might have a form of cognatic descent, although he was accurate in supposing that they

---

3. When the villagers lived across the Sand River in the 1950s, they had three hamlets and three *irons* but when they moved back to their present site with a single hamlet, they eventually built a single large *iron* for all the men, which was abandoned before I arrived in 1971.
4. I never collected convincing data to indicate that this was either a traditional custom or a post-contact innovation. My hunch, based on the flexibility in Lujere culture, is that it was always a possibility but has become more prevalent in recent times. However, youths and bachelors today, as before, always sleep in the *iron*.

don't conform to the traditional ideal of patrilineality, a point which further strengthens my own analysis.[5]

The Lujere's descent groups were all patrilineal; however, the tie to Ego's mother's group was usually a strong one. In Wakau, many marriages were within the village or the neighboring villages and this facilitated affective and instrumental interaction between related families and patriclans. Fortes (1969: 98) used the term "complimentary filiation" to characterize matrilateral relations that were pervasive and strong; however, the Lujere had gone a step farther by creating an individual's bilateral alliance to both parent's patriclans albeit the character of the alliance was not symmetrical. So, if the ethnologist takes informants at their word—and s/he should—they were declaring that Ego belonged to two different patrilineal descent groups: his mother's and his father's. While a son, for instance, was affiliated with both his father's father and his mother's father's descent groups, his membership rights and obligations were not coequal. Nothing in Wakau society, material or virtual, was transmitted by tradition from a mother to her sons or daughters in the way that economic assets were transmitted from a father to his sons. The son inherited "basic resources," to use Fried's (1967: 186) term, from his father's line just as his mother's brother's son did from his father's line. Of course, a boy's maternal grandfather or maternal uncle might opt to privilege him with some of their resources, thus honoring his close tie to them via his mother. The same kind of sharing could be extended to the boy's sister as well, but it was always an optative act and not a prescriptive one.

I think my Wakau informants just took it for granted that a person belonged to both his or her mother's and father's patriclan, just as we unconsciously acknowledge our bilateral tie to both our parent's families. Certainly, no one ever talked about it until I started asking questions. I had never heard a word about this idea of dual clan membership until I gave the example of the Wape patriclans, that a person at birth is a member of only his or her father's descent group, and they disagreed. I later realized Oria's emphasis on only naming the Wakau men's father's clan was because the mother's clan is relatively insignificant to her sons. While a man or woman may belong to the mother's clan, there are no strong jural or economic rights and obligations stemming from this maternal tie as there are to the father's clan. The tie to the mother's clan for either a girl or boy is more accurately characterized as a titular one with the potential for a usufruct relationship. However, even then he or she must ask permission if one wants a favor related to the mother's patriclan's resources.

Thus, while a person's clan affiliation at birth is bilateral, that is, filiation is both matrilateral and patrilateral, it is significant that (1) the determination of a man's *iron* is by his patriclan, and (2) the transmission of wealth in basic resources was always patrilineal, father to son. For a male, it was the patrilateral affiliation to his father's patriclan that was highly significant in everyday life, as it was also for a female until she married, and her sago was now processed from her husband's palms.

---

5. In a June 14, 2000 email replying to my queries, Barry Craig wrote,

> Always bear in mind that I was doing survey material culture ethnography, not in-depth research, and I wrote down what I elicited from informants but am quite conscious that the information could be individualistic or even that I misunderstood what I was being told. It is certainly random! So more than a grain of salt is in order.

When I began making genealogical charts of the villagers' kinship relations, I was concerned that they seemed to be a collection of disparate little groups with no genealogical depth and often lacking demonstrable connections between alleged patriclan members. They reminded me of Ian Hogbin's shallow genealogies for Wogeo Island off Wewak and his comment that "the Wogeo are not good genealogists" (Hogbin 1970: 22). But I also was learning that the deep past was insignificant to the Lujere, especially when compared to many other New Guinea societies whose lengthy genealogies are of paramount importance for establishing status, claiming ownership, or reckoning marriages.[6] When I would press for an explanation on how the scattered collateral kin segments of a local clan were related, my informants—sometimes a bit impatient and distressed by my concern for irrelevant minutia—told me that they must have had a common clan ancestor in the past but it was too far back for them to know. And, seeing the lineal shortness of their genealogies, who could argue with that?

Whether or not the kin tie of some local clan members was fictive, having grown up together they demonstrated in myriad ways their close affective tie to one another. When I saw several men leaving or entering the village, they were usually patriclan brothers or, when Mowal and his wife lost their infant daughter to cerebral malaria, it was his patriclan brother Nauwen who initiated her burial. Undoubtedly, men usually were closer to their patriclan-mates than to other village men. In former times they were warriors together, and today they still usually chose men among their patriclan to hunt with or go as families together to their bush camps. For example, when the Wakau men first gathered to build my house, Mowal, Mari, and Oria—all Apilami clansmen—were together with their families at distant bush camps across the Sand River hunting, fishing, and making sago.

The reason my informants could not trace their lineal genealogical connections was, as indicated, that the necessary knowledge didn't exist. I collected the villagers' kinship charts onto wide, long sheets of brown wrapping paper, and I was fortunate if they had knowledge of their grandparents, as some didn't. Klowi, however, had more kin data than most. Lertau, Klowi's maternal grandfather, had six married siblings. One of Lertau's four sisters and her two children were ambushed in the forest and killed by Tsila men, and one of his two brothers was also killed in a Tsila raid. Although Klowi had information about Lertau's other four siblings, he had no information about their parents, his great grandparents, not even their names. This was typical; lineal data stopped abruptly, but Klowi got further than most.

All informants had extensive lateral and lineal descending knowledge of kin who were mostly the people they knew or had known face to face. But the dead kin one never knew personally were, literally, non-existent. And this made sense in personal terms. All a man really had to know to prosper in Lujere society were the locations of the economic resources held by his father that he and his brothers would inherit to help feed themselves

---

6. The genealogies of the Enga people of the Papua New Guinea Highlands provide a startling contrast to the Lujere. Wiessner and Tumu (1998: 28) found that the "Enga genealogies extend back approximately ten generations, the shortest that we collected being eight and the longest fourteen." While not as extensive as the Enga genealogies, the genealogies of the Gnau in the Torricelli Mountains had a range of five to fifteen generations with an average depth of nine generations (Lewis 1975: 17).

and their families. The mother's clan also had an important role as a kind of safety net to be utilized when needed if, as I explain below, one had maintained an active relationship with some of its members.

As postmarital residence among the Lujere was usually virilocal, when a woman married a man from another village, she left the male members of her paternal clan like her father and brothers to whom she was more closely related than the males of her paternal clan residing in other villages. Importantly, members of a person's mother's or father's patriclan living in another village could be approached for help or a favor if—and it is an important tactical "if"—one had sustained the relationship through time. Maintaining an active positive relationship was emphasized to me when, for example, a man wanted to hunt on his father-in-law's land, plant a stand of sago on his mother's brother's land, or move to his brother-in-law's village. The extent of the favor requested, and chance of a positive response was very much dependent upon the nature of the relationship.

When Kaiera wanted to move out of his *iron* in his natal Mauwi because of 'sanguma' fears and the lack of bathing water on the hilltop, he chose to move to the *iron* in his mother's natal village, Wakau, as he had maintained good relationships with his mother's paternal kin since childhood. When Samaun was harassing Sakone for sex after her husband left as an indentured laborer, she and her five children moved to her nearby natal village of Mauwi to live with her brother's family. There sometimes was a special push for a Wakau male to reside in the village where *both* his mother and wife were from, that is, to reside both matrilocally and uxorilocally. Such was Lean's case; he was a young man born in Wakau but moved to Iwani's Sepik River hamlet of Aukwom where his wife and mother were born. He was a friend of Nauwen's and, as Nauwen and Oria's mother also was from Aukwom, he had encouraged Nauwen and Oria to come to Aukwom to live. But the brothers declined the invitation, preferring to continue hunting and fishing in their father's bush than that of their mother's father's and her brothers.

Another example of the flexibility dual clanship provided regarding residence was Sakrias, a youth born in Papei whose mother came from Wakau. When I moved to Wakau, Sakrias was living in the upper *iron* with men of his mother's patriclan. However, before I returned home, he had moved back to his father's village. His was a typical example of a young male temporarily living with his mother's patriclan. From my data, the converse temporary residence pattern for a young female apparently doesn't occur.

A girl at birth, like her brother, was filiated byboth her parent's patriclans but when her mother's father died, his strategic resources would be transmitted to her mother's brothers as they would be to her own brothers when her father died, bypassing her. However, her father could opt to give a line of sago palms to her and her husband to cut and process into sago starch. Or, if she had no brothers and her father had access to large hunting grounds and owned extensive holdings of food trees, he might invite her and her husband to come live in her natal village and use his holdings. Then their sons, having lived in an *iron* amid her mother's local clansmen, would be the legitimate inheritors after their grandfather's and parent's deaths. These anomalous situations regarding postmarital residence, the prevalence of adoption, and the gifting allocation of resources, all made Wakau's clan-held lands a kind of patchwork quilt of practice. My attempt to understand local ownership and usage, like clanship, defied quick and easyunderstanding.

Adoption

The Lujere's many clans were scattered among the villages; five, as described earlier, had corporate sections in Wakau. Members were affiliated with a clan through their father or mother at birth, or by adoption. Adoption had no associated rituals but was acknowledged when others raised an orphaned child. Death of young parents was not uncommon, resulting in the adoption of the children by cognatic or affinal kin. When a boy's father died, for example, he might be (1), adopted affinally by his older sister's husband or his mother's new husband, or (2), adopted cognately, by his mother's brother or a much older brother. Only in the last instance would he not necessarily become attached to a new clan. Unless he were very young, he would sleep in his new patron's *iron* and hunt with him in his bush. Only if he moved to another village and ignored his agnatic ties would he lose privileges in his father's clan, though not in the harvesting of his father's resources, regardless of where they were planted. He could also give some or all of his strategic resources to another person, especially those that were difficult to access from his new locale.

For example, I was told that Pewal, whose father had died and his mother remarried, was not fed well, so his mother's brother from Tsila came to Wakau to take him home as a youth to raise him. Now grown, he had remained with his mother's brother in Tsila, never visiting Wakau. Some assumed he had probably forfeited membership in his father's clan as he had leveraged his membership in his maternal brother's patriclan. Here are a few more examples of adoption, all by Wakau villagers. Unei was a young orphan living in the lower *iron*. (His father had died while he was still small, and his mother remarried Mithaki who in turn died, and then his mother also died.) Unei's mother's brother in Pabei did not offer to care for him, so Klowi assumed responsibility for Unei because Mithaki, Unei's stepfather, was Klowi's mother's brother. Klowi and his wife Wawenowaki also had taken in Yamai, a girl, whose father Newai, a Wakau man, was Klowi's mother's younger brother, after both of her parents died. Another case is Kunai's. He was the youngest of seven siblings; the eldest was his sister Areawane married to Kaboi, a Wakau man. When Kunai's parents died, his sister and brother-in-law raised and fed him along with their own four children that included their two young sons, Arakwake and Nakwane.

When Oria and Nauwen's mother died, their father Limeritjo married Ariawani, the widow of Walpi of Gwidami. She had one son, Yaope, who came with his mother to Wakau as Limeritjo's adopted son. Yaope could at any time return to Gwidami where he was born and his inherited resources were located, but he remained in Wakau. Because early death and adoption were so pervasive among the Lujere, other instances of both appear at random throughout the text.

This common custom of adoption partly explains the cognatic disconnect among local sections of a Wakau clan. With such a convincing lack of knowledge of, or interest in, their genealogical past, it only takes a few generations for an adopted boy to disappear from the collective kinship memory and for his progeny to appear as clan members but with no visible tie to another clan segment. Men who helped me with the kinship charts were to a person blissfully unconcerned with these "discrepancies." I eventually learned—too slowly for them I am sure—not to press my search for an apical ancestor as no one cared a whit; it only bothered me.

Economic Resources

Wakau's five clans controlled the village's extensive land holdings, which extended in all directions from the village. The largest property (belonging to Oria; see map 7) was in the vast fens extending westward from the Sand River. The land across the river was divided among the village's clans into three huge tracts extending east to west from the river. The lower tract bordering Wagu's land to the south belonged to local members of the Elamoli clan (lower village men), the middle tract to the Naroli clan (Luritsao and Enewan, who were upper village men), and the upper tract bordering Tsila's land belonged to members of the related Apilami, Iwaridami, and Waro clans (other upper village men). These tracts were the villagers' primary hunting, gathering, and gardening grounds with creeks of diverse size for obtaining fish, plus numerous stands of both wild and domestic sago palms.

The Lujere identify two types of economic resources, those that are *enduring*, and those that are *transitory*; all are inherited in the male line, that is, patrilineal. The *enduring* resources are like the land areas described above, which, in Tok Pisin, are composed of 'bus,' 'baret,' and 'tais,' that is, forest land, creeks and ponds, and swamp land. A man's *transitory* resources are those that are more permanent than a banana tree but eventually expended like palm trees such as sago, coconut, betel, and 'limbum.' Breadfruit trees, 'galip' nut trees, 'tulip' trees, and domestic pigs, for example, are also transitory resources but are usually fewer in number and not of the same significance in providing food for descendants. The sago palm grows in freshwater swamps up to fifty feet tall and takes from ten to fifteen years to mature; it is usually cut down just before it matures to maximize the amount of sago starch processed (Lea 1972:14). A coconut palm must be planted on higher ground, begins to bear in its sixth year and may continue for as long as eighty years (Shand 1972:187). A good father plants sago and coconut palms for his progeny to assure they will have food to eat when they grow up. He plants on his father's clan's land or, with permission, that of relatives and friends. A man may own palms on another man's land, perhaps his father's 'wanwok' who gave him permission to plant, or on his mother's brother's land if he had secured permission. Unlike among the Wape, Lujereland has a surplus of land, so obtaining permission is seldom a problem. Importantly, the fact that land is not a scarce resource in Lujereland as it is for many New Guinea groups, such as in the Highlands, helps facilitate the society's flexible nature.

A clan's forestland is extensive and is the primary hunting ground for its members and where their small, unfenced gardens are planted. If a man's mother is also from his village, he may seek hunting privileges on his mother's father and brother's hunting ground as well. Within these lowland areas are numerous creeks whose waters eventually empty into the Sepik River. The larger ones are named and divided into sections that are owned by members of the clan for their exclusive fishing use, not unlike how a prime Quebec salmon river might allot fishing rights when the fish are spawning. Most of the large swampy areas are also named where wild or planted sago grows. I despaired, however, of ever getting a proper map of a clan's 'bus,' 'baret,' and 'tais.' The idea of a map, essentially a "bird's eye" view of a man's natural resources where he hunted, fished, collected, and planted was a puzzling concept to some. I did, however, prevail upon Oria to make me a map of his natural resources from the perspective of being in an airplane, something he had experienced. Choosing a green pencil, he made two drawings: one of his 'bus' near Wakau and the other larger 'bus' across the Sand River (map 7).

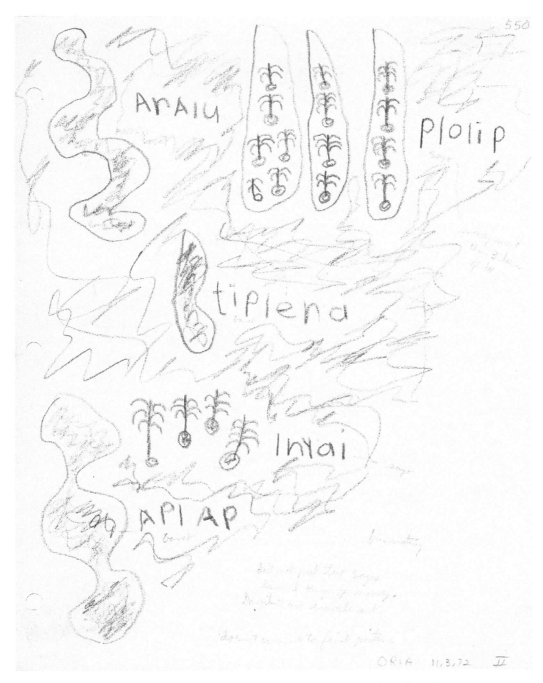

Map 7. Oria's map of his land across the Sand River with sago stands and creeks.

The three creeks on his land, Araiu, Tipiera, and Apiap, appear more like ponds but may just represent to him the part of the creek that is his. The swampy land where his sago stands are pictured are Plalip and Inyai. The other areas are hunting grounds. When

I asked him why the lower right corner was blank, he replied, "'em i bus nating,'" that is, it's just wild forest. But 'bus nating' is a relative notion; this area, he said, belonged to the Tsila people and was not one where he roamed. He did make the point, however, that hunting boundaries were more amorphous as feral pigs and cassowaries move through the 'bus' irrespective of local boundaries, and he added that they aren't planted like sago palms.

Resource Transmission

If a man has several sons, his resources are inherited jointly but the eldest son has the responsibility of their management, a fact reflected in the kinship terms. Primogeniture among brothers was one of the stronger Lujere organizational principles they usually adhered to. A father might divide his arboreal resources and water fishing rights before he died if he anticipated quarreling among his sons. If he died when his sons were small, his wife supervised his resources. A woman, who since childhood had set fish traps and processed sago with her mother, usually loses access to her father's resources when she marries but gains access to her husband's resources. However, it is common for fathers to extend specific resource privileges, for instance, to hunt on his land or plant sago palms in a swampy area, to his new son-in-law and daughter after their marriage. But if a father-in-law is hostile, as old Leno was to Tsaime, he may, as discussed later, specifically forbid his son-in-law access.

A man's arboreal resources may not all be on his clan's land but, as already indicated, by invitation or with permission, he can plant on any man's land. For example, Poke's father, Lumuria, had planted sago palms on Oria and Nauwen's father's land. Poke, as noted, was an older bachelor in the upper *iron* with no siblings or living agnates. He told Oria that when he died his sago palms were to go to him and his infant son Nakwane. Oria also said that Poke had other sago palms near Waniyo's holdings and believed Waniyo and his brothers would claim these palms when Poke died, probably because Waniyo and his younger brother Nimo were two of the five married men whose wives fed Poke. In the meantime, he was very protective of his resources, as were most men. Poke had a stand of sago palms in a Mauwi swamp and, when he discovered that one of his palms had been cut down and was being processed into sago starch without his permission, he destroyed the processed sago and demolished the processing apparatus. Likewise, when he discovered an errant fish trap in his section of a creek, he took it out and wrecked it. Kunai, another bachelor with no brothers or descendants, also had given a couple of lines of sago to his older sister's sons, Arakwake and Nakwane, whose mother raised him and whose wives helped to feed him.

Kinship Terminology

The idea of "kinship terminology systems" —a society's systematic arrangement of kinship terms, as conceived by Lewis Henry Morgan (1871)—is one of the oldest and most original inventions of anthropology (Trautmann 1987). Morgan, a nineteenth-century lawyer in upstate New York, ethnographer of the Iroquois (Morgan 1851), and natural historian of the American beaver (Morgan 1868), realized that the terms the Iroquois called their relatives formed a patterned system very different from his own society's. For one thing, one's father and one's father's brother were referred to using the same term. Moreover, Morgan found it peculiar that all of the Iroquois clans traced descent through females, not males. His insight was that these and other unusual findings stimulated him to make a comparative study of kinship around the globe. This being the mid-nineteenth century, Morgan sent queries to far-flung missionaries, government officials, and travelers by sea. Logistic difficulties notwithstanding, he amassed an astonishing array of findings from his cooperative informants about the world's kin terminology systems. In 1865 he had completed a first draft of his findings, but publication was initially refused by the Smithsonian Institutions on the grounds that "in proportion to the conclusions arrived at, the quantity of your material is very large" (Resek 1960: 97). It was only after he revised the manuscript in terms of a then-fashionable evolutionary hypothesis—it was a time of Darwin's (1859) greatest influence—that it was published (Morgan 1871).[7] Thus began the scientific study of "Kinship as an analytical category" (Godelier, Trautmann, and Tjon Sie Fat 1998, 2). While Morgan's evolutionary views were later discredited, his discovery of kin term systems has continued to be a relevant topic among anthropologists despite Schneider's (1972) attempts to make kinship a non-subject.

Morgan was especially interested in the kin terms for a person's (or "Ego's" in kinship parlance) parents and their siblings and he discovered that his data fell into either "Classificatory" or "Descriptive" kin term systems.[8] Robert Lowie (1928) built on Morgan's initial insights and, surveying even more native kin term systems, found that they fell into four categorical types determined by whether kin terms on the parental generation were merged or not, namely, *generational, bifurcate merging, bifurcate collateral,* and *lineal.* Then, George Peter Murdock (1949), based on data in his cross-cultural files at Yale, postulated six typologies centered on Ego's children's and sibling's children's terms. His "cousin" term categories were Hawaiian, Iroquois, Sudanese, Eskimo, Crow, and Omaha.

The field of kinship study, especially that of kin terminologies, however, has had its critics who have found it arcane and tedious and have questioned its relevance. Even Robin Fox in his admired book on kinship and marriage acknowledged that kinship terminologies remained an "esoteric" subject (Fox 1983: 1). One of its most caustic critics was Bronislaw Malinowski "who complained of 'the bastard algebra of kinship' that Morgan had created" (Trautmann 1987: 258). While Malinowski railed against the subject, David Schneider (1972: 50) more majestically simply defined it out of existence. As Marshall Sahlins (2013: 12) has slyly commented regarding Schneider's, "Long study of 'kinship' had convinced him that there was no such thing," adding that, "Indeed, by the logic of Schneider's argument, there would be no such thing as anything" (Sahlins 2013: 15).

---

7. It is ironic that the later rejection of Morgan's evolutionary hypothesis regarding the human family by men like Kroeber (1909) in turn, for a time, negatively impacted recognition of Morgan's major contribution to the scientific study of the world's kin nomenclature systems.

8. An example of a "Classificatory" system of kin terms is where on Ego's parental generation there is a single term for *father, father's brother,* and *mother's brother,* and a single term for *mother, mother's sister,* and *father's sister.* An example of a "Descriptive" system is one like ours where Ego's *mother* and *father* each have a term, but *father's* and *mother's sister* share a term (aunt), as do *father's and mother's brother,* (uncle).

Regardless of one's measure of enthusiasm for kinship studies or kin term systems, the status of the latter as a field of inquiry within anthropology began to pall toward the last phase of the twentieth century as colonialism gradually ended and access to study kin-based societies became more difficult. Graduate students increasingly viewed the exotic fieldwork site as politically incorrect, even exploitative, while the study of the here and now, even as close as one's own disability, was favored. Certainly, the required kinship course for many US anthropology majors has disappeared from the curriculum, as it did from ours at the University of Vermont.[9] Nevertheless, a culture's kin terms are real and of ethnographic interest as they document how the actual people, in our case the Wakau villagers, see their relatives. *Homo sapiens* is physiologically wired to make sense of things; so, through time, every society has created a system of kin terms.

One might think that collecting kinship terms would be a simple, straightforward charge. Anyone who has tried knows it isn't. There are "terms of address"—what you call someone, for example, Dad, Gramma—and "terms of reference"—how you refer to someone, for instance, my father, my grandmother. There are even further distinctions: "elementary," "derivative," and "denotative" terms. Interviewing in Tok Pisin about your informant's Namia kin terms, leaves a lot of room for slip-ups and wiggle-waggle. Also problematic was that, although the Wakau villagers have kin terms, they don't usually use them; more often they call a relative, even a parent, by their personal name. So, kin terms, as evidenced by their general dislike in using them, were not of importance or interest to the Wakau, which is so different from the Wape. I worked with several Wakau men on kin terms but, to a man, they found it confusing and gave me blatantly contradictory data they couldn't explain that were not only exasperating, but were driving me nutty, and the fact that I was so obsessive in trying to make sense of their answers, was obviously driving them nutty too. I never did succeed in getting across the difference between terms of address and terms of reference to the point that I had full confidence in what I was getting. This was, by leagues, the most exasperating and inconclusive of my data gathering experiences, so what I am providing here is, at best, provisional. Oria was the only man who could stick it out with me and at least bring the illusion of occasional clarity, so what I submit as "Wakau kin terms" are primarily my understanding of his understanding. All terms are from a male Ego's perspective, and I *think* these are terms of reference.

Wakau Kin Terms

A male Ego's grandparents and their siblings are all referred to as *ajuwa*, while kin terms for Ego's first ascending generation—the parental generation—are "generational," that is, all of Ego's mother's and father's brothers and sisters have the same term as Ego's mother and father: mother = *mo* and father = *aja*. Although the same kin term refers to Ego's mother as well as to her and her husband's sisters, there is no doubt in the son's mind, or anyone else's, regarding who is his biological mother and who nursed, fed, and cared for him as he grew. But the classificatory term *mo* does connote the kind of maternal

---

9. But only after Carrol Pastner and I, who both cherished teaching the course, had retired.

relationship he can expect from his parent's sisters, regardless of where they live. The same is true in a paternal way for the classificatory term *aja* for his parent's brothers.

Logically consistent with this "generational" pattern on the parental generation, in Ego's generation the kin terms for matrilateral and patrilateral cousins are the same as for Ego's brother and sisters, that is, the "Hawaiian" type. Thus sister = *elae* while brothers are distinguished by age; that is, older brother = *awa* and younger brother = *nanwa*. This finding of Generational and Hawaiian type kin terms will strike some readers as strange, as it initially did me, because the theoretical models for Hawaiian and Generational kin terms are assumed to be incompatible with the unilineal descent groups that the Lujere have. But, once again, I eventually surrendered to their ethnographic facts. And, if you think about it, by not distinguishing kin on the mother's and father's sides, their kin term system is complementary to their view of descent.

Interestingly, none of the societies proximal to the Lujere for whom data exists have Hawaiian cousin terms. To the north, Abrau village (Awun lang.) has Dakota type cousin terms and Kwieftim village (Ak lang.) has Omaha type cousin terms (Kelm and Kelm 1980: 269–272); to the east, Magaleri village (Amal lang.) has Omaha type terms;[10] to the west, Wagu village (Abau lang.) also has Omaha type cousin terms. To the south cross the Sepik River, both the Iwam (Iwam lang.) (Rehburg 1974: 211) and the Sawiyano (Ama lang.) (Guddemi 1992, 112) have forms of Iroquois type cousin terms.

It gets even more interesting when we examine the kin terms on the generation of Ego's grandchildren. A terminological distinction exists between a female and a male cousin's children. The children of male patrilateral and matrilateral cousins are termed *tsana*, the same term for Ego's and his sibling's children. But Ego has a special relationship with his female patrilateral and matrilateral cousins' children (his parent's siblings' daughters) who are termed *mamaru*—it is a reciprocal term—and whose patriclan is different from his. There are more *mamaru*s, but first, as already indicated, on the second ascending or grandparent level, Ego's parent's parents and their siblings are all termed *aitdwa*, while on the second descending or grandchild level, all children of a *tsana* are termed *inani*, and children of a *mamaru*, in turn are also termed *mamaru*.

As the reciprocal *mamaru* relationship is unique, it demands further attention. The senior male *mamaru*, that is, Ego, has a responsibility to occasionally bring food to his little male or female *mamaru* that could include sago, grubs, game meat, and fish, as well as firewood. In response the child's parents (Ego's patrilateral and matrilateral female cousins and their spouses) are required to give him money or traditionally shell "money."

If the junior *mamaru* dies, its parents must give shell "money" to the senior *mamaru* as well as pig or game meat; this is not reciprocated. Or if the junior *mamaru* is sick or has a baby, again food must be brought. Overall, the senior *mamaru* has a nurturing and protective role towards the junior *mamaru* who, in turn, has a supportive role to his senior *mamaru*. This *mamaru* reciprocal relationship continues throughout life, as in the relationship between Yaope and Klowi shown in the next chapter. Also, if the senior *mamaru* goes away to work and returns with presents for his *mamaru*, these must be reciprocated

---

10. Based on my interview at the Yellow River Base Camp on April 9, 1972, with Makau of Magaleri on his village's Amal language kin terms.

with shell "money." Finally, for the kin terms for the second descending generation from Ego, all his and his sibling's grandchildren are termed *inani* as are the grandchildren of his bilateral male cousins, but the children of his *mamaru* are also termed *mamaru*.[11]

This exchange between a senior *mamaru* and his junior *mamaru* and its parents was the main kin regulated exchange system I found among the Lujere. Because the Lujere prescribe patriclan exogamy, a senior *mamaru's* junior *mamaru* would belong to a different patriclan from his. In this way the reciprocal relationship between a senior *mamaru* and his various male and female junior *mamarus*, encourages a positive tie between the nuclear families of different patriclans in different villages.

Some New Guinea societies have rules against calling certain relatives by name; to unwittingly say the name is a cause for shame. This was true for some groups, such as the Wape and the Baruya (Lloyd 1974: 98) of the Eastern Highlands District. But for the Lujere, again indicating the comparative openness of their society, there were no constraints against using an individual's personal or kinship name either face to face or indirectly. In the same way, there were no culturally required avoidance relationships among kin as sometimes occurs with in-laws. However, there is a joking relationship custom, often ribald, between brothers-in-law.

Joking Relationships

A male Ego has a reciprocal joking relationship, frequently of an obscene nature, with his classificatory sisters' husbands. Nimo was married to Aria's classificatory sister. and I had been in the village only a few weeks and still naive regarding kinship terms and behavior when they began teasing each other in Tok Pisin. Nimo was laughing and saying to Aria in Tok Pisin, "You are my woman. I'm an evil man. I'm going to fuck you!" and the other men around, including Aria, were all laughing. This bawdy, even lewd, joking, I quickly learned, is only between brothers-in-law and seems to occur primarily in the presence of males. A man has a milder type of joking or teasing relationship with his female *mamaru*, and his wife jokes with his male *mamaru*. These would be in Namia, and if they occurred in my presence I was unaware of it. I do not recall any casual playfulness between the sexes as I noted occasionally between males or between several laughing females. With Ego's own sister, her husband, and their children, joking or 'tok pilai' is banned as with other cognatic or affinal kin except the ones described.

In summation, despite wealth transferred exclusively in the male line, the overall bilateral symmetry in the Wakau kin term system is, not so oddly, complementary to the Wakau practice of bilateral patriclan affiliation.

---

11. The Namia linguists Thomas and Becky Feldpausch (1988: 2011) include some Lujere kinship terms in their publications; I have checked their spelling against what I got in Wakau and I have tweaked a few kin terms to be in compliance with their spelling. An important difference, however, is that the bilateral cousin terms they collected in Yaru village are not the same terms as for Ego's siblings; thus, female cousin = *aripae* and male cousin = *aripa lu*. Consequently, the cousin terms they collected would be classified as an "Eskimo" system, not a "Hawaiian" one, although both kinds of cousin terms are theoretically incompatible with unilineal descent groups

Love and Marriage

The expression of love and affection was easily observed within most Wakau families. The tie between parents and small children was especially affectionate and both fathers and mothers appeared dedicated to succoring not only their own children, but others as well. However, outward displays of affection between husbands and wives were less easy to discern.

"Romance" is not a word in either the Tok Pisin or Namia lexicon but young Lujere men and women, like the young everywhere, were actively, flirtatiously, aware of the other sex. But the signs were usually subtle and mostly beyond my awareness, especially as the young women of the village spoke only Namia. However, Nauwen, as an eligible single young man, was helpful in orienting me to some of the ways a young man could charm a young woman with magic to want him. He also volunteered that women had no magical way to entice a man, but in my original notes I typed, "A woman might have another version regarding this." (WN440)

A man can charm the attentions of a woman in three main ways. The first two are traditional; the third is a more recent invention. A man going to a 'singsing' (festival) who wants a girl to be attracted to him, usually sexually or at least for marriage, secretly spits ginger on the side of his hand drum. He does not incant a charm; he just spits the ginger on it. Again, in its simplicity, a very Lujerian ritual act. A second way to entice a girl is to take some of the earth where she has left a footprint, mix it with ginger, then rub a bit of the mixture around the base of a partially trimmed cockatoo feather. The feather is attached to a house so it points to the girl's village and as it waves in the breeze, her heart will turn to the boy. Interestingly, when I later repeated the feather charm custom to Aria and Iwi, neither had heard of it. The third way is to take a girl's bamboo tube for smoking tobacco and put into its mouth a bit of ginger and 'senta' (something that smells good) but only a tiny bit as she may smell it. This will bring the girl to the boy. Throughout the book I have cited the magical powers of ginger, but there is yet another deliberate usage shared with the Wape: some ginger placed under a boss's or 'kiap's house ladder will cool any potential angry outburst as he crosses over it.

As there was no language the Wakau women and I shared, I mutely wondered how they felt about their marriages that, to me, appeared to be mostly arrangements made by men, albeit not covertly. Because of the relatively high status of Lujere women and the public nature of marital arrangements, a woman could intervene if she wished. Among all of the Wakau marriages past and present that I knew about, divorce was unknown. At times of marital stress, however, a wife could stay with her brother and sister-in-law as Oria's sister did; a wife's absence could remind a churlish and hungry husband of his dependency on her processed sago and evening meal.

I earlier stated that marriage was usually virilocal, but there was no strong feeling that it had to be. If the wife's situation looked better than the husband's and her family wanted them to join them, then they might make the move to her village. Klowi's father's younger brother Tone married a woman from the Weari region and they settled there with her family. However, his son Lumai made the occasional visit to Wakau maintaining his tie to his father's Wakau kin and resources. His son Emiyano was away at work but, Wakau men said, when he returned and wanted to get married, his *home* village must find him his wife, not them. The negative sentiment voluntarily voiced to me was that

Emiyano's future wife was of no concern to them as neither he nor his father had ever lived in Wakau. The implication was that although Emiyano's father had planted sago and other food trees for him here that he had the right to harvest and, that while he also had clansmen here, he was not a son of Wakau, thus there were no marital obligations to him. This also illustrates a related point: the politics of marriage was the responsibility of a man's village, as well as that of his clan. Another example of this principle was Engwe's marriage, discussed later.

For a Lujere male, "sister exchange" was the choice for finding a mate, not that it was a hard and fast rule, but that it was the easiest way to get a wife—if you had an eligible sister. Two men exchanged sisters, what could be simpler? If a man did not have a sister, there might be other female relatives, perhaps a young widow, who could be exchanged for a wife. As always, a lot depended on the attributes of the young man—was he a skillful hunter and industrious?—as marriages were usually negotiations between families as well as individuals. Finally, if no woman was available for exchange, traditionally shell valuables and pigs or, today, money might be given for a bride. Although a man should not marry a woman he terms sister, and that includes his female cross and parallel cousins, I saw instances where the restriction was ignored without any consequences that I could discern.

Yaope Takes a Bride

I was in Lumi with my family for Christmas when Yaope and Yaowitjha were married, and I got most of the story from Arakwaki. He told me that he had expected it, as the two had been very friendly and playful with one another. One evening, neither was in the village so everyone knew that they were at a bush camp together. In the absence of a formal Lujere nuptial ritual, when they returned, they would be considered husband and wife. His bride was Yaowitjha, the spurned wife of Karol. Here is the backstory.

Karol (Waro clan) and Ariawani (Iwaridami clan), both Wakau men, exchanged sisters. When Ariawani's wife, Karol's sister, died he remarried and moved to the Iwani hamlet of Iwarwita, his mother's hamlet, the same hamlet that Joyce and I visited briefly where they were mourning a dead man. Karol and Yaowitjha had a baby that died and then later he abandoned her when he didn't return home after completing his indentured laborer contract. Instead, he got a job in a Wewak store, remarried, had two children and, having been gone for eight years, was not expected to ever return, thus liberating Yaowitjha in villagers' eyes to remarry. When I moved to Wakau, Yaowitjha lived with Akami and Eine's wives and their children.[12] One of her eyes was impaired, but she was described as having the oft-voiced male Lujere criteria for female youthfulness: a lively and energetic woman with upright breasts.

When Iwani's 'tultul,' Ariawani learned of his sister's marriage to Yaope, he twice stormed into Wakau demanding a woman in exchange for his sister. This in spite of the fact that the exchange was consummated years ago and his exchange wife, Yaope's sister, had died. Both times he came with a blackened face carrying a bow and arrows, striding

---

12. While Yaowitjha's husband Karol belonged to the Waro patriclan and Akami and Eine to the Iwaridami patriclan, the two clans were associates in the upper village *iron* and in the large upper land tract across the Sand River, thus providing a tactical link among their wives.

through the village loudly claiming they owed him a woman. He also threatened to cut down his coconuts in Wakau if they did not comply with his wish to which their response was simply "he can cut his trees if he wishes." The Wakau men expected him to reappear and laughed as they recalled his storming through the village, adding that in former times he might have shot at them. As he was a *nakwolu*—although supposedly reformed when he became 'tultul'—their levity barely masked their anxiety regarding any future covert actions. However, his demanding public incidents were not repeated, the gossip faded away, and Yaope and Yaowitjha quietly settled into domesticity during my stay.

Threatening Female Abduction

Abducting a woman to be a wife is a last act of desperation when (1) a man has no sister to exchange, and (2) when a woman has been given but the return has not been honored. In the first instance, I learned of no actual cases in the past or present. I did hear it being threatened by frustrated bachelors who, like Samaun, were sisterless. Late one night when I returned to my office screen room to type up notes, Samaun was standing just outside and began talking to me. At that time, it was most unusual for him to speak to me at all, let alone at 10:00 p.m. Eine and Wolwar were outside nearby and what he had to say was undoubtedly for their benefit too. He said the villagers were starving him; none of the women would bring him food. He was very angry with all of them and threatened to kidnap one of the local girls for his wife. He had had enough, and he did sound very upset and, obviously, was very hungry. The withholding of food, I knew, was the villagers' punishment for his alleged bringing the 'kus sik' [severe colds] upon the village. Poor Samaun; now he needed a wife not only for the pleasures of sex but to keep from starving to death. He did not, however, abduct a wife as he knew that was a sure path to the 'kiap's jail.

Again, I was struck with the powerful sanction of food the married men had over the single men in a hamlet where so few of their mothers were living. Once Oria's five-year-old daughter Womkau was horsing around in my 'haus kuk' with her uncle Nauwen. Finally, he told her to take off, he had work to do. Then, totally aware of his gastronomic dependence upon her mother for food, she laughed and said they wouldn't give him any sago! That was the place to get a single man—his belly, and little Womkau already knew the point well.[13]

Were women ever abducted for a wife or was it just macho posturing? One old case I learned about involved K____'s daughter, K____, who lived in Mauwi, by mutual agreement married a Wakau widow, but he did not offer a woman in exchange to her male Wakau kin. Then early one morning before people were awake, a group of Wakau men went up to Mauwi and, demanding K____'s little daughter, carried her crying down to Wakau. Eventually she ran back to her father but, after she had grown, she returned to Wakau as Nakwani's wife, the exchange finally completed.

---

13. The controlling of a village's bachelors' access to food by the married men is a common way to keep younger men in their place. Gell, who worked with the Waris speakers in the Border Mountains west of the Lujere, cites a situation similar to the Lujere noting, "The fact that the bachelors were economically dependent on the married men was the fundamental sanction in social control within the hamlet" (Gell 1975: 108).

Tsaime and Nemia: A Turbulent Nuptial Scenario

The events leading up to Tsaime and Nemia's marriage and the associated community fallout including the 'kiap's intercession that set up two more marriages was the fodder for much village gossip and the impetus for new events that I struggled to keep up with. Ethnologists don't usually think of themselves as "gossip mongers" but, as crass and ugly as that expression sounds, that is what we are. Gossip, that is, talk about people's personal matters and life events, is the quintessential stuff of good fieldwork. "Gossiping is a thing that humans do" (Stewart and Strathern, 2020: 21).[14] The only way to learn about a society and its culture is to move in, make friends, ask questions, keep your eyes open, and hang out. It is an immersive experience like few others, and certainly not for everyone. In the field, your quotidian quest is involvement in the minutiae of other people's everyday lives—minutiae that would both bore and embarrass you back home. Your role is one of a shameless snoop prying into other people's business, constantly eavesdropping on conversations, asking personal questions, and generally being a busybody, hopefully a tactful one.

As social scientists, we professionalize this as "participant observation." The *art* of fieldwork is to carry this off without alienating your hosts while gaining insights into their lifeways to write about when you return home. Fortunately, in nonliterate societies like the Lujere's, ethnologists are such weird, ignorant aliens that they exist as one to be helped and tolerated at times, rather like a slightly annoying child. Anyway, that is the way I think my Wakau neighbors sometimes perceived me.

The extended scenario of Tsaime and Nemiai's marriage began on a Friday morning. At least it was Friday to me and some of the men who, more or less, still kept track of days and, by the moon, months (but rarely years) from the Western calendar they had learned about while away at plantation work. Before then the Lujere, other than tracking days, had neither the interest nor way to divide time into the named seconds, minutes, hours, weeks, and years, that for a civilized society are a ceaseless obsession.

An aborted elopement

At 10:10 A.M., while I was working in my office screen room, Waniyo's wife Elewe came into the upper village exclaiming to all that Tsaime had tried to elope with Leno's daughter Nemiai earlier that morning. Nemiai had lived with Elewe and Waniyo since her father forbid her to get married. Elewe was en route to work sago with Tsaime's little sister Womie, who also lived with her. Earlier, Tsaime had taken a route across the 'kunai' then doubled back through the forest to meet the two. He grabbed ahold of Nemiai's arm but she broke loose. He told her to go back home, that he was going to the Yellow River Base Camp to see the 'kiap.' He continued alone and swam the swollen creeks both going and again, coming home.

---

14. Stewart and Strathern's article is important as it unapologetically takes on gossip and rumor as important categories of action, distinguishes between them and, while noting they may lend themselves to harmful actions, they "are not *necessarily* malicious" (Stewart and Strathern 2020: 20; my emphasis).

Old Leno was in the upper village's *iron*, and as soon as he heard Elewe's alarm, he emerged from the *iron* swinging a bush knife and hollering like a pig being blinded. I immediately turned on my Uher tape recorder and watched Leno storm past my house where Oria and I were standing, and on down into the lower village plaza to in front of Tsaime's *iron*. Then round and round he went in a counterclockwise circle, stopping to shout, to chop the air with his knife, then stop again completely to get his breath, as he was an old man who had just recovered from pneumonia the week before. Grabbing my Leica, I went down to the *iron*, and was surprised to see Meyawali inside. I took some photos of Leno still yelling and circling (as in fig. 30). Then, seeing Ai'ire sitting by some betel nut trees west of his wife's house, I joined him to learn what was going on. Just then the sun came out blazing and we crossed the plaza to find some shade in front of Klowi's wife's house. Leno, with a new spurt of energy, renewed his tirade, and I asked Ai'ire to translate.

Figure 30. Leno striding angrily by the lower *iron*, bush knife in hand.

Leno declared that when his wife was sick and dying and they lived in a bush house under Mauwi hill, no one from Wakau came to help him, that he had to do all of the work and caretaking just like a woman. When he first raged into the plaza he was yelling about sago, saying that Klowi and his clansmen didn't have any sago of their own—that they cut the sago palms of others for food. Thus, he fumed, if his daughter went to live with Tsaime, where would they get their sago to eat? This was a big status insult indicating that their fathers didn't provide for them, so they allegedly had to steal others' food trees. Leno, exhausted, despondent, and breathing heavily, switching to Tok Pisin said to no one in particular, "'Mi lapun nogut!'" that is, "I'm a worthless old man!" Ai'ire turned to me saying, "Bipor em i bikhet tru,'" meaning he used to be a truly stubborn and arrogant troublemaker; and I was reminded of the stories I already had heard about his temper, his fighting, and his exploits as a feared 'sangumaman.'

I took a few more photos, including one of Yaope's new wife, Yaowitjha, crossing the plaza in a native skirt, then returned home. Leno eventually came by, exchanged a few quiet words with Oria, and went on up to the *iron*. Early in the afternoon I decided to wander up towards the *iron* to see what was up if anything. It was almost too quiet. Leno was sitting on the *iron's* veranda, and he acknowledged my presence, but we didn't talk. My friend Kaiera came to the doorway, his pitiful eyes shifting around looking in the wrong direction. We visited a bit then I went down to the lower *iron*, but none of the men were there. Aria had followed me down and we watched a mother hen with her clutch of six-day-old baby chicks. They belonged to Klowi's wife, Wawenowaki. Someone had broken a big ant's nest into five sections, skewered them onto a stick, which the hen vigorously attacked to make food for herself and her brood.

Around 3:30, I was working intently in my office screen room tent on my blasted, fouled-up Hitachi tape recorder when I sensed a body standing by the tent screen. Glancing up I saw Tsaime, his face painted completely black and holding out an envelope toward me. I was surprised, startled really. I quickly went outside; he was breathing heavily and seemed very upset. A short while before Eine, who was on my porch, said he had heard someone cry out and thought it must be Tsaime. The envelope contained a note to me from Ray, the 'kiap,' that said he had instructed Tsaime to bring all of the parties to the marital dispute to the base camp tomorrow and wondered if Tsaime had had sex with the girl. Tsaime was actually shaking, I didn't know if it was anger, emotional trauma, or what. I finally got a brief smile from him—he usually was an extremely pleasant and positive young man whom I liked a lot—and knew things were under control. Then he showed me a wooden baton embedded above the handle with a bright silver coin bearing the Queen's portrait (fig. 31). None of the men or youths who had gathered had ever seen anything like it, nor had I. Tsaime was instructed to give it to Leno who was to personally return it to the 'kiap' tomorrow; it was apparently a kind of bush subpoena to assure Leno's presence. There was no discussion of the events by the men around me, just that the 'kiap' would have court tomorrow and hear the sides.

Earlier Oria told me that Nemiai had wanted to marry Tsaime when he returned from his contract work, but Klowi would not allow it. The reason was that Klowi's brother's son, Ai'ire, earlier had eloped with Leno's stepdaughter, Miwali, without an exchange. It would be wrong for them to take his very own daughter too. Tsaime, much against his will, had obeyed Klowi—his father's younger and only living brother—who had helped raise him after his parents died. Around 5:00, Klowi arrived carrying his shotgun, apparently back from hunting, saying that Leno had just threatened him with burning down his house. Oria reminded him about the importance of the gun and hunting game for us all; it was obvious that Klowi was trying to behave himself and not put his gun license in jeopardy. Klowi, looking at me laughingly, said, 'Mi man nogut' (I'm a bad man). Nauwen came up on the porch, saw his friend Tsaime's blackened face and, beaming widely,

Clanship, Kinship, and Marriage

Figure 31. Tsaimi, face blackened to express his powerful emotions, holds the 'kiap' baton inlaid with the Queen's coin portrait to give to Leno.

reached out to shake his hand. It was a poignant gesture because all the others who had come to see Tsaime had a questioning gaze when they saw his fiercely blackened face connoting frighteningly strong feelings. After everyone was gone, I hurriedly began typing up my notes before something else occurred.

Glancing up just after 6:30, I saw Klowi marching strongly past my house carrying an axe over his shoulder, then on up past the *iron* where Leno was sitting on the veranda, on towards the top of the village, turn around, and head back down towards the old, dilapidated *iron*. All the time he was talking out loudly to Leno, declaring that these problems are because Leno would not exchange his daughters in marriage. Next, I noticed Tsaime walking towards the front of the old *iron* and quietly standing there. Leno then swung into action, lecturing Tsaime that it was *his* sago that his mother fed him when he was growing up, that it was *he*, Leno, who was responsible for his food, growth, and eventual maturity.

Noticing Klowi's axe, Leno announced that Klowi wanted to cut him with it, but Klowi answered, no, he used it to cut 'hap pos.' This was meaningless to me; later I asked Mangko what Klowi was talking about. As he explained, I gradually began to understand that this was all an extension of an old family feud and, at the same time was also gaining insights into why the Wakau men abandoned their big common *iron*. According to

Mangko, who was the eldest son of Klowi's dead big brother, the 'hap pos' was a piece of a post of Klowi's father's house in the old settlement across the Sand River, that Oria's father Limeritjo with Luritsao had burned down. Exactly why, he didn't explain. But at least I was learning that this was a society that expressed ultimate anger by torching property. A burning house is a terrific inferno; thus, most of the villagers, seeking safety from the flames of the blazing house and escalating tempers, had taken off for their bush camps. But there was another even larger firestorm. Leno had set fire to the big *iron* of Klowi's father's Elemoli clan, because Tsaime's father, Iwak, had married Leno's sister Mamau, without a woman to offer in exchange. In other words, just as Tsaime's father eloped with Leno's sister, Tsaime now wanted to elope with Leno's daughter. The difference, and it was a major one, was that Tsaime's father had no sister to offer in exchange, but Tsaime did.

Leno and Klowi were still engaged in an extended back and forth shouting match, but it was getting too dark to see them easily, so I stayed with a few men who had gathered on my veranda, taking notes while Nauwen translated. At almost 7:00, old Aiyuk, totally ignoring the shouting men, walked within a foot or two of Leno and past several unflappable children still playing on the dirt plaza. Nimo, Waniyo's younger brother, walked up to where Tsaime was still standing and, talking with him, seemed to disapprove of Tsaime's actions and was supporting Leno. Tsaime explained that the reason he tried to elope with Nemiai was that everyone was saying that she was bringing him sago to eat—a public sign that she favored him—and that they were married, so he decided that he would marry her!

Nimo walked up to my house smiling; his older brother Waniyo and younger brother Engwe were still hunting in the big bush. Leno, now extremely agitated, began dancing around snapping his fingers as if shooting arrows from a bow and shouting. Klowi's irate wife was standing in front of my house emphatically exclaiming to Leno that she gets her sago from her own mother, not from him! Tsaime, his face still blackened, had retired to my 'haus kuk' where we could hear him softly singing a love lament like a gracious obbligato to all the squabbling.

It was now quite dark, but still light enough to write as a shaft of dying sunlight hit where I was sitting. Leno had gone back towards the upper *iron*, children were still playing around, and Wolwar's wife was breaking some firewood, when Klowi came up on my veranda. He commented that he shot no game today; there was too much village dissension. It was the same, Nauwen added, when the Mauwi 'tultul' stormed into the village angry over Yaope's marriage; Klowi's gun misfired then too.

Klowi returned to the plaza and, walking towards the upper *iron*, called out to Leno to strike Tsaime; he was granting Leno permission to give his paternal nephew a beating. It was not a taunting suggestion, but genuine, telling him to strike Tsaime with a stick, but Leno declined, saying he didn't want to be jailed if he bloodied his head. Throughout, and in the background, Tsaime continued softly singing, over and over again, his love lament.

Nauwen told me that just before the argument this evening, Tsaime said that he was keeping Nemiai regardless! He added that Nimo also told Leno that he couldn't support him anymore; that it was he, Nimo, who should have married Nemiai, not Tsaime. His complaint was that he had given Leno's daughters gifts of game many times, yet Leno would not let him marry Nemiai. Instead, although a young man, he had to marry a middle-aged woman (Anwani's twice-widowed sister Aidwapi) and that was not right!

I was getting dizzy trying to follow all the unexpected permutations that kept arising. It was now seven-twenty and completely dark; Leno was at Mowal's house quietly visiting and a few men were still at my place chatting and discussing the confrontations. It seemed like a good time to go inside, have a strong shot of dark rum, and a warm shower.

Later that evening I visited a bit with Tsaime and Nauwen at the 'haus kuk.' Tsaime had made our place his headquarters during this time of strain. He told Nauwen that he told Klowi that he would burn down their *iron* if Klowi forbid him to marry Nemiai; he was the one who built it and the others just moved in. Speaking to both of us, he said that Leno had gone to his bush house for the night but it was just so he could work 'sanguma' on him. He declared that every time that Leno was angry, he left the village to do his 'sanguma,' then added, "I'm not afraid."

I wondered aloud if Leno ever got the "Queen's baton," but they said that he would not accept it; that he would not go to the Yellow River court tomorrow. Tsaime stayed the night with Nauwen in my 'haus kuk'; that was unusual, but it had been a very unusual day for Tsaime. It was late and I was in my office typing when at 10:30, Eine came by. I thought he probably had new developments. I wasn't sure I wanted to hear, but it was just village gossip. He blamed Samaun's 'poisin' for the return of his bad cold. After he worked in his garden the day of the big rain, it was severe again. He added that Samaun is disgusted because Tsaime is getting a wife and he still has not been given one. But, Eine added, who would want him as a husband? He can't hunt or find food; all he can do night and day is to sleep!

By 8:35 A.M. on Saturday, Tsaime, Oria, Mangko, and I had left the village and were crossing the 'kunai' on our way to the base camp for the 'kiap's hearing. I had stressed that I was going along for the hike, and that this was their concern and I would stay out of it. Just before we left the village, Leno came to my house to say he had 'sotwin' and couldn't go. Then just as we were leaving the lower plaza, Klowi came up to me saying he had sores and couldn't go, showing me an old one on his rear and a supposedly new one on his inner thigh. I was noncommittal to both men, but it was obvious that Tsaime was the only man who wanted his day in the 'kiap's court.

A stick fight

From out on the 'kunai' we saw Tsaime's sister, Wabe, starting down the hill from Wakau towards us, then a figure left the distant 'kunai' house, Waniyo's and Nimo's wives' home, and it was Nemiai. Looking back and up toward the village, I saw Leno waving a long stick rushing down the incline to the 'kunai,' yelling loudly for his daughter Nemiai to stay where she was. Tsaime called out once telling her to keep coming, but it would be easy for Leno to cut off her path to us. Nemiai turned around and started back to Waniyo's house. Oria did some yelling, but it looked like Leno had won the day. Then I saw a man carrying his bow and a big clutch of arrows approaching us on the Mauwi path. It was Kowali, the man who had distributed the food at a Mauwi *na wowi* healing festival I had filmed. As he approached, he called out that he knew all about our troubles and that he would straighten out Leno, adding that the problem was that he prevented his daughters from marrying. Leno was now out of sight and, Kowali and the little boy with him, continued on toward Wakau. Kowali was on his way to see his sick niece Sakome who lived alone with her five children and whose husband Waripe was away working.

It was the first I had heard that she was delirious with fever. Nauwen later told me that when Kowali met up with Leno in the village, Leno tried to grab Kowali's weapons, but Nauwen held him firm, telling him that if he fought him, he would take him to court and send him to jail. Someone held Kowali's weapons for him, then he started down the other path to the 'kunai' house where Nemiai was, shouting all the way.

My little group was still standing out on the 'kunai' when we saw Kowali leave the 'kunai' house followed by Nemiai and Wabe; Nemiai walked with her left arm raised and her hand to her forehead, looking down as she walked along towards us. Leno now really incensed and hollering again came charging down the incline with his stick heading directly for Kowali. Nakwane had appeared and went down the other path to the 'kunai' house. Leno, running across the 'kunai' to Kowali, began to strike him with his long stick but Kowali grabbed it and the two men began to grapple with it. The girls, obviously alarmed, started back towards the 'kunai' house. Too far away to intervene or photograph, we continued to watch, as did a group of villagers from Wakau. I wished for my zoom Leica lens to record this unusual encounter, the first and only traditional stick fighting I saw during my stay.

Nakwane was now on the path with the girls; Kowali and Leno had ceased their struggle with the stick and Kowali began walking towards us while Leno went towards the 'kunai' house. As we continued observing, Newai, a bright-eyed youth that Mangko looked after, joined us. His parents lived in Mauwi, but he came as a child to live in Wakau with his mothers' kin. Then with the girls and Nakwane in the lead, we continued across the 'kunai' plain until we met its edge and Nakwane turned back toward Wakau. Moving into the forest we proceeded in a line: Nemiai, Wabe, Mangko, me, Oria, Newai and Tsaime last. It was now 9:00 A.M.; the "stick fight confrontation" had taken twenty-five minutes. We proceeded to the base camp without further incident, except that with much of the path under water, it was sloppy going.

The patrol officer's court

We arrived around 11:00 and Ray was conducting an adultery trial of a young man from Aukwom who had sex with a young married woman in the back of her house. Phillip appeared a bit later and it was one of his Bible students; he was very discouraged. "It is always the same," he said. I told him that White Christians are adulterous too, but that was scant consolation to him. After I had lunch with Ray, Tsaime and the others gathered with the 'kiap' in an informal session on the steps of his office but without Leno's presence, Ray could not proceed. Since the authority of the "Queen's baton" had failed to bring in Leno, Ray decided to send his corporal with Mangko to Wakau to fetch him and set the following day to hear the dispute.

The next morning, Sunday, we were all back on or near Ray's office steps, including Leno, for an informal arbitration session, but to the Wakau group this was 'kot' ("court") and the decision of the 'kiap' would be binding (fig. 32). The session lasted about fifteen minutes; but first, Ray asked Mangko to interpret for Leno. Ray began with a reprimand to Leno for not returning the baton as he was told to do. When Leno said that he didn't see it, the 'kiap' knew that was a lie and angrily yelled at him. Ray had little to ask Tsaime, Nemiai, and Wabe as he had questioned them earlier; he knew they wanted to marry and that Tsaime's sister, Wabe, was available as an exchange. Ray tried to draw out Leno but had little luck beyond Leno's comment that when his first daughter eloped, a woman was not returned in exchange.

Figure 32. Leno and Tsaime at PO Lanaghan's informal court.

Having heard the parties' views, Ray concluded there was no reason why Tsaime and Nemiai should not be married, then gave Leno a gentle lecture. "'Mi givim lik lik tok long yu papa,'" saying that Leno can't fight Tsaime or others regarding this marriage, that it is a time to be happy, not to fight. It was cold, rainy, and windy on Ray's small porch and Leno, standing in front of the 'kiap,' was shaking. Ray noticed and recommended that he visit the aid post before he returned home, which he did. Then he gave Leno a stick of coveted twist tobacco as a kind of consolation prize. (Later Ray told me he does this so it "doesn't leave a man stripped"; this was his idea, not 'kiap' policy.) Looking at Tsaime, Ray told him he can't 'bik het long Leno,' that he must respect him, as Leno was his father now.

Ray then discovered that the man to marry Wabe didn't yet know about the arrangement and, Tsaime added, that they could not complete the marriage exchanges until next week. Ray approved as that gave Leno time to get used to the idea of his daughter's marriage and to cool down his anger. Tsaime, Nemiai, and Wabe then left for Wakau, but Mangko, Oria, and I decided to wait until the drizzle stopped and the sun came out. But this was New Guinea, and finally, with no sign of sun and the drizzle turning into a slight rain, we started for home. At a bush camp on the Inarlit River we met Tsaime's group, then together, contented if wet, we tramped over the felled tree bridge, and on to Wakau.[15]

Colonialism was a paternalistic, exploitative, authoritarian and, vis-a-vis the Lujere, often totalitarian system that, regardless of my dislike of it, I could inveigh against only in silence as the administration controlled both my presence in the country and access to do research. In spite of how I sometimes felt regarding Ray's actions to the locals, today I was impressed with how he, a young foreigner to the Lujere, had carefully used his imposing authority to resolve a community problem that he didn't seek out, but was brought to him by a frustrated young man. And his gift of a twist of coveted trade tobacco to old Leno was a genuine stroke of compassion.

Once home and removing my water-soaked boots, I heard a loud voice from the lower village and inspecting, saw Waniyo parading back and forth grasping his bow and some arrows and declaring loudly in Namia. Yesterday his wife had gone into the bush to tell him about Tsaime's attempt to elope with Nemiai, hence his return. Now he was angry with Nemiai as she had been living with his family for several years since running away from Leno's home; it was he, he said, who had given her a home and taken care of her. He threatened to beat her—or at least Nemiai thought so—and had furtively run away from the village.

I was reviewing these events with Oria and Nauwen later on my back veranda when Waniyo and Nimo's younger brother, Engwe, unexpectedly joined us. I had heard gossip that Engwe was to be Wabe's husband but now I learned it wasn't just gossip. In his quiet, withdrawn, odd way, Engwe surprisingly said, "No," he didn't want to marry Wabe. He explained that they had more or less grown up together; that their relationship was too close. He wanted, he said, to use her to exchange for a wife, that is, to exchange her as if she were his sister. The idea apparently originated with Klowi. I could only think, where will this saga go next? And who will be his bride?

Earlier when Tsaime learned that Nemiai had disappeared he asked to borrow a flashlight as I had the only ones in the village or, at least, the only ones with batteries that worked. He wanted to try and find where she had gone. Of course, I agreed. He found her alone at Leno's house out of the village and they spent the night, their wedding night, there together.

Klowi's stern lectures

Life in the village, however, continued to be unpredictably eventful. The next evening after dark, Monday, I heard a commotion down in the lower plaza and went to investigate. As discussed in chapter 11, Ai'ire, to my surprise, had struck his wife Miwali. But the big commotion in the lower plaza was Klowi's peripatetic lecture with several things on his mind. The primary subject was his disapproval of Tsaime's attempt to marry Nemiai; he repeated that his younger brother's son Ai'ire already had eloped with one of Leno's

---

15. When I first moved to Wakau there was no passage over the Inarlit; after heavy rain, the small river rose perceptively preventing my exit in case of an emergency or carriers accessing mail and supplies from the base camp area. Mangko, ever resourceful and helpful, cut a large 'erima' tree (*Octomeles sumatrana*) on its banks to bridge the flowing water.

daughters, and now his nephew, Tsaime, went after the last one. Besides, he was insulted that Leno said they stole his sago and were squatting on his land; only the last allegation was new to me. Oria said Klowi also had a few things to say about young people today who thought only about sex, especially boys who get an erection and the girls who then let them have intercourse. He railed on in the plaza, striding as he spoke, while the men sat in the *iron*, and the women in Ai'ire's wife's house. His tone was not of ranting anger, something he was certainly capable of, but that of a stern self-righteous lecturer.

Having completed his rebukes for the lower village, Klowi came up the rise to the upper village and, standing near my house, gave a second lecture that could be easily heard by both sections of the village. This one was to remind everyone the negative effect that the current village bickering and arguing had on hunting with his shotgun. That was why he had no luck hunting again today. Unei already had told me that yesterday Klowi shot at two wild pigs and did not kill either one.

Later, I asked several men regarding the impact, if any, that village arguments had on bow-and-arrow hunting and was not surprised to receive different diffident answers. This obviously wasn't a topic that had a codified belief attached to it and fit my developing view of the culture as "loose" in terms of the number of normative constraints explaining and shaping everyday life. This was very different from the Wape who firmly believed that in village arguments the wronged protagonist's ancestor's intervened to ruin the other man's hunt, be it with a bow or shotgun (Mitchell 1973). In just the few weeks since the gun had arrived, Klowi had espoused this "guns and village goodness" perspective; perhaps this was the way societies evolved their theories of behavior. I seemed to be observing the creation of a new belief about "guns and goodness" and the negative consequences of village dissension on the food supply.

The bow-and-arrow confrontation

Tuesday morning started quietly with the exception that, Nauwen and Oria's sister, who was married to the allegedly lazy licensed gun owner in Mauwi, had an argument with her husband and leaving him in anger, had come down the hill to Wakau. Shortly before 11:00 A.M., Klowi came out of the upper *iron* talking crossly and proceeded through the village to the lower *iron*, returning with an axe (again? I thought); he was undeniable furious and yelling fiercely. My small 16 mm camera lay nearby loaded with film and I wanted to follow and film him, but I was hesitant as I was unclear about what was happening. He also seemed unpredictably angry, and I recalled an early murderous story, later unsubstantiated, I had heard about him: that he had killed his first child when she was about five, ate her lower lip, and drank her blood in connection with assuming some of his 'sanguma' powers.

Marching up to Yaope's new house, Klowi began chopping at the house posts, continuing his enraged shouting, then went to the front of the *iron* and swung his axe at the log steps. Tsaime appeared and quietly took his uncle's axe from him. By this time, the men in the *iron* were coming outside and soon everyone in the village was out of their houses to see what was happening; some had gathered in front of my house. The next thing I noticed was Klowi marching with his bow and arrows. It was 11:05 A.M. and, finally emboldened, I grabbed the cine camera, a notebook and, throwing the strap of my Leica camera around my neck, joined the confused throng and began filming. The atmosphere was ominously charged, unlike anything I had experienced in fieldwork before. Then I saw the brothers Waniyo, Nimo, and Engwe aggressively entering the plaza carrying their bows and clutches of arrows amid a din of men's voices shouting and arguing. The shouting was mostly in Namia so I could only guess that it was more emotional fallout from Tsaime's marriage.

Klowi was now on the *iron*'s porch and the three irate brothers surrounded Tsaime. Nimo threateningly pulled his bowstring back slightly marking Tsaime's feet with an arrow. Nakwani gesticulating, approached Tsaime; Klowi had gone inside and then more men, including the armed and angry brothers, also went inside the *iron*. By eleven-eighteen, the shouting had died down; the angry confrontation was ended. Nakwane came over to me declaring that I must notify the patrol officer in Yellow River and have the men put in jail. I told him it was not my fight, I just lived here and besides, I didn't even know what was going on! He said that the brothers Waniyo, Nimo, and Engwe wanted a different sister exchange than the one decided on, and that when Klowi heard this, it angered him.

When the angry men, both inside and outside, calmed down, the mood around the plaza was unexpectedly mellow, like a crowd after a boxing match. More people than usual were still outside, so on my way home I took photos of the smiling girls sitting on Kwaien's house porch, then of Mari and his family at his house, and old Leno going up the men's house ladder that Klowi had chopped at. Some of the men had come back outside the *iron* and I saw Klowi, Kaiera, Tsaime, Yaope, Aiyuk, Aria, and Alomiaiya all on the porch. Luritsao was standing on the ground below them with his toddler jauntily on his shoulders. Klowi and Leno were arguing—of course—but in a controlled way. Little Menetjua, playing near where I was standing, fell down hard but didn't cry. I snapped a quick photo then brushed the sand off his face. I finished the movie film on the three young girls on Kwaien's porch and it ended with little Menetjua suddenly running towards the camera and me.

As I was walking home, Luritsao joined me, saying I must not listen to Nakwane's talk to report the men's argument to the 'kiap.' I assured him that I would not, that I didn't come to live with them to cause trouble but to learn their ways. Klowi followed me to my 'haus kuk' where he sat down smiling, relaxed and happy; Mari was already there quietly smoking his two-piece Lujere pipe.

Tsaime came by a few days later, as I was finishing typing up my notes on the "bow-and-arrow" confrontation, so I interviewed him on his views of what had happened, and they jibed with Oria's. In brief, Klowi was at the upper *iron* when Yaope told him that some of the men were saying that Engwe should marry Wewani (Ai'ire's half-sister) and that Engwe preferred this too. This incensed Klowi as he already had said that Tsaime's sister Wabe would be given in exchange for Nemiai, Leno's daughter. When Klowi came with the axe, Yaope told him to chop down the *iron*, as it was his anyway. The chopping was not to express anger at Yaope but to the other men; as Yaope was Klowi's *mamaru* he had to support Klowi whose argument was that Wewani was not yet a grown woman, hence could not get married to anyone. It was Wabe and that was that! The reason the three brothers surrounded Tsaime was because they had not expressed their anger at him for "stealing" their mothers' brother's daughter, Nemiai. Nimo was especially incensed over this. Feeling cheated with a twice-widowed middle-aged wife, he aimed, but didn't shoot, an arrow at Tsaime's feet. Nakwane then got into the act telling them to all calm down and get this thing settled.

A rained-out political meeting

Early the same evening, a young, handsome, and compelling man from Tipas, also named Yaope, came to Wakau to campaign for an Ambunti man running for the House of Assembly. He called a meeting and the villagers gradually gathered by gender in the lower village shortly before dark; the males on the *iron's* narrow veranda and in near proximity while the females were mostly sitting randomly in the plaza. While waiting I chatted with Nauwen, who said that Engwe's wanting Wewani for a wife was impossible as she was Unei's sister and must be exchanged for *his* wife. Smiling, he added that Leno told Nakwane that he wanted Wabe to go to Kunai, of all people, but everyone agreed that he was too old for her.

The meeting began with Yaope inferring that he had been sent by the 'kiap,' (not true) and that he could arbitrate our marriage problems that he had heard about, adding, arrogantly I thought, that if we don't get this Tsaime matter settled, he would report us to the 'kiap,' and that, if we don't settle this matter now, it will end up in court and some of us will go to jail. He exclaimed that he found Tsaime's 'lain' in the clear; that he personally had many sisters and did not demand an exchange or money for them; he just let them get married as they wished. Then he intimated that the 'kiap' will 'kot' Gwidami village because they did not show up for his meeting but were all away in the bush. By then, I was beginning to find this self-important guy to be a royal pain. He also tried to get Nauwen's sister to 'kot' her husband, but she replied she wouldn't do it; she felt sorry for him.

During Yaope's arrogant speech making, I finished a roll of black-and-white film on our gathering. It started to rain, then heavily, and everyone ran for cover. I dashed up the wet incline towards home in my flip-flops, slipped, fell awkwardly, and was splayed across the muddy path, unhurt but a mess. When I had cleaned up, I joined Nauwen who was cooking dinner. He said that Mari once told him that Yaope's new wife, Yaowitjha, desired him but he didn't want her because of her bad eye. Klowi, just the day before, also told Nauwen that Nemiai had wanted him and had brought him sago. Nauwen was surprised that Klowi mentioned this to him. Regardless, Nauwen said that he had forbidden any woman to come to the 'haus kuk' at night (where he liked to sleep instead of the *iron*) because he was afraid of the gossip that would be directed towards him. Marriage, as it often did, occupied Nauwen's mind, but unfortunately, he had no sister to exchange.

The closing nuptial exchange

Finally, Engwe's marital exchange was established; his wife would come from Mauwi, not Wakau, so in all, there were three couples married, not just two. Here is how it worked. Instead of Engwe accepting Tsaime's sister Wabe, he gave her to Waien of Mauwi and Waien gave his sister, Warare, to Engwe. Although all three marriages were affected by the sister exchanges, the ritual 'ring-moni' exchange would be between just Engwe's and Kwaien's brothers. It was agreed that rather than the traditional exchange of shell wealth, each side would collect about twenty dollars from kinsmen and villagers and, after the exchange of coins and bills, each contributor to the exchange would receive back the exact amount he had "donated." This kind of exchange—where wealth changes hands while assuring the maintenance of the status quo—was a clever way to economically involve the grooms' kinsmen and friends as supporters of his marriage but without anyone actually giving away anything of value. In American slang, these were wedding gifts, "not."

I was told that the money exchange for Engwe's marriage would probably occur the following day, but it didn't. It was just over a month later before it happened. The day before, Nauwen and Oria took our contributions down to Waniyo's house. I gave two dollars, Oria five dollars, and Nauwen five dollars and ninety cents: a total of twelve dollars and ninety cents or, 'sikispela paun na nainpela siling.' When they returned, Oria said that Waniyo was very impressed and pleased. He told Oria, "Bill's boys gave the most!"

The exchange would be the following day in Mauwi; I wanted to go but Betty Gillam, the CMML missionary nurse based in Lumi who earlier with Jalman had conducted the health clinic and, at my request, weighed and measured all the Wakau villagers, was making her last hike out to Wakau and returning back to the mission before dark. For that earlier visit I had put her up in my office tent on one of the children's comfortable cots. This time she had planned to come out Saturday and return Sunday but had received a note before she left from one of the mission women asking her, please not to. She didn't want Betty's Wakau visit to harm the "witness of the mission" in the area by staying overnight in my house. If she did decide to stay over, her colleague asked her to sleep in a native house. But if she did that, having been a guest in my house before, villagers might wonder what happened that I had thrown her out! I marveled that all of this moral hectoring out in the middle of "nowhere" was about villagers with not a single Christian among them. It was what my Kansas mother would have called being "nasty nice"—an old expression indicating that a speaker's moral rectitude did not mask her dissolute thoughts.

Initially I was more amused than affronted by the mission's self-righteous prudery, but Betty was very provoked and probably hurt that her colleagues would so seriously question her judgment. As a result, she had decided to come out just for the day and would do no more infant welfare patrols in the area. Betty arrived the next morning around 9:00 and, as planned, we spent most of the day discussing the Lujere; she was seeking information to use as a participant in an upcoming missionary culture conference in Lumi. Just then, it seemed there were no two foreigners who knew more about the Lujere than we did, she clinically, me ethnographically, and who never tired talking about them. In spite of the mission's officiousness, it was a day of delight for each of us. In the meantime, while Betty and I were conferring about the Lujere, the less abstract exchange of Engwe's marriage money happened up in Mauwi without a hitch. The system worked and, eventually, I even got my two dollars back.

Nauwen and Kunai's Marital Woes

When Nauwen returned from his second term as an indentured laborer the year before I arrived, old Nanu of Iwani's Aukwom hamlet on the Sepik, sent word to him that he had a daughter Nauwen could marry if he would send him 'bilas,' that is, new clothes or ornaments, apparently as an act of good faith. Nauwen gave Nanu a small amount of money, a good knife, and a new waistcloth, among a few other items. Then later the word came back to him that the deal was off, that only another woman in exchange would be satisfactory. Nauwen was disgusted because he had been swindled. He showed me a letter he had written to the licensed gun owner in Aukwom asking him to find out Nanu's intentions. He periodically talked about taking Nanu to court to get his money back but for some reason, seemed very cautious. When I left Wakau, nothing had happened.

Kunai, slight, funny-faced, and humorous, was also vexed by Nanu's behavior as he was the 'waspapa' or foster father of Leaurwe, a Mauwi woman Kunai wanted to marry. She was originally married to a Mauwi man in a sister exchange, but he did not like her, went off as an indentured laborer, and never returned. Kunai had no respect for Leaurwe, called her a 'bladi puk puk meri,' that is, a bloody ugly woman, who was almost an old woman to him as her breasts had just recently fallen down. Kunai was clear that he didn't want to marry her so much for sex, but to have someone to prepare his food for him. But neither Nanu nor her brother Kowlie would give her to him. Kowlie was so disgusted with Kunai's constant badgering him regarding marrying his sister that a Mauwi woman reported that he wouldn't visit Wakau anymore.

One day in December after lunch, Kunai came by and, as I was visiting with Nauwen and Kunai, each explained their "girl" problem; they wanted me to know as each hoped to bring it up to the 'kiap' if he came on patrol. Kunai then launched into a negative lecture—as only he would do—on how backward the Iwani villagers were, that all of the other villages both trade and buy women, but we only want to trade sisters like our ancestors. And, if you try to buck the system, you might get killed by 'sanguma.' Now really wound up, he self-abusively exclaimed, "Mipela kanaka yet; mipela no savi gut, no sindaun gut; no harim tok bilong misin nau ol masta; mipela no skulim gut yet," in other words, "We are just bush Natives, we don't understand how to behave, we don't listen to what the missionaries or other White men tell us, we are uneducated."

No anthropologist wants to hear colonialist-inspired self-deprecating remarks from his informant friends. Fortunately, Kunai quickly switched expressive gears into a humorous, even silly, mode. He began making funny but disparaging remarks about the woman he desires, that her skin was like that of a snake, then tops that with, that it was more like the leg of a cassowary! Nauwen and I couldn't help but laugh at his outrageous descriptions of the woman he wanted to marry—but never would. Informants like Kunai are somewhat rare in my New Guinea experience. If they appear a bit unhinged, it's as if they lack the usual censors to keep the culture's id in check. If you listen, sometimes you can learn a lot.

CHAPTER THIRTEEN

Into the Bush: The Quest for Food

> *The Lujere people literally subsist by interaction within their forest.*
> Elizabeth "Betty" Gillam, CMML nurse (1983: 8)

> *They live on a diet of sago and game with small quantities of green vegetables collected from the bush.*
> PO R. K. Treutlein, (1962: 14)

The Lujere's iconic ecological niches, 'bus,' 'baret,' and 'tais' (forest, creeks, and swamps), are each a significant food source.[1] The forest was the primary location for Lujere gardens and the game and birds they hunted. The creeks and ponds contained fish and frogs and the swampland was the thriving domain for sago palms. As the Lujere had a surfeit of land to exploit, a relatively industrious family should never go hungry. Still, the nutritional value of much of their diet was often sorely lacking. The two staple foods of the Lujere were sago (*na*), processed from the sago palm, and bananas (*nar*). Almost every meal was based around one or the other; thus, if you ate bananas with a meal, you would not also eat sago, like we don't eat rice with potatoes. Although more meals were centered on sago starch, it is notoriously lacking in food values excepting carbohydrates where it excels. Betty Gillam, one of the CMML nurses during my fieldwork that you already have met and who later made two important studies on Lujere nutrition (Gillam 1983, 1996), nicely summarizes the Lujere approach to food getting:[2]

---

1. The fourth important ecological niche, the 'kunai' or expansive wet grasslands, were not a significant source of food. However, during a dry period, a section of a 'kunai' might be set afire to rout out any small animals for slaughter.
2. This section has benefited from Betty Gillam's (1983, 1996) detailed Lujere nutritional studies plus our conversations about her understanding of their food ways gleaned from her numerous maternal and childcare health patrols to their villages.

When the Lujere people work at obtaining food they do not divide their time equally among tasks. If the weather pattern is not too hot and fine they will go hunting. When the rivers are low they fish; they will prepare a garden when it has not rained for a while. Gathering seems to persist in all weathers, as does the processing of sago. (Gillam 1983: 82)

Sago, the Lujere Staff of Life

Classifying sago is a rather slippery act as it has an ambiguous identity. Is sago horticulture, foraging, silviculture, all of these, or perhaps something else? I once seriously raised this question (Mitchell 1991), but here my interest is solely in the place of sago in the Lujere food chain. As it has a unique and major role in Lujere food practices, how it is classified is immaterial. More significant is that the Lujere recognize seventeen named varieties of domesticated sago as well as the wild sago palm, each identifiable according to a palm's color, size, thorns, leaves, and ecological setting, for instance.[3] Digging up a shoot and transplanting it in a wet area propagates any variety. Pests avoid it and it has no known diseases. A palm takes from ten to fifteen years to mature at which time it is felled just before efflorescence when the starch within the trunk is at maximum. A single sago palm will produce from 200 to 700 pounds of sago flour and, while it is superlative as an energy provider, it fails as a nutritional source (Lea 1972: 14–15). In the Sepik region men usually fell the palm and women process all sago varieties the same way. Here is a classic and succinct description of sago processing:

> Men fell a sago palm, and when the trunk is lying on the ground the bark is removed to expose the pith which is dug out from the trunk. The men or their wives then carry the pith to a washing trough set up at the edge of the nearest stream. In the trough the pith is kneaded with water to release flour from the fibre. Suspended in water, the sago flour passes through a crude filter lower down the trough into a container below. It settles to the bottom, and the water flows away over the sides. The flour is wrapped in leaves, then baked or smoked prior to being stored. (McArthur 1972: 444)

The wrapped sago can be stored under mud and water for a couple of months. Kairapowe, the good-natured wife of Nauwen and Oria's father's brother Ukai, showed me how the sago pith was broken up and washed. Her sago trough apparatus (fig. 33) was ubiquitous in lowland New Guinea. A culinary bonus is sago grubs, a succulent delicacy, harvested later from the log's exposed pith.

The Lujere had several ways of cooking sago: wrapped in a long leaf cooked in a fire, cooked raw on an open fire, wrapped around a very hot stone ('hatwara' described earlier), and in a tin over fire.[4] If the fruit of a citrus tree were available, its juice might be used

---

3. For a demographic study of sago in another Sepik society, see Townsend (1974).
4. In the Torricelli Mountains larger species of bamboo grew that I did not see in Lujereland. A favorite way for some Wape people to eat sago, and definitely mine, was to put the sago into a large empty bamboo node and cook it on the fire; this solidified the gelatinous texture, and the bamboo imparted a flavor that reminded me of popcorn.

Figure 33. Kairapowe washing sago by the Sand River with Oria's daughter Womkau.

to flavor the sago. The amount of sago eaten at a meal was large in comparison to the meat, fish, or greens that might accompany it. While raw sago cooked on a fire or in a leaf might be eaten alone as a snack on the trail, the gelatinous dumpling ('hatwara') needed to be eaten with other foods to make it more palatable. The former patrol officer and coast watcher, Erich Feldt, gives sago this negative culinary review.[5]

> The sago palm grows in profusion, its rough trunk crowned by repulsive, spine-covered fronds, its roots in the mud. . . . However cooked, it is glutinous and tasteless and, to those not inured to it by years of consumption, unsatisfying, leaving the belly distended but with the feeling of hunger unappeased. (Feldt 1946: 172)

The Lujere believed that three of the domesticated sago varieties caused older people 'sotwin' or shortness of breath and regardless of age, if a person had 'sotwin,' eating these varieties would exacerbate the condition. According to Eine, Luritsao got his 'sotwin' from breaking this taboo. As a consequence, Eine, although younger than Luritsao, also observed the taboo to avoid getting 'sotwin' as he aged. Furthermore, if a close relative dies, a person will not eat 'hatwara' for many months, the length of time depending upon the mourner. The death of parents, their siblings, and one's own siblings are especially honored with this mourning practice. Then there is the taboo mentioned earlier that a man is forbidden to eat sago from the palms he has planted because sickness, specifically

---

5. Gill (1996) provides a succinct biography of his colorful life.

'sotwin' and body aches, will follow. But sago palms aren't just utilized for food, they also provide important building materials. The roof thatch for Lujere houses is made from sago palm leaves and house walls often are made from their strong hard stems.

Relentless Gatherers

The gathering of food—almost anything anywhere—was a perpetual incidental activity that was carried out by adults and children alike. Whether moving through the bush or across grasslands, regardless of the intent of the journey, they were also casual gatherers with an alert eye for some or all of the following, for example, grasshoppers, crickets, caterpillars, tadpoles, frogs, bush rats, snakes, turtles, lizards, bush turkey eggs, nuts, ferns, wild greens, fungi, and leaves for wrapping food. As Knauft (1985: 18) observed for the Gebusi of Western Province, "In general, anything that is digestible—and almost everything over an inch long that moves—is eaten." The item collected might be cooked and eaten as a snack or used to augment a meal. Scanning the terrain when afoot for any wild food source to gather was a generic Lujere trait learned at an early age and practiced throughout life. Betty Gillam was especially impressed with the gathering zeal of children.

> Usually the boys went off in one direction with small bows and arrows and a bush knife between them. The girls would go in another direction with a bush knife and string bags. . . . The ages ranged for these groups from approximately two and a half years to ten to twelve years of age. (Gillam 1983: 55)

Reluctant Gardeners

Compared with many New Guinea societies, especially in the Highlands, that plant large, fenced gardens, it is a stretch to call the Lujere "gardeners." That certainly was the finding of PO Treutlein on his patrol of the Lujere villages:

> Often they will plant a small garden with taro and kaukau, and then they will leave it to its own devices, unfenced. When, after a couple of months they return, pigs have usually rooted out all the plants and they are left with nothing. As a result they say that there is no use in gardening. This attitude is the chief problem that will have to be overcome, if these people are ever to have a sound economy. (Treutlein 1962: 21)

Nevertheless, the small slash-and-burn fenceless gardens that are prepared by the men do provide a variety of foodstuff that augments their swamp-grown sago. At best, they might be called indifferent shifting horticulturalists.[6] Bananas were the most prevalent planting in almost every Wakau garden I saw. Depending on the variety, banana plants

---

6. The one part of Lujereland I did not visit was the northwest with the villages of Yawari and Mantopai, about seven hours' walk north up the Sand River from Wakau. These Lujere may not garden but subsist exclusively on gathering, processing sago and hunting. Betty Gillam, who visited the area four times on health patrols, wrote that she always met villagers returning from

bear fruit in between four and eight months while a few varieties take as long as ten months. Thus, the planting of banana shoots is a constant activity to assure a steady supply of the fruit as bananas, unlike sago, cannot be stored. In Wakau, there was no ritual involved in planting either bananas or sago palms. A stick is thrust into the ground, worked around a bit, withdrawn, the plant inserted, and then the ground tamped down. Hoeing, tilling, and composting were not practiced. Bananas, while primarily planted in gardens, were also sometimes planted on the edges of the village. Gardening for my Wakau hosts was, at best, a tedious job; certainly no one got credit for being a good gardener the way men were singled out for esteem if an excellent hunter. Betty Gillam, who had spent far more time in numerous Lujere villagers' gardens than I, had the same impression flatly stating, "Gardening for the Lujere is a chore, no-one enjoys it much" (Gillam 1983: 78).

Gardening tools consisted of an axe, a bush knife, and a digging stick. A garden was often planted in an old garden area that had reverted to secondary forest thus lessening the felling of large trees. Once an area had been more or less cleared of trees with an axe and the underbrush slashed away with a bush knife, the residue was dried in the sun and set afire. When the smoke, embers, and ashes were completely dissipated, a digging stick was easily cut with a bush knife and planting could begin. Both banana and sago shoots were planted this way and no ritual was involved. A ritual accompanied only tobacco planting.

The Lujere recognized thirty named types of banana plants—not that surprising, as the banana was first domesticated in Southeast Asia and New Guinea. "Recent archaeological and paleoenvironmental evidence at Kuk Swamp in the Western Highlands Province of Papua New Guinea suggests banana cultivation there goes back to at least 4000 BCE, and possibly to 8000 BCE."[7] Wakau villagers ate nineteen banana varieties cooked on a fire, nine varieties were eaten raw, and three varieties were eaten both ways. Twenty-two varieties were said to have originated with their ancestors, while returned laborers introduced the other eight varieties. Regardless of the variety, bananas were never mixed with other foods but eaten separately alongside grubs, fish, or meat. There were no taboos associated with the eating of bananas. Babies, I was told, were never fed bananas because of the fear of it catching in the throat and strangulation. However, if a baby were sick, it might be given a little masticated banana for added nourishment.

Some of the little gardens I visited contained only bananas and tobacco. Others also were growing a few sweet potato plants (*ipomeoa batatas*). The bachelors Aria and Meyawali had a joint garden plot, but their plants were clearly separated. It had more diversity than most with sweet potatoes, several yam vines growing up long sticks, and one pumpkin vine. In another garden I also saw a single taro plant (*xanthosoma*); occasionally sugar cane (*sacchrun officinorum*) was planted, but all gardens had multiple banana plants. I was most surprised to see a few corn stalks—a new world plant far from home—with several small mature ears. With no fences, the pigs, as Treutlein recorded, could easily dig up the root crops but ignored the bananas, sugar cane, and corn. In some of the village gardens nearer to the mission a wider variety of food products were grown, such as melons, papayas, beans, and pandanus.

---

hunting "with full game bags. Also, the bush rang with the chorus of birds like hornbills, parrots and pigeons" (Gillam 1983: 142). She saw no gardens and locals told her they did not garden.

7. "Banana," *Wikipedia*, https://wikipedia.org/wiki/Banana, accessed October 26, 2016.

An important green to accompany a meal was the fresh leaves and seeds from the 'tulip' tree (*gnetum gneom*) whose Tok Pisin name attests that its leaves grow in pairs. It's found wild in the primary forests and is planted in secondary forest near a village. Women also use the bark to make string for their skirts, bags, fishnets, and rope. Other food trees sometimes found near or in a village were the breadfruit (*artocapus altilis*), which takes three to six years to produce fruit and whose big leaves, if handy, made an improvised umbrella for the copious rains. The fruit of the papaya tree (*carica papaya*), so deliciously moist and a favorite of mine, was a rarity in Wakau. Coconut palms, of course, were the most prominent botanical feature of every village, towering over the houses, and a reliable beacon from the air signaling human habitation. A green coconut was valued for its cool liquid and both green and ripe coconuts were valued for their meat. When villagers went into the bush for extended periods, they usually warned others not to molest a tree, like a coconut or betel nut, by tying dry palm fronds around the trunk at eye-level or higher. Similar taboo signs were also sometimes seen in the gardens as warnings against stealing.

Most Lujere like to smoke either using their traditional *mero* or tobacco rolled in newsprint. Tobacco is very valuable and was carefully cultivated and cured. It was grown in small amounts in a garden area and often near a person's house where it could be more easily tended—or pinched, as old Leno tended to do. After the leaves are large and full, they are picked and seeds are sometimes saved for later planting. Leaves are dried in various ways, such as being hung in the sun to dry, hung on a stick near a fire, or placed under the roof over a fire. Once they are more or less dry, the leaves are often crumpled then placed outside in the sun or over an open fire to get even drier. McCarthy observed on his 1936 patrol that the Yellow River villagers smoked their tobacco on the green side but, at least in Wakau, they seemed to prefer a crisper cut.

The Fervor of the Hunt

While the grasslands were distinctly bounded, the forests and swamps at times lapped into each other and weren't as clearly delineated. But to a hunter pursuing a pig or cassowary, as long as he was within his or an approved territory, it mattered little, as it was the chase and killing his quarry that was important, not the locale. In men's quest for food, hunting was the most important and exciting activity, and it was the killing of wild pigs and cassowaries that earned a man the highest prestige as an expert hunter (see fig. 34). It was also the topic among men that assured both participants and listeners. Gilbert Lewis' statement about the Gnau he lived with in the Torricelli Mountains could just as well be applied to the Lujere: "Talk about hunts was drawn out, animated and assertive: it was perhaps the most congenial subject at gatherings of men" (Lewis 1975: 342).

A man's longbow and his clutch of broad-blade bamboo arrows for killing large game, unchanged since McCarthy first described them, were the largest and most impressive Lujere artifacts created, once fight shields and 'garamuts' were no longer made.[8] Little boys made their own little bows and arrows and went into the nearby 'bus' and 'kunai' to hunt

---

8. Unlike the medieval longbows, which were made of fibers, the Lujere bowstring was made from a strip of cane whose comparative rigidity lessened its draw force. While medieval arrows had feather fletches, the Lujere arrows had none.

Into the Bush: The Quest for Food

Figure 34. Men carry a wild boar shot by Klowi to the 'kunai' house.

for small animals and edible insects. As soon as they were big enough and knew how to escape an attacking wild boar by clambering up a tree, they joined their father or other close clansmen on a hunt, perhaps carrying a torch if it were night. The other weapon sometimes used in hunting larger game was the spear, but it was not as common as the bow and arrow. Before the mission came, according to Mangko, when a man killed a pig, he put some of the pig's blood on his bow before putting it away in the *iron*. They discontinued this practice, but Arakwaki volunteered it was their decision to stop, not a taboo from the mission.

Techniques for finding game were mainly tracking or taking a stand, sometimes in a tree, especially if hunting birds, or on the ground near a tree to quickly climb if attacked by a wild boar. There were stories of men being gored by pig tusks or lethally eviscerated by a swipe of a cassowary's spreading claw. Whenever I was with the men on a bush trail they usually spoke out if they saw pig or cassowary tracks, sometimes with detailed information on the age of the track and the size and speed of the animal. As Gillam notes, the Lujere men liked to hunt.

> In the dry season they will light fires on the grasslands and drive the wild life to waiting hunters. At night time, they use torches and flares to hunt flying foxes [large fruit bats], bandicoots and marsupials. They will patrol at night time, watching gardens, fresh pith from sago processing, fallen berries and bait for pigs to come and feed. They will climb trees and wait for birds to come and feed on berries. They will hide behind cut branches and wait for those birds that eat at ground level. For all the time and energy used in this, the catches are usually small, but this recreation is always enjoyed. (Gillam 1983: 64)

All birds were hunted, including parrots, cockatoos, bush hens, and the Victoria crowned pigeon as well as the large fruit bats that flew into the village at night. One night I was on my back veranda with Arakwaki and several boys when we heard fruit bats screeching around the trees. I shined my big flashlight up into the towering arima tree near my house and before we knew it, Klowi was there with his shotgun. He neatly shot one dead through the neck; earlier in the day he said he had killed two cassowaries and one Victoria crowned pigeon (fig. 35).

Figure 35. Klowi in the upper village with a recently shot Victoria crowned pigeon.

It was considered taboo for anyone to eat bat meat unless they had killed game. Unlike the Wape who considered the bat wing a delicacy, the Lujere ate only the flesh. While Klowi had his shotgun, other village men had only their bow and arrows for hunting birds. One of their favorite tactics was to take a stand in the forest and await their luck. It was also taboo for a father to eat any game his son killed. If he did, he would go blind and his son would have no luck in hunting. A father also risks getting sick if he helps his son butcher a pig he killed. A son with a successful kill might trade a bit of the meat for fish that he would then give his father.

As important as hunting was to the male ethos, Oria said that there were six Wakau men who had never killed a pig or cassowary, namely, Meyawali, Poke, Kunai, Aria, Mari, and Unei, although Unei was still trying. The village's most successful hunters were Arakwaki,

Waniyo, Kwoien and Ukai. Of the younger men, Oria said he and Mangko had good success, adding that while many of the village men had killed pigs, it was more unusual to kill a cassowary. Eine, for example, who was an excellent hunter, had never killed one. Mangko killed the only one I actually saw with his bow and an arrow (see fig. 36). The Lujere, like numerous other New Guinea societies including the Wape, tabooed the successful hunter from eating any of his kill. To do so could jeopardize his hunting prowess. It was explained that the spirit of the killed animal would cause the hunter to aim badly in subsequent hunts. To avoid such a disastrous consequence, the hunter always divided his prey among others. It is an interesting custom that redistributes protein among a group, while assuring the hunter that the men who have eaten from his kill will reciprocate in kind.

Figure 36. Mangko with boys and the cassowary he shot with his bow and arrow.

Sometimes, the distribution of a hunter's game is a point of disagreement, as related in chapter 11 regarding Oria's award of a pig's tail. If a man or woman, for whatever reason, is angry about the portion of game given to them and scolds the hunter or similarly makes a rumpus, it can also ruin the hunter's prowess. The angry accuser can rectify the jinx only by mixing shavings of his or her fingernails with betel that is given to the hunter to chew.

Compared to the Wape, the Lujere had little ritual regarding the actual hunt. There was no ritual in the butchering of a pig, just a general procedure for cutting it up. But when a youth kills his first pig, his father performs an important ritual: he cuts out the pig's heart and gives it to a close male relative who is a successful hunter to cook and eat. This custom is related to a similar one among the Wape men. The difference was that whenever *any* Wape man killed a pig—not just a youth's first pig—the heart was always given to an old successful hunter. Another Lujere custom associated with a youth's first pig kill was, if his father knew the ritual words—Oria's father didn't—to make cuts on the tendon side of the pig's four legs with a new 'hapmambu' (small bamboo knife) that he then gave to his son. Although Oria wasn't sure, he suspected that some of the older men, like Klowi, Menetjua, and Kwoien, knew the ritual words. This rather indifferent approach to ritual was unlike the Wape, whose approach to ritual, any ritual, was with a sense of sureness and vital necessity.

Ginger's Magical Power and Use

One day I noticed that Klowi had a cord around his neck with three strands of ginger attached to it. In a whisper he told me that it was for success in hunting. Before he goes hunting, he must rub his eyes and joints with it. This would give him success in killing many pigs; it also blinds the pig to his presence. Mangko, he added, also uses this ginger when he hunts. It was secretly planted near Klowi's house but the women in his house didn't know about it. Once while I was interviewing Oria on some of the magical uses of ginger—there are a lot—he mentioned the same ginger-related hunting custom indicating that it was widespread. The Lujere recognize four ginger varieties: *kwere*, a low growing plant—lots grew around my house— with small leaves and a lovely small orchid-like flower; *aiewa*, a common wild ginger that also was around my house and looked like what the Wape called *kaflaf* in Olo; *yuwowi*, that grew near the Sand River; and *lamari* (Nauwen said the correct pronunciation was *lama*, that his brother's was wrong), which grew in the forest. There was no single variety dedicated to a particular kind of magical work; rather it was the efficacy of a particular plant that was important. Thus, if my father's father told me that the *kwere* plant near a certain coconut was for hunting success I would use it for that, while a man who owned another *kwere* plant might use it to make himself ferocious and fearless when faced by an adversary.

Ginger had other uses in hunting. When hunting for birds the hunter puts ginger on the bird's track to assure success. One way of hunting for pigs was to cut down a sago palm, as pigs like to eat its pith. After a section of its bark is stripped away a hole is made in the pith with a stick. The hunter then mixes ginger with sago, spits this into the hole, and closes the hole with pith. A blind of leaves is made near the felled sago palm and after four or five nights, the hunter returns at dusk to wait for a pig to come and eat. When it does, Oria said, you can't miss. Among ginger's multiple magical uses is also the power to cure, discussed in chapters 15 and 18.

Hunting Dogs and Wild and Tame Pigs

Hunting crescendos during the rainy season, which is when I lived in Wakau. There could be days when the only people in the village were the sick and their caretakers. Once, late in March, Mowal, Kworu, and Nauwen were still in the village when Nakwane reported seeing pig tracks and they all took off with a dog to hunt it down. Left in the village were Aria, who was in the old *iron* with a painful boil on his upper inner thigh, and Ukai, who was at home caring for his wife Kairapowe, sick with pneumonia. The men returned later, flushed with success; but it was the dog that got the pig. Dogs are primarily kept for hunting, and all have names; some names are humorous and remind the owner of an incident about a person the owner dislikes, while others are descriptively common, for instance, in translation, "Spot" or "Blackie."

One day Eine was sitting with his hunting dog, and I uneasily watched as he hesitantly lifted his bush knife over the dog's tail and then suddenly dropped it, cutting off about three inches of its tail. Although the dog was fully grown, Eine explained this would make the dog stronger and heavier. His wife picked up the rather dazed dog and carried him to Oria's abandoned house next door and fed him a fetal pig she had stored. . The same tail surgery was also supposed to make a pig get bigger, as was castration. I was intrigued with their notion that losing something physically induced strength and growth; then I learned that a man can get bigger if he shaves the hair of his legs and arms. This, however, was not an Indigenous idea. Unei had picked up this idea from "Sepiks" in Wewak when he and Oria were rejected from signing as contract laborers; both he and Nauwen were staunch adherents of the new custom.

Talking with Mowal later, I learned it was not taboo to discuss a planned hunt or to ask questions of others regarding a hunt, which were all forbidden by the Wape. The only time you couldn't ask was when a Lujere man was going to take a stand at a blind by a fallen and rotting sago palm. Then it was tabooed, but not when going on other hunts or when going to a bird blind. My assumption was that the Wape, unlike the Lujere, had a scarcity of game and had created numerous hunting taboos to both abet a successful hunt and to explain a failed one.

While most of the pigs the Wakau men killed were wild, the villagers also had domesticated pigs identifiable by cutting off part of the ear that easily distinguished them in the bush from a wild pig. All village male pigs were also castrated when young, but they mercifully did not blind their pigs with a smoking firebrand the way the Wape did to keep them from wandering away. I was once commandeered along with several other Wape men to help hold down a thrashing pig (huge in my memory) as it was being blinded—a vivid fieldwork experience I didn't need. A number of Wakau men had been skilled in castrating a pig but, with the deaths of Oria's father and his two brothers, only Waniyo, Klowi, and Ukai were considered competent during my stay. Village sows mated with the wild boars, so all pigs were of a single gene pool. Some of the village's domesticated pigs were originally young wild piglets captured in the bush and brought to the village. The piglet was bound in a net bag with just its head free and fed sago, insects, fish, banana, and other foods until it was tamed. When it got older it had to forage for itself in the bush, but occasionally was given food by its owner, usually the scraps of a meal. Families that went to the bush for several weeks or months left their pigs at home to fend for themselves. As they got bigger, they came to the village less and less, becoming semi-wild; eventually they were killed and eaten. Unlike the Wape's food-challenged blind pigs, a Wakau pig never came to its owner's house and bawled for food. When villagers returned to the village after being in the forest all day, they might report on a village pig they had seen; but if a village pig hadn't been seen more or less regularly, there was no serious search for it as among the Wape who had a lack of pigs, both wild and domesticated. As there was so much conversation, both casual and serious, about pigs among the men, I easily added the following terms to my auditory Namia lexicon: *dwai* (pig), *waladwai* (village pig), and *manudwai* (wild pig).

Wakau's domesticated pigs numbered ten, all males except one. Five were considered semi-wild and rarely, if ever, came into the village. Women owned two of the pigs. All the pigs had names and, in a few cases, were called to come by name but more frequently by a guttural "aaak!" I got the pigs' names from Mangko—along with some laughs—and they ranged from the ordinary such as the pig's color, *Olku* (black), *War* (white); or a geographic name like *Laritja* (a creek), *Wakau* (the village); to "joke" names, such as *Adlowawe* (a woman's hymen, referencing a story of a man who tried to have sex with a certain woman but her hymen was too strong), and *Parupowe* (an expression for 'no gat' or "all gone," for when a man is distributing pig meat and comes to the end and says *"parupowe!"* to those still waiting). There were several other joke names and, like the other two, they were based on some form of deprivation.

The sometime levity about a village pig's name was indicative of the relative unimportance of domestic pigs in Lujere exchange. Pigs or pig meat were not part of Lujere marriage exchanges but were important in the curing festivals described in chapter 15. An exchange of pig meat and traditional wealth between a man and his mother's brother once had been important but, according to Oria, was rare today. In this exchange a man with a pig must wait for his mother's brother to mark the pig as his, signaling that later he will give rings—now rings and money—for the pig. In buying the pig the mother's brother was helped by his relatives who, in turn, would get a portion of pork. Oria had a large male pig over six years old that no maternal relative had asked for—and was not likely to, because it was now worth so much. These exchanges were usually done when the pig was young, about two years old. As the going rate for a pig was fourteen dollars for each year of its life, no one, Oria assured me, would buy an old pig, his or anyone else's.

Finding Fish

Wakau villagers, although near the Sand River, did no line fishing although the people of villages located directly on the Sand, Yellow, and Sepik Rivers occasionally did. There were many creeks of diverse sizes in Wakau's domain, as well as ponds and lagoons left when rivers changed their course, all homes of fish and other aquatic creatures. When ponds were low, the woody derris vine (*derris elliptica*) was used to obtain fish, as its roots contained rotenone, an odorless crystalline substance used commercially as the active ingredient in some insecticides. Two methods were used. The simpler method was to pound the derris root in the water; the other method was to dry the root, grind it into a powder, and throw it into the water. Either method stunned the fish, which were easily scooped up as they floated to the pond's surface. Those not eaten while fresh were smoked and kept up to six weeks for later consumption.[9] One night I saw several burning torches

---

9. The use of the derris root to stun fish occurred throughout the Papua New Guinea mainland; I even saw it used successfully in the Bismarck Sea by locals on Ali Island off Aitape.

crossing the open grassland beyond the village and learned that these were women returning from night fishing. They had visited a shallow pond and, as a fish became visible, clubbed it with a knife or sliced its head off. Both women and men fished this way.

Stretches of some creeks, as noted earlier, were the property of individual men and fished only by family members unless permission was given. But the very small creeks leading into the larger appropriated ones could be fished by any of the men attached to that area. When a creek or brooklet was not in flood, it could be partially dammed and a fish trap set in the dam. This was the most popular way to fish in Wakau. A dam was made by sticking sticks upright across the creek and, for example, affixing sago leaves to keep the fish from escaping while allowing some of the water through. Towards the bottom of the dam, a long weir woven from split cane was placed with its open mouth pointing upstream and its terminus, narrow and long, on the other side of the dam pointing downstream. The fish swam into the weir and were trapped in the narrow end, unable to turn around and swim out. The size of the weir varied according to the size of the creek and the number of fishes to be entrapped. On the larger Iwop Creek the weirs were longer—perhaps five feet or so—than on the small creeks, where they might be just over two feet in length. The smaller the weir the more frequently it should be monitored. Weirs were often checked when family members returned from the bush in the hope of providing a substantial dinner. There was no separate word to distinguish rivers from creeks; all were called *iju*.

The Sepik River, as I noted in my patrol with Joyce, is a lucrative source of fish for those Lujere who live on the river. Betty Gillam observed on one of her health patrols to Tipas,

> There were about forty people milling around the area. Six canoes were noted each with two to four people. They all brought from their canoes as much fish as they could carry. The varieties of fish they carried were 'kol pis,' a herring 'maus gras,' and 'bik maus,' (pidgen terms) varieties of cat fish. That night the village had a strong aroma of fish being cooked and smoked. No other village was ever seen to have such an over abundance of fish, and their catches were much smaller. (Gillam 1983: 110)

Ginger was also used in fishing, as in hunting, to promote success. Women sometimes used a small round net to scoop up fish. However, to ensure that the fish would not hide, ginger was first spit into the net. 'Savolim pis,' a favorite way for both men and women to fish, was to first scoop out a lot of water in a little swamp pond several feet across. This was done with the stem part of a sago palm leaf but first, ginger was spit onto the "shovel" to ensure success in finding fish after much of the water was scooped out. Only men or boys speared fish. Their weapon was a multipronged spear, and to be successful, they had to first spit ginger into the water. Frogs, and there often were lots of them, were a relatively easy quarry.[10] I once saw Oria shortly after he had shot ten of them with his bow in a small pond near the Sand, and I photographed one, a brilliant green, which filled his hand. He wrapped them individually in leaves, put them on a fire to cook, then ate the entire creature—stomach and all—with sago. I love frog legs but never worked up the appetite to try frogs Wakau-style.

---

10. See the myth "The Origin of Frogs" in chapter 14.

To sum up the Lujere approach to the food quest: they are a society that relentlessly processes sago and plants banana shoots, avidly gathers what is available, fishes and hunts with gusto, and dutifully practices a little gardening on the side.

The Omnipresence of Food Taboos

For many New Guineans, food usually has complicated cultural implications. Gilbert Lewis noted,

> For the Gnau few foods are neutral, just food and always food to all persons. Nearly all have valencies which make their use right or wrong for certain kinds of persons or for persons in particular relationships or for persons in particular situations. . . . Such views on susceptibility make one person's food another's poisin. (Lewis 1995: 172)

It was the same for the Lujere. The Wakau villagers had many food taboos; I have already mentioned some in passing, but there were so many that I was still learning new ones when I departed. A food taboo could depend on a variety of factors, particularly the person's sex, age, and health. Betty Gillam's (1983, 1996) nutritional studies of the Lujere were especially concerned with how food taboos affected nutrition, noting that, "Food taboos are many and varied. They affect pregnancy, child bearing, child rearing, puberty, illness, death and some aspects of hunting and gardening" (Gillam 1996: 28). Among the Lujere, there were two main types of food taboos: (1) *deprivation* taboos that usually honor a dead person and (2) *debilitating* taboos that may affect a person's well-being (Ego's or another's) if the proscribed food is eaten.

The primary example of a *deprivation* taboo was that the death of a close relative, as mentioned earlier, imposed a taboo on eating sago dumplings. If the deceased were a parent, the self-imposed taboo might extend to six months or more. Most food taboos, however, were of the *debilitating* type. For example, boys at puberty knew that if they ate any big fish or eel, they would be failed hunters as men. Girls at puberty were at risk of later malnutrition if they ate any opossum or tortoise meat. A pregnant woman's diet was restricted to sago dumplings, ferns, leaves, small fish, and small pieces of pig meat; the eating of other foods could cause the infant's death. During the woman's postpartum period, the whole family had a diet restricted to sago dumplings and greens until her lochia discharge had ceased and the infant was washed. To ingest other foods then would threaten the baby's life. Gillam (1996: 30) also notes during this brief postpartum period that the males of the household who left on a food quest risked becoming emaciated and sick. To assure that the infant would grow strong, it was washed in a new 'limbum' filled with water in which a small bundle of ginger leaves had first been swished about. Lactating mothers in need of good nutrition nevertheless risked their baby's death if they ate any meat, large fish, eels, and leaves from the 'tulip' tree; and drinking coconut milk could cause the infant to have breathing problems. These perceived risks persisted until the baby left the breast at two or three years old or a sibling was born. Children not suckling had few restrictions, but an illness could impose a food taboo.

Men could not eat the products of palms (e.g., coconuts or betel nuts) they planted for their progeny or else they would get backaches, have weak knees, and body and stomach aches. The penalty was even worse for a man who ate sago from a sago palm he planted: he would go blind. Young men couldn't eat cassowary eggs, though older men with children can; nor could they eat fetal pigs, though women can. Violating this taboo meant his skin would become old and flabby, although Nauwen told me that Poke ate cassowary eggs and was healthy. According to Oria, most of the food taboos were for young unmarried males and females: for instance, young women couldn't eat wallaby meat, or they would continue to lose weight until they were skin and bones and would never gain the weight back. There were fewer taboos for a couple with children, but here is an example of one: Oria's beautiful year-old son Nakwane had a fever for a couple of days so his mother, Pourame, took him down to the Sand River where her brother, an *imoulu*, was to treat him at his camp. When he finished, he told her that a lizard was causing the fever. Although it was taboo for parents with young children to eat lizard, Oria said he had done so, hence his son's illness. It appeared that almost any food, in particular circumstances, could cause illness or death. Old people, however, could eat almost anything they wanted. The cruel irony was that few lived long enough to enjoy their gastronomic license.

PART THREE

Magic, Murder, and the Lujere Imagination

*The imagination of man knows no limits, and we must expect
great varieties of form in mythical beings and happenings.*
Franz Boas (1914: 380)

*If the whole community does not believe in the efficacy
of a group of actions, they cannot be magical.*
Marcel Mauss (1975: 19)

CHAPTER FOURTEEN

Stories from an Imaginary Past

*Memory creates the chain of tradition which passes
a happening from generation to generation.*
Walter Benjamin (2007: 98)

Mental Worlds

One of the distinct privileges of living with the Wakau villagers in the early 1970s was that their ideas about how life was organized and should be lived were primarily their own, as were their notions about the composition of the world they inhabited. Importantly, their colonial masters had not dispossessed them of their Indigenous beliefs and attitudes. Their cosmological, ontological, and epistemological propositions and practices remained primarily those of their parents and grandparents. "Conquered and colonized societies, to take the obvious example, were never simply made over in the European image" (Comaroff and Comaroff 1993: xi). In two probing papers contrasting African traditional thought and Western science, Robin Horton wrote:

> It is that in traditional cultures there is no developed awareness of alternatives to the established body of theoretical tenets; whereas in scientifically oriented cultures, such awareness is highly developed. It is this difference we refer to when we say that traditional cultures are "closed" and scientifically oriented cultures "open." (Horton 1967: 155)

For the Wakau villagers, the penetrating lances of doubt and skepticism that can puncture an intellectually sealed society were not present. Although they had been under foreign hegemony for almost ninety years, they had dwelt, both literally and figuratively, in a remote New Guinea in cerebral and behavioral worlds unexposed to missionary beliefs in God, sin, heaven, and hell. While they had adjusted some customs to satisfy a patrol officer's demands during rare visits, such as digging latrines (which they then ignored) or burying their dead, their one major moral adjustment in response to colonial domination was to abandon revenge killings with enemy villages, a change they welcomed and which complemented their basically pacific ethos.

Explicit in the concept of magic is that it refers to phenomena that, like the Lujere spirit beliefs considered in chapter 15, cannot be scientifically validated.[1] Magic is real only to those who believe it is real; to others, it is at best spurious, not physically actual or even possible. Like beauty, magic is in the eye of the beholder. While the Lujere and I shared a world of ordinary village life, for them that world of explicable everydayness was interspersed with another world of magical possibilities that I found inexplicable. This included talking animals, humans living in the earth, spirits and animals transforming into and out of human beings, and 'sanguma,' men we both knew but whom they believed could fly through the air or slash a victim's flesh without scarring, then set the day for their death. It was a florid magical world I had once intimately known and deeply believed in—but in a very different cultural version—from my early Kansas childhood of tooth fairies, the Easter Bunny, and Santa Claus to my later childhood and young adulthood of Sunday school and church stories of spectacular biblical miracles.

Although the villagers and I were, in a daily sense, physically alone together, our enormous mental domains of information, knowledge, and experience were vastly different. More important for our mindfulness, while we each were initially socialized into intellectual and emotional worlds where magic and supernatural beliefs passed as "natural," I had gradually discarded them while growing up in a society of contested belief systems.[2]

To attempt an appreciation of the individual consciousness of a Lujere person is a radical undertaking: one must eliminate words like "magic" and "occult," as they have no matching concepts in their worldview. For example, I viewed the *wowi* curing rituals discussed in the next chapter as a form of magical treatment whose efficacy existed only on a symbolic level, but a Lujere man would perceive them as acts with genuine efficacy and as real as a conversation with me. Gilbert Lewis, who has written a searching essay on magic, writes, "An act may look like magic from the outside, but you cannot tell the thought behind an action purely by the look alone" (1986: 421). It is important, he adds, to know "about personal attitudes or convictions or beliefs" as well. So, if I watch a *wowi* ritual that is alleged to cure, I perceive it as a magical act—that is, one that implicates the supernatural; whereas Nauwen or Oria watching alongside me would perceive the ritual as practical behavior intended to cure. Their belief system is not saturated with leeriness of the paranormal like that of a secular Westerner. Evans-Pritchard in his pioneering ethnography on Azande witchcraft and magic similarly noted,

> There is no incentive to agnosticism. All their beliefs hang together. . . . In this web of belief every strand depends upon every other strand, and a Zande cannot get out of its meshes because *this is the only world he knows.* The web is not an external structure in

---

1. Books and definitions regarding magic are almost unlimited. For a big book that deals with a big subject, see O'Keefe (1982). See also Schultz (2017) for a fascinating article that challenges our ontological assumptions about the real and the imagined.
2. Peter Pels's introduction to *Magic and Modernity* (2003), is one of the best critical summary explorations of the anthropological history of magic in all of its semantic guises.

which he is enclosed. *It is the texture of his thought and he cannot think that his thought is wrong.* (Evans-Pritchard 1937: 194; my emphases)

It is the same for the Lujere or anyone else, whether a villager in a staunchly traditional society or a charismatic Christian in a postmodern society, when one's belief system is closed to challenge. We will have occasion to return to this problem of altering perceptions of what is "real" and "not real" in the following chapters.

My Lujere fieldwork was before the digital age of computers and cell phones that are now commonplace. But today both the Lujere and Wape have cell phone towers while the little Vermont valley where I live is still awaiting one. My cell phone is useless at home but ironically, they can call my landline from a cell phone in New Guinea's forests and swamps. In the 1970s, mechanical and analogue electronic technology was sparse and spotty in New Guinea. Other than face-to-face contact, Europeans primarily accessed information and knowledge via *paper* media—books, letters, newspapers, magazines, journals, telegrams, and files—as well as radios and, less frequently, via movies and telephones. Even in the bush I had lots to read, cassette tapes of my favorite music, Tok Pisin's Radio Wewak in the daytime and, if I chose, erratic shortwave Australian radio stations at night for international news and music. Most days after lunch I read a bit in an escapist novel—Somerset Maugham was perfect—just to jump momentarily into another cultural and emotional world and meet new people. It was almost as delightful as taking a shower.[3] But none of the above-mentioned modes of communication, with the exception of face-to-face contact, were available to Wakau villagers. It made me curious to know what it was like to carry, as they did, everything in your head and to have only people, mostly one's family and neighbors, for information and entertainment.

Another irony was that, while my primary reason for being in Wakau was to seek entry into and understanding of the villagers' mental and behavioral worlds, they seemed little interested in mine beyond how it might impact my immediate behavior towards them. It was almost comic: while I exhibited a blatant non-stop curiosity about them, they were singularly incurious about my previous life and where I came from. Although I know that they were astute and studious observers of my behavior, once I had explained why I wanted to live with them and they had met Joyce and the children, they seemed content to just accept me without questions—I mean no questions at all. It still puzzles me.[4]

---

3. While looking for examples of 'sanguma,' I chanced on my original edition of F. E. Williams's *Orokaiva Society*, which I bought for a few dollars when a graduate student, and was delighted to read in the preface the pleasure he took, back in the early 1920s, in lunchtime escapist literature. Thus, after a few hours' work, "an *alfresco* lunch spread out on a banana-leaf tablecloth; and beguiled by some reading (always, I confess far removed from anthropology and Papua)" (1930: vi). My copy of Williams's book once belonged to J. G. Frazer of *The Golden Bough* fame, and throughout the three hundred and fifty pages are his tiny, exquisitely penned marginalia.
4. In 1961–63, Karl Heider lived with the Dani in the Central Highlands of then West Irian Province of Indonesia and had a similar experience. He notes that the Dani "had no touch of the ethnographer in them. . . . They were just not curious about other ways of life" (1979: 12). The people, while friendly, were singularly uninterested in his past or even his possessions.

This, did, however, cause me to also wonder about the Lujere imagination and their creative sensitivities because, unlike many New Guinea societies, they had not invested thought or time in creating, for example, elaborate artistic constructions, complex initiation cycles, millenarian and messianic movements, or systems of intricate exchange. True, they had once carved slit gongs and made handsome fight shields, but those artistic activities were gradually abandoned with the arrival of the 'kiaps' and Australian rule in the early 1930s.[5] Unlike the Middle Sepik River societies of the Iatmul or Abelam that enthused in creating material and ceremonial complexity and competitiveness, to the extent of sometimes approaching that of a ranked society, the Lujere, other than their small curing festivals, appeared to have simplified existence by concentrating their energies on subsistence and family. Of course their language, being a Papuan one, was very complex, but it was invented many hundreds of years ago. From my outsider's perspective, their recent creativity seemed to be specially channeled into (1) traditional stories—*walkali*—told in the men's *iron,* and (2) combating sickness and death related, in part, to an obsession with the terrors of 'sanguma'. This chapter will explore the Lujere imagination in terms of their traditional stories, content that will overlap, and in some ways prefigure, the book's concluding chapters that explore the cultural and personal queries inherent in 'sanguma,' the vagaries of sickness, and the inevitability of death.

The Storytellers' Tales

Most of the Wakau males were very interested in their stories and more than willing, often unasked, to relate them to me.[6] They seemed to approach the task with the same keen attention that a film-buff friend might exhibit when relating the plot of a new or favorite movie. Of course, an individual's skill in telling a Lujere story and the narrated detail could vary. I usually tape-recorded these stories, and several other males often were hanging around listening. If an important detail or story section were omitted, someone quickly interjected a correction. But if there were just the two of us and the storyteller was a youth, I might hear a (mercifully) short "shaggy-dog story" with no apparent point, as if something were left out. But regardless of the storyteller, there were some conventions each observed.

There is a custom among all Sepik area informants I've worked with to make the time line of the story itself isomorphic with the time line of its telling.[7] Thus, instead of saying "they went a long way up the Sepik River," they might *slowly* say, 'ol i go, i go, i go, i go, i go, i go, i go, i go, long wara Sepik.' While it produces an almost ritual cadence of attenuation, it usually triggered in me an acute sense of impatience I had to squelch before

---

5. Unfortunately, slit gongs were never collected or photographed nor, from what I can determine, did any of the early Western visitors to Lujereland, including Robinson and McCarthy, mention them.
6. Four other ancestors' stories are in chapter 8 ("A Man, His Son, and a Dog Go Up the Sepik" and "Male Initiation"), chapter 9 ("Tsila Village Massacre"), and chapter 17 ("The Origin of 'Sanguma'").
7. See Fortune (1942: 147), translating from the Arapesh: "'Not yet' he waits he stays he stays he stays."

trying to surrender to the tale. I admit I was not always successful. Another convention was that a section of a story might be repeated several times; for example, if a protagonist must return to the village for different reasons, the return trip itself was narrated in detail each time. Boas, who had a deep interest in traditional stories, noted that the convention of repetition was worldwide. He also noted its "intolerable" quality to a European but the pleasure it gave the Indigenous listener.[8] Since I also took notes during the storytelling, those pages are occasionally littered with weird doodles and goofy faces to keep me in the game. So, to hear these stories properly, one should be lying around at night in a dark and smoky *iron*, tired after a day in the bush, and with nothing else to do. In 1936, Walter Benjamin wrote a provocative essay called "The Storyteller," setting up the atmosphere in which he thinks storytelling flourishes and then marking its decline in the modern world. To remember a story, he writes,

> requires a state of relaxation which is becoming rarer and rarer. If sleep is the apogee of physical relaxation, boredom is the apogee of mental relaxation. Boredom is the dream bird that hatches the egg of experience. A rustling in the leaves drives him away. His nesting places—the activities that are intimately associated with boredom—are already extinct in the cities and are declining in the country as well. With this the gift for listening is lost and the community of listeners disappears. . . . The more self-forgetful the listener is, the more deeply is what he listens to impressed upon his memory. (Benjamin 2007: 91)

If boredom, as Benjamin avers, is a precursor for remembering stories, the *iron* at night is the archetypical setting for mental relaxation. And, if a story were repetitive and drawn out, that was fine; after all, it wasn't as if there were other TV channels to switch to. Benjamin, I am sure, would be dismayed by our preoccupation with our multiple digital devices.

Anthropologists have always been interested in people's oral stories, and there is a varied vocabulary that refers to them—myths, tales, folklore, fables, yarns, sagas, legends, and anecdotes, not to mention the related massive and oft-controversial critical literature on the various terms. A fable, for instance, is didactic, as it is always making a moral point. But "definitions of myth have been debated since primitive religion became a topic of scholarly attention" (Lessa and Vogt 1972: 249). Anthropology's seminal pioneer Edward Tylor, in mentioning the problems historians have had with myths, notes, "Myth is not to be looked on as mere error and folly, but as an interesting product of the human mind" (1881: 387). But he wants to be clear that in his use of the term, myth does not represent

---

8. Here is how Boas explained it:

> I believe the liking for the frequent repletion of single motives is in part due to the pleasure given by rhythmic repletion. For example, the tales of the Chinook Indians are always so constructed that five brothers, one after another, have the same adventure. The four eldest ones perish while the youngest one comes out successful. The tale is repeated verbatim for all the brothers, and its length, which to our ear and to our taste is intolerable, probably gives pleasure by the repeated form. (Boas 1925: 330)

actuality; rather, "It is sham history, the fictitious narrative of events that never happened" (1881: 387).[9] For Tylor, and many others, myth is fiction.[10] Most Lujere think otherwise.

If you recall the Iwani's bloody raid on the Tsila hamlet in chapter 9, I raised questions concerning Kaiera's story. While there is little doubt that the Iwani men, including the Wakau men, attacked Tsila more than once, the detailed story account of the specific raid that Kaiera told me is probably not a good example of Tylor's "sham history," though it does contain some mythic elements, such as raiders knowing things they could not have known. To avoid the thorny ontological problem of determining if a story is mythic or not, for the Lujere tales I use the more inclusive neutral term, "traditional story."[11] In Tok Pisin, the storytellers classified their tales as 'stori bilong ol tumbuna,' that is, a story from the ancestors or in Namia, *walkali*. As far as I could tell, no modern tellers purposely created new stories. Certainly, the stories told to me describe a precontact era; no colonial characters or events are portrayed in them. One story, however, does mention a modern dug grave, an innovation stipulated by the colonial powers, although the dead spirit (*aokwae*) that disappeared into it was their own concept.

None of the stories I listened to, regardless of how unbelievable to me, were presented as sham history but as real events of the past, in the same way that some miraculous stories in the Old and New Testaments are literally true to many Christians. Some stories are concerned with the Lujere spirit world that is discussed in the following chapter. What follows is a sampling of the stories—I like to think of them as Lujere short stories—that the males of Wakau told me. More precisely, they are really "men's adventure stories," created by males for male diversion. Most stories feature violence, especially murder and/or forced sex, and there is a pattern of who violates whom and how, but this is not the place for a detailed analysis of the stories or their relation to other world story genres. The intent here is only to present the Lujere imagination at play to attain a richer understanding of the villagers' expansive humanness in one of its varied guises.

Thirteen different storytellers recorded their tales in Tok Pisin on tape at various times during my fieldwork. The thanks I offered was usually a piece of coveted newspaper from my copy of the weekly *Papua New Guinea Post Courier* that they then used for rolling their cigarettes. Most of the stories were recorded during the day but occasionally, when

---

9. Myths and folktales, like humor (Mitchell 1992: viii), today occupy the periphery of anthropological studies. Nevertheless, a contentious literature has developed through the years over the proper referent for the first two terms. The British classicist G. S. Kirk (1969: 34) notes, "there is no greater agreement on the nature of folktales than on the nature of myths." The disagreements between and among the folklorists, classicists, and anthropologists are myriad. Kirk (1969) has a lucid chapter, "The Relation of Myths to Folktales," which cuts through some of the semantic brush, and Carrol (1996) on myth and Cohen (1996) on folktales also clarify some of the controversies. For a succinct critical review of myth's relation to ritual, see de Waal Malefijt (1968: 172–95).
10. The anthropologist's viewpoint is epitomized by Leach's comment (1969: 7): "The non-rationality of myth is its very essence, for religion requires a demonstration of faith by the suspension of critical doubt."
11. Kirk's (1970: 37) cogent discussion of myth and folktales uses the term "traditional tales" as a lumping term for myths and folktales and Colby and Peacock (1973: 615) employ "traditional prose narrative" in a similar way.

most of the village had gone to bed and I was typing up my notes late at night in my screen tent under the welcoming glow of an Aladdin lamp, a restive villager, maybe Eine or Nakwane, joined me and wanted to tell me a story. I never refused, as it was a welcome change from my lonely typing on a mechanical typewriter to turn on the tape recorder, grab my notebook, and be entertained, Wakau style.

Several of the men had a large repertoire of stories and liked to go immediately from story to story. As I've indicated, their ability to captivate my ear varied. Most were interesting storytellers while others like Kunai, who possessed a seemingly endless font of fantastic tales, spoke them in a rapid and non-expressive style, or Kaiera, whose lagging cadence amid the afternoon heat and the cicadas' slow rhythmic droning, set my eyelids aflutter. But regardless of the raconteur, the stories were always told in the present tense and, almost always, were long, drawn-out affairs, even when the plot was simple. There were numerous untranslatable filler terms like 'orait' and 'olsem,' often used in a pause or to signal a change in action, that might pepper a taped rendition. In translating the stories from Tok Pisin, I have stuck to the story line using informal, even vulgar English in an attempt to capture the flavor of the original, but I have spared the reader the tedious repetitive sections, only occasionally indicating where they occurred. The storyteller sometimes initially suggested what the story was about but more often didn't and, even when I was told what it was about, the subject often seemed to be tangential. At any rate, the titles of the oral short stories presented here are mostly my creation.

In terms of its cast of characters' whereabouts and their comings and goings, a story was not always logical; for example, a couple might return to the village when you never knew they had gone away. These small logical inconsistencies never bothered the storyteller or other listeners (as they did me) who, I assumed, already had heard the story multiple times and mentally provided the connection. When confused I avoided stopping a storyteller with a query, in the hope that clarity would come as the story unfolded; sometimes it did and sometimes it didn't. The occasional question mark in my notebook or scribbled "I don't get it" documents that I was trying to relax and go with the flow. The main problem was that spoken Tok Pisin is often quite rapid, so a pronoun may get separated from its persona and, in a story with multiple persons, if one's attention wanders, confusion reigns.

These Lujere oral short stories, presented here in their near-natural state, are best enjoyed in lazy leisure—preferably in the dark—and are not for the compulsive logical nitpicker, the hurried, or the harried. It also helps if schadenfreude humor enlivens you. Story interjections from my field notes are in parentheses, while comments made when writing this chapter are in brackets.

Why Dogs Eat Shit

Storyteller: Yaope

A wallaby and a dog were arguing about food. The wallaby asks the dog, "What do you eat?" The dog answers, "I eat nuts, I eat these," and points to some shit on the ground and the surprised wallaby says, "You eat what?!" The dog, annoyed, says, "You can't keep asking me what I eat, you go find your own food!" The wallaby suggests they go into the forest and look for some food together. They come to a breadfruit tree with some fruit on the ground but the wallaby doesn't tell the dog. The dog sees some shit and begins to eat it while the wallaby eats the breadfruit. The wallaby says, "You find your food on the path!" and begins to laugh as he watches the dog eat more shit. The dog looks up and wonders, "Why does he always laugh at me?" Then he says to the wallaby, "Why are you laughing at me!? We've both eaten, what are you laughing about?" The wallaby explains that while he is eating *good* food, the dog is eating *bad* food. This angers the dog and the two begin to fight. They fight and fight and fight [many repeats] and finally the wallaby runs away and the dog chases after him. They run up and down three mountains and the wallaby is so exhausted he is about to die, but the dog then runs out of breath and never catches him. That is why dogs eat shit and the wallaby is to blame. [The logic of this moral still eludes me.][12]

A Pond Python Eats a Mother and Her Baby

Storyteller: Kunai

A woman is pregnant and she and her husband go to cut down a sago palm. Two very large snakes live in the pond. A big rain- and windstorm comes up and one of the big snakes comes out of the water, kills the woman, then eats both her and her baby. The husband sees what has happened and rushes back to the village to tell them what happened. A group of villagers returns to the pond with him and they put hot stones into the pond until the water boils. One by one, the two snakes die. They cut open the snake that had eaten the woman and her child and she is still alive, but the baby is dead. They then burn the snakes and the reunited couple eats of them. [Kunai ends the tale saying,] "We don't have snakes that big now."

Filial Love: The Cassowary Mother and Her Human Son

Storyteller: Nakwane (Listeners: Eine and Nauwen)

A man named Skruma and his wife go to the forest to have sex. When they finish, they see a nearby fig tree whose fruit is ripe, so she climbs the tree to get the figs while he waits below. She is still naked with no skirt to cover her vulva. One of the figs has fallen to the ground. As she moves around, unbeknownst to the couple, some of Skruma's ejaculate seeps out of her and lands on the fallen fig. She climbs down the tree with the picked fruit and they return home. Later a cassowary comes along, sees the fallen fig and swallows it whole.[13] The cassowary becomes pregnant and has a baby boy, a Black baby boy.

---

12. In Mead's (1940: 366) second version of an Arapesh story, "The Dog and the Rat," the rat mocks the dog for eating feces and, after other humiliating misadventures, the dog kills the rat and eats it. (True to myth form, this story demonstrates that Mead, like her mentor Boas, had to listen to a lot of repeats. Also, in Mead's story, the rat *tricks* the dog into eating feces; if the wallaby had similarly tricked the dog into eating feces, that would help provide the logic I seek for the Lujere story's final sentence.)

13. The cassowary is an important character in the stories and rituals of many Sepik area societies, for example, among the Wape in the Torricelli Mountains (Mitchell 1988). Among the

When she hears the baby's loud cry, she is frightened and runs away but comes back. She takes care of the baby as its mother and they go everywhere together. The baby grows and learns to walk.

One day Skruma is in the bush and sees a small child's footprints alongside a cassowary's. When he returns home, after eating and while smoking and chewing betelnuts, he tells the villagers and his wife what he saw. They decide to try and catch the child. The cassowary and her son are sleeping in the wild sugar cane, so the next morning the villagers get up to go hunt for them. But both escape. The villagers return three successive days to surround the wild sugar cane (repeated in detail) and each time the cassowary and child elude them. Finally, on the fifth day, they capture the little boy but his mother escapes. After the villagers eat, they start back to the village but they keep the boy surrounded so the cassowary, who follows them, is not able to rescue her little son. She doesn't go back to her home but remains in the area.

Back in the village, Skruma and his wife and his old father watch the boy so he won't run away. They give him food but he doesn't know how to eat. In the forest, he and his mother only ate nuts. After he learns how to eat human food like meat, sago, and cooked insects, his parents go to make sago in the bush and leave him with his grandfather and his two older siblings. But his siblings won't give him any meat or sago and he is very hungry. They tell him, "This isn't your kind of food, you just eat the nuts from the forest!" While they are away, he gathers together some food and climbs up to the top of the house and calls out to his mother. He calls and calls. Finally, he hears an answer from the Sand River. He continues to call to her. Each time she answers his call she is closer. Finally, she is as near as Waniyo's house. When she arrives at Skruma's house, he climbs up her leg, puts his things on her neck, sits on her back as he is still a little boy, then they run away. The grandfather grabs a stick to strike the cassowary, but she and her son have already escaped.

When the couple returns from making sago and hear what has happened, she cries and cries at the loss of her new son. The boy and his cassowary mother come to a small pond by a little hill like Mauwi. He makes a little temporary house with one bed, gets some fish from the pond and some wild sugar cane for his mother. They go to sleep and the next day get up and travel until they come to a mountain. The cassowary tells her son to make this his place. He makes a shelter to sleep but the next day he builds a big house and, with his two stone adzes, cuts down the little trees, then the big trees, and sets them all on fire. Now he makes a garden, as it was dry-weather time. Then he makes a ritual for wind and rain. His mother sleeps under his big house. The garden comes up overnight and his two dogs, one male and one female, are now full grown. Then he makes an even bigger house. He also makes weapons for hunting and shoots two pigs and two cassowaries. He brings them home, butchers them and smokes them. The next day he kills one pig and three cassowaries.

His mother finds two girls near the Sepik River by a pond. The girls' skirts are hanging up so she eats them. The girls want to strike her but she runs away and they follow her. They come to the boy's mountain home and the three of them go on top to the house.

Waina (Gell 1975) and Amanab (Juillerat 1996) in the Border Mountains, it evoked a provocative discussion on a cassowary-related ritual cycle (Juillerat 1992). See also Tuzin's (1980: 1–8) Ilahita Arapesh myth of the cassowary/woman.

The boy is out hunting so the cassowary hangs up the girl's things and gives them food. The boy returns from hunting with one pig and one cassowary and, coming inside, sees the two girls. [They think he is a spirit boy and he thinks they are spirit girls and they ask each other what they eat to assure the other is not a demon or spirit.[14] It is a standard verbal exchange in many stories, among the Wape too.] They tell him how they met the cassowary at the pond and came back here with her and that she carried all of their things. He then explains that the cassowary is his true mother. He decides to marry both of the girls and they all first eat, then chew betel and smoke tobacco.

The next day he goes hunting while the two girls, who are sisters with the same mother, make sago. In time, one sister has a baby boy, the other a baby girl. The sisters continue to have children and when they grow up, the boys marry their own sisters. They can't exchange sisters with other men because there are no other villages nearby.

One day the cassowary goes to a pond but a hunter is hiding in wait and he kills her. Her son is waiting for her to come home but by dark she does not appear. The next day he gets his weapons and, on finding the man that killed his mother, he kills him. Once back home, he beat the slit gong to announce his victory over his enemy.

[This story wound down rather rapidly. It had started to rain unusually hard, was almost 11:00 P.M., and I know that Nakwane got soaked dashing home.]

The next story was the first one I collected from the Lujere; at eighty minutes, it was also the longest.

The Turtle Moon and the Naughty Children

Storyteller: Oria (Listeners: Nakwani, Nauwen, Yaope, Iwi, and Kairapowe)

A woman finds a turtle by the river, puts a hole in its shell, then hangs it up. She had no sago to eat with it, so she and her husband go to the bush to cut down a sago palm and make sago flour but their small son and daughter remain at home with their father's mother. The children go to the river to bathe and play with the turtle, then bring it back to the village and place it at the base of a big black palm. It climbs up the tree but the grandmother sees it and climbs after it, catches it, then takes it back to the river and fastens it with a strong vine. Two more times the children take the turtle to the village and each time the grandmother climbs up the tree, catches it, and returns it to the river where she fastens it with a strong vine. But the fourth time when the grandmother sees the turtle going up into the fronds of the palm, she does not go after it as her chest and breasts are so badly bruised from climbing up and down the tree. The turtle continues to climb, goes up into the clouds, and then becomes the moon. The grandmother then makes a false turtle out of a wild taro leaf and puts it by the river.

The parents come home in the afternoon and the mother makes sago dumplings from the new flour. The grandmother says nothing about the turtle. When the mother finishes the dumpling, she gets the turtle, breaks it open and cooks it on the fire. When it is cooked she tastes it but it tastes awful. She tries it again and it is still terrible and she throws it away in disgust. The grandmother then tells her the story of what happened to

---

14. Mark Pendergrast (2017: 155–210) interestingly deals with demons in contemporary society as aspects of psychiatry and psychotherapy.

the turtle, how she caught it three times after the children released it but the fourth time it got away because her chest was too badly scraped to climb the palm again. The mother does not say anything about this to the children.

Early the next morning the father goes hunting for pigs in the wild sugar cane with some other men. The children and the two women stay home. The mother says that she wants to pick some breadfruit and the two children want to go with her. She says as soon as it is light they can go with her. They set out together and the mother cuts the flower sheaths from three big palms for three big baskets and also cuts some vines. She collects shoots of coconuts, bananas, breadfruit, sago palms, and tulip trees, as well as yams and all the other kinds of food they plant to eat. She also has a female and male puppy. She then climbs a breadfruit tree and throws the fruit down, chops some firewood, cooks the breadfruit, removes the skins and feeds the breadfruit to her children. She asks them if they are sleepy and suggests they rest in the baskets. She has them lie down, each with a head at either end; soon they are sound asleep.

The mother takes the vines and ties the children into the baskets, then makes a raft and puts it into the river. She places the sleeping children on the raft, then puts all of the plants and trees aboard with the two puppies. She also puts some sago and meat on board and ties everything down securely. She walks with the raft towards the middle of the river, pushes it downstream, and returns to the shore.

The children float down the river on, and on, and on, and on, and on, and on, and on, and on, [etc.]. For four days and four nights they drift down the river then, towards evening, they are washed ashore by a wave (Oria wonders how a wave got into the story; there are only waves on the ocean!). The boy wakes up and with a shell in his net bag cuts a hole in the basket and gets out. He wakes his sister and tells her what their mother has done to them. But she says, "We can't cry; we ruined her turtle so she has ruined us!" They eat the food she provided for them, smoke, then make a shelter.

Their father returns from his hunt after killing five pigs and asks, "Where are the children?" His wife answers that they are out playing and he tells her to call them to come and eat his meat. She says she doesn't know where they are and for him to call them. He becomes annoyed and tells her strongly to go and find his children. She goes outside and pretends to look for them. When she returns, she says she could not find them. The man's mother then tells him what his wife did with the children. The father says nothing. He gets his bow and shoots his wife dead with an arrow.

The children wake up the next morning at 6:00 and find themselves at the base of a big mountain. They look at the mountain and decide, "This is our place!" There are no people there but lots of wildlife: pigs, cassowaries, bush fowl, [etc.]. The children eat, feed the dogs, then climb up the mountain to find a place to make a house. They find some cassowary eggs and a place for the house. He cuts down all of the trees, then they return to their shelter. But first they put poison in a brook to kill the fish. They stay up all night smoking the many fish. In the morning he tells his sister, "You smoke fish today and I'll go and make our little house [myriad details of his getting the supporting posts, crossbeams, etc.]. At five o'clock he goes back home. He asks his sister, "Have you eaten?" and she answers, "No." The two eat together, feed the dogs, and go to sleep. At six o'clock the boy gets up and cuts some branches of the wild coconut palm to enclose the top front of the house while his sister remains to smoke more fish. His sister makes the clay hearth in the house and a place to smoke the fish. Both are now big and robust; "We're all right now!" (Oria makes an aside here, saying they cannot eat cassowary eggs; only a married man with children can. They can just eat the eggs of the bush fowl.) They go down to the raft and bring all of the things on it up to the house. They then clear land for a garden and burn it off with a very bright fire. The fire is so big that people from far away see it burning on the mountain and wonder. It burns steadily for six days and goes out on the seventh.

The children make a rain ritual and the rain comes down. Now they plant all of the plants and trees they brought with them [all are named individually, one by one, and planted one by one]. At dusk they eat some sago dumplings and eggs and, when it is dark, they go to sleep. But during the night, the boy gets up and, looking at the garden, sees that everything [all are named one by one] has grown big. He gets his sister up, the dogs wake up too, then they eat a bite, have a smoke, and go back to sleep. The boy is up with the sun and, as he looks around, again sees how everything they planted has come up. Then he gets his sister up, "This is different from our place; there we didn't have plenty of everything like here." The sister gets a stone to cut a flower sheath for washing sago and dries it in the sun. They cut some bananas to eat and cut some tobacco leaves to dry. They try everything. They make a big house that is larger than our [Wakau's] old men's house and move in.

The boy goes pig hunting with his two dogs that are good hunters. The boy and girl are in the bush and he shoots a pig. There is another man pig hunting, shoots a pig, and the boy sees him and asks, "Where do you come from?" [Then the usual back and forth, are you a man or a demon questioning.] The two males have a smoke and make a fire. The man that shot the pig butchers it and gives him a front and hind leg and a shoulder, then asks him, "Are you single or married?" The two males separate and when the boy gets home, his sister comes from washing sago and he tells her that a bush demon gave him the pig parts. Earlier, the hunter told the boy to come to his place in four days. He goes to his house, then they mark the day for the hunter to go to the boy's place. When he arrives, the boy says that the woman is his sister, not his wife. The hunter says that his place is no good, that he lives in the fens, doesn't have a garden; it is all forest. He wants to exchange sisters, saying they can do it. "We will collect food first then, after the third night, exchange sisters." He says on the fourth day they will meet at the boy's place; it is a good place. They make a big feast, and each shoots two pigs. They decide to live on the boy's mountain. After the two couples marry, numerous children are born and they decide they need a men's house and build one.

[The Wape have a similar moon story with disobedient children exiled by their mother. I tried to explore this with Oria and his listeners, but they weren't interested.]

The Selfish Husband and a Magical Skirt

Storyteller: Kaiera

A village was having a 'sing-sing', but a husband told his wife that he would go alone because they did not have the shell rings to give them for meat and sago.[15] His wife, however, protested; it was her birth village and she wanted to go, too. "No!" he said, "Only

---

15. The festival referred to is the more important of the two *na wowi* festivals where a village accumulates a large amount of smoked meat and sago for the exchange of the visitors' shell rings.

I will go and you cannot follow me!" So, she made a new skirt for herself and that night, after fastening the door tight, she made a hole in the roof of the house. She then put on her new skirt and was transformed into a bird of paradise. When her husband returned home the next morning from the all-night 'sing-sing,' he tried and tried to get in. He called out repeatedly for her to open the door but she had flown away.

[After the story was over, Kaiera added that men can no longer make their wives stay at home when there is a 'sing-sing'; now they go with them.]

A Cannibal Demon and the Villagers' Revenge

Storyteller: Yaope (he learned the story from his father, old Menethua)

One night a man named Ilemelo was alone at his bush camp when he heard a pig, then went outside and shot it. With a lighted torch, he followed its blood and eventually found it dead. He fastened its legs together, then covered it over with some leaves. He was hungry and wanted a frog to eat so he killed two little green ones and brought them back to his bush camp to cook and eat. He looked for his sago but it was gone because a demon named Souku had eaten it. Souku did not hide but called out, "Sago! Sago! Sago!" Ilemelo answered, "Who ate my sago dumplings and sago cakes?" Ilemelo sees Souku and they begin to fight but Souku wins. First he rips off Ilemelo's balls, then his penis, and immediately eats them; he then proceeds to eat the rest of him until nothing is left but his bones.

It was almost dawn when Souku went into a rotten black palm tree and stood up inside of it. Back in the village, Ilemelo's wife wonders why her husband has not returned and if a wild pig has killed him. She tells the villagers that her husband is missing and goes to find him with their young son who didn't want to go with her. They arrive at their bush camp but when she sees no smoke, she knows he is not there. "Where is he?" She hasn't yet seen his bones. Then on the veranda she sees his bones and begins to wail, as she knows a demon has killed and eaten him. Then their son also begins to wail.

The two of them now go to look for the demon. He walks like a crocodile and they follow his tracks to the black palm tree. From inside, Souku asks, "Who are you looking for?" and she answers, "My husband," and wants to know who ate him. "See my stomach?" he says, "I ate him!" She says she is going back to the village and tells him to come with her but he says, "This is my house, I am not going anywhere! I'm too full to walk." She and her son begin wailing again and head for home where the villagers hear them approaching. The villagers ask why are they wailing and she tells them that she saw her husband's bones and that a demon had eaten him. "Did you see the demon?" they ask. "Yes," she answers, "I saw him and talked to him. He is in a black palm tree." All of the village men get their weapons and go back with her to the camp, and then she takes them to the dead black palm. Souku sees them and begins to laugh, saying, "I can eat all of you!"

The village men take sago and wild coconut leaves and pile them up around the palm then they cut it down. The demon in the top of the palm falls and begins to fight with the men. But the men win and kill the demon. They take his body and put it on the leaves and set it all ablaze. His stomach explodes and they throw some frogs and ants into the fire. Only the ashes remain. The village men return to the camp but Ilemelo's wife wants to find out if her husband shot a pig so she goes to the sago tree [?] and sees the pig's blood.

She returns and tells the men about the pig. The men cut up the pig and carry it back to the village and present it to their mothers' relatives to eat.

Wararu and the Spirit Woman

Storyteller: Oria

This story is about a man, Wararu, from Wakau and a woman named Wetabe from Gwidami village. Gwidami is having a *na wowi* curing festival, the one you saw in Mauwi [an aside to me], and Wararu goes to it because he lusts for Wetabe and assumes she will be there. Both are single. He doesn't eat; he just lusts for this girl. He says, "Just give me tobacco and betel nuts, that is my kind of food!" The next day Wetabe sleeps until the afternoon and plans to go netting for fish with a girlfriend. A man in the village warns her not to go as Wararu lusts for her and might try to abduct her. She disagrees and goes off with her friend to a local pond to catch fish. Wararu sees their footprints and follows them to the pond. Wararu talks with Wetabe and tells her to come with him. She asks him to wait awhile longer so she can catch more fish. [He repeats his request numerous times with the same avoiding answer.] Now Wararu is furious with her and taking his bow, shoots an arrow into her stomach and she dies.

Wetabe's spirit follows him and materializes into her physical self. She is now the same as a real woman. She tells him to wait for her but he sees a red tree, breaks the bark open and goes inside of it to hide from her. When she looks for him and can't find him, she calls, "Where are you hiding?" and then finds him. He comes out and says, "You are a spirit!" but she denies that he shot her and says that he missed! Meanwhile her girlfriend ran back to the village and told how Wararu had shot and killed Wetabe. [Oria retells the story to here as the girlfriend would tell the villagers what happened.]

They return together to the village and he tells everyone that she is really a spirit but she says that she is not a spirit but really Wetabe. The two of them have sex and she has a baby boy and they settle down in her village. Their next baby is a girl. Wetabe has a younger sister and she and the spirit Wetabe are at another *na wowi* curing festival. The spirit Wetabe asks her sister to come with her to the privy, as she has to shit. The sister is carrying Watebe's baby and on the way, she shows her sister where they buried her, whereupon the spirit leaves her and goes down into the grave. When the sister returns to the festival, they all are angry with her and tell her that now she must care for the baby and become Wararu's wife. So she becomes his wife and they move back to his village.

The Origin of Frogs

Storyteller: Kaiera (Listener: Oria)

There was a single man named Manu with an older married brother and a woman named Tabilyeh. Once Tabilyeh went to cut firewood but when she cut it, it called out, "Manu, Manu!" She started to cut the firewood again, and again it called Manu's name. Manu heard his name being called, went to where the woman was and they had sex; then each went home. The next day the same thing happened and this was repeated many times, day, after day, after day, after day. Finally, Tabilykan'eh got tired of having sex with Manu so she took the fruit of a tree, stuck a long sago thorn into it, and placed it in her vagina. Manu hears his name being called, goes to Tabilyeh but when they have sex, the thorn goes up into his penis's opening and causes great pain. "What are you doing to me?" he cries, "What did your vagina do to me?" (Oria is here and he is helping out with this story, making it a little more dramatic than quiet Kaiera would.) Tebilyeh stood up, picked up her firewood, and went home but Manu's penis began to swell. It continued to swell up to the size of a tree.

Manu's brother's wife always gave food to Manu but his penis was too big now for him to wear a gourd or walk about so his brother brought him his food. This continued for two months with her calling out to Manu that his food was ready, his answer that he can't walk with this terrible boil, then his brother would bring him the food. Finally, Manu's brother told his wife to make two 'limbums' of sago dumplings, then call Manu to come get them but to leave her string skirt very loose so it would expose her vagina, explaining that when his brother came for the food, he would see her, then get an erection that would break the swelling in his penis. She did as her husband instructed, then called to Manu to come but he resisted, exclaiming about his bad boil. She kept calling for him to come then, after saying her husband said it was all right for him to come, he did. He watched her make the second batch of sago dumplings and he saw her exposed vagina. Manu's penis immediately becomes erect and breaks the swelling with the sound of a gun. (Oria adds the gun metaphor.) The pus splatters all over the sago dumplings, the fire, and all over Manu. But his brother's wife said, "Don't be embarrassed, your brother himself asked me to do this because you have been sick for such a long time."

After Manu's sore healed, he decided to get even with Tabilyeh for causing him so much distress. He takes an old piece of bamboo and puts it up in the roof of the house above the fire to dry thoroughly then sharpens it. He hears Tabilyeh's firewood calling his name and taking his piece of sharp bamboo, goes to where she is breaking firewood. He goes up to her and says, "All right, you and I can have sex again." She replies, "What's the matter, why did you go away for so long? My firewood kept calling out your name but you never came." But he doesn't answer her; he was thinking, "You caused me a great deal of pain before and I have no sympathy for you." Then he said, "You can lie down now." Manu told her to open her legs wide so that he could get a good look inside her vagina adding, "I'm not taking any chances that you repeat what you did to me before!" Tabilyeh replied, "I only did that once. I wouldn't do it again". So she lay down and opened her vagina for him. But Manu took his bamboo knife and slit her open from her vagina up to her stomach, killing her. Then he dug a hole and buried her in it. Tabilyeh's mother and father waited for her to come home but she never did. They searched for her day, after day, after day, then decided she had been killed and began to mourn her.

A village was going to have a curing festival and the men went hunting for the meat. Both Manu's and Tabilyeh's villages knew about the festival and Tabilyeh's parents go to it. Manu tells his brother that he is going to the festival alone and his brother's wife made a very long piece of twine from the bark of the tulip tree for him. He fastens one end of it to a post of his house and then, carrying the rest of it wound up, starts for the festival village atop a hill. The villagers sing and dance all night long, then at daybreak, Manu begins his own song (Kaiera sings it for me) and it mentions the name of Tabilyeh. Her parents hear Manu singing and hurriedly sharpen some sago bark, then using a magical spell, begin to cut down the hill. The hill breaks down and water gradually rises but the villagers continue dancing, wondering where all the water is coming from. The water covers up all of the villagers but Manu escapes with four girls who had been dancing with him by holding the twine to his penis sheath. Manu flies into the air with the four girls and returns to his brother's house. Once home, his brother asks him where he got the four girls and he gives him one for a wife and takes the other three for his wives. Back in the flooded village, the dancers have all drowned and have been transformed into frogs.

Kaiera explained that some of the frogs were very noisy, others less so, and it was related to how noisy they were as people. He then gave me the Namia name for different kinds of frogs and imitated each one's croaking sounds. He added that a villager who had been away during the festival returned home but saw that the place had been transformed into a pond. He heard all the frogs croaking and, rather sadly, departed to start another village.

A Tale of Two Brothers

Storyteller: Nauwen

Two brothers live alone in the forest. The big brother makes a bird blind up in a tree. He goes into his blind and kills many birds. The last one was a cockatoo and it fell to earth. An old woman nearby is washing sago. She sees the bird fall, gets its, plucks out it feathers and puts it in her bag. The big brother climbs down and is surprised to see the old woman. "Oh," he says, "I think you are a spirit woman!" "No," she replies, "I am a real woman! I think you are a spirit man!" He assures her that he is a real man and won't eat her, then she asks, "Are you hungry?" He is and they both eat some sago. She sees a snake and the brother kills it. A nearby pandanus tree is ripe with fruit. He mentions this to the woman and she tells him to get two of the fruits but not to throw them down. He climbs up in the tree and brings two of the fruits back to her. She puts the two fruits by a tree and they become two young women, real women. They wrap some of the sago the old woman has made, then the two girls go home with the big brother. When the little brother sees the two girls, he asks his big brother for one of them. He says no, but tomorrow morning you can hunt from my bird blind.

The next morning, the little brother gets up early and goes to the bird blind and shoots a cockatoo like his brother and it falls to the ground. The old woman gets it, plucks its feathers and puts it into her bag. He climbs down to get his bird and sees the old woman washing sago.

Alarmed, he says, "Oh, I think you are a bad spirit. You mustn't eat me!" She replies, "I can't eat you, I'm not a spirit woman!" Then he asks her, "Did you see a cockatoo fall down around here?" "Yes," she replies, "You can have it." Then she asks, "Are you hungry?" "Yes, I'm hungry," he replies. She cooks some sago and they eat it. The little brother sees the pandanus tree with its ripe fruit. She tells him to climb up and get two, but not to toss them down. He climbs up and returns with the fruit. He then kills a snake just like his big brother. Again, the two pandanus fruits become young women. They tell the little brother that the old woman is their mother. He then takes the two women home with him. Once home, the little brother says to his big brother they should exchange women, but the brother doesn't want to.

The little brother goes hunting for fruit bats. The big brother makes a very large hole in the ground to make a new house under the ground. His two wives make sago and collect food while he makes the house underground. He repeatedly calls out to them from down in the hole but they don't hear him. He comes up and says, "I called and called to you. I called very loud!" But they tell him they never heard him calling. The big brother is worried that his little brother wants to harm him.

The two brothers go hunting early in the morning for fruit bats. The big brother's wives finish making sago, then go into the hole down to the house he has made for them. The little brother kills some bats and his big brother climbs into an ironwood tree to kill some more. He puts his hand in a tree hole but it becomes firmly stuck. The little brother calls up to him that he will now marry his two wives. The little brother collects all of the dead bats, breaks his brother's bow, and goes home. Once home, he asks his two wives where his brother's wives are and they say they haven't come home yet. He sends his wives to look for them but they go to where they were washing sago but come back without them. He accuses them of trying to fool him, but they deny it.

A man named Tsamu, a stranger [I found out later he really is a fruit bat], finds the big brother with his hand stuck in a hole up in the tree. He asks Tsamu to get him some betel nuts, lime, and betel pepper vine but Tsamu returns with wild betel nuts, fire ash, and another vine. The brother tells him these aren't right, then tells him where to get the real items and Tsamu returns with them. Hungry for a banana, he asks Tsamu to bring him a ripe one but he returns with not a true banana. He tells Tsamu where a good banana tree is and Tsamu gets a ripe one for him. Tsamu tells the brother that if something happens, he mustn't be afraid. The brother assures him that he won't be. Tsamu then calls for all of the birds and snakes to come and they gather together on the ironwood tree. One very large bird comes and breaks the tree and releases the brother's hand. All the little snakes make a ladder so the two men can climb down out of the tree. On the ground, the big brother talks out to all the birds and snakes and says, "When my hand is healed, I'll repay you." In the meantime, his two wives mourn for him in their house in the ground.

Tsamu and the big brother go down into the hole to his house to tell his wives what has happened and show them his badly injured hand. His two wives feed them meat and sago dumplings then Tsamu treats his hand. He tells his wives that they must no longer eat birds and snakes. Tsamu tells the big brother that he will stay and take care of him until his hand is good again. He treats the brother's hand many times until it is completely healed. After his hand is healed, he goes to see his little brother who says, "I thought you were dead!" The two brothers go fishing but the wives first get together all the sago, meat, and sago grubs. Tsamu speaks out to all the birds and snakes. The brothers begin to try and scoop up the fish. The little brother keeps trying to scoop up the fish. Two big snakes come up out of the pond. The water rises and the little brother thinks it is a big fish. But he is getting tired and decides to rest. Now the big brother and his two wives begin fishing. But the two big snakes attack the little brother, wrap around him and kill him. All the fish and snakes become very active.

The big brother tells the little brother's wives that they can't feel sorry about his death. After all, "He was to blame for my badly injured hand." All the little snakes come out of the pond. Then the big brother takes his little brother's two wives to be his.

Water-Snake Woman Is a Good Wife

Storyteller: Kunai

Twenty men go to a mountain, one is as young as Iwi, the rest are adults. They make a house, make sago, and hunt game. The boy goes hunting, makes a bird blind and sees twenty women in a bamboo grove. The next day he again goes to hunt birds from his blind and again sees the women. They are getting water; he runs away to the men's house. The women then all go up to the men's house and all of the men get a wife. But the boy's wife doesn't like him. Even when he is fully grown, his wife still doesn't like him. She won't cook for him or accept the game that he brings her.

In a nearby pond, there is a black poisonous snake that turns into a woman. He goes to the pond to get water and catches the snake-woman. He goes with her down into the water. There she cooks food for him and makes him stay with her. But after a year he goes back up to visit everyone. He asks for his wife; now she wants him but he doesn't want her. He makes a slit gong and strikes it and his parents and all his relatives come. Then he and his snake-wife go back down into the water. His first wife never did remarry but he and his snake-wife had many children.

CHAPTER FIFTEEN

The Lujere Curing Festivals

> *Magical practices are not entirely without sense.*
> Marcel Mauss (1975: 60)

> *Magic in general is a very blind fool.*
> Reo Fortune (1932: 289)

Modes of Therapeutic Intervention

It is a truism that cultures are never neutral about human existence. Inasmuch as cultures are arrangements for living, each has opinionated beliefs about what is acceptable and good and what is unacceptable and bad.[1] It is this strong ethical stance about what constitutes a good life that permeates cultural behavior. It is also the human ability to arrive at varied and conflicting community mores that so vividly distinguishes humans from other primate species. Within any one culture the "good" and the "bad" are polarized opposites yet, paradoxically, therein lies the intimacy of their ontological relationship. For knowledge of what is good and bad is a contrasting process; one helps to define and determine the other.

In any society, remedial actions directed towards individual human beings tend to take one of three therapeutic modes: to *instruct*, to *punish*, or to *heal*. The three are alike only in their goal—to change the bad to good, the negative to the positive. But their strategies for inducing change are radically different. As indicated, a positive change is attempted by (1) corrective teaching, (2) inflicting suffering, or (3) alleviating suffering. These therapeutic modes are not necessarily mutually exclusive and two of them, or all three, may be implemented simultaneously. In our own society a person may be jailed (punishing) but

---

1. This section draws extensively from my paper, "Culturally Contrasting Therapeutic Systems of the West Sepik: The Lujere" (Mitchell 1975).

while in jail may attend vocational training classes (instructing) and participate in group psychotherapy (healing), all in an effort to make her or him over into a law-abiding citizen. And always, as Gilbert Lewis has observed, "Meaning is present not in things but in people's minds" (1980: 222).

The therapeutic mode chosen to correct a perceived problem will depend upon the specific circumstances and the culture's values. Always, it is the intervention's cultural rationale, not the intervention itself, which classifies the therapeutic act. For example, amputation may be a healing intervention in an American hospital but a punitive intervention in Libya, when a thief's hand or an armed robber's left foot is amputated (Peck 1973: 16). So, it is not enough to know just the therapeutic act; its intent must be known as well.

But what happens when two cultures, for example, colonial Australia and the Lujere, with contrasting traditions about the "good" and the "bad" come into continued contact? Are the remedial systems for changing the bad to the good—always a major cultural concern—complementary or in conflict? And what is the intrasystemic nature of this relationship? Is it a simple and separable interface, or do discordant values and behavior become intermeshed in the lives of the people and, if so, with what consequences for the individual as well as the culture? These were some of the broad questions on culturally contrasting therapeutic systems I asked as a way of orienting my research while living with both the Wape and Lujere.[2] We have seen partial answers to some of these questions for the Lujere in the previous pages. But my basic finding was that in the early 1970s, the Lujere, especially the Wakau villagers that I knew best, were only modestly impacted by the value systems of colonial Australia, except for the welcomed suspension of warfare. They mostly just ignored Christianity but some appreciated and used the introduced health services as adjunctive amenities. Other than a shared idealistic desire for a 'kiap'-staffed patrol post that would suppress alleged 'sanguma' murders and provide work when they needed money, Lujere villagers tended to look culturally inward, not outward. As A. D. C. Broadhurst astutely wrote, "The people show a complete lack of interest in anything that is going on in the outside world" (1970: 2). Families actually looked forward to spending weeks, if not months, out of the village and in their forest hunting camps.

Of the three modes of remedial action I have outlined, I will have little to say regarding the mode of *corrective* instruction, usually a non-traumatic form of intervention that I did not deliberately pursue. Here, however, are a few examples. The Australian 'kiaps' on village patrol spent considerable time, as already suggested, instructing villagers on Western notions of order such as laying out a neatly arranged village, and notions of hygiene, for example, the digging and use of latrines. You might recall how PO Hutchins found Iwani village in shambles, then remained three nights to instruct and talk with them. As far as examples of villagers' corrective instructions towards others are concerned, I have little data. I was only occasionally aware of a parent quietly redirecting a child's behavior but more often of a raised voice or body slap. Among adults in an egalitarian society like the Lujere without a tradition of developmental initiatory grades for either sex or a

---

2. For a probing book that deals with these questions using the concept "medical pluralism" in a dozen Papua New Guinea societies, see Frankel and Lewis (1989).

plethora of hierarchical statuses that can validate corrective intrusions, the observational challenge of citing examples obviously was even greater.

But there is no lack of data on *punitive* interventions on both the administration and village level. Many of these involving the administration were presented in chapter 11 in a discussion of "colonial offenses" and cited the specific transgression and penalty imposed. But regardless of the nature of the offense, the administration imposed only two forms of negative sanction: the denial of freedom and/or hard labor. Physical punishment was outlawed and fines, although an important form of reprimand in Australia, were disallowed in the Territory. Consequently, the most common forms of punishment imposed by the local 'kiap' for a Lujere's perceived transgression of Administration policy were jailing or cutting grass around the base camp.

Within the village, punitive sanctions included women withholding food from a strong young man like Samaun to chastise his laziness and alleged sorcery, or an enraged villager setting fire to the house of a man whom he believed had wronged him—a practice less common than in the past but still used as a threat—or a dueling stick fight over a disagreement, like that between old Leno and Kowali in chapter 12. But of the three therapeutic modes I have mentioned, *healing* concerns us the most. The principle thrust of my Lujere research was to identify and understand both Indigenous healing therapies and those of scientific medicine introduced by Australian colonizers. Of the two, the former is the more challenging undertaking so that is where we will begin.

The Lujere View of Sickness

How do the Lujere perceive sickness? What are their abiding views about the causes of bodily injury and illness? While a minor injury or illness might be discounted as 'sik nating' or "not really sick,"[3] a graver situation is usually attributable to one of three causes: 'sanguma,' sorcery, or spirits. 'Sanguma,' a death from which there is no recourse, is, as you know, executed by men, *nakwolu*, who are believed to physically and lethally attack their lone victims. *Nakwolu* are also believed to travel furtively, either afoot or flying, through the forest and might sneak into a village at night to shoot small items, such as bits of a razor blade, into a victim's body, causing sickness and probable death if not removed.

Examples of sorcery ('posin,' *paumei*) are spells, hexes, or charms that anyone can perform if they know the process. There are however, many conflicting local beliefs regarding sorcery. Tsaime believed that only the person who made the sorcery could undo it, while other men thought that was wrong. In Wakau, some men blamed S____ for working a spell to give villagers a bad cold with coughing. Both 'sanguma' and sorcery are considered more fully in the following chapters.

The third important cause of illness was believed to be spirits. This brings us to the focus of this chapter—the *wowi* curing festivals—that are centered on malevolent spirits. In Tok Pisin, they are called 'masalai,' "malevolent spirits," but this was not a term the Lujere seemed to use, preferring the Namia term *aokwae*, a concept elaborated on in the

---

3. But see Roscoe's (1989) nuanced discussion of 'sik nating' among the Boiken of the Yangoru Subdistrict of the East Sepik Province, where the concept is more complex than among the Wakau villagers.

next section. I characterize the Lujere's traditional curing ceremonials as "curing festivals" because they involve (1) specific curing rituals, (2) the coming together of the patient's family and close relatives from other villages, and (3) the provision of food. However, before we can describe them, we must first examine the Lujere beliefs about spirits, those unseen, incorporeal entities that inhabit and/or activate aspects of a villager's physical and perceptual domains.

The Lujere Spirit World

On a stormy morning late in January, I finally got a breakthrough into Lujere spirit beliefs and practices, a topic I had been dancing around since I arrived. Among the Lujere, heavy rain is perfect for data collection as men who happened to be in the village preferred to stay put rather than get drenched going to the bush. While working with Oria, I asked him an offhand question, whether the *nakwolu* were possessed by *aokwae*. "Oh, yes!" he eagerly replied and the data began to tumble out. Oria was the perfect informant; in appreciation of my vast ignorance, he seemed to delight in filling the void with local knowledge. After our long interview he went home, luckily nearby, as the rain continued to noisily strike my 'morata' roof. Soon, Tsaime and Yaope eagerly climbed the ladder steps to my 'ofis' to escape the downpour. It was perfect timing. I could run by my visitors some of what I had just learned from Oria for confirmation and/or elaboration. But neither that day nor later did I succeed in resolving all of the spirit-belief inconsistencies among my data.[4] However, the logical niceties I sought were as irrelevant to my informants as those I mentioned earlier on "kinship." The Lujere's preternatural beliefs and concepts were not as neatly distinct as those I had found among the Wape.[5] Here, I was constantly challenged by the uncanny. What follows, then, is a wary distillation of my understanding of the Wakau version of Lujere spirit beliefs and magical practices.

Souls, Spirits, and Ghouls

A person's spirit or soul is called *poketaiyup* (pronounced quickly). It is what animates a person and departs the body at death via the anus, when the sphincter and bladder muscles relax, expelling feces and urine. Once freed of a person's body, it is called an *aokwae* with, at times, some monstrous characteristics, discussed below, of a ghoul. After a villager's death, a *nakwolu* must perform a private ritual before the *aokwae* is free to leave the area. At night and alone he goes to the village's open plaza and, holding out his hand,

---

4. Gilbert Lewis identifies a similar problem with Gnau ideas about spirits in the person of "Malyi," who perhaps had afflicted a sick villager, when he asks, "Is the sickness Malyi itself or caused by Malyi?" (2000: 127). For an article that plays imaginatively with the idea of the supernatural and plumbs its ontological problems by citing research on the ranking of fantastic beasts, see Schultz (2017).
5. Nils Bubandt has a footnote in his witchcraft book (2014: 249, n. 10) where he cites Evans-Pritchard's (1937: 540) frank admission that the coherency he found in Zande witchcraft beliefs was of his own creation and ". . . that order and coherence were actually an effect of his academic inscription."

the *aokwae* comes and licks it, then, after also licking his legs, it is freed to wander. If the *nakwolu* neglects to perform the ritual, the *aokwae* will come to his house at night and throw little stones and sticks against it.[6]

A new *aokwae* is called an *aokwae naki* (spirit new) and many of the old spirits (*aokwae bidami*), especially those of her or his dead parents and relatives, come into the village to meet it. First, they ask it, "Are you really dead and have come to join us or are you playing tricks on us?" The *aokwae naki* answers, "I have really come to join you, this isn't a trick. Now give me some food! You must feed me as I am hungry." If you imagine all the village's *aokwae* flying into the village to meet and greet their new dead relative and neighbor, it is an almost sweet "welcome wagon" image, but to the living residents it is a terrifying one to consider. *Aokwae* can be menacing. They have sharp fingernails several inches long that can easily rip apart a person's flesh, teeth set in a creepy grimace, and big protruding eyes. Informants loved to imitate an *aokwae*'s scary expression but those watching became immediately anxious, squirmed and yelped with a true shudder. They enjoyed the burlesque but the laughter was tinged with fear. *Aokwae* were real.

Here, I again want to emphasize the nature of the phenomenological world of the Lujere. The preliterate societies of New Guinea for tens of thousands of years were geographically and socially isolated from the world's complex civilizations. For these societies, as Goode observed, "The supernatural is as real as what we call the empirical, and the world does not stop at the borderline of the Western scientist's senses" (1951: 50). This includes their dead family members and even their ancestors whom they didn't know personally. The challenge for the fieldworker, as it is for the reader, is to float over that borderline and wander into the Lujere consciousness where the unseen, like electricity and Wi-Fi beams, are active and alive.

As the stories in the last chapter demonstrated, *aokwae* relish eating humans and their habit of eating flesh raw is considered especially odious. They are also versatile in changing into and out of human form—hence the standard query on meeting a total stranger, whether they are human or an *aokwae*—and a sure sign of the latter is being seen eating raw meat. Another ominous trait of an *aokwae* is fire coming from under the arms, the groin, and the area behind the knees. A frequent event in a traditional story is for an *aokwae* to trick a villager to hunt or work sago with him or her by saying he or she is another villager. Then when the two are walking along the path with the *aokwae* in front, the victim suddenly notices the fire from the *aokwae*'s legs or armpits.

If a villager was in the bush when they learned that someone died, it was imperative to return to the village. If found out there, or even while out walking alone at night in a sleeping village, an *aokwae naki* might rip off a man's genitalia and gouge out his eyes and eat them or, if a woman, her vaginal area would be attacked and eaten as well as her eyes. Even in the village, after a person dies people tend to stay in their houses at night for at least a month, not that they wander nocturnally much otherwise. The dual threat of *aokwae* and *nakwolu* potentially menacing a village results in individuals rarely being alone in the bush, night or day, or on foot in the village at night. My village presence might have modified that custom a bit as my 'ofis' was open on three sides and, as I spent most nights there until almost midnight typing up data from my note books, my Aladdin lamp thrust a welcoming light in what otherwise was a darkened village. But even on a

---

6. This is the only licking ritual I recorded among the Lujere or the Wape.

bright moonlit night, when Wape villagers would be visiting and laughing on their roomy verandas, Wakau villagers were mostly securely indoors.

Because of an *aokwae*, and especially an *aokwae naki*'s possible murdering vengeance, it was of upmost importance for villagers to be particularly cautious if they had offended or were ungenerous to the recent dead. Thus, a son who had not given sufficient food to his old father might be attacked by his father's angry *aokwae naki* and devoured. The fact that no one could supply an instance of such an act did not diminish the belief. It was the same with parental neglect of a child: if it died its *aokwae naki* would try to kill its mother and father. This fear of the recent dead was a strong motive in the attention given to the sick and dying, especially when genuine affection was lacking. Moreover, for a people who seemed to spend as much time, if not more, out of the village than in it, the probability of these frightful attacks helps to emphasize the importance of the village to its residents as a place of refuge and solidarity, not only against the homicidal enemies of yore, but also against the unseen *aokwae* and *nakwolu* that continued to threaten a villager's life.

There is, however, a very comforting belief regarding *aokwae*. The *aokwae* of one's parents, or perhaps of an elder brother, can be entreated to help you. If you have been a good son, your father's *aokwae* might come and dwell in your house (my informant looked up to the roof when he said this) and occasionally make a noise or soft whistle to signal that he was there and, if a *nakwolu* came to harm you, he would chase him away. Or it could be the *aokwae* of your mother, or a grandparent (*aokwae aitwa*) you knew; these people never can forget you. They must stay and look after you forever. So there are always these beneficent *aokwae* who have your back while the others are mostly out to do you in.

In an interview with Alomiaiya and Yaope,[7] two bright and affable youths who were hanging out at my 'ofis' one day, I was trying to discover the extent of the requests you could make of family *aokwae*. I knew they were important in hunting but these young men also emphasized that when seeking a wife your *aokwae* could help turn a girl's affection towards you or, more instrumentally, help you cut down a big tree. When I asked about gardens, Yaope replied with an interesting example (here translated from Tok Pisin):

> Suppose your mother and father die at the same time. Your mother's *aokwae* will go to your garden and look after it. If any person comes to steal, she will hit them and make them vomit and they will become very sick. All right, the *nakwolu* that treats this sick person will ask him if he has been in someone's garden and if he says, "Yes," the *nakwolu* will say, "Well, that's what it is; you were in his garden and his *aokwae* has made you sick." Then the *nakwolu* will talk out to the *aokwae* and tell it to make the sickness go away."

When I asked them both if my father's *aokwae* didn't hear my pleas or answer my requests, could I be cross with him or must I remain silent, the answer, as I had predicted, was that I could be cross with him but, they cautioned, you never can hear it speak, you only hear it whistle. Then, pressing to see if *aokwae* thinking had been extended into modern and introduced materials, I asked in Tok Pisin, "What if I want some new

---

7. The youth Yaope, the son of Walbi, died when he was little and is not to be confused with the older Yaope whose marriage was described in chapter twelve.

clothes, can I ask my *aokwae* to help me get them?" The thoughtful reply was, 'Mi no harim gut yet,' or, "I haven't yet heard about this."

In many societies that believe in ancestor spirits, it is necessary to offer them food but, according to my two young informants, this is not the case with the Lujere. "No, you give them nothing. He isn't like you and me sitting down here. You only see him *in your dreams*. In the morning you might get up and tell your wife, 'Oh, last night I saw my *aokwae*, we talked together" (my emphasis). I also wanted to know if these benevolent family or ancestral *aokwae* we had talked about were the same *aokwae* that (1) shoot little spears into people and break their small bones that I had watched *nakwolu* either remove or mend, as well as those *aokwae* that (2) sit atop big tress and terrorize people like in the ancestral stories. Yes, I was assured, they are all the same *aokwae*, it just depends if they are friendly, or not, to you.

The most ubiquitous of the several kinds of *aokwae* are those of the villagers' dead relatives that inhabit and protect their descendants' lands and waters. There are a lot of beliefs regarding the nature of *aokwae*, and, depending to whom you are talking, some of the beliefs appear contradictory; for example, if a stranger is hunting on someone else's bush, a resident *aokwae* might help him find a pig or a murak but it also might make the intruder sick and induce vomiting. If a man has been on another's land and is vomiting, he will go to the owner and ask him to rub his skin with stinging nettles and speak out to his *aokwae*. Kin-*aokwae*, as noted, will aid a relative in the hunt and in getting fish, but they might also turn against a living relative. Some *aokwae* like to sit in the tops of big trees and if a man, whether a relative or not, happens to cut down the tree where it is sitting, it might shoot him with a little arrow causing his chest to pain or to make him vomit. To cure his illness, he must seek a *nakwolu* or, more correctly, an *imoulu* for treatment.

In the Lujere consciousness, *aokwae* are everywhere and the explanation for myriad phenomena. A child's crying for no discernable reason might be attributed to a dead grandfather visiting his grandchild or other small children he knew. Oria gave me this example. His father who was a *nakwolu*, died several months before I arrived, and his *aokwae* might go to a villager's house and unwittingly scare the resident baby, making it cry. Then Oria must go to the baby and, blowing gently into its ear, speak out telling his father's *aokwae* to leave the child alone. Once when Eine's daughter Imani was wailing loudly for food, Nauwen joked that he thought she was an *aokwae*'s child. But Oria said that there were no *aokwae* involved in her constant crying; she just wanted meat The other form of crying, he explained, was episodic or unusual.

In usage, the term *aokwae* is a multivalent term with multiple referents. Besides the kin-*aokwae* are those spirits in service to a *nakwolu* and assumed to have been his victims. They help empower his treatment stratagems, look after him, and protect him from the attacks of other *nakwolu*. The next chapter focuses on the beliefs about and the behavior of *nakwolu* both as alleged killers and recognized curers, *imoulu*, and reviews their presence in other societies including Aboriginal Australia. The more I learned about *aokwae* the more unstable the concept became. Another kind of *aokwae*, unrelated to dead humans, are the *aijan aokwae*, spirit entities associated with natural phenomena like ponds (*ena aokwae*), streams (*iju aokwae*), swamps (*lei aokwae*), or anything of unusual size, for example, a very large coconut tree with lots of coconuts or a very large sago palm. There were also *aokwae* associated with specific places like a hill, or who dwelled underfoot, down in the ground.

But regardless of the kind of *aokwae*, they all have the power to cause sickness. Thus, if a woman beats derris root into a pond to kill the fish, a resident *aokwae* might be angered and shoot something into her body, causing a sickness. As a sick person she usually would initially go to an *imoulu* for a diagnosis and treatment. In my observations of many *imoulu* treatment sessions, they were persistently extracting bits of this or that, usually not shown, shot into the body by an *aokwae* or *nakwolu*.

Any *aokwae* also has the potential to steal a person's *poketaiyup*, an act resulting in sickness. To return the *poketaiyup*, an adept must dream they have gone to secure it from the *aokwae* and brought it back to the person. In Wakau, Klowi once had this skill but since obtaining a gun has lost the ability. Tsaime explained that the loud noise of the gun's firing had chased "it" away, "it" apparently being the skill. The youth Yaope's widowed mother also had this soul-procurement dreaming skill but she left Wakau when she remarried a Gwidami man. When a Wakau villager thought, or was told by an *imoulu*, that soul loss was the cause of a sickness, he or she either went to Yaope's mother in Gwidami or to one of several individuals in the Edwaki area who had the skill. When the adept dreamed that the soul had returned, they either told the person or sent a message regarding the success. But my favorite reference to *aokwae* was that a colorful rainbow (*aokwae nebu*) arched across the sky was the road of the *aokwae*.

Tracking Down the Wowi *Spirits*

I had lived in Wakau only two weeks and was still a neophyte in terms of understanding what was happening around me—especially regarding the magical spirit world—when I saw my first curing festival. This was a *na wowi* curing festival in Mauwi near the end of November. Then in February, I observed two *aewal wowi* (stinging nettles *wowi*) curing festivals, one in neighboring Mokadami and the other in Wakau, and in early March, another in Wakau. But try as I would, I could get no translation for the generic term *wowi*. Finally, near the end of my fieldwork when Kaiera began telling me the old Lujere stories of their forefathers, I got an answer. Like so much of fieldwork, it was a serendipitous event and, being in the form of a story, somewhat implicit. Also, it appeared to be a story not as widely known in Wakau as in Mauwi, where Kaiera had lived most of his life.

Kaiera's story began with a Kwieftim woman in the bush being bothered by two flying insects that buzzed around her head as she was making sago. They were two *wowi* who, after transforming themselves into men, murdered her. Her son, who was hiding, watched as they cut up her body, drank her blood, and then wrapped her parts in a 'limbum'. Finally, they carried it to a tree with a hole near its base into which they all disappeared. The tree was filled with *wowi*. The boy hurried home, told his relatives what he had seen, and they returned together to the *wowi*'s tree and built a great fire at its base. Threatened by the raging flames, the *wowi* all flew away to different villages. *Na* (sago) *wowi* went to Tsila; *ithu* (water) *wowi* went to Marpel [?]; *anapi* (bow) *wowi*[8] flew away

---

8. I was unsuccessful in discovering the cultural significance of the qualifying terms, *na*, *ithu*, and *anapi* in the *wowi* names.

to Kelnom; *piaba* (untranslatable) *wowi* stayed in Kwieftim; and *yokwar* (untranslatable) *wowi* flew to Maurom.[9]

Once in Tsila, *na wowi* put his erect penis into a long gourd and began to dance. Two women working sago heard, as he danced, the noise of the gourd striking the Job's tears seed necklace on his chest. They liked the sound and wondered what made it but, every time they approached the sound, it would stop. Finally they sneaked around behind the noise and saw him dancing. When he saw the two women, he immediately dropped his gourd and flew away.

The women went to the spot from where he had flown away and found the gourd on the ground, ginger that gave him a continuous erection, and the paint with which he had decorated his legs. One of the women stuck the front of her skirt into the gourd and began to perform, but it wasn't the same. Then the other woman tried and she also failed. But when one of their husbands donned the gourd and began to dance, he was very good. The women decided it was something for men, not for women. Their finding was confirmed in a dream when the *wowi* told them the same thing. Finally, in the ashes of the *wowi*'s burned tree, three kinds of banana plants came up and some *wowi* ginger.[10]

As Kaiera finished the story, he said the two women felt that the *na wowi* still belonged to them as they had found it! Interestingly, the *na wowi* curing festival is the only one of the *wowi* curing ceremonials I observed that women could witness in its entirety, a seeming confirmation of male acknowledgment of the women's rights by discovery. In the two *aewal wowi* festivals I observed, there were strategic times when women had to cover their heads to protect themselves from the harm that visual knowledge of the proceedings would incur.

Although Kaiera's story about the vicious *wowi* finally established for me a Lujere referent for the term, it was obvious that the story wasn't well known; as mentioned, my Wakau informants, couldn't tell me what the word "wowi" meant. As an example, one informant told me, 'em i samting nating,' in other words, of no importance. As this evil entity called a *wowi* who could change from a flying insect into a human was not a part of my Wakau informants' consciousness I, like my informants, focused my attention on the *na wowi* and *aewal wowi* phenomena and, although no one seemed to know where they came from, what they were, or even cared, there was agreement that it was their *aokwae* that made people sick. Thus, when Oria's wife became sick, as will be reviewed in chapter 18, it was clear to him that it was the *aokwae* of the *aewal wowi* that had shot something into her.

The Ways of Ritual

While knowledge of a society's beliefs about the supernatural is necessary for an overall grasp of their way of life, it is just as important to know about the related ritual practices.

---

9. Maurom was located in the Torricelli foothills just north of Lujereland. I had visited the village earlier in 1971 when seeking a new research site and saw masks in the men's house called "Yokwar" or a term very close to that. Marpel seems to have been a hamlet or village that no longer exists.
10. Kaiera explained that they are tabooed from eating one of the bananas during a *na wowi* festival but could give no rationale.

Ritual, which Wallace (1966: 233) characterized as "stereotyped communication," in the most general sense connotes a customary repetitive action. More specifically, it can denote social etiquette such as greetings, the repetitive obsessive acts of a neurotic person, the mating performances of some insects and animals (including *homo sapiens*), secular acts like the morning brushing of one's teeth, and routinized actions towards supernatural beings. Already I have used the term multiple times in the previous pages, mainly in the latter sense.[11] The rest of this chapter examines Lujere curing rituals performed in a festival context. These are community shared curing rites whereby villagers relate and/or appeal to preternatural forces—unseen but presumed to exist—with the intent of effecting a change in a victim's life status from sickness to health.

The *Wowi*-Spirit Curing Festivals

The Wakau villagers celebrate three kinds of curing festivals: *na wowi*, *aewal wowi*, and *aokwae wowi*. All are primarily but, in practice, not exclusively concerned with a certain kind of affliction, specifically, *na wowi* with sores; *aewal wowi* with 'skin i lus' or, in American vernacular, being "run down" or "sickly"; and *aokwae wowi* with 'sot win' or pulmonary disorders. Festival rites are dedicated to restoring health to the afflicted and are, in Geertz's terms, "a kind of religious psychodrama" (1966: 19).

There are two kinds of *na wowi* festivals, but only the second kind involves sickness. The first, and communally more important, was performed in the western area, mainly in Mokodami, Aiendami, and Mantopai, but Oria said he saw it once in Mauwi. This festival has nothing to do with sickness but is involved with the trading of smoked meat for shell rings or money. The village giving the festival goes to the bush to hunt for several months; when they return laden with smoked meat, they stage their festival with other villages coming to trade their rings for the meat.[12] This festival lasts several days, with all-night celebrating. *Na wowi* masks participate but perform only in the daytime. I never saw this festival but while living in Wakau I later heard that Norambalip staged one and that Ces Parish had attended.[13] This sounds similar to a festival celebrating a new men's *iron* that the Feldpauschs (1988: 30–31) report on for Yaru village. The other kind of *na wowi* festival that involves curing is discussed below.

Curing festivals are small-scale communal events that usually include a few relatives of the afflicted person from other villages and the offering of food. The sponsor of the curing festival is usually a close relative of the sick person and must provide a meal,

---

11. The anthropological literature on ritual is enormous and controversial; for an array of critical data on approaches, see, for example, Van Gennep (1960), Leach (1968), Turner (1969), La Fontaine (1972), Vizedom (1976), and Lewis (1980). I have chosen to stay out of the "bitter arguments in the social sciences over the nature and meaning of ritual" (Jean and John Comaroff, 1993: xix).
12. "The Selfish Husband and a Magical Skirt," a story in chapter 14, was about this type of *na wowi* festival.
13. Unfortunately, I have no details regarding this festival or know if they still used rings or, as I suspect, substituted money. There was a good motorbike track from the mission up to Norambalip, the main reason I didn't consider it for a research site.

usually with help from relatives, for all the participants in the ritual plus visiting guests. In Wakau, this would include sago dumplings and cakes, and meat, either fresh and/or smoked. Usually they would try to kill a wild pig or cassowary but, if they had no luck and owned a pig, it might be butchered. If no meat were available, at the very least, cooked insects and/or fish would have to be offered.

None of the three kinds of curing festivals was their own invention but borrowed from cultures west of them, although some of the related chants they considered their own. Interestingly, they continued to borrow, as Mokadami did for the *aewal wowi* curing festival described below. Eine said that the *aewal wowi* 'sing-sing' was new in his father's time, that their ancestors did not know it and it came from Tsila village before the Yellow River missionaries arrived (that is, before the mid–1950s), adding, 'mi lik lik yet,' that he was a little boy.[14] Earlier, they already had imported the *na wowi* 'sing-sing' from apparently both Tsila and Wagu.

When I asked Eine about the *aokwae wowi* 'sing-sing' that I had never seen, he replied that it was given for individuals who were sick with sores or had difficulty in breathing. It was performed in the afternoon, food was distributed, and it ended before dark with no all-night 'sing-sing.' The mask was similar to the *na wowi* with the same big gourd phallus. This curing festival also came from Tsila, whose villagers got it from further west. Sometimes the *aewal wowi* and *agwai wowi* curing festivals were combined in a conjoined festival.

The *aokwae wowi* festival was the only one where I received an unequivocal statement that, if you had 'sot win,' an *aokwae* had gone *inside* of the sick person, grabbed its heart, shook it over and over and pulled it about so violently that it became increasingly difficult to breathe; eventually the person would die. To my questioning, Oria said that this *aokwae* was tiny and that only an *imoulu* could see it. As I knew that Luritsao had serious 'sot win,' I wondered why his brother Enewan didn't have an *aokwae wowi* curing festival to exorcise the malicious *aokwae* threatening his life. The answer was that Enewan had had no luck in finding game for the festival and his *Naroli* clansmen didn't seem interested in helping him. From Oria's data, this curing festival was rarely given. He had seen it in Mokadami when he was still single and another time for his father's brother, Ukai. I photographed, filmed and tape-recorded all of the curing festivals I attended and villagers were usually keen to hear any play-back of the proceedings that I offered (see fig. 24).

After I had listened to Kaiera's tale about the evil *wowi*, I thought I would hear a lot about them as I interviewed and asked questions regarding the various curing festivals. But no one ever mentioned the insect-flying, human-transforming, blood-drinking murderous *wowi* that terrorized the villagers in Kaiera's *wowi* story. In fact, the term *wowi* was never mentioned as a catalyst in causing illness. Almost always, it was the *aokwae* who was blamable for the malady.

Mauwi's Na Wowi *Curing Festival*

I had moved into my new house the night before and was still disorganized when I heard that a curing ceremony would occur that afternoon in nearby Mauwi hamlet. I only knew

---

14. As this was about the same time that Wakau village was first visited by a patrol officer (1956), it indicates that at least some Lujere had peaceful ties to Tsila village, perhaps in trade, like documented in chapter nine for the Lujere and their foes across the Sepik, the Sawiyano.

that it involved a *na wowi* mask—whatever that was—so, after paying off the men at noon for building my house, at around one thirty we heard the beating of 'kundus' coming from Mauwi signaling the ensuing *na wowi* curing ceremony.[15] In my rush to prepare my recording gear and get men to help carry it up the little mountain, the afternoon heat and humidity seemed unusually oppressive. We set out just after 2:30 p.m. for the steep ascent and arrived on top in the Mauwi plaza at 3:20, at which point I was panting and in a sweat. A Mauwi man, seeing the little group from Wakau approaching for the ceremony, yelled out in Namia that I was coming and to dress up good.

This is not the first time that I have mentioned the top of Mauwi hill: the Mosstroops had a base up there for a time during 1943; CPO Orwin visited in 1951 while searching for a Yellow River air strip site, as did PO Oakes for his pioneering 1956 census; Barry Craig collected artifacts there in 1969 and had men paint their artifact designs for him; on a 1970 visit PO Hutchins 1970 found the "place in shambles" and stayed three nights to shape it up; Joyce's and my July 1971 visit; and finally, Kaiera's origin story of the Lujere when Walwin, his son, and their dog Mauwi first arrived atop the hill in legendary times.

Once my friends and I were in Mauwi, as I looked around, I couldn't help but notice that a number of houses were in such miserable repair that PO Hutchins would have despairingly shaken his head. The sick man was Lijeria, a Mauwi bachelor who was born mute. He used a sign language for talking with people but most of it was simply pointing. Although orally disabled, he was very alert and an excellent hunter. His brother was a few years younger than he and had cared for him during his illness. Lijeria had been sick for about three months and his complaints included a swollen arm, an unsteady and/or very fast heart beat ('klok I tanim tanim nabaut') and pains in his back. He also appeared emaciated, walked with a staff and, during the two days of the rituals, I never saw him without a mournful expression. He had been in the 'haus sik' in Edwaki then, about a month before, had returned to the village. It was brotherly concern that prompted the organization of this *na wowi* curing festival to end Lijeria's sickness.

While the phrase "curing festival" is appropriate, in "festival" parlance this was a small one. The concept of "ritual drama" (Radin 1957: 289–306) is also a fitting description of the *na wowi* ceremonies that were divided into five parts over two days: (1) The *na wowi* masks were made in the forest; (2) The masks, joined by village celebrants, entered the village in late evening to prance around the sick person while food for the ritual feast was brought, piled up, and distributed; (3) An all-night chanting, drumming and parading vigil was held by the young people; (4) Final curing rituals were enacted at daybreak, then the masks were thrown into the forest; and (5) A purifying ritual bathing was performed by the mask carriers.

---

15. Feeling challenged by the disorder around me, I decided not to take my large awkward tripod-bound sync-sound Bolex 16 mm camera with its Tandberg recorder or my Leica camera with Kodachrome film. Keeping things simple, I would take instead the smaller hand-held Bell and Howell 16 mm camera, the Uher tape recorder with its light windproof mike, the Leica camera with b/w film, and, as always, my notebook. I regret not taking the Kodachrome-dedicated Leica but, just then, not strapping another small but heavy camera around my neck seemed like a wonderful idea.

Day one: Preparations

While the stoic patient and the prancing masks were the ritual center of the curing festival, it was also a time for feasting, chanting, and dancing (more akin to parading), particularly enjoyed by the young people. But when we arrived midafternoon in Mauwi's dirt plaza, not much was happening, although it was obviously a holiday as far more villagers were about than usual. Front verandas were peopled with mothers and children, and other villagers were moving about on errands or just killing time standing around or sitting visiting. The skies remained cloudy and overcast all day. After setting up my Tandberg recorder and microphone by the platform of a partially demolished house where Nauwen, Tsaime, and the other Wakau males had settled down, I went into the forest just under the top of the hill to where the *na wowi* masks were made earlier that day. They were created by a group of youths, some just boys, whose faces were thickly painted white across the entire forehead, down the sides of the face and under the chin (fig. 37). The white paint was from a mixture of ashes and water and paint from red mud was around their eyes. Several had 'kundus' that they occasionally struck. When I later asked why only boys and youths were involved in the ritual preparations, Klowi explained that boys were not vulnerable to the *na wowi* mask the way men were.

The mask was comprised of two long pieces of sago spathes painted in designs and laced to two pieces of soft 'pangal' sticks to which lengths of 'kanda' had been stuck. Attached to the kanda sticks were feathers attached to small sticks. Most of the feathers appeared old and those of the lesser bird of paradise predominated. The mask designs were painted with three colors: white, store bought; black, from batteries; and brown, from red earth. The rather disordered designs had been painted with sticks about five inches long with unwieldy pithy ends that, along with the youth of the painters, accounted for the untidy results.[16] The masks still had to be dressed with a nearby long skirt of shredded sago leaves but, overall, compared to Wape masks I was disappointed with their ordinariness. Later, examining my developed photos with several Wakau men, I tried to discover the iconography of the designs but learned little beyond that the white dots were stars and the wavy lines were snakes; there was nothing uniquely referencing the *na wowi* persona and exegesis was nil.

When I returned to the village some of the youngest boys came too, and I set to work recording the scene, taking casual pictures with both my still and movie cameras of things like visiting men smoking their unique pipes, mothers with their inquiring babies, the mask-making boys horsing around beating their 'kundus,' and far below, the area where Wakau lay hidden in the forest just off the 'kunai.' Throughout this activity, Lijeria now sat, silently waiting on a 'pangal' mat (fig. 38). He was wearing a bright white, obviously new 'laplap'.[17] I noticed a man, one of only a handful wearing a penis sheath, with a

---

16. Barry Craig, you might recall, complained about how some of the Mauwi men executed their designs for him. With this foreknowledge about the designs themselves, when he saw my photograph of the *na wowi* mask he commented on its "rather disorganised design" and wondered—correctly—if the painters were "unskilled" (personal communication, November 28, 2016).
17. Without money for soap, white cloth was unusual; Lujere clothes mostly looked as if they had been dipped in tea.

Figure 37. The boys and youths who created the *na wowi* masks.

Figure 38. Lijeria quietly awaits the beginning of his *na wowi* curing festival.

swollen hand and asked him how it happened. He said that he had given Klowi some cartridges and went hunting with him and they got a pig but when he returned home his hand, which had been slightly swollen earlier, was then very swollen. He saw a curer who removed a part of a razor blade and a piece of spear and appeared satisfied with the treatment.

Shortly after four-thirty, Aiyuk strode into the plaza yelling and accusing the villagers of killing his hunting dog. Mauwi, of course, was his natal village, but his continuing anger with their 'sanguma' had motivated him to move his large family to Wakau, where his mother had been born. By five o'clock the daylight was beginning to fade and I was told that the masks would soon enter.

Lijeria, supported by a long narrow staff, was already standing alone in the plaza. Then eight boys ran nosily across the plaza, with one youth holding a bow drawn up towards the sky, another blowing a wooden trumpet (*waniwan*i), and others beating hand drums (*tiramli*). A group of girls running in string skirts with blouses or towels on top against the evening dampness were followed immediately by a group of youths in shorts as they ran back and forth across the plaza crying, "Wo, wo!" over and over. Amid this sudden uproar, the two masks came prancing in on flattened bare feet, preceded by their giant gourd phalluses (*meru*) tossing majestically up and down. Throughout the excitement, Lijeria continued to stand silently, moving only if a roving pig came too close or when a boy spat healing ginger upon him. Only when they arrived did he sit (fig. 39). Transformed by such dramatic action, the masks that had seemed to me as disappointedly ordinary in the bush were now exotically spectacular.[18] The towering feathered and painted headdress hid the mask carrier's head and the long body skirt of shredded sago leaves covered him except frontally. Holding his drum high, he struck it repeatedly as the gourd phallus simultaneously soared up towards his chest, striking a brace of Job's tears seeds with a clack, the sound that had intrigued the two legendary Kwieftim women. When a masker felt he was losing his erection, he left the clearing and another youth assumed his costume and returned to play his role. Mothers warned their children not to stare at the oscillating phalluses to ensure the masks would dance longer. Kaiera once laughingly told me that his mother had thus warned him and how, as a child, he felt constrained to only look at the towering headdress.

Near six o'clock, the masks paraded three times around Lijeria, then left the clearing. Someone told me that it was Mangko's mother's sister's son who spat the ginger on Lijeria reminding me, once again, of the multiple ties among the villagers. Men, women, and children then began bringing large bundles of food wrapped in leaves, mostly sago dumplings, to Lijeria's brother. The food was roughly stacked along an unfinished house's platform with portions of meat placed on top. The masks reappeared for a while in the plaza to circle Lijeria, then departed again. When the food was distributed, all thoughts had turned to dinner and the only noise was that of multiple conversations with an occasional shout for someone. Throughout the day's activities I had been filming and taking photos, not just of the masks and the youthful revelers, but also of the bystanders, men conversing and smoking their extraordinary pipes and women playing with their babies as the masks came and went.

---

18. See Craig (1975: 421) for his sketches of two Yegerapi village *na wowi* masks, each with a different sago-spathe design.

Figure 39. One of the *na wowi* masks approaches Lijeria, seated.

By a quarter after six the light was beginning to fade and I stopped filming. As I began to put the equipment away, I visited with Mangko and Nauwen about the day's events. Oria appeared with a large bundle of food, but this was not like an American picnic; there was no communal eating of the gift food. Like the others, Oria would take the food home. One mask surprisingly reentered the plaza, but did not linger and departed almost as quickly to a very fast drumbeat. Other men of our Wakau group gradually appeared with gift food. Mangko and Unei decided to stay in Mauwi and 'sing-sing' all night, which would entail a lot of running back and forth across the plaza with other young people in gender segregated groups. There would be chanting and drum beating, but no ritual; the masks would not appear. The rest of us would return to Wakau, then come back in early morning for the reappearance of the *na wowi* masks and Lijeria's final curing.

None of the chants for any of the curing festivals I attended or recorded were translatable *in toto* and some not at all. At best, a Namia word was identified here or there, but the overall meaning of the chant was left to speculation. Once when recording various chants by Oria, I asked him for translations. Here is an example of the level of translation available for one chant: He identified a word for a leaf that grows along the Sepik River that sago dumplings are laid upon. Another word was for a flying tree insect that he imitated. The chant ended with the words, "turning, turning." What it all meant, he didn't know. Villages sometimes have their own chants for a common curing ritual like the *na wowi*; Mauwi and Wakau have different chants for the *na wowi* curing festival. The one Oria chanted for me was untranslatable. The chant Wakau does for their *aewal wowi* curing rituals, he said, was learned from Green River men of the Upper Sepik River during plantation work. But Nakwane, who was with us, then recorded for me another *aewal wowi* chant that came from Tsila. All he knew was that it was about a bird called *arame* or, in Namia, *koworo*.

Sometime after 6:30 p.m.—it was almost dark—we left the plaza, but on the steep forested path down to Wakau it was night and I stumbled along, following Nimo. Later that night, as I prepared the film for the morning climax of the rituals, Klowi stopped by. He said that Wakau would soon have a curing 'sing-sing' for Ukai, the brother of Nauwen and Oria's recently dead father. However, they first must make the sago and kill the game to be distributed. He said it would be the *aokwae wowi* 'sing-sing' that had a similar but smaller mask than the *na wowi*. But even after Ukai fell dangerously ill, I heard no more about it and left Wakau without having seen it. Lying in bed, not quite asleep, I could faintly hear the distant all-night revelers up in Mauwi chanting and drumming.

Day two: The exorcism

At five forty-five A.M. I had finished breakfast and was ready with the equipment and helpers to return up to Mauwi. A slight pervasive fog hung in the air. When I arrived in Mauwi about an hour later, the young were still celebrating but they were no longer running back and forth across the plaza; the fact that they were even parading at a walk was impressive. I counted sixteen youths and twenty-two girls; like the day before, the groups, while adjoining, were gender segregated. Only the males were chanting as they struck their 'kundus.'

Figure 40. *Na wowi* mask carriers, Iwowari, Purkenitobu, and Katweli, practicing their moves.

The masks had not appeared and I, interested in talking with their carriers, went "backstage" to the steep ascent where the masks were hidden behind a screen of palm fronds, a taboo area for all females. I quickly knew why. Three young men— Purkenitobu and Katweli from Papei, and Iwowari, from Mauwi but currently living in Papei, all incongruously wearing shorts and long gourd phalluses, were practicing the *na wowi*'s pelvic thrusting movements on the steep path. Even in New Guinea it was an astonishing scene to run into, especially so early in the morning.[19] I photographed them practicing and learned some secrets of their art (see fig. 40). There was no cult involved with the *na wowi* rituals and any male could carry the mask, providing he could sustain an erection and do the phallic moves; one way to get and maintain the erection was to drink a lot of water and avoid urination. Unfortunately, there was no magic *wowi* ginger as in the story to help them out. While participating in the ritual the mask carriers were restricted from the village unless masked and could not be with women or children. After the rituals were concluded and the masks thrown into the forest, they must bathe in a stream to be purified before returning to normal life. There was an easy camaraderie amongst the three young men who were having fun with their ritual tasks.

---

19. The big bouncing phalluses had a clownish quality to me, but not to the villagers. I was reminded of a photo in Ronald Berndt's (1962: 299) book of two naked youths in body paint at an Eastern Highlands festival ostentatiously exhibiting their eighteen-inch bark phalluses in a ceremonial farce.

By seven-twenty I was back in the village visiting with Iwani's 'luluai,' who held gently in one hand a very small, beautifully colored parrot he caught in the forest. He offered it to me but I declined the gift, not seeking another responsibility. Near us were two men who were joking with one another. One grabbed the other and said in Tok Pisin, "You're my wife!" as his companion laughingly responded by grabbing his "husband's" buttocks. The 'luluai' explained that the two men could joke because the first man was married to the second man's sister, that is, they were brothers-in-law. It was the first ritual joking I had seen and, without even trying, I had received some insight into Lujere joking relations (considered earlier in chapter 12).

Lijeria already was in the clearing sitting motionless on a 'pangal' mat. I was told that he stayed up all night, then someone else said he didn't think so. Regardless, it was obvious he was sitting down and taking it easy that morning. The fog had lifted a bit and just after seven-thirty the two masks came prancing into the village but their entrance was not as noisy as the day before. The masks and the faithful, if tired, young celebrants raggedly circled Lijeria, and I filmed a long sequence. The mask carriers did not have good visibility and when one started to go astray, a nearby boy guided him back in line. Finally, at ten minutes to eight, the climaxing curing ritual began (see fig. 41). While one mask looked on, Lijeria was almost surrounded by the celebrants as the other mask approached him from behind and, kneeling down, bent over with its ornate headdress next to him. The top of the mask continued to shake slightly as those around Lijeria took the mask's still fresh paint and swabbed it on his back and head with their fingers. These were the moments when the sickness was fated to leave his body, an action validated to onlookers by the patient's slight trembling.[20] I was told that Lijeria did shake but many months later, when I reviewed the film footage back in Vermont, I detected no bodily tremors.

After the curing, the masks advanced separately toward the edge of the clearing, followed by yelling celebrants, the horn blowing, and energetic drumbeating. I followed the masks into the forest where they were eagerly tossed over the carriers' heads into the bush. I returned to the clearing where, with the festivities finished, my Wakau mates were ready to go home. They told me that Lijeria would now be all right—'sik i pinis' is the stock phrase. However, about two weeks later three *imoulu* curers from the Weari villages visited Wakau for two days of healing sessions at the lower *iron*.[21] I was filming the procedures with my hand-held camera when I suddenly realized the patient in my lens was Lijeria. The *na wowi* curing festival apparently was not the success he and his brother had hoped for.

An outsider's perspective

The purpose of a *na wowi* curing festival is to cure a sick person via a series of rituals. As close kin of the afflicted person, the sponsor/producer of the festival has multiple responsibilities, including: (1) selecting males to create the *na wowi* masks; (2) selecting men to carry the masks; and (3) providing feast food, especially meat, for the creators,

---

20. The Wape had a similar custom of the patient trembling when exorcised.
21. This curing session is discussed in chapter eighteen.

Figure 41. A *na wowi* mask kneels next to Lijeria for the curing climax.

performers, and guests. It is interesting that those concerned with the *na wowi* mask creation and performance were young single men, youths, or even boys, because the intimate involvement of older married men with *na wowi* endangered their health.

David Napier, in an absorbing book on masks that ranges deep and wide, writes, "Masks are hypothetical and make-believe. They are paradoxical" (Napier 1986: 4). The *na wowi* masks were all of that. Each was a mask without a face, a towering prancing presence preceded by an enormous phallus bouncing skyward to rhythmically strike a necklace of hard seeds. It was an arresting and strange creation. Its dancing phallus appeared to my Western eyes as more suggestive of a fertility rite than a curing one. The *na wowi* story Kaiera told me was the festival's single piece of Indigenous exegesis I obtained. However, at least amongst my informants, the evil *na wowi* character of the tale did not appear as a personalized force causing sickness but more as an amorphous negative power.

Some summarizing comments on the festival with Kaiera's story in mind could include the following: The murdered woman as well as the women who found the *wowi*'s gourd were all making sago or *na*, hence the mask's name, *na wowi*. The myth acknowledges *na wowi*'s erection-sustaining ginger, but the only ginger in the curing was some spat by a boy on the sick man. While the mythic *na wowi* left behind paint for his legs, the Mauwi, Kwieftim, and Abrau *na wowi* did not use body paint. The important paint in the Mauwi curing was the paint from the *na wowi*'s headdress that the youths rubbed on Lijeria as part of the cure. Regarding the three banana plants that emerged from the tree's ashes, they apparently had no explicit or symbolic significance for the festival beyond, perhaps, a banana's phallic shape. At least to me, the *wowi* myth as exegesis for the curing festival provided little beyond identifying the destructive features of the three villages' *na wowi* festivals.

I wasn't surprised that local exegesis for the *na wowi* curing festival was virtually nonexistent. There wasn't much mystery to explain if you believed that the *na wowi* mask represented malicious forces that afflict humans. Thus, it would make sense to create an attractive, even awesome mask and bring it prancing into the village with ceremonial regard amid trumpet calls, drums beats, energetic chanting, and the tireless parading by young people in the village plaza (see front cover, lower right figure). The ensuing exchange was a reciprocal one: villagers showed their enthusiastic deference to the *na wowi* mask and in response the detrimental grip on the patient was released, an event that was actualized at dawn the following morning when the *na wowi* knelt over the sick man and paint from its body was smeared on the patient's body as a possible form of immunization. Finally, the *na wowi*'s hyper-masculine effigy was characterized by his big thrusting phallus as a declaration of his supremacy over humans, men as well as women; in a similar way, the traditional Lujere male's penis-enhancing phallocrypt signaled his supremacy over females. At least one can make those assumptions, but a Lujere's response might be either wry or puzzled bemusement.

Ritual phallocrypts in the upper Sepik Basin

When New Guinea's early twentieth century German explorers reached the Upper Sepik Basin, they observed that the standard costume for most men was the gourd penis sheath, while nut and shell phallocrypts were also worn in some locales; a finding later substantiated and ethnographically augmented by patrolling 'kiaps' and anthropologists. Although the Star Mountains and the Border Mountains bounded the Sepik Basin to the west and turned the ascending river back on itself, the penis-sheath custom extended over the mountains, westward along the island's Central Cordillera towards the neck of the Vogelkop (Doberai), and northward along the coast of the Bismarck Sea (Gell 1971: 166)[22]. A Lujere man's gourd phallocrypt might be oval, straight, curvy, or curly depending on local style or the wearer's whim and was serviceable for several months. It was, however, a relatively modest penile accessory compared to the large tubular gourd (*Lagenaria sieceria*) so theatrically carried on a masker's erect penis in the *na wowi* curing rites and, while also useful as a food as well as a partial smoking device, was sartorially restricted to a ceremonial context. As the *na wowi* ritual with its huge phallus seemed not to have originated with the Lujere, I was curious about its origins and regional distribution.

Prime suspects were the ritually elaborate fertility and regeneration ceremonials of the Border Mountain societies. If Thurnwald had visited them during his pioneering patrols, he probably would have included them with the Green River people whom he found had "greater vivacity, curiosity and interest," in contrast to the "dullness" of the other Upper Sepik people. Both the Administration and missionaries were slow to establish their influence in this geographically isolated, jurisdictionally ambiguous international border area, inhabited by a people with few metal tools. The political transfer of West Irian to Indonesia by the Netherlands in 1962 transformed the region into a politically sensitive area, especially after the border was fixed and agitation for independence from Indonesia became an issue for some villagers on the Indonesian side. The Australian political response was to build a couple of airstrips and patrol posts in the Border Mountains area. Anthropological fieldwork began in 1969, followed by publications of highly imaginative fertility-regeneration ritual festivals by Alfred Gell (1975) for Umeda village (Umeda language), Bernard Juillerat (1996 [1986], 1990) for Yafar village (Amanab language) and Peter Huber (1980, 1990) for the Anggor language villages. It is striking, for example, the difference in ritual elaboration between the twenty named and masked figures in Umeda village's *ida* festival, compared to the two identical ritual figures in Mauwi village's *na wowi* festival. Unlike the relative simplicity of Lujere's *wowi* curing festivals, the reproductive cultural dramas acted out in the Border Mountains were of great ceremonial and dramatic complexity.

When I lived with the Lujere, they were the only society I knew firsthand with a masked performer sporting a ritual phallocrypt of long tubular proportions. In the same year that I first wrote about the Lujere *na wowi* curing festival (Mitchell 1975), Antje and Heinz Kelm's book (1975) appeared in German, with a section titled "Das Wowi-Fest." It documented *wowi* curing festivals in the two villages they studied in 1969–70, namely Abrau (Awun language) and Kwieftim (Ak language). Their descriptions of the *wowi* curing festival were versions of the one described above. According to the Kelms, the Abrau people had recently acquired their *wowi* curing festival from neighboring Maurom village (Pouye language), located slightly to the northwest. Their *wowi* costume was essentially the same as the one I had seen in Mauwi, except that it was taller, more carefully painted, festooned with numerous feathers including the lesser bird of paradise,

---

22. For a detailed article on the worldwide distribution of penis sheaths with close attention to New Guinea, see Ucko (1970).

Victoria crown pigeon, and cockatoo, and topped with a large plume of cassowary feathers (fig. 42). Around the skirt-top was a circle of orange fruit. The masker wore a long dark phallic gourd that, as he performed, noisily struck a belt.[23] The masks arrived in the village at dawn then, at the sick man's house, they smeared his feet with mud and encircled his wound with pale ochre mud. There were three males to alternate the carrying of the masks; from time to time a mask would leave the village to return with a fresh performer. The patient was a clan and village elder whose son was one of the mask carriers, and whose youngest son was the principal mask maker. Instead of throwing both masks into the forest to rot at the end of the festival, one was sold to the Lujere village of Nami (located on Ljuereland's eastern border) for seven Australian dollars, adding yet another village to the spread of this curing custom. The authors contend that the sick man's health, unlike Lijeria's in Mauwi, improved after the ritual (Kelm and Kelm 1980: 381–85).

Kwieftim's *wowi* curing festival reportedly came from the Upper Sepik area and was more elaborate; for example, up to ten masks might participate in a curing festival, each with a hand drum. Another difference was that the mask wearer's dancing phallus made no percussive noise as in the *wowi* myth and at the performances in Abau and Mauwi. The patient was treated with a paste of earth and ground-up plants, then was struck a couple of times with stinging nettles. The climax of the treatment was also different. The masked performer carried a bow and, fastening the nettles to a war arrow, pulled back the arrow to prance in a circle around the patient before suddenly shooting it high into the air to land in the forest beyond the village. Thus, the cause of the sickness was removed from the patient's body and sent back whence it came.

The shooting of an arrow into the forest to end the ritual in Kwieftim is reminiscent of the climax of the *ida* festival in Umeda, where the strategic *ipela* red bowmen end the festival by sending their arrows high into the air above the forest (Gell 1975; 206-7)[24]. The *wowi* ritual, of course, is concerned with sickness and the *ida* ritual with fertility and regeneration so, while the rationales for the two festivals are different, there are ritual acts like the arrow maneuver that are the same. Besides the shooting arrow in Kwieftim and Umeda that separately ends the *wowi* and *ida* festivals, a dancing ritual gourd phallocrypt is worn as an important festival feature in both the Border Mountain villages of Yafar and Umeda and the Sepik plains villages of Mauwi, Kwieftim, and Abrau. A difference, however, is that the phallocrypt in the Border Mountains' fertility festivals are large ovoid gourds that noisily strike a waist high decoration, whereas the long tubular gourds in the Sepik plains curing festivals strike at chest level. In both instances, the two types of gourds are worn exclusively in ritual situations and never for everyday use (see also Gell 1971: 174).

Leaving the lowlands, there is also a *wowi*-like curing ceremony among the Au speakers in the Torricelli foothills north of Abrau village. Lewis describes a ritual told to him that was performed by Winalum villagers (Au language) who came to Rauit village (Gnau language) to treat a man named Kantyi:

---

23. See Kelm and Kelm (1980: 186) for a drawing of an Abrau ritual gourd or "Kult-Peniskalebasse."
24. See Juillerat (1992: 44–45) for photos of the *ida* bowmen.

Figure 42. A *na wowi* mask parades across the village plaza, followed by chanting children and women.

For the treatment rites, they brought big 'limbums' of water and put them down, began their Au songs . . . then two by two they came out of the men's house dancing with gourds (*tu'anit*, a dried Cucurbit squash) tied on their penises so that, as they danced, the gourds clicked against the shells or dogs' teeth on their belts. They said that the men dancing were either "cassowaries" or "pigs"—if tall, cassowaries, and if short, pigs. One of the "cassowaries" held a spear and threw it to split a round orange *dapati* [a decorative inedible fruit] fixed under water in the big 'limbum'. The split *dapati* bobbed up to the surface. Kantyi did not in fact get better until they had carried out this ritual. (Lewis 2000: 163)

It is significant that in another publication, Lewis describes the ritual gourds as "long phallocrypts which are made to bounce up and down clicking against the belt. In this respect they resemble the dancing described by Alfred Gell from the Waina Sawonda" (1975: 193). Thus, based on the documented evidence reported by the Kelms and myself, the *wowi* curing rite may have a regional significance. It is present in Tsila (Yale language); Wagu (Abau language); Mauwi, Wakau, and Nami (Namia language); Kwieftim (Ak languge) Maurom (Pouye language) and Abrau (Awun language), all in the Sepik plains of the Upper Sepik Basin,[25] as well as among the nearby Torricelli Au speakers, for a total of six language areas. The idea for the *wowi* curing rite's long tubular ritual gourd may have come from the Kwomtari language area located in the Sepik plains just east of the Border Mountains. The data are in a letter that Juillerat wrote to Gell after the latter had returned to England. It concerns ritual phallocrypts he saw in the Oweniak village (Kwomtari language) area located on the Sepik plains east of Amanab. He writes,

In the ritual house of the Wongu I have seen the penis sheaths used in "phallic" dancing; these sheaths are *very long oblong gourds*, brown and without designs, with holes at both ends and measuring at least 30–35 cm [12–14"]. It is interesting to note that they serve at other times as cigarette-holders, being held between the smoker's lips and the cigar which is rolled in a leaf and held at the other end.[26] (Juillerat 1971: 180; my emphasis)

Unfortunately, Juillerat does not identify the gourd's ritual context, but it was likely a curing ritual like the *na wowi* curing festival as none of the Sepik plains societies, as far as we know, have anything resembling the Border Mountains' multifaceted and attenuated

---

25. For total geographic accuracy, Maurom village at 200 meters is just off the Sepik plains in the beginning broken country of the Torricelli Mountains.
26. A hole in the gourd big enough to hold an erect penis would necessitate a rather large cigar composed of clumsy native tobacco and I think unlikely. The Upper Sepik Basin smoking tubes I have seen were composed of two tubes: first, an apical tubular gourd for sucking in the smoke, and a secondary thin bamboo tube inserted at the gourd's terminal end that climaxed with a small clutch of tobacco. The dual use of the same gourd in both ritual and quotidian contexts would be highly unusual and, identifying the gourd's extremities as both penile and oral, even alarming. Further evidence that Juillerat's assumption regarding a dual performing ritual/smoking gourd was in error is that Barry Craig collected a tubular ritual phallocrypt (43 cm x 6 cm diameter) *and* a tubular smoking gourd (47 cm x 4.5 cm diameter) in Biaki village south of Oweniak village, both Kwomtari language.

fertility and regeneration festivals. Seeking data to test this supposition, I consulted the material culture collections digitized in Barry Craig's excellent "Upper SepikCentral New Guinea Project" website that provides a color photograph and measurements for each artifact. I found at least one long tubular ritual phallocrypt collected in each of the following villages: Biaki village (Biaki language, a sub Kwomtari language); Yenabi village (Kwomtari language); Hogru village (Abau language); and Bamblediam village (Abau language).[27] Thus, it is very possible that a *wowi*-type curing ritual is also prevalent in some Kwomtari villages, as well as being more extensive amongst Abau speakers than originally indicated. If true, that would locate the *na wowi* curing ritual not only in some Ak, Awun, Abau, Pouye, Namia, and Yale villages, but also in Kwomtari villages, giving the ritual a Sepik plains regional provenance as well as a foothold in the Torricelli foothills among the Au speakers. That would be an interesting finding, but more research is necessary to establish it.

Mokadami's Aewal Wowi *Curing Festival*

There was no masked figure in the *aewal wowi* curing festival to personify what had stricken its victims, but there were bamboo ritual horns gaily festooned with white feathers—the first I had ever seen or even heard about in a New Guinea ritual—that were intimately associated with the *aewal wowi* ritual, the same as the *na wowi* mask was with its ritual. In other words, the horns had the same association with sickness that characterized the *na wowi* mask, a difference being that women and small children were especially vulnerable to the horns' strong ritual powers and, for their safety, remained out of their physical and visual proximity. The only exception was the afflicted women involved in the curing rituals. Of necessity they had physical proximity to the horns, but they covered their heads to avoid visual contact.

Preparations

The middle of February I went to Mokadami (Gwidami) for my first *aewal wowi* curing festival; Nimo's and Eine's brother-in-law, Anwani, was one of the ailing. I would need most of my recording equipment to chronicle the event so I recruited the youthful males, Akami, Unei, Akau, Newai, Iwi, and Warajak to help carry it and Oria and Nauwen also came along. Mauwi and Mokadami were the two geographically closest villages to Wakau and the ones with which they had the most marital ties. Mokadami lay on the east bank of the Sand River about two hours' walk upriver. The Mokadami track crossed two large beautiful 'kunai' meadows that CPO Orwin would have visited in his 1951 search for an airstrip site. The first 'kunai' had a few poles still visible from a hamlet that burned down in a grass fire. Nearer Wakau there were several gardens of mostly bananas including Oria's and Nakwane's, then a couple of Arawaki's gardens further on. Much of the walk was heavily forested, mostly secondary growth. It was a typical lowland level track but with enough interesting contrasts, like several tricky slippery fallen-tree bridges

---

27. Barry Craig collected the ritual phallocrypts except the one for Yenabi village collected by Bernard Juillerat.

across swampy brooks. As long as I was wearing a pair of spiked canvas golf shoes that the Catholic mission sold in Lumi, the log bridges were almost fun.

Mokadami had three hamlets and the one we stayed in was Mokwebe. It had the government rest houses, one for the 'kiap' and another for his 'polis,' and we claimed the latter for the night. The abandoned old village was across the Sand to the west. Mokadami's main hamlet was about the size of Wakau, probably one hundred or so people, with about fifteen houses in various states of disintegration and situated in a pleasantly haphazard way around a very large central plaza where the curing festival would be held. The houses, however, appeared makeshift in design with most walls of 'pangal' stems tied with 'kanda,' unlike Wakau houses that usually followed a more traditional design.

Just four days earlier I had made my first visit to Mokadami with Kworu and Eine and we immediately went to Eine's sister's house and I met her husband Anwani with whom I visited, off and on, during the next several hours. We were there because Eine was sick; he already had been treated by three different *imoulu* and was still feeling bad, so while he was at his sister's house a local *imoulu*, Oriak, would try his hand.

Anwani was an impressive and somewhat peculiar man. He was in his early thirties with a strong physique and was an important *nakwolu*. He certainly did not look as if he were on his deathbed as some proclaimed. His ailment was not only a puzzle to me, but to some of the villagers as well. Several months earlier he had been released from his indentured job in New Ireland and seemed to have some form of epilepsy. I was told that his legs could go weak and sometimes he would become unconscious and tremor. He also slept a great deal and needed support when walking.

When I came in, Anwani was sitting on a typical man's elevated bed and never moved from it. He sat on a long plastic bag and said that was all he brought back with him, except for two blankets and fifty dollars he distributed to relatives. After he was released from his labor contract, he said he was in a New Ireland hospital for several months but they found nothing wrong with him. Then in Wewak on the way home, he was examined at the regional hospital and they told him the same thing. As both were modern Western hospitals, his ailment apparently was 'sik nating,' indicating some behavioral disturbance. But Anwani told me his illness was due to the sorcery of a New Ireland man—he gave me his name—who worked 'posin' on him but no local treatments had cured him. Already his family had mounted two *aewal wowi* curing festivals for him, one around Christmas and another in January, and numerous *imoulu* had treated him, all to no avail.

The house was filled with people sitting with him, men, women, and children. Anwani was obviously a respected man and, according to comments, he and his brother had taken care of a number of orphans, much as Klowi had done. His big concern speaking to me was what would happen to his family when he died. His face was continuously serious and everything he talked about was in the negative, especially his sickness, but he did, at one point, take pains to show me his two wives—the second was Warajak's mother—and the two children each wife was holding.

I left for a short time to make a first visit to neighboring Aiendami hamlet, a fifteen-minute walk and, arriving unexpectedly, I startled the women in their Native skirts and several men in penis sheaths who all scurried into their houses. Seeing men run from me was a new experience. The men immediately reappeared wearing either shorts or 'lap laps' but one man had slapped his 'lap lap' around without removing his penis sheath, creating an amusingly lewd costume. After a visit to their flimsy *iron*, which was open at both ends, I returned to Mokadami; Anwani's position was unchanged, his visage still tragic. It was the only time in New Guinea when someone told me they were physically sick that I clearly thought that they were not. It was usually just the opposite; New Guineans endure pain and fevers with astonishing fortitude and stoicism. I did, however, think that Anwani was clinically depressed with the same type of blunted affect that had sometimes characterized Samaun, but Samaun's despair seemed to make more sense than Anwani's. Samaun was a strong young man with no prospect of a wife or children and a projected lifetime of dependency on other males' wives for food. Yes, sleeping his life away was a convenient escape. The only times I saw him take initiative and join in with creative enthusiasm was in all-night curing festivals when he would lead the chanting. But these were infrequent affairs. Anwani's despair was less fathomable to me. In Lujere terms, he appeared to have everything: good looks, a strong-appearing body, two wives, children, supporting kin, and a valued healing skill. Perhaps the New Ireland sorcerer was the actual source of his illness; at least if the victim accepts the victim role and surrenders his personal autonomy to a belief in the pernicious power of the other, the affliction is real.

That initial visit to Mokadami had been instructive, but now I was back again, four days later in the midafternoon, this time with my Wakau friends for an *aewal wowi* curing festival. The ritual curing climax with the horns would be in the evening, followed by distribution of food, then an all-night 'sing-sing.' Although Anwani was not one of the central sufferers in this curing festival, he would be a participant. We again went immediately to Anwani's wives' house as they had fed me on my recent visit and I wanted to reciprocate with some coveted trade store tobacco. Anwani was lying down when we entered; he looked strong and healthy but there was no smile. He said that the day before he had started again with diarrhea.

The main recipients for the planned curing ritual were Orana, the wife of the *imoulu* Oriak who earlier had treated Eine, and a man called Loku. Both Orana and Loku had become afflicted in the same way. While having intercourse with their respective spouses, some of their sexual fluids apparently fell to the ground and was stolen by *aewal wowi*'s *aokwae*, who then made them sick. Loku and his wife had had sex in their house and Orana and her husband in the bush near the river. Anwani and another woman, Mane, with a chronic condition, would also participate in the curing but tangentially. Mane had been sick with the *aewal wowi* for a very long time; for both Anwani and Mane, this ritual curing would be more like a "booster shot" to reinforce their earlier *aewal wowi* curing rituals.

As usual, things seemed slow to get underway. I took some photos of a young father in traditional dress bathing his two small children in the village stream emptying into the Sand, then of several girls washing pig entrails downstream, and of boys gingerly crossing the log bridge over the stream into the village. Earlier I watched the licensed gun owner enter the village carrying his shotgun followed by a man carrying a huge pig on his back, literally piggyback. For the curing festival, two wild pigs and one village pig already had been butchered. I wandered back to check my filming equipment set up on the plaza; fortunately, I had an excellent Angenieux zoom lens on my cine camera so, regardless of where the center of activity was—and with the Wape it rarely was where they said it would be—I could zoom in and out to catch the action. The goal for my field recording, whether with pen and paper, tape recorder, or still and cine cameras, was to be

A Witch's Hand

as nonintrusive as possible to record an event in its authenticity without any direction or interference from me, the exact opposite of a Hollywood film or TV shoot. As I wandered about, Newai and Warajak kept me company. I had noticed that the Mokadami women's skirts were different from Wakau and they explained that here, although hips were bare in both villages, the women put yellow strands made from the tulip tree over the common brown strings made from the sago tree.

The *aewal wowi* ritual horns

I had not yet seen the *aewal wowi* horns that were at the ritual center of the curing rites, so around 5:00, Nauwen and a couple of Mokadami men and I went a short walk away into the forest between the village and the Sand River. There they lay, already decorated, on the grass in a small clearing near the bank of the river with about a half dozen men sitting around smoking and chewing betel. Four of the men would carry the horns and all were friendly except one older, very small man, the only one not in cloth but in traditional dress that included arm bands, a phallocrypt, and a "Daniel Boone"–style cap I had not seen before, made from the mottled fur of a wallaby. He neither spoke nor smiled and later when I took some Kodachrome photos, he frowned and moved away quickly, to the other men's amusement. It was obvious that, while accepting him, they considered him a 'buskanaka,' a man of the bush who had never left home, did not speak Tok Pisin, and had not even marginally adapted to modern ways.

Earlier in the day the men, newly following Tsila village custom, had made four ritual horns—Wakau only made three—from green bamboo; each was two feet or so long, with a small hole in the apical end and open at the terminal end. All but one was decorated, and that was the "grandfather" horn—the older unsmiling man would carry it—and the others were the "children" horns (see fig. 43). These were numbered one, two, and three, and the amount of decoration declined as the number increased.

Figure 43. Men playing *aewal wowi* horns encircle afflicted victims. The "grandfather" horn is the undecorated one and the others known as the "children."

The first horn was an extraordinary looking construction that terminated in a large squarish "parrot's nest" made by winding the aromatic under-bark of a particular tree around four corner sticks, then spitting betel nut juice over it. Finally, feathers, mostly white ones, including the lesser bird of paradise, were attached to sticks and stuck vertically around the nest. The bird's-nest decoration for a horn was new and came from Tsila village. No one knew what the nest stood for or, as usual, cared. As I have mentioned before, the Lujere were not big on exegesis; they simply liked the nest idea and adopted it. The same under-bark was wound around the ends of horns two and three, bespat with ginger, then decorated with many mostly long white feathers, some well-used.

When the men learned I had not seen bamboo horns played before, they offered to give me a demonstration. The person playing the grandfather horn would not participate and walked sourly away as another man wordlessly took his place. Like the performers in the *na wowi* festival, there was no special ritual status involved with playing the horns, just the ability to perform the relevant routines. The men lined up numerically left to right, legs wide apart, holding the horns to their mouths with two hands—horn one with the nest looked awkwardly heavy—and bent over from the waist with heads tilted leftward. Hopping sideways to the left on flat feet, they emitted a yelping sound each time then, after several hops, stopped completely and made two consecutive, drawn-out, and descending "woooo" sounds as they raised their horns. They then returned to their original positions and repeated the sequence several times.

It was about five-twenty when the men heard a certain bird's call, indicating it was time to bring the horns into the expansive village plaza, already empty of women and children. I returned to my filming and recording equipment, then heard a commotion under Loku's house. Men struck the supporting house posts to scare away any *aokwae*, then dug up some earth under the area of the house where Orana and her husband had had intercourse. Some dirt previously dug up from the spot would be used in their curing rituals. Later in an interview with Oria on the Mokadami festival, I questioned him on the significance of the dug-up earth. Oria said it was just the husband's semen that the *aokwae* were after in the earth, while Nauwen insisted it was the sexual fluids of both. But I already had learned that in Lujereland, where the unseen was concerned, versions of "truth" could vary greatly.

Around five-thirty Orana, her head shrouded, took her place sitting on a pad of 'pangal' laid on the ground, and I took my first cine shot as others gathered around the curing site. Less than fifteen minutes later, I saw the men with their horns approach the plaza from the right. I had set up my equipment thinking they would approach from the riverside where I'd seen the horns earlier. Anwani was there standing in a 'lap lap' holding the wrist of his his second wife—Warajak's mother—apparently for physical support, and Loku was standing near the seated Orana. Mane had been there but left before the horns entered, then reappeared for the final ritual curing.

For almost a half hour, the horn men performed the basic ritual routine they had shown me while at least two men struck their hand drums. About a dozen local men began to circle the victims counterclockwise, voicing the untranslatable *aewal wowi* chant. At the same time, the horn men would approach the victims, back off, approach again, back off, and each time take a different position. At one point they gradually circled the victims clockwise, always "yipping" into their horns as they hopped, and then wailing after they stopped. When they finally circled the victims and were actually facing me, I got the best-filmed sequence of their ritual performance and the lifting of the horns. However, their actions as a chorus were ragged at best, as at times they bumbled back and forth into each other. The grandfather horn especially appeared to feel the tempo differently.

The concluding rituals

At 5:55 p.m., my camera jammed but the horn men had just finished their performance and placed their horns on the ground near where the victims sat and stood. The chanting men continued to circle them, then gradually stopped. Several final rituals (see fig. 44) were performed on the victims in the presence of the horns; sweat from the hornist's bodies was transferred to the victims and a small leaf-packet of betel nut was pressed against their bodies. I also watched as the grandfather hornist rubbed Loku's back and between his knees with his horn.

Young boys then picked up the horns and carried them out of the village so the women and children could safely return, but there was a final important ritual only for Orana and Loku. It was just after six o'clock, Mane and Anwani and his wife had left the curing arena, and Orana had uncovered her head. Separate muddy pastes had been made from the sexualized dirt collected earlier and with it, circles were painted on Orana's hips, elbows, and knees. The painting of circles on Loku was more extensive, eleven in all: two each on his chest, knees, elbows, shoulder blades, upper buttocks, and one on his belly.

The curing rites were over and I packed up my gear. As we headed back to the 'haus polis,' I noticed a pile of sago dumplings wrapped in leaves with a few pieces of pork placed on top—a reward for the men who performed the rituals—near where Orana was still sitting. Visitors, like my little group of Wakau males, also were separately gifted with food. It was getting dark but there was still time for Nauwen, Iwi, and me to have a refreshing plunge in the Sand River before dinner. We still had to attend an all-night 'sing-sing.'

Around eight thirty we could hear the men's *aewal wowi* chanting and we returned to the plaza. Orana was still on her 'pangal' bed but lying down and five of her women relatives had joined her; a small fire burned nearby. Villagers were walking counterclockwise around her in a big spread-out circle, men and youths first, followed by women and children in a strung-out group. It was a large contingent of villagers, probably seventy or eighty. The males walked in darkness with no fire or lanterns, but several of the women carried blazing torches made from the stems of sago leaves tied together with vine; some were five or six feet long. Periodically a torch was put to the ground to clear away the burned material and keep it ablaze, sending brilliant sparks flying. All of the women were in traditional skirts, some carried babies or had toddlers on their shoulders, and other babies were in cloth slings. None of the women or little girls were holding hands as the Wape do but, to my surprise, some of the men were walking hand in hand, something Wape men never did. Traditionally, the men would have paraded carrying their weapons but only a few did. Occasionally, five or six little boys would run ahead of the men with glowing, not burning, torches, waving them wildly around sending sparks flying into the night, like American children with their Fourth of July sparklers. The children generally were livelier than the adults who walked round and round in the incessant circle at the same rather poky gait. Several times while I observed, the circle would begin to crumble

Figure 44. Orana and Anwani are treated near the four *aewal wowi* placed on the ground.

apart as some took a rest, but always some of the men continued and eventually the large circling group would re-form.

At one point I went into the unfinished house where my equipment was stored and my right leg crashed through a partially covered hearth hole; I was down and shaken but uninjured. More annoying was being covered with little flying insects crawling all over my bare skin. Earlier I had begun a sound recording on my Uher as the men's chanting was haunting and a fascinating juxtaposition to the women's very high "wup, wup, wup" that reminded me of the chirping of baby chicks. I was impressed how community-focused this curing festival was compared to the *na wowi* one in Mauwi that only the young really celebrated. Here, almost everyone except the very old were staying up and parading thorough the night. Also, in this curing festival, there was no "moment of truth" when the victim was supposedly "cured" of his or her affliction. Instead there was a series of ritual actions each of which, if I understood the logic of what was explained to me, could be curative.

By 10:30 p.m., the bugs were getting worse, but some Mokadami men had joined me; one was home from Wewak where he now lived, and he hoped I could make a recording for Radio Wewak to play. He also knew by name all of the participants in the ritual and he verified or clarified my earlier spotty data. By 11:00, the bugs were intolerable. I watched a mother carrying a baby leave the group to walk towards her six-year-old son sitting on the sidelines with other little boys and men. Forcefully taking his hand, she pulled him, struggling and yelling, into the circle to join her in the parade.

Orana's fire was dying and someone brought firewood to rekindle it. It was almost 11:30 p.m., and the circling, drumming, and chanting continued unabated. Sometimes I could surrender to the repetitive monotony and slip into a trance-like state like the celebrants, but not that night. I yearned to escape the bugs and for just a half-note change in the men's repetitive chanting. When my tape finished recording, I packed up and stored the recorder with the rest of my gear in the house where I had crashed through the floor and, with Nauwen and Newai, left the village by the log bridge and returned to the 'haus polis.' Then they and the others, with the exception of Warajak who slept at his mother's house, cooked some of the gift pork. But I eagerly crawled into my blissful mosquito net and soon was asleep.

When we awakened the next morning the 'sing-sing' had ended and by 8:00 a.m., we all were on our way home. By the time we reached Wakau, I had a rare raging headache. I immediately fell into bed and slept most of the day. That evening I felt better and different conjectures were floated by my local friends as to what had struck me down in Mokadami. What it was that hit me, I would never really know.

Wakau's Aewal Wowi *Curing Festivals*

Not all *aewal wowi* curing festivals were as large as Mokadami's. A week after I had returned from Mokadami, Wakau had a small *aewal wowi* curing festival for Marawami, the daughter of the widow Debrai, who lived with the brothers Waniyo and Nimo's families in the house on the 'kunai.' Marawami was married to a Mauwi man who was away as an indentured laborer and, as she lived in Mauwi, I didn't personally know her. Unei told me she became sick in a bush camp and was so ill that Mangko and old Menetjua, both *nakwolu*, were going out to treat her. The next morning, I heard that Menetjua didn't go but that Mangko and Poke did. There was also talk about carrying her back to the village but no one knew for sure. I was busy with Ces Parrish who had surprised me with a visit but had made cursory notes about her illness.

Debrai's two older sons were away as indentured laborers, but her four young sons lived with her, as well as the wife of an older absent son. So, when Marawami became seriously ill in the bush, it was easier to carry her to Waniyo's 'kunai' house where her mother lived, rather than up the steep hill to her husband's family in Mauwi. She had been sick for four nights and became delirious, spurring Waniyo and Nimo to organize her rescue. They, rotating with Mangko, Poke, Unei, and Kunai, would carry her back on an improvised stretcher. Shortly before four, I started walking towards the 'kunai' house to see if they had arrived and saw them approaching on the plain.

The first curing festival

The 'kunai' house was larger than most, with four cooking hearths; the rear male section was raised. When they came in, Marawami was prostrate and wearing just a small traditional pubic cover. Her temperature was 101.5 and I gave Nimo some sulpha tablets and two aspirin to give her. I suspected pneumonia. Kaiera came in with Marawami's husband's father Klene wearing a phallocrypt, followed shortly by Oria, but no one went toward her. Then Enewan, Nauwen, and Alomiaiya come in, but Alomiaiya immediately went to her side and, taking sweat from under his arm, gently wiped her with it.

When some water arrived, they helped her sit up and Nimo gave her my medicine then poured some water in her mouth from an old tin cup. She coughed but swallowed it. Around 4:30 p.m., I started for home, joined briefly by Klowi who told me that Aiendami men had threatened to kill him with 'sanguma' because he wants them to give Mangko a wife. Once on the path, I heard the plane chartered by the 'kiap' take off from Yellow River for Mageleri.

Around 8:30 p.m., the now familiar *aewal wowi* chanting came drifting through the village from the vicinity of the upper *iron*. I returned to the 'kunai' house to give Marawami more medicine; this time it was Waniyo who supported her. Although her mother and other women were around, I was heartened to see men other than very close kin in such a personal and caring role. Only later did I learn that Waniyo and Nimo were her *mamaru*.[28] Klowi and Menetjua both had treated her during the afternoon. She was still sick, but her temperature was down and her skin cool. Marawami's case was a good example of the Lujere eclectic temperament with its penchant for things useful, whatever the source. Engwe was in the room asleep but Mangko pointed out to me Engwe's new wife. Although an *aewal wowi* curing festival for Marawami was definitely under way, tonight she would eschew the chanting and parading and sleep at home.

The following evening a hefty bonfire was built in front of the upper *iron* and a handful of males chanted and circled around it, counterclockwise. Samaun was definitely the lead singer, joined by Akami, Iwi, and Kworu, and preceded by a number of lively little boys. No women participated, but two little girls followed the men and another little girl carrying a torch joined them as she pulled a much smaller little naked girl to bring up the

---

28. The *mamaru* kin term is described in chapter 12.

end. I visited with Eine on the *iron*'s veranda while tape recording but by eleven o'clock I was home. Before I went to sleep, I listened briefly on my wireless radio and learned that Nixon had begun his famous trip to China.

The next morning when I visited Marawami with antibiotics, she was sitting up but her temperature had climbed a bit and Waniyo and her mother were still concerned. On the way home, I stopped in the lower *iron*, where Tsaime was being treated for a big boil on the right side of his back—it had been cut open and was a mess. He had hung a strap from the house roof so he could gently pull himself up and down. He said that Warajak, Newai, and another youth had gone to the bush to cut the bamboo horns and their wild decorations. Then early in the afternoon Mangko reported that Marawami had put on a skirt, was eating and talking more, but was still sick. By 5:30 p.m., village men were beginning to gather near the upper *iron*. I set up my filming and recording equipment, then strung a string around it and announced to the boys watching me that the inside area was now 'tambu' (taboo). It was a Tok Pisin word as well as an Indigenous concept they all understood; even if I left the village, I knew nothing would be touched. As I waited for some action, I watched two boys skin the wings of a big fruit bat. Finally Akami and Turai, the controversial Mauwi licensed gun owner married to Oria's sister, arrived carrying Marawami on her stretcher. Once it was lowered to the ground, Klowi began to treat her. The village already was devoid of women and children.

Eventually the assembling men and youths began to parade and chant against the fast beat of several hand drums. Klowi continued her treatments until we got the word that the *aewal wowi* horns were arriving and Marawami covered her head.[29] To my surprise, four, not three men with their charmed *aewal wowi* horns dramatically entered the area, performing the musical and movement routines I had witnessed and described for Mokadami. Apparently Wakau also was adopting Tsila's four horns, with the principal difference that the first horn did not terminate in a parrot's-nest design but in an effusion of white feathers and greenery. The chanting men paraded counterclockwise and the *aewal wowi* horns clockwise, when they weren't moving in and out, towards and away from Marawami.

Marawami was carefully helped to her feet. As she stood assisted, the ritual horns—elaborately decorated with white bird feathers, stinging nettles, and aromatic leaves, then bespelled with a mixture of spittle, chewed betel nut, and *aewal wowi* ginger, and the aromatic inner bark of a special tree—moved in closer and closer, while a small packet of heated pungent leaves was put on the ground beneath her.

According to the youth Yaope, one of the most powerful of these leaves was from a type of rree called *lami*, but it was the *lami aokwae*, or the tree's spirit, together with its pungent aroma, that made it powerful. Yaope almost whispered the names, as they are especially detrimental to females; just to hear the words could cause severe sickness in a

---

29. Oria told me in an interview on the Mokadami *aewal wowi* festival that it was custom to begin the festival by burning bamboo for its explosions just before the horns appeared. But the Mokadami festival I saw was following current Tsila custom, hence the four, not three, horns, and the lack of exploding bamboo. However, at the first *aewal wowi* festival for Anwani they did set off firecrackers from Wewak. No bamboo was exploded at either of the Wakau *aewal wowi* festivals and I neglected to ask why. Oria thought the rational for the exploding bamboo was to frighten away the *aokwae* of the *aewal wowi* causing the sickness.

female. Interestingly, it is the extremely strong aroma of the various ritualized substances that is believed to waft into and cure the sick person's body, rather like a bush form of trendy Western aromatherapy. Then the patient might shake slightly, verifying the cause of the sickness, as Marawami apparently did. In a final rite, Klowi chewed some special betel nut and spat a symbolic amount on her head.

By 6:40 p.m., the horn-men had departed but the local men continued their parading and chanting. Klowi and Newai helped me pack up the cine equipment and I headed home for a respite. When I got home, I found that Nauwen was very sick with a high fever. Earlier in the day I had given him some chloroquine as we both thought it was malaria but now his chest hurt when he coughed and that sounded like pneumonia. It was interesting that during the year and a half that I lived with the Wape, I seldom intervened medically as they had easier access to aid-post and hospital services. But living with the Lujere was very different. Here, acute respiratory infections—the commonest cause of morbidity New Guineans experience (Riley et al. 1992: 281)—especially pneumonia, could be a death sentence without antibiotics.

When I returned to the festival after 9:00 p.m., the 'sing-sing' was going strong. It just happened to be Saturday night, an American's night to party, and here I was with fifty or so village celebrants, almost all locals, parading and vigorously chanting the same three-note interval, over and over and over. Marawami was wearing a skirt and blouse and lying on a 'limbum' mat in front of Akami's new house where I had filmed the curing rituals earlier. There was a small fire by her and sitting nearby were her mother, Waniyo, and others from his family. The chanting males led the parading, passing in front of her, not around her; most carried their bows and arrows. They were followed by the women and girls carrying their babies and a few torches. As usual, the men carried no light. I had brought a small kerosene lantern and had set it down as I wandered around. I had essentially abandoned the lamp and Klowi, forever enterprising like few others, hung it on a stick in the middle of the circling celebrants. I was delighted, as no one else, including me, would have thought to do that. When I walked around to where Marawami was lying, Kunai came up to me and earnestly insisted that I give her medicine again tonight, as she wasn't yet well. Sitting by her now were both Waniyo and Nimo, her nurturing *mamaru*. At about 10:30 p.m., I took a short break to go home and unload the two heavy Leica cameras hanging around my neck and get Marawami's medicine while checking on Nauwen.

Eine had joined me and he talked about the 'sing-sing' as we walked. Then he added that next Monday Mokadami was having another *aewal wowi* curing festival for Orana, and her husband already had the 'binatangs'—probably the grubs found in rotting sago palm logs and considered a delicacy—to reward the performers. It would not, however, include any of the other victims as before.

Marawami's curing festival was dwindling in size although the chanting and drumming continued unabated; two more small fires had been started where several women and children rested. Marawami sat up with difficulty and Waniyo gave her the medicine. When my last tape recording ended at 11:24 p.m., I went home with my recording gear, but my kerosene lamp would remain to cast long shadows of the circling celebrants until the kerosene was gone and the flame finally died.

After midnight I was still up and heard loud talking and shouting up at the 'sing-sing.' Nauwen, who had been sleeping in the 'haus kuk,' was awake and explained that it was

Samaun accusing Klowi of making 'kawawar nogut', that is, casting an evil spell with ginger, while Klowi protested that he didn't want to make any one sick or die; that he wanted us to stay strong. Then he reminded any listeners that if Klowi threw away the cartridges the villagers gave him, there would be no more meat from his gun!

At 6:30 the following morning, the festival was over, and I gave Klowi the medicine to give to Marawami. Later Oria explained that the reason he didn't participate in all night 'sing-sings' was because his uncle Ukai's adopted son died at station last year and that if your brother, real or classified, were to die, you could never again 'sing-sing' in your own village. Around 8:00, I heard that Mowal's wife was in labor; then just before 10:00, Klowi told Eine and Nauwen at the 'haus kuk' that Mowal's wife had a baby girl and named her Kairapowe. He had been there and helped with the delivery. Such an incident defies interpretation as childbirth is anathema to Lujere men and can endanger their hunting prowess, not to mention their lives. But it documents the extent of Klowi's unique character and his unassailable belief in himself that, while very much a part of his community and culture, he epically transcended both.[30]s

The second curing festival

Marawame's health quickly improved and within a week she had resumed her normal activities, though she remained living with her mother and Waniyo's family. Was her recovery because of the tetracycline I was giving her, or the magical curative powers of the *aewal wowi* ritual horns? Such an either/or question was not a relevant one to the pragmatic Lujere; both interventions were accepted as instrumental but there was no question that the ritual of the *aewal wowi* festival was the curative one. However, there was still some question as to just how well she was, so I wasn't completely surprised when, two weeks later, I heard talk of a new festival for her; Waniyo's household was large enough that it could easily sponsor another one soon after the first. I was, however, convinced she no longer had pneumonia.

On a Friday, Yaope told me that a new *aewal wowi* curing festival for Marawami would begin that day and Engwe and Poke had gone to the forest to cut the bamboo horns. That evening Klowi, Yaope, and Samaun energetically began the chanting and drumming, but Waniyo heard them from the 'kunai' house and sent word for them to stop, as he had not given them permission to begin. They reluctantly stopped, but Klowi and Yaope said that if Waniyo wanted them to shut up, then they would stay shut up, truculently adding that they wouldn't join the 'sing-sing' when it did start! The following day, Saturday, Waniyo gave his approval for Marawami's curing festival to begin, and by ten P.M. it was underway, but a ten-thirty rainstorm aborted it as everyone ran for shelter.

Early Sunday evening women were bringing food to the men's *iron* for their husbands' dinners, Nakwane and Kunai returned from the bush, and Newai killed a local pig. At 6:25 p.m., Arakwaki arrived, having just killed a large wild boar with his bow and arrow, followed shortly by Nauwen carrying it piggyback. Women began bringing food to be distributed to the performers and arriving guests from Mokadami, Aukwom, and Mauwi,

---

30. He was one of the most fascinating and enigmatic persons I have ever known and, if I had remained in the community longer, I would have collected data for a biography to see if I could understand his exceptionalness.

Figure 45. Decorated *aewal wowi* horns perform for Maruwami's curing rituals.

including Sakome and her children, whom I hadn't seen since she fled to her brother Kowali's house in Mauwi to escape Samaun's harassment. K____ and his family also had come.

By six forty-five, the women and children had disappeared and Marawame arrived in a traditional string skirt and took her place on a 'limbum' pad. Men, including Klowi and Yaope, were already chanting and drumming, with most carrying a bow and arrows or an adze over the shoulder. The bamboo horns, some elaborately decorated with bird of paradise feathers, bright fruit, shell bands, and greenery (fig. 45), entered and began their ritual performance as the men circled, chanting and drumming, and the curing rites were performed.

This time there was no night rain and, once the ritual horns had departed, the women returned and the energetic 'sing-sing' went until dawn. The Wakau men that chanted and paraded off and on all night were Klowi, Nimo, Samaun, Meyawali, Engwe, Alomiaiya, Akami, Kunai, Unei, Warajak, Newai, Poke, Mangko, Kwoien, and Iwi. A number of boys also lasted all night and I was astonished mid-morning to see five of them having a high-energy mock fight in the lower village. But most of their fellow male celebrants were dead asleep in an *iron*.

CHAPTER SIXTEEN

'Sanguma': The Terror of Magical Ritual Murder in Oceania

> *It is not the practice of sorcery that does the harm,*
> *but rather the belief in it, and especially the fear of it.*
> F. E. Williams (1928: 215)

> *Who or what is sangguma?*
> Georg Höltker (Koster and Höltker 1942: 213)

Many societies, including the Lujere, are culturally enmeshed in beliefs in magic and the supernatural[1] It was my curiosity about 'sanguma,' a logically puzzling form of magical ritual murder sometimes called "assault sorcery" that had lured me from the pleasant, but rainy, Torricelli Mountains down to the Yellow River swamps where I met the Lujere. They, and tens of thousands of others in New Guinea and the adjoining islands, were terrified by the possibility of a violent 'sanguma' attack that marked its victim for certain death. In this chapter and the next, based on what I learned about 'sanguma' from my fieldwork and from what others have written, several questions will be considered. This chapter is the more wide-ranging one; it is an inquiry into the extent of geocultural distribution of 'sanguma.'

'Sanguma' as Magical Ritual Murder

'Sanguma' is the Tok Pisin term for a form of magical ritual murder of an extreme transgressive type that is widely distributed in Oceania but called by its own Indigenous term in

---

1. Kapferer (2002) provides an excellent yet short historical and critical review of magic and sorcery in anthropology.

each culture.² On Dobu Island it was called *mawari*, in the Southern Highlands *maua*, and among the Motu and Koita of the Port Moresby area *vada*, a term used by some early ethnographers (e.g., Fortune 1932: 284), to discuss the phenomenon cross-culturally. However, because of Tok Pisin's prevalence in much of Papua New Guinea and its status as one of the country's two official languages, for my comparative discussion in this chapter I will use 'sanguma' while cogently aware it is synonymous with *vada*. Regardless of where 'sanguma' is known, "it inspires horror; it provides the bogeyman for small children; it is feared, reviled and despised. Its use is always antisocial and illegitimate" (Lewis 1987: 998).

While many ethnographic categories and their vocabularies are straightforward and unambiguous—no one argues about the types of hunting or fishing—the vocabulary pertaining to the supernatural is slippery and often contested. Hence, I will define my terms to help find our way through the lexical haze confronting most inquiries about the occult. First, analytical terms like "supernatural" or "occult," which identify our subject, are not Indigenous concepts in New Guinea languages. Unlike English, New Guinean languages do not have a special term equivalent to "occult." Something I might identify as inexplicable or unfathomable, indicating there is no explanation short of the supernatural, for many Indigenous persons *is* fathomable, because they don't question its authenticity. Thus, in my usage, *magic* is a set of beliefs and actions that can't be objectively validated and is a characteristic of nonmodern societies like the Lujere, whereas modern societies tend towards secularism.³ I say they "tend towards secularism" because, under some conditions, as Jones reminds us, "occult phenomena have not only persisted but proliferated under the postmodern, postcolonial, postsocialist conditions of global capitalism" (Jones 2017:17). Pioneer ethnographers such as W. Lloyd Warner also distinguish between "black magic," which allegedly kills (like 'sanguma' and sorcery), and "white magic," which allegedly cures, a central concern of chapter 18.

Sorcery and Witchcraft

While the spirits, ghosts, and ghouls discussed in the last chapter are intangible, sorcerers and witches are human beings, albeit with reputations for dealing with the intangible and supernatural. I define *sorcery* as an individual's actions or thoughts intended to magically bring harm to others. Here are some Lujere examples: placing in house thatch bespelled leaves whose aroma is believed to cause illness; heating something associated with the victim's mouth, such as a small piece of their leftover food, cigarette, or betel cud that first must be enclosed in some dried mud. In the latter method, the encased item is placed on a cooking hearth. With the many hearth fires, the victim becomes sick, and after losing much weight, will die. The antidote is for the victim to repeatedly send his brother to the

---

2. It is puzzling that two such experienced researchers as Peter Lawrence and Mervin Meggitt (1965) make no mention of 'sanguma' in the introduction to their multiauthor exploration of Melanesian religious beliefs, including witchcraft and sorcery.
3. The decline in magic and the supernatural has been steady since the Enlightenment and many writers have documented and commented on this change. Here I will cite only one influential study (Thomas 1973) relevant to English-speaking countries.

suspected sorcerer and eventually the sorcerer might relent and accompany the brother to wipe his curative sweat upon the victim's body.

Another old sorcery practice is to isolate your victim's footprint on a path and thrust a spear into it, then put the spear in the 'morata' of your house, above the hearth to make it hot. The victim will first have a pain in the legs that becomes more diffused, then will continuously lose weight and die. The antidote is the same, with the addition that the offending spear must be thrown into a brook or pond. A sorcery technique some men learned as indentured laborers was to place a small personal item of a victim on the fan or fan belt of an automobile or airplane. When the motor starts the victim will become sick and die before the night is over. There is no antidote for this.

One need not be labeled a sorcerer to do sorcery; anyone can. All that is needed is knowledge of the spell and/or to think the damaging thought. Witchcraft, as defined by a committee of the Royal Anthropological Institute of Great Britain and Ireland, is very different, however, as discussed by Seligman: "*Witchcraft is distinguished from sorcery in that it is generally believed to be a power, more for evil than for good, lodged in an individual himself or herself (the witch)*. It may be inborn, hereditary or acquired by undergoing special rites" (B. Seligman 1954: 189).[4]

Thus, once initiated, Lujere *nakwolu*, in anthropological analytical terms, are witches—the only ones in Lujereland. "Witch beliefs," as Monika Wilson has written about Africa, are "the standardized nightmare of a group" (1951: 313) and 'sanguma' was the Lujere's number one nightmare. Writing about 'sanguma,' however, presents epistemological problems for the ethnographer who, as an experientially oriented scientist, is challenged to write about actions in X society that appear to be miraculous and empirically impossible, while the members of X society accept the same actions as real and truthful. In other words, the referenced actions do not contest the sense of the real and plausible for the locals as they do

---

4. Glick's understanding of sorcery and witchcraft is similar:

    "A sorcerer's capacity to harm . . . depends on his ability to control powers *extrinsic* to himself: whereas a witch, who can inflict sickness or death on others simply by staring at them or willing evil on them, possesses powers—inherited or acquired—as an *intrinsic* part of his or her person (1972: 1080; my emphasis).
    Seemingly diametrically opposed to this is Kapferer's statement, "Sorcery is the work of specialists, whereas witchcraft may be practiced by anyone and everyone" (1997: 6). Some anthropologists, following Evans-Pritchard's (1937) influential description of Zande witchcraft beliefs restrict the term "witch" to someone who is *innately and involuntarily* possessed of evil and mysterious powers. In reviews of Evans-Pritchard's work, Middleton and Winter (1963) suggest it is a witch's possession of evil supernatural powers, not how they were acquired, that is the essential characteristic of a witch. This is the usage I have followed. A cogent example of the referential diversity regarding witchcraft is made by Aletta Biersack (2017) in her afterward to an edited volume on Pentecostalism and witchcraft in Melanesia (Rio, MacCarthy, and Blanes 2017), where she notes "the distinction frequently drawn between sorcery, which involves *conscious* acts of malevolence, and witchcraft, which bears on *unconscious* attempts to harm" (my emphases). However, she then records that the editors of that volume "adopt the term witchcraft to mean acts of occult malevolence, conscious or not" (2017: 294). For a detailed discussion of sorcery and witchcraft with multiple examples, see Stephen (1987) and Mitchell (1989).

for the ethnographer. Mead, in an early comment on *vada*, was well aware of this problem: "The whole nature of the practice [*vada*] is such that it is very difficult for the field-worker to distinguish between phantasy and myth, on the one hand, and the actual practice resulting in the death of specific persons on the other" (1938: 174). One solution, and the usual one, is for the ethnographer to describe the event from the local perspective, being careful not to let one's own disbelief skew the account. Adam Ashforth, who has written perceptively on witchcraft in South Africa and Soweto specifically, lays out the challenge:

> Perhaps the most difficult challenge I have faced in dealing with issues of spiritual insecurity has arisen from the necessity of taking seriously (and by this, I mean treating as literal statements) propositions about witchcraft that seem evidently absurd and nonsensical without thereby denigrating the people who utter them as idiotic or stupid. . . . Tolerant secular humanists, such as myself, find it extremely difficult to accept that otherwise reasonable people really believe as literally true impossibilities such as propositions about virgin birth, spaceships behind the Hale-Bopp comet, or healers living seven years under the water of a lake. . . . But unless we make the imaginative leap to treat propositions about invisible forces seriously, the social and political dynamics of vast portions of humanity will remain incomprehensible. (Ashforth 2005: xiv)

Nils Burbandt, in his book *The Empty Seashell: Witchcraft and Doubt on an Indonesian Island*, takes exception with the approach to witchcraft beliefs exemplified by Evans-Pritchard, who accepts witchcraft as "explanation." Fatefully, contends Burbandt, "When witchcraft becomes belief and meaning, doubt is sidelined" (2014: 7). While Burbandt is undoubtedly correct that there are societies with witchcraft, as the one he studied, where some challenge the belief in it, the Lujere are not one of them. Their beliefs in 'sanguma' were as solidly grounded and unchallenged as their beliefs about sago and pigs. For them, 'sanguma' does explain sickness and death. Yes, there might be debate and doubt regarding which 'sanguma' witch killed a neighbor but rarely regarding the cause of death, as most adults are thought to be killed by a 'sanguma' attack.

In my reading of many anthropological accounts of 'sanguma,' I was often aware of the tension between the writer accepting that the 'sanguma' witch was not a phantom spirit but a living and breathing human being, yet preposterous and unbelievable events were ascribed to him. How could a real person kill another person then restore him or her to life? How could a real person remove another person's muscle tissue or organs without scarring? Or even more mind-boggling to me, how could a Lujere witch himself believe that he actually did such things? Remember the young Tolai policeman, William, at the Yellow River Base Camp who told me that 'sanguma' men weren't like Jesus and could cut up people, then seal them back together like nothing had happened? Well, if you *believe* that 'sanguma' men can do that, from your point of view, they can! Just as in my society many evangelical Christians believe that Jesus literally fed a crowd of five thousand from five loaves and two fishes and raised a very dead Lazarus back to life, not to mention that he himself rose from the dead. They would agree that these were miraculous events, but insist on their actual occurrence. I will return to the paradoxical phenomenological dilemma inherent in 'sanguma' in chapter 17.

The phenomenon I have identified as 'sanguma' is, according to informants, performed by a human being and not by the likes of a spirit, ghost, or forest demon. While varying in detail, the usual features of this magical murder are: (1) one or more 'sanguma' witches attack the lone victim and render him or her unconscious; (2) the skin is cut and bodily properties removed; (3) the incisions are closed without scarring; (4) the victim is returned to consciousness without memory of the event; and (5) is sent home to a doomed death, typically in a predetermined number of days. There is no counter magic against 'sanguma'; death is inevitable. The only steps that are not indisputably magical are one and two. It is this unusual mixture of physical *and* magical brutality that has influenced some, such as Glick (1972: 1029), to call it "assault sorcery," and that made it paradoxical to a critical thinker. The above complex of descriptive behaviors is what I am concerned with in the following section, irrespective of what it is called locally. The Tok Pisin word 'sanguma' references this way of magical killing; the fact that a *Lujere* 'sanguma' witch is *also* a curer is irrelevant, as some 'sanguma' men in other societies are not.

Geocultural Distribution of 'Sanguma'

The thrust of this chapter is to indicate the geocultural distribution of 'sanguma' as a cultural belief system, starting with the earliest accounts I could find in the literature. This is not an exhaustive catalogue of where 'sanguma' occurs but is intended to show the extensiveness of its distribution cross-culturally, primarily in Oceania, and how researchers have written about it. The term "description" used in the headings means that the researcher has given a general description of 'sanguma'; the term "account" means that the writer has given an informant's first-hand account of a 'sanguma' incident. Most of the examples of 'sanguma' are from the colonial era; the single example from the twenty-first century is to document that 'sanguma'—albeit redefined—is still perceived as a menace, further elaborated in the next chapter. In these ethnographic examples, what the perpetrator of the deadly deed is called—witch, sorcerer, wizard, or a local name—is irrelevant; it is the 'sanguma' features of the magical ritual murder outlined above that are analytically significant. The geocultural data will be presented in the following sequence: Papua New Guinea, Indonesia, and Australia.

Note: Readers should be forewarned that much of the content in 'sanguma' accounts is extremely disturbing; those who are sensitive to descriptions of violence and assaults may do well to avoid reading these accounts.

Ethnographic Descriptions of 'Sanguma' in Papua New Guinea

The first descriptions by Codrington and Seligman

The British Anglican missionary R. H. Codrington, pioneering ethnographer of the Melanesian islands east of New Guinea, was the first to describe in his 1891 (1969) book, *The Melanesians: Studies in their Anthropology and Folk-lore*, a form of magical murder similar to 'sanguma' as the Lujere understood it.[5] He mentions it by different words

---

5. Codrington, son of an Anglican priest, schooled at Oxford, ordained in 1857, an immigrant to New Zealand, joined the Melanesian mission in 1866, and worked as a missionary mostly in the Solomon and Banks Islands and on Norfolk Island in mission schools until 1877.

in his sketchy descriptions for the Solomon Islands, naming it *vele* for Florida and Savo, and *hele* for Guadalcanal and Malanta. He gives a more focused account from the nearby New Hebrides Islands where it is called *gagaleve*:

> At Lepers' [Aoba] Island, in the New Hebrides [today Vanuatu], . . . The wizard overcomes his victim with his charms, so that the man cannot distinctly see him or defend himself; then he shoots him with a little bow and arrow made of some charmed material, and strikes him with the arrow. *The man does not know what is done to him, but he goes home, falls ill, and dies; he can remember nothing to tell his friends*, but they see the wound in his head where he was struck, and in his side where he was shot, and know what has happened. (Codrington 1969: 207; my italics)

All that is missing for an apt description of Sepik 'sanguma' is cutting into the victim's flesh to remove some aspect of the body and closing the incisions without a scar.

The other pioneering ethnographic survey work on New Guinea was by C. G. Seligman. Trained as a physician, he volunteered for the famous Cambridge Anthropological Expedition to Torres Straits in 1898 led by A. C. Haddon, and became enamored with anthropology. He returned to New Guinea in 1904 with the Daniels Ethnological Expedition to New Guinea and in 1910 published his classic book, *The Melanesians of British New Guinea*. His main informant for the Koita in the Port Moresby area was Ahuia Ao, the hereditary chief of his group and literate in English. Ahuia gave the following account of one method of killing people by magic, the sorcerers practicing this method being called *vada*, though they were clearly not spirits or other nonhumans:

> One or more (often two or three) men who were sorcerers would follow their intended victim to his garden, or into the bush. There he would be speared and clubbed, and when dead cut to pieces. One end of a length of rope is then looped round the dead man's hand or knee, while the opposite end is steeped in certain "medicine" (*gorto*). This 'go along rope make man get up,' [badly rendered Tok Pisin] i.e., the virtue in the medicine passing along the rope to the dead man would restore him to life. . . . The dead man on his revival is dazed, 'he mad,' and knows not where he is, or what has befallen him. He is told that he will die shortly; he does not subsequently remember this, but manages to return to his village [obviously reassembled], where his friends know what has happened to him by reason of his feeble, silly condition, though the victim himself does not know, and can give no account of what has occurred. (Seligman 1910: 170–171)

Seligman doesn't affirm that the victim dies, but we can assume that he does. Interestingly, Sir Hubert Murray (1912: 216), who was British New Guinea's first Lieutenant Governor from 1908 until his death in 1940, also published a brief description of

---

Although not a trained linguist, in 1885 Oxford University Press published his *The Melanesian Languages*. In 1888, at fifty-eight years old, he returned to England where in 1891 he published his pioneering ethnography, *The Melanesians*, quoted here. Ernest Beaglehole (1968), in a précis of his biography, notes that "Codrington's erudition is both powerful and impressive. . . . The master of Melanesian ethnography died suddenly—old in years [92], wise in theology, honored in scholarship—on September 11, 1922."

'sanguma' with the term *vada* for the Koiari people just interior of Port Moresby.[6] *Vada* quickly became the first term used by different researchers to identify this form of magical murder (that I gloss as 'sanguma') and was used by Patterson (1974–75: 142–43) in her seminal study that describes in detail one of the three types of "sorcery techniques" used in Melanesia. What follows are field workers' examples of 'sanguma' arranged by geographic area, first Papua New Guinea, then Indonesia and Australia.

'Sanguma' in the eastern islands

Hogbin's Guadalcanal description

In 1933, the Australian anthropologist Ian Hogbin (1937) visited the hill people of northeastern Guadalcanal. He spent ten days in an inland hill village and learned about another more complicated form of 'sanguma' sorcery called *vele*:

> *Vele* differs from *piro* [sorcery] in that it is always fatal. . . . The victim looks in the direction from which the sound came, and as soon as the sorcerer catches his eye, he begins to wave the charm in front of his face. The man's head begins to swim at once, and in a few moments he falls to the ground unconscious. The sorcerer then takes the bone of a flying fox[7] and, bending over him, makes a small incision at the tips of all his fingers and toes. Next he recites a spell which causes a bird to fly down from a tree nearby and perch on his shoulder. He puts a portion of the blood from each wound in its beak and then rubs the man's skin with a smooth shell, reciting a spell as he does so with the result that all the holes close up at once, leaving no trace. All is now ready for the awakening of the victim. His eyelids flutter, and soon it sits up. He always has an unpleasant taste in his mouth, and his nose is filled with an abominable stench. This makes him spit, and as soon as he does, he forgets everything that has occurred.
>
> He returns home as if nothing had happened, and for a few days continues in perfect health until one morning he hears the sorcerer calling him. He goes to meet him, suspecting nothing, and receives from him a small package, the contents of which he eats. This is the real *vele* poison. At once he begins to feel ill, and within a few days he is dead. (79–80)

What with the waved charm, blood-eating bird, bad smells, spitting to forget, and actual poisin, this was one of the most unusual magical murders I found in the literature. Consequently, I wasn't surprised to read that when Hogbin returned to the coast from

---

6. Murray, a thoughtful colonial administrator, still took a typically jaundiced view of native culture. He wrote, "I must confess that, to me, many of these customs seem unutterably foolish, just as even the best of native art appears to me crude and entirely lacking in inspiration; but probably if I were less ignorant I should be more appreciative" (Hides 1936: xiii). As this book is primarily oriented to the section of New Guinea that became German New Guinea, the history of British New Guinea has been slighted. For an authoritative but short history see Legge (1971).
7. This is a large fruit bat that, as Coiffier (2020) explains, is an important icon in New Guinea art, especially that of the Sepik region, and is often intimately related to food, human sexuality and procreation.

the village, he "was able to investigate the subject of sorcery thoroughly and came to the conclusion that, despite native beliefs, it was never carried out (Hogbin 1937: 80).

Ludvigson's Espiritu Santo Island description

In 1974–76, anthropologist Tomas Ludvigson spent seventeen months with the Kiai-speaking people of the upper Ari valley in central Espiritu Santo, Vanuatu, gathering data for his Auckland University doctorate. In this unusual version the victim is not physically attacked by a real person but by his spirit and spirit helpers.

> *Patua* is a form of assault sorcery. The sorcerer has two little spirit children (patua), invisible to others, who come to him when he is asleep. The *patua* want liver and entrails to eat, and will go hunting with their master. Together with his spirit they enter a house where someone is asleep and cut open his stomach. After the *patua* have eaten the victim's insides, they stuff the cavity with leaves and seal up the wound so that it does not show. In the morning there is no trace of the operation, but the victim will be dead within a day. (1985: 57)

In almost every case of death, *patua* was thought to be the cause. The sorcerer also can assume the shapes of animals and, if he is killed when in his animal appearance, he will be dead within a day.[8]

Fortune's Dobu account

For the first ethnographically authenticated "eyewitness" description of 'sanguma,' or *vada* as it was then characterized in the anthropological literature, we must jump back to the early 1930s and Reo Fortune's New Guinea field work from before he was married to Margaret Mead. They had met on shipboard in 1926 after her first fieldwork in Samoa on her return home to her husband Luther Cressman, and Fortune was en route from his native New Zealand to England for a two-year graduate fellowship in psychology at Cambridge.[9] As Mead remembers the voyage, "we were falling in love" (Mead 1972: 161). At Cambridge, Fortune was uninspired by his psychology professors and gravitated towards anthropology and Professor A. C. Haddon, with thoughts of fieldwork in New Guinea. "He had decided to leave Cambridge and hoped to get an anthropological grant through A. R. Radcliffe-Brown, who was developing a lively research center at the University of Sydney in Australia" (Mead 1972: 164). He succeeded, and in 1927–28 Fortune spent six months on tiny Tawara and Dobu Islands in the D'Entrecasteaux Islands, north

---

8. Knut Rio (2002: 141) also describes a 'sanguma' magical murder called *abio* for Vanuatu's Ambrym Island.
9. Fortune (1927) published in England his book *The Mind in Sleep* that examines personal ambivalence via dreams that contradict one's waking opinions. See Lohmann's (2009) insightful article on Fortune's dream study. In 1928 he married Margaret Mead followed by their 1930's fieldwork together in the Sepik region of New Guinea. For more on their relationship, see Dobrin and Bashkow (2010).

of New Guinea's northeastern tip, followed in 1932 with the publication of his classic *Sorcerers of Dobu*, where he gives the first full description of a 'sanguma' murder.

Once Malinowski had published his celebrated first book (1922) on his extended stay with the Trobriand Islanders, the peripatetic survey work in which Codrington and Seligman excelled was largely abandoned. Fortune lived in a village and stridently avoided contact with all Europeans, especially missionaries and government officials. One night, when Fortune and his most reliable and trustworthy informant Christopher (Fortune's pseudonym) were alone in his hut conversing in Dobu,

> Christopher let fall a hint of a piece of work in the black art quite accidentally. I followed it up and with some pressure got it out of him. He began with reluctance, but soon his eyes were half starting from his head and he was rolling and writhing on the floor of my hut in active description of a thing too vigorous for words to do justice to—obviously re-living the scene he described with a thoroughly ugly intensity. (Fortune 1932: 161)

The incident begins with a man insulting Christopher's wife's mother's brother, a noted sorcerer who in Fortune's story is called Y. In seeking revenge for the insult, Y, on the basis of his affinal kinship tie to Christopher, persuaded him to accompany him as his assistant and lookout.

> The intended victim, all unknowing, went alone to his garden in the early morning. Y and Christopher set out. . . . The two performed the *logau*, a charm which is believed to make the man who utters it invisible. Christopher circled three times round the foot of a convenient coco-nut palm while he did the *logau*. Y and Christopher could see each other, being both charmed together. Others could not see them. Nevertheless, Christopher climbed the palm to keep watch against possible intruders. From this height he also directed the movements of Y by signs towards the unconscious solitary gardener.
>
> Y moved in concealment, charming with spells towards the gardener and charming his sorcerer's lime spatula. Then with the gardener facing him, and nearby where he crouched concealed, he burst forth with the sorcerer's screaming shout. Christopher saw the gardener fall to the ground and lie writhing convulsively under the sorcerer's attentions. (Christopher had a painful filarial swelling in his groin approaching bursting point—but here he hurled himself down on the floor of my hut and writhed, groaning horribly—re-living the scene in his excitement.)
>
> The sorcerer feinted to rap his victim gently over the body with his lime spatula. The body lay still. He cut open the body with the charmed spatula, removed entrails, heart, and lungs, and tapped the body again with the spatula, restoring its appearance to apparent wholeness (here my informant speaks from what he apparently believes his own eyes saw in the cleared garden space below). The sorcerer's attentions here left the body of the victim, and transferred to charming the lime spatula anew. The body rose. Y said, "You name me." The body mumbled incoherently and received a feint at a gentle rap on the temples from the spatula. Again, "You name me," aggressively. Again an incoherent mumble, and another feinted rap. So a third time. Y said, "You go." The man went to the village and arrived raving, leaving his personal goods and tools in the garden. His children went to bring them. The man lay down writhing, groaning, and

calling on his abstracted vital parts by name—by this time it was mid-day. So he lay that day and night. Next day the sun climbed to its zenith and he lay dead. (Fortune 1932: 162–63)

Fascinated by Christopher's account, Fortune adds, "So firm was his [Christopher's] belief that he used the language of an eye witness of the removal of the entrails, heart, and lungs of the victim." As a commentary on the sorcerer and victim's behavior he notes, "It is clear the sorcerer's procedure is hypnotic in nature, the fear apparently being paralysing [to the victim]" (1932: 163). [10] Then Fortune writes,

> I believe that Christopher's account of his adventure . . . was no fabrication. He had no need to implicate himself so closely if he was spinning a tale. I have never seen a human being so possessed with emotion as my informant, yet retaining his sanity. He appeared to see everything that he described once again, and I felt toward him much as I did towards a man that ran amuck with a spear in my village and raved, threatening to cut my throat and eat me, stuffing rubbish into his mouth to illustrate his intention, after I got him disarmed and was proceeding to truss him up. My informant was equally ugly in manner, and more powerfully so in that he was not in any pathological state. He was, however, so strongly excited that I would be inclined to connect running amuck . . . with the state of mind engendered by witchcraft and sorcery. (Fortune 1932: 163)

In the Dobu language that's spoken on both Tawara and Dobu islands, 'sanguma' is called *mawari* because the sorcerer shouts, "*Mawari!*" as he attacks his terrorized victim. Fortune, however, titles his analytically provocative eleven-page Appendix II "*Vada*," which I will later discuss in relationship to the territories' laws against sorcery and witchcraft.

'Sanguma' in the Sepik region

Bateson's Iatmul account

Four years after Fortune published his informant's allegedly eyewitness 'sanguma' account, Gregory Bateson published one too, but it is less emotional than Christopher's narrative. Bateson's Iatmul informant was Tshava of Kankanamun village whose mother, Nyakala, had died of sorcery. Her brother was Malikindjin, a renowned sorcerer who Bateson said was the greatest man in Kankanamun village. Intensely hated by some and feared by all for his sorcery, Bateson admired him as "an astonishingly vivid dramatic orator" (1936: 164–65). Regarding Nyakala, Tshava told Bateson in some detail about the incident where he and his uncle Malikindjin brutally avenged her death:

---

10. Patterson (1974–75: 143) takes exception to the assumption that the victim is hypnotized, as Wright (1959: 209) claims, since there was no custom of hypnosis among Fortune's islanders.

> When Malikindjin was mourning for Nyakala he came to me and said to me, "We will go down to such and such a piece of bush." We went there and found a man named Tamwia. Malikindjin said, "Now we are going to take vengeance for your mother on this man." He told me to hide myself and he used magic to make Tamwia unable to see him. Tamwia was "in the dark" and Malikindjin made him "cold." He did not cry out. Malikindjin came straight up to him and broke his neck and head with an adze. He killed him. He cut off his head and put in its place a head made of *nggelakavwi* (a tuberous plant, *Mymecodia* sp.). He threw the real head away.
>
> We each took an arm and hid the body in the elephant grass. Malikindjin said, "Don't talk about this, but there is no fear of trouble. We are only taking vengeance." Then I went away to work on Malikindjin's garden, and came back to find the man Tamwia lying sick and groaning. Malikindjin woke him up and said, "Are you asleep?" and Tamwia said, "Yes." Malikindjin said, "What have I been doing to you?" and Tamwia said, "I was asleep and you woke me up." Malikindjin said, "Right. That is the way to talk. Now go away."
>
> Malikindjin also told him, "You cannot cry out with sickness soon. You will stay awhile first," and he gave him a date—five days thence. "You cannot mention me. It is not good for you to live in Kankanamun. You had better die." . . . The poor man, Tamwia, soon died. (Bateson 1936: 59–60)

In a footnote, Bateson alludes to the similarity of Fortune's account, noting that both of their informants participated as lookouts and that "the magic was of the type called 'vada.' In it the victim is first killed and then brought back to life only to die later" (Bateson 1936: 59, n. 2). Bateson also observed that in Fortune's account, it was the heart that was removed instead of the head. He was impressed that "Dr. Fortune's informant was moved almost to hysteria in the narration of the story, whereas my informant described the events in as cool and as detached a manner as he would have described a magical procedure for the improvement of yams" (1936: 59, n. 2).

Roscoe's Yangoru Boiken description

In Roscoe's account, alien young married men from eastern Boiken who are secretly initiated in occult rites to carry out homicidal magical attacks are called *maiyire*:

> In choosing a victim, *maiyire* are said to make no distinction by age, sex, or skin color, picking on anyone who happens to be alone. . . . They immobilize their hapless prey by pointing at them or breathing on them with their magically potent breath. . . . The *maiyire* then split open the body to feast on the heart or smash the arm and leg bones, before magically resealing the flesh to mask the destruction. . . . The victim is revived and a time and date appointed in the near future for their death. . . . The victim is then set free and returns home remembering nothing of the attack. (Roscoe 1986: 182)[11]

---

11. Roscoe's paper is of special interest as it reports a much more complex set of beliefs and behaviors related to *maiyire* than in most other 'sanguma' descriptions including, for example, seasonality of the attack, cannibalism, giving an emetic to a collapsed victim, trance-like states, and *maiyire* as a culture-bound syndrome.

Gesch's Yamuk village (Middle Sepik) description

This is a contemporary account of 'sanguma' in the Middle Sepik. Yamuk (Yamok) is an Ndu language village located inland, directly east of the Sepik River village of Pagui. Patrick F. Gesch, a Divine Word Mission priest who spent many years in the Sepik region and received his doctorate at University of Sydney with a thesis (1985) on a movement in the Sepik similar to a cargo cult, describes 'sanguma' as follows:

> The *sanguma* knock the victim out, generally expressed as "killing" him, and then operate on him by removing some of his internal organs, parts of his major muscles, his penis or other meat. This meat will be kept and dried as a powerful agent of *sanguma* work. When the *sanguma* next wants to work, he will scrape this piece of meat with his teeth or breathe his spells over it. The *sanguma* will revive the man they have "killed," and ask him if he recognizes them. If he does recognize them and what they did, he will be knocked out again and revived until finally he does not know the *sanguma* who have terminated his life. The victim is then sent away with knowledge of the day and the circumstances under which he will finally die, but with no recognition of the *sanguma* men who have killed him. (Gesch 2015: 118)

Kulick's Gapun and Juillerat's Yafar descriptions

Bateson's early account of 'sanguma' was for the Iatmul in the Middle Sepik. Here, from more recent fieldworkers, are two more descriptions at opposite ends of the Sepik River. In 1986–87, Don Kulick worked in Gapun village between the mouths of the Sepik and Ramu Rivers and gives a succinct description of 'sanguma' as it was presented to him. He attests that the Ramu River villages

> are feared for their powerful sorcery and *sangguma* men (aŋgwar). These *sangguma* men are considered to be especially horrific because of the way they kill their victims. First they ambush and mesmerize them. Then they rip out the victims' entrails with their fingers, which are long and clawed. The entrails are replaced with leaves and grass, and the still-dazed victim is sewn up and sent back to his or her village. Before the victim goes, the *sangguma* men whisper in his ear the exact day and time when he will die. And, at the appointed time, he dies. (Kulick 1992: 31)

Kulick, who was focusing his fieldwork on language shift and not sorcery, makes only one other allusion to 'sanguma,' regarding its use as a frightening threat to keep young children within or near their home, the equivalent to my childhood's "boogeyman." I heard the same threat while living with the Lujere, but using the local term. This scare technique to control a child's behavior provokes a fright internalized at a tender age and helps to account for the overwhelming dread of *vada, gagaleve, numoin*—or whatever it is locally called—that is carried into adulthood and old age with such tenacity by so many New Guineans.

The French anthropologist Bernard Juillerat found a variant form of 'sanguma' while working in 1970–71 among the Yafar in the Border Mountains next to Indonesia's Papua Province:

> The sorcerer or sorcerers surprise their victim, usually in a lonely spot (clearing, forest) where he may be with his family. The *sysiri* [sorcerer] holds a piece of *nefôkêg* [magic plant] clenched in his teeth, having tied some of its leaves to his bow and arrow. This makes the sorcerer and his weapons invisible to any witnesses who may be with the victim, but not to the latter, who is nevertheless incapable of crying out, paralysed by both the action of the [magic plant] and by fear. The oncoming arrow will therefore be visible to him, but will quickly vanish into his body without leaving a wound and without causing immediate death or incapacity: the wounded person will not dare say a word about what has happened for fear of retaliation and will go back home—not without having lost consciousness for a time—and die a few weeks later of illness. As he is about to die—and only at that moment—the victim may reveal that he has been killed by an *aysiri* and identify the sorcerer if he has recognized him. (Juillerat 1996: 467)

Scorza's Tumentonik village (Torricelli Mountains) description

David and Jackie Scorza lived in Tumantonik for fifteen years and translated the New Testament into the Au language. The following description is from a letter he wrote to me on February 28, 1974:

> There are at least one or two ['sanguma' men] left, but the real feared ones were almost all gone when we got here, and the last two of those died about 1970. . . . We have what is called *Hiwak* (sanguma) who never disclose if they are this type or not. . . . The *Hiwak* are usually in numbers of four or more, and they grab the victim, hold him down and jam something into his mouth so he can't scream out, then they squeeze the testicles and rub them between their hands til he loses consciousness. They stick him with the thorns, then when he regains his senses, they make him dance. If he dances well, they club him until he is senseless, then they send him back to his village [to die]. You only do this to someone who isn't related.

Morren's Telefolmin description

The Miyanmin at the headwaters of the Sepik River apparently had no 'sanguma' men but their neighbors, the Telefolmin, did. George Morren, who worked with the Miyanmin in the late 1960s and again in 1980–81, writes,

> The Miyanmin identify two varieties of lethal sorcery, one a Telefolmin patent, the other practiced among the Miyanmin themselves. The Telefolmin type, which the Miyanmin call *usem*, is widely reported in New Guinea and Australia and resembles felonious assault. Typically, the male or female victim is ambushed alone in some isolated bush location, wrestled or beaten to the ground, and held while bamboo or (now) steel needles are driven into the body. The victim returns home with no memory of the attack, sickens, and dies. . . . an adult death in a southern Miyanmin parish sets off a hysteria of phantom Telefolmin sightings, and numerous suspected sorcery attempts are brought to public notice. (Morren 1986: 211)

'Sanguma' in Papua (former British New Guinea)

Knauft's Gebusi (Western Province) description

The Gebusi, who were studied by Bruce Knauft and his wife Eileen Cantrell in the early 1980s, are a cultural and linguistic group of 450 persons living on the Strickland Plain east of the Strickland River. Knauft says that "*ogowili* is a variant of classic 'sanguma' or *vada* assault sorcery."

> An ogowili is a semi-invisible warrior form taken on by a real man. . . . Ogowilis, either singly or in groups, are said to stalk a victim in the forest until they find him or her alone. . . . When ogowilis find a person who has been careless or unwise enough to stray from his or her companions, the attack is swift. The victim is said to be shot with arrows or hit over the head until dead. The body is believed to be butchered by the ogowilis, with the flesh removed and the skin flayed and wrung out over leaves so that the blood does not leave telltale marks on the forest floor. . . . The attackers then replace the victim's skin, make him or her whole again, and give him or her amnesia so that the attack is forgotten. . . . The ogowilis return home with their bags full of human flesh to eat. Meanwhile, their victim goes weakly back to his or her own settlement and soon becomes very sick. When the ogowilis excrete the eaten meat of the victim, he or she dies. . . . ogowili afflictions cannot be diagnosed prior to death itself; a genuine attack is always swift and fatal. (Knauft 1985: 104)

Burton-Bradley and Julius' Motu village (Port Moresby) description

The psychiatrist B. G. Burton-Bradley and ethnologist Charles Julius describe an urban form of 'sanguma.' They do not, however, indicate that death is inevitable; apparently, they just assume that it is.

> In the Motu village of Tatana (Port Moresby), side pains . . . are attributed to a type of sorcerer known as *vada*. Such men are believed to work in groups of three. . . . One group renders the victim unconscious; the next group opens his body, removes some internal organ and replaces it with some other substance; the third group closes the wound and revives the man, making him forget what has happened. (Bradley and Julius 1965: 14)

Malinowski's Mailu description

Like Bateson and Fortune, Malinowski also found 'sanguma' on his first field trip in 1914–15 to tiny Mailu Island, off New Guinea's southeast coast:

> Sorcerers throughout the Massim are called *Bara'u*, and the same word is used in Mailu, while the Motu [Port Moresby area] use the reduplicated *Babara'u*. The magicians in these parts use such powerful methods as those of killing the victim first, opening up the body, removing, lacerating or charming the inside, then bringing the victim to life again, only that he may soon sicken and eventually die. (Malinowski 1922: 42)

Under the heading "Nature of the Dreaded Beings; the Babará'u,"[12] Malinowski gives early evidence of his later dedication to the ethnographic detail in his Trobriand books as he discusses multiple aspects of the Mailu form of magical murder, first noting that it was "the exact counterpart of the *Váda* of the Central District." While he clearly establishes that the islanders believed the *Babará'u* was a man, not a spirit, he also notes that "he smears himself all over with some magical herbs, and mutters some spells and becomes invisible." Adding that the *Babará'u* is invisible only from the front but remains visible from behind, this explains "why people see often mysterious shadows moving in the dark." More than some writers, Malinowski highlights discrepancies among his "informants' statements in respect to details" and provides examples. *Barbará'u* are present in all villages but travel away for their killings; going great distances, "They come like the wind, quickly and invisible," but there is no consensus among his informants as "to the exact method of these aerial flights" (1988 [1915]: 647 passim).

As is common for fieldworkers in New Guinea, information about the dark side of Mailu culture was initially withheld from Malinowski. His research base was a disused mission house where his cook-boy and some village lads also slept until the news spread that the house had ghosts. One night when Malinowski was listening to some Mailu men and his cook-boy was visiting in Motu, the conversation veered to the house's resident ghosts. Malinowski, "seeing that they took the matter very seriously and expressed views very valuable to the ethnologist," eventually entered the conversation. He "asserted emphatically that, as a white man, I was afraid only of ghosts, but I added that, not knowing the habits of the local evil powers, I would like to know what I had to fear and how I should best protect myself." His companions, aware of Malinowski's concern for his safety, began to explain and describe what, until then, he had no knowledge of. Ghosts, he was told, "are absolutely innocuous" and can neither talk nor make noise. But footsteps and noises had been heard in his house; to sleep alone as he did, and in the dark without a hurricane lamp, "was a plain invitation to the *Bará'u* to come and do his horrible work" (1988 [1915]: 273).[13]

---

12. Malinowski's 1915 study of the Mailu was reissued (Malinowski 1988) with light editing by Michael Young and a masterful introduction.
13. On Rossel Island at the eastern end of the Louisiade Archipelago off the eastern end of New Guinea, W. E. Armstrong gives an interesting account of a custom of ritual assault without magic done at night. Armstrong got the data from PO Bell who, in 1908, had conducted a patrol of about three weeks on Rossel.

> It depends on the strength of the person to be killed whether the party consists of one or more. They enter his house, and if four are in the party one will hold the lower limbs, another grasps the throat, another holds his hands over the person's mouth to prevent him calling out, and the other breaks two or three ribs with his hands. It appears the trachea or the gullet in most cases is injured, as the person complains of his throat afterwards. They do not attempt anything beyond this, apparently being quite satisfied the person must die, which of course must take place, the native himself realising it. Death occurs usually the next day, the man suffering great pain and unable to take any food. (Armstrong 1928: 222)

'Sanguma' in the north coastal region

St. Lehner's Markham-Ramu plain description

In an article translated from the German, Höltker refers to a Divine Word missionary by the name of St. Lehner, who wrote an article in a German journal about the Azera people on the Markham-Ramu Plain, where men called *garam opa* practice *Todeszauber* or death magic:

> The *garam opa* always sees to it to impede the person only when he is alone without any escort. After the first physical contact the person loses consciousness immediately, then the *garam opa* opens his body, deprives him of his liver and fills the gap with foliage which will immediately heal in such a way, that one cannot even see the slightest scar. The person wakes up, but has no recollection of the incident, walks into the village where he will die the next day or the day after. (Höltker 1942: 215)

Hogbin's Wogeo Island description

Wogeo is one of the Schouten Islands located off the coast of Wewak and where Ian Hogbin spent the whole of 1934 and again for a few weeks in 1948. He was the first and only European resident on the island during his stay. Assault sorcery on Wogeo is called *yabou* and according to Hogbin (1970: 14), was allegedly so common in the Sepik area "that the residents have coined a term in pidgin English for it, *sangguma*." His account includes the sorcerer and assistants finding a victim, then,

> the assistants at once take him (or her) from behind and blindfold him with a strip of barkcloth. The sorcerer thereupon emerges from the bushes and recites a spell that has the effect of rendering the person unconscious. He falls backwards on the ground with eyes rolled upwards beyond the lids; but he still breathes, and his heart continues beating. The sorcerer then removes the clothing from the prostrate body and places it on the ground behind. Next the assistants hammer the neck, shoulders, chest, back, and legs with a stone till these are black with bruises. They move to one side, and again the sorcerer takes over. He drives his needle into the person's left side under the ribs; or he may push it into the anus or urethra; and he may even remove some vital organ, such as a lung or kidney, and replace it with a stone, earth, or leaves. He also cuts the ligament under the tongue. Any blood he wipes away before rubbing the wounds with bespelled "medicines," an action that causes them to close up or disappear—not a single cut is visible, not a single bruise. Finally, standing behind the victim, he places other 'medicines' on the eyes and mouth and recites further spells to restore him to life and destroy all memory of what has taken place. Sorcerer and assistants then hide behind bushes. If the victim, however dizzy, goes straight to the pile of clothing and replaces the garments the sorcery is working—he will attend to the day's task as usual and probably make plans for the future. But if he is so ill as to be indifferent to his nakedness, this means that he is aware of having been bewitched and of the identity of the assailants. Then the whole process has to be repeated. . . . The victim completes his (or her) work, but that night begins to feel ill. . . . All too soon he dies. (Hogbin 1970: 149–50)

Hogbin, unlike some ethnographers, goes out of his way to point out the logical impossibility of such attacks being real.[14]

Koster's Banara (Bogia area) description

During much of the 1930s, Father G. J. Koster served at the missionary station of Banara on New Guinea's north coast, about eighteen miles east of Bogio and southeast of the volcanic island of Manam. Besides hearing reports about 'sanguma,' Father Koster also had occasion to examine a victim of 'sanguma' shortly after an assault, described in chapter 17 of this volume. Below he summarizes his understanding of 'sanguma'.

> The sangguma men unexpectedly attack an isolated native either in the forest, traveling, or in his gardens, or any place where he happens to be, as long as there are no witnesses nearby, and then maltreat him in such a way that death must occur within a couple of days. In order to make themselves unrecognizable the sangguma killers paint themselves all over with a black pigment. . . . the murderers know how to orchestrate their maltreatment in such a way as to allow the victim after the attack to reach of his own accord his closest friends and next of kin, or the nearest village after which he will die within several days. (Koster 1942: 218) [15]

Koster is vague regarding the nature of the "maltreatment," and thus downplays the magical elements related in other accounts. I believe this is because of an attack for which he has factual evidence. However, he does recount what one informant told him regarding physical abuse of a victim:

> One man named Pake, about forty years old (in 1936) and originating from Monumbo, told me a lot about sangguma. He also told me that at times the sangguma men would insert a long object into the victim's anus. In order to do so they would take a pointed dry stem of a coconut leaf, from which they removed the foliage, leaving only the tough stem. The stem was then inserted through the anus into the intestines, turned around, and taken out again. No need to say that the intestines suffered greatly. He told me that in these modern times iron wire is also used. After this gruesome maltreatment, they would try to make the victim regain consciousness, in case he fainted. If they do not succeed, the actual sangguma is considered a failure. People will then say that the victim was murdered. (Koster 1970: 149–50)

---

14. Hogbin's account of *yabou* is much more culturally nuanced than most, including data on how a sorcerer learns to kill this way and that it is the Headmen who are the alleged sorcerers, but not the one in your own village. But *yabou* men are only allegedly about magically killing; there is no concomitant magical curing role. Hogbin (1935a; 326–28) earlier gives a much simpler description of 'sanguma' for Wogeo.
15. Father Koster's 'sanguma' paper is translated from the Dutch. I am indebted to Dr. Risto Gobius who sent me a taped translation from New Guinea in 1973. Later my brother-in-law, John Slayton, who was living in the Netherlands, sent me a typescript translation by a Dutch friend.

'Sanguma' in the Highlands

Berndt's Jate (eastern Central Highlands) description

'Sanguma,' defined as a form of assault sorcery, does not appear to be as prevalent in New Guinea's Highlands as it does in its lowlands and the islands to the east. However, Ronald Berndt (1962) reports its presence in the Eastern Highlands where in the early 1950s he worked with the Jate and adjoining groups. He describes several cases of 'sanguma' (*tunakafia* in Jate) told to him but in none of them does he describe in detail the cutting into the body and the restoring of the flesh without scarring. However, he notes, "We are not dealing solely with magic but with a physical operation under the *guise* of magic," and footnotes the sentence with Seligman's and Fortune's accounts of *vada*, adding, "To account for this type of sorcery [including the Jate], I am postulating a form of hypnosis or suggestion used in conjunction with aggressive physical action" (1962: 224). Below is one of Berndt's cases concerning five 'sanguma' men from Ifusa village. (Note: this account may be especially disturbing for some readers.)

> It is said that, setting out for Keniju [village], they . . . found a young woman named Jogulgakiza at work. They dragged her into the long grass, threw her upon the ground, and tore off her skirts ready for *sangguma*. But as they looked at her, they changed their minds and instead copulated with her in turn. Then they told her to return the following day for the same purpose but not to tell anyone else or they would work *sangguma* on her. Next day she again came alone to the garden and was soon joined by the five Ifusa men, who proceeded to behave as before. This continued for several days until one of the men became impatient. "We are *sangguma* men," he told the others, "Do we not shoot with *tunakafiagaijona* (nails)? Or do we use only our penes for this sorcery? We must kill people! All you do is to copulate with this woman. But I shall kill her, alone." On the following morning he left without his companions and found her waiting. He took her into the grass, choked her into unconsciousness, and proceeded to carry out *sangguma*. The victim walked back to her house; as she was dying, she described what had happened but without revealing the men's identity. This was discovered only afterward. (Berndt 1962: 227–28)

Stewart and Strathern's Wiru and Hewa (Southern Highlands) descriptions

In the Southern Highlands province, Pamela Stewart and Andrew Strathern write that among the Wiru speakers in the Pangia area,

> The sorcerer waylays his victim, projecting an aura of heat which stops the victim in his or her tracks. Numbers of *maua* men may "hunt" victims together. If they find a woman in her garden, they call to her from the bush, she goes over, and they copulate with her repeatedly before killing her. . . . The sorcerer simply cuts open the victim's stomach, pulls out the kidneys, places one in the victim's mouth, stuffs the exposed insides with leaves, sews the skin up by magical touch, and sends the person home, telling him or her to cook the kidney and eat it. Where the relatives recognize the signs of maua, they will not even attempt medical treatment nor is there any Indigenous ritual care

available. The victim will simply die within the period stated by the sorcerer. (Stewart and Strathern 2010: 111)

Regarding the Hewa people also of the Southern Highlands province, Stewart and Strathern comment that "The Hewa witch (*pisai*) was said to cannibalize the viscera of the victim by opening the body, eating the organs, and closing the body again so that the attacked person died several weeks later" (Stewart and Strathern 2004: 126).

Ethnographic Descriptions of 'Sanguma' in Indonesia

'Sanguma' in North Maluku province

'Sanguma,' called *suangi* (*suanggi, suwangi, swangi*) in eastern Indonesia, is the comparable Malay term that, according to anthropologist Nils Bubandt (2014: 26), is known and feared along an arc that stretches from the islands of Sumba, Flores, Roti, and Timor, across North Sulawesi, Maluku, and North Maluku provinces, east to the Bird's Head region of West Papua province, and into the borderlands between Papua province and Papua New Guinea. When I discovered that 'sanguma' was in eastern Indonesia, I wondered if it were also in western Indonesia and the southern Philippines. I made a cursory search but did not find it in those areas.

Bubandt's Halmahera Island description

Nils Bubandt's recent book (2014) about witchcraft and doubt centers on the Buli village area on the east coast of Halmahera in the northern Moluccas. In earlier days it was under the rule of the Sultan of Tidore, then the Dutch, and today it is called North Maluku and is Indonesia's poorest province. Witches are a community scourge; they are human and anyone might be one and not even know it—so witch fear, like 'sanguma' fear, is a pervasive state. One lives among witches but never knows exactly who they are.[16] Villagers say that they are greedy, stingy, and arrogant.[17] What follows is Bubandt's description of a *gua* (witch) attack that in most respects is similar to classical 'sanguma'. (Note: readers should be aware that this account contains disturbing sexual violence.)

> The *gua* approaches its victim stealthily, and almost always from behind. It then knocks the victim unconscious by kicking or punching him—evicting the person's *gurumin* (the human shadow-cum-awareness). Victims are also said to lose their "inside"—their emotions and feelings—at the mere sight of the *gua*. With both his protective shadow and his 'inside" (*ulór*) gone, the victim is helpless and essentially lifeless in the hands of the witch. The *gua* then proceeds to open the victim's abdomen to get at his liver (*yatai*). Squatting on top of the inert body, either in its human shape or in the shape of one of its animal familiars (a dog, certain birds, a pig, or an insect), the gua feasts on the raw and bloody liver before molesting the body, sexually as well as physically.

---

16. While this is true for some societies, among the Lujere the 'sanguma' witches are known to all.
17. This view is very reminiscent of that of the Kaguru of central Tanzania, as reported by Beidelman (1986: 156): "Witches epitomize selfishness, greed, and contempt for others."

After extracting the liver, it seals the wound with water, or by licking it with its long tongue. The wound closes completely and becomes invisible to the human eye. The *gua* may also spear its victim with whatever is at hand—a piece of wood, a sago branch, or a spear brought along for that purpose—and such a wound will later cause a piercing pain (know as *lebet*). In its frenzy, it may even beat the victim, causing black-and-blue marks where the punches have fallen, choke it, or try to drown it in a pool of water, which will result in breathing problems during the subsequent illness. A frequent *gua* hallmark is sexual molestation directed at the victim's genitals (*nyawa*). A male *gua* will often rape a female victim and sometimes does so very violently, which is why one frequent sign of a *gua* attack is said to be the laceration of the rectovaginal septum. The genitals of male victims are also often beaten and molested. Swollen and painful testicles are therefore also a frequent symptom of a *gua* attack. (Bubandt 2014: 120)

Although believed to be humans, *guas* are said to be faceless or unrecognizable.[18] "Victims of witchcraft attacks report that the face of the witch was 'clouded' (*cocomá*) or 'dark' (*dororam*)" (Bubandt 2014: 121). It is interesting, however, that this fear of the attacking witch, hungry for flesh, is thematic in Indonesia while absent or negligible in the culture areas of Micronesia and Polynesia to the north and east of Melanesia and Australia. Here is Bubandt's brief summary of a local account of a nine-year-old girl's death. (Note: the violence described is especially graphic and disturbing.)

Witchcraft is nothing if not horrible; and a large part of its horror is visceral. Hilda's death after a female *gua* [witch] had assaulted her, eaten her liver, and forced a piece of firewood through her body from her private parts to her mouth—preventing her from urinating and from speaking during the last day of her life—was a total destruction of Hilda's embodied being. (Bubandt 2014: 119)

'Sanguma' in West Papua province

Held's Waropen description

Garrit Jan Held took his PhD at Leiden under Josselin de Jong and soon after went to Dutch New Guinea with his wife, never to return. He was initially sponsored by the Netherlands Bible Society at Amsterdam and settled among the Waropen on Geelvink Bay to study their language and culture. Unlike the Sepik missionaries whom the Japanese killed, the Helds, as well as his manuscript for *The Papuas of Waropen* completed in 1942, all survived the Japanese occupation; the book was published posthumously two

---

18. Sulawesi, the wonderfully strange shaped island with four wandering peninsulas, lies just west of the Moluccas and is where Jane Atkinson found a 'sanguma' among the Wana that was a "demon," not a human, that was reminesent of a *s* witch's attack. Explaining a young man's death, she writes,

    The posthumous explanation was that a demon had attacked the youth in the forest, cut open his chest, and eaten his liver, then closed up the wound. The victim, not remembering what had transpired, lived on for a while. On the day of his death he went out birdhunting, returned to the house, and cooked his catch, but he did not live to eat it. (Atkinson 1989: 110–11)

years after his death in 1957. The interest for us is that the version of 'sanguma' he records is related to the sorcery beliefs of the Molluca Islands, or "Spice Islands," immediately west of New Guinea.

> The most dreaded form of evil magic is the "suangi" (*sema*) which is feared throughout the Moluccas. Here the *sema* are true specialists whose sole object is to kill others. It is said of them that they have an insatiable desire after human flesh. . . . They are able to approach their victim unobserved, quickly making a cut in his body and then proceeding to devour him inside. Then they touch the wound with their leaves (*sema-rana*), whereupon the wound is closed and becomes invisible. The victim is completely unconscious of these happenings and from then on, he is completely at the mercy of the *sema*, who compel him, for instance, to dance for them or to have sexual intercourse with them. In the long run the unfortunate person cannot continue to live, his body being devoured from inside.
>
> Often the *sema* tries to divert people's attention by seemingly reviving his victim, after having emptied him inside, and ordering him to drown after some time, or to fall out of a tree. This is the reason that even in these cases the Waropen do not think in the first place of a fatal accident, but rather try to establish which *sema* could have caused this death. Another result of this attitude is that the Waropen set little store by rendering first aid, as they argue that of course nobody can have an accident if he had not been first killed by the *sema*, being alive in appearance only when the accident occurred. So what sense would there be in treating somebody who is actually dead? (1957: 258–59)

'Sanguma' in Papua province

Wirz's Marind-Anim description

The notable Swiss anthropologist, collector, and photographer Paul Wirz provides an early description of 'sanguma' from his fieldwork between 1916 and 1922 among the Marind-Anim living in the southeast part of today's Indonesian Papua province bordering Papua New Guinea.[19] The Dutch anthropologist Jan Van Baal's (1966) single bulky volume on the Marind-Anim is a reformulation with other material from Wirz's two bulky volumes in German. He writes,

> Wirz's informants gave the following description of the act of *kambara* . . . Then, from behind, they hit him on the head with a club. He falls down, unconscious, his heart "being small," i.e. beating faintly. Presently, without damaging the skin, they cut his muscles and intestines. With the thorny tail of a sting-ray they tear shreds of flesh out his body. Throughout, his heart keeps beating faintly. When they have finished, they bring him to again by beating him with croton-twigs, by blowing in his ears and by calling *ku, ku, ku, ku!* to his heart so as to quicken its beat. Finally he wakes up. The *kambara-anim* have disappeared and without realizing what has happened to him he continues on his way. That very night he feels indisposed. He has a headache, develops

---

19. Also see related descriptions of 'sanguma' in Papua Province by Hans Nevermann (1941: 33) for the Je-nan people located on the international border above coastal Merauka and by J. W. Schoorl (1993: 62) for the Muyu people in the plains and hills of the Digul and Star Mountains.

a fever, cannot get any food down and before long he has a bout of diarrhea. He spends a restless night and the next day he is dead. (Van Baal 1966: 906)

Ethnographic Descriptions of 'Sanguma' in Australia

Benjamin R. Smith's (2016) article on "Sorcery and the Dividual in Australia" indicates the extent of the data available on 'sanguma' in the country's Aboriginal societies.

> Other forms of ['sanguma'/*vada*-type] sorcery recall those described by Keen and other Arnhem Land ethnographers (e.g., Reid 1982; Thomson 1961; Warner [1937] 1958). These attacks by shadowy, often semi-human figures . . . held to lurk in uninhabited areas or along deserted stretches of road, waiting to 'catch' those who are foolish enough to venture there alone. These malevolent figures feature in disturbing accounts of magical assaults in which the *wapa* hypnotizes his victim, operating on his or her body to remove blood, organs, and other substances, stitching the wounds and reviving the victim. Unable to tell others what has happened, victims are said to have collapsed and died several days afterwards as a result of such attacks (cf. McKnight 1982: 498; Taylor 1984: 242-3). (Smith 2016: 670–87)

'Sanguma' in South Australia

Spencer and Gillen's Arunta description

Those who know the Australian Aboriginal cultures will recognize the following account of Kurdaitcha magical murder among the Arunta tribe as a form of 'sanguma.' The description is in Baldwin Spencer and Frank Gillen's classic ethnography of the Central Australian tribes. In their account the murder is to avenge a death and is carried out by two men; one is the avenger or Kurdaitcha—referred to by some ethnologists as "featherfeet killers" (Tonkinson 1974; 80) —who must wear shoes formed of a thick pad of emu feathers matted together with human blood to disguise their tracks, and the other is a medicine man with magical powers. Both carry shields, spears, and Churingas; the last is believed to give them strength and courage plus make them invisible to their victim.

> Followed by the medicine man the Kurdaitcha takes the lead until the enemy is sighted. Then the medicine man falls into the rear while the Kurdaitcha stealthily creeps forward towards his quarry and suddenly rising up, spears him before he is aware of the presence of an enemy. Both the medicine man and Kurdaitcha have meanwhile put the sacred Churinga between their teeth and when they are thus armed the spear cannot fail to strike the victim. As soon as this is done the Kurdaitcha man goes away to some little distance from the fallen man and from which he cannot see the operations of the medicine man who now approaches and performs his share in the work. By aid of his magic powers and by means of the *Atnongara* stones he heals the victim. These *Atnongara* stones are small crystalline structures which every medicine man is supposed to be able to produce at will from his own body. . . . Into the spear wound he rubs a white greasy substance called *Ernia* which he obtains by pressure of the skin glands on the outside of the nostril. After all external traces of the wound have disappeared, he goes quietly away and, together with the Kurdaitcha man returns to his own

country. Having been touched by the *Atnongara* stones, the victim comes to life, but is completely ignorant of all that has taken place. He returns to camp and in a short time sickens and dies. (Spencer and Gillen 1968 [1899], 480–81)

'Sanguma' in Western Australia

Tokinson's Jigalong description

Fieldworkers among the aborigines throughout Australia have reported extensively on this Australian form of 'sanguma.' Robert Tonkinson, working among the Jigalong of Western Australia writes,

> Many deaths are attributed to the malicious and deadly activities of featherfeet ritual killers. . . . Featherfeet are said to be men, not spirits, who come from distant areas and lie in wait for their victims, whom they ambush, kill, revive magically, then send back to Camp. The victim is said to remember nothing of the attack and has no visible wounds, yet dies within days and is unable to name his attackers. (Tonkinson 1972: 79–80)

'Sanguma' in the Northern Territory

Reid's and Warner's Murngin accounts

The Stanford-trained Australian anthropologist Janice Reid has worked in the Aboriginal land of the Northern Territory. Termed Arnhem Land, it is where W. Lloyd Warner studied the Murngin people in 1926–29. Reid's fieldwork almost fifty years later found that the *galka* were still feared for their 'sanguma'-style homicidal assaults; she summarizes the attack's stages:

> First of all the *galka* either waylays his victim in a secluded place or draws him there. Second he puts the victim to sleep, cuts his body open, removes or mutilates his organs and drains away his blood. Third, he induces amnesia in his victim to ensure that he is either unable to remember or unable to tell anything about the attack. Fourth, the victim dies, usually within hours or days of returning home. (Reid 1983: 37)

Warner ([1937] 1958) succeeded where all other Oceania researchers have seemingly failed in obtaining firsthand accounts of a sorcerer's murderous assaults. His informant for the account below of the killing of Bom-li-tjir-i-li's wife was Laindjura who, as a practitioner of "black magic," was one of the most famed "killers" in the southeastern Murngin country. He had several wives and numerous children and was both a good wood carver and an excellent hunter. Warner emphasizes that in everyday life he was an ordinary man, "There was nothing sinister, peculiar, or psychopathic about him; he was perfectly normal in all of his behavior" (1958: 198). Below is his translation of Laindjura's detailed account of a magical killing, obtained on his second field trip. (Note: readers are warned about the violent content in what follows.)

> All of us were camping at Marunga Island. We were looking for oysters. This woman I was about to kill was hunting for oysters that day, for the other women had gone another

A Witch's Hand

way to search for oysters. I carried a hatchet with me and watched her. The woman gathered her lily bulbs, then left the swamp, went back on the sandy land and lay down in the shade. She covered herself with paper bark to keep warm because she had been in the lily pond and felt cold. Only her head came out from the bark. She could not see me.

I sneaked up and hit her between the eyes with the head of a tomahawk. She kicked and tried to rise up but she couldn't. Her eyes turned up like she was dead. I picked up under the arms and dragged her to a mangrove jungle and laid her down. She was a young girl.

I split a mangrove stick from off a tree and sharpened it. I took some djel-kurk (orchid bulb) first and got it ready. I did not have my spear-thrower with me, so I took the handle off my tomahawk and jabbed about the skin on her Mount of Venus which was attached to her vagina and pushed it back. I pushed the skin up to her navel.

Her large intestine protruded as though it were red calico. I covered my arm with orchid juice. I covered the killing stick with it, too. I put the stick in the palm of my hand so that I could push the point upward with my thumb. When she inhaled I pushed my arm in a little. When she exhaled I stopped. Little by little I got my hand inside her. Finally I touched her heart. I pushed the killing stick with my thumb up over the palm, which pressed the stick against my fingers, into her heart. She had a very large heart and I had to push harder than usual.

I pulled the stick out. I stood back of her and held her up with her breasts in my hands. She was in a squatting position.

Her heart's blood ran in to the paper-bark basket I had left to catch it in. It ran slower and slower and then stopped. I laid her down and took the blood away. I hid it. I came back and broke a net of green ants off a tree. I laid it near her. I put the live aunts on her skin. I did not squeeze them, for I was in a hurry because I was afraid her relatives would come looking for her. The skin, when bitten by the ants, moved by itself downward from her navel and covered her bones over her Mount of Venus.

I then took some dry mud from an old lily pond. I put my sweat on the mud and warmed it over the fire. I put it against her to heal the wound so that no trace would be left of what I had done. I was careful none of her pubic hair would be left inside her vagina so that it would be felt by her husband or seen by the women. I kept up the mud applications until the vagina looked as it did before. I put blood and sweat in the mud and warmed it and put it inside the uterus. I did this again, using the mud, sweat, and blood. I did this six or eight times. The inside now was like it was before.

I turned her over. Her large intestine stuck out several feet. I shook some green ants on it. It went in some little way. I shook some more on, and a little receded. I shook some more, and all of it went in. Everything was all right now. There was no trace of the wound.

I took the tomahawk handle which had the heart's blood on it. I whirled it around her head. Her head moved slowly. I whirled it again. She moved some more. The spirit that belonged to the dead women went into my heart then. I felt it go in. I whirled the stick again and she gasped for breath. I jumped over her and straightened her toes and fingers. She blew some breath out of her mouth and was all right.

It was noontime. I said to her, "You go eat some lilies." The woman got up and walked away. She went around another way. I said to that woman, "You will live two days. One day you will be happy, the next day you will be sick." The woman went to the place where I found her. She went to sleep. I took her blood and went away. The other women came from where they had been gathering oysters. They were laughing and talking. They awakened the girl. She picked up her lily bulbs and went to the camp with the women.

The next day she walked around and played, laughed, talked, and made fun and gathered a lot of oysters and lilies. She came back to camp that night. She brought the things she had gathered into camp. She lay down and died that night. (Warner [1937] 1958: 199–200)

This is quite an astonishing report told by an informant to his ethnographer friend. What is more astonishing, this is but one of several equally detailed firsthand reports of killings that Warner recorded and published. What is the ethnographer—and the reader—to make of such firsthand reports told by the informant, whether it is Fortune's Christopher, Bateson's Tshava, or Warner's Laindjura? Warner is acutely aware of this conundrum and comments on the ontological problem that bedevils all purportedly firsthand accounts of magic:

It is impossible definitely to evaluate how far Laindjura and other killers believed the case histories which they gave me. There was no doubt in my own thinking that Laindjura believed a great part of them. Since he was constantly credited and blamed by friends and enemies for certain deaths, he may at first have taken an attitude "as if" if he had done these things and ultimately have come to believe that he had actually performed the operations he claimed he had. A black sorcerer who is credited with many killings has a rather difficult time among the people surrounding his own group, and under most circumstances it is more difficult and unpleasant to be so classed than as an ordinary man; hence a man would not practice such complete duplicity as these stories might indicate unless the setting were extraordinary from our point of view. (Warner [1937] 1958: 198–99)

I think Warner is saying that, since Laindjura's stories are *not* "extraordinary" from his culture's point of view, at least for Laindjura they could certainly *be* true, I would add, because they *feel* true. This brings me to a very insightful article by Victoria Burbank (2000), where she relates the act of a serial sex killer in Western society to Warner's sorcerer Laindjura's account of his lustful murder of the "young girl." She also emphasizes the role of fantasy and daydreaming to each genre. The role of fantasy is obvious in Laindjura's account and Burbank cites research indicating that fantasy is the prime motivator in serial sexual homicide. "The primary difference", she observes, "between this serial killer [Laindjura] and the Western variety is that one murders in fantasy, whereas the other murders in fact" (Burbank 2000: 415). To summarize, I would argue that fantasy, illusion, and imagination are significant personal elements in perhaps all of the previous detailed descriptions of 'sanguma,' a point we will return to in the next chapter.

Conclusion: The Cultural Extent and Mapping of 'Sanguma'

Heretofore, the cultural and geographic extent of 'sanguma' as a form of sorcery or witchcraft was not known or even explored. I have documented here the extensive distribution of 'sanguma' as a major belief system from Eastern Indonesia across the island of New

Guinea into eastern Island Melanesia and south into and across parts of Australia. From this geocultural mapping, it is not possible to determine where the 'sanguma' belief originated or how it spread. However, we do know from ethnographic accounts in Melanesia and Australia that 'sanguma' has been present there since the late nineteenth century and that the north-central coast of Papua New Guinea appears to have been an important twentieth century distribution point via indentured laborers from diverse cultures and the facility of Tok Pisin. Hopefully, from these beginnings, other researchers eventually will be able to augment and deepen our historical understanding of the origins of 'sanguma' and ethnographic odyssey.

CHAPTER SEVENTEEN

'Sanguma' and Society

This area is notorious for Sanguma.
Lumi ADC A. S. Wright (Wafingian 1972: 5)

Sanguma beliefs are absolute rubbish.
PNG Prime Minister Peter O'Neill (2018)

In the last chapter, 'sanguma' as a form of magical murder was shown to have a cultural distribution from Indonesia's eastern islands, through New Guinea, to the islands of eastern Melanesia, and south to the continent of Australia. This chapter continues the examination of 'sanguma' with the following questions: (1) What are the Lujere 'sanguma' traditions? (2) What is the etymology of 'sanguma'? (3) Is 'sanguma' real or a cultural fiction? (4) What are the Territory's laws regarding sorcery and witchcraft related to 'sanguma'? and (5) What is the influence of these laws on villagers' behavior?

Lujere 'Sanguma'

I had lived in Wakau almost two and a half weeks before I decided to ask about 'sanguma.' My first tasks, as you already know, had been to map and census the village house by house, start learning the villagers' names, and build a house to create a comfortable camp for my research. I initially was randomly told that Wakau had no 'sanguma' witches, not that surprising as the government had outlawed the practice of both witchcraft and sorcery. So, my tentative hypothesis that 'sanguma' might be just magical beliefs unsubstantiated by observable facts remained untested. However, before I began my questioning about 'sanguma,' I thought it prudent to first get a feel for the village and the individual men. This also gave them time to help evaluate my trustworthiness. After all, just before moving to Wakau I had lived at base camp, in the house belonging to the 'kiap' while he was on patrol, and I occasionally visited with the resident police.

The time seemed right one night when Arakwaki stopped by my 'ofis' to visit. As we chatted, I asked him how a man becomes a 'sanguma'-man, and he seemed perfectly at ease with the question. Right then I thought it was because we were alone, but now I know differently. There seemed to be no community secrets about 'sanguma'; the beliefs about it were widely shared in a very matter-of-fact way. It is, rather, the Westerner who is initially hesitant. I believe the magical aspects of a cold-blooded 'sanguma'-murder spook the Westerner and cause the intellectual tension that make it so disturbing. Astute villagers must have sensed this and, hoping that this American would bring wealth in the form of jobs to Wakau, dissembled regarding their own 'sanguma' men; they didn't want to scare me away. It is one thing to describe 'sanguma' to me as Arakwaki did, or to dismiss the witches as alien to reassure the newcomer—like my first night in Wakau in the old abandoned *iron*—but quite another thing to tell me outright that Wakau has its own resident 'sanguma' men and that some are my close neighbors.

The Apprenticeship of a 'Sangumaman'

Arakwaki's answer to my question, "How does a man learn to be a 'sanguma' man," was a very basic answer and unlike more detailed ones I later heard. First the novice needs a teacher, a 'sanguma' man, a *nakwolu*, to instruct him. This can be anyone qualified in his own or another village who will take him on as an apprentice; often it's a man's father or a relative. Unless a man teaches his son, a fee of around two Australian dollars is expected. At night the two catch a lizard, cut it, remove some of the flesh onto a leaf, say an incantation to close the cuts, say another incantation to mark its death for tomorrow, then release it. The next day they return to the tree and find the lizard dead. Good, now they will try to kill a dog. They repeat the same steps and if they return and find the dog dead, they will kill an old woman, except that blood is taken from the human victim. If that death is a success, the novice's training is finished. 'Em i savi olgera nau!' Arakwaki exclaimed, "He understands how to kill by 'sanguma'!"

Arakwaki then explained the important ritual value of the victim's blood to village men. First it is poured into small bamboo tubes; when dried it is mixed with other ingredients, an egg of the bush hen, grubs, aromatic leaves or a bit of eel or catfish. It is then packed into small leaf packets. Now a valued commodity, it is sold to men to feed to their hunting dogs for hunting success and, I later learned, may be eaten by the hunter himself to give him prowess with his weapons. Pleased with Arakwaki's explanations and feeling I was "on my way," I didn't press for further information. But I was beginning to think that maybe these Lujere 'sanguma' witches were real.

Two days later Joyce and the children flew down to Yellow River for a four-night stay to see my new Wakau digs and to say goodbye before they went to Australia to await the completion of my fieldwork. Just after they had returned to Lumi, T___, a bright-eyed boy from Mauwi whom I knew, came by my 'ofis' to watch. I was typing up an interview and we chatted sporadically as I worked. He had attended some of the mission's Tok Pisin Bible literacy classes and was fluent in Tok Pisin. I had remembered him from Joyce's and my earlier visit to Mauwi as he stood out from the other children for his alert attractiveness. T___ was one of several children, and his older sister was married to a Wakau resident. Sometimes I took advantage of these moments of quiet intimacy to ask about troubling research problems. Winging it, I asked him who were the *nakwolu* in one of the villages. Counting them on his fingers he said, "J___, M____, B____, and H____." Then he mentioned P____, who had died a few months earlier.[1] I think I expressed surprise regarding one of the men who was much younger than the others. He continued with the names of the *nakwolu* in another village: T____, W____, W____, and E____.

Off-handedly he then said that a *nakwolu* had two kinds of work: 'Mekim sik nau wokim skin.' The men who were reviled for their brutal attacks and for causing sickness and death were the same men that villagers sought for treatment when they and their children were sick. It struck me as a bizarre, maybe cruel, cultural oxymoron, but there it was: the men the Lujere believed to be heinous killers were also their life-saving curers.[2] It was a major bit of knowledge that I knew would help shape the rest of my Lujere research.

A few days before Joyce and the children visited me, Ai'ire was sick with diarrhea, looked terrible, but no one alerted me when W____ came to the village Mauwi to treat him. I found out after it was over but Wami, a strong, animated man who knew I had not seen a local treatment, explained to me in detail what he had done. Then, just before T____ found me typing in my 'ofis,' I had been watching J____ treat a woman, totally unaware of his and W___'s related but oppositional *nakwolu* role, namely, murdering their victims by the dreaded 'sanguma' magical ritual.[3]

For the next couple of days, though I did not reveal where I got my new knowledge, it was obvious to those who knew me best by my comments and questions that I knew the names of some *nakwolu*. I had treated my new knowledge casually as ordinary information, the same way they did among themselves. In the next weeks, by observing and ceaseless questioning, my information and understanding of 'sanguma' flourished. But it all began thanks to T____'s revelations that the magical rituals for killing, curing, and hunting were all in *nakwolu* hands. At least I was still assuming that the killings were magical but kept it as an open question; there were those packets of a supposed victim's flesh and blood used in hunting. When I typed up T____'s information, I added, "What would one do without children to fill you in? Because once you begin getting details, you can drop these around the grown men and they, seeing you already know, a lot feel freer to talk. Odd, but it always works."

It was S____ who gave me a deeper understanding of a *nakwolu* initiation. First, he said, you have to apprentice to an established *nakwolu*, the way M____ did with J____. The relationship is kept confidential. The novice accompanies his tutor on three private killing exploits in the forest. On all three killings, the novice does not make the person

---

1. Later I learned that P___ as a sometime *nakwolu*; he had received some instruction but never completed his ritual initiation in magical killing. I never saw him cure and rarely heard him referenced as a curer or *imoulu* when someone was sick and seeking help.
2. Just as killing and curing were seen as complementary, not competing opposites in much of Melanesia, Whitehead observes that for Amazonian shamanism, "Killing and curing are complementary opposites, not antagonistic or exclusive possibilities" (2002: 203).
3. Since information about alleged practitioners of 'sanguma' has recently led to vigilante attacks on them, I opt to protect the identity of these men, who may well be entirely innocent of such accusations, by withholding their names and using arbitrarily chosen initials instead.

unconscious, perform the bloodletting, or cut slices of flesh from the victim. He does, however, put his hand on the *nakwolu's* elbow to follow his motions. He described six places where the cuts are made for the slivers of flesh, specifically the fleshly portions of the lower arms, the inner thighs, and the calves of the leg. These incisions are made with a razor or a small knife or, as formerly, with a piece of razor-sharp bamboo. I drew different lengths for him to select from and the cuts were about one half to an inch long. Small portions of flesh are removed from these incisions and placed in a bamboo tube or, today, maybe a small bottle or tin. Then two separate incisions (one on each side) are made in the area between the nipple and the underarm and blood is drained into a small container.

On the first two exploits, only the *nakwolu* drinks the blood and eats the flesh, but on the third exploit, they are given to the novice. The initiator stands with his legs apart behind the novice who squats or sits facing away from him. The novice then lifts his head facing skyward and the *nakwolu* drops into his open mouth a small bolus of the victim's flesh and blood mixed with a bit of a ginger leaf from a plant designated for this purpose. It must be swallowed whole immediately, without chewing. From then on, the novice is able to treat the sick. It is a skill he can never lose even as an old man, although when old he will give up the ritual killing of victims. (Others told me that it was the spirits of his multiple victims that gave him his magical powers.) The novice's initiation to his new *nakwolu* status as a killer-cum-curer remained a secret until he treated his first patient. That public act drastically changed his fellow villagers' perception of him; he was now also a feared killer.

Yaope had joined S____ and me and they both were surprised that I did not know that *nakwolu*s could fly, that they could fly from one place to a distant one if they wanted to. I specifically asked about J____ and M____; S____ said that J____ had given up flying as well as killing after having been in the Lumi jail so many times. (Some men from the upper *iron* still greatly feared him as an active 'sanguma' killer.) Flying was achieved by eating another bit of ginger leaf just for obtaining this skill. S____ thought that M____ couldn't fly as we have lost this plant but he assured me that J____, M____, and T____ still could fly. L____ and M____, he said, would be too old.

Positive Roles of a 'Sangumaman'

The Lujere primarily associated the Tok Pisin term 'sanguma' with killing, not curing. They were adamantly against it and, in their contacts with the colonial administration, missionaries, and other expats, wished it were eradicated. Hence their long hours of volunteer labor to build a base camp that promised a resident 'kiap' and policeman who would act against the 'sanguma' scourge. From a local perspective, the major cause of death was the vicious attacks of *nakwolu* on unsuspecting villagers. Namia does not have a comparable word for "evil" but if they did, I'm sure that they would declare the *nakwolu* as its personification.[4] Yet these men who were believed able to secretly kill their immediate village neighbors as well as anyone else they privately encountered, including relatives—witchcraft is "the dark side of kinship" (Geschiere 2013, xvi)—played several strategic and

---

4. David Parkin's (1985: 125) introduction to his book *The Anthropology of Evil* cogently explores the nature of evil and its conceptual usefulness to anthropologists as exemplified in their wide-ranging studies.

positive roles in village life that tempered their negative status. First, these also were the men, the curers, the *imoulu*, who could save you or your child from sickness and death. This was a very powerful and effective role that marked the villagers' dependency on the same men who, at the very least, might shoot deadly objects into your body without your knowing or, at the other extreme, magically attack you when alone, ensuring your death.[5]

The *nakwolu* had other positive functions besides the healing role they offered the community. It was they who protected the village when foreign *nakwolu* hid in the village's peripheral brush for a daytime stealth attack on a lone child or adult, or attempted to furtively enter the village at night. Three different people told me how M____ had frightened away a *nakwolu*. It was in May 1971, a few weeks after he had returned to the village from his indentured labor. One night, M____ heard a *nakwolu* moving along in the bush below the village's knoll. He ran down to the 'kunai' to head him off and shot an arrow in pursuit. One account by a Mauwi youth was that he hit the intruder, as there was blood on the arrow. Someone told me this might be true, but if so, the rain had washed off the blood by the time M____ had retrieved the arrow. He added that a *nakwolu* might fight another one, as he wouldn't be afraid like an ordinary man. In the same way, only a *nakwolu* would be wandering alone in the forest at night; an ordinary man almost never.

The third way a *nakwolu* is helpful to his community I have already mentioned. His little packets of victims' flesh and blood, described by A____, were of great importance to hunters. When imbibed by a man and/or his dog they empowered success in the hunt. The value of these affirmative services to a village was deeply appreciated by all. S____ emphasized to me that a village without *nakwolu* was in a bad way, adding that the inhabitants wouldn't have game to eat or men to cure their ills and protect them from foreign *nakwolu*, thus making them dependent upon other villages.

These locally esteemed cultural roles of the *nakwolu* help to explain the tenacity of 'sanguma' as a social institution among the Lujere, even as they wish it expunged. Although the *nakwolu* are witches believed to have an inherent power to magically kill, they are unlike the witches in societies who are are exclusively evil, with no redeeming community merits.

The Origin Story of Lujere 'Sanguma'

This was the only origin story I heard about 'sanguma.' Kaiera related it and it concerns two mythical men, Abanaki and Awamoliait, from the Iwani hamlet of Iwarwita (Iwariyo).

Abanaki had built a blind in a tree for shooting birds. One night he dreamed that a lizard crawled along a branch of the tree and came into his blind. He broke the neck of the lizard but did not kill it as its body was still warm. The name of this kind of lizard is *ili*, which means "yellow." Abanaki cut out pieces of the lizard's flesh and also took some of its blood. He broke the neck of the lizard through a spell that a spirit had given him. Then he worked another spell to bring the lizard back to life. He sent the lizard on its

---

5. Although I tried, I never succeeded in getting a good grasp on how this dependency on a curer who could also kill you would personally feel. Thinking analogously was no help: what seriously sick American man would go to a doctor he knew was a vicious serial killer? Yet, if that were your only option . . .

way and it ran out on the branch it had come in on. It went to sleep on the branch and Abanaki went to sleep in his house. The lizard and Abanaki slept for two nights. On the third night Abanaki returned to the tree and went up into his blind to hunt birds. Entering, he said, "What is that bad smell in my blind?" Then he saw the dead lizard. "Why it's that lizard, I thought I sent it out of here and it ran away on that branch. What's it doing here?" On reflection, he mused, "I think it is something good! I think it is something truly good! I think I'll try this again".

He tried it one more time with the same results; when he looked, he said, 'Yes, em i samting tru,' that is, it really works. Abanaki then told Awamoliait what had happened, adding, "I have tried this two times and it has worked." Then the two began making 'sanguma.' They killed many people. Finally, Abanaki killed a brother of Awamoliait. Then Awamoliait, wherever he would go, would call out Abanaki's name. (Here, Kaiera said, "We still hear him crying out in the bush all the time," and imitated Awamoliait's cry.) However, the angry villagers then took off after the two men and surrounded them, but they flew away and came down at the hamlet of Lawou that is behind Bapei. The reason they can fly is because they now understood all about 'sanguma.' Those are the two men who originated 'sanguma,' Abanaki and Awamoliait.

When I asked Kaiera who it was that taught these two men the art of 'sanguma', he said that it wasn't anyone. That it was all in their dreams. He wondered if it was the spirit of the tree that caused the dream and showed them how to work 'sanguma.' To my question if it were a new or old story, he replied it was a very old one.

An Iwani Sorcery Trial in Lumi

While in the field, I was able to collect data on two very different Iwani trials involving, in one way or another, 'sanguma.' One was a criminal sitting of the Supreme Court held at Lumi in 1960, where three Iwani male defendants were tried on charges of willful murder, found guilty, and sentenced to death (it is discussed later in this chapter). The other trial, described below, was in the District Court at Lumi for two accused Iwani *nakwolu*. It was by chance that in late June 1971, I attended this trial held four months before I had decided to study the Lujere. Here are the circumstances.

I still lived in Taute village when I hiked one morning into Lumi to meet the afternoon plane of an anthropologist friend, Ann Chowning, who planned to visit Joyce and me. This was a few weeks after I had accompanied ADC Peter Broadhurst on his flying inspection of the Edwaki Base Camp described in chapter 6. Knowing I was interested in the Yellow River area as a research possibility, when he heard that I was in Lumi he thoughtfully sent a note saying, "Bill, I am doing this sorcery case now and it looks interesting. Would you like to come up? Cheers, Peter." Of course, I immediately replied, "Yes!"

The courtroom was in a small two-room rectangular wooden building right on the Lumi airstrip. One room serviced the court, the other was a cargo storage room; a narrow covered porch along the front connected the two rooms. The courtroom had a single door and window facing the strip and was sparsely furnished with three file cabinets, a couple of chairs, an incongruous freezer, and a desk for the magistrate (the ADC) towards the far wall with shelving behind it. Although I was blissfully unaware of it at the time, this court case would be some of the first data I collected on the Iwani villagers. Those present at the trial were the ADC, four policemen, Iwani's 'luluai' and 'tultul', the two accused defendants, and myself as an observer. I never learned the details of how the case originated. There had been accusations that W____ and A____, both Iwani 'sanguma' men, two months earlier had allegedly used 'sanguma' to kill a young woman from the Iwani hamlet of Aukwom on the Sepik, which Joyce and I had visited. They were arrested by the police and flown from Yellow River to stand trial for, from what I could make out, committing sorcery; it was not a murder trial, as that required a higher court. There was a pretrial session with the parties in the morning and, after a lunch break, the trial.

When I arrived just before eleven, Peter welcomed me and gave me permission to record the proceedings on my small portable Hitachi cassette recorder. He was neatly dressed in the colonial tropical male work-a-day costume of the time: a short sleeve shirt, shorts, de rigueur knee socks, and shoes. Four policemen lined up informally along the window wall stood guard throughout the proceedings. They symbolized the majesty and authority of the administration's court in their uniform of a light blue shirt, navy shorts, a big black belt with an embossed coat-of-arms silver buckle, blue knee socks topped with a red design, and black shoes with black gators. I set up towards the other end of the room opposite the door in the only other chair. I wore a clean T-shirt and the shorts I hiked in, but I had washed the mud off my legs and exchanged my muddy but prized Australian canvas spiked golf shoes that kept me upright on the slippery trails for some flip-flops.

The four Iwani men—two defendants and the administration's two village officials—were barefoot; the former sat on the floor opposite the ADC's desk towards the window wall and the latter stood in front of his desk. The pretrial session of about an hour that I attended was spent mostly with the ADC interviewing his Iwani officials in detail about 'sanguma.' It was a back-and-forth process with most of the initial questions directed towards the Iwani 'luluai,' Biauwi, sporting his official cap with one red stripe and wearing old green shorts with an ivory plastic belt. The 'tultul,' Ariawani (whom I described in chapter 11 as angrily stomping into Wakau with blackened face and bow and arrows protesting his sister's marriage to Yaope) was diminished in this setting in spite of his official cap with two red stripes, a long-sleeved striped shirt, shorts and big side burns. He, too, helped in replying to the ADC's persistent questions that moved on to a 'sanguma' man's hunting charms made, they said, with the victim's flesh.

During the ADC's interview a plane landed, roaring down the grass runway, and a tractor rumbled noisily by a couple of times. I usually could understand the ADC's rapid Tok Pisin but the official's replies, also rapid, were spoken in a softer, less resonant tone. Based on what I had learned about 'sanguma' from living in Wakau, and then listening to the trial's tape recording and reviewing my notes, the only new twists I got were that, according to the 'luluai,' after the victim dies a mark appears on the body, that 'sanguma' men either work in threes or twos—one man is not enough—and that they drink the blood of the victim by sucking it from the cuts. The ADC paused at least once to write down the 'sanguma' information he was eliciting. Towards the end of the interview, he asked for the Namia word for 'sanguma'. It was the first time I had heard the word *nakwolu* spoken. I took the liberty to ask if that was the same as 'posin,' the Tok Pisin term for sorcery, and was told "No." It was noon; Peter said we would adjourn until 1:30. I turned off my tape recorder and left to have lunch with Joyce and the children.

Earlier in the month Joyce, Ned, and Elizabeth—after a year in the bush with me in Taute village—had moved to Lumi, into a small timber house that Don McGregor of the

Lumi CMML had built for us on mission land, with the proviso that the house would become the mission's when we returned to America. The house seemed loaded with luxuries, including running water from a tin roof catchment area, a flush toilet that delighted the children, a fauceted sink, and electric lights several hours each evening. This would be Joyce's base as I finished my work among the Wape and then would study a second culture solo.

After a hot bucket shower and lunch, I returned to the courtroom for the trial. It was the same cast as in the morning but the focus was now on the two accused Iwani men. The ADC began by asking them some of the morning questions regarding 'sanguma.' There was no oath taking and the ambiance was informal but authoritative.[6] There was no doubt to anyone in the room regarding the ADC's dominance; it was he, and he alone, who would hear the case, ask the questions, make a decision of innocent or guilty, and set the sentence that could extend up to six months in jail; in other words, "The kiaps were the gods of law" (LiPuma 2001: 157).

A____, the first defendant questioned, was a skinny man in old brown shorts hitched up with a leather belt. The ADC began by asking him about the alleged attack on the young woman Nieni. Then W____ was similarly queried. He wore only a black 'laplap' and was as powerfully built as A____ was slight; his face was drawn, his unkempt hair had grass in it, and his right earlobe was slit and carried several small black rings. Earlier that morning, as the ADC interviewed the 'luluai' and 'tultul,' he had caught my attention with his alertness to his surroundings. Several times in apparent response to outside sounds, he stood up as if to hear and see better. Now the tractor appeared to be parked in front of the courtroom, roaring as if the motor were going to fly apart, but the questioning continued; eventually the tractor moved away. When Dr. Lynn Wark appeared, the ADC called a recess as they conversed on an unrelated matter.

Back in session, both men stood in front of the ADC's desk and were asked a series of questions about cutting the victim. The case appeared to have got to the court because the men had insinuated publicly that they had killed her with 'sanguma' in revenge for the death of relatives. The ADC continued to elicit information on how they had attacked her, including cutting her skin, but he seemed aware of the impossibility of 'sanguma' magic and accused them of 'tok giaman,' that is, of lying. This was followed by another questioning period of the men mostly denying what they had just attested to. The ADC then forcefully asked them, "Did you kill this woman, true or false?" They both answered, "False." He then asked them if others had killed her, and they replied, "Yes."

A plane roared onto the landing field and the ADC asked his police sergeant to see if a witness from Yellow River was on it, then he began writing up his report. Soon a local man wearing a black 'lap lap' with a black belt came in and walked straight up to the front of the room where the ADC was still writing. He had slightly bulging eyes, shaved sideburns, and wore a string around his neck and an ornament in his right ear, maybe a paperclip. No sign of recognition passed between him and the four Iwani men but when our eyes met, we both smiled. As the ADC continued to write, the plane's motor revved up for departure, then roared down the airstrip and into the sky. When the ADC finished writing he looked up and began to question the witness, the victim's brother, but soon

---

6. For detailed information about the law and legal authority of Administration field officers or 'kiaps,' see Barnett (1972).

established that he had neither seen his sister after she died nor was there for her burial. Aware that there was nothing to be gained by talking with him, he told the police to feed him and send him back. With the plane now gone, I assumed he would have a very long walk home.

It was just after 3:00 when the ADC began speaking to the defendants with a resume of his findings. He noted that first they said they had attacked the woman but later renounced their admission. In other words, they had lied to the court. His sentence was three months in jail: 'Yu kalabus pinis'! (you're going to jail!). Both men quietly nodded. Now standing, the ADC looked directly at them and began an avuncular lecture: 'Dispela pasin no gut long giaman long govman; olosem yu mekim rong, yu mas i go long kalabus tripela mun' (It is wrong to lie to the government; you did something wrong and must go to jail for three months). By 3:20, the court had finished its work.[7]

I was convinced that Peter had tried to make it clear to both W____ and A____ that the reason they were going to jail was that they initially told a story to the court that was untrue, that they had lied. But to the Lujere villagers of 1971, it was a subtle point and, in terms of this case, those outside of the courtroom undoubtedly would never hear about it or understand it if they did. Although I did not follow up on this trial as I should have, I would be surprised if villagers didn't think that W____ and A____ got off with very light sentences for their 'sanguma' "murder" of the woman.

Etymology of 'Sanguma' and Its Conflicting Referents

Leonard B. Glick's article (1970) on "Sangguma" in the *Encyclopedia of Papua New Guinea* cogently distinguishes between two types of sorcery: "projective" and "assault." The former is where the sorcerer and his victim do not come into direct physical contact but the quarry is magically stricken from a distance; the latter is where the victim is physically attacked and allegedly killed in an extended magical ritual. To Glick, 'sanguma' is a form of assault sorcery and "the attack is personal, immediate, and uncompromisingly vicious. The assailants . . . jab poisons directly into his body, sometimes twist or rip out organs . . . They are not satisfied until he is thoroughly befuddled, unable to remember who or what has afflicted him (Glick 1970: 1970: 1029).

The victim returns home and death is inevitable, but Glick omits a critical action in his account: that after the attack, the victim's body is magically restored without evidence of bruising, cutting, or scarring from the assault. Hence a 1970s standard reference description of 'sanguma' for Papua New Guinea was incomplete and misleading.

The Australian linguist Don Laycock was in the Sepik area during much of the time that I was in the early 1970s, and we met several times to discuss our research, usually over a few beers or Queensland dark rum. He was interested in 'sanguma' both as a linguistic term and as a form of "sorcery"—or, as we both agreed, better identified as "witchcraft," since 'sanguma' men were differentiated from other villagers by an intrinsic quality that in anthropological parlance marked them as witches.

---

7. For a fascinating comparison in which "Due process had no more meaning for the 'kiap' than it had for the Maring," see Edward LiPuma's (2001: 174–80) account of a formal 1980 sorcery trial, convened independently from the authorities by Maring villagers.

Don Laycock and 'Sanguma'

In 1975, with Laycock back at ANU and me back at UVM, I sent him a letter about 'sanguma' with a copy of my first paper on the Lujere (Mitchell 1975). In the kind of long, single-spaced snail-mail letter that scholar friends back then used to send, he wrote,

> Now, on your Lujere article. I was quite impressed with your account of the YR [Yellow River] sanguma, as it fits in with my own observations—and, as you are perhaps aware, runs counter to the views of some anthropologists who do not have Sepik experience (and even some who have).[8] What I maintain is:
> (1) While many (all?) societies in the New Guinea area have some form of sorcery, and some go in for secret killings vaguely resembling sanguma, there is a specific variety of witchcraft which is endemic to the Sepik (and Western Madang) region, for which the term sanguma should be reserved. . . . That is, *'sanguma' as akin to vada.* (my emphasis)

He continued by laying out in envious outline form his provocative thoughts on 'sanguma' and Sepik cultural history, including the Lujere's, interspersed with myriad details from his extensive knowledge of the Sepik area and New Guinea.

Laycock's (1996) article on 'sanguma' was published posthumously. One of its aims was to tie down the etymology of the word, which is Tok Pisin. He traced its origins to Monambo of the Torricelli Phylum, a small Papuan language on the Bogia coast west of Madang (Lewis et al., 2015: 232).[9] However it was Georg Höltker (1942: 213) who much earlier noted that 'sanguma' is derived from *tsangumo* in the Monumbo (Monambo) language, which refers to the type of supernatural ritual murder already described.[10] I'll return to Höltker's 'sanguma' research shortly. 'Sanguma' is unique as the only Tok Pisin word derived from a Papuan language; this is what provoked Laycock's linguistic curiosity regarding its spread throughout the Territory. He wrote,

> I can hazard a guess that the transmission process was related to the German plantations (many of them mission-plantations) along the Bogia-Madang coastline. . . . The further extension of plantation labour from Madang to the Gazelle [Peninsula] would have carried it to that area, and the Sepiks—who had the extensive Sepik Labour-recruiting following World War II . . . The concept, if not the word . . . is, I think, related to the spread of Tok Pisin, via the plantations. (Laycock 1996: 278)

---

8. He may have been thinking of Margaret Mead's early Arapesh definition of "segumeh" or of Leonard B Glick's (1972) "Sangguma" article and, while not an anthropologist, perhaps of Fr. Mihailic's idiosyncratic dictionary definition. These definitions are presented and discussed further in this chapter.
9. McCallum (2006: 199), who also wrote on 'sanguma' etymology, agrees with Laycock's finding.
10. The nearby Tangu language has a similar term for sorcery and sorcers, *ranguma*. Burridge, who spoke Tangu and wrote in detail about *ranguma*, discusses killing in this context but not the particular kind of magical assault murder of 'sanguma' (1960: 59–71; 1965: 224–249).

Laycock notes that he wasted a lot of time unsuccessfully tracking down the term "sanggoma" from South Africa with an imputed similar meaning to 'sangoma' but could not "find words even remotely like it in a score of African language dictionaries" (1996: 277). Maurice McCallum (2006) was similarly interested in the etymology of 'sanguma' but was more successful in finding an African word that is similar in pronunciation but different in meaning. "Sangoma" is a Zulu word but with no connotations of magical homicide:[11] "It means, not magic itself, but a traditional healer, a person, who uses magical means more than herbal means—a divine-healer who consults the ancestors and not just the symptoms and soul of the sick person, and the hundreds of products of the herb sellers (2006: 196).

It appears to be a quirk of linguistic history that the Zulu and Monambo terms—worlds apart geographically and culturally—are so similar, as their referents are decidedly different. Ashforth (2005), as earlier noted, writes in considerable detail about traditional healers and witchcraft in South Africa and specifically Soweto. However, he identifies no tradition of a 'sanguma' type of magical murder; furthermore, as far as I can tell from library research and conversations with knowledgeable African researchers, there is no New Guinea–style 'sanguma' in the whole of Africa. 'Sanguma,' as a form of ritualized magical murder, appears to be a cultural tradition limited to the islands of the South Pacific with a very deviant cousin, *kanaimà*, in South America.

Margaret Mead and 'Sanguma'

While Laycock and I agreed that 'sanguma,' as a vicious form of magical ritual murder akin to *vada*, was a widely distributed belief in the Sepik region in the early 1970s, there were some older, conflicting meanings of the term. Margaret Mead, in the first volume of her pioneering study of the Mountain Arapesh based on her 1931–32 fieldwork with Reo Fortune, defined a phenomenon called "sagumeh":

> *sagumeh* (P.E.) [Pidgin English] A form of combined sorcery and divination, associated with pointing bones, burial of exuviae, and possession by a spirit of the dead; contains many work-boy elements and *is rapidly diffusing through the work-boy population of the Madang Aitape coast*. (Mead 1938: 345; my emphasis)

Mead, who saw the Arapesh as a society with a modicum of Indigenous traditions, characterized them as "an importing culture" (not unlike the Lujere). The example of the imported "sagumeh" she gives in the text are of a diviner—there were two in her village of Alitoa—in a faked trance:

> The diviner chewed bone dust and ginger, ran about as if possessed, and finally sank on the ground in an imitation stupor, out of which he was able to answer questions in a

---

11. Also see Tomaselli (1989: 6–7), who cites film and video research by Professor Len Holdstock—who has worked with sangomas, that is, Indigenous healers, of Soweto—as well as Holdstock's films, *On Becoming a Sangoma*, and *Indigenous Healers of Africa* that also feature sangomas.

strained voice, using many tricks to make the occasion seem eerie, such as referring to usually unmentionable subjects. (Mead 1938: 345)

Mead's 'sagumeh' as being linked to pointing bones clearly refers to a form of trance divination. A more confounding description of 'sanguma,', published a year earlier in the *Official Handbook of the Territory of New Guinea*, attests that

> In the Wewak area, the natives believe in a malign spirit called *Sanguma*, whose aid is sometimes invoked by sorcerers. The best-known method of invoking the *Sanguma* is to point a dagger of cassowary shin bone at the intended victim. The *Sanguma* works in a most mysterious way, and is believed to assume many disguises, human and animal, to overcome his victim. When he slays all that is left of the victim is a little blood. The body is never found. (*Official Handbook of the Territory of New Guinea* 1937: 417)

In this rendition, 'sanguma' is a "malign spirit" capable of manifest transformations to slay a victim whose body disappears. And then there is Stanhope's (1968:139) report that 'sanguma' for the Rao of the Madang District is a term for "demon-induced illnesses." Even as late as 1962, variant understandings of 'sanguma' were around. POTreutlein included in his patrol report that villagers found one of their group dead in the bush: "They told me that the Yawari men [eastern Lujere] had 'marked him with an arrow' thus putting a wound in his neck, from which he died. . . . quite adamant that he had not actually been touched at all, the arrow had only been pointed at him from a distance, and Sanguma had done the rest" (Treutlein 1962: 12).

Exactly *how* "sanguma had done the rest," we are not told. Mead (1973), in a paper on "A Re-Examination of Major Themes of the Sepik Area, Papua, New Guinea," uses regionally shared Tok Pisin words to indicate common themes or traits. She does not mention "sagumeh," a form of trance divination described in her Arapesh work, as a regional Sepik trait, apparently conceding its areal limitations and/or datedness. Nor does she cite 'sanguma' as a common trait. She writes,

> It is also important to recognize that the same term may occasionally cover widely different practices. For example while poisin is widely used as a general term for sorcery, *sanguma*, the name for a particular sorcery practice, is sometimes used *specifically* but *sometimes also encompasses the entire supernaturalistic practice of a people*. (Mead 1973:14; my emphases)

Mead's methodological problem here is that she acknowledges two referents for 'sanguma': one as a specific practice of magical ritual murder, and the other as a compendium of cultural beliefs and practices related to a specific practice of magical ritual murder. The latter sense of 'sanguma' is in reference to my work with the Lujere, and one that we will return to. She then quotes Mihalic's unusual dictionary definition of 'sanguma':

> *sanguma*, (sang-guma) (Melanesian) secret murder committed by orders from sorcerers. The victim is waylaid, short poisoned thorns are inserted into the base of his tongue, causing swelling and loss of speech. Then other thorns (usually from the wild sago plant) are pushed into vital organs, where they cause infection and eventual death. (Mihalic 1971: 169)

This, however, is neither sorcery nor witchcraft. It is just plain murder. It is not 'sanguma,' the "magical murder" that Laycock and I encountered as a fervent belief in the multiple Sepik societies we separately visited in the early nineteen seventies. Although the Mihalic dictionary was the most scholarly and authoritative source for "Melanesian Pidgin" when published in 1971, its definition of 'sanguma' was, at best, very idiosyncratic, and in terms of the popular meaning of the term at the time, simply wrong. Steinbauer's Neo-Melanesian dictionary of the same time frame as Mihalic's, while lacking details, is more accurate, but still wanting: "*sanguma*, ritual and secret murder by means of sorcery; telepathic sorcery," and "*sangumaman*, secret ritual murderer (often on hire by sorcerers)" (1969: 166). Mead, commenting on Mihalic's definition of 'sanguma,' says, "Writing in 1935 I used the term *vada*, which had already been widely used in the literature on Papua, to discuss this practice ['sanguma'], but without giving it the naturalistic, matter of fact explanation [i.e., devoid of magic] which Fr. Mihalic gives it (1973: 14).

Here Mead indicates her recognition of the contemporary equivalence of 'sanguma' to *vada*. Mead visited Joyce and me in Lumi in 1971 (as she also did Rhoda Metraux in Tambunum and Don Tuzin in Ilahita), just before I moved to the Lujere, and knew from me the current Sepik understanding of 'sanguma' as a dreaded form of magical murder akin to *vada*. Early on, she clearly understood the special problems of *vada* noting, "The practice is such that it is very difficult for the field-worker to distinguish between phantasy and myth, on the one hand, and actual practice resulting in the death of specific persons on the other" (1938: 174). In my post-fieldwork conversations with her, I described the way the Lujere 'sanguma' man or *nakwolu* was not just a sorcerer that anyone could be, but, once magically initiated, became a witch with unique intrinsic powers to magically kill, cure, fly, make hunting charms and, some said, to become invisible. It was probably based on this understanding of Lujere 'sanguma' that she wrote,

> Among the Lujere of the Yellow and Sand Rivers Mitchell found that the term *sanguma* characterized the entire complex of supernatural practices of sorcery, healing and hunting. . . . Here we move from a disavowed phantasy to a full time preoccupation, and to a widespread usage in which the referent does not have the same thematic consistency as the terms that I have selected. (Mead 1973: 15)

While I never used the term 'sanguma'—and never would—to "characterize" the nature of Lujere society, Mead is correct in acknowledging its interrelations with multiple parts of their culture. Within a societal context, the extent to which a belief in 'sanguma' articulates with other parts of a culture's beliefs and practices varies enormously, as documented in the last chapter. I would also question her use of the term "disavowed phantasy," as without phantasy, there is no conversation regarding 'sanguma.' Unfortunately, when the conference paper was published in a revised version as "The Sepik as a Culture Area: Comment," Mead (1978) chose not to include 'sanguma' as a regional trait. In the 1970s, there were few men or women born in the Sepik region who were not alarmed by the frightening features of 'sanguma.' Indeed, even today it remains "a matter of concern in most areas" (Gesch 2015: 112) that is expanded on in later sections. We will also see how the term 'sanguma,' especially in the Highlands provinces, has morphed from the specific form of magical ritual murder examined here to become a common synonym for "sorcery."

Is 'Sanguma' Real?

This is the question that Father Gesch (2015: 115) asked, as has anyone else who has dealt with the phenomenon. As Ian Hogbin writes,

> The account of *yabou* is so fantastic that one would imagine no European could possibly accept it as true. Many residents in New Guinea, nevertheless, are so prone to believe any native tale dealing with the occult that sorcery of the *yabou* type—the pidgin term is "sangguma"—is in some quarters solemnly believed in. Amongst the natives, of course, there are no sceptics. (Hogbin 1935b: 13)

What made 'sanguma' initially so insidious for me was its admixture of the implied physical or "real" violence, and the magical or "unreal." Near the beginning of this book, I cited my skepticism of whether 'sanguma' even existed as real events. Now I know that 'sanguma' magical murders are sometimes *attempted* but, to date, no credible data exists to substantiate a single successful one that includes a killing assault of the victim, the removal of flesh or organs with no scarring, resurrection to life, and a final death soon following. I have, however, attempted to gather information on authenticated actual attacks and present this below. In some of these cases, the victim died from the initial assault while in others the victim survived. These data establish that 'sanguma' ritualized attacks are in some circumstances actually attempted and serve to help validate a belief in them as "real" and the sense of terror that 'sanguma' engenders.[12]

Father G. J. Koster's Accounts

The fathers and brothers of the Society of Divine Word (*Societas Verbi Divini* or SVD) were one of the most important missionary groups in the Sepik area before World War II. An early, if not the first, attempt to identify, describe, and critically discuss 'sanguma' was by two SVD priests: G. J. Koster (1942), a missionary who served in the Bogia area on Papua New Guinea's north coast just opposite Manam Island, and Georg Höltker, editor of the international anthropology journal *Anthropos*. Koster's article, written in Dutch, has a preface by Höltker, who was fascinated with 'sanguma' and intended a future publication.[13] Höltker writes,

> On the occasion of my three-year expedition in New Guinea (1936-39) I have been able to gather with the aid of competent missionaries from the Bogia district a considerable amount of material on the *sanguma* subject. . . . To complete my material I

---

12. The terror I am referring to is strictly psychological, the result of hearing and internalizing the myriad tales of 'sanguma' atrocities and is very different from the terror engendered by the *physical* pain from the "rites of terror" that Whitehouse (1996) finds in some Melanesian initiations.
13. Dr. Risto Gobius generously translated the article for me from the Dutch. Höltker's later (1963) publication on 'sanguma' (*Todeszauber*) is in German. See Rüegg (2018) for a review of Höltker's work in New Guinea. For another account in German of 'sanguma,' see Schmitz (1959).

also asked the Banara missionary, Father G. J. Koster to report his experiences in the *sanguma* field. . . . Immediately it was clear to me that his observations were of special significance and therefore earned a separate publication. (Höltker 1942: 214)

The reason Höltker was so interested in Koster's material is that he had first-hand experience with 'sanguma' attacks, thus firmly establishing that 'sanguma' is sometimes more than Indigenous imaginings. It is Father Koster's data that concern us next:

The first case dated from around 1936 and involved a young man who is approximately 25 years old. He originated from the coastal area of the Uligan region. He married a woman from the village of Dalua in the Banara district and lived with her in Dalua. Another man, approximately 30 years old, happened to fancy that woman, although he was already married. He used to serve the state as a police-boy. . . . Both men were Catholics. Therefore, he wanted to operate cleverly. He thought that first the legal spouse must be dead. Then the woman would be free. Consequently a *sanguma* attack was arranged in order to do away with the young man. Regarding the above I heard and witnessed the following.

In the morning a white stranger happened to drive through the village of Dalua. When the Dalua women saw him they ran into the forests and fields. Dread and anxiety about the white stranger caused this hasty departure. For someone who knows the New Guinea people, this was not surprising . . . The women who fled into the forest all at once saw a number of men painted black. They were *sanguma* men. . . . The men realized they had been caught red-handed by the women and fled. Their black shapes shocked the women. The women fled in another direction and eventually returned to the village. There they reported to their men that they saw *sanguma* men in the forest. At once, the men ran to the described spot in the forest and found the young man, moaning and complaining. The men picked him up and took him to the village of Dalua. Mr. Johnson, a planter who lived close to Dalua, soon learned of the *sanguma* attack and immediately went to Dalua, where he heard and saw what happened. He had the young man taken to his home at his plantation.

I arrived at Mr. Johnson's plantation that very afternoon while I was on my missionary journey. . . . We examined the young man and actually found some of the famous little pointing bones in his body. They were in his upper arm and above the knee. One little bone was sticking out of the skin. We were able to pull that one out rather quickly. It appeared to be a fishbone and was rough on both sides and denticulate. Out of his arm we pulled another similar bone that was smooth; both were approximately 5 cm long. I had both of the bones for a long time. With our fingers, we also sensed even more bones that were stuck deeper in the flesh. . . . Later those areas started to ulcerate and as a result those little bones simultaneously came out. (Koster 1942: 221–22)

The fleeing women had taken the 'sanguma' men by surprise while they were attacking the young man, who was able to give a rough report to the authorities of what had happened to him. He even had an idea who the 'sanguma' men were. The suspects were sent for, tried in court, found guilty, and sentenced to six months in jail. After the victim recuperated, he and his wife left for his native area of Malala. Koster's other case, however, is riddled with hearsay and is not worth reporting on.

F. E. Williams's Accounts

Francis Edgar Williams (1893-1943), an Australian educated at University of Adelaide and Oxford, had the unusual career of being Government Anthropologist for the Territory of Papua. Appointed initially by Hubert Murray in 1922, he completed studies of a commendable seven distinct and geographically separated societies before dying in a plane crash in the Owen Stanley Mountains during World War II. His academic cohorts rarely gave his ethnographies the accolades they deserved; they are knowledgeable, lucid, wryly reflexive and, however long, gratifying to read. In a paper titled, "Mission Influence Amongst the Keveri of South-East Papua," he also describes two cases of substantiated 'sanguma' attacks. Williams notes that the local term was *mimi* and gives a concise summary of the process.

> The distinctive character of the method is that the assailant is believed to kill his victim first; then bring him to life again; and then send him off more or less dazed and doomed to die in a short space of time. Many accounts possess such unbelievable features as cutting out the liver, even cutting the body to pieces and sewing it up again, and there is no difficulty in dismissing most of them as figments of imagination. But on the other hand there are some grounds for supposing that *vada* sorcery of a less anatomistic kind may sometimes be actually put into effect. It was especially to test out this possibility that I devoted some time to the subject among the Keveri. (Williams 1944: 106)

The first case he describes is not one of the substantiated ones but based on hearsay. What he says about the case, however, is interesting:

> What seems incredible is that the *mimi* sorcerers should actually render their victim unconscious and then revive him. The foregoing case hardly proves that they do so. It is no more than a typically straightforward case, allegedly successful, as narrated by two sorcerers who have a reputation to keep up. For it is the theory of *mimi* that the sorcerers kill their victim and bring them back to life; the man in the street believes they can do so; and the sorcerers themselves may say anything to keep this impression alive. (Williams 1944: 107)

Williams writes, "To appreciate the fact that *mimi* is actually put into practice, it is only necessary to examine certain cases in which it has been tried and failed" (1944: 108). This was the situation in a case where the informant he calls "B" took part.

> B is a very fine type of Papuan, vigorous, intelligent and purposeful; a Christian, of course, and, I have little doubt, a very sincere one. On the whole I took him to be pretty honest. Some years ago he had gone out on a *mimi* expedition with five confederates. He was to play the part of resuscitator and was equipped with all the necessary spells and medicines, as well as a sheet of bark-cloth with which the victim was to be gagged. But the party failed to take their man entirely by surprise. Instead of being immediately over powered he struggled most manfully, and succeeded in wounding the leader with his knife. Perhaps the sight of blood was too much for their nerve. At any rate one of their assistants cried out that they had messed up the whole thing, and forthwith drove his spear clean through the unfortunate man's body. Naturally the idea of *mimi* was abandoned without further ado, and the victim was killed then and there in a most

thoroughgoing manner—all to the intense disgust of B, who was bent on trying his skill as a resuscitator.

B seems to have had no luck as a *mimi* man. Long before this he had been taken out on his first expedition by O of Uiaku. He was then a mere lad, and this was to be his initiation. O had instructed him beforehand in *mimi* methods and he went out in the full expectation, no doubt mingled with pleasant curiosity, of seeing them put into effect. But when it came to the point O, instead of proceeding with the half-methods appropriate to *mimi*, had delt the victim a blow on the head with his club of such violence as to crack his skull. In answer to his pupil's expostulations the master could only reply that he had lost his head. (Williams 1944: 108)

In reviewing the literature on 'sanguma,' I was intrigued when a writer accepted it as "real" or appeared ambivalent regarding its actuality. Missionaries sometimes appeared to accept the possibility of its reality as genuine; ethnologists less so. But Williams, who disparaged aspects of *mimi* as being possible, totally surprised me in his reporting on one case by apparently accepting the resurrection of a victim as valid. However, the attackers obviously had not killed the victim but only stunned him to unconsciousness.

Then again, the victim, so far from dying may live and remember and inform against his assailants. A case of this nature was recounted by Ma'u of Amau. In company with another he had waylaid a man named Abanapu from a neighbouring village, allegedly because he was constantly thieving from their gardens. They had carried out their *mimi* and *brought him back successfully to life;* he . . . apparently failed to recognize them; and they had gone so far as to assist him part of the way home. But Abanapu was not so stupefied or stupid as he seemed. On reaching home he revealed who had attacked him, and his people came to Ma'u's village on the lookout for vengeance. It appears they were worsted in the fight which ensued and the matter was allowed to rest. (I see no reason to disbelieve this story, which was volunteered by my informant; though I do not feel quite so ready to believe the sequel, that Abanapu died "two days later.") (Williams 1944: 109; my italics)

William's last documented case is a revenge *mimi* killing in which several of the attackers went to jail. It begins with a man R and his wife going to buy tobacco at a local plantation, Kauru, and on their way home they were attacked by five Mekeo laborers who drove off the husband then raped and killed the woman. R then arranged for some *mimi* men to avenge his wife's murder. The group consisted of men from several different villages and two plantation laborers, totaling nine men including R. They met at dusk at an old garden where they made a banana-leaf shelter and camped for the night. Some men had blackened faces veiled with cassowary feathers.

The two local labourers, Y and D, who were in the plot, used to spend their week-ends at an old house in this garden, and they used to bring with them a Mekeo man (a signed-on labourer) named W. This man had been selected as the victim (whether he was actually one of the five rapers I do not know), and now a private message was sent on to Y and D at Kauru: they were to be sure to visit the garden house next afternoon (Saturday) bringing W with them; there would be a bunch of bananas in the house for their supper. . . . After a suitable lapse of time the *mimi* party crept up in the darkness while the victim and the two betrayers were busy eating their bananas. The two leaders fell on W from behind, a man to each arm and leg. It was [another's] appointed duty to hit him about the body while he was held down on the ground. He did so with a stone club, striking him on the back of the neck, the shoulder blades and the ribs, "till they were soft," while another man twisted his head and "broke" his Adam's apple with his teeth. W, by now apparently dead, was carried into the house and laid on a bed of banana leaves near the fire.

The next business was to restore him to life, and this was in the expert hands of R, himself. But he tried in vain. He used all his spells and medicines, but when they raised the victim up he just fell limply back. R pulled all his fingers one by one; there was no response. Then he gave up, saying only, "We must have killed him properly." (Williams 1944: 111)

One of the laborers confessed when questioned and six of the men were imprisoned—R, the instigator, for four years. When he returned to the community, he finally paid his accomplices for their help. Williams was satisfied with his research, commenting "it seems clear that *mimi* was sometimes at any rate put into practice—though we may be sure that it was supposed to be put into practice far more often than it really was" (1944: 111). *Mimi*, *vada*, 'sanguma,' or whatever one calls it, is always more than just an initial brutal assault that kills. The alleged resurrection of the dead victim and his subsequent death a few days after returning home—both magical acts—are important identifying features.

Dr. Becker's Surgical 'Sanguma' Patient

In Lumi, Dr. Lyn Wark told me that a doctor in Port Moresby had slides of x-rays related to a 'sanguma' attack. I wrote to him soon after returning home and received an immediate answer. The physician was Dr. S. C. Wigley, a fellow of London's Royal College of Physicians, and stationed at the General Hospital in Port Moresby as an advisor in tuberculosis. Earlier, however, he worked at the hospital in Wewak where he obtained the slides (see fig. 46 for an example).[14] His letter, dated July 19, 1973, says, in part,

> The request was for concrete evidence of sanguma activities in the Sepik area. I enclose three photographs of x-ray films of a man admitted to the Wewak General Hospital in 1956 from Ambunti with a story of chest and abdominal pain.
>
> The x-rays speak for themselves. One of the more sophisticated sangumamen on the River had used sharpened casing wire instead of the traditional bamboo slivers or saksak thorns.
>
> The wires were removed successfully from the mediastinum and the abdomen by Dr. A. A. Becker who was at that time the Medical Officer at Wewak, and who left New Guinea two years ago. He gave me the x-rays years ago. The films have long disappeared but I still have the slides.
>
> The patient recovered uneventfully from what was in fact a most formidable surgical intervention in the circumstances which obtained in Wewak in 1956.
>
> To my knowledge no "longterm follow-up" was done, and it is not known whether he is still alive or whether the sangumaman had "another bite at the cherry."

---

14. Later he wrote an important paper on tuberculosis and New Guinea (Wigley 1990:167-204).

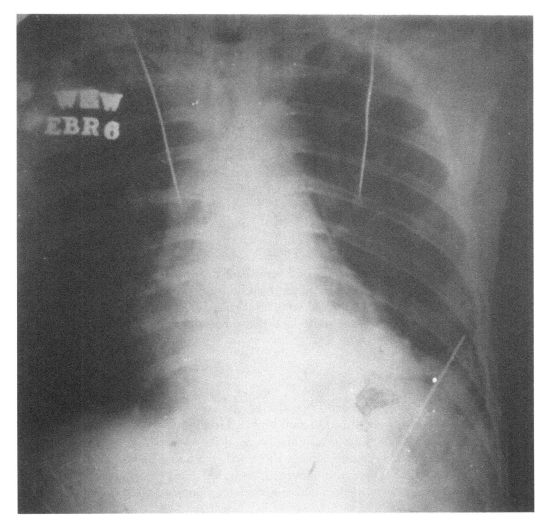

Figure 46. Chest x-ray slide of victim's thoracic cavity with three casing wires.

In spite of the seventeen-year hiatus between the victim's hospitalization and Dr. Wigley's letter, I hoped to get more background data on the victim, especially his village in the Ambunti area, but was unsuccessful.[15] So, without hospital records, we have a man from the Ambunti area attacked by 'sanguma' men, probably knocked unconscious and

---

15. I wrote to the then-current medical officer at the Wewak hospital, Dr. Risto Gobius, whom I first befriended on my 1967 stay, and he explained as follows in a letter dated September 19, 1972:

> There are only two persons in this Hospital who could possibly remember this particular event, both being operating room orderlies and though they do remember vaguely an event of this sort, they are unable to place this particular individual in their memory. In view of the fact that Dr. Wigley had his X-rays and the move from the old hospital

held down as the various wires were inserted into his body. The patrol officer at Ambunti probably arranged for his transfer to the regional hospital in Wewak, where Dr. Becker operated to remove them. Although I sometimes had heard allegations that 'sanguma' men inserted sharpened wire, such as umbrella ribs, into a victim's body, here was undisputed proof that such assaults did actually occur.[16]

Iwani's Double 'Sanguma' Murder

The innocent victims of the killings in this incident were two older Iwani women, Prai and Ilowa, who were murdered by three local *nakwolu*, namely K____, A____, and S____.[17] Two were from Mauwi hamlet and one was from Wakau. Of the three, only K____ was living during my fieldwork. The killers eventually were apprehended, tried, found guilty, and sentenced to death, though the sentence was commuted by the Administrator to four years in prison. The case is interesting as I have three kinds of information to reconstruct the story: Two I collected in the field, the villagers' account of the murders and data from the Lumi Gaol Record. The other data were from the presiding judge's detailed report of the trial he submitted to the Administrator in Port Moresby, which I accessed much later.[18] Of special interest is the way the village and Government accounts of the murders differ, especially the alleged motives for the killings.

The Queen v. three 'sangumamen'

The case was heard in September 1961, during the criminal sittings of the Supreme Court held at Lumi in the Sepik District, by His Honour, the Chief Justice Sir Alan Mann; presumably in the courtroom by the Lumi airstrip where ten years later Broadhurst heard the Iwani sorcery case, already discussed. The Supreme Court of Papua and New Guinea, regardless of where it convened, respected court conventions: "The robed judge and counsel may be sitting in a native-material temporary courthouse on the banks

---

in 1956 to a new Hospital in 1961, I am afraid that any records pertaining to this particular period have also been lost.

16. Also see Pulsford and Cawte (1972), who write as follows: "Sanguma is sometimes plain murder. Post-mortem examinations conducted by modern medicine have revealed lengths of wire pushed into the chest, the point of entry camouflaged by a club wound. Alternatively, a fine sharp bamboo is passed through the anus, perforating the bowel but not marking the anus" (1972: 95).

    The book was written in part as an introduction to medical anthropology for students at the University of Papua and New Guinea and the Papuan Medical College in Port Moresby. At the time, Pulsford was Lecturer in Sociology and Anthropology at the Papuan Medical College and Cawte, with both a M.D. and Ph.D., was Associate Professor at the University of New South Wales and Director of the New Guinea Islands Psychiatric Research Project.
17. To lessen confusion among the diverse local and formal spelling of the victims' and accused names, I have used the spelling as recorded in the chief justice's trial record, quoted later.
18. I am especially grateful to Peter Broadhurst for helping me gain access to the chief justice's official report of the trial.

of the Sepik River, but they maintain the same formality of address and the same rules of evidence and cross-examination as their counterparts in Brisbane. The only major break with Queensland tradition has been the abolition of jury trials" (Barnett 1972: 627).

The following quotations are from Chief Justice Mann's two-page, single-spaced British foolscap report of the three Iwani men's trial prepared for the Administrator, dated September 14, 1961.

> Mr. McLoughlin appeared on the trial to prosecute for the Crown and Mr. O'Regan appeared as Counsel for the accused. . . . The facts were not in dispute, and the accused have all been perfectly frank about their conduct from the outset. S____'s case came on first and I entered a plea of Not Guilty to enable the facts to be investigated. When the second case of K____ and A____ was reached, I accepted a plea of Guilty, as charged . . . The three accused in the present case . . . all come from the area to the north and west of the Sepik River. . . . Much of this country is uninhabited and is very poor and rugged. . . . These people live beyond the area where there is any real Mission influence, and apart from occasional contact with the Patrol Officer at the Amanab [should read Lumi] Patrol Post, they do not enjoy much Government influence. . . .
>
> The trouble in the present case was that there were two very old women named ILOWA and PRAI living together in a house owned by WAIBUKEI. NAMINORO, who helped to look after the old women, left the village for a period of about six days to visit a relative. During his absence it appears that WAIBUKEI sent word to the accused and to at least one of the other men that they should come and kill the two old women. The men came as instructed, had some sort of discussion amongst themselves, and then proceeded to the house where the two old women were living. S____ entered the house first and strangled ILOWA and he was closely followed by the other two accused, K____ and A____, who killed the other old woman, PRAI. The three men emerged from the house bearing the bodies of the old women and they threw the bodies into some rough scrub country about thirty yards away from the house. The party of people then left, and nobody appeared to be concerned to arrange for any funeral or other ceremonies for the deceased.
>
> It appears that during the absence of NAMINORO the two old women spent most of their time sleeping, and they were asleep when the three accused entered the house to kill them. They were in extreme old age, helpless and unable to look after themselves, . . . had been making a most objectionable mess inside the house so that the smell was offensive to other people in the vicinity. . . .
>
> Perhaps the intensity of local feeling in the matter is indicated by the fact that WAIBUKEI, who has since died, but who was the owner of the house and who was most probably a relative of the old women himself, made his complaint to the accused, A____, who was in fact the tul-tul of the village. The group of men who discussed the problem and finally did as WAIBUKEI requested, were all responsible men, and it seems quite likely that they acted in a matter in which WAIBUKEI, because of some relationship or obligation, might have felt himself precluded from acting. Nevertheless he took a leading part in organising the whole excursion, although he did not himself at any stage touch the victims or their bodies. . . . I respectfully recommend that His Excellency may be pleased to commute the sentence of Death which was recorded in respect to the three accused and to substitute a sentence of imprisonment in its place. If asked to suggest a term which might be suitable, I would respectfully suggest a

period of four years for each accused, which in the circumstances under which these people are living at the present time would be regarded as a substantial period of time.

The villagers' version of the murders

I first learned about the murders when I went to Lumi from Wakau to spend Christmas with my family and copied all the offenses of Iwani villagers from the Gaol Register for the Lumi Correctional Institution (discussed in chapter 11) that was essentially a lockup. Later I did interviews regarding the men's offenses—there were no female offenders—and asked Oria for the details of the murder of the two Iwani women. To the villagers, these were two botched 'sanguma' murders as the three men, all *nakwolu*, could not resurrect the women after the initial attack and strangulation. The circumstances from the villagers' perspective follow.

It was the dry season when hamlets are even emptier than usual as the low ponds and streams and a less bogy countryside facilitate fishing and hunting. The women Ilowa and Prai lived in Iwarwita hamlet and everyone was going down to the Sepik and Aukwom hamlet on the river to fish but the walk was too far and arduous for them to attempt. They were supplied with food plus 'limbum' containers for toilet needs and were told under no circumstances to let anyone in until someone returned. The day of the crime, A____ went to get S____ then, according to Oria, A____'s wife, went to the women's door and told them she had climbed a coconut tree to collect nuts and would give them some. When the old women eventually opened the door, K____ and A____ rushed inside and K____ immediately strangled Ilowa, then S____, who also had entered, strangled Prai. A____ cut the women under the arms to collect the blood then cut bits of flesh from their legs for use in hunting amulets. When they tried to make the magic ritual to get them up, neither rose; both women were dead. Leaving the bodies where they fell, they left the hamlet of the murders and returned home, S____ to Wakau and K____ and A____ to Mauwi.

When Nanimoro returned from Aukwom, he found the two dead women in the house and thought they had probably been killed the day before. He dragged the bodies out of the house and threw them into the bush near the present *iron*. About three months later Enwan, a nephew of one of the women, returned from plantation labor near Madang. He was angry about the killings and with a Papei man went up to Lumi, he said to buy a knife, and reported the murders. Three police and the police sergeant were sent to investigate and found the bodies still exposed, now mainly bones. The residents of the murder hamlet were mostly in Aukwom but the police got all of the Mauwi men together and eventually A____ confessed that he had cut the bodies but that S____ and K____ had killed the two women. After A____'s wife was sent to Wakau to get Saime, the three accused *nakwolu* returned with the police to Lumi to be indicted and await trial by the Supreme Court.

I also heard stories that K____ had escaped and disappeared into the great fens to the west of the Sand River but was eventually captured.[19] Indeed, the Lumi Gaol Register first shows that he was given a month's sentence for "theft in gaol awaiting Supreme

---

19. R. K. Treutlein, an Australian patrol officer, devotes a single-spaced typed page to his searches for K____ and S____ after they escaped from the Lumi Correctional Institution. He organized two secret raids on Mauwi village at dawn with the police but both failed. He notes,

Court case for murder," then collected another six months jail time for two escapes awaiting trial. All of this notoriety assured him of a fearsome reputation when he returned to the community after his imprisonment. Even when I lived in Wakau, he was not a man the villagers would want to run into when alone. I recall once when strong and healthy Nauwen met K____ alone on a path near the village and was badly shaken when he reached our 'haus kuk.'

In comparing the court's and the villagers' versions of the murders, several points are of interest. First, the court version makes no mention of the deaths resulting from a 'sanguma' attack by 'sanguma' men. The four Lumi police who made the investigation in situ would have known that the accused were 'sanguma' men and that villagers considered both deaths to be 'sanguma' murders. With no transcript of the trial, I can only assume that there was a major cultural disconnect between the Lumi police and the Administration's imported attorneys, Mr. McLoughlin for the Crown and Mr. O'Regan for the accused men. The court's motivation for the murders was by inference: that the Native people involved were from a remote area with little mission or government influence, that the two old women were helpless and a filthy and smelly nuisance to their neighbors, therefore spurring the owner of the house, an inferred relative, to ask the men to kill the women while the villagers were away.

Although my village informants did not mention Waibukei who allegedly owned the house, it is more probably that he hired the three *nakwolu* to murder the old women. According to Oria, the women were not helpless and the reason they were defecating in the house was their fear of a 'sanguma' attack if they left the house while their neighbors were absent. There also is no agreement between the two versions regarding who killed whom, but because of the court report's timeliness, it is assumed accurate on this specific point.

All in all, the homicides appear to have been a classic case of a double 'sanguma' ritual murder, albeit a failed one, inasmuch the three *nakwolu* could not magically seal the victim's cuts or return them to life to meet their subsequent "real" deaths. The details of the women's botched deaths verified once again that 'sanguma' as ritualized *magical* murder was not a reality but just a Lujere belief.[20] At the same time, the case documented that there were *nakwolu* who attempted such magical murders but failed.[21] However, such incontestable evidence regarding the impossibility of returning a murdered dead person to

---

The Iwani's unwillingness to help in apprehending the two escapees is due to the death of their Luluai at Lumi last year. He died at the Lumi Hospital and they are convinced that he died as a result of Sanguma. They are afraid that the same thing will happen to K____ and S____. (Treutlein 1962: 18)

20. In 1969, the year before I went to New Guinea, Jeanne Favret-Saada moved to the Bocage region of rural Western France to study witchcraft. Her finding regarding the prevalence of actual witchcraft practice was similar to mine regarding actual 'sanguma' assaults among the Lujere. She writes that, in spite of the regional prevalence of witchcraft beliefs, "I nevertheless got the impression that there are no witches actually performing the bewitchment rituals attributed to them, or that they are extremely rare" (1977: 135).

21. Lastly, Mary Patterson reports without detail that "I have a number of accounts of attempted but failed *vada*-type sorcery from my own fieldwork in . . . the New Hebrides," and also that "[Ruth] Craig volunteered the information that in a Telefomin village where she worked a number of men of the village assaulted a victim in the bush to try out a sanguma (the New

life was locally ignored or understood as an error in ritual. All of my Wakau informants believed that K____ could and did commit 'sanguma' murders at will. Magical thinking is an all-pervasive and mentally enveloping way to interpret one's experiential world, and in that kind of closed world, a culturally entrenched belief, however logically dubious or ridiculous to the non-believer, always trumps hard evidence that challenges it.

'Sanguma' and the Law

The laws against sorcery were an important feature of colonial Papua New Guinea. Reo Fortune, more than most early anthropologists, was deeply concerned about them, as his six-and-a-half-page Appendix III, "Administration and Sorcery" in *Sorcerers of Dobu* attests. It is a revealing documentation of the thinking that he surprisingly and challengingly shared with the Australian Territory of Papua's top official, Lieutenant-Governor J. H. P. Murray, in a series of testy exchanges that Geoffrey Gray (1999) has highlighted and clarified. Here I am not concerned with Fortune's challenge to the lieutenant governor, as historically critical as it was, but more directly with Fortune's critique of the Administration's sorcery laws in terms of villagers' beliefs.[22]

Reo Fortune's 1932 Critique of the Sorcery Ordinance of 1893

According to Fortune, "The Native Ordinance declares: 'Sorcery is only deceit, the lies of the sorcerer frighten many people; therefore, the sorcerer must be punished'" (1963 [1932]: 288). He notes, however, that a conviction was usually less than a year's imprisonment. Fortune was strongly critical of the law in a country where "sorcery is an integral part of the supernatural system of the people" and where most everyone knows at least a destructive spell or two (1963: 288). He thought the law should be rewritten: "If the Ordinance were amended to 'sorcery is a part of a supernatural system which causes much social damage and fear, but which is practiced in secret by all members of a Papuan community,' the truth would be more fairly represented (1963: 289).

The most damning part of the original ordinance was that it made the Administration an accessory to the crime by elevating magic to a reality.[23] As to how to diminish or eradicate the universal belief in sorcery, he felt that ridicule was the way and that "This is gradually happening in some areas exposed to civilization" (290). Nevertheless,

---

Guinea pidgin term) technique [for *vada*] and succeeded in sticking needles in the man before he managed to escape" (1974–75: 143).

22. According to Gray (1999), Murray initially was well disposed to anthropologists but, after his negative experience with Fortune, only permitted his government anthropologist, F. E. Williams, to work on the mainland and never sent any patrol officers to Radcliffe-Brown's applied anthropology course in Sydney.

23. Hogbin, aware of Fortune's critique, writes, "Finally if we do wish the belief in sorcery to be eventually eliminated are we not defeating our own ends by punishing sorcerers? The natives do not realize that these men are paying the price of their deceit, but imagine instead that we regard them as evil-doers because we also believe in the efficacy of their rites and spells" (1935b: 31).

so long as sorcery is a crime, as murder, assault, rape, theft, and the like are crimes, it will hardly prove possible to ridicule the natives away from it [i. e., sorcery]. Does not the Administration treat it seriously! There is no doubt that it does, and there is equally no doubt that Administration is a powerful ally of the native sorcerer against all would-be educative agencies (Fortune 1963: 290).

This is a very commanding and convincing argument against *any* sorcery law. But Fortune is not finished. Here's his coup de grace: "A native imprisoned for sorcery will never learn to take the view that he is imprisoned for creating bad social feeling. He and all others inevitably take the view that *the white man shares in his conception of sorcery as actually and directly powerful*" (1963:290; my emphasis).

Here, I agree completely with Fortune. When I lived with the Lujere I saw that the men who were accused, tried, or jailed in relation to sorcery by Administration officials had their reputations enhanced as men to be feared. Fortune's defaming charge is that "the worst aspect of the law against sorcery is . . . that it tends to strengthen the practice of sorcery" (1963: 289). Further, he advances that "it is not questionable that Administration supports belief in it [sorcery] by treating it so seriously as to hold long court cases upon suspected instances of it, and to convict supposed sorcerers to a term in gaol" (1963: 293). From the villager's viewpoint, can you think of a better way to empirically validate the mythic power of sorcery than the colonial administration's jailing those who allegedly practice it?

The Sorcery Act of 1971

In 1971 an Indigenous elected member of the House of Assembly introduced a new Sorcery Ordinance that was aimed at punishing "harmful" sorcery and compensating the victims.[24] It passed with little debate although its implications for the future were significant. In order to demonstrate proof of an act of sorcery, it took account of the victim's belief but the onus was placed on the alleged perpetrator to establish his innocence, standing, as it were, Western justice on its head. T. E. Barnett, an expert on Papua New Guinea law, critically commented that if the alleged perpetrator

> fails to discharge this onus he is to be punished severely and, if some harm subsequently does occur to the intended victim or one of his relatives, it can be deemed to result from the sorcery and the accused must pay compensation. . . . As unexplained death, sickness, and disaster are attributed to sorcery, the fear of it is regularly reinforced by natural events. *For the law to be so locally oriented, however, as to reflect these beliefs is to*

---

24. It needs to be emphasized how much the concept of 'sanguma' was a part of the national culture in the 1970s. For instance, in 1977, in the University of Papua New Guinea's Music Department, "Eight students, calling themselves *Sanguma* (magic sorcery men), created PNG's first grass roots rock band. Performing in traditional dress (*bilas*), they won acclaim in PNG and overseas for their quintessential sound of modern PNG, combining contemporary musical forms with traditional words, melody, and beat" (Rossi 1991: 21). Their music may be sampled at https://www.youtube.com/watch?v=jZGu8OxPFT4.

grant sorcery official recognition. The beliefs will be confirmed when courts imprison 'sorcerers' who are 'deemed' to have caused harm by magic. (1972: 627–28; my emphasis)

Forty years after Fortune's Appendix III exposed how the administration was in bed with sorcerers and their bogus spells, Barnett had to reiterate the point after the House of Assembly passed a new and even more absurd law about magic. Until the '71 Sorcery Act was passed, the law recognized sorcery only as nefarious but now there was a distinction between "evil" and "innocent" sorcery (black and white magic) to complicate litigation. The Preamble's following sentence, written in wonderland legalese, sets forth the law's dubious logic:

There is no reason why a person who uses or pretends or tries to use sorcery to do, or to try to do, evil things should not be punished just as if sorcery and the powers of sorcerers were real, since it is just as evil to do or to try to do evil things by sorcery as it would be to do them, or to try to do them, in any other way. (Zocca and Urame 2008: 175)[25]

By this specious reasoning, it is as bad to wish someone dead as to murder them outright, but even Jimmy Carter knew the difference between committing adultery in one's heart and committing it in bed.[26]

'Sanguma' Witch Hunts in Papua New Guinea Today

The hunting down and killing of alleged witches occurs sporadically in the contemporary world. At the turn of the present century, in a small corner of eastern Java, "Over a three-month period, some 120 villagers were accused of sorcery and summarily killed by their neighbors, their mutilated bodies left by roadsides" (Hefner 2007). Today, Papua New Guinea also has become notorious for the proliferation of 'sanguma' witch hunts, especially against women accused of sorcery, that is, 'sanguma' or 'posin'.[27] This contemporary use of the term 'sanguma', particularly in the Enga and Western Highlands provinces, is as a vague blanket term equivalent to sorcery or 'posin' and used to label individuals accused of magically killing or injuring other humans and/or their possessions, both living and inanimate. The brutal public murder and burning of innocent women as witches unjustly blamed for local deaths by lawless mobs played a major part in finally repealing the controversial 1971 Sorcery Act. One of the most active and nationally well-connected web sites focused on preventing violence emanating from these 'sanguma' sorcery accusations against Papua New Guineans, especially women, is

---

25. A copy of the Sorcery Act 1971 appears as an appendix in Zocca and Urame (2008:175–188).
26. "I've looked on many women with lust. I've committed adultery in my heart many times. God knows I will do this and forgives me."—Jimmy Carter, *Playboy* magazine, November 1976, 86.
27. There are many books on witch hunts, from generalized histories to witch hunts in specific countries. For witch hunts in Europe, see especially Goodare (2016), Pavlac, (2010), and Barstow (1994). In our own time there have been "witch hunt" allegations of large-scale child sexual abuse in England (Webster 2005) and the United States (Pendergrast 2017), with legions of unsubstantiated claims that condemned innocent individuals to terrible ordeals. For a recent collection of articles on Pentecostalism and witchcraft, see Rio et al. (2017).

www.stopsorceryviolence.org/the project/. This usage of 'sanguma' is usually unrelated to the term as I have defined and explored it in this book.

The 2015 Repeal of the Sorcery Act

After years of dissention, the 1971 Sorcery Act was finally repealed in 2015.[28] One murder that figured in its repeal was the beheading of an older former PNG teacher by a mob accusing her of witchcraft in the killing of a colleague that, in turn, provoked international condemnation and embarrassment to Prime Minister Peter O'Neill's government. The '71 law recognized the accusation of sorcery or 'sanguma' against the victim as a defense in murder cases but this was revoked under the 2015 amendments. Now the killing of an alleged sorcerer is considered murder and, like rape and robbery, could draw a death sentence. While many applauded the repeal of the Sorcery Act, others reviled it as augmenting the death penalty. The *New York Times* reported on the following sorcery incidents from the Western Highlands province:

> Papua New Guinea has come under increased international pressure to end a growing trend of vigilante violence against people accused of sorcery. Last July, police officers arrested 20 members of a witch-hunting gang who were killing and cannibalizing people they suspected of being sorcerers.
>
> The killing in February [2013] of Kepari Leniata, 20, who was stripped, tortured, doused with gasoline and set ablaze, caused an international outcry. The United Nations said it was deeply disturbed by her killing, which was reportedly carried out by relatives of a 6-year-old boy who, they claimed, had been killed by her sorcery. . . . Amnesty International, which has campaigned loudly against sorcery-related violence in Papua New Guinea, praised the repeal of the Sorcery Act but assailed the reintroduction of the death penalty. ("Papua New Guinea Acts to Repeal Sorcery Law after Strife," May 29, 2013)

Many educated Papua New Guineans are deeply concerned regarding the existence and increase of "witch hunting" and 'sanguma' killings within their country. Several probing books with multiple authors and case descriptions address both the seriousness and geographic extensiveness of the problem, for example, Zocca (2009), Zocca and Urame (2008), and Forsyth and Eves (2015). To graphically dramatize that the problem of witch hunting and killing continues, in 2017, the martyred Kepari Leniata's six-year-old daughter was accused of 'sanguma' and maimed and tortured. On January 4, 2018, *The Guardian* reported that

> In Sirunki, Enga Province, a six-year old girl was accused of *sanguma* and tortured with hot knives. She survived after Lutheran missionary and Highlands resident Anton Lutz convinced the community to release her and her guardian. She was taken to hospital and treated for her injuries. Pictures of her tiny burned body shamed the populace. Politicians stepped up and condemned the attack. Newspapers wrote strident editorials. Enough was finally enough. The prime minister, Peter O'Neill, labeled the alleged torturers "cowards

---

28. For excellent historical reviews of New Guinea's sorcery laws see, Keenan (2015) and Forsyth (2015).

who are looking for someone to blame because of their own failure in life. Let's be clear *sanguma* beliefs are absolute rubbish," he said.... The last time PNG had been this upset about a sorcery-accusation was in 2013, when the young girl's mother, Kepari Leniata, was burned alive on a stack of tyres. "Because of the mother, they believed the child was a probable suspect for anything that happened in the village," Lutz says. "So when there were repeated illnesses in the village, and even a death, it was blamed on the child." The mother's death prompted a long overdue change in PNG law—until that year suspecting someone of sorcery was a legitimate legal defence for murder. But since then little has changed. In fact the frequency of attacks appears to be increasing. ("'Bloodlust Hysteria': Sorcery Accusations and a Brutal Death Sentence in Papua New Guinea")

The report of the child's torture in *The Diplomat* ("Why Is Papua New Guinea Still Hunting Witches?," January 17, 2018) said that the locals believed she had used sorcery to remove the victim's heart to eat but, when the man recovered, they believed their torture had incentivized her to return his heart, thus prompting them to release her to the missionary. He, of course, did not return her to the community.

By far, the majority of Papua New Guineans believe in sorcery, making it difficult for police—who may also believe in sorcery—to cooperate in making arrests among a vigilante group of perpetrators. In one study at Australian National University of perpetrators cited in the newspapers, Dr. Miranda Forsyth said, "Looking at all of those cases, about 15,000 perpetrators have been involved and of those only 115 individuals received sentences." The extent of the national problem is indicated not only geographically but socioeconomically by the fact that a few days after the above account of the child tortured as a witch was published, *The Guardian* reported that Papua New Guinea's Chief Justice had been threatened at a roadblock and his car stoned because an alleged sorcerer's killing by his tribe had not been compensated.[29]

---

29. In an article entitled "Papua New Guinea Chief Justice Attacked as Sorcery-Related Violence Escalates" (January 10, 2018), Helen Davidson reported that:

> Chief Justice Sir Salamo Injia was traveling from his home in Enga province's Wapenamanda district on Monday when he and his police escort were stopped at a makeshift roadblock. The acting police commander, Epenes Nili, said both vehicles were attacked by a large group of men in what he believed was a preplanned ambush. They didn't listen to the police (trying to move the crowd on) and started attacking the police vehicle and throwing stones and rocks at the Chief Justice's vehicle, he told Guardian Australia. The cars fled the scene and returned to Injia's home, Nili said. The Chief Justice was not hurt but was shaken after the incident. Injia was targeted because his tribe had not paid compensation for the death of a man said to have been killed with sorcery, Nili said.
>
> On June 2, 2018, the BBC put up a new web site, www.bbc.com/news/av/world-asia-44333447/the-witch-hunts-of-papua-new-guinea about a Papua New Guinea woman who can magically identify a sorcerer who performs Sanguma, a policeman who tries to prevent the maiming or killing of people accused of Sanguma, and a school teacher who tells how his sister-in-law killed his daughter by destroying her insides with Sanguma. In 2019, Philip Gibbs and Maria Sagrista put their 58-minute film (https://www.youtube.com/watch?v=12AnEwRIF90) on 'sanguma' in the PNG Highlands on YouTube, but readers should be warned that it contains scenes of actual torture.

CHAPTER EIGHTEEN

The Afflicted and their Curers

> *It is true that the magic of healing often goes*
> *hand in hand with that of killing.*
> F. E. Williams (1936: 338)

> *In Melanesia this mode of production of disease by the projection*
> *of material objects into the body seems to be exceptional.*
> W. H. R. Rivers (2001 [1924]: 12)

Patients' Curing Options

When a Wakau villager was self-described as sick, he or she had access to three kinds of therapeutic intervention: (1) traditional "home" remedies; (2) Indigenous therapies based on magic, like curing festivals and *imoulu* (a.k.a. *nakwolu*) curers; and (3) Western therapies based on biomedical research, like those available at an aid post or through infant welfare nursing patrols, both introduced by the Australians. As Rivers (1924: 76) notes, for most societies, home remedies, if applicable, are resorted to first. In Lujereland, If the health problem persisted, an *imoulu*, or a succession of them, would be visited or brought to the patient to identify and remove the cause of the sickness. Depending on the patient's wish and the nature of their health issue, they also at any time might seek treatment at an aid post, but in Wakau, it was seldom a first choice. The aid post orderly's explanations and diagnoses of sickness and disease were foreign and unrelated to the local cultural beliefs regarding illness etiology and curing. To the villager, the *imoulu* were the only culturally authentic diagnosticians and practitioners. As they and the villagers shared the same theory of sickness and disease, only the *imoulu* could identify the root cause of an illness and remove it; they alone got credit for the cure.[1] While most villagers did not believe that the aid post worker could cure serious ilness, they acknowledged he had powerful medicines that could alleviate suffering, even keep a person alive until a cure by an *imoulu* was achieved. Thus, in the history of a person's illness there was often a weaving back and forth in the implementation of the three different types of therapeutic intervention. Appendix documents over months one such case history—that of Ai'ire of Wakau village.

The last resort for a local healing intervention was a curing festival, as described in chapter 15. It was also the most infrequent as it depended on concerned family members, not the patient, for its organization and sponsorship. Similarly, among Western forms of medical intervention, transfer of a patient to a regional hospital was unusual as the transfer in a MAF plane was dependent on the mission's arrangement.

Medical Services through the Administration and Mission

In these pages I have, on occasion, citedthe introduced role of medical practitioners in Lujereland whose services are based on scientific medicine. Thus, (1) the two local aid posts in Akwom and Yegerape provided villagers with access to limited medical treatment; (2) Rosemary Ace offered clinical nursing skills at the CMML Mission; (3) the Admin sponsored maternal and child care village patrols carried out by visiting CMML missionary nurses; (4) the administration established Native people's hospitals, in Lumi under CMML missionary Dr. Lyn Wark and in Anguganak under Dr. John Sturt, and (5) the administration had a large coastal back-up hospital in Wewak and a smaller one in coastal Vanimo for patients requiring medical services the bush hospitals couldn't provide. For infrequent peripatetic attention, the 'kiap' might be accompanied on patrol by a medical technician, or an aid post orderly might offer a village medical patrol. Below is an account of a medical patrol to Wakau by the Yegarapi aid post orderly, Litabagi.

Litabagi's Wakau Medical Patrol

This was the only medical patrol Yegerapi's aid post orderly, Litabagi, held in Wakau while I lived there. He arrived just before noon with one of his wives who spoke fluent Tok Pisin and an adopted son. A man with sartorial style—something unusual in Lujereland—he wore a colorful shirt, neat shorts, sported an Aussie-style felt hat decorated with a clutch of beautiful dusty blue feathers from a Victoria crowned pigeon, and proudly carried his shotgun. It was a one-day patrol; after examining the Wakau families he would repeat the process in Mauwi hamlet, then return home.

Litabagi and I had a friendly, almost jocular, relationship but he still surprised me with a gift of two coconuts from trees in Wakau that were planted for him years earlier by Nauwen and Oria's father.[2] After a brief rain shower, the shout 'ol i lain' was heard,

---

1. An exception to this generality were a few women who took their sick infant directly to Rosemary Ace at the mission for help as she was known to save an infant's life.
2. Litabagi and Oria, as of course their fathers, all belonged to the Apilami patriclan.

and villagers began assembling in front of my house where Litabagi was situated, since I had set up my Bolex movie camera to film the action and take photos with my Leica. As usual, without direction males including boys fell into a staggered line in front and women with babies and daughters several yards behind (fig. 47).

Figure 47. Partial lineup of Wakau families for Litabagi's medical patrol; Mowal far left, next to Mangko and Kairapowe chatting.

Reviewing the film and photos so many years later was far more interesting and informative than my originally being there. As Litabagi sauntered down the two spread-out lines, first past the males then the females, he would have known most everyone by name, how he was related to them, if at all, and would have rapidly read how they stood, looked, and acted for signs of illness. Like a practiced physician who can tell as you walk into his space what might be wrong, Litabagi asked questions, answered a few, touched some, took a child by the hand as he spoke, all while making a mental list of who needed his attention.

He told Enewan and Eine they both had pneumonia and must come to his 'haus sik' for medicine. Eine's daughter Emani and Mari's daughter Lelaware both had sores that needed treating. A few others he treated in situ, as Oria's sister's baby (see fig. 48). Then I went with him to see Ime, Sakome's daughter who was too sick to attend the clinic. He immediately diagnosed pneumonia, started her on sulpha tablets and gave me a supply to continue her treatment to assure her recovery. Three days earlier, she had suffered a brutal *imoulu* curing session with K____, described later in this chapter. Ime's illness was one of the first serious cases that I became involved with. Although I was trying not to give villagers medicine because of my research design, I relented after witnessing Ime's pain-fraught curing session with K____ and knowing she was too sick to walk to the aid post for Litabagi's help. I had been told that her sickness began with a fever and shaking so I misdiagnosed malaria and started her on chloroquine, but her temperature remained high. Fortunately, Litabagi surprisingly arrived the next day with his practiced clinician's eye and modern medicines. With Litabagi, Ime lucked out with a more expert bush diagnostician than either K____ or me and gradually recovered. Several days later, Eine and the two girls went to the aid post for treatment, but Enewan never did.

Figure 48. Aid post orderly Litabagi gives oral amodiaquine to Oria's sister's baby.

Home Remedies, Physical and Ritual

When a villager had an unusual physical condition or felt rotten, they sometimes resorted to home remedies before seeking professional help, such as going to the aid post or an *imoulu*—whom they usually must pay—to treat them. The Namia vocabulary regarding sickness is small; there are no names for specific types of afflictions, just descriptions. The word for sick is *pai*, but they did differentiate between a sore, *ila*, and an abscess or boil, *wan*. Home treatments were performed by the patient or by a family member for minor ailments, or before a progressive sickness became grave. The Lujere distinguished those illnesses that were external and visible to the eye, like sores, wounds, and injuries, from the more mysterious internal illnesses, like pains, fevers, vomiting, diarrhea, and malaise. The former usually were treated by home remedies, at least initially, and the latter by *imoulu*. When men went away as indentured laborers, they took their local treatment notions with them but might not always have the correct item at hand. Ginger, for example, was used in many treatments but not just any ginger; it must be a specific species, often growing in a specific place. While Waripe was away working, having left his wife Sakome with five children to care for, only to be harassed by Samaun, he sent a letter to Alomiaiya saying that he was very sick and to send some *aiwar wowi* ginger as soon as possible. Oria said that the ginger plant belonged to Kwoien and he thinks he got it from Gwidami village.

Here are a few examples of home treatments. When Yaope was sick all week with a headache his only remedy was to tie a piece of cloth tightly around his forehead. He also had a cold. He blamed his condition on the 'ton' tree (Pometia pinnata) and its small fruits he had eaten. When the 'ton' tree bears its fruit, he explained, 'em i taim belong kus,' that is, colds become prevalent. But other villagers had been eating 'ton' fruit for a couple of weeks, and Yaope was the only one apparently affected.

Another remedy for pain was bleeding—for instance, making small cuts in one's forehead to cure a headache. One night when visiting the lower *iron*, I noticed caked rivulets of blood on Klowi's right leg. Before I could ask, he explained that his legs had ached while he was hunting and he had asked his wife to make small incisions on the lower part of his right calf. Letting the bad blood out, he added, eased the pain. Another of the most common remedies for aching muscles was applying a counterirritant of stinging nettles.

Boils, a type of painful abscess, are infections of a hair follicle or oil gland, and were an occasional complaint of males in the lower *iron* where I was a frequent visitor. Their treatment usually was to endure the discomfort and eventually lance it to drain the pus. Tsaime had a particularly bad one and, once he had lanced it, he went to the aid post to have it bandaged. Oria explained to me that the reason the males in the lower village have boils is from stepping on a species of wild ginger that flourishes on the 'kunai' near the Sand River, an area they frequently visited.

Ringworm or tinea is a contagious fungal infection of the top layer of the skin and was especially disliked by both males and females. In some cases, it could cover much of a person's body and was considered disfiguring. In Wakau, there were nine men, six boys, seven women, and three girls afflicted, totaling twenty-five villagers. There was no belief regarding its origins; they thought some skins resisted it while others succumbed. Oria said that as children, he, Nauwen, and their sister were afflicted. Their father's treatment for it was to rub the affected skin with part of a pig's or fish's liver; this worked for his sons but his sister was still covered with tinea. Another local treatment was to rub the affected areas with pig blood or to take a shoot of the *moru* shrub, crush it and mix it with lime. This turned it red and the residue was spread over the tinea.

I was surprised how often a sick villager would not resort to an alleviating treatment but just suffered it through, especially if the ailment were not considered life-threatening. For about a week I observed Enmauwi suffering from what looked like pinkeye or conjunctivitis. He carried an old rag to occasionally wipe his eyes or shield them from the bright light. Most of the day he stayed inside. Eventually he went to a woman in Gwidami for a cure but on his return, he wasn't in a mood to give me any details so I let it drop. His eyes cleared up in a few more days, but this is also about the length of time pinkeye lasts. There were a few more cases of pinkeye but no one else visited the Gwidami woman nor did I ever elicit a cause for the ailment. It also was one of several very annoying minor illnesses that weren't taken to an *imoulu* for diagnosis and treatment—no one ever died of pinkeye.

Other than physical home treatments there were also ritual home treatments. A father—in this case Oria—with a baby screaming in the middle of the night might cut down a black palm because earlier he inadvertently stepped upon a branch that fell from it. Then at night, when the wind blew and shook the palm's branches, the baby would cry; only by felling the palm could he quiet his child. Another reason for a crying baby might be that a dead grandparent's *aokwae* had returned to the village to see his or her grandchild. Then the baby's parent must blow into each of the baby's ears while imploring the *aokwae* to leave it in peace.

Once when Oria's wife Pourame was sick and running a fever, and already had been treated by Mangko and another *imoulu*, Oria decided to try something one of the Mokadami curers had advised him to do for her when we attended their *aewal wowi* curing festival. The day after our return, Warajak and I accompanied Oria a short way down the slope behind my house into the bush to collect the prescribed potent botanical items for an *aewal wowi* curing packet. As he collected each specific item, he described it, then gave me its Namia word, thus: layer under a tree's bark *laumi*; vine leaf, *awoiwai*; a tree leaf, *miwai*; small plant leaf, *monawanu*; tree shoot, *naulere*; moss from a 'kwila' trunk, *naminami*; white betel pepper, *pulakari*; ginger, *iwowi*; aromatic bark, *yaparna*; swamp leaf, *anabirnakiewai*; and a mushroom, *unware*. He then assembled the items on a large leaf and neatly tied the bundle together (fig. 49).

Figure 49. Oria makes an *aewal wowi* curing bundle for his sick wife.

After Oria went to get his wife, they arrived with Oria carrying one-year old Nakwane and Pourame looking very sick and weak. Giving his wife the baby, he covered their heads with a cloth to protect them from seeing the powerful packet (fig. 50). He then held Nakwane as Warajak rubbed the packet on different parts of her body.

Figure 50. Oria covers Pourame for the curing ritual.

Oria then returned their son to Pourame, knelt, and gently stroked her legs (fig. 51) before making several small cuts on her left foot—she didn't flinch—with a new razor blade I had loaned him. Seeing the blood, Oria said to me, 'Blut i kapsait, nau sik i pinis,' that is, "the blood flowed, now her sickness is cured." The entire ritual took about ten minutes and throughout Pourame said nothing. After Oria removed the cloth from her head, they left for home. Later he optimistically commented to me how dark her blood had been; it was a good sign for a recovery.

Pourame and Oria's Family Health Crisis

But Pourame did not get better. Two days later I was tape recording Oria about his curing ritual for Pourame and Tsaime happened to join us. I already had learned that she was still sick and had only eaten a small amount of sago dumpling. I asked if there were other ritual cures for her sickness and he replied, "No, just the *aewi wowi* and we have tried that and it didn't work." Then he startled me by coldly saying, "Let her be; suppose she dies, it is alright!" Alarmed, I wondered who would feed and care for the children if she died and he replied, 'Wantoks,' friends. Tsaime laughed lightly, then protesting, said, "No way, friends won't look after the children the way a mother would!" and I immediately agreed. Oria's apparent callousness was troubling to both Tsaime and me; Tsaime looked at me with a worried look and slightly shook his head as if to say, "Man, what is he doing!" Then Oria abruptly admitted that he was very worried and, talking rapidly, outlined a plan as if Pourame were dead, saying that he would first find a woman to take care of the children, then find himself another wife so he could take the children back and care for them himself. He also said something about going to the 'haus sik' with his children but that he would tell Nauwen and me first. Speaking non-stop, he admitted he would like to sit down and talk with his wife but that now she just wanted to die. Tsaime, now visibly upset, exclaimed, "I don't want her to die!" I asked if her brother (married to Oria's sister) in Mauwi had been down to see her and was told, "No," and Tsaime added that he didn't think they knew she was so sick. Then I recalled that her brother was in Wakau well over a week ago when Pourame was sick and he did not go into her house but visited me to see if I had a job for him, which I didn't. Oria added that he had sent a message to him yesterday to come see them, but so far, he hadn't.

Oria then began to get more distraught. He was disgusted with this kind of sickness. Plenty of men had tried to cure her and she was not one bit better. He wants a sickness to be cured after at least two *imoulu*, or at the most three, have tried, but that her kind of sickness seemed to be incurable; it won't go away. I agreed that Pourame now seemed seriously ill. Oria exclaimed that he didn't know what caused her sickness; he can't look inside of her, and then indicated that it was 'sanguma,' that a *nakwolu* had ruined her. He thought they had taken a part of her backsides then cooked and eaten it. When I asked how, he replied it's just like you take the hindquarters of a pig and cook them. Tsaime seemed uncomfortable regarding this entire discussion and smiled nervously. Oria knew it was her backsides because since she had been sick, she could not sit down. All she could do was lie down but couldn't sit up. She was, however, able to go outside for bodily needs. The conversation then shifted to Ai'ire's sickness as he had gone to the 'haus sik' because his urine had turned red.

Figure 51. Warajak helps Oria complete the *aewal wowi* curing ritual for Pourame.

I had decided that Pourame had pneumonia and, as she was now too sick to go to the aid post, started her on a regime of sulpha and she gradually recovered. But Oria's anxiety regarding Pourame's illness and how he handled it has never left me; his initial chilling response, then the almost panic he experienced at the thought of her death. Tsaime's response, which so mirrored mine, was probably why I liked him so much; we shared a similar affective reaction to life.

Magical Curers

While magical curing prevails in many nonlliterate societies like the Lujere, it is still a part of some contemporary Western societies' religious groups, although greatly diminished in importance from the seventeenth century, when healing by magical touch, especially by the monarch, was prevalent. Charles II is known to have ministered to over ninety thousand persons in the twenty years, 1669–64 and 1667–83 when 8,577 entries appear in the King's Register of Healing. Queen Anne (1665–1714), whose patients included the infant Samuel Johnson, was the last English ruler to heal by touch. (Thomas 1971: 228.) The Lujere also have an impressive roster of male healers or *imoulu* who are locally renowned for their magical hands; we will now turn our attention to them.

Male Magical Curers

Earlier I identified the *nakwolu* as witches and described the vicious 'sanguma' murders attributed to them that the Lujere believed were real, although no one had actually witnessed one. It was always a surprise assault on a lone person. Although unseen, the terrifying verbal descriptions of a brutal 'sanguma' battering with strangulation, flesh slashing, blood collection, and a doomed death flooded the awareness of every man, woman, and child in Lujereland. Ironically, and to me a tragic irony, 'sanguma' in its detailed florescence of evil was usually no more than a frightening but magical linguistic trope. The complex acts of a 'sanguma' killing—especially the several impossible magical ones—were just factually unsubstantiated beliefs; the primary existence of 'sanguma' was in the Lujere imagination. While the murderous magic of the *nakwolu* was mostly imaginary, what was highly visible and made them essential in everyday life was their status as a valued curer, an *imoulu*.[3] It was a peculiar dual status they uniquely held in Lujere society, a Janus-faced, Jekyll-and-Hyde persona, lauded for one skill and damned for the other. Within a village context he was respected as an *imoulu* and pursued for his curative skill. At the same time, when out of sight he was believed to perform heinous murderous attacks as a *nakwolu* on the unsuspecting. Thus, a 'sanguma' man in Lujere society was both a *nakwolu* and an *imoulu*; there was no doubt in his patient's mind that his power to cure was related to his vicious clandestine murders.

---

3. The verb for his curing moves is *imoure*. Kelm (1990: 450), in her fieldwork with the Lujere's northern neighbors, the Kwieftim (Ak language) and Abelam (Awum language) villagers, also found that 'sanguma' men doubled as curers. As Hau'ofa notes for Mekeo society, "The attacker is the healer" (1981: 243) and Malinowski for the Trobriands, "The art of killing and curing is always in the same hand" (1922: 75).

Precolonial Lujere society had only one important male specialist status: the *imoulu* as a healer. Other specialists, for example, the 'luluai,' 'tultul,' licensed gun owner and aid post orderly, were all colonial statuses. *Nakwolu*, in spite of their bad reputations as malicious secret killers, in their *imoulu* status were the desired diagnosticians and curers in Lujereland and enjoyed the prestige that physicians have in Western society. Their curing role, besides being greatly valued, was ethically transparent and as highly public as their alleged magical murders were clandestine. Some curers were so renowned that they visited distant villages to treat the sick. Still, regardless of where the *imoulu* was welcomed and esteemed for his curing skills, his healing performance remained shadowed by his reputation as a murderous *nakwolu*.

Female Magical Curers

Although most curers were male, a few villages also initiated female curers. There were no female curers in the western Lujere villages I knew best but I observed three who had come to Wakau with three *imoulu* from the eastern Weari–area villages. Unlike the male curers, who as 'sanguma' witches were both curers and killers with intrinsic powers to perform magical murders, to cure, and to fly, these female curers had only the power to cure.[4] To receive that power, they underwent a special initiation: The initiate first entered a river with her husband or close male relative while men upriver ran yelling through the forest, frightening *aokwae* who fled into the river and were swept downstream. If the waiting woman was entered by one of the *aokwae* she began to shake violently and was held by her male attendant to keep from drowning. Leaving the river, they returned to the village to celebrate. She now had the power to assist an *imoulu* to cure but remained subject to mild, if infrequent, shaking fits caused by the *aokwae* within her. Like the male curers, the women were paid with money but proportionally lower. While male curers performed their therapeutic actions as they squatted, sat, or stood next to their patient, the female curers I observed always worked while standing upright or bending over from the waist.

Magical Curing Practices

When a Wakau villager felt really sick and a home remedy, if tried, didn't help, an *imoulu*, not the aid post orderly, was usually approached for treatment.[5] But, I was told, you should be very sick. One evening I was at the upper *iron* and found Kwoien lying on a blanket in a corner with a raging fever, barely talking, and he had been this way for two nights. No *imoulu* had treated him. As Akami explained it, 'sik i nupela yet,' meaning he hadn't been sick very long, adding that if you get treatment too early, the curer just has to do it over again.

---

4. I did not learn if there was a distinct term for women curers.
5. If a sick person lived in a village with an aid post, as in Yegarapi or Akwom, there was perhaps a better chance that they first sought the free help of an orderly before accessing an *imoulu*, whom they usually must pay.

An ambulatory patient might seek out an *imoulu*, even if he lived in another village. I had recorded numerous instances of patients coming to Wakau for treatment, as well as Wakau villagers going to neighboring villages for healing. Whether the patient went to the curer or the curer came to the patient, the treatment usually was in a house or an *iron*. A sick person might see numerous different curers or even the same one repeatedly before he or she recovered, died, or as in some cases, more or less settled for a chronic condition, as the woman Mane did in chapter 15. Moreover, a curer might decide not to treat a patient. Arakwake had a bad stomachache and asked K____ to treat him but he declined. Earlier Arakwake had accosted K____ in Wakau's bush, looking for his dog, and told him he didn't want him coming onto our bush to kill us with 'sanguma.' Arakwake thought K____ was retaliating by refusing to treat him. There was also the possibility that it was K____ who made him sick, as a *nakwolu* does not treat someone he has attacked. Depending on the relationship to the patient, a small monetary payment, at most a few shillings, was expected. Only K____, I was told, treated members of his own family. All others sought out other curers for themselves and family members; as an example, one morning Wami, an important *nakwolu* and *imoulu* from Mauwi, came down to Wakau with his feverish son and had both Menetjua and Meyawali treat him.

In Lévi-Strauss's (1949) classic paper on "The Sorcerer and his Magic," he calls attention to the three essential elements in the "shamanistic" curing complex that cannot be separated: the shaman curer, the sick person, and the observing public. He also emphasizes that "in treating his patient the shaman also offers his audience a performance" (1949: 180). That certainly was the histrionic situation among the Lujere. In my reporting on the *imoulu* curing practices below, I follow his lead by including the same contextual triumvirate.

First, unlike a visit to a doctor in America, there is nothing private about a Lujere sick person's treatment session; often the venue is filled with women, men, and children talking, sleeping, cooking, eating, or just looking. Watching a patient's treatment is often a break in a wearisome day as the curer performs his different curing procedures in the presence of oft random others. There is no undressing; the patient is examined in what they were wearing: if a woman, a sarong or Native skirt; if a man, shorts, a sarong, or penis sheath. The *imoulu* usually asks his patient a few questions about the problem before the patient sits or lies down on the floor for him to begin examining his or her bare skin with his exploring hands. Hence the title for this book, *A Witch's Hand*; these are the same magical hands that are believed to kill or cure. No herbs or medicines are used or administered.

If the patient is seen in an *iron*, there are often a number of men sitting around smoking, chewing betel nut, and visiting, as well as a few curious boys and a sleeping dog or two. As the men talk, handfuls of sago-leaf fibers are pressed into loose balls and passed among them as the men chewing betel nut spit repeatedly into them until they are almost dripping with the bright red spittle. In this way part of the audience are active participants in the curing performance. But there was no rationale behind the use of the spittle-coated leaf bundle. Their explanation for this custom was the phrase, tiresome and unhelpful to me, "It's what our ancestors taught us."[6]

---

6. A betel-bespat sago frond bundle was not a requirement for treatment but always occurred if a group of men were present. A treatment in a person's home might forego it without comment or concern; this was not a society that obsessed over procedures.

Squatting next to his patient, the curer does much probing and kneading of the skin as he attempts to find the cause of the sickness. Most curers are fairly careful, but if the probing is done roughly or too deeply, it can be a painful process; children and young women sometimes scream in pain and fright as the curer's strong fingers probe deeply into and under tender body areas. Relatives then restrain and try to comfort a protesting patient as the treatment and cries continue. While the curer attempts to identify and isolate a lethal object shot into the patient by an *aokwae* or *nakwolu*, he tightly pinches the skin together with his fingers, pulling it inches aloft. When he locates an offending entity under the skin, he grips it tightly within his fingers and, taking the betel-bespat fibers in the other hand, grasps the affected skin and by pinching, pulling, and shaking the skin he magically expresses the noxious substance, whatever it is, into the fibers to be taken outside for disposal. This overall process may be repeated numerous times until he is satisfied that he has removed the causes for the sickness, or at least done all he can right then. Sometimes the curer will report that the object was, for instance, a piece of razor blade or a bamboo sliver; more rarely he might momentarily display it, but he usually shows and says nothing.

Another frequent and sometime concurrent cause of sickness is "broken bones," especially the bones in the upper body that may be cracked or broken by invisible arrows shot into the body by an *aokwae* or *nakwolu*. These he repairs by pushing the fractures or broken bones together with his fingers. A curer may perform other therapeutic actions like simple massage for muscle soreness, or try to turn a baby in an improper position for birth by massage and external manipulation. Klowi, however, was the only curer I knew who actually assisted at a birth. For ordinary men, anything to do with childbirth was taboo, as it negatively affected their health and ability to hunt.

Magical Curers and Their Patients

I observed twelve male curers and three female curers from a total of six different Lujere villages performing treatments. From the many curing sessions by these fifteen curers that I watched, I have selected a sampling to give the range of patients and curers, including the differences in the latter's temperament and treatment style.

Klowi Treats Iwanauwi of Mauwi Hamlet

The first *imoulu* I watched was Klowi treating the young girl Iwanauwi of Mauwi. Just before lunch Nauwen mentioned that Weame was here with his sick daughter for Klowi to 'wokim skin,' (curing with hands). I immediately went to the lower *iron* where the two men and Ai'ire were visiting. Klowi seemed a bit surprised when I asked if I could watch him treat Weame's daughter, but Ai'ire smiled and said he would call out for me when he did; right then she was with her mother at Klowi's wife's house. I returned home for lunch but by one ten, not hearing from Ai'ire, I returned to the *iron* with my notebook and Leica. Klowi was sitting on the floor kneading the skin of a girl around twelve years old held in her mother Pokeni's arms. Ai'ire lay on the floor fast asleep.

Her father Weame, who was sitting to the side smoking his beautiful two-piece traditional pipe, looked up and smiled. Klowi was rubbing the girl's stomach and chest and addressing me said, 'banis i bruk,' 'het i pen,' that is, her rib cage was injured and her head ached. Klowi felt around Iwanauwi's head and neck while she securely gripped her mother's arm. Her father continued to quietly smoke and watch. It reminded me of Joyce and me visiting the pediatrician with one of our children; the caring affect of all was the same, only the situation was startlingly alien. Iwanauwi began to whimper—she was afraid as Klowi began pressing her head strongly with his fingers. I had been taking photos but now moved my position so the four faced me and sat with my back against a welcomed house post. Her mother abruptly had a brief coughing fit; the treatment was interrupted, and we all smiled and laughed.

Klowi then carefully kneaded her back and her chest. He was not exploring for objects shot into her by *nakwolu* or evil spirits; earlier he had told me, 'Em i sik nating,' implying there was nothing to be removed from her body. Then he began feeling around under her jaw. He pushed rather hard with his fingers and she did not like it; she began to squirm away but her mother continued to hold her firmly. Klowi looked at me occasionally and smilingly told me what he was doing. He then pushed very strongly on the frontal bone above her left eye—he had chosen this area for special attention—now I began to mentally squirm as he pressed extremely hard. Iwanauwi screamed; but he kept pressing even as he tried to sooth her. I glanced at my watch; it was one-twenty.

Iwanauwi was still sobbing from the pain she had endured so I was relieved when he began making a blowing motion, over and over, on the very top of her head; Klowi seemed to be finished. My cynical thought was that the treatment was more painful than her symptom. The young patient and her mother arose and left the *iron*—the terminal phase of the treatment session I watched was just ten minutes long—then I stayed to visit with the men. Enewan came in and reminded me that he was picking up my supplies from Yellow River tomorrow when the MAF plane came in. Back home, I asked Nauwen about Klowi's blowing on Iwanauwi's head. He said that it was to finish her sickness, he didn't know the details but that she would be all right and her headache would stop. The community's optimism regarding an *imoulu*'s treatment still impresses me, since I privately saw it as, at best, only as an honest yet bogus remedy.

Menetjua Treats Tschorai

One morning early in February after Eine and his family had moved into Oria's wife's house, Eine came over, all seriousness, to say that his son had become sick during the night and that his skin was hot. Tschorai, about eleven, had little of the energy and loquaciousness of his father. In fact, unlike other boys his age, he hadn't picked up any Tok Pisin and showed no curiosity about his foreign neighbor across the way. Early in the afternoon I went over to see how he was; my less compassionate ethnographic self also was curious to see how the two families had merged in their one-room accommodations after Eine's family moved in uninvited as noted in chapter 11.

There were two clay hearths in the middle of the floor of the house, one on each side, and two elevated traditional beds, one each in the upper right and back left corners of the room with no hearth beneath them as in the *iron*. The back bed was

Oria's, the front one Eine's and his son's. The women and other children slept on the 'limbum' floor. When I arrived, Oria was cooking a sago pancake on a piece of metal taken from a kerosene drum. Sitting on the floor near him was his wife holding their sleeping baby son, Nakwane. Eine was sitting on the side of his bed by Tschorai who was lying naked on his belly with Oria's old white tomcat curled up next to him. Eine's young daughter Imani was standing on the other side of the bed watching. I sat down on the bed next to Eine and felt Tschorai's head and back, both very hot. He was very lethargic but Eine finally got him to sit up and said that his lower back ached and he had a headache. When Tschorai turned towards me I saw that his lips were dry and a bit puffy and that his right cheek was flushed and badly swollen. He looked miserable, but was stoical.

Eine said he was going to take his son to the upper *iron* so Menetjua could treat him, so I went home for my notebook and tagged along with them, slowly, as Tschorai was unsteady walking and Eine held his arm. When we entered the *iron*, Samaun was asleep—as usual—and Kaiera was sitting quietly on the floor near Menetjua's bed eating sago. Alomiaiya and Kworu were lazing around and Enewan, who was sick, was lying in the sun on the narrow back veranda; seeking the sun when ill was an uncommon habit here, but very common among the Wape. Eine and Tschorai followed me to the back of the *iron* where I sat down near the door; it was two-thirteen.

Menetjua slowly got off his bed, appearing very sleepy. He neither looked at nor spoke to me but sat down on the floor opposite me. Nor did he speak to his patient who lay down with his head on his father's legs while the latter swatted at flies annoying his son. Tschorai moaned slightly when Eine tried to swish his body with nettle leaves, so he stopped. Eine and Menetjua exchanged a few words then Menetjua scooted up closer to the boy and at two-fifteen began to treat him. First he felt around the small of his back and his upper buttocks, then pressed on his spine in various places with his thumbs and the first few fingers of each hand. His motions were gentle but Tschorai had his eyes tightly shut and at no time did he look at the *imoulu*. I visited a bit with Alomiaiya and Enewan while Eine got his son to turn onto his back and Menetjua felt around his frontal area, then his neck. Tschorai coughed and pulled away—this boy did not want to be there—but Eine coaxed him to turn back towards his healer by holding both of his son's arms.

Menetjua pulled on Tschorai's neck skin and when he began to press, the boy cried out, but Menetjua continued, moving around to the side of the neck. Then Tschorai forcefully turned onto his side away from Menetjua, who stopped. It was now two twenty-six. With Eine still holding his son, Menetjua continued by putting his fingers on the swollen neck area, but gently. Tschorai had a very sore boil that had yet to abscess. Eine told me that Aiyuk and Leno previously both had children with boils on the head area. Menetjua moved his hands momentarily to the boy's stomach area, then at two twenty-seven, he lifted them, scooted back, slowly stood, and got back up on his bed. The twelve-minute treatment was over. I asked Alomiaiya, standing next to me, what Menetjua had done and he replied that he had fixed the boy's broken bones in his back but that the boil was just an ordinary boil, and that is why he was sick. I glanced out the rear door and Enewan was sleeping. I stood to leave but Eine and Tschorai remained, the latter with his eyes still closed and maybe blessedly asleep.

Eine's and Tschorai's Curer Treatments

Because I lived so near to Eine and his son, I was able to record their recourse to treatment for a few days when both were in physical distress. Eine had been sick for about a month when he took his son on a Friday to see Menetjua, as just reported. A few days earlier, Eine had been diagnosed with pneumonia on Litabagi's medical patrol to Wakau and was ordered to visit the aid post for treatment. His son, who didn't like any kind of practitioner, did not attend. Eine was not satisfied with Menetjua's treatment for his son and later that same day had Klowi treat him. On Saturday Tschorai was still feverish so Ulwau came down from Mauwi to treat him, then later in the day Mangko did too. As he still had a fever the next morning, Eine decided to take his son to Mokadami where his brother-in-law Anwani lived, so a few others and I went with them. Once there, both Eine and his son were treated by different local *imoulu*. Oriak began by massaging Eine's stomach, searching for lethal objects to be removed, occasionally pulling up his pinched loose belly skin by several inches then, having located something, was handed the usual betel nut spittle-soaked bundle of shredded sago fronds wherein he put it over his clasping hand before carrying it outside to discard the object. He did this four times in the ten minutes I watched. Before I left to make a quick visit to nearby Aiendami village, Oriak, on our host Anwani's instructions, showed me a slender ivory-colored object he had removed that appeared to be a tooth, maybe filed down. Before we all returned to Wakau, I watched Tschorai being unhappily treated by Mankani. Eine told me that since a small child, his son had protested any and all curing treatments. Yet in the three days of Tschorai's acute sickness, his caring father had arranged for him to be treated by five *imoulu* from three different villages.

The following morning Eine and his daughter Emani went to the aid post as advised by Litabagi, but not Tschorai. In spite of his abscess, Eine said Tschorai did not want to go, adding that Mankani had successfully cured his son's fever.

A 'Sangumaman' Treats Ime

K____, as we know, was a convicted murderer, having ten years earlier strangled to death the old woman, Prai, in a failed 'sanguma' magical ritual murder. As one of the most feared *nakwolu* in Lujereland, he also was considered a powerful curer. Before Sakome had moved to Mauwi with her children to live with her brother Kowali's family to avoid Samaun's harassment, her oldest child Ime became sick and K____ was sent for to treat her. Ime was physically mature but still very young. This became the most personally disturbing treatment session I observed.

Ime's treatment occurred in Klowi's wife Wawenowaki's house, just down the rise from my house that, as usual, was active with people. Ime's mother's brother, Kowali, who had a close relationship with his sister and her children, arrived in Wakau from Mauwi just before noon with two other Mauwi men. He was convinced that Meyawali (a *nakwolu*) and his brother Samaun had caused his niece's sickness. At twelve-thirty I went down to the treatment house with my notebook in hand and Leica around my neck and sat on the floor towards the head of Ime's prone body. To her immediate left sat her mother Sakome with a small child and, to her left, her husband's older brother's widow, Baruboi. To Ime's right K____ squatted and down by her legs was her mother's brother, Kowali. Others sat and stood around, still occupied with their own concerns, except for the numerous children who, welcoming this diversion, crowded in around the door behind me. Walwin, a Mauwi man I didn't know well and the husband of Baruboi's daughter Elamwari, squatted a short distance down from Baruboi. At the far end of the house Oria stood near the other door.

Ime lay on her left side and Walwin and K____ lightly stroked her legs, then her arms with nettles. Walwin pulled her finger, placed his hand on her face, then helped her sit up and felt her back. Sakome was nursing her baby but continued to watch her daughter. When K____ put his hand on Ime's head, she opened her eyes and appeared rational if not steady. Earlier Warajak told me she had been delusional. K____ helped her stand up as he spoke with Baruboi, but Ime was almost immediately helped back down, coughed, and I noticed a line of new decorative burn scars on her upper right arm as K____ resumed his squatting position. Looking around, I realized that most of the men and boys were towards the other end of the house and I was at the end with the women, girls, and toddlers. Hence, I was minus a young friend to keep me informed of what was happening and to translate, a tradeoff for the bright light streaming behind me into the dark house and the photos I was hoping for. I saw that Tsaime and Nauwen had entered the back door; everyone was visiting, smoking or chewing betel nut as Baruboi continued to soothingly rub Ime's back. Meyawali came in the front door and stood watching. Little was happening and I wondered, is it all over? Then men gradually began to pass the sago frond bundles around, each spitting his betel juice into them while K____ began his treatment (fig. 52).

It was now one o'clock. K____ felt around her stomach then appeared to grab something into his bundle before exiting the front door to return almost immediately to repeat the process. K____ probed deep into her abdominal cavity as Ime moaned in anguish and he made a grunt as if he had caught something in his bundle, pulled her skin up, and again immediately exited to return quickly and continue his abdominal explorations. Her moans of distress persisted as he pressed inward, then moved his attention to her bare left breast. When Ime emitted a loud moan, he momentarily let go, then returned his tight grip. As she began to resist the treatment, loving hands restrained her arms and legs.

I noticed Oria was now near me confining her right arm. They turned her over onto her left side as K____ accelerated his intrusive moves poking his hand painfully deep into her armpit; she moaned pitifully. I wrote in my notebook, "I'm upset!" They moved her onto her back and when K____ continued his probing she now screamed out in pain. Her family and friends continued to restrain her as K____ searched for something; she screamed again and he left with the bundle. I scribbled, "Thank God"—but he immediately returned and began pulling her stomach skin apart. I could sit there no longer and had to stand up but continued to take notes and photos.

At one twenty-two, he turned her over on her stomach, flipped her G-string and pulled her skirt down exposing her upper buttocks and began pinching the skin at the base of her spine. Kowali appeared to have come to his limit too and had pulled back from the treatment area. Ime was now sobbing but K____ continued to work on her exposed buttocks area. He pulled her skirt up half way and they turned her again on her back, and K____ returned to his intrusive abdomen motions pressing up under her rib cage. Amid her sobbing she occasionally moaned in pain. Her mother said something funny—emotional relief?—and they all laughed. Walwin held her left breast then pulled her skirt back down as K____ returned to working over her left breast. He moved his

Figure 52. Ime with K____ and Kowali, her mother's brother, holding a betel bespattered bundle.

hands to her head, but just feeling, not pressing, then to her neck. But some of the action had moved to me: I was standing and several little girls were stroking and playing with the strange blond hair on my legs.

It was one twenty-eight when they helped her sit up and K____ straddled her sideways feeling around her back; this time I scribbled, "When will this torture stop?" For another fifteen minutes he continued to explore her skin down to her legs doing pressing repairs but there were no more painful intrusions into her body with a betel be-spat bundle of frayed fronds. Pausing, K____ offered Ime some water to drink from a plastic bowl then at one forty-four he pushed back. Ime, obviously sick and exhausted, sat quietly; the curing session had ended, as everyone turned to new interests. I counted twenty-five people still in the house and then, looking up for the first time, I saw the roof overhead swarming with animated cockroaches. Fortunately for Ime, two days hence, Litabagi arrived as already described on his medical patrol, diagnosed her sickness as pneumonia, and prescribed the medicines that cured her.

Ime's horrific hour-long curing session with K____ had been both physically painful and emotionally wrenching. K____'s session might have seemed of heroic proportions to some as he magically cornered and removed the deadly things causing her serious illness. To me his actions seemed more sadistic abuse than curing and I, as a passive observer, felt complicit in Ime's nightmare ordeal. Yet these actions were publicly performed before a local community that included her closest and most loving kin.

Late that evening Tsaime stopped by and I asked a few questions. K____ had removed a part of an arrow and mended her many broken and fractured bones, one of the painful parts of his work. Her family, he said, wanted another *imoulu* from Gwidami to treat her tomorrow and also wanted to consult a woman who could dream back her soul.[7]

A Curing Clinic

I was just beginning to learn about the curing practices of the *imoulu* when on a Sunday afternoon in mid-December, six Weari-area curers—three men and three women—arrived at the lower *iron* for an extended curing session with Ai'ire. I was startled because I thought only men were curers. That was true for the western part of Lujereland where I lived but, as already noted, not for some of the eastern villages.

Shortly after 5:00 p.m., I went to the lower *iron* where the visiting male curers and about twenty men and youths were sitting and lying around smoking or chewing betel nut, plus two asleep stretched out along the wall. Some of the men were visiting while others seemed to be in a private zone. It was hot. With evening approaching, I had left my cameras at home. Ai'ire, who was there for treatment, sat near the entrance; his primary symptoms seemed to be gastrointestinal, with stomachaches and recurrent bouts of diarrhea. Ai'ire stretched out on his back and one of the visiting male curers began kneading and rubbing his stomach. Some of the men were preparing the sago strands by splitting them apart and bundling them, then passing the bundled fibers to be spat into

---

7. This was the closest the Lujere got to creating what some witch-prone societies call a "dewitcher"—a specialized person who is consulted by those who believe a witch has used his or her powers to impair their health or luck in life, as Favret-Saada (2015) describes for the Bocage region of northern France.

with betel juice. Another man rubbed a bundle vigorously between his hands as the red juice colored it.[8] The male curer working on Ai'ire's stomach made a big mound of flesh in the middle, pinched it together as one of the female curers grasped it with a bundle, tugged upward, then took it outside. The other two female curers were now by the door. Ai'ire's primary curer had immediately resumed his ardent belly kneading, rubbing, and pinching the flesh together. Ai'ire seemed stoical; no one had spoken to him, or he to them, since I had arrived.

Bending down in her faded skirt, Ai'ire's female curer had again placed her bundle on his belly where her partner had gathered and held his flesh in a very high mound. Grasping, she tried and tried to extract something, then her partner spoke and, in another yank, succeeded, but almost fell over backwards as Ai'ire smilingly grunted in relief. The male curer had removed his hands and leaned back; Ai'ire first lifted one knee then gradually sat up. I wrote in my notebook, "God, he looks sick!" The male curer started smoking as did two of the female curers. Oria, who was sitting near me, now also was spitting betel juice into a bundle. Pulling its dripping strands widely apart, he crushed them back together as he rubbed them briskly between his stained hands. Ai'ire, now sitting cross-legged, slowly scratched his back then stared down at his belly. Looking directly across at me he silently raised his eyebrows in a quizzical gaze. Touched, I wrote, "He is in bad shape. What a terrible way to deal with a man's 'bel'" [stomach]. Oria rubbed his hands on a nearby post to get rid of the betel juice then, reaching into his 'bilum,' (a string bag) took out a traditional white shell ring, saying he wanted to send it to Amanab where he could get two 'paun' (Australian dollars) for it, then replaced it. Within my view the Wakau men in the room were Kunai, Menetjua, Yaope, Oria, Nakwane, Mangko, and Mowal.

Just after 6:00 p.m., one of the other curing women standing by Ai'ire leaned over, lifted high one of his arms and rubbed down on it over and over, then repeated the process on his other arm. Ai'ire, now standing, extended an arm upwards to grip an overhead rafter as she rubbed his sides and his rib cage. The male curer returned and simultaneously began working on Ai'ire's stomach, trying to locate something in his belly as his other hand pushed strongly up on his shoulder. Ai'ire tightly gripped the rafter to maintain his balance. The woman now addressed his stomach, pushing repeatedly inward with the heel of her hand. The male curer had Ai'ire turn towards the door and also began rubbing his belly. Then all three of the female curers began working on his stomach as the man put his arms around Ai'ire for physical support. One of the women brought in a 'limbum' of water and placed it on the floor near Ai'ire while another leaned over to rinse her be-spat bundle. A third man—the first time he had touched Ai'ire—stood behind him with his arms around his waist and began kneading his belly. All now were working away and I turned my attention to the men around me, and learned how the women became curers and who they were. Nawerie was from Naum and Nabtho and Inaru were both from Alai. The women talked among themselves as they worked, occasionally going out with a bundle, returning to rinse it, then back to work kneading, pulling and squeezing Ai'ire's belly flesh.

At six thirty-two one of the men had returned to work on Ai'ire, still clinging to the rafter with one hand and the other on his head to keep it out of their way. Oria asked

---

8. When I asked what utility the bespat bundles had in the treatment, I was told it was their custom, always a lame explanation to the curious ethnologist. To my eyes, the primary function of the bundles was in grasping the noxious entity then removing it to the outside.

me if I wanted to go and when I said, "No," everyone laughed but I didn't grasp why. However, amid the Namia talk around me, several times I had heard the word 'masta,' obviously referring to me. Then when one of the male curers said to me that the treatment was about over; I wrote wondering, "Trying to get rid of me?" When living submerged in a language you don't really know, paranoia is a recurrent risk. Conversation continued and Oria said that Klowi had shot a cassowary today. Ai'ire now was lying on his back and the interminable stomach kneading had resumed. Oria again, atypically, tried to get me to leave with him but I declined. Around six forty-five, Oria left alone, Ai'ire sat up and I noticed that Nimo was here too.

The three female curers ceased working on Ai'ire, then left together to stay overnight with women relatives. I asked the male curers if they planned further curing that evening but they said no; they would remain the night and go home tomorrow. One of them, for no pertinent reason, added that Ai'ire would go to the aid post tomorrow, making me wonder if they assumed that I disapproved of their traditional treatments like the missionaries did. Mangko, probably in need of newspaper for his cigarettes, wanted to come that evening to tell me stories but I suggested tomorrow. As much as I usually enjoyed his company, he was a deadly dull storyteller. In the evening, if my energy lagged, he would put me to sleep. Back home I reviewed the curing session with Oria and Nauwen, who avowed that as onlookers, they didn't know what the curers were removing except that it was not good and that they can see it even if we can't. *Nakwolu*, I already had heard, were clairvoyant.

It rained hard all night and next morning the village was soaked and dripping. The skies remained cloudy and a four-foot python was killed behind my house before breakfast. When I later visited the *iron*, the Weari *nakwolu* were just eating. As all the waterways were swollen from the heavy rains, they planned to return home tomorrow and treat more patients today, including Ai'ire, who obviously wasn't going to the aid post. I went home and readied my equipment to film with my hand-held Bell and Howell movie camera—the *iron* was too crowded with participants for the bigger tripod-mounted Bolex camera—and to take photos with my Leica. When I returned shortly after noon with my filming gear, the usual lower *iron* men and youths, about twenty, were visiting and smoking or napping, like Klowi stretched out along a wall. Ai'ire was sitting near the entrance and one of the men already was working on him, and I began filming his treatment. This seemed to both please and slightly amuse the men and youths hanging out there.

Iwi came in with some sago fronds and gave them to Kunai, Engwe, and Tsaime to shred and prepare for the customary curing bundles. Mangko had a champagne bottle filled with kerosene, the bottle left over from when Joyce and I had celebrated with my family, who came down to see my new camp. He tipped out a bit of the kerosene to rub on a couple of small sores, then passed it around so men with lighters could fill them. The *imoulu* Ari focused his kneading attention on Ai'ire's stomach while two of the female curers took turns in grasping into their bundle whatever Ari had obtained and carrying it outside. In the meantime, I was both filming and photographing the process.

By one forty-five, Ai'ire's curing had ended and the next patient was Yabowe, the little daughter of Nakwone of Mauwi. Her symptoms were also abdominal; later Warajak told me that an *aokwae* had shot something into her and from his description it sounded like she had parasitic worms. Yabowe, wrapped in an old sarong too big for her, stood for her treatment supported under both arms by her father (see fig. 53). Ari felt all around her abdomen, then on locating something, his helper grasped it in her curing bundle and

Figure 53. Yabowe, supported by her father, is treated by Ari.

Figure 54. As Klene clings to a rafter for support, Ari tugs on his belly skin.

carried it outside. It was noticeable that Ari's moves were not as intrusive in his thrusting and pinching as with Ai'ire, and the patient did not struggle to get loose or cry. While Ari continued to treat Yabowe, his helper began working on Klene, also from Mauwi, who had symptoms in both his neck and his stomach.

Finally, Ari began treating Klene's abdominal problems. Klene stood with his right arm grasping a rafter and his other behind his head as Ari grappled with his belly skin (fig. 54).

It was after two o'clock, and the next patient was one of my favorite little Wakau boys. Manwe's father was Wolwar but it was his mother, Nauware, who brought him for treatment. Manwe was one of the few small children who, if I were in his vicinity, always looked up at me and, one way or another, made it a point to emotionally connect with me. Now he lay on his back and, like all little boys, was naked. Almost immediately his mother had to hold down his two arms while Ari, squatting down by him, began feeling over his belly with his long fingers (fig. 55).

Figure 55. Little Manwe is held down by his mother as Ari treats him.

Manwe started to scream and babble incessantly in Namia. It was a panic reaction hard to watch from such a sweet child. As he struggled for freedom, I admired Ari's professionalism and compassion—but he had certain procedures to complete just as any pediatrician must when examining a panicked child. However, it was Ari's female helper that terrified Manwe the most. Towering above him, she repeatedly thrust her soggy curing bundle down on his quivering belly with the chilling complacency of a Nurse Ratched (fig. 56).

Figure 56. Ari explores Manwe's belly as his helper leans down with a curing bundle.

I finished the roll of film on Manwe's curing as he screamed "iiiiiiii!" when his skin was pinched together. I loaded in another roll but was so distraught by my little friend's anguished screaming I somehow, unwittingly, even crazily, put the cover *on* the lens, thereby losing the next eleven photos. I didn't notice the mistake until after my little friend had been liberated; that set me musing regarding the mysterious power of the unconscious. By then it was two-twenty and Iwani's 'luluai' Bauwi came forward and sat down with his legs outstretched as Ari, squatting by him, began to probe and pinch his stomach. He, too, had problems with his gastrointestinal functioning, but this would be a short ten-minute session. After his helper made just two trips outside with her curing bundle, Ari relaxed his hands; for now he was finished.

Ari had been relieved by Enaru, the other *imoulu* from Alai, whose patient would be Lijeria, the mute bachelor and subject of Iwani's *na wowi* curing festival a month earlier, described in chapter 15. Lijeria rose slowly from the floor then stood listlessly, his skinny arm gripping a rafter as Enaru probed and squeezed his wasted body (fig. 57). His floppy shorts were sizes too big for him and made him look even more emaciated than he obviously was.

I used the end of the film in both the Leica and Bell and Howell cameras on Lijera's curing, then packed up and went home where Mangko was waiting to tell me some ancestor stories.

Mangko Treats Kaukobu of Gwidami

Towards the middle of January at the lower *iron*, I saw for the first time Mangko, who was the village's youngest *imoulu*, treat a sick person. His patient, Kaukobu, was from

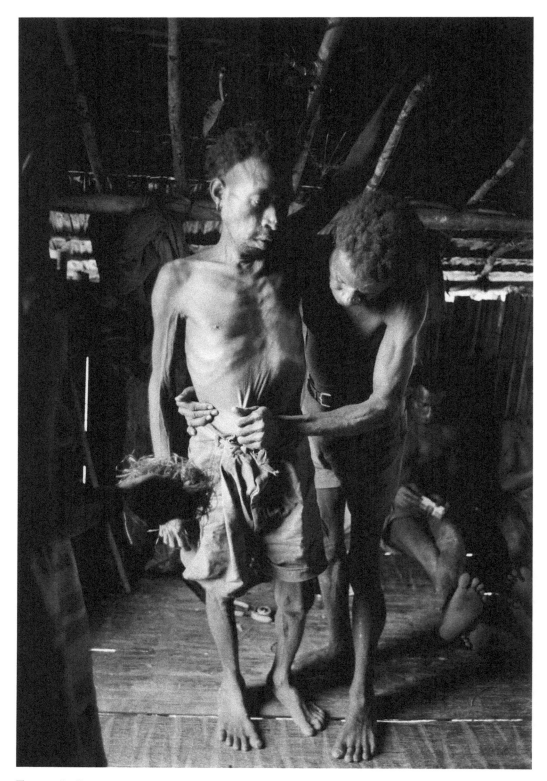

Figure 57. Enaru squeezes Lijeria's flesh as his helper waits with her curing bundle.

Gwidami and had returned from plantation labor just a few weeks before. Like his fellow villager Anwani, Kaukobu's plantation boss sent him home because he was sick too often. His major complaint was chronic chest pains. Mangko's treatment lasted fifteen minutes. His patient lay on his back wearing shorts and he primarily kneaded Kaukobu's stomach. He did not use a betel juice bespattered curing bundle but just his bare hands manipulating the skin. His healing style was highly informal. He rarely looked at what he was doing but was talking and joking with the patient and others including me. As Mangko was working, Kaukobu also was talking to me telling me about his trip home. I did not see Mangko remove anything from Kaukobu's body or comment that he did. When he finished, Kaukobu sat up and began smoking and Mangko went outside to eat some sago. Iwi and some boys came inside with pieces of pork and put them on the hearth's fire to cook. The action over, I went outside in the bright sunlight and up the short rise to home.

Three Weari Curers Treat Klowi

In the last week of February five men, of whom at least three were *imoulu*, came to Wakau from the eastern Weari villages. Previously Ai'ire had visited them for curing his little girl and they had marked the date they would return the visit. The morning of the day they arrived in Wakau, Ai'ire's wife had taken their daughter to the aid post because of a fever; Ai'ire told me he would go tomorrow and also take a pumpkin to trade for salt at the mission. At my house Nauwen had been seriously sick but my regime of vitamins and tetracycline had him finally up and looking more alive although Oria, who himself had a headache, was still helping him out with household tasks. It was Monday and Nauwen planned to go to Papei on Saturday to see an *imoulu* because neither Menetjua nor Mangko would treat him, apparently miffed at him about aspects of the younger Yaope's marriage I hadn't sorted out. Mangko wasn't even in the village, having gone on an overnight hunt with Klowi's gun accompanied by Warajak and Newai.

I had spent most of the day laboriously working on genealogies with Mari, Mowal, and Oria when the Weari men arrived midafternoon at the lower *iron*. By the time I joined them, some cooked 'aupa' leaves had been brought to them from Klowi's wife's house and men from both *irons* were scattered around the four sides of the room including Ai'ire, Aiyuk, Ukai, Klowi, Alomiaiya, Iwi, Kaiera, Enewan, Menetjua, plus Oria and Nauwen who arrived with me. Shortly after four o'clock, the little boys who were clustered in the center of the room were told to clear out so the visitors could start curing there. At four-twenty, Klowi stood up and walked quietly to the center and lay down with his head on his folded blanket, loosened the belt on his shorts and the three visiting *imoulu* joined him on the floor. I was informed earlier that two Aiendami *imoulu* told Klowi that he had a piece of a metal sickle in him and these men had come to remove it. As I already had exhausted Oria with the genealogy work, I looked around for Tsaime—always a helpful and tactful informant— to join me, but he was at his wife's house. So, with no names for the visiting curers, they would only be numbers—*Two*, *Three*, and *Four*—in my notes. I watched as a couple of clusters of betel juice-soaked sago fronds were passed among the men when Four first put his hands on Klowi's stomach, then felt under his back as Three stroked his legs and Two felt of his head. This, I thought, was going to be interesting; it was the first time I had seen an *imoulu* treated by his professional peers. It was obvious that Klowi believed in an *imoulu*'s power to cure or he wouldn't be stretched out before me. I was fascinated: how did Klowi and his curers rationalize their moves, like the bodily removal of an object, albeit usually unseen by the ordinary observer like me? More to the point, what was their personal understanding about those objects that they *actually* removed?

Three held both of Klowi's hips while Two held his arms. I wanted to take a photo but it was far too dark. Amid much talking amongst themselves, all three began working on his frontal area, including under his belt. They were a rather grubby-looking bunch but they also had made a grubby two hour or so hike to get here. Four was now sitting on Klowi's left, Two on his right, and Three near his feet. Four did the most exuberant work, pursing his lips tightly together as he pulled up tautly on Klowi's belly skin. At four forty-five, he finally found something, pulled strongly with his betel-red bundle to quickly take it outside and, in less than a minute, resumed his exploration of Klowi's belly. A clutch of young girls watched from the front door. Again, Four appeared to yank something from Klowi's belly and headed outside the door as the girls jumped out of his way. (I wondered out loud what happened to the noxious invisible substance when it was released, where did it go? But no one else cared; apparently it was just another of my irrelevant or inane questions.) Two had stopped to eat some 'opa' on a leaf while Four and Three continued to feel and probe. By five o'clock, Three had both hands in Klowi's shorts on either side of his genitals as Four pulled up his belly skin, yanked hard, and went out the door with the curing bundle. As he came back inside, a young woman, Wabe, threw in some nettles to old Menetjua. Another curing appeared to be happening: I watched our curer Menetjua stand behind one of the other two visiting Weari men, lean over to stroke his stomach with the nettles, blow gently into his right and his left ear, then stepped over him astride his head before enigmatically returning to where he was sitting.

When I returned my puzzled attention to Klowi's curing session, all three men busily focused on his abdomen. One of them was rubbing it up and down while emitting a soft continuous sibilant sound. At eight minutes after five, Three turned Klowi onto his left side amid mild laughter, and Two began exploring and pulling at the skin on his back. The sun was now streaming in the door and I took some photos of the three curers with their prone patient. Two was now having success and he went outside two more times as I took two more photos.

Finally they put Klowi onto his belly and Two worked on his back and lower spine as the other two curers watched; then it ended. At five-fourteen, Ukai was the first to leave, then I left momentarily for some tasks at home, but returned to watch Two treat Ai'ire for thirty minutes. The Weari men began to work on both Nauwen—whom Klowi and Mangko had declined to treat—and Oria, but I went home; I had had a surfeit of magical curing and wanted to clear my head with a warm bucket-shower and a shot of my favorite dark rum over a few tiny ice cubes, whose appearance from my small kero fridge in the middle of a steamy tropical jungle was the only magic I could truly believe in.

Oria later said the *imoulu* told him that the reason his head ached was that he had been shot in the back of his head with a wire that extended to the front. He had paid them thirty cents, twenty for himself and ten for Nauwen. He added that they did not say what they removed from Ai'ire's or Nauwen's stomachs and I forgot to ask if they removed the piece of a sickle from Klowi. Later that night Nauwen, after a few miserable days of real sickness when no *imoulu* he trusted would treat him, was almost jubilant he felt so good, enthusing to me how the Weari *imoulu* had removed bad things from his stomach. Although I was just as delighted to see his energy and spirits returning, I totally lacked his faith in the magical cures of a visiting curer and wished I were able to distinguish the difference between the placebo effect of a local hands-on cure and the proven efficacy of the powerful drug tetracycline I was giving him. I envied my colleague and friend, Gilbert Lewis, who had lived in a remote village like Wakau with doctorates in both anthropology *and* medicine. Though Nauwen protested that he already was cured, I insisted that he still complete the tetracycline regimen he had agreed to. Not surprisingly, it was the Weari *imoulu* magic that was credited for his cure.

Early the next morning Oria awakened me across the way loudly yelling in pain from an intense headache. Later I went across to see him and his head was wreathed in a long rope. All I could think of was the wire the *nakwolu* said had been shot into his head. Meyawali was with him gently rubbing his head. While he was a *nakwolu*, he only knew the hands-on techniques of curing, not how to remove lethal objects. I had brought with me some aspirin so by midafternoon Oria felt better and had come over to my office. Earlier Ai'ire and his wife had gone to the aid post as their daughter's fever had returned, and Tsaime had gone because he wanted a bandage for his lanced boil. Oria and I went to work and he taught me everything I should know about why the lower *iron* men were so susceptible to the boils that I earlier described.

Sickness, Curing, Placebos, and the Male Curers

When a Lujere villager was sick, their fervent hope was that an *imoulu* treatment would return them to health. I had seen the worried anxiety of a sick person who could not get the treatment of a curer, then the calming—on Nauwen it was exuberance—of the body when finally being treated by *imoulu* hands. Because there are so many *imoulu*, if a patient did not get better after a curer's treatment, he or she had only to seek out another one, thus maintaining a sense of hopefulness. However, regardless of the dramatically convincing physical details of a curer's treatment, from the perspective of scientific medicine, any healing effect was only psychological. An *imoulu* had none of the remedial implements, skills, or pharmacopeia to cure disease. As Gilbert Lewis writes,

> For nearly all man's time on earth, he has had almost no power to combat disease in the way we do now. Largely lacking effective somatic treatments, lacking microscopes and chemistry and knowledge of the intimate, intrinsic characteristics of disease, most people's decisions about treatment have made probably little, or random, difference to the natural outcome of their ailments. In terms of evolution, disease was mostly left to work on human populations like the wolf among the caribou, taking the infirm, leaving the rest—the healthy—to run free. (Lewis 1977: 233)

Yet these healers, the *imoulu*, were not charlatans or quacks: what we call magic, they perceived as real. Via the confidence villagers placed in a curer's healing hands, the hope of regained health was kept alive by the patient and their family. However, to a scientifically trained observer, an *imoulu* curing treatment was at best a placebo, a treatment with no active therapeutic agency. In this sense, to me their treatments, like the curing festivals, were just theater, but to the local believer they were genuine. In fact, from the outside, the entire *imoulu*-curing syndrome could be conceived as a culturally embraced placebo.[9]

In recent years the placebo effect has had extensive study as researchers have discovered that patients who erroneously think they are receiving a curative agent often show signs of improvement. While that obviously was not a part of my thinking when I lived with the Lujere, I was impressed that their Indigenous forms of curing like the *imoulu* and curing festivals were significant in maintaining a community sense of viable optimism—up to a point—when faced with sickness. While these Indigenous interventions couldn't realistically save lives, they could provide a thrust of hopefulness until death became inevitable. Then villagers were as skilled as an elderly GP in recognizing the clinical signs of dying; with unsentimental pragmatism they abandoned their cherished curing traditions and sought only to provide emotional support and physical comfort.

The Curer Paradox and Self-Referential Magic

At various points in this book, I have paused to consider the nature of the phenomenon I was writing about, especially if I identified it as magical or fantastical. By now it is clear that I perceive Lujere magical beliefs as specious; however, my modus operandi generally has been to write about occult phenomena with the field-oriented ethnographer's suspension of disbelief, just as I behaved when I lived with them.[10] My primary responsibility is to present the Indigenous view, not to contest it.

I also have occasionally focused on the disjunction between the consciousness of the Wakau villagers and my consciousness. While we more or less inhabited the same everyday physical world for month after month, our perceptions, how we experienced and interpreted the enveloping events, were often light years apart. My professional task—not theirs—was to lessen this disjunctive gap by looking, listening, questioning, and learning; theirs (if they wished), was to teach and explain.

What my Wakau friends taught me about 'sanguma' was that they—unlike what Burbandt (2014) reported for the Indonesian village of Buli—had no doubts regarding their witchcraft beliefs. Never did I hear a villager question the authenticity of 'sanguma' or

---

9. It was Michael Specter's (2011) article that stimulated my thinking regarding the Lujere's Indigenous forms of curing therapy as placebos and introduced me to the pioneering placebo research of Ted Kaptchuk (Kaptchuk and Miller 2015) and his colleagues.

10. Bubandt has a very thoughtful discussion regarding the "anthropological exhortation to suspend disbelief as a general rule" as it relates to modern and pre-modern or traditional societies, finding it problematic as it "upholds the illusion that disbelief is the monopoly of modernity" (2014: 15–17). Also see Bruno Latour's (2010) book, that even more radically explores "belief" in modernity and his critical and creative takes on "fetishes" and "facts." For another searching view of the significant difference between "literate and oral cultures" see Jack Goody's historical essay on agnosticism in relation to the ethnographer's holistic approach that "tends to exaggerate. . . . and to neglect absences or failures of belief, and the existence of doubt" (1996: 677). Holding these caveats in mind, I still aver that the Wakau villager, even with a succession of failed treatments by *imoulu*, rarely lost faith in their eventual efficacy. Ai'ire was the only villager I knew who explicitly did.

what a *nakwolu*-cum-*imoulu* did, or was alleged to have done, regardless of how logically impossible to me. Never! Not even Litabagi who, while a practitioner of Western medicine, totally believed in their killing and curing magic. At the political meeting I attended at the base camp before I moved to Wakau, it was Litabagi who scathingly proclaimed to the group that all of the 'sanguma' men should be captured and thrown into jail for life. That was the only way—for him, and many other Lujere—to end the secret murdering scourge of the *nakwolu*.[11]

I had no problem appreciating—if not accepting—the villagers' fantastic beliefs about the *nakwolu*; I had been raised in the Kansas Bible belt with a plethora of wildly inexplicable supernatural beliefs I believed in when young, so personally knew the inherent power of socialization. Still, there were some Lujere occult actions I initially could not find a way to easily fathom. My main problem was with the *nakwolu*-cum-*imoulu* themselves: it was one thing for villagers to attribute to them magical powers, but quite another for them to claim the capability to personally perform such logically impossible acts. How could they believe in (1) the magical, even bizarre murderous actions individually attributed to them, and (2) the magical curing treatments they performed on their patients? This was the paradox that for a long time was constantly gnawing at me. It wasn't until writing this book that I came to more deeply grasp the impact that magical thinking had not only on the *imoulu's* patients but, even more extensively, on the *imoulu* themselves.

While still in the field I was convinced *nakwolu-imoulu* were not frauds but believed in their own magical powers. Why else would they go, or bring family members, to each other for treatment when sick? As skepticism or doubt regarding a *nakwolu's* magical powers was almost unknown within the culture, it makes it easier for a *nakwolu* to be convinced of them himself.[12] Magical thinking, as I have documented repeatedly, was endemic among the Lujere. It shouldn't take much imagining for an *imoulu* to believe that what he had corralled within a curing bundle was real and lethal and, as he had the power to see what others couldn't, know from his *thoughts*, his imagination, what it was. Likewise, he could fantasize, like Warner's murderous Murngin informant Lainndjura (chap. 16), a gruesome magical 'sanguma' murder if he wished. If you live in a society where magical thought is universally credible, who is to challenge your fantasies as not really real? Even in our secular modern society, many Christians believe that the Eucharist's wafer and wine are Christ's body and blood. Belief in itself makes it genuine.[13]

From the point of view of an empirically oriented rationalist like myself, the Lujere mentally inhabited a perceptual world steeped in magical thoughts not verifiable in a space/time continuum, as did the Christian Brethren missionaries who felt the Lord

---

11. This, of course, also would have exterminated access to their prioritized form of curing, but that was ignored.
12. I recorded only a single instance of doubt, when Oria told me that K____'s wife, in anger, called him a fraud as a cure
13. Fortune provides another example among the Dobu where a sorcerer removes crystals from a person's body:

    This removal is like a trick in appearance, but actually the sorcerer does not think of it as a trick. The presence of the crystal in his hand after he has projected it magically at a victim, or before he has ejected it from a patient is immaterial. The immaterial on the contrary is material effecting his purpose. That is all there is to it. (Fortune 1963: 298)

was divining and guiding their and others' decisions (Thorp 2004). When *imoulu* or their family members were sick they, as indicated, sought out each other for treatments just as Western physicians do when ill. I assumed they believed their curing happened on an unseen level they could see, and was therefore real. No one questioned the integrity of their curing or its effectiveness and neither did they. If your metaphysics includes the imagined as real, then it is.[14]

In the history of ethnographic research, shamans (Balzer 1996) are famed as mediators between the worlds of spirits and of humans, with trance being a strategic aspect of their performances that, for our interests, includes curing with the use of miraculous acts or tricks. Michael Taussig (2003) has written a searching article about shamans, stimulated by Boas's research among the Kwakiutl and his informant–shaman collaborator, George Hunt (Boas and Hunt 1966). A Kwakiutl shaman's curing is much more given to tricks or chicanery, often elaborate, than is the Lujere *imoulu*, who never goes into trance and who can at most can produce, for example, a bit of razor allegedly removed from his patient's abdomen.[15] Taussig cites Stanley Walens as to how the Kwakiutl understand their curing tricks as a form of mimesis, thus the shaman performs his curing trick, but the spirits imitate it exactly: "The tricks turn out to be models or scenes for the spirits to follow, and it is the spirits who ultimately supply the cure" (Taussig 2003: 288), therefore preventing the shaman from being accused of deception. That is fine for the Kwakiutl, but the Lujere do not have a similar belief of curers and spirits in a magical, symbiotic relationship.

It is significant that I never saw an *imoulu* show an actual object he extracted in the many curing sessions I observed. Nor was there any onlooker curiosity to view the unseen objects removed and quickly disposed of outside. I was the exception. I once casually followed a woman curer out and saw her lean over and slightly shake the bundle near the edge of the cleared area absent of people, and immediately return inside. In my cursory assessment, I saw nothing unusual. Once, I did see a single object that allegedly was removed from a patient when in Mokadami at Anwani's house and described earlier in this chapter. This was when Anwani wanted the *imoulu* Oriak, who was treating Eine, to show me the thing he had removed: a slender ivory colored object that appeared to be a filed tooth of some kind.

When a cultural practice is trusted without question by the populace, there is no need for the curer to validate his prowess with actions such as Oriak's. As Boas and Hunt

---

14. This line of argument may shed light on the self-acceptance of a *nakwolu*'s curing prowess, but it does not provide a convincing explanation of how a novice understands his training to magically kill victims with a *nakwolu* and then revive them to go home and die. If it were a solo fantasy activity, I could perhaps grasp it, but how do two men, a novice and his teacher, work together to create a fantasy about an alleged actual event involving killing, cutting, closing cuts, and returning a victim to life (unless, perhaps, it is a form of *folie* à *deux* in which they somehow share the same homicidal fantasy)? Athough ethnographers strive to understand the consciousness of those they live with, I confess that the consciousness of the *nakwolu* and *imoulu* I knew remains a troubling conundrum to me.
15. Also see Graham M. Jones's (2017: 115) unique book that considers European "entertainment magicians" or "illusionists in relation to the "magical thinking by ritual experts at conjuring tricks" in less developed societies.

observed for the Kwakiutl, where shamanistic practice was oft challenged and the shaman himself could be doubtful of his powers, he "is always ready to bolster them up by fraud" (Boas and Hunt 1930: 121). But the Lujere belief in magic is so thoroughgoing that the idea of "fraud" is an inoperable one. Nevertheless, my unremitting abjuration of all forms of magic makes me wonder if Oriak, by documenting his cure with the "removed" tooth, may have raised personal skepticism in his own powers while Anwani, who also was a curer, on seeing the tooth may have questioned his own abilities. Likewise, Eine, as well as the observers to the treatment, may have questioned the efficacy of the powers of curers in subsequent treatments if the nature or the object were either ignored or just verbalized, rather than being expressly shown. Concrete facts can have a way of destabilizing the status quo. However, the above scenario is of *my* skeptical imaginative devising in opposition to the Lujere imagination rife with magic. Consequently, "concrete facts" are open to interpretation, thus raising slippery questions about what's real. These, however, are ontological questions that can't be answered definitely here, if indeed anywhere.

Psychosis or Devil Possession?

We can, however, examine what happens when one's sense of what is real gets tangled or goes off the track. I only saw one psychotic person while living with the Lujere.[16] I first saw him at the mission when I was removing my boots and he walked by alone, talking loudly and incessantly in Tok Pisin, never Namia. I glanced quizzically at a nearby local man and he said he was 'long long,' psychotic. He had been 'long long' before and only recently had returned from indentured labor. Later I was down on the airstrip waiting for a mission plane to Lumi and saw him again with two men who were trying to escort him back to his hamlet in Yegerape. Another man was shouting at him for insulting his wife, having said he wanted to have sex with her. He reeled around awkwardly like a drunk and headed out onto the airstrip, but was neatly dressed in fresh clothes. Eventually his handlers got him headed homeward, still walking unsteadily.

While I was in Lumi, he flew up on a government-chartered plane I met with Betty Gillam in the hospital's pickup. He was standing on the airstrip with two policemen and a small crowd around him. His wrists were tied together in front of him with bark, as were his knees and ankles. He was again in a manic state, laughing and talking continuously in Tok Pisin about praying, declaring there was a Satan inside of him, ranting on and on, while raising his hands together up and down as if praying. Addressing the police, he kept saying, 'O tenkyu, O tenkyu,' "Oh thank you," over and over, mixed with more Christian-inspired religious talk, again all in Tok Pisin. Betty said that he had religious books that Ces Parish had given him and that at one time he was a Bible teacher. Along with five other men including the police and me, he was driven in the back of the pickup to the hospital where his legs were freed but not his hands. Betty gave him an injection and he gradually quieted down. I mention this man because he was the only psychotic person I knew about and, as an intimate associate of the mission at one time, a completely atypical Lujere person. Whether it was personal instability, his involvement with charismatic

---

16. I heard only about two other people who were 'long long' and in other villages.

Christianity, a combination of these, or other factors that provoked his psychosis, I had no way of knowing. What I did know, however, was that the closed stability of his parents' magical Lujere world he knew as a child had been shattered.

Philip Ace visited his disturbed friend at the Lumi Hospital but when he tried to kneel in front of Philip he said no, they would kneel together, then his friend began preaching nonsense and speaking vulgarities, so the CMML nurse Shirley Stephens with them had to leave. Later Philip prayed with the man's brother, a Christian, regarding his brother's madness, as Philip was convinced, and the patient himself believed, that the devil was inside of him. When Philip and his wife Rosemary returned to Yellow River, as a testament to their faith they flew back with the disturbed man and his medication so they could look after him and pray with six others for the devil to release him. The man wanted to return home and they felt this was God's will because when the Lumi Hospital tried to transfer him to the larger Vanimo Hospital, the doctor in charge would not give his permission as they did not have the necessary funds. While both the missionaries and the Lujere believed in the supernatural, the Lujere were not also divine fatalists.

Exorcism, the casting out of evil spirits residing in a person, is a common action in those societies with strong beliefs in supernatural powers. In chapter 15, we learned about the Lujere beliefs and curing rituals related to exorcism.[17] Both CMML charismatic Christianity and conservative Catholicism have ardent beliefs regarding the evil powers of the devil that can corrupt a person's morality. But the Lujere belief system is very different. The traditional Lujere belief is that an evil spirit can make you sick, not make you bad; theirs is a mechanistic connection and unrelated to ideas of morality or a person's ethical character.[18]

---

17. On April 20, 2018, *The New York Times International* carried an article on a Catholic exorcism conference in Rome with the headline, "Amid Fears That Evil is Winning, Learning to Cast Out il Diavolo." Goodman (1988) also explores the nature of exorcism in "the modern world."
18. A sometime point of linguistic confusion is that the Tok Pisin term for "spirit" is 'tewil,' which a Westerner may misconstrue as "devil."

CHAPTER NINETEEN

Death in Wakau

> *Pneumonia is not among the sicknesses they recognize,*
> *and they blame the death on Sanguma.*
> PO R. K. Treutlein (1962: 14)

The last weeks of my village fieldwork included dismantling my camp to return home—a wearying task I conducted with mixed emotions—and a glimpse of Ray Lanaghan's 'sing-sing' to celebrate the official opening of the Edwaki Base Camp; in importance and meaning however, both events paled in comparison to the deadly attacks of pneumonia occurring in Wakau. This final chapter examines the disease's tragic consequences within the cultural context of the Lujere's comparative use of Indigenous (magical) and introduced (medical) curing techniques that are then contrasted to indicate some of the factors inherent in each that kept them inviolate. Finally, I summarize my findings on the veracity of 'sanguma' killings and curings, acknowledging the extraordinary power of the human imagination to shape our beliefs and, consequently, our lives.

Rampant Pneumonia

With Ces Parish and a visiting missionary, I flew up to Lumi on the mission plane the day before Joyce and the children were to return from Australia. In spite of the fact that all three arrived in Lumi with bad colds, we had a joyous reunion. It was a busy few days: Joyce and I hiked out to Taute village to say our farewells, my Wape artifacts got partially packed, hours were spent hand copying records in the office of the Lumi 'kiap,' and more hours spent organizing cargo to be sent home and given away. My days in PNG were now literally numbered. On April thirtieth we would fly from Port Moresby to Hong Kong on the first leg of our roundabout trip home. But my work in Wakau was not yet finished.

A Witch's Hand

I flew back to the Edwaki Base Camp with Tony Wright, the new ADC who replaced Peter Broadhurst. We had lunch with Ray, then I saw Mary Parish at the mission who told me that Mowal's infant daughter had died at the aid post of cerebral malaria, the third infant they had lost to that fateful disease. Oria told me it was an *aokwae* of Arakwake's that killed Mowal's baby, as they had stolen a papaya from him. Oria also told me that Kairapowe, Ukai's wife and Oria and Nauwen's paternal aunt, was seriously sick so we stopped in Yegerape at the aid post to get some sulpha and quinine medicine from Litabagi who, with his Tok Pisin–savvy wife, were busily treating people. It was still the rainy season; on our way home, we pushed through one swift brook that was waist deep. In Wakau, the village was almost empty, as many families had departed for their hunting camps with no intention of a hurried return.

Oria and I found Kairapowe sitting by a burning clay hearth, moaning occasionally but surprisingly talkative, apparently pleased to see her nephew. She had become sick while I was gone and had been delirious off and on the past two nights. She had a high fever and, from her pain in breathing, probably pneumonia. I had a long-standing affection for Kairapowe, as early on she had shown me how to wash sago; it was an amusing encounter, she with no Tok Pisin and me with no Namia. Following Betty's regime, I gave her three quinine and four sulpha tablets. Oria said that both Mangko and Klowi had treated her earlier that day; an *aokwae* had broken some of her chest bones causing the pain and they had fastened them back together.

Later that evening, I told Oria and Nauwen that in two weeks I would be moving out of the village to Lumi in preparation for returning home with my family. What I didn't know then was that they would be the two most stressful weeks of the fieldtrip. As I predicted, they both took my announcement with matter-of-fact calmness. New Guinea men have a wonderful way of taking events—excepting death—in stride. Nauwen and Oria did express regrets that I was leaving and I thought and hoped it had to do with me as a person, not just what I gave to people. With the Wape, I sometimes felt that I was just a commodity dispensing commodities and was judged by the amount I was dispensing. But in Wakau I had felt real warmth from the people, even from the women with whom I couldn't communicate verbally, and that I was appreciated as a fellow human— different to be sure, but not just as a rich white man.

The following day Kairapowe took more sulpha tablets and, when I stopped by that evening, she was lying down with Ukai sitting near her; visiting her were Oria's family, Yaope and his wife, and Nakwane's wife Auwe. Also present was a young daughter of Mowal's dead older brother who had come from Bapei to live with Ukai and Kairapowe. It was a happy setting with casual visiting and laughter. Regarding Kairapowe, Oria said that she was much better now, that her heartbeat was slower and, if I had been gone two weeks, she would have died; but I still found her feverish. Ukai, in his limited Tok Pisin, spoke to me twice. He told me how he had built the house by himself and that there was a bit left of the canned fish I'd given Kairapowe. She had requested the fish because of a pork taboo; it was thought to be lethal for the sick.[1] Yaope said he was sorry I was leaving

---

1. While the Lujere denied pork to the sick, Li Puma observed that for the Maring in the mountains behind Madang, "feeding ritual pork to the sick may add quality protein to their diet at a critical time, helping to replace nutrients and to assist the body's natural defenses" (2001: 324).

so soon, adding jokingly that some of the men alleged that they would then return to the bush and go wild. The day before Oria had told me that when I left he would 'go long bus' [go into the bush for a long time] for seven months, then that day he said that when I left he and Nauwen would go to Wewak.

The following Wednesday was a pivotal day as the pneumonia cases increased; in my field notes it became "The Day of the Big Sick." The day's only good news was that just before seven A.M. a thumping sound from someone striking the keel of a forest tree signaled that a pig had been killed. Later Ino's wife arrived to see Kairapowe, bringing the news that Nimo had killed a pig from a blind by a felled sago palm. He also put an arrow into another pig, but being alone and at night, did not follow it. Three Tsila villagers stopped briefly en route home after being sent by the 'kiap' to Litebagi's aid post to cure their tropical ulcers.

Late morning, I went up to Ukai's house to see Kairapowe but found her in Ukai's half-finished new house sitting in a dark corner and Ukai on the narrow veranda. She was still feverish with labored breathing and a haunting wild look in her eyes that distressed me. The sulpha that usually changes the progress of pneumonia was not being effective, so I returned home for some tetracycline from my dwindling supply. While I was helping Kairapowe, Ukai said he had become sick the previous night and it was obvious that he too had pneumonia so I began him with sulpha tablets and aspirin.

I was still at Ukai's house when three Gwidami men transported Eine, too sick to walk, to Wakau on a trapeze-type bar strapped to their back that they carried in turn. He had gone to them three days previously where two *imoulu* had treated him. His carriers had literally dumped him on the upper *iron's* veranda and then gone inside. His family followed a short time later. I stopped to see him and his eyes were haunted as if he were dying. His breathing was the most labored I had ever seen and he could not really talk, although he was rational. It was the first time I had seen him since he left the village weeks earlier, angry with Oria and bitter towards me because I did not give him everything he asked for. Oria and Nauwen finally went up to see him midafternoon, but it was no great reunion. Oria still was aggravated by the advantage Eine had taken of their kinship tie and said he couldn't feel that sorry for him. Once home for lunch, I sent up some tetracycline for him to take, but when I went to the *iron* around 4:00 p.m., I learned he could not swallow them. One of the men who had carried him in said something was wrong with his throat; they had stopped once to give him some water but he couldn't swallow it. And they wouldn't carry him to the aid post. Earlier that day Oria said they never carry anyone to the aid post; if they don't get well in the village, they die. I recalled when his wife Pourame was so sick and he had no intentions of carrying her to the aid post; and his father, who was related to the aid post orderly Litabagi whose penicillin might have saved him, died of dysentery in Wakau only months before my arrival in the village.

Just before four o'clock, Klene of Mauwi trudged into the village with his family from their camp across the Sand River. Too sick to climb the hill home, they settled at Akami's house where Eine's family also was staying. Klene lay on his back, a small belt strapped around his chest, with the same vacant stare as Eine. He too had pneumonia and I offered him medicine but he said through Nakwane—he spoke only Namia—he would wait for an *imoulu* to treat him. I heard that Mangko also was sick and had been in bed all day with back pains but when I looked in the lower *iron*, he was asleep. Nakwane, seeing my red tetracycline capsules for Eine, told his wife that they were to replace blood. What a good example of how we humans tend to process the unknown; it was a hypothesis but stated as a fact. Nakwane also had some physical complaints but nothing serious so I gave him two aspirin, joking that I had become Wakau's personal medical assistant. Nauwen stated he had diarrhea so I gave him some Lomotil. Kaiera and Samaun were also sick but not with pneumonia. The sun was fast sinking out of sight when Alomiaiya approached me; Mangko was now very sick and had sent him to me for some medicine. It seemed that everyone was falling apart and I, fatefully, had become a central player in the therapeutic systems I had come to study.

I went down to the lower *iron* and Mangko came out from under his mosquito net, one of the few in Wakau. His body was burning and his eyes glazed; he was seriously sick. I gave him Betty's treatment regime. He said it was only this morning that he became ill; however, I thought he had looked sick the day before when he went to the base camp to pick up my kerosene, but I said nothing and neither did he.

It was a beautiful, bright, moon-lit night when around eight o'clock I began my medical rounds. Mangko was sweating profusely and had strong chest pains. If not better by the next day, I would start him on tetracycline. I found Ukai and Kairapowe now sleeping at Akami's house and they were about the same. Akami greeted me outside; he had not been inside all day because he didn't want to get their sickness. Although the diagnosis of a serious sickness is usually explicitly related to the occult, the Lujere also have an amorphous sense of sickness as contagious even to the extent that, occasionally, a village must be abandoned. Litabagi's sulpha was almost gone and with so many sick—there were five with pneumonia—I started publicizing that someone needed to go to the aid post for more.

In the upper *iron*, Eine seemed a bit better in spite of still being unable to swallow any medicine; his face was expressionless when he tried to talk. He said he had been 'long long' three successive nights in Mokodami and again last night was unable to sleep and wandered around. He believed it was a 'sanguma' man who had made him sick and named him but his speech, never clear to my ear, was now even more garbled. He also was upset because an *imoulu* who had treated his daughter Emani in Mokadami performed the treatment too hurriedly as dark was settling in. When he looked for him the next day to finish the treatment, he had left the village. Now he wanted Klowi to return from his bush camp to treat her. I saw Emani earlier and, although she might not have felt well, she wasn't seriously sick. Eine was a solicitous father, but it was observable that he wasn't well liked; no one was attending him or visiting him, not even his wife.

Thursday morning at seven forty-five I was at Akami's house and saw Kairapowe chucking my precious tetracycline through the limbum floor. I was both irritated and surprised as she had taken her meds eagerly before. But I already knew that as soon as a villager feels better, they stop taking medicine. Their thinking is the same when seeing a curer; if you felt a lot better after seeing one *imoulu*, why would you pay to visit another one? It wouldn't make sense. They have the additional judgment that too much medicine makes you sick. Exasperated by Kairapowe's behavior, I lectured her briefly that medicine was money and you don't throw it away, but I knew right then that my days of giving medical assistance were probably over. Rather than get caught up with negative emotions towards the villagers' slack attitude to Western medicine, I abandoned my nursing role, a role I had reluctantly assumed only when I saw people deathly sick with pneumonia. If villagers no longer wanted my medicine that was their right, just as villagers didn't have to visit the aid post when sick. It was also clear by now that no one was going to fetch more sulpha from Litabagi.

Ukai seemed about the same, coughing but no big fever. He was my last pneumonia patient; I offered him his sulpha and he took it but Nauwen later asked me not to give him medicine because his aunt and uncle would just throw it away. Samaun and Kaiera looked fine and I gave them their last medications, then looked in on Eine. Although he still had trouble swallowing, his skin was cooler and he seemed over the worst, apparently cured by his own strong immune system. Mangko must have felt better as he had gone with Alomiaiya across the Sand River to be treated by Klowi at his camp. What with my retirement from giving medical assistance and Mangko gone, Wakau still had one active curer in the village: Poke, who was such an unlikely *nakwolu* I often forgot he was one, had done a lot of curing the past few days including of Eine, Ukai, Kairapowe, and Mangko.

Having done what I could with what I had for Wakau's five pneumonia cases, I tried to turn my attention elsewhere. Although I had a lot to do, it wasn't easy. It haunted me that the aid post had plenty of penicillin and sulpha if a person were motivated to go there for treatment, thus making it ridiculous for any adult but the truly weak and aged to die in Wakau. However, the villagers I knew, and that you have come to know, lived in another logical world with different ideas about sickness in terms of etiology, diagnosis, and treatment. Although I knew this better than anyone, it was still a stretch to accept that my medical help to Wakau's pneumonia victims was useful only up to a firm cultural line, really more of a cultural wall, they could not venture over. Even then, it was wrenching to accept the cold reality that they were unwittingly trading cultural fealty for a potential early death.

With my time in Wakau limited now to days and not weeks, I had a lot to accomplish. I still had several professional obligations to complete; most important was a collection of Lujere artifacts I had promised to Margaret Mead for the American Museum of Natural History in New York where she was a curator. I purposely had left this to my last days in the field as, once the word goes out that you are now a buyer of traditional items, your days can be obsessed with locals coming from everywhere to sell things. This had been a huge task when leaving the Wape but I knew the Lujere culture was not as rich in traditional material culture so the task would be, as I predicted, not as onerous. I also had a commitment to Alan Lomax's Cantometric Project for tapes of the Namia language and I had yet to adequately measure and map the village, not to mention the gradual breaking down of my camp and packing of supplies and equipment for transshipment by sea back to the States. My two treasured mosquito-proof tents, however, would be left in Wewak for colleagues Rhoda Metraux and Nancy McDowell to collect for planned Sepik River anthropological fieldtrips. Last, but not least, carriers had to be enlisted for transporting my cargo to the base camp but, with so many men happily away in their hunting camps, Oria was concerned, as was I.

Thursday morning after making my decision to retire from active doctoring, I returned home, took some village footage with the Bolex, and then when Kori of Mauwi brought me a few interesting old artifacts to buy, the day mushroomed to one of buying and cataloguing. It was also a day of learning, as I was seeing and asking questions about some traditional articles for the first time. Fortunately, there weren't the masses of things thrust at me as in Taute. It was busy but manageable—they had none of the pottery and wooden pieces the Wape make—and my prices seemed fair, as there was no haggling. The villagers were intrigued with my new role as artifact collector and enjoyed the excitement that a market atmosphere always generated. I did hear that Kairapowe was not doing well and Eine sent someone saying he wanted me to give him a blanket and some canned fish. He obviously had recovered; it was his same old annoying demanding behavior. While asking for something from a rich white man was a common occurrence in New Guinea, among the Lujere it was done with a sense of humor. If the answer were no, the response was a smile or a laugh and, 'Em i orit, mi traim tasol!' ("That's ok, I just thought I'd ask!"). There is no term in Namia, Tok Pisin, or even English for Eine's personality type, but the Yiddish term "shnorrer" nicely nails it.[2]

A Hunting Camp Visit

The visit to Klowi's hunting camp described in chapter 10 occurred just two days after Wakau's "Day of the Big Sick." As indicated, Mangko and Ai'ire were there, both ill. There was talk that there might be a curing festival for Ai'ire, Eine, and Kairapowe, and Ai'ire told me he still wanted to go to the Wewak hospital as neither the aid post orderly nor the *imoulu* had cured him. I told him I had learned that the mission had almost completed plans for that to happen. He also said that the *imoulu* were removing little snakes from his stomach, but the problem was that they kept coming back! There was a lot of talking and commotion in the house and Mangko, obviously not well, moved out onto the quieter veranda. Sago and cooked green leaves were served to us guests and, after more visiting, some of us including Oria, Nauwen, and Samaun got up to leave. Outside we met Klowi just arriving with a big Victoria crowned pigeon that, as described earlier, he generously gave to me.

On our way home, I was sloshing through a swamp with precarious footing and concentrating on not falling when a sharp twig suddenly jammed into my ear and I cried, "Ouch!" Then I heard Samaun who was following me giggle. I realized it was the first time I had used that term with the Lujere, as I had learned and always used their term for sudden pain or being startled, "Aii!" Nauwen ahead of me was also giggling and, on my questioning, they said what made my term funny was that it was the nasalized cry of a baby crocodile and that, of course, made me laugh too.

We had crossed the Sand River when Oria heard the cry of a bird they called a 'mok mok' and announced that it meant a big sickness was coming. My jaundiced thought was that it already *was* here. Superstition or not, it wasn't what I wanted to hear just then. My other concern, fast becoming an obsession, was that in spite of the rare chance for local men to earn money, I did not have the carriers to transport my cargo to the base camp. Akami said it was because they were sorry that I was leaving and that they wanted me to stay until my house fell down indicating, I guess, if my cargo stayed, I would have to stay too. As I discussed the cargo carrying dilemma with Oria that evening his suggestion was to apply economic sanctions: "If you don't carry cargo, Bill won't buy any of your artifacts!" Creative, yes, but I needed both carriers *and* artifacts.

---

2. For more on "shnorrer" with some amusing usage, see Rosten (1970: 364-7).

A Graveyard Ritual

Saturday morning Oria and I, with the help of some boys, began measuring the village and houses with my long tape for an eventual proper village map more to scale; in two hours we were finished and I began buying artifacts from waiting villagers. My house was adjacent to the cemetery and in the afternoon Oria reported that Ukai's 'sot win' (or pneumonia) was worse and that he needed to dig up some of the dirt atop his father's nearby grave, which he proceeded to do (see fig. 58). His father was the village's last adult death, and his hunting bow and arrows set atop his grassy grave—the only indication this area was a grave yard—I easily viewed from my dining tent. He explained that Ukai held his brother Limeritjo in his arms as he died and the sweat and dirt of his dying brother got on Ukai's skin and, as Limeritjo's body was still hot in its grave, this heat was going to Ukai's heart, giving him 'sot win' and making his heart beat too fast. Opening the earth atop the grave would allow the heat to escape and Ukai would be able to breath easily. Also, the rain could now go down through the opened ground to cool his father.

When I saw Ukai on Akamai's veranda later in the morning as Oria and I measured the village, I hesitated to offer him medicine but when I did, he tacitly agreed. I didn't get back to him immediately but got sidetracked buying artifacts villagers were bringing to Wakau for me to buy. Sometime after lunch I gave Nauwen four sulpha and two aspirin for Ukai as Nauwen was leaving to carry Kairapowe to Mari's house. There were *aokwae* in Akamai's house who were making the couple sick, although now it was Ukai, not Kairapowe, who was sickest. Nauwen then went to bathe, but at 5:15 p.m., I saw Kwoien and learned that Ukai did not want the medicine. On further questioning he said 'nek i pas,' that Ukai had trouble swallowing. A little after six o'clock Kworu walked fast past my 'ofis' looking serious and said he was going to Klowi's camp across the Sand River to get him to treat Ukai. Then Poke went by with his bow and arrows, obviously accompanying him. Later Nauwen also told me that Ukai declined the medicine. This was disheartening but not surprising. Once I had shown my concern and tried to help but was declined, I was still learning to let it go, regardless of how dangerously misguided I felt they were.

Yet a bit after 6:00 p.m., when Oria and I started for the upper *iron* where Ukai was, I carried some tetracycline, just in case. While there I learned that Ukai oddly had been left alone at Akami's house, had gone out to defecate and then, wanting company, had walked naked across to the *iron* where, too sick to climb the ladder, they pulled him up onto the veranda where he now lay. On our way we met Aria whose dire remark was, "He won't get up again."

The Death of Ukai

We found him naked on the *iron's* veranda, lying in Kwoien's lap, conscious but with his eyes partially closed. Soukene and her baby were next to him and she occasionally, gently nudged him, trying to keep him from slipping into a coma. Ukai's testicles were very painful and he asked Kwoien to bind them, which he did with thin tree bark as he explained his actions to me. Then Ukai took the thin bark and bound his penis to his testicles. Oria and K____ were also outside, as were two women who began to wail but faintly. However, it stimulated Kwoien and Oria to carry Ukai inside and for me to dash home for the notebook I had stupidly forgotten. I momentarily thought about also getting my Uher tape recorder but somehow, just then, it seemed too crass. When I returned, I saw Kairapowe, observably sick, sitting stoically inside. Kaiera and Samaun, whose home it was, were also inside, Kaiera sitting on his bed and Samaun soundly asleep, maybe dreaming about a new young and appealing wife preparing his evening meal. Ukai asked for water to be poured on his testicles, which Kwoien did, but the pain was not abated. A bit later K____ brought a glowing firebrand to heat his testicles but that also did not ease the pain. It was now dark both inside and outside of the *iron* but my two lanterns, one I brought and the other I had asked K____ to fetch from Nauwen, gave a soft glow of light with big looming shadows. Ukai asked for Kairapowe's hand and gently held it, but he was restless. Aria, who had moved to the old *iron* because he was afraid of 'sanguma' in this one, had come in and was sitting nearby. Ukai sat up suddenly, then lay back down and shouted, "Oh, Oh!" Aria leaned towards me, saying it was the pain from his testicles. Then he told me a story I didn't really follow about sleeping alone in the bush for two nights. He also said that in the afternoon Mowal had put mud on Kairapowe's chest and also a circle of mud around Ukai's nipples, both healing rituals.[3]

    Our little group was just inside the front entrance of the nearly empty *iron* and outside, the village itself was almost as empty of life. Kwoien and Ukai were in the middle of the 'limbum' floor between two vacant beds and their hearths on opposite sides of the room. Aria and I sat against the wall just left of the entrance and Kairapowe was up nearer her husband. She remained silent and finally lay down. Once Ukai exclaimed, "*aokwae!*" but it was the mosquitoes, legions of them—not *aokwae*—that were unmercifully attacking us, in spite of the smoldering fires Kaiera had made in several of the hearths. At 7:10 p.m., Kwoien got up and Oria took his place supporting Ukai and, at my suggestion by pointing to the tetracycline in my hand, Oria asked him if he wanted medicine, then K____ also asked him, but he softly replied, 'Maski,' "Never mind," a polite Tok Pisin "No," apparently aware I was there too.

    I went home for a shower and some food as it looked like a long night's vigil. Refreshed by my bucket-shower, I had some rum and then the delectable bird that Klowi had given me. Nauwen had cooked it in boiling water and made some brown rice grown in the Nuku area east of Lumi. Occasionally we could hear Ukai call out in pain. Pourame and her children were at home across the way joined by a young woman friend, as Oria would sleep at the *iron*. Oria had asked for his flashlight so Pourame, who wanted to see Ukai, took it to him and then returned.

    Shortly after nine, Nauwen and I went up to the *iron* where he joined Oria, Kwoien, and the youth Kairapowe in attending to Ukai. Samaun and Kaiera were still there and so was K____. Kwoien and Nauwen sat down together, both supporting Ukai; Kairapowe, seeking intimacy with her husband, lay her thin legs astride his. I joined Kaiera and K____ who said Ukai had drunk water twice while I was gone. (Either Ukai or Kwoien earlier had dissembled regarding his inability to swallow.) A bit later he drank again. K____ told me a rather rambling story about when he was sick at Boram; he had been

---

3. These were similar, but only grossly, to the curing rituals done at the Mokadami *aewal wowi* curing festival, reported in in the "Concluding Rituals" of chapter 15.

given some tablets by someone he worked for, took four of them, and was cured. He saved the rest and gave them to his children when sick and they recovered every time! I was impressed how this infamous traditional curer gave modern medicine to his children and had encouraged Ukai to take some too.

Kairapowe had changed her position to sitting next to Ukai, whose breathing now was very heavy. The rain had started soon after Nauwen and I came to the *iron* but by now it was a raging storm with flashing lighting and roaring thunder. Ukai, eyes closed, remained in Kwoien's and Nauwen's enfolding arms while K____'s flashlight was focused on his heavily breathing torso. It was beautiful, and deeply human, the way this dying person was so intimately held within a comforting clasp. There were two deep breaths, then nothing, just the claps of thunder and flashes of lightening.

Kwoien was the first to wail, crying out as he rubbed Ukai's body then Kairapowe, grasping his left leg, also began but she was so sick, there was scarcely a sound. It was ten o'clock, Ukai lay dead, and the storm continued to rage. The men's wailing grew in intensity and the *iron* shook with sorrow, even as the storm quieted and began to move on. Their wailing was very private and self-absorbed, each seemed lost in a rapturous world of grief. Oria's cry was a profound tenor and K____'s a high rich baritone, but Nauwen's a meager murmur, and Kaiera did not cry at all; it was indicative of the two older men's commitment to their culture and, despite different personalities, bold self-confidence.

When the rain slackened, I started home to get the Uher to record the wailing. The black village seemed lifeless but as I passed Mari's house, I heard gentle wailing that was hauntingly beautiful. Pourame, her house shut tight, had heard Oria's wailing announcing Ukai's death and the two women were quietly lamenting his demise. When I started back the strap to the Uher came unhooked and it fell heavily to the ground. As I fixed it the rain began again so I gave my lantern to Aria, who had tagged along and didn't wail, to take to the *iron* and I returned home and recorded from there; I could hear Oria's voice, loud and clear. But the rain got heavier and louder making recording impossible, so at a bit before midnight I went to bed. It was still April Fool's Day; just two years ago we had left our Vermont home for New Guinea.

I slept fitfully, something unusual for me, and the wailing was so compelling that I got up twice in the night to record it. I was surprised to see on my calendar that it was Easter Sunday. At six-thirty Nauwen arrived, undoubtedly relieved to be away from the mourning and I, after some hot tea, walked over the rain-soaked earth up to the *iron*. Eine was sitting under the house, his eyes listless and his body emaciated, but without fever. He almost demanded that I give him a blanket. In the *iron*, Ukai's body lay on the floor with Kairapowe's legs astride his; exhausted and skirt less as tradition demanded, she stared trance-like. Sakome sat with her baby across from Kairapowe, wailing quietly, and sometimes touched Ukai's arm as she cried. Lujere women wail unobtrusively, it is the men who are the belters. I noticed Klene in a 'lap lap' and Oria wore only his under pants, having removed his shorts, but no men were naked. There were two other women by Ukai's feet, also mourning. I was surprised not to see either Samaun or Kaiera—they were probably in retreat to the quieter old *iron*—but I spoke to K____ who was hoarse from wailing; he had a wonderful voice and, for all his faults, was an impressive man. K____ told me that a 'sanguma' man had killed Ukai and cut his testicles. The bark that had bound his testicles now lay across his genitals.

Ukai's wake

At 7:00 p.m., Kwoien and Oria put 'limbum' flower sheaths under Ukai's body, then carried him to his own house to continue the mourning. I helped them down the *iron's* ladder then went home for some breakfast. Around nine o'clock, Oria was with me in my 'ofis' and we discussed the events around Ukai's death. The forty cents I saw on Ukai's chest was something about appeasing relatives that had brought him food in the past; a widow must destroy all her sago tools; only men without small children can do the burial; the two women mourning by Ukai's legs were Ino and Klene's wives; they wanted Klowi to treat Kairapowe when he arrives; the *nakwolu* had attacked and killed Ukai when he went alone to get sugar cane for Kairapowe last Saturday. Most surprising, Oria said that K____ had stopped curing. His wife was angry with him because he accused her of infidelity and she now proclaimed that he was a fraud as a curer. Oria also had brought with him from Ukai's house a strong old spear that I bought for the New York museum.

Late morning Tsaime arrived from the bush camp and said they had found Warajak and he was fine. Then Kori, naked, charged out of the upper *iron* and ran around the plaza yelling. Tsaime said he had marked Tsetsuwani of Mauwi as Ukai's killer and was exclaiming that we should go get him. He explained that Mauwi believed Wakau had killed Tsetsuwani's younger brother Poiani before I arrived, and now he and the 'tultul' had reciprocated by killing Ukai. It made me aware of how few mysteries, if any, there were in the Lujere consciousness; sickness and death, for example, was always explainable if sometimes contestable. What wasn't contestable was *Homo sapiens*'s obsession with intellectual closure. Kaiera told me that the burial for Ukai would be tomorrow and the village would grieve again tonight but that mourning a death used to be for several nights. Nauwen added that they were waiting for Arakwaki and Engwe to arrive before the burial. Arakwaki told Tsaime he wanted to see me before I left Wakau and all were expected later that day. I still desperately needed carriers to transport my cargo to the base camp so told Nauwen privately that when Klowi and Arakwaki arrived, we needed to have a meeting about the carrier crisis.

The day before, Mowal had gone to Edwaki to get an *imoulu* to come and treat Ukai. Midafternoon Mowal and four Edwaki men were reported on the 'kunai' approaching Wakau. Klowi and his wife as well as Meyawali already were back but Klowi and his wife left almost immediately for a garden to get some bananas. A short while later Engwe, Nimo and Nakwane arrived and another group were seen on the 'kunai' coming to mourn. Visiting male mourners usually circled Ukai's house counterclockwise, carrying weapons. At about 5:00 p.m., Mowal came to me with a short note from Litabagi and a few pills I didn't recognize for Kairapowe but no directions regarding their use. The villagers coming to mourn were, as required, in their shabbiest clothes and one woman was naked. I was told that sometimes mourners rolled in the dirt or mud to express their grief. During the day, other than the death, I had been preoccupied with taking my camp apart and organizing trunks and buying artifacts. I had only four days remaining in Wakau. Throughout the day villagers continued to return, usually wailing as they entered, and at almost 6:00, Akami and Yaope appeared. Many of the village men had returned but several, including Aiyuk, Enewan, and Luritsao, were still away. Everyone, however, was expected to return to mourn Ukai's death.

Early evening, I went up to the *iron* where a visiting *nakwolu* named Narape from Mantopai, the Lujere village far up the Sand River, had stopped. His father's father had come from Wakau. Ai'ire hadn't given up entirely on the *nakwolu* curing techniques and had Narape treat him, but I was still buying artifacts and taking my camp apart so did not stay. After dinner, Nauwen and I went to Ukai's house where he would spend the night in mourning. Except for the lanterns Nauwen and I brought, the house, filled with mourners, was dark. Men and women were wailing and Kori strode around naked as he wailed; Poke was also naked sitting with his legs astride Ukai's legs. I sat down towards the back with Mowal and Wolwar, both genial men, and the wailing gradually died down, but I heard snippets of conversations all around me and knew I was being discussed. Then Kori, knowing Nauwen would be mourning, spoke in Tok Pisin about who would stay with me tonight, that I can't be left alone, that Samaun and Kworu should sleep in my 'haus kuk' tonight, and on and on. Lujere villagers don't like to be alone at night, but especially not on a night when a fresh corpse's horrifying *aokwae naki* was amok in the village, not to mention the dozens or hundreds of threatening, long departed *aokwae bidami* who had flocked into the village to greet it. I appreciated Kori's concerns about my safety but I presumed that the the others were less concerned for my safety from a ravaging ghoul and more about their own.

From the semi darkness it was impossible to know, other than Kori and Poke, who might be naked among the seated throng as women were always topless. But there were many visitors, especially women, in the crowded room to whom I was at best, if known at all, still an alien white man. Out of the darkness behind me I heard Nauwen's voice, unusually brisk, say, 'Bill, yumi tupela i go nau,' "Bill, we must go." I was being dismissed, expelled, ousted, booted out of Ukai's wake. My initial response was a weird mixture of embarrassment and anger, a classic response to a status insult. I gradually stood, said only, 'Lam em i ken stap' "The lantern can stay," and walked to the entrance to join Nauwen outside.

Nauwen, who disliked confrontational situations, would have been irritated that he was assigned the task of ousting me from the wake, and just as aware of my irritation at being sent home. When I asked him why, he initially tried to avoid answering—that really did irritate me—but I kept my cool. Pressed, he said that the visitors were embarrassed to wail in front of me, then added that it was just the women, not the men, as they had worked away on coastal stations, implying they were more familiar and comfortable with white men. Then after seeking my assurance that I was not afraid to sleep alone, I gave him my lantern and he returned inside as I slowly wandered home through the dark village without benefit of a flashlight, moon, or single star. As I walked along, my anger intensified at being thrown out; then I became even angrier with myself for not making a scene. However, by the time I climbed the ladder to my house, reason had gradually returned. But, had I not been leaving for good in a handful of days, I think my impulse to express self-righteous umbrage might have prevailed. Back in my own cultural cocoon with lanterns lit, I had a shot of rum on several precious tiny ice cubes and returned to organizing and packing for my departure. Throughout the night as I worked, I would now and then hear the wailing drift towards me from Ukai's house at the far end of the village. But by midnight, all was quiet.

Ukai's burial

Nauwen arrived early the next morning. Yesterday Oria had been focused on his uncle's death, but I was unaware he also had been recruiting carriers as men returned to the village to mourn Ukai. Then at eight, the last two carriers volunteered. I wrote in my notebook "WHEW!" The long indecisive nerve-wracking hassle of looking for carriers was over. My joyful relief was tempered, however, by knowing that only a death made it happen. It was a cruel irony that the mortality of kindly Ukai was making it possible to wrap up my work with the Lujere and head for home.

Arakwaki and Nimo had returned in the night and Aiyuk and Enewan entered the village wailing Ukai's death even as Engwe, Kworu and Nimo were digging his grave. Six Mauwi women filed past my house in tattered skirts, wailing but not sobbing as they headed home. Eating breakfast, I watched the men prepare the gravesite and saw the brothers Samaun and Meyawali down on the 'kunai' going to their garden. By custom a grave was not usually dug by men of the dead person's patriclan, but by members of other village patriclans. For Ukai, it was primarily the men of the lower village Elamoli patriclan, including Engwe, Nimo, and Klowi. I spent the next hour or so in and around the gravesite, taking photos and making notes.

The grave was about five feet deep by five feet long and three feet wide. In a sense it was an earthen tomb, a small underground room where the body was placed off the ground, an adaptation of their traditional burial scaffold where the body was left to decompose in the elements. The difference in the underground tomb was that it eventually would collapse in on itself and become an ordinary grave. The platform for the body was laid five or six inches from the bottom, where four poles were inserted in small holes a few feet apart along the width of the grave. On these were placed ten 'limbum' strips running the length of the grave, on top of which the body would be placed about a foot above the grave's floor.

At 11:35 a.m., six men, including the three gravediggers Engwe, Kworu and Nimo, two men from Mokadami, and Klowi carried Ukai's body on 'limbum' flower sheaths past my 'ofis' to the neighboring cemetery. His body was swollen, his face and genitals were covered with cloth, and the stench was tangible. Several small boys followed at a short distance and, once the entourage was at the grave, two young women arrived with 'limbum' baskets full of water (fig. 59) for the men to wash the body.

Klowi removed the two cloths and the body, held sitting up, was brushed with garlands of ginger unavoidably removing some skin then washed with the ginger infused water. Watching from a fair distance were Meyawali, Arakwaki, several children, the water carriers who stayed the farthest away, and little Womkau who had joined me as I moved around taking photos. Children watched as ginger was thrashed in a 'limbum' of water, and Klowi, facing Ukai's body, stroked it with ginger. Five mourners stood in the distance on the 'kunai' path to the village. Just before the remaining ginger infused water was poured over the body, Oria arrived to observe; then the men together lowered the body into the grave as the children gathered up close to watch.

Klowi, who had done much of the cleansing, rinsed his hands and Akami arrived with more 'limbum' sheaves to cover the grave. The body, now lowered in place, was covered with sheaves; then a series of small but strong poles was laid horizontally and lengthways atop the grave. Finally, several large palm branches were placed lengthwise on the poles

Figure 58. Men plan and prepare Ukai's gravesite.

Figure 59. Two young women bring water to the gravesite for the men to wash the body.

to be covered with more sheaves that, in turn, were covered with some light dirt, closing the underground tomb.

By eleven-thirty in the morning, the burial was complete and the participants gradually dispersed. I returned to my house where I continued packing, but was interrupted by two Mauwi couples wailing and approaching the new grave. I stopped work to record the restrained blending of their male and female voices. At 1:45 p.m., I was interrupted again when I heard that Mangko had just been carried in from Klowi's camp and went to the lower *iron* to see him. His skin was red hot. He was obviously now seriously sick and I offered him medicine but he, like Ukai, said, 'maski.' I told him if he changed his mind to send for me, as I would be home packing all afternoon. Feeling both dejected and aggravated by Mangko's obliviousness to his fatal plight and the lifesaving medicine I offered, I eagerly returned to packing up my belongings, a wonderful distraction for frustration. Then something poignant happened that changed my miserable mood. Wolwar's wife, just in her G-string, came to Ukai's grave alone; she quietly sat down in the grass under the palms in the afternoon heat and began softly wailing her soothing lament. Later Kunai brought Ukai's bow and arrows and placed them atop his grave.

Just at dark, Oria went to the grave with a lighted torch so Ukai's *aokwae* could take the light to the village of the *nakwolu* who killed him. Litabagi had agreed he would be up at the base camp where he could see Wakau and follow the path of the *aokwae's* fire to the killer. That night I visited with Oria who, the mourning finished, had moved back to his wife's house. He said that Ukai's body began to swell up last night and that was why

Nimo began digging the grave early this morning for the burial. Regarding why I was banished last night, he said, as Nauwen had earlier, that the visiting women were embarrassed by my presence, adding that if I hadn't been in Wakau, they would have come wailing naked into the village and put on their G-strings later. Regarding the washing of the body with water and ginger, there were two reasons. One was to remove the smell of those who had touched him, to prevent their children from getting sick; the other was so his dead relatives would welcome him and not be angry at the living for sending him off unwashed. All of these were old traditions.

The following morning, Tuesday, six carriers arrived as scheduled and I was elated to send them off with the first three trunks ready to go. I was now in countdown mode to leave the village. Mourners were still arriving; at eight-thirty, three strange women were wailing near the grave, and a man with just a sash around his waist carrying his bow and arrows circled the grave to the left. One of the women came forward, sat lightly on the grave, patted the surface, then got off. She must have had some tender memories of Ukai, but I didn't know their relationship. The man, I learned, was related to Ukai by marriage. Those were probably my last thoughts about Wakau for the day: the darkness of death was behind me as I threw myself into the task of dismantling my 'ofis,' packing supplies and gear except for my cameras and the back-up typewriter I never had to use, a lightweight portable Olivetti.

That night at around eight-thirty I stopped for a break and, over a cup of instant coffee, enthusiastically scribbled in my notebook with a number of atypical capital letters,

> What a day! Finally got my office tent cleared out and the tent DOWN and packed—Hallelujah! I'M GOING HOME! Letter from JM [Joyce] tonight and she is just as desirous as I to take off. Problems with our reservations but who gives a shit! As long as we've got those air tickets we'll find a place to sleep.
>
> My *fabulous* adventure is coming to an end. But I'm not sad—there is an odd sadness about leaving these people who never really knew a white man before—but I'm ready to go. I need a switch; just like I needed one when I came to NG. But it's been two of the greatest years of my life. TOTAL INVOLVEMENT!
>
> That's *thrilling*. To be a sensitive instrument recording a culture—what more could a man like me want to do? *Nothing*—How lucky I found anthropology.
>
> But—let's get back to packing—You're not home yet baby!

There was a final note regarding Ai'ire. This was the day he would fly to Wewak in the mission plane for a checkup at the government's regional hospital. The Mission had made all the arrangements; hopefully the physicians there could successfully diagnose his abdominal malady and provide a cure. After I left Lumi for home with my family, we had to stop in Wewak to complete numerous tasks and there I was able to talk with my friend Dr. Gobius. He told me that the clinicians who examined Ai'ire had found nothing. This seemed to me inexplicable, but such was the disappointing medical finding after Ai'ire's inpatient tests and examination.[4]

---

4. See Appendix for a case study of Ai're's magical and medical interventions.

The Death of Kairapowe

The next morning the carriers, smiling and fresh, arrived to carry the second group of trunks to the base camp. For me it was just another day of endless packing, and I was still buying artifacts, mostly from visiting mourners. Neither of my two precious Aladdin lamps was packed, but today one would have to go. Late afternoon I took a break and went to the lower *iron* to see Mangko, as I'd had no feedback from him regarding medicine. He was draped in a towel and sat cross-legged facing the wall. He looked ghastly. With him were his younger sister Wabe, Klowi with his wife and son Pipia, and Weyuro. Without asking, I successively handed Mangko four tetracycline and two aspirin that he swallowed with difficulty. He seemed thankful that I was there. Then Klowi told me that Kairapowe had just died at Kwoien's house, that 'sanguma' men had killed both her and Ukai. He added that K____ and Meyawali had treated her but, to my surprise, called them 'rabisman' [a worthless person]. Later I was told that K____ did not treat her because she was too sick and would die.

Back home I could hear the wailing from Kairapowe's house and felt both thwarted and despondent about two such futile deaths. Neither Nauwen nor Oria were with her when she died; if they were aware she was dying, as they must have been, neither mentioned it to me. When I spoke to Nauwen about her death, he seemed oddly cold and unaffected. I asked him if the mourning would deter my cargo going out and he said it wouldn't. I went up to the house briefly but Oria did not go until much later.

In the early evening I gave Mangko more tetracycline and aspirin; already his fever had receded some. In the interim both Klowi and Meyawali had treated him and Warajak told me they removed a one-inch "spear," which he saw. Mangko was still in pain, so gladly took the medicine. K____, Kwoien, and Kori were there and the conversation was about death and 'sanguma.' Arakwaki told me later that he never had heard of a couple—a husband and wife—being killed like that, almost at once. He added that they, the *nakwolu*, would probably keep killing until the entire village was dead. Kwoien said that Kairapowe's *aokwae* had spoken to Sakome and that she was 'long long' or disturbed.

When I went up later that night to Kairapowe's house to record the wailing I saw Sakome and, while some agreed she had been affected, she was not crazed. The dark house contained mostly women wailing, but I also saw Yaope, Kwoien, K____, and Poke, naked except for his mourning sash. Nauwen came to mourn, then Oria and his family. Of the carriers for the morning, only Yaope was committed to mourning and he had found a replacement. Outside were Klowi with his shotgun, Nimo, and Iwi, all guarding against Kairapowe's new reality as a terrifying *aokwae naki*. I earlier had been told that outside mourners would come as for Ukai's wake, but by the time I had finished my recording, my last in Wakau, and gone home, no mourners had arrived from the neighboring villages or Iwani hamlets, not even Mauwi except for K____. It made me wonder if it was because she was a woman or, having mourned two successive nights for her husband Ukai, with her death only three days later; if it was excessive to mourn all night once again. Or maybe it was a bit of both. Still, I couldn't help but feel it must be a kind of status insult to both Kairapowe and Wakau.

This time I left the wake voluntarily to address the myriad tasks awaiting me at home, including organizing the trunks to be taken in the morning. Then I wrote a long letter to Rhoda Metraux citing in detail the supplies and gear I was packing for her return to

Tambunum Village on the Sepik, with special details on how to carefully maintain the kerosene refrigerator that not only had given me a few miniature ice cubes for my nightly rum on the rocks—sheer luxury—but kept cool the meat and eggs ordered from Wewak.

At seven A.M. I heard Klowi in front of the lower *iron* giving a yelling lecture condemning Mokadami and Aiendami for not coming to mourn Kairapowe's death and felt justified for my last night's feelings of pique. Not a single outside mourner had entered the village crying since she had died. It was another instance where the action belied the talk, a familiar occurrence for any fieldworker. Around nine o'clock, Meyawali and a couple of helpers began digging the grave for her burial and I went into high gear as this was my last full day in Wakau; tomorrow the final cargo would go to the base camp, then I, too, would say goodbye.

At one o'clock I watched Meyawali, Mowal, and Poke carrying Kairapowe's frail body towards my house and the cemetery. I followed them, and this time a larger group of children, nine or ten including a few girls, had come to watch. The only other adult present was Klowi's wife, Wawinowaki, who was helping the men prepare Kairapowe's body for burial. Once the body, so slight, was washed, it was placed in the grave and covered with a cloth, then the burial was completed as for her husband.

My last black and white Wakau fieldwork photograph was Mowal placing 'limbums' over the palm branches he and Meyawali placed atop Kairapowe's grave (see fig. 60). I had yet to make the promised Cantometric recordings for Allen Lomax's project, so I turned to that task with Oria and Nauwen's linguistic help. Afterwards, Oria and I talked about the funeral customs. The reason they put articles of the dead on the grave is to placate the deceased and prevent them from becoming angry at the survivors and attacking

Figure 60. Meyawali and Mowal closing Kairapowe's grave with palm branches.

them or their children. The women wailed while their husbands circled the grave. The 'limbum' palm that I saw cut by Ukai's house was used in the wood for his grave. For Kairapowe's grave a betelnut tree was cut, but any small tree could be used. Wawenowaki had cut Kairapowe's waist string so that when her body swelled, it wouldn't cut into her. Even after death, the Lujere knew compassion.

Saying Goodbye

Late afternoon, feeling more pensive than sad, I took my final walk through the quiet and almost empty village. One little boy I knew but not by name looked up at me and wistfully said, "Oh, Beal!" Once home, I returned to completing and checking off my diminishing to-do list. At nine o'clock I grabbed a flashlight and went down to the lower *iron* to give Mangko his last tetracycline tablets. His fever and chest pains were gone. He didn't want them, 'sik i pinis!,' "Sickness is cured!" he exclaimed. But Klowi and Arakwaki were both there and prevailed on him to take them. Back home, I gave gifts to those men who had made this adventure in Wakau possible, and lastly cleaned the refrigerator and secured it for transport in the morning. Small but heavy, it would be lashed to two poles and carried, sedan-chair style.

The next morning, I awakened at eight o'clock, annoyed that I'd overslept an hour with so much yet to be done. After we dismantled and folded the big Abercrombie and Fitch "house" tent I'd occupied on the Sepik in 1967, it was a wild morning of final packing. A light rain was falling. There was an abundance of stuff, stacked, ready, and waiting to be carried to the base camp but I couldn't seem to get the cargo moving out. I mused: Why is it relatively easy to move into a village and always such a royal pain to get the hell out? By early afternoon everything was ready to go, but we were still waiting for the carriers to get organized. I was frustrated by just standing around then, so after a promise that they would bring the cargo today, I suppressed my disgust and anger and took off with Oria for the base camp. It was a crummy way to leave a village I had come to deeply appreciate as a welcoming home. Nauwen remained at the empty house to stand guard over the gifts I had given him for his friendship, hard work, and loyalty.

Once on the trail, striding through the familiar marshes and brooks, I began to calm down. After experiencing the acute tensions inherent in dismantling and packing up my camp, finding carriers, the rampant pneumonia, and the tragic and absolutely senseless deaths of Ukai and Kairapowe, I didn't realize what a mess I was until the steady tempo of the trail began to straighten me out. I had learned to love hiking in New Guinea; even today it takes only a good hike to restore my equanimity when personal events or the world kicks me off balance. Ray was waiting for me in his big airy house where I began my Lujere adventure with that alarming wind and rain storm—now seeming years ago—and we enjoyed a few welcoming beers. I relaxed. What a fantastic relief to be successfully out of the village! Then, at about five-thirty, the men began arriving, laden down with every last bit of the cargo. I was thrilled and finally could rejoice with both an emotional and physical sense of closure on my Wakau fieldwork. As I paid each man, I added a twist of coveted tobacco as a bonus, then thanked him as we shook hands and smilingly said goodbye. But it was harder to say goodbye to Oria. Without his help as a resourceful teacher, his generous friendship, and fine intelligence, this would have been a very different book—if indeed there could have been a book at all. By six o'clock my Wakau friends Yaope, Akami, Alomiaiya, Engwe, and Oria wearily started down the mountain towards home, probably arriving just after dark.

My chartered flights to Lumi were three days hence so I had two days to unwind and write up data from the patrol reports and other administration records in Ray's office, and to learn more from Makau about Magaleri village's culture and the killing of his father. Extremely aware of the unpredictable exigencies of life in New Guinea, I had prudently scheduled the two buffer days as rescheduling a missed charter could take weeks.

On Monday morning, rested by two carefree days, I was on the airstrip with all of my cargo and eager to go (fig. 61). The MAF Cessna first took two loads to Wewak that would continue by sea, and then returned to take a final small load, including the Lujere artifacts and me, to Lumi where I met Joyce, Ned, and Elizabeth to celebrate the end of my Lujere fieldwork. Joyce already was busy collecting things to be given away while packing other things to be shipped to America, and our bags for the trip home; whereas I got busy readying the Wape and Lujere objects for shipment to the museum in New York.

Figure 61. The author with his cargo and two local boys on the Yellow River airstrip awaiting his MAF chartered plane to Lumi. Photo by Ray Lanaghan.

I actually had one more bit of Lujere fieldwork to complete: to attend Ray's big 'sing-sing' celebrating the official opening of the Edwaki Base Camp the following Saturday. He had requested that as many local people of the South Wapei Census Division who could attend come in traditional dress. When I arrived shortly after lunch in the Franciscan's plane with the Lumi patrol officer Bill Swan, his wife Margaret, and baby son Jim, the airstrip was lined with colorfully decorated local people (the splendid yellow and white plume of the lesser bird of paradise was the favored adornment) who thronged the field. There seemed to be two groups, one with bows and arrows, obviously Lujere men and women, and the other with spears that someone said were from Magaleri and Yawa villages, the latter a village far to the east of Magaleri. In the evening the action moved atop the hill by the base camp buildings and it went all night, making sleep a spotty difficult option. A very large palm leaf–screened area was the backstage for the Lujere's *nawowi* men who performed in the morning with their flamboyant dancing phalluses. I had brought color film for both my Leica and small cine camera and took colorful photos and film of the celebration.

Ray, as he should have been, was delighted with the locals' turnout and the genuine success of his planned festivities. After lunch, although the 'sing-sing' was still going strong, my Franciscan plane ride returned to take me to Lumi. Not too surprisingly, none of my Wakau friends had come to the party thrown by the 'kiap,' nor had I seen anyone from Mauwi among the crowds. After Kairapowe's burial they had started returning, family by family, to their bush camps to hunt, fish, and make sago. The Iwani villagers remained, as when I arrived, more aloof than intimate with the base camp's life. It seemed improbable that just days before, for month after month, they had been my only regular companions, but had now, suddenly, physically vanished. Already they lived only in my memory and in the generous amount of rich and varied research materials I had collected. Writing this book, however, was mostly an excursion into the Lujere's past as I knew them. Reconnecting with my Wakau friends via vivid memories, scribbled notebooks, color and black-and-white photos, tape recordings, films, and most importantly, detailed notes banged out on a mechanical typewriter, night after night, in a village asleep, was like returning to the Lujere for a long rewarding visit—but without the jet lag.

Magical versus Medical Curing

In the previous pages you have come to know the Lujere as I came to know them via their colonial history and my fieldwork among them in 1971–72. One important focus of my research and this book was curing; in this concluding section, I pull together some things we know about the different techniques of curing intervention we've encountered among the five therapeutic modes to which the Lujere had access.[5] Discrete examples of these interventionist techniques appear throughout the text, but are presented in tabular form in table 10. The Lujere's three Indigenous therapeutic modes were home remedies, curing festivals, and treatment by their Indigenous practitioners, the *imoulu*. The immediately available, introduced, or Western therapies were aid post clinics, maternal and child health (MCH) clinics, and Rosemary Ace's nursing care at the mission. The following analysis and discussion include the perspective of the Lujere people, in particular the residents of Wakau, and concludes with my observations on the relationship between the Lujere's Indigenous (magical) and introduced (medical) therapeutic systems.

---

5. This section is based in part on an earlier paper, Mitchell (1975).

Curing Modes and Techniques

The major types of healing or curing interventionist techniques that were available to the Lujere are briefly identified as follows:[6]

1. *Medicinal*: introduction of *materia medica* into or on the patient's body, such as pills, injections, inhalations, ear and nose drops, ointments, poultices, nettles, and ginger.
2. *Surgical:* cutting into the patient's body, for example, lancing, bloodletting, amputation, and suturing.
3. *Physical*: manipulation of the patient's body, through massage and/or grappling to remove objects, mending bones, and applying tourniquets.
4. *Ritual*: appeal to a supernatural agent, for example, *aokwae*, *wowi*, and God, via patterned acts of exorcism and prayer.
5. *Avoidance*: abstaining or avoiding certain foods, substances, organisms, or places.

Table 10. Variability in Lujere curing modes and techniques, 1971–72

Curing techniques	Lujere curing mode			Western curing mode	
	Home remedies	*Imoulu*	Curing festivals	Aid posts	MCH clinics
Medicinal	X			X	X
Surgical	X			X	X
Physical	X	X		X	X
Ritual	X		X		
Avoidance	X			X	X

Table 10 shows the different patterns of curing techniques according to the therapeutic modes available to Lujere villagers. The therapies with the most similar profiles are Lujere home remedies, aid posts, and MCH clinics. All three employ a wide variety of healing techniques, except that the Western therapies, grounded as they are in experimentation and clinical empiricism, exclude ritual techniques, whereas certain Lujere home remedies consist of private ritual treatments in which a spirit (an *aokwae* or *wowi*), is invoked and asked to depart the afflicted person's body. And, just as the Lujere's curing festivals use only ritual techniques to heal, *imoulu* use only physical techniques. *Imoulu*, via physical techniques on the patient's body, are believed able to remove lethal objects intruded into a patient by other witches or spirits.

Also of interest is the fact that Lujere home remedies and curing festivals were performed by ordinary villagers; there was no apprenticeship to learn the techniques as required for *imoulu*, aid post orderlies, and MCH nurses, each a trained professional. Of the three kinds of professionals, it was the *imoulu*, as explained earlier in this chapter, who enjoyed the greatest prestige in terms of villagers' faith in their diagnostic skill and treatment. As in many societies, it is not technical versatility but diagnostic skill that is

---

6. I am indebted to Rena Gropper's classification (1967) for inspiring mine.

ultimately valued. Finally, though lacking reliable counts, my observations on the usage of the five therapeutic modes suggested that home remedies, *imoulu* treatments, and the aid post were used most frequently and in that order. Just as we do not feel a pressing need for a definitive diagnosis for every sore muscle, diarrhea attack, or headache, neither did the Lujere. They treated themselves much as we do, perhaps with rest or a remedy learned from their parents; or they went to the aid post because they knew the orderly had medicine that could, for example, heal an ulcerating sore or eradicate a feverish headache. As already emphasized, however, it was usually only ambulatory patients who visited the aid post, possibly a girl with a badly abscessed hand, a man with recurrent diarrhea, or a mother who could easily carry her sick baby. As we saw in the pneumonia cases of Ukai and Kairapowe, the reason that the severely sick, at least from Wakau, were not carried to the aid post was because the orderly was not considered an appropriate therapist for a critically ill person.

Remembering that the MCH clinics made occasional village patrols focusing on mothers and their babies, the aid post stood alone among the available therapies with ready access to powerful antibiotic and malaria drugs to treat illnesses in patients of all ages. But the germ theory of disease (i.e., microorganisms) that the orderly Litabagi had learned and on which his treatments were based was alien to Lujere culture and irrelevant to Lujere beliefs about the violent *nakwolu*, *aokwae*, and *wowi* who were ready and eager to cause lethal sicknesses. Although Litabagi was valued as a dispenser of free Western medicines that were often considered very helpful in curing or at least relieving the symptoms of minor illnesses, if not the cause of a major one, when a loved one's life was endangered by sickness, the family turned to a proven expert, an *imoulu*—not an aid post orderly—to provide a sensible and definitive diagnosis in Lujere cultural terms to eradicate the noxious agent.

Western and Lujere therapies also differed in the frequency of treatment for serious illnesses. According to Lujere belief, if one received the correct diagnosis and treatment, then one treatment was all that was needed. The exception I've observed is that when two curers were readily available, they both might be utilized. But the more general principle was, if the patient didn't improve after an initial treatment by an *imoulu*, the latter might modify his treatment, or the patient might seek out another *imoulu*. Thus, K____, having failed to cure Ai'ire in the daytime, told him he would try to treat him at night, which he did, but still unsuccessfully. Or, again focusing on Ai'ire, he was treated successfully when "little snakes" were removed from his stomach, only to have others reappear, necessitating further treatments. But treatment with Western medicines like antibiotics may involve taking pills several times a day and over a successive number of days. Obviously, such an attenuated approach to treatment does not inspire local confidence in the prowess of the practitioners of Western medicine.

Linked to the Lujere belief that any truly effective treatment for eradicating the cause of a serious sickness should be a single one was the belief that, although Western medicines may at times be dramatically helpful, they are potentially lethal as well; swallowing too many pills or capsules could destroy the inner body. As we saw in my doctoring efforts towards the end of my fieldwork, as soon as patients began to feel better, further medicine was tragically refused. Mangko was the exception when two important senior men, Klowi and Arakwaki, insisted that he continue the tetracycline after he felt he was cured.

This study of the Lujere was made in the twilight of the colonial era, when the society was still in vassalage to Australia. Thus, it is instructive to review the relationship of the Lujere Indigenous and Western-introduced curing systems at this point in time to provide a baseline for future studies on how a society's therapeutic systems change. In 1971–72, the Lujere's cultural contact situation was one of mutual autonomy of the Indigenous and introduced curing systems; each had remained inviolate. Neither had been altered noticeably by contact with the other, as each continued to follow its own rationale and treatment schema as conceived by the originating culture. Only in the person of Litabagi, the aid post orderly, were both therapeutic systems—the Lujere magical one and the Western medical one—enacted. Nor had the Wakau villagers innovated any alternative therapies based on cultural syncretism as described for the Manus of Papua New Guinea (T. Schwartz, 1962; L. R. Schwartz 1969). There, Christian cosmology and moral concepts about the good and the bad had extensively influenced therapeutic beliefs and practices in a succession of cults and the Paliau political movement.

The Lujere Separation of Local and Introduced Curing Systems

Some of the factors contributing to the persisting cognitive and structural separateness of the Lujere Indigenous and Western-introduced curing systems have been alluded to, but let me summarize them here. Marked change in any group's Indigenous curing system through cultural contact is often slow to transpire. Concepts and beliefs about sickness and its treatment are learned at an early age through intense experiences of sickness and suffering, and these fears and hopes of childhood imprint the personality, inhibiting change. More directly relevant, although the Lujere had been under the direct political influence of Westerners since the 1930s, actual intercultural contact had been very sporadic and slight. The Lujere were a small and scattered population, geographically isolated mostly off the Sepik River in inhospitable and economically destitute swamps, a society of zero interest to Western entrepreneurs once exotically feathered hats went out of vogue. Before the establishment of the Christian Brethren mission and the more recent Public Health Service's aid posts, the only contact with Western medicine occurred every year or so, when a government patrol including a health officer or medical orderly set off from Lumi to visit the distant Yellow River villages. Then sores were dressed, injections given, and an occasional order given to take a child to Lumi for treatment. But the patrols made little impact on local healing techniques and health practices, beyond the obligatory burial of the dead. The mandated latrines were still rarely used during my stay.

Similarly, the influence of Christian teaching had been culturally insignificant in the western Lujere villages I knew best, so that basic ideas about life, sickness, death, and a person's relationships to others remained basically unaltered. One or two missionary couples, however ardent their faith and energetic their effort, can have only limited influence on a widely dispersed population of thousands who, for much of the year, abandon their villages for scattered family hunting camps. Another argument, not pursued here, is that the relative simplicity of Lujere culture itself has a structural and cognitive resiliency that tends to ignore or minimize the threatening dissonances that occur when radically divergent cultures meet.

'Sanguma': Some Final Thoughts

When I had finished my fieldwork with the Wape in 1971, it was my curiosity about the terrors of 'sanguma' and its fearsome male practitioners that had lured me down to the Yellow River swampland. I wasn't disappointed. The *nakwolu* and their infamous magical 'sanguma' murders were a challenging and fascinating topic to study. However, these secret 'sanguma' murders—according to villagers they accounted for almost all adult deaths—eventually mostly evaporated into air as magical scenarios unsubstantiated by facts grounded in reality. Examining the entire Sepik area, I could only locate a few actually documented killings by 'sanguma' men, and those that I did, like K____ and his two accomplices, could not magically revive their physically slain victims. There was no magic; they were simply murderers, a fact recognized by the territory's Supreme Court when it initially sentenced them to death for their crimes.

As for the ritual scenario of a 'sanguma' man's magical murder—killing the victim, cutting the flesh to remove tissue or organs and magically sealing the wounds without scarring, then returning the dead victim to life and sending him or her home without memory of the attack for an eventual, final death—these procedures were all illusory, little more than fantasized heinous acts. In studying the Lujere, my private approach to their occult practices and beliefs was as a scientist; thus I couldn't accept their unseen and unsubstantiated supernatural phenomena as tangible or real, but instead as demonstrable features of the Lujere imagination. If you are similarly negatively disposed towards undocumented problems of evidence, good luck in discounting 'sanguma' as a reality without also calling your own supernatural beliefs into question.

What I did discover about the Lujere's *nakwolu* that was both culturally and ontologically grounded was the role of the *imoulu* as the society's principal curer. As dedicated therapists wielding white magic to pull mostly unseen deadly objects from their patients' bodies, I found them compelling to study and a unique part of their society. Probably for centuries, the *imoulu* had been the principal source for the relief of suffering caused by sickness. But as their curing was anchored in magic, it was as unreal as their alleged *nakwolu* killings, thus medically incapable of curing physical sickness. With the coming of the aid post and the modern availability of powerful antibiotics and drugs that could eradicate death-dealing sicknesses, the *imoulu* had become a part of the past no longer crucial. But cultural icons as affectively formidable as the Lujere's *nakwolu* cum *imoulu* don't disappear overnight. In the meantime, when serious sickness threatens life, many Lujere will continue to find explanatory comfort in their ancient beliefs—beliefs that promise surcease from suffering by the extraordinary powers of a witch's hand.

APPENDIX

Ai'ire's Chronic Abdominal Illness

A Case-Study Log of Magical and Medical Interventions

Ai'ire battled abdominal distress during my stay in Wakau and I followed as best I could his use of therapies that were readily available to him: the aid post clinic in Yegerape; Indigenous curers, that is, the *imoulu*; and curing festivals. Of these, he availed himself only of the first two. I have no record of self-applied "home" remedies because I heard of none. While there were rumors of a curing festival for Ai'ire, it never materialized. The following is a chronological log account of Ai'ire's recourse to diagnosis and/or treatment based on the incomplete and intermittent evidence I collected during 1971–72.

According to Ai'ire, he first became sick while away as an indentured laborer and was temporarily in his employer's 'haus sik.' Back in Wakau, he was occasionally ill with diarrhea and stomach pains from early October 1971. His closest kin and friends were concerned about his illness, but Ai'ire appeared to take the initiative seeking treatment. Below are his treatments that I happened to know about and my brief comments; in no way is it a definitive account of his symptoms and treatments. Nevertheless, it is an interesting record of a chronically sick man's recourse to local treatments by *imoulu*, whose magical rationale he clearly grasped, and to the foreign treatments by the aid post orderly, whose biomedical rationale he understood little. He was often discouraged that his symptoms persisted but at other times he voiced confidence that he was cured—even when he seemed sick to me—and throughout, he never physically retreated from the community into depression. How his illness progressed after I left the village, I do not know.

November 11–13, aid post: Ai'ire went to the aid post the day before I moved to Wakau because of diarrhea and stayed two nights. He had a single shot of penicillin on two successive days; white round pills, probably sulpha; and some cough syrup.

November 29, the villagers' diagnosis and etiology: I visited the lower *iron* in the morning; the night before Ai'ire again had diarrhea. Sitting around a hearth were Klowi, Aiyuk, Oria, Tsaime, and some boys including Warajak, seeming to be in deliberation; Ai'ire sat apart from them, his legs crossed, eyes sunken and looking sick. They believed that Ai'ire's sickness was caused by old Leno, his father-in-law and a *nakwolu*, who disapproved of his daughter's marriage and was openly angry with Ai'ire. To them it appeared obvious that Ai'ire had been ensorcelled by Leno. (Some believe that only the sorcerer himself can nullify his sorcery.)

Oria was convinced that the aid post did not have strong enough medicine to cure Ai'ire's sickness and that eventually he would have to go to a regional hospital in Anguganak or Wewak. The local consensus was that Ai'ire had the same sickness that had killed a Mauwi man and recently Oria's father, that is, dysentery, except Ai'ire's sickness hadn't moved to the bloody stage.

November 30, Wami, *imoulu* from Mauwi: Ai'ire's treatment is mentioned in chapters 16 and 17; Wami treated him at the lower *iron* and described it to me after the fact.

December 9, aid post: Ai'ire sought treatment for diarrhea and cramps and went with Eine and his daughter and Wauripe's wife; all except Eine had diarrhea.

December 10, Oriak, *imoulu* from Gwidami: The same group that had visited the aid post the day before went to Gwidami for a local curer's treatment. Oriak told Ai'ire that he should have come to him sooner as he has cured others with the same complaint. He removed some fibrous slivers from his stomach by kneading, slivers that were smaller and different from those Wami had removed. Ai'ire had paid each curer five shillings.

December 11, My medical lecture: On December 9, Litabagi had given Ai'ire some pills that appeared to be sulpha to take home and directed him to take one in the morning and another in the afternoon. But on December 10, he had taken only one and, as of my visit to him the next day, he hadn't taken any. I found him after lunch stretched out on his stomach and obviously sick, still with diarrhea. He said that since the *nakwolu* had removed the things from his stomach he was cured; his only remaining problem was diarrhea. In other words, he felt that the cause of his illness had been removed, but discounted the fact that his symptom of diarrhea remained. I prevailed on him to take one of the pills and gave him a little lecture on the importance of taking Western medicine consistently to make it strong enough to work. My note ends with, "I can see that hospitalization is really the only form of treatment that can succeed with such illnesses. They don't take medicine at home." (WN437).

December 12, *imoulu* from Weari: Chapter 18 includes a brief description of his treatment by one of the six visiting Weari curers (three men and three women) in the lower *iron*. [See WN598–600 for verbatim description.]

December 13, *imoulu* from Weari: Ai'ire was again one of the patients the visiting curers treat.

December 15, aid post: Ai'ire left with the Weari men and women but also stopped at the aid post for treatment.

December 15, *imoulu* in Alai: Finally arriving in Alai village, he was further treated by the six Weari curers.

December 16, aid post: On his way back to Wakau, he stopped again for Litabagi's medical help at the aid post. I talked with him the following day and he said his diarrhea was gone, that it cleared up after the December 13 treatment in Wakau.

December 21–January 4: I was away in Lumi and Wewak during this time period. I only knew that Ai'ire had stayed at the aid post's 'haus sik' for several days. While there, K____ talked to him about treating him at night instead of during the day on his return to Wakau to trick the elusive substance that was making him sick.

January 20: Ai'ire sent Unei and Tsaime to find K____ to request that he come treat him.

January 22, K____, *imoulu* from Mauwi: K____ had the idea that the reason his treatments for Ai'ire had not been successful was that the noxious "whatever" ran away in the daytime but maybe they could trick it at night. I wasn't there but Ai'ire explained what had happened. Ai'ire was in the lower *iron* and, after it was dark but before everyone had gone to sleep, K____ grabbed the upper part of Ai'ire's stomach as Mangko grabbed the lower part to trap the noxious agent. Using sago fronds K____ kneaded Ai'ire's stomach and extracted a couple of razor blade fragments and a bit of ginger. He said they had been shot into him with a tiny bow by an *aokwae*. K____ also told him that if they had remained in his stomach, they would have cut it to bits.

January 25, aid post: Ai'ire had gone to Norambalip the day before, then to the aid post to "drink medicine" on his way back home. He told me he was all right then but he did not look good; he had lost weight and his face was very drawn.

January 31, *imoulu* at K____'s camp: Ai'ire had gone to K____'s camp across the Sand River for treatment on a Monday but stayed until Saturday, February 5, when Mangko, Oria, and I went to Klowi's camp to see why he was staying there so long and he returned home with us. Klowi had only treated Ai'ire on his arrival. On February 7, his diarrhea returned. I spoke with him the following day and he said that if K____ had just treated him one more time, he would probably be all right. My note says, "He looks like hell."

February 13, I give Ai'ire medicine: I gave him a course of sulpha treatment. I visited the lower *iron* in the morning and gave Ai'ire three sulpha tablets; he only wanted to take one but finally took all three. No diarrhea that morning.

February 29, aid post: Litabagi treated Ai'ire when he was accompanied by his wife and daughter who also were treated because their legs felt weak. He told me this on March 2; my note says, "Ai'ire's famous stomach is at it again! It was gurgling away tonight and he has slight diarrhea again. He said he might go to the 'haus sik' with me when I go to YR this Saturday."

March 13, Ai'ire sick again: While I was visiting the lower *iron*, Ai'ire said he was having stomach pain,

> this time mid and left lateral: no diarrhea. Just a constant pain. . . . I talked with him about going to the Wewak 'haus sik' [hospital] and he said he would; if he doesn't do something like that he thinks he won't make it. I talked with Betty [Gillam] about him Sunday [when she visited] and she thought it might be cancer; there are a few cases she said. I will check with Ces [Parish] Thursday and with the 'haus sik' in Lumi for procedures to get him shipped out to Wewak. If something isn't done while I am here, I am afraid he is going to keep losing weight and then get pneumonia that would finish him off. (WN555)

March 31, I visit with Ai'ire at Klowi's camp: Ai'ire told me that there was talk of a curing festival for him, Eine, and Kairapowe. I told him that Ces Parish was working on getting him admitted to the Wewak hospital. He added that since neither the aid post nor *imoulu* had cured him, he wanted to go to the big hospital. My skeptical note is, "We will see, when it gets down to it, if he really will go or not." Ai'ire said that the *imoulu* treating him from Alai and Bapei told him they were removing little snakes from his stomach but the problem was that they kept returning.

April 4, Ai'ire flown in the CMML plane to Wewak hospital: The Yellow River CMML mission had arranged for Ai'ire's transfer to the Admin's regional hospital for diagnosis and treatment.

April 22, I meet with Dr. Risto Gobius in Wewak: Dr. Gobius told me that the hospital staff's clinical results found nothing physically amiss with Ai'ire. This was a very discouraging and befuddling finding; to me he had appeared clinically ill and I had monitored the deteriorating process of his illness over many months and hoped for a definitive diagnosis. It was not the terminus of the case study I had expected. When I returned briefly to the Lujere in 1982, I sadly learned that Ai'ire had died.

References

Allen, Bryant J. 1982. "The Pacific War 1941–1945." *Papua New Guinea Atlas: A Nation in Transition*, edited by David King and Stephen Ranck. 14–15. Bathurst, Australia, and Port Moresby, Papua New Guinea: Robert Brown & Associates in association with the University of Papua New Guinea.

———. 1983. "A Bomb or a Bullet or the Bloody Flux? Population Change in the Aitape Inland, Papua New Guinea, 1941–1945." *The Journal of Pacific History* 18 (4): 218–35.

———. 1990. "The Importance of Being Equal: The Colonial and Postcolonial Experience in the Torricelli Foothills." In *Sepik Heritage: Tradition and Change in Papua New Guinea*, edited by Nancy Lutkehaus, Christian Kaufmann, William E. Mitchell, Douglas Newton, Lita Osmundsen, and Meinhard Schuster. 185–96. Durham, NC: Carolina Academic Press.

———. 1992. "The Geography of Papua New Guinea." In *Human Biology in Papua New Guinea: The Small Cosmos*, edited by Robert D. Attenborough and Michael P. Alpers, 36–66. Oxford: Clarendon Press.

———. 2005. "The Place of Agricultural Intensity in Sepik Foothills Prehistory'. In *Papuan Pasts: Cultural, Linguistic, and Biological Histories of Papuan-speaking Peoples*, edited by Andrew Pawley, Robert Attenborough, Jack Golson, and Robin Hide, 585–623. Canberra: Australian National University Press.

———. 2006. "Remembering the War in the Sepik." In *The Pacific War in Papua New Guinea: Memories and Realities*, edited by Yukio Toyoda and Hank Nelson, 11–34. Tokyo: Rikkyo University Centre for Asian Area Studies.

Anonymous. 1945. "Operations–Moss Troops." *National Archives of Australia*: A3269, C4/C.

Arens, W. 1979. *The Man-Eating Myth: Anthropology and Anthropophagy*. New York: Oxford University Press.

Armstrong, W. E. 1928. *Roussel Island: An Ethnographic Study*. Cambridge: Cambridge University Press.

Asad, Talal. 1991. "Afterword: From the History of Colonial Anthropology to the Anthropology of Western Hegemony." In *Colonial Situations: Essays on the Contextualization of*

Ethnographic Knowledge, edited by George W. Stocking, Jr., 314–24. Madison: University of Wisconsin Press.

Ashforth, Adam. 2005. *Witchcraft, Violence, and Democracy in South Africa.* Chicago: University of Chicago Press.

Atkinson, Jane Monnig. 1989. *The Art and Politics of Wana Shamanship.* Berkeley: University of California Press.

Bachelard, Gaston. 1969. *The Poetics of Space.* Translated by Maria Jolas. Boston: Beacon Press.

Balzer, Marjorie Mandelstam. 1996. "Shamanism." In *Encyclopedia of Cultural Anthropology*, vol. 4, edited by David Levinson and Melvin Ember, 1182–85. New York: Henry Holt.

Barnes, J. A. 1962. "African Models in the New Guinea Highlands." *Man* 62: 5–9.

Barnett, T. E. 1972. "Law and Legal System." In *Encyclopedia of Papua New Guinea*, vol. 2, edited by Peter Ryan, 617–29. Melbourne, Australia: Melbourne University Press.

Barry, J. V. 1945. "Report of Commission of Inquiry into the Suspension of the Civil Administration of the Territory of Papua in February, 1942." Produced for the Australian Commonwealth Government. Unpublished manuscript.

Barstow, Anne L. 1994. *Witchcraze: A New History of European Witch Hunts.* London: Harper Collins.

Bateson, Gregory. 1932. "Social Structure of the Iatmül People of the Sepik River." *Oceania* 2 (3–4): 1–101.

———. (1936) 1958. *Naven: A Survey of the Problems suggested by a Composite Picture of the Culture of a New Guinea Tribe drawn from Three Points of View.* Stanford, CA: Stanford University Press.

———. 1972. *Steps to an Ecology of Mind: A Revolutionary Approach to Man's Understanding of Himself.* New York: Ballantine Books.

———. 1978. "Towards a Theory of Cultural Coherence: Comment." *Anthropological Quarterly.* 51 (1): 77–78.

Baxstrom, Richard, and Todd Meyers. 2016. *Realizing the Witch: Science, Cinema, and the Mystery of the Invisible.* New York: Fordham University Press.

Beaglehole, Ernest. 1968. "R. H. Codrington." *International Encyclopedia of the Social Sciences.* Edited by David L. Sills and Robert K. Merton. New York: Free Press.

Bean, Ian. 1971. "Agricultural Patrol Report: Lumi Sub District." Lumi Patrol Report #1 of 1971/72. University of California, San Diego, Mandeville Special Collections Library.

Behrmann, Walter. 1917. *Der Sepik (Kaiserin-Augusta-Fluss) und sein Stromgebiet: Geographischer Bericht der Kaiserin-Augusta-Fluss-Expedition 1912–13 auf der Insel Neuguinea.* Berlin: Ernst Siegfried Mittler und Sohn.

———. 1922. *Im Stromgebiet des Sepik: Eine deutsche Forschungsreise in Neuguinea.* Berlin: August Scherl.

———. 1924. *Das Westliche Kaiser-Wilhelms-Land in Neu-Guinea* (with three folded maps). Berlin: Gesellschaft für Erdkunde.

Beidelman, T. O. 1986. *Moral Imagination in Kaguru Modes of Thought.* Bloomington: Indiana University Press.

———. 2012. *The Culture of Colonialism: The Cultural Subjection of Ukaguru*. Bloomington: Indiana University Press.

Benjamin, Walter. (1955) 2007. *Illuminations: Essays and Reflections*, edited by Hannah Arendt. New York: Schocken Books.

Beran, Harry, and Barry Craig. 2005. *Shields of Melanesia*. Honolulu: University of Hawaii Press.

Berndt, Catherine H. 1972. "Myths and Tales." In *Encyclopedia of Papua and New Guinea*, vol. 2, edited by Peter Ryan, 822–29. Melbourne, Australia: Melbourne University Press.

Berndt, Ronald M. 1962. *Excess and Restraint: Social Control among a New Guinea Mountain People*. Chicago: University of Chicago Press.

Biersack, Aletta. 2017. "Afterword: From Witchcraft to the Pentecostal-Witchcraft Nexus." In *Pentecostalism and Witchcraft: Spiritual Warfare in Africa and Melanesia*, edited by Knut Rio, Michelle MacCarthy, and Ruy Blanes, 293–305. London: Palgrave Macmillan.

Biskup, Peter. 1969. "Hahl at Herbertshoehe, 1896–1898: The Genesis of German Native Administration in New Guinea." In *The History of Melanesia*, 77–99. Papers from the Second Waigani Seminar, May 30–June 5, 1968, Port Moresby, University of Papua and New Guinea. Canberra: Australian National University Press.

Blackwood, Beatrice. 1935. *Both Sides of Buka Passage: An Ethnographic Study of Social, Sexual, and Economic Questions in the North-Western Solomon Islands*. Oxford: Clarendon Press.

Boas, Frantz. 1914. "Mythology and Folk-Tales of the North American Indians. *Journal of American Folk-Lore* 27: 374–410.

———. 1925. "Stylistic Aspects of Primitive Literature." *Journal of American Folk-Lore* 38: 329–39.

Boas, Franz, and George Hunt. 1966. "Religion." In Franz Boas, *Kwakiutl Ethnography*, edited and abridged by Helen Codere, 120–70. Chicago: University of Chicago Press.

Bowden, Ross. 1983. *Yena: Art and Ceremony in a Sepik Society*. Oxford: Pitt Rivers Museum.

Bracken, Christopher. 2007. *Magical Criticism: The Recourse of Savage Philosophy*. Chicago: University of Chicago Press.

Bridges, John G., ed. 1945. *Displaying Australia and New Guinea*. Sydney: Australia Story Trust.

Brightwell, M. 1957a. "Report of Investigation of Massacre of Yellow River Natives." Archives #CRS A518, Item EU 840/1/4. Canberra: National Archives of Australia.

———. 1957b. "Patrol Report–Ambunti No. 3 of 1956/57." Port Moresby: National Archives of Papua New Guinea.

Broadhurst, P. T. K. 1970. "Patrol Report–Lumi No. 8 of 1970/71." University of California San Diego Libraries, Mandeville Special Collections.

———. 1971. "Lumi Patrol Report #4 of 1971/72." University of California San Diego Libraries, Mandeville Special Collections.

Brookfield, H. C. 1972. *Colonial, Development and Independence: The Case of the Melanesian Islands in the South Pacific*. Cambridge: Cambridge University Press.

Brown, C. A., ed. 2011. "SRD Operations in New Guinea: Mosstroops, Sepik District, Aug–Dec 43." *The Official History of Special Operations–Australia*, vol. 2 *Operations*, 124–28. Canberra, Australia: SOA Books.

Brown, W. T. 2012. "Reminiscences of Rough Times: May River and the Mianmin." http://asopa.typepad.com/asopa_people/2012/09/remininscensces-of-rough-times-may-river-mianmin.html. Accessed March 2, 2016.

Bubandt, Nils. 2014. *The Empty Seashell: Witchcraft and Doubt on an Indonesian Island*. Ithaca, NY: Cornell University Press.

Burbank, Victoria Katherine. 2000. "'The Lust to Kill' and the Arnhem Land Sorcerer: An Exercise in Integrative Anthropology." *Ethos* 28 (3): 410–44.

Burridge. K. O. L. 1960. *Mambu: A Melanesian Millennium*. London: Methuen.

———. 1965. "Tangu, Northern Madang District," in *Gods, Ghosts and Men in Melanesian*, edited by P. Lawrence and M. J. Meggitt, 223–49. Melbourne: Oxford University Press.

Burton-Bradley, B. G., and Charles Julius. 1965. "Folk Psychiatry of Certain Villages in the Central District of Papua." South Pacific Commission Technical Paper no. 146. Nouméa, New Caledonia.

Buschmann, Rainer F. 2000. "Exploring Tensions in Material Culture: Commercialising Ethnography in German New Guinea, 1870–1904." In *Hunting the Gatherers: Ethnographic Collectors, Agents and Agency in Melanesia, 1870s–1930s*, edited by Michael O'Hanlon and Robert L. Welsch, 55–102. New York: Berghahn.

———. 2009. *Anthropology's Global Histories: The Ethnographic Frontier in German New Guinea, 1870–1935*. Honolulu: University of Hawaii Press.

Calaby, J. H. 1972. "Finsch." In *Encyclopedia of Papua Ned Guinea*, vol. 1, edited by Peter Ryan, 404–5. Melbourne, Australia: Melbourne University Press.

Campbell, I. C. 1989. *A History of the Pacific Islands*. Berkeley: University of California Press.

———. 2000. "The ASOPA Controversy: A Pivot of Australian Policy for Papua New Guinea, 1945–49." *Journal of Pacific History* 35 (11): 83–99.

Campbell, James. 2007. *The Ghost Mountain Boys: Their Epic March and the Terrifying Battle for New Guinea–The Forgotten War of the South Pacific*. New York: Crown.

Cantwell, Anne-Marie and Diana diZerega Wall. 2001. *Unearthing Gotham: The Archaeology of New York City*. New Haven, CT: Yale University Press.

Carey, Matthew. 2017. *Mistrust, An Ethnographic Theory*. Chicago: Hau Books, Chicago Distribution Center.

Carroll, Michael P. 1996. "Myth." In *Encyclopedia of Cultural Anthropology*, vol. 3, edited by David Levinson and Melvin Ember, 827–31. New York: Henry Holt.

Charlton, Peter. 1983. *The Unnecessary War: Island Campaigns of the South-West Pacific 1944–45*. South Melbourne, Australia: Macmillan.

Cheesman, L. E. 1941. "The Mountainous Country at the Boundary, North New Guinea." *The Geographical Journal* 98 (4): 169–88.

———. 1949. *Six-legged Snakes in New Guinea: A Collecting Expedition to Two Unexplored Islands*. London: George G. Harrap.

Codrington, R. H. (1891) 1969. *The Melanesians: Studies in Their Anthropology and Folk-Lore*. Oxford: Oxford University Press.

Cohen, Alex. 1996. "Folklore." In *Encyclopedia of Cultural Anthropology*, vol. 2, edited by David Levinson and Melvin Ember, 501–2. New York: Henry Holt.

Coiffier, Christian, 2020. "Chauves-souris et roussettes en Papouasie Nouvelle-Guinée. Leune représentations dans la région du Sepik." *Journal de la Société des Océanistes* 150: 43–56.

Colby, Benjamin N., and James L. Peacock. 1973. "Narrative." In *Handbook of Social and Cultural Anthropology*, edited by John Honigmann, 613–35. Chicago: Rand McNally.

Comaroff, Jean, and John Comaroff,. eds. *Modernity and its Malcontents: Ritual and Power in Postcolonial Africa*. Chicago: University of Chicago Press.

Conrad, Sebastian. 2011. *German Colonialism: A Short History*. Cambridge: Cambridge University Press.

Cotlow, Lewis. 1966. In *Search of the Primitive*. Boston: Little, Brown.

Counts, Dorothy Ayers, Judith K. Brown, and Jacquelyn C. Campbell, eds. 1999. *To Have and to Hit: Cultural Perspectives on Wife Beating*, 2nd ed. Urbana: University of Illinois Press.

Craig, Barry. 1969. "Houseboards and Warshields of the Mountain-Ok of Central New Guinea." MA thesis, University of Sydney.

———. 1972. "Report of Upper Sepik Ethnographic Expedition, 1969." Unpublished manuscript.

———. 1975. "The Art Style of Yellow River, West Sepik District, New Guinea." *Bessler-Archiv* n.s. 23: 417–45.

———. 1988. *Art and Decoration of Central New Guinea*. Aylesbury, UK: Shire.

———. 1990. "Is the Mountain Ok Culture a Sepik Culture?" In *Sepik Heritage: Tradition and Change in Papua New Guinea*, edited by Nancy Lutkehaus, Christian Kaufmann, William E. Mitchell, Douglas Newton, Lita Osmundsen and Meinhard Schuster, 129–49. Durham, NC: Carolina Academic Press.

———. 1997. "The Fate of Thurnwald's Sepik Ethnographic Collections." Special issue: *Gestern und Heute-Traditionen in der Südsee. Festschrift zum 75 Geburtstag von Gerd Koch*, edited by M. Schindlbeck. *Bessler-Archiv* n.s. 45: 387–408.

———. 2008. "Sorcery Divination Among the Abau of the Idam Valley, Upper Sepik, Papua New Guinea." *Journal of Ritual Studies*. 22:(20), 37–50.

Craig, Barry, Ron Vanderwal and Christine Winter. 2015. *War Trophies or Curios? The War Museum Collection in Museum Victoria 1915–1920*. Melbourne, Australia: Museum Victoria Publishing.

Craig, Barry and Christine Winter. 2016. "Richard Thurnwald and Thomas James Rodoni in the Upper Sepik Region of New Guinea 1914." http://www.usncngp.com/papers. Accessed November 28, 2016.

Dalton, Doug. 2000. "Melanesian Can(n)ons: Paradoxes and Prospects in Melanesian Ethnography." In *Excluded Ancestors, Inventible Traditions: Essays Toward a More Inclusive History of Anthropology*, edited by Richard Handler, 284–305. Madison: University of Wisconsin Press.

Darwin, Charles. 1859. *On the Origin of Species by Means of Natural Selection or the Preservation of Favored Races in the Struggle for Life*. London: John Murray, Albemarle Street.

Dawes, Allan W. 1936 reprinted 1943. *Official Handbook of the Territory of New Guinea*. Canberra, Australia: L. F. Johnston, Commonwealth Government Printer.

De Groot, Nick. 2008. "Foreword." In *Papua New Guinea Tok Pisin–English Dictionary*, edited by C. A. Volker. South Melbourne, Australia: Oxford University Press.

de Martino, Ernesto. 2015. *Magic: A Theory from the South*. Translated and annotated by Dorothy Louise Zinn. Chicago: Hau Books.

Denoon, Donald, with Kathleen Dugan and Leslie Marshall. 1989. *Public Health in Papua New Guinea: Medical Possibility and Social Constraint, 1884–1984*. Cambridge: Cambridge University Press.

de Waal Malefijt, Annemarie. 1968. Religions *and Culture: An Introduction to Anthropology of Religion*. New York: Macmillan.

Dexter, David. 1961. *The New Guinea Offensives*. Canberra: Australian War Memorial.

Dobrin, Lise M. and Ira Bashkow. 2010. "'The Truth in Anthropology Does Not Travel First Class': Reo Fortune's Fateful Encounter with Margaret Mead." In *Histories of Anthropology Annual*, edited by Regna Darnell and Frederic W. Glesch, 66–128, Lincoln: University of Nebraska Press..

Dobson, Denis, n. d., "Aitape Mission." Unpublished typescript manuscript.

Dornstreich, Mark D. and George E. B. Morren. 1974. "Does New Guinea Cannibalism have Nutritional Value?" *Human Ecology* 2 (1): 1–12.

Dozier, Edward P. 1956. "The Concepts of 'Primitive' and 'Native' in Anthropology." In *Current Anthropology: A Supplement to Anthropology Today*, edited by William L. Thomas, Jr., 187–202. Chicago: University of Chicago Press.

Drea, Edward J. 1984. *Defending the Driniumor: Covering Force Operation in New Guinea. 1944*. Fort Leavenworth: Combat Studies Institute, U. S. Army Command and General Staff College.

Duggan, Stephen J. 1979. "The Passing of the 'Good Time:' A History of the People of North-Central Papua New Guinea During the Second World War, 1942 – 1947." Thesis submitted as part of the Final Honors Examination in the Department of History, La Trobe University.

———. 1983. "In the Shadow of Somoro: The Franciscan Experience in the Sepik Region, 1945–75." MA thesis, La Trobe University.

———. 1989. "Franciscans in the Sepik: A Spiritual Conquest or a Quest for Acceptance?" *The Journal of Pacific History* 24: 70–88.

Eliade, Mircea. 1972. *Shamanism: Archaic Techniques of Ecstasy*. Princeton, NJ: Princeton University Press.

Errington, Frederick K., and Deborah Gewertz. 1995. *Articulating Change in the "Last Unknown."* Boulder, CO: Westview.

Evans-Pritchard. E. E. 1937. *Witchcraft, Oracles and Magic among the Azande*. Oxford: Clarendon Press.

Farlow, Raleigh Monash. 1944a. "Report on Operations: Moss Troops." Copy one, *National Archives of Australia*, digitized item, Series no. A3269, Control symbol C4/B, barcode 235119.

———. 1944b. "Mosstroops: "Report on Food Packs, Equipment, Weapons, Etc." *National Archives of Australia*, digitized item, Series no. A3269.

Favret-Saada, Jeanne. 1980. [1977] *Deadly Words: Witchcraft in the Bocage*. Translated by Catherine Cullen. Cambridge: Cambridge University Press.

———. 2015. *The Anti-Witch*. Translated by Matthew Carey. Chicago: HAU Books.

Feinberg, P. E. 1951. "Lumi Patrol Report No. 2 of 1950/51." University of California San Diego Libraries, Mandeville Special Collections.

Feldpausch, Becky, compiler. (2001) 2006. *Namia, Tok Pisin and English Dictionary*. Ukarumpa, PNG: Summer Institute of Linguistics Papua New Guinea.

———. 2011. "Introduction to the Namia Dictionary." Unpublished manuscript. Ukarumpa, PNG: Summer Institute of Linguistics Papua New Guinea.

Feldpausch, Thomas, and Becky Feldpausch. 1988. "Background Study: Working with the Namia People of the West Sepik Province PNG." Unpublished manuscript. Ukarumpa, PNG: Summer Institute of Linguistics.

———. 1992. "Namia Grammar Essentials." Ukarumpa, PNG: Summer Institute of Linguistics. http://www.sil.org/pacific/png/abstract.asp?id=34683

———. 1993. Updated 2009. "Phonology Essentials of the Namia Language." Ukarumpa, Summer Institute of Linguistics. Accessed August 22, 2016. http://www.sil.org/pacific/png/abstract.asp?id=51230

———. 1999. "Dialect Survey of the Namia Language." Manuscript. Ukarumpa, Summer Institute of Linguistics. http://www.sil.org/pacific/abstract.asp?ic=51809 Accessed March 7, 2015.

———. 2000. "Namia Orthography Paper," Manuscript. Ukarumpa, Summer Institute of Linguists. Accessed March 7, 2015. http://www.sil.org/pacific/png/abstract.asp?id=51229.

———. 2003. updated 2007. "TAM [tense, aspect, mood] Marking in Namia (nnm)." Manuscript. Ukarumpa, Summer Institute of Linguists. Accessed August 24, 2016. http://www.Namia_Tense_Aspect_Mood(1).pdf

Feldt, Eric. (1946) 1967. *The Coast Watchers*. Sydney: Angus and Robertson Pacific Books. Citations refer to the Pacific Books edition.

Firth, Stewart. 1983. *New Guinea under the Germans*. Melbourne: Melbourne University Press.

Fowke, J. E. 1968. "Lumi Patrol Report No. 21 of 1967/68." University of California San Diego Libraries, Mandeville Special Collections.

Foley, William A. 1986. *The Papuan Languages of New Guinea*. Cambridge: Cambridge University Press.

Forge, Anthony. 1970. "Prestige, Influence, and Sorcery: A New Guinea Example" in *Witchcraft, Confessions, and Accusations*, edited by Mary Douglas. Oxford: Clarendon Press.

Forsyth, Miranda. 2015. "A Pluralist Response to the Regulation of Sorcery and Witchcraft in Melanesia." In *Talking it Through: Responses to Sorcery and Witchcraft Beliefs and Practices in Melanesia*, edited by Miranda Forsyth and Richard Eves, 213–240. Canberra: Australian National University Press.

Forsyth, Miranda and Richard Eves. eds. 2015. *Talking it Through: Responses to Sorcery and Witchcraft Beliefs and Practices in Melanesia*. Canberra: Australian National University Press.

Fortes, Myer. 1953. "The Structure of Unilineal Descent Groups." *American Anthropologist*, 55: 17–41.

———. 1969. *Kinship and the Social Order: The Legacy of Lewis Henry Morgan*. Chicago: Aldine.

Fortune, R. F. 1927. *The Mind in Sleep*. London: Kegan Paul, Trendh, Trubner.

———. 1942. *Arapesh*. Publications of the American Ethnological Society, Franz Boas editor, vol. 19. New York. J. J. Augustin.

———. (1932) 1963. *Sorcerers of Dobu: The Social Anthropology of the Dobu Islanders of the Western Pacific*, 2nd ed. London: Routledge & Kegan Paul.

Fountain, Jenny. 1999. *…To Teach Others Also: The Bible Schools of the Christian Brethren Churches of Papua New Guinea*. Palmerston North: Osjen Ministries Trust.

Fowke, J. E. 1967. "Lumi Patrol Report No. 21 of 1967/68." University of California San Diego Libraries, Mandeville Special Collections.

Fowler, F. R. 1960. *Aid Post Medical and Hygiene Training Book*. Port Moresby: Department of Public Health, Territory of Papua and New Guinea.

Fox, Robin, 1964. "Witchcraft and Clanship among the Cochiti." In *Magic, Faith and Healing: Studies in Primitive Psychiatry Today*, edited by Ari Kiev, 174–200. Glencoe, IL: Free Press.

———. 1983. *Kinship and Marriage: An Anthropological Perspective*. Cambridge: Cambridge University Press.

Frankel, Stephen, and Gilbert Lewis, eds. 1989. *A Continuing Trial of Treatment: Medical Pluralism in Papua New Guinea*. Dordrecht, Netherlands: Kluwer Academic Publishers.

Franklin, Karl J. 2010. "Comments on Sorcery in Papua New Guinea." Graduate Institute of Applied Linguistics electronic notes. http://www.gialens/vol4num3/. Accessed October 30, 2017.

Fried, Morton H. 1967. *The Evolution of Political Society: An Essay in Political Anthropology*. New York: Random House.

Fulton, E. T. W. 2005. *No Turning Back: A Memoir*, edited by Elizabeth Fulton Thurston. Canberra, Australia: Pandanus Books.

Fyfe, Andrew. 2006. "Progress Report, June 2006." Upper Sepik–Central New Guinea Project. http://uscngp.com/reports. Accessed September 9, 2017.

Gailey, Harry A. 2004. *MacArthur's Victory: The War in New Guinea, 1943–1944*. New York: Presidio Press.

Gamble, Bruce. 2006. *Darkest Hour: The True Story of Lark Force at Rabaul—Australia's Worst Military Disaster of World War II*. Minneapolis: Zenith Press.

———, 2010. *Fortress Rabaul: The Battle for the Southwest Pacific, January 1942–April 1942*. Minneapolis: Zenith Press.

———. 2014 Target: *Rabaul, the Allied Siege of Japan's Most Infamous Stronghold, March 1943–August 1945*. Minneapolis: Zenith Press.

Gardner, Don. 1999. "Anthropology, Myth, and the Subtle Ways of Ethnocentrism." In *The Anthropology of Cannibalism*, edited by Laurence R. Goldman, 27–49. Westport, CN: Bergin & Garvey.

Gardner, Robert and Karl G. Heider. 1968. *Gardens of War: Life and Death in the New Guinea Stone Age.* New York: Random House.

Geertz, Clifford. 1966. "Religion as a Cultural System." In *Anthropological Approaches to the Study of Religion*, edited by Michael Banton, 1–46. London: Tavistock.

Gell, Alfred. 1971. "Penis Sheathing and Ritual Status in a West Sepik Village." *Man* 6 (2): 165–81.

———. 1975. *Metamorphosis of the Cassowaries: Umeda Society, Language and Ritual.* London: Athlone Press.

Gesch, Patrick F. 1985. *Initiative and Initiation: A Cargo Cult-Type Movement in the Sepik Against Its Background in Traditional Village Religion.* St. Augustin, West Germany: Anthropos-Institut.

———. 2015. "Talking *Sanguma*: The Social Process of Discernment of Evil in Two Sepik Societies." In *Talking it Through: Responses to Sorcery and Witchcraft Beliefs and Practices in Melanesia*, edited by Miranda Forsyth and Richard Eves, 111–29. Canberra: Australian National University.

Geschiere, Peter. 2013. *Witchcraft, Intimacy, and Trust: Africa in Comparison.* Chicago: University of Chicago Press.

Gewertz, Deborah. 1983. *Sepik River Societies: A Historical Ethnography of the Chambri and their Neighbors.* New Haven, NJ: Yale University Press.

Gibbs, Phillip, and Josepha Junnie Wailoni. 2008. "Sorcery among the Plains Arapesh." *Anthropos* 103: 149–58.

Gill, C. H. 1996. "Feldt, Eric Augustas (1899–1968)." *Australian Dictionary of Biography*, National Centre of Biography, Australian National University. http://adb.anu.edu.au/biography/feldt-eric-augustas-01063/text17953. Accessed March 26, 2016.

Gillam, Elizabeth A. 1983. "Cultural Aspects of Infant Undernutrition Among the Lujere People of Papua New Guinea: A Nursing Perspective." MA thesis, Massey University, Palmerston North, New Zealand.

———. 1996. "The Nutritional Practices of the Edwaki Sub District, Sandaun Province, PNG: An Investigation into What is Eaten, What is not Eaten and the Reason Why." Postgraduate thesis, Department of Human Nutrition, University of Otago, Otago, New Zealand.

Glasse, R. M. 1969. "Marriage in South Fore," In *Pigs, Pearlshells, and Women: Marriage in the New Guinea Highlands*, edited by R. M. Glasse and M. J. Meggitt, 16–37. Englewood Cliffs: Prentice Hall.

Glick, Leonard B. 1972. "Sangguma." In *Encyclopedia of Papua and New Guinea*, vol. 2, edited by Peter Ryan, 1029–30. Melbourne, Australia: Melbourne University.

Godelier, Maurice, Thomas R. Trautman, and Franklin E. Tjon Sie Fat, eds. 1998. *Transformations of Kinship.* Washington, DC: Smithsonian Institution Press.

Goldman, Laurence R. 1999. "From Pot to Polemic: Uses and Abuses of Cannibalism." In *The Anthropology of Cannibalism*, edited by Laurence R. Goldman, 1–26. Westport: Bergin & Garvey.

Goodare, Julian. 2016. *The European Witch-Hunt.* London: Routledge.

Goode, William J. 1951. *Religion Among the Primitives.* Glencoe. IL: The Free Press.

Goodman, Felicitas D. 1988. *How about Demons? Possession and Exorcism in the Modern World.* Bloomington: Indiana University Press.

Goody, J. 1996. "A Kernel of Doubt." *Journal of the Royal Anthropological Institute* 2 (4) 667–81.

Gordon, Robert. 1981. "The Myth of the Noble Anthropologist in Melanesia." *Bikmaus* 2 (1): 10–20.

Gray, Geoffrey, 1999. "'Being Honest to my Science': Reo Fortune and J. H. P. Murray, 1927–30." *Australian Journal of Anthropology* 10 (1): 56–76.

Greenop, F. 1944. *Who Travels Alone.* Sydney: K. G. Murray.

Grey, Jeffrey. 2008. *A Military History of Australia*, 3rd ed. Cambridge: Cambridge University Press.

Griffin, James, Hank Nelson, and Stewart Firth. 1979. *Papua New Guinea: A Political History.* Richmond, Australia: Heinemann Educational Australia.

Grimshaw, Peter J. 1972. "Police." In *Encyclopedia of Papua New Guinea*, vol. 2, edited by Peter Ryan, 916–21. Melbourne, Australia: Melbourne University Press.

Gropper, Rena. 1967. "Toward a Universal Comparative Medicine." Unpublished manuscript.

Grosart, Ian. 1972a. "Australian School of Pacific Administration." In *Encyclopedia of Papua New Guinea*, vol. 1, edited by Peter Ryan, 50–52. Melbourne: Melbourne University Press.

———1972b. "House of Assembly." In *Encyclopedia of Papua New Guinea*, vol. 1, edited by Peter Ryan, 531–40. Melbourne, Australia: Melbourne University Press.

———1972c. "District Administration." In *Encyclopedia of Papua New Guinea*, vol. 1, edited by Peter Ryan, 266–69. Melbourne, Australia: Melbourne University Press.

Guddemi, Phillip Vickroy. 1992. "We Came from This: Knowledge, Memory, Painting and 'Play' in the Initiation Rituals of the Sawiyanô of Papua New Guinea." PhD diss., University of Michigan, Ann Arbor.

Haberland, Eike. 1965. "Tasks of Research in the Sepik Region, New Guinea." *Bulletin of the International Committee on Urgent Anthropological and Ethnological Research* 7: 33–44.

Healy, A. M. 1972. "Goldfields." In *Encyclopedia of Papua New Guinea*, vol. 1, edited by Peter Ryan, 499–501. Melbourne, Australia: Melbourne University Press.

Hefner, Robert W. 2007. Review of *Naming the Witch* by James Siegel in *American Anthropologist* 109 (2): 420–21.

Heider, Karl G. 1970. *The Dugam Dani: A Papuan Culture in the Highlands of West New Guinea.* Chicago: Aldine.

———. 1976. *Grand Valley Dani: Peaceful Warriors.* New York: Holt, Rinehart and Winston.

Held, Gerrit Jan. (1947) 1957. *The Papuas of Waropen.* Hallstrom Pacific Collection, Translation Series 2. The Hague, Netherlands: Martinus Nijhoff. (Originally published in Dutch as *Papoea's van Waropen*. Leiden, Netherlands: E. J. Brill.)

Herskovits, Melville J. 1948. *Man and his Works.* New York: Alfred A. Knopf.

Hides, J .G. 1936. *Savage Patrol.* New York: Robert M. McBride.

Hinkle, L. E., N. Plummer, R. Metraux, P. Richter, J. W. Gittinger, W. N. Thetford, W. E. Mitchell, H. Leichter, R. Pinsky, D. Goebel, I. D. J. Bross, and H. G. Wolff. 1957. "Factors Relevant to the Occurrence of Bodily Illness and Disturbances in Mood, Thought and

Behavior in Three Homogeneous Population Groups." *American Journal of Psychiatry* 114: 212–20.

Hogbin, H. Ian. 1935a. "Native Culture of Wogeo." *Oceania* 5: 326–28.

———. 1935b. "Sorcery and Administration." *Oceania* 6: 1–32.

———. 1937. "The Hill People of North-Eastern Guadalcanal.'" *Oceania* 8 (1): 62–92.

———. 1943. "Developing New Guinea and the Future of the Natives." *Australian Journal of Science* 5 (5): 133–35.

———. 1952. "Sorcery and Succession in Wogeo." *Oceania* 23: 133–36.

———. 1970. *The Island of Menstruating Men: Religion in Wogeo, New Guinea.* Scranton, PA: Chandler.

Hogbin, H. Ian, and Camilla H. Wedgwood. 1943. "Development and Welfare in the Western Pacific." Sydney: Australian Institute of International Affairs.

Höltker, Georg. 1963. "Neue Materialien über den Tedeszauber in Neuguinea." *Anthropos* 58 (3–4): 333–71.

Horton, Robin. 1967. "African Traditional Thought and Western Science." *Africa: Journal of the International African Institute.* 37 (2): 155–87.

Horowitz, Jason. 2018. "'Shut Up, Satan': Rome Course Teaches Exorcism, Even by Cellphone." *New York Times*, April 19: A6.

Huber, Peter B. 1975. "Defending the Cosmos: Violence and Social Order Among the Anggor of New Guinea." In *War: Its Causes and Correlates*, edited by Martin A. Nettleship, Dale Givins, and Anderson Nettleship, 619–61. The Hague, Netherlands: Mouton; Chicago: Aldine.

———. 1980. "The Anggor Bowman: Ritual and Society in Melanesia." *American Ethnologist* 7: 43–57.

———. 1990. "Masquerade as Artifact in Wamu." In *Sepik Heritage: Tradition and Change in Papua New Guinea*, edited by Nancy Lutkehaus, Christian Kaufmann, William E. Mitchell, Douglas Newton, Lita Osmundsen, and Meinhard Schuster. 150–59, Durham, NC: Carolina Academic Press.

Huber, Mary Taylor. 1990. "The Bishops' Progress: Representations of Missionary Experience on the Sepik Frontier." In *Sepik Heritage: Tradition and Change in Papua New Guinea*, edited by Nancy Lutkehaus, Christian Kaufmann, William E. Mitchell, Douglas Newton, Lita Osmundsen, and Meinhard Schuster, 197–211, Durham, NC: Carolina Academic Press.

Hudson, W. J. 1971. "Introduction." In *Australia and Papua New Guinea*, edited by W. J. Hudson, 1–7. Sydney: Sydney University Press.

Hutchings, R. 1968. "Patrol Report No. 22, 1967/68, Lumi Sub-District, West Sepik District." National Archives of Papua New Guinea, Port Moresby.

———. 1970. "Patrol Report No. 3, 1970/71, Lumi Sub-District, West Sepik District." National Archives of Papua New Guinea, Port Moresby.

Jack-Hinton, C. 1972. "Discovery." In *Encyclopedia of Papua New Guinea*, vol. 1, edited by Peter Ryan, 246–57. Melbourne, Australia: Melbourne University Press.

Jacobs, Marjorie, 1972. "German New Guinea." In *Encyclopedia of Papua New Guinea*, vol. 1, edited by Peter Ryan, 485–98. Melbourne, Australia: Melbourne University Press.

Johnson, L. W. 1983. *Colonial Sunset: Australia and Papua New Guinea 1970–74*. St. Lucia, Australia: University of Queensland Press.

Jones, Graham M. 2017. *Magic's Reason: An Anthropology of Analogy*. Chicago: University of Chicago Press.

Jorgensen, Dan. 1996. "Regional History and Ethnic Identity in the Hub of New Guinea: The Emergence of the Min." *Oceania* 66 (3): 189–210.

Joyce, R, B. 1972. "Exploration." In *Encyclopedia of Papua New Guinea*, vol. 1, edited by Peter Ryan, 385–89. Melbourne, Australia: Melbourne University Press.

Juillerat, Bernard. (1986) 1996. *Children of the Blood: Society, Reproduction, and Cosmology in New Guinea*. Translated by Nora Scott. New York: Berg.

———. 1990. "Male Ideology and Cultural Fantasy in Yafar Society." In *Sepik Heritage: Tradition and Change in Papua New Guinea*, edited by Nancy Lutkehaus, Christian Kaufmann, William E. Mitchell, Douglas Newton, Lita Osmundsen, and Meinhard Schuster, 380–84, Durham, NC: Carolina Academic Press.

———. 1992, ed. *Shooting the Sun: Ritual and Meaning in West Sepik*. Washington, DC: Smithsonian Institution Press.

———. 2000. "Do the Bánaro Really Exist? Going Back After Richard Thurnwald." *Oceania* 71: 46–66.

Kaberry, Phyllis M. 1941–42. "Law and Political Organization in the Abelam Tribe, New Guinea." *Oceania* 12 (1, 3, 4): 79–95, 209–25, 331–63.

———. 1967. "The Plasticity of New Guinea Kinship." In *Social Organization: Essays Presented to Raymond Firth*, edited by Maurice Freedman, 105–23. Chicago: Aldine.

Kapferer, Bruce. 1997. *The Feast of the Sorcerer: Practices of Consciousness and Power*. Chicago: University of Chicago Press.

———. 2002. "Introduction: Outside all Reason—Magic, Sorcery, and Epistemology in Anthropology." In *Beyond Rationalism: Rethinking Magic, Witchcraft, and Sorcery*, edited by Bruce Kapferer, 1–30. New York: Berghahn.

Kaptchuk, Ted. J., and Franklin G. Miller. 2015. "Placebo Effects in Medicine." *New England Journal of Medicine* 373: 8–9.

Kaufmann, Christian. 1990. "Swiss and German Ethnographic Collections as Source Materials: A Report on Work in Progress." In *Sepik Heritage: Tradition and Change in Papua New Guinea*, edited by Nancy Lutkehaus, Christian Kaufmann, William E. Mitchell, Douglas Newton, Lita Osmundsen, and Meinhard Schuster, 587–95. Durham, NC: Carolina Academic Press.

Kaufmann, Christian, Philippe Peltier, and Markus Schindlbeck. 2018. "Le Sepik: Société et production matérielle." *Journal de la Société de Océanistes* 146: 5–14.

Keenan, Mel. 2015. "The Western Legal Response to Sorcery in Colonial Papua New Guinea." In *Talking it Through: Responses to Sorcery and Witchcraft Beliefs and Practices in Melanesia*, edited by Miranda Forsyth and Richard Eves, 197–211. Melbourne: Australian National University Press.

Kelm, Antje. 1990. "Sanguma in Abrau and Kwieftim." In *Sepik Heritage: Tradition and Change in Papua New Guinea*, edited by Nancy Lutkehaus, Christian Kaufmann, William E. Mitchell, Douglas Newton, Lita Osmundsen, and Meinhard Schuster, 447–51. Durham, NC: Carolina Academic Press.

Kelm, Antje and Heinz Kelm. 1975. *Ein Pfeilschuss für die Braut: Mythen und Erzählungen aus Kwieftim und Abrau, Nordostneuguinea*. Wiesbaden: Franz Steiner Verlag.

———. 1980. *Sago und Schwein: Ethnologie von Kwieftim und Abrau in Nordost-Neuguinea*. Wiesbaden: Franz Steiner Verlag.

Kelm, Heinz. 1966. *Kunst vom Sepik II*. Berlin: Des Museums für Völkerkunde.

King, Charles. 2019. *Gods of the Upper Air: How a Circle of Renegade Anthropologists Reinvented Race, Sex, and Gender in the Twentieth Century*. Doubleday: New York.

Kirk, G. S. 1970. *Myth: Its Meaning and Functions in Ancient and other Cultures*. Cambridge: University of Cambridge Press.

Knauft, Bruce M. 1985. *Good Company and Violence: Sorcery and Social Action in a Lowland New Guinea Society*. Berkeley: University of California Press.

———. 1999. *From Primitive to Postcolonial in Melanesia and Anthropology*. Ann Arbor: University of Michigan Press.

Koster, G. J., and Georg Höltker. 1942–45. "'Sangguma' of de Sluipmoord op de noordoostkust van Nieuw-Guinea." *Anthropos* 37–40: 213–24.

Kroeber, A. L. 1909. "Classificatory Systems of Relationship." *Journal of the Royal Anthropological Institute* 39: 77–84.

Kulick, Don. 1992. *Language Shift and Cultural Reproduction: Socialization, Self, and Syncretism in a Papua New Guinean Village*. Cambridge: Cambridge University Press.

———. 2019. *A Death in the Rainforest: How a Language and a Way of Life Came to an End in Papua New Guinea*. Chapel Hill, NC: Algonquin Books.

La Fontaine, Jean. Editor. 1972. *The Interpretation of Ritual: Essays in Honour of A. I. Richards*. London: Tavistock.

———. 1973. "Descent in New Guinea: an Africanist View." In *The Character of Kinship*, edited by Jack Goody, 35–51. Cambridge: Cambridge University Press.

Langdon, Robert. 1971. "A Short History." In *Papua/New Guinea: Prospero's Other Island*, edited by Peter Hastings, 42–59. Sydney: Angus and Robertson.

Lanaghan, R. F. 1971. "Patrol Report LUMI No. 9 of 1970/71, South Wapei Census Division, Establishment of Base Camp." University of California San Diego Libraries, Mandeville Special Collections.

———. 1972. "Patrol Report LUMI No. 9 of 1971/72, South Wapei Census Division." University of California San Diego Libraries, Mandeville Special Collections.

Latour, Bruno. 2010. *On the Modern Cult of the Factish Gods*. Durham, NC: Duke University Press.

Laycock, Donald C. 1973. *Sepik Languages: Checklist and Preliminary Classification*. Canberra: Australian National University.

———. 1996. "Sanguma." In *Papers in Papuan Linguistics*, vol. 2, 271–81. Pacific Linguistics Series. Canberra: Australian National University.

Lawrence, P. and M. J. Meggitt. 1965. *Gods, Ghosts, and Men in Melanesia: Some Religions of Australian New Guinea and the New Hebrides*. Melbourne: Oxford University Press.

Lea, D. A. M. 1972. "Sepik Districts, East and West." In *Encyclopedia of Papua New Guinea*, vol. 2, edited by Peter Ryan, 1030–36. Melbourne, Australia: Melbourne University Press.

———. 1972. "Agriculture, Indigenous." In *Encyclopedia of Papua New Guinea*, vol. 1, edited by Peter Ryan, 10–18. Melbourne, Australia: Melbourne University Press.

Leach, Edmund R. 1968. "Ritual." *International Encyclopedia of the Social Sciences*, vol. 13, edited by David L. Sills and Robert K. Merton, 520–26. New York: Free Press.

———. 1969. *Genesis as Myth and Other Essays*. London: Jonathan Cape.

Legge, J. D. 1971. "The Murray Period: Papua 1906–40." *Australia and Papua New Guinea*, edited by W. J. Hudson, 32–56. Sydney: Sydney University Press.

Lessa, William A., and Evon Z. Vogt. 1972. *Reader in Comparative Religion: An Anthropological Approach*. New York: Harper and Row.

Lévi-Strauss, Claude. 1949. "The Sorcerer and His Magic." In *Structural Anthropology*, translated by Claire Jacobson and Brooke Grundfest Schoepf, 167–15. New York: Basic Books.

———. 1976. "Anthropology, History and Ideology." *Critique of Anthropology* 2 (6): 44–55.

Lewis, Gilbert. 1975. *Knowledge of Illness in a Sepik Society: A Study of the Gnau, New Guinea*. London: Athlone.

———. 1977. "Belief and Behavior in Disease." In *Health and Disease in Tribal Societies*, 227–41. Ciba Foundation Symposium 49. Amsterdam, Netherlands, New York: Elsevier/Excerpta Medica/North-Holland.

———. 1980. *Day of Shining Red: An Essay on Understanding Ritual*. Cambridge: Cambridge University Press.

———. 1986. "The Look of Magic." *Man, the Journal of the Royal Anthropological Institute* 21 (3): 414–435.

———. 1987. "Fear of Sorcery and the Problem of Death by Suggestion." *Social Science and Medicine* 24 (12): 997–1010.

———. 1995. "Revealed by Illness: Aspects of the Gnau People's World and their Perception of It." In *Cosmos and Society in Oceania*. Eds. Daniel de Coppet and André Iteanu. Oxford: Berg.

———. 2000. *A Failure in Treatment*. Oxford: Oxford University Press.

———. 2021. *Pandora's Box: Ethnography and the Comparison of Medical Beliefs*. Chicago: Hau Books.

Lewis, M. Paul, ed. 2009. *Ethnologue: Languages of the World*, 16th ed. Dallas, TX: SIL International.

Lewis, M. Paul, Gary F. Simons, and Charles D. Fennig, eds. 2015. *Ethnologue: Languages of the Americas and the Pacific*, 18th ed. Dallas: SIL International.

Lindenbaum, Shirley. 2013. *Kuru Sorcery: Disease and Danger in the New Guinea Highlands*, rev. ed. Boulder, CO: Paradigm.

———. 2004. "Thinking about Cannibalism." *Annual Review of Anthropology* 33: 475–98.

Lindstrom, Lamont. 1990. *Knowledge and Power in a South Pacific Society*. Washington, DC: Smithsonian Institution Press.

Lipscomb, Adrian, Rowan McKinnon, and Jon Murray. *Papua New Guinea*. Hawthorn, Australia: Lonely Planet.

LiPuma, Edward. 2001. *Encompassing Others: The Magic of Modernity in Melanesia*. Ann Arbor: University of Michigan Press.

Lloyd, Richard. 1974. "Baruya Kith and Kin." In *Kinship Studies in Papua New Guinea*, edited by R. Daniel Shaw, 97–124. Ukarumpa, Papua New Guinea: Summer Institute of Linguistics.

Lohmann, Roger Ivar. 2009. "Dreams of Fortune: Reo Fortune's Psychological Theory of Cultural Ambivalence." *Pacific Studies* 32: 273–298.

Lomnitz, Claudio. 2014. *The Return of Comrade Ricardo Flores Magón*. New York: Zone Books.

Long, Gavin. 1963. *The Final Campaigns*. Canberra: Australian War Memorial.

Losche, Diane. 2011. "The Anthropologist's Voice: Margaret Mead and Donald Tuzin." In *Echoes of the Tambaran: Masculinity, History and the Subject in the Work of Donald F. Tuzin*, edited by David Lipset and Paul Roscoe, 297–311. Canberra: Australian National University.

Loving, Richard and Jack Bass. 1964. *Languages of the Amanab Sub-District*. Port Moresby, Papua New Guinea: Department of Information and Extension Services.

Lowie, Robert. 1954. "Richard Thurnwald, 1869–1954." *American Anthropologist* 56 (5): 863–67.

Ludvigson, Tomas. 1985. "Healing in Central Espiritu Santo, Vanuatu." In *Healing Practices in the South Pacific*, edited by Claire D. F. Parsons, 51–64. Honolulu: Institute for Polynesian Studies.

Lutkehaus, Nancy C. 2008. *Margaret Mead: The Making of an American Icon*. Princeton, NJ: Princeton University Press.

———. 1995. *Zaria's Fire: Engendered Moments in Manam Ethnography*. Durham, NC: Carolina Academic Press.

Lutkehaus, Nancy, Christian Kaufmann, William E. Mitchell, Douglas Newton, Lita Osmundsen, and Meinhard Schuster, eds. 1990. *Sepik Heritage: Tradition and Change in Papua New Guinea*. Durham, NC: Carolina Academic Press.

Mair, L. P. 1970. *Australia in New Guinea*. Melbourne, Australia: Melbourne University Press.

Mair, L. P., and Ian Grosart. 1972. "Local Government." In *Encyclopedia of Papua New Guinea*, vol. 2, edited by Peter Ryan, 657–73. Melbourne, Australia: Melbourne University Press.

Malinowski, Bronislaw. 1915. "The Natives of Mailu: Preliminary Results of the Robert Mond Research in British New Guinea." *Transactions and Proceedings of the Royal Society of South Australia* 39: 494–706.

———. 1922. *The Argonauts of the Western Pacific: An Account of Native Enterprise and Adventure in the Archipelagoes of Melanesian New Guinea*. London: Routledge & Kegan Paul.

———. 1988. *Malinowski among the Magi: The Natives of Mailu*, edited with an introduction by Michael W. Young. London: Routledge.

Mar, Tracy B. 2016. "Performing Cannibalism in the South Seas." In *Touring Pacific Cultures*, edited by Kalissa Alexeyeff and John Taylor, 323–31. Canberra: Australian National University Press.

Marshall, Alan John. 1938. *The Men and Birds of Paradise: Journeys through Equatorial New Guinea*. London: William Heinemann.

Matthiessen, Peter. 1969. *Under the Mountain Wall: A Chronicle of Two Seasons in the Stone Age*. New York: Ballantine Books.

Hau'ofa, Epeli. 1981. *Mekeo Inequality and Ambibivalence in a Village Society*. Canberra: Australian National University Press.

Mauss, Marcel. (1902–03) 1975. *A General Theory of Magic*. Translated by Robert Brain. New York: Norton.

McArthur, Margaret. 1971. "Men and Spirits in the Kunimaipa Valley." In *Anthropology in Oceania: Essays Presented to Ian Hogbin*, edited by L. R. Hiatt and C. Jayawardena, 155–189. Sydney: Angus and Robertson.

———. 1972. "Food." In *Encyclopedia of Papua New Guinea*, vol. 1, edited by Peter Ryan, 433–47. Melbourne, Australia: Melbourne University Press.

McCallum. P. Maurice. 2006. "'Sanguma'—Tracking Down a Word." *Catalyst* 36 (2): 183–207.

McCarthy, John Keith. 1936. "Report of Patrol to the Yellow River Base Camp. Sepik Division – J. K. McCarthy." Department of Territories, Patrol Report from Territory of New Guinea. Commonwealth Archives Office: Accession AS13/26 item No. 20.

———. 1963. *Patrol Into Yesterday: My New Guinea Years*. Melbourne: F. W. Cheshire.

———. 1964 "Establishment of Government Stations, New Guinea." Circular memo file No 2–1–0, 9 September, Department of Native Affairs.

McDowell, Nancy. 1991. *The Mundugumor: From the Field Notes of Margaret and Reo Fortune*. Washington, DC: Smithsonian Institution Press.

McKnight, D. 1982. "Conflict, Healing, and Singing in an Australian Aboriginal Community." *Anthropos* 77: 491–508.

Mead, Margaret. 1938. The Mountain Arapesh, part 1: An Importing Culture. *Anthropological Papers of the American Museum of Natural History* 36 (3): 139–349.

———. (1935) 1963. *Sex and Temperament in Three Primitive Societies*. New York: William Morrow.

———. 1947. "The Mountain Arapesh, part 3: The Socio-Economic Life." *Anthropological Papers of the American Museum of Natural History* 40 (3): 163–232.

———. (1938, 1940) 1970. *The Mountain Arapesh: Arts and Supernaturalism*. Garden City, NY: Natural History Press.

———. 1972. *Blackberry Winter: My Earlier Years*. New York: William Morrow.

———. 1973. "A Re-examination of Major Themes of the Sepik Area, Papua, New Guinea." Paper presented at the Ninth Congress of Anthropological and Ethnological Sciences, Chicago.

———. 1978. "The Sepik as a Culture Area: Comment." *Anthropological Quarterly* 51 (1): 69–75.

———. 1977. *Letters from the Field, 1925–1975*. New York: Harper and Row.

Mead, Margaret, and Rhoda Metraux. 1978. *An Interview with Santa Claus*. New York: Walker.

Melk-Koch, Marion. 1989. *Auf der Suche nach der menschlichen Gesellschaft: Richard Thurnwald*. Berlin: Dietrich Reimer Verlag.

———. 2000. "Melanesian Art or just Stones and Junk? Richard Thurnwald and the Question of Art in Melanesia." *Pacific Arts* 21–22: 53–68.

———. 2010. "Remembering Bernard Juillerat. Visiting the Bánaro after Richard Thurnwald." *Journal de la Société des Océanistes*. 130–31: 29–40.

Merlan, Francesca. 2016. "Women, Warfare and the Life of Agency: Papua New Guinea and Beyond." *Journal of the Royal Anthropological Institute*. 22: 393–411.

Métraux, Rhoda. (1954) 2001. "Themes in French Culture." In *Themes in French Culture: A Preface to a Study of French Community*, edited by Margaret Mead with Rhoda Métraux, 3–73. New York: Berghahn.

Middleton, John, and E. H. Winter. 1963. *Witchcraft and Sorcery in East Africa*. London: Routledge Kegan and Paul.

Mihalic, F. 1971. *The Jacaranda Dictionary and Grammar of Melanesian Pidgin*. Milton, Australia: Jacaranda Press.

Mikloucho-Maclay, Nikolai. 1975. *Mikloucho-Maclay: New Guinea Diaries 1871–1883*. Translated and edited by C. L. Sentinella. Madang, Papua New Guinea: Kristen Press.

Mitchell, William E. 1968. "The *Doktaboi*: A Medial Medical Role in New Guinea." Paper presented at the Eighth International Congress of Anthropological and Ethnological Sciences, Tokyo.

———. 1971. "Use and Abuse of Pidgin." *Man in New Guinea* 3 (3): 17–19.

———. 1973. "A New Weapon Stirs up Old Ghosts." *Natural History* 82: 74–84.

———. 1975. "Culturally Contrasting Therapeutic Systems of the West Sepik: The Lujere." In *Psychological Anthropology*, edited by Thomas R. Williams, 409–39. The Hague, Netherlands: Mouton.

———. 1977 "Sorcellerie chamanique: 'Sanguma' chez les Lujere du cours supérieur de Sépik." *Journal de la Société des Océanistes* 3 (56–57): 179–89.

———. 1978a. *Mishpokhe: A Study of New York City Jewish Family Clubs*." The Hague, Netherlands: Mouton.

———. 1978b. "On Keeping Equal: Polity and Reciprocity among the New Guinea Wape." *Anthropological Quarterly* 51 (1): 5–16.

———. 1988. *Magical Curing*. VHS Film and Film Guide. Prospect Heights, IL: Waveland.

———. 1989. Review of *Sorcerer and Witch in Melanesia* by Michele Stephen, ed. *American Ethnologist* 16 (3): 591–92.

———. 1991. "Bus, Baret and Tais: A Lujere View of Ecological Resources in Terms of Kinship and Subsistence." Paper presented at the 90th Annual Meeting of the American Anthropological Association, Chicago.

———. 1992. ed. *Clowning as Critical Practice: Performance Humor in the South Pacific*. Pittsburgh: University of Pittsburgh Press.

———. 1999. "Why Wape Men Don't Beat Their Wives: Constraints Towards Domestic Tranquility in a New Guinea Society." In *To Have and to Hit: Cultural Perspectives on Wife*

Beating, 2nd ed., edited by Dorothy Ayers Counts, Judith K. Brown, and Jacquelyn C. Campbell, 100–36. Urbana: University of Illinois Press.

———. (1987) 2012. *The Bamboo Fire: Field Work with the New Guinea Wape*, 2nd ed. London: Routledge.

Molnar-Bagley, Emese. 1980. "West Sepik Handbook – 1980." Produced for the Sandaun Provincial Council, Papua New Guinea. Unpublished manuscript.

Monckton, C. A. W. 1921. *Taming New Guinea: Some Experiences of a New Guinea Resident Magistrate*. New York: John Lane.

Morgan, Lewis Henry. 1851. *League of the Ho-de-no-sau-nee, or Iroquois*. Rochester, NY: Sande & Bros.

———. (1868) 1970. *The American Beaver and his Works*, reprint ed. New York: Burt Franklin.

———. 1871. *Systems of Consanguinity and Affinity of the Human Family*. Smithsonian Contributions to Knowledge 17. Washington, DC: Smithsonian Institution Press.

Morrell, W. P. 1960. *Britain in the Pacific Islands*. Oxford: Oxford University Press.

Morren, Jr., George E. B. 1986. *The Miyanmin: Human Ecology of a Papua New Guinea Society*. Ann Arbor, MI: UMI Research Press

Moses, J. A. 1969. "The German Empire in Melanesia 1884–1914: A German Self-Analysis." In *The History of Melanesia*, Canberra: Australian National University Press, University of Papua New Guinea.

Murdock, George Peter, 1949. *Social Structure*. New York. Macmillan.

Murray. J. H. P. 1912. *Papua or British New Guinea*. London: T. Fisher Unwin.

Mwakyembe, H. G. 1986. "The Parliament and the Electoral Process." In *The State and the Working People of Tanzania*, edited by Issa G. Shivji, 16–57. Dakar, Senegal: Council for the Development of Social Science Research in Africa.

Napier, A. David. 1986. *Masks, Transformation, and Paradox*. Berkeley: University of California Press.

———. 2003. *The Age of Immunology: Conceiving a Future in an Alienating World*. Chicago: University of Chicago Press.

Needham, Rodney. 1967. "Blood, Thunder, and Mockery of Animals." In *Myth ad Cosmos: Readings in Mythology and Cosmos*, edited by John Middleton, 271–85. Garden City, NY: Natural History Press.

Nelson, H. N. 2000. "McCarthy, John Keith (1905–1976)." Australian Dictionary of Biography, National Centre of Biography, Australian National University.

———. 1985. "European Contact and Administrative Control." *Papua New Guinea Atlas: A Nation in Transition*, edited by David King and Stephen Ranck, 2–3. Bathurst, Australia, Port Moresby, Papua New Guinea: Robert Brown & Associates in association with the University of Papua New Guinea.

Nevermann, Hans. 1941. *Ein Besuch bei Steinzeitmenschen*. Stuttgart: Kosmos.

Oakes, George D. 1956a. "Patrol Report Sepik District, Lumi No. 1, 1956/57." University of California San Diego Libraries, Mandeville Special Collections.

———. 1956b. "Patrol Report Sepik District, Lumi No. 2, 1956/57, University of California San Diego Libraries, Mandeville Special Collections.

Oakley, E. W. and S. Eve. 1932. "Patrol Report No. A3/32–33., South Wapi Extending to the Sepik River." Accession AS13/26 item No. 21. Canberra, Australia: Commonwealth Archives Office.

Obeyesekere, Gananath. 2005. *Cannibal Talk: The Man-Eating Myth and Human Sacrifice in the South Seas*. Berkeley: University of California Press.

Odgers, L. 1942. "The J. A. Thurston Expedition Across New Guinea via Sepik and Fly Rivers—April to September, 1942." Australian Archives: Accession No. AS13/26, Box 34–79, item 59.

Official Handbook of the Territory of New Guinea. 1936. Canberra, Australia: L. F. Johnston, Commonwealth Government Printer.

O'Hanlon, Michael and Robert L. Welsch. 2000. *Hunting the Gatherers: Ethnographic Collectors, Agents and Agency in Melanesia*, 1870s–1930s. New York: Berghahn.

O'Keefe, Daniel Lawrence. 1982. *Stolen Lightning: The Social Theory of Magic*. New York: Vintage.

Orwin, R. 1951. "Sepik (Wewak) Patrol Report No. 2 of 1950/51." University of California San Diego Libraries, Mandeville Special Collections. Assen: Van Gorcum.

"Pacific Islands – Sepik River Expedition, 1919." Department of Home and Territories, Correspondence File, NG Series (Old File). Commonwealth Archives Office: CRS A4 item NG 40. Canberra, Australia.

Pappenhagen, Ronald W., and Doris J. 1981. "A Sociolinguistic Survey of Namie." In *Sociolinguistic Surveys of Sepik Languages*, edited by Richard Loving, 163–76. Work Papers in Papua New Guinea Languages 29. Ukarumpa, Papua New Guinea: Summer Institute of Linguistics.

Parkin, David. 1985. "Introduction." In *The Anthropology of Evil*, edited by David Parkin, 1–25. Oxford: Basil Blackwell.

Patterson, Mary. 1974–1975. "Sorcery and Witchcraft in Melanesia: An Ethnographic Survey." *Oceania* 45 (2): 132–60; *Oceania* 45 (3): 212–34.

Paulsen, Rune. 2003. "Fighting Hierarchy: Relations of Egality and Hierarchy among the May River Iwam of Papua New Guinea." In *Oceanic Socialities and Cultural Forms: Ethnographies of Experience*, edited by Ingjerd Hoëm and Sidsel Roalkvam. 29–49. New York: Berghahn.

Pavlac, Brian A. 2010. *Witch Hunts in the Western World: Persecution and Punishment from the Inquisition through the Salem Trials*. Lincoln: University of Nebraska Press.

Pawley, Andrew, Robert Attenborough, Jack Golson, and Robin Hide, eds. 2005. *Papuan Pasts: Cultural, Linguistic and Biological Histories of Papuan-Speaking Peoples*. Canberra, Australia: Pacific Linguistics.

Payne, G. F. 1972. "Ambunti Patrol Report No. 2 of 1972/73, Rocky Peaks Census Division." University of California San Diego Library, Mandeville Special Collections Library.

Peck, Susan L. 1973. "Ethics and the Public." *Hastings Center Report* 3: 16.

Pels, Peter. 2003. "Introduction." In *Magic and Modernity: Interfaces of Revelation and Concealment*, edited by Birgit Meyer and Peter Pels. 1–37. Stanford, CA: Stanford University Press.

Peltason, Ruth A. 2005. *New Guinea Art Masterpieces from the Jolika Collection of Marcia and John Friede*. Vol. 2. San Francisco: Fine Art Museums of San Francisco.

Pendergrast, Mark. 2017. *Memory Warp: How the Myth of Repressed Memory Arose and Refuses to Die*. Hinesburg, VT: Upper Access Books.

Philsooph, Hushang. 1971. "Primitive Magic and Mana." *Man* 6 (2): 182–203.

———. 1990. "Open Structures: Aspects of Cross-Cultural Influence in the Sepik in Relation to Southeast Asia, India, and the Middle East." In *Sepik Heritage: Tradition and Change in Papua New Guinea,* edited by Nancy Lutkehaus, Christian Kaufmann, William E. Mitchell, Douglas Newton, Lita Osmundsen, and Meinhard Schuster, 87–115. Durham, NC: Carolina Academic Press.

Powell, Alan. 1996. *War by Stealth: Australians and the Allied Intelligence Bureau, 1942–1945*. Melbourne, Australia: Melbourne University Press.

———. 2003. *The Third Force: ANGAU's New Guinea War, 1942–46*. Oxford: Oxford University Press.

Prinz, Jesse J. 2007. *The Emotional Construction of Morals*. Oxford: Oxford University Press.

Pulsford, R. L. and J. Cawte. 1972. *Health in a Developing Country: Principles of Medical Anthropology in Melanesia*. Milton, Australia: Jacaranda Press.

Radford, Anthony J. 1971. "The Future of Rural Health Services in Melanesia, With Particular Reference to Niugini." Presented at the Fifth Waigani Seminar on Change and Development in Rural Melanesia, Port Moresby, Papua New Guinea.

Radin, Paul. (1937) 1957. *Primitive Religion: Its Nature and Origin*. New York: Dover.

Reed, Stephen Winsor. 1943. *The Making of Modern New Guinea*. Philadelphia: American Philosophical Society.

Ray, Herbert. 1892. "The Languages of British New Guinea." Sidney *Transactions of the Ninth International Congress of the Orientalists* 2: 754–70.

Rehburg, Judith. 1974. "Social Structure of the Sepik Iwam." In *Kinship Studies in Papua New Guinea*, edited by R. Daniel Shaw, 211–22. Ukarumpa, Papua New Guinea: Summer Institute of Linguistics.

Reid, J. 1983. *Sorcerers and Healing Spirits: Continuity and Change in an Aboriginal Medical System*. Canberra: Australian National University Press.

Resek, Carl. 1960. *Lewis Henry Morgan: American Scholar*. Chicago: University of Chicago Press.

Richmond, Keith. 2004a. "'Locust,' 'Whiting' and New Britain: Guy Black's Covert War with M and Z Units." *The Free Library*. Military Historical Society of Australia. https://www.thefreelibrary.com/%22Locust%22%2c+%22Whiting%22+and+New+Britain%3a+Guy+Black%27s+covert+war+with+M...-a0126849912. Accessed July 17, 2014.

———. 2004b. "Nakano Agents and the Japanese Forces in New Guinea, 1942–1945." *The Free Library*. Military Historical Society of Australia. http://www.thefreelibrary.com/Nakano+agents+and+the+Japanese+forces+in+New+Guinea%2c+1942-1945.-a0123162110. Accessed July 17, 2014.

Riley, Ian D., Deborah Lehmann, and Michael P. Alpers. 1992. "Acute Respiratory Infections." In *Human Biology in Papua New Guinea: The Small Cosmos*, edited by Robert D. Attenborough and Michael Alpers, 281–88. Oxford: Clarendon.

Rio, Knut. 2002. "The Sorcerer as an Absented Third Person: Formations of Fear and Anger in Vanuatu." In *Beyond Rationalism: Rethinking Magic, Witchcraft, and Sorcery*, edited by Bruce Kapferer, 129–54. New York: Berghahn.

Rio, Knut M. and Bjern Enge Bertelsen. 2018. "Anthropology and 1968: Openings and Closures." *Anthropology Today* 34 (2): 9–13.

Rio, Knut, Michelle MacCarthy, and Ruy Blanes, eds. 2017. *Pentecostalism and Witchcraft*. Cham, Switzerland: Springer.

Rivers, W. H. R. (1924) 2001. *Medicine, Magic, and Religion*. Reprint ed, New York: Routledge.

Robinson, Eric D. 1931. "Annual Report of Sepik District 1930–31." Territory of Papua and New Guinea Archives. Canberra, Australia: Commonwealth Archives Office.

———. 1932. "Patrol Report: Ambunti to the Sepik–Dutch Border, and approximately 10 Miles of the Yellow R. No. A4 of 1932–33. Sepik District. E. D. Robinson." Accession AS13/26 item no. 14. Canberra, Australia: Commonwealth Archives Office.

———. 1934. "Special Patrol Report No. S.D. 1/1934–35." Territory of Papua and New Guinea Archives. Canberra, Australia: Commonwealth Archives Office.

Roscoe, Paul B. 1986. "The Emergence and Development of a Sepik Culture-Bound Syndrome." *Ethnology* 25 (3): 181–93.

———. 1989. "Medical Pluralism among the Yangoru Boiken." In *A Continuing Trial of Treatment*, edited by S. Frankel and G. Lewis. 199–215. Dordrecht, Netherlands: Kluwer.

———. 1996. "War and Society in Sepik New Guinea." *Journal of the Royal Anthropological Institute* 2 (4): 645–66.

———. 2005. "Foraging, Ethnographic Analogy, and Papuan Pasts: Contemporary Models for the Sepik-Ramu Past." In *Papuan Pasts: Cultural, Linguistic, and Biological Histories of Papuan-Speaking Peoples*, edited by Andrew Pawley, Robert Attenborough, Jack Golson, and Robin Hide. 555–84. Canberra, Australia: Pacific Linguistics.

Rosi, Pamela C. 1991. "The Role of the National Arts School in the Creation of National Culture and Identity in Papua New Guinea." Paper presented at the Annual Meeting of the Association for Social Anthropology in Oceania, Victoria, Canada.

Ross, Malcolm D. 2005. "Pronouns as a Preliminary Diagnostic for Grouping Papuan Languages." In *Papuan Pasts: Cultural, Linguistic, and Biological Histories of Papuan-Speaking Peoples*, edited by Andrew Pawley, Robert Attenborough, Jack Golson, and Robin Hide, 15–66. Canberra, Australia: Pacific Linguistics.

Rosten, Leo. 1970. *The Joys of Yiddish*. New York: Pocket Books.

Rowley, C. D. 1954a. "Native Officials and Magistrates of German New Guinea 1897–1921." *South Pacific* 7: 772–82.

———. 1954b. "The Area Taken Over from the Germans and Controlled by the A.N.M.E.F." *South Pacific* 7: 824–39.

———. 1958. *The Australians in German New Guinea 1914–1921*. Melbourne, Australia: Melbourne University Press.

———. 1966. *The New Guinea Village: The Impact of Colonial Rule on Primitive Society and Economy*. London: Pall Mall Press.

Royal Anthropological Institute. 1954. *Notes and Queries on Anthropology*. London: Routledge and Kegan Paul.

Rüegg, Francois, ed. 2018. *Ethnographie und Mission: Georg Hölker und Neuguinea.* Sieburg, Germany: Franz Schmitt Verlag.

Ruhen, Olaf. 1963. *Mountains in the Clouds.* London: Horwitz.

Rutherford, Danilyn. 2012. *Laughing at Leviathan: Sovereignty and Audience in West Papua.* Chicago: University of Chicago Press.

———. 2018. *Living in the Stone Age: Reflections on the Origins of a Colonial Fantasy.* Chicago: University of Chicago Press.

Ryan, Peter. 1969. *The Hot Land: Focus on New Guinea.* Melbourne, Australia: Macmillan.

———. 1972a. "World War II." In *Encyclopedia of Papua and New Guinea*, vol. 2, edited by Peter Ryan., 1211–24. Melbourne, Australia: Melbourne University Press.

———. 1972b. "ANGAU (Australian New Guinea Administrative Unit)." In *Encyclopedia of Papua and New Guinea*, vol. 1, edited by Peter Ryan, 21–23. Melbourne, Australia: Melbourne University Press.

Sack, Peter, and Dymphna Clark, eds. 1979. *German New Guinea: The Annual Reports.* Canberra: Australian National University Press.

Sagan, Eli. 1983. *Cannibalism: Human Aggression and Cultural Form.* New York: Psychohistory Press.

Sahlins, Marshall. 1965. "On the Ideology and Composition of Descent Groups." *Man* 65: 104–7.

———. 1978. "Culture as Protein and Profit." *New York Review of Books* 25: 45–53.

———. 2013. *What Kinship Is—And Is Not.* Chicago: University of Chicago Press.

Salisbury. R. F. 1964. "New Guinea Highland Models and Descent Theory. *Man* 64: 168–71.

Sanday, Peggy Reeves. 1986. *Divine Hunger: Cannibalism as a Cultural System.* Cambridge: Cambridge University Press.

Scaglion, Richard. 1990. "Reconstructing First Contact: Some Local Effects of Labor Recruitment in the Sepik." In *Sepik Heritage: Tradition and Change in Papua New Guinea*, edited by Nancy Lutkehaus, Christian Kaufmann, William E. Mitchell, Douglas Newton, Lita Osmundsen, and Meinhard Schuster, 50–57. Durham, NC: Carolina Academic Press.

Schindlbeck, Marcus. 1997. "The Art of the Head-hunters: Collecting Activity and Recruitment in New Guinea at the Beginning of the Twentieth Century." In *European Impact and Pacific Influence*, edited by Herman J. Hiery and John M. Mackenzie. London: German Historical Society, I. B. Tauris.

Schmitz, Carl A. 1959. "Todeszauber in Nordost-Neuguinea. *Paideuma* 7: 36–67.

Schneider, David M. 1972. "What is Kinship All About?" In *Kinship Studies in the Morgan Centennial Year*, edited by Priscilla Reining, 32–63. Anthropological Society of Washington. Washington, DC: Smithsonian Institution Press.

Schoorl. J. W. 1993. *Culture and Change among the MuYu.* Leiden, Netherlands: KITLV Press.

Schultz, Kathryn. 2017. "Fantastic Beasts and How to Rank Them." *The New Yorker* (November 6): 24–28.

Schuster, Meinhard. 1967. "Vorläufiger Bericht über die Sepik–Expedition 1965–1967 des Museums für Völkerkunde zu Basel." *Verhandlunger der Naturforschenden Gesellschaft Basel* 78: 268–82.

———. 1969. "Die Maler vom May Rivers." *Palette* 33: 2–19.

Schutt, Bill. 2017. *Cannibalism: A Perfectly Natural History*. Chapel Hill, NC: Algonquin Books.

Schwartz, Lola Romanucci. 1969. "The Hierarchy of Resort in Curative Practices: The Admiralty Islands, Melanesia." *Journal of Health and Social Behavior* 10: 201–9.

Schwartz, Theodore. 1962. "The Paliau Movement in the Admirality Islands, 1946–1954." *Anthropological Papers of the American Museum of Natural History* 49: 211–421.

Scott, Michael W. 2007. *The Severed Snake: Matrilineages, Making Place, and a Melanesian Christianity in Southeast Solomon Islands*. Durham, NC: Carolina Academic Press.

———. 2016. "To be Makiran Is To See Like Mr. Parrot: The Anthropology of Wonder in Solomon Islands." *Journal of the Royal Anthropological Institute* 22 (3) 474–95.

Seligman, Brenda Z., ed. 1954. *Notes and Queries on Anthropology*. London: Routledge and Kegan Paul.

Seligman, C. G. (1910) 1976. *The Melanesians of British New Guinea.* New York: AMS Press.

Serjeantson, Susan W., Philip G. Board, and Kuldeep K. Bhatia. 1992. "Population Genetics in Papua New Guinea: A Perspective on Human Evolution." In *Human Biology in Papua New Guinea: The Small Cosmos*, edited by Robert D. Attenborough and Michael P. Alpers, 198–233. Oxford: Clarendon Press.

Shand, R. T. 1972. "Cocoanut Industry." In *Encyclopedia of Papua and New Guinea*, vol. 1, edited by Peter Ryan, 187–90. Melbourne, Australia: Melbourne University Press.

Shaw, R. Daniel. 1974. "Introduction." *Kinship Studies in Papua New Guinea*, edited by R. Daniel Shaw, 11–21. Ukarumpa, Papua New Guinea: Summer Institute of Linguistics.

Silverman, Eric K. 2018. "The Sepik River, Papua new Guinea: Nourishing Tradition and Modern Catastrophe." In *Island Rivers: Fresh Water and Place in Oceania*, edited by John R. Wagner and Jerry Jacka, 187–221. Acton, Australia: Australian National University Press.

Smith, Benjamin R. "Sorcery and the Dividual in Australia." *Journal of the Royal Anthropological Institute* 22 (3): 670–87.

Souter, Gavin. 1963. *New Guinea: The Last Unknown*. Sydney: Angus and Robertson.

Specter, Michael. 2011. "The Power of Nothing." *The New Yorker* (December 12): 30–36.

Stanhope, 1968. "Competing Systems of Medicine among the Rao-Brerik, Lower Ramu River, New Guinea." *Oceania* 39: 137–45.

Spencer, Baldwin, and F. J Gillen. (1899) 1968. *The Native Tribes of Central Australia*, reprint ed. New York: Dover.

Stanley, G A.V., S. W. Carey, J. N. Montgomery, and H. D. Eve. 1935. "Preliminary Notes on the Recent Earthquake in New Guinea," *Australian Geographer* 2: 8–15.

Steadman, Lyle. 1975. "Cannibal Witches among the Hewa." *Oceania* 46: 114–21.

Steer, Martin. (2005) 2011. "Languages of the Upper Sepik and Central New Guinea." *Upper Sepik–Central New Guinea Project* (website). Paper no. 33. Unpublished manuscript. http://uscngp.com/papers. Accessed October 26, 2015.

Steinbauer, Friedrich. 1969. *Concise Dictionary of New Guinea Pidgin (Neo-Melanesian) with translations in English and German*. Madang, Papua New Guinea: Kristen Pres.

Stephen, Michele. Ed. 1987. *Sorcerers and Witch in Melanesia*. New Brunswick, NJ: Rutgers University Press.

Stevens, David L. 1972. "Patrol Report Ama No. 33, 1972–1973." National Archives of Papua New Guinea, Accession 496.

Stewart, Pamela J., and Andrew Strathern. 2020. "Gossip—A Thing Humans Do." *Anthropology News* 61 (1) 18–21.

———. 2004. *Witchcraft, Sorcery, Rumors, and Gossip*. Cambridge: Cambridge University Press.

Stocking, George W. 1996. *After Tylor: British Social Anthropology 1888–1951*. Madison: University of Wisconsin Press.

———. 1992. *The Ethnographer's Magic and Other Essays in the History of Anthropology*. Madison: University of Wisconsin Press.

Strathern, Andrew. 1972. *One Father, One Blood: Descent and Group Structure among the Melpa People*. Canberra: Australian National University Press.

Strathern, Andrew, and Pamela J. Stewart. 2010. *Curing and Healing: Medical Anthropology in Global Perspective*. Durham, NC: Carolina Academic Press.

Strathern, Marilyn. 2017. Book Review of *A Practice of Anthropology: The Thought and Influence of Marshall Sahlins*, edited by Alex Golub, Daniel Rosenblatt, and John D. Kelly. *Journal of the Royal Anthropological Institute* 23 (1): 226–27.

Swadling, Pamela. 1981. *Papua New Guinea's Prehistory: An Introduction*. Boroko, Papua New Guinea: National Museum and Art Gallery; Port Moresby, Papua New Guinea: Gordon and Gotch.

———. 1990. "Sepik Prehistory." In *Sepik Heritage: Tradition and Change in Papua New Guinea*, edited by Nancy Lutkehaus, Christian Kaufmann, William E. Mitchell, Douglas Newton, Lita Osmundsen, and Meinhard Schuster, 71–86. Durham, NC: Carolina Academic Press.

———1996. *Plumes from Paradise: Trade Cycles in Outer Southeast Asia and Their Impact on New Guinea and Nearby Islands until 1920*. Boroko, Papua New Guinea, Coorparoo, Australia: Papua New Guinea National Museum in association with Robert Brown & Associates.

Taaffe, Stephen R. 1998. *MacArthur's Jungle War: The 1944 New Guinea Campaign*. Lawrence: University Press of Kansas.

Taussig, Michael. 2003. "Viscerality, Faith, and Skepticism: Another Theory of Magic." In *Magic and Modernity: Interfaces of Revelation and Concealment*, edited by Brigit Meyer and Peter Pel, 272–306. Stanford: Stanford University Press.

Taylor, J. C. 1984. "Of Acts and Axes: An Ethnography of Socio-cultural Change in an Aboriginal Community, Cape York Peninsula." Doctoral diss., Cook University.

Terrill, Angela. 2007. Review of *Papuan Pasts: Cultural, Linguistic and Biological Histories of Papuan–speaking Peoples.*, edited by Andrew Pawley, Robert Attenborough, Jack Golson, and Robin Hide. *Oceania Linguistics* 46 (1): 313–21.

Thomas, Keith. 1971. *Religions and the Decline of Magic: Studies in Popular Beliefs in Sixteenth and Seventeenth-Century England*. London: Weidenfeld & Nicolson.

Thompson, D. F. 1961. "Marrngitmirri and Kalka—Medicine Man and Sorcerer—in Arnheim Land. *Man* 61: 97–102.

Thorp, Dennis, and Barbara Thorp. 2004. *Christian Brethren Churches in Papua New Guinea 1951–2004: How Did It All Happen?* Auckland, Australia: Castle.

Tonkinson, Robert. 1974. *Aboriginal Victors of the Desert Crusade*. Menlo Park, CA: Cummings.

Thurnwald, Richard. 1914. "Entdeckungen im Becken des oberen Sepik." *Mitteilungern aus den deutschen Schutzgebieten* 27: 338–48. English translation: "Discoveries in the Basin of the Upper Sepik." Annotations and footnotes by Barry Craig, 2010. *Upper Sepik–Central New Guinea Project* (website). Paper no. 26. http://uscngp.com/papers. Accessed October 26, 2015.

———. 1916a. "Vorstösse nach dem Quellgebiet des Kaiserin-Augusta-Flusses, dem Sand-Fluss und dem Nord-Fluss bis an das Küstengebirge." *Mitteilungen aus den deutschen Schultzgebieten* 29: 82–93. English translation: "Dash to the Source of the Sepik River and to the Sources of the Sand and North Rivers as far as the Coastal Range." Annotations and footnotes by Barry Craig, 2010. *Upper Sepik–Central New Guinea Project* (website). Paper no. 27. http://uscngp.com/papers. Accessed October 26, 2015.

———. (1916b) 1974. "Bánaro Society: Social Organization and Kinship System of a Tribe in the Interior of New Guinea." Reprint ed. *Memoirs of the American Anthropological Association*. Millwood, New York: Kraus.

———. 1921. *Die Gemeinde der Bánaro. Ehe, Verwandtschaft und Gesellschaftsbau eines Stammes im Innern von New-Guinea. Aus den Ergebnissen einer Forschungsreise 1913–15. Ein Beitrag zur Entstehungsgeschichte von Familie und Staat*. Stuttgart, Sonderausgabe aus der Zeitschrift für vergleichende Rechtswissenschaft, vol. 38 and vol. 49.

———. 1936a. "Review of Sex and Temperament in Three Primitive Societies." *American Anthropologist* 38 (4): 663–67.

———. 1936b. "Studying Savages in Melanesia." *The Yale Review* 36, 313–32.

Tomaselli, Keyan G. 1989. "Visual Anthropology in South Africa: A Survey of the Turbulent '80s." *Commission on Visual Anthropology Newsletter* (May).

Tomlinson, M. E. 1969. "May River Patrol Report No. 5 of 1968/69." University of California, San Diego, Mandeville Special Collections Library.

Tonkinson, Robert. 1974. *The Jigalong Mob: Aboriginal Victors of the Desert Crusade*. Menlo Park, CA: Cummings.

Townsend, George Wilfred Lambert. 1968. *District Officer: From Untamed New Guinea to Lake Success, 1921–46*. Sydney: Pacific Publications.

Townsend, Patricia K. 1974. "Sago Production in a New Guinea Economy," *Human Ecology* 2 (3): 217–36.

———. 1971. "New Guinea Sago Gatherers: A Study of Demography in Relation to Subsistence." *Ecology of Food and Nutrition* 1: 19–24.

Trautmann, Thomas R. 1987. *Lewis Henry Morgan and the Invention of Kinship*. Berkeley: University of California Press

Treutlein, R. K. 1962 "Lumi Patrol Report No. 1 of 1962/63." University of California, San Diego, Mandeville Special Collections Library.

Trollope, C. A. 1962. "Lumi Patrol Report No. 8 of 1962/63." University of California, San Diego, Mandeville Special Collections Library.

Tudor, Judy. 1968. "Introduction." In *District Officer: From Untamed New Guinea to Lake Success 1921–46*, by G. W. L. Townsend, 1–14. Sydney: Pacific Publications.

Turner, Victor W. 1969. *The Ritual Process: Structure and Anti-Structure*. Chicago: Aldine.

Tuzin, Donald F. 1976. *The Ilahita Arapesh: Dimensions of Unity*. Berkeley: University of California Press.

———. 1980. *The Voice of the Tambaran: Truth and Illusion in Ilahita Religion*. Berkeley: University of California Press.

———. 1983. "Cannibalism and Arapesh Cosmology: A Wartime Incident with the Japanese." In *The Ethnography of Cannibalism*, edited by Paula Brown and Donald Tuzin. Washington, DC: Society for Psychological Anthropology.

Tylor, Edward B. 1881. *Anthropology: An Introduction to the Study of Man and Civilization*. New York: D. Appleton.

Ucko, Peter J. 1970. "Penis Sheaths: A Comparative Study." *Proceedings of the Royal Anthropological Institute of Great Britain and Ireland for 1969*, 24–67. London: Royal Anthropological Institute of Great Britain and Ireland.

Vargyas, Gábor. *Data on the Pictorial History of North-East Papua New Guinea*. Budapest: Ethnographic Institute of the Hungarian Academy of Sciences.

Van Baal, J. 1966. *Dema: Description and Analysis of Marind-Anim Culture (South New Guinea)*. The Hague, Netherlands: Martinus Nijhoff.

Van Gennep, Arnold. (1908) 1960. *The Rites of Passage*. Translated by Monika B. Vizedom and Gabrielle L. Caffee. Chicago: University of Chicago Press.

Vargyas. G. 1986. *Data on the Pictorial History of North-East Papua New Guinea*. Occasional Papers in Anthropology 1. Budapest: Ethnographical Institute of the Hungarian Academy of Sciences.

Viveiros de Castro, Eduardo. 2014. *Cannibal Metaphysics for a Post-Structural Anthropology*. Translated and edited by Peter Skafish. Minneapolis: Univocal.

Vizedom, Monika. 1976. *Rites and Relationships: Rites of Passage and Contemporary Anthropology*. Beverly Hills, CA: Sage.

Volker, Craig Alan. 2008. *Papua New Guinea Tok Pisin English Dictionary*. South Melbourne, Australia: Oxford University Press.

Wafingian, F. J. 1972a. "Lumi Patrol Report No. 13, 1971/72." University of California San Diego Libraries, Mandeville Special Collections.

———. 1972b. "Lumi Patrol Report No. 15, of 1971/72." University of California San Diego Libraries, Mandeville Special Collections.

Wallace, Anthony F. C. 1966. *Religion: An Anthropological View*. New York: Random House.

Wark, Lynette, and L. A. Malcolm. 1969. "Growth and Development of the Lumi Child in the Sepik District of New Guinea." *Medical Journal of Australia* 2: 129–36.

Warner, W. L. (1937) 1958. *A Black Civilization: A Social Study of an Australian Tribe.* New York: Harper & Brothers.

Webster, E. M. 1984. *The Moon Man: A Biography of Nikolai Miklouho-Maclay.* Berkeley: University of California Press.

Webster, Richard. 2005. *The Secret of Bryn Estyn: The Making of a Modern Witch Hunt.* Oxford: Orwell.

Weiner, Annette B. 1984. "From Word to Objects to Magic: 'Hard Words' and the Boundaries of Social Interaction." In *Dangerous Words: Language and Politics in the Pacific,* edited by Donald Lawrence Brenneis and Fred R. Myers, 161–91. New York: New York University Press.

———. 1992. *Inalienable Possessions: The Paradox of Keeping-While-Giving.* Berkeley: University of California Press.

Wells, Roberta. 1999. "Sidney Herbert Ray: Linguist and Educationist." *The Cambridge Journal of Anthropology* 21 (1): 79–99.

Welsch, Robert L. 2000. "One Time, One Place, Three Collections: Colonial Processes and the Shaping of Some Museum Collections from German New Guinea." In *Hunting the Gatherers: Ethnographic Collectors, Agents and Agency in Melanesia, 1870s–1930s,* edited by Michael O'Hanlon and Robert L. Welsch, 159–79. Oxford: Berghahn.

Wenke, P. B. 1953. "Report on Patrol to Yellow River passing through the Lower Mai-Mai and the Lower Wapi Area." Ambunti Patrol Report No. I of 53/54.

West, Francis. 1972. "Townsend, George Wilfred Lambert." In *Encyclopedia of Papua and New Guinea.* vol. 2, edited by Peter Ryan, 1141. Melbourne, Australia: Melbourne University Press.

West, Harry G, 2005. *Kupilikula: Governance and the Invisible Realm in Mozambique.* Chicago: University of Chicago Press.

White, Geoffrey M., and Lamont Lindstrom, eds. 1989. *The Pacific Theater: Island Representations of World War II.* Honolulu: University of Hawaii Press.

White, John. "Patrol Report May River No 3 of 1970/71." University of California San Diego Libraries, Mandeville Special Collections.

White, Osmar. 1965. *Parliament of a Thousand Tribes: A Study of New Guinea.* New York: Bobbs-Merrill.

Whitehead, Neil L. 2002. *Dark Shamans: Kanaimà and the Poetics of Violent Death.* Durham, NC: Duke University Press.

Whitehead, Neil L., and Robin Wright. 2004. *In Darkness and Secrecy: The Anthropology of Assault Sorcery and Witchcraft in Amazonia.* Durham, NC: Duke University Press.

Whitehouse, Harvey. 1996. Rites of Terror: Emotion, Metaphor and Memory in Melanesian Initiation Cults." *Journal of the Royal Anthropological Institute* 2 (4) 703–15.

Whiting, John W. M. 1941. *Becoming a Kwoma: Teaching and Learning in a New Guinea Tribe.* New Haven, CT: Yale University Press.

Wiessner, Polly and Akii Tumu. 1998. *Historical Vines: Enga Networks of Exchange, Ritual, and Warfare in Papua New Guinea.* Washington, DC: Smithsonian Institution Press.

Wigley, S. C. 1990. "Tuberculosis and New Guinea: Historical Perspectives with Special Reference to the Years 1871–1973." In *A History of Medicine in Papua New Guinea*, edited by B. G. Burton-Bradley. Kingsgrove: Australian Medical Publishing.

Williams, Francis Edgar. 1928. *Orokaiva Magic*. Oxford: Oxford University Press.

———. 1930. *Orokaiva Society*. Oxford: Oxford University Press.

———. 1936. *Papuans of the Trans-Fly*. Oxford: Clarendon Press.

———. 1944. "Mission Influence Amongst the Keveri of South-East Papua." *Oceania* 15 (2): 88–141.

Wilson, Monika. 1951. "Witch Beliefs and Social Structure." *American Journal of Sociology*. 56 (4) 308–13.

Winkelman, Michael James. 1992. *Shamans, Priests, and Witches: A Cross-Cultural Study of Magico-Religious Practitioners*. Anthropological Research Papers 44. Tempe: Arizona State University.

Wolfers, E. P. 1971. "Political Development." In *Papua New Guinea: Prospero's Other Island*. edited by Peter Hasting, 142–68. Sydney: Angus and Robertson.

Wright, E. J. 1959. "Taboo." *Papua and New Guinea Medical Journal* 3 (3): 108–9.

Wronska-Friend, Maria. 2015. "From Shells to Ceramic: Colonial Replicas of Indigenous Valuables." *Journal of Museum Ethnography* 28: 50–69.

Yoshida, Shuji. 1987. "Migration Routes of the Iwam, East Sepik Province, Papua New Guinea." *Man and Culture in Oceania* 3: 177–89.

Young-Whitford, D. 1946. "Aitape District Patrol Report No. 6 of 46/47." University of California San Diego Libraries, Mandeville Special Collections.

Zocca, Franco. 2009. *Sanguma in Paradise: Sorcery, Witchcraft and Christianity in Papua New Guinea*. Goroko, Papua New Guinea: Melanesian Institute.

Zocca, Franco and Jack Urame. 2008. *Sorcery, Witchcraft and Christianity in Melanesia*. Goroko, Papua New Guinea: Melanesia Institute.